THE PORTABLE MBA IN ENTREPRENEURSHIP

The Portable MBA Series

THE
PORTABLE MBA
IN ENTREPRENEURSHIP

Second Edition

William D. Bygrave

John Wiley & Sons, Inc.
New York • Chichester • Weinheim • Toronto • Singapore • Brisbane

Library of Congress Cataloging-in-Publication Data:

Bygrave, William D., 1937–
    The portable MBA in entrepreneurship / William D. Bygrave. — 2nd
ed.
      p.   cm.
    Includes bibliographical references and index.
    ISBN 0-471-16078-4 (cloth : alk. paper)
    1. New business enterprises.   2. Small business—Management.
  3. Venture capital.   4. Entrepreneurship.   I. Title.
    HD62.5.B94   1997
    658.02′2—dc20
                                  96-43971

Printed in the United States of America

10 9 8 7 6 5 4 3 2

CONTENTS

PREFACE TO THE SECOND EDITION

The three years that have passed since we published the first edition of this book have been one of the most spectacular periods in the annals of entrepreneurship in the United States. The crucial role that entrepreneurial companies play in keeping the U.S. economy dynamic and vibrant has become more and more apparent.

Consider one example, the World Wide Web, which was barely a faint blip on the radar economic screen when we were preparing the first edition of this book in 1993. The Web was invented by Tim Berners-Lee to make the Internet more easily accessible for his colleagues at CERN, the European high-energy research laboratory in Geneva. The possibilities of the Web immediately fired up the imagination of young computer users. In just three years, a host of Web entrepreneurs have transformed the Internet from an exclusive network for technically-savvy academics and researchers into a powerful global communications and computing medium for anyone with a personal computer.

Today, the Internet affects everything . . . the computer industry, telecommunications, media, semiconductors, publishing, software, distribution, political campaigns, travel. It is generating a tidal wave of opportunities that will rival the one created by the personal computer almost fifteen years ago. When a 23-year-old University of Illinois computer programmer, Marc Andreessen, can start a company, Netscape Communications (originally

Mosaic Communications), that is at the forefront of a revolution that is changing our work and leisure habits, anything seems possible in this land of entrepreneurial opportunity.

WILLIAM D. BYGRAVE

Babson College
November 1996

INTRODUCTION TO THE FIRST EDITION

I am at INSEAD in France on sabbatical leave from Babson College. As I write this introduction, it is a glorious spring day. The nearby Fontainebleau forest is teeming with life. Everything is budding and sprouting. Fresh green shoots are everywhere. Nature is busily renewing herself, unaware that the economy lies in deep winter, frozen in an economic recession. Unemployment, already too high, is on the rise. In Europe entrepreneurial springtime, with its green shoots of economic growth, seems a long way off.

What a contrast with the United States. Across the Atlantic the East Coast is paralyzed by the "storm of the century," but entrepreneurial spring is in the air. New jobs are being created. Productivity is at a 20-year high. Stock prices of small companies are the highest they have ever been. Long-term interest rates are falling. And the cost of capital is the lowest in the industrial world.

Entrepreneurship is what America does best, bar none. No other advanced industrial nation comes close. In the United States entrepreneurial companies created the personal computer, biotechnology, fast food, and overnight package delivery industries; transformed the retailing industry; overthrew AT&T's telecommunications monopoly; revitalized the steel industry; invented the integrated circuit and the microprocessor; founded the nation's most profitable major airline; and the list goes on. Indeed, every sector of the economy feels the influence of entrepreneurs.

Just to keep up with population growth, the U.S. economy must generate about 10,000 jobs every working day. That amounts to 2.5 million new jobs each year. Just to keep level with the number of births, let alone the number of new immigrants, the United States will need to generate something like 20 million new jobs between now and the year 2000. Where are those jobs going to come from? If the trend of the 1980s continues, small, entrepreneurial firms will generate most of the new jobs. Projecting present trends on the birth, survival, and job creation rates of startup firms, we estimate that the nation will need at least 15 million new entrepreneurs between now and the end of the century.

Consider these employment statistics produced by David Birch, the MIT business demographer: The U.S. economy created 21 million jobs in the 1980s. Just 5% of the young and rapidly growing companies accounted for 77% of those jobs, and 15% accounted for an astonishing 94%. There were approximately 500,000 small companies growing by 20% per year. But while small businesses were putting Americans to work in the 1980s, giant corporations were laying them off in droves. *Fortune* 500 companies eliminated more than 3.5 million jobs in the 1980s. In one year alone, 1988, 3.6 million new jobs were added, while 400,000 jobs were eliminated by the *Fortune* 500. And the pace continues unabated into the 1990s: *Fortune* 500 companies are laying off 400,000 workers annually. Nowhere has the carnage been more bloody than in the manufacturing sector, where almost one million jobs were lost between 1988 and 1990. In contrast, small manufacturers with fewer than 20 workers added more than 200,000 jobs. Today only 5% of the U.S. work force are employed in *Fortune* 500 manufacturing plants.

It is not just blue-collar workers who have been hit hard by unemployment. In the five years ended January 1992, 2.8 million white-collar workers lost their jobs. And since January 1992, four pillars of the *Fortune* 500—Citicorp, Digital Equipment, Sears Roebuck, and IBM—have laid off 100,000 white-collar workers. Small wonder that increasing numbers of recent MBAs are unable to find management positions commensurate with their qualifications: large corporations that traditionally hired new MBAs have fewer openings.

Never before in the history of business schools has there been such a demand from students for entrepreneurship education—a demand that most business schools have not met satisfactorily. True, 317 four-year or graduate U.S. institutions (304 of them business schools) reported having entrepreneurship courses, according to Karl Vesper's survey; and virtually every ranked business school now offers courses in entrepreneurship or related fields, according to another survey. However, the quality or depth of coverage of most programs is thin. A survey of entrepreneurship education in America's major universities found that only 31% of undergraduate and 13% of graduate schools teaching entrepreneurship offer courses beyond the introductory level. And less than half of those schools (44%) have any full-time entrepreneurship faculty. It seems to me that a business education without entrepreneurship is as incomplete as medical training without obstetrics. After all, without the conception, birth, and growth of new enterprises, there would be no businesses.

The Portable MBA in Entrepreneurship is a book for would-be entrepreneurs, people who have started small firms and want to improve their entrepreneurial skills, and others who are interested in entrepreneurship, such as loan officers, lawyers, accountants, and consultants—indeed, anyone who wants to get involved in the birth and growth of an enterprise. The chapters are written by leading authorities on new business creation. They include professors, consultants, and entrepreneurs with extensive experience in teaching the art and science of starting a business. These authors practice what they teach. They have started businesses, served on boards of venture capital funds, been directors of high-growth businesses, raised startup and expansion capital, filed patents, registered companies, and, perhaps most important of all, have created new products and many new jobs. What's more, they are tireless champions of entrepreneurship. They believe that entrepreneurs are America's best hope for an eternal economic springtime.

1 THE ENTREPRENEURIAL PROCESS

William D. Bygrave

This is the entrepreneurial age. Entrepreneurs are driving a revolution that is transforming and renewing economies worldwide. Entrepreneurship is the essence of free enterprise because the birth of new businesses gives a market economy its vitality. New and emerging businesses create a very large proportion of innovative products that transform the way we work and live; products such as personal computers, software, the Internet, biotechnology drugs, and overnight package deliveries. They generate most of the new jobs. According to some estimates a thousand new businesses are born every hour of every working day in the United States. From 1990 to 1994, small, growing firms with 100 or fewer workers generated 7–8 million new jobs in the U.S. economy, whereas firms with more than 100 workers destroyed 3.6 million. In central and eastern Europe as many as 7 million entrepreneurs are striving to transform the command economies of the postcommunist nations into free markets. Even China, the last major bastion of communism, is encouraging entrepreneurs. The People's University of Beijing is dropping its Marxist courses and replacing them with courses dealing with free enterprise and entrepreneurship.

There has never been a better time to practice the art and science of entrepreneurship. But what is entrepreneurship? Early this century, Joseph Schumpeter, the Moravian-born economist writing in Vienna, gave us the modern definition of an entrepreneur as the person who destroys the existing economic order by introducing new products and services, by creating new forms of organization, or by exploiting new raw materials. According to Schumpeter,

1

that person is most likely to accomplish this destruction by founding a new business but may also do it within an existing one.

Very few new businesses have the potential to initiate a Schumpeter-ian "gale" of creation-destruction as Apple computer did in the computer industry. The vast majority of new businesses enter existing markets. In *The Portable MBA in Entrepreneurship,* we take a broader definition of entrepreneurship than Schumpeter's. Ours encompasses everyone who starts a new business. Our entrepreneur is the person who perceives an opportunity and creates an organization to pursue it. And the entrepreneurial process involves all the functions, activities, and actions associated with perceiving opportunities and creating organizations to pursue them. Our entrepreneur's new business may, in a few rare instances, be the revolutionary sort that destroys the global economic order. But it is much more likely to be of the incremental kind that enters an existing market.

- An *entrepreneur* is someone who perceives an opportunity and creates an organization to pursue it.
- The *entrepreneurial process* involves all the functions, activities, and actions associated with perceiving opportunities and creating organizations to pursue them.

But can the art and science of entrepreneurship be taught? Or is the birth of a new enterprise just happenstance and its subsequent success or demise a haphazard process? Although ten years ago—even as recently as five—many business school gurus maintained that entrepreneurship could not be taught, entrepreneurship is today the fastest-growing subject in the business school curriculum. That transformation has come about because a whole body of knowledge about entrepreneurship has developed during the past decade or so. The process of creating a new business is well understood. Yes, entrepreneurship can be taught. However, we cannot guarantee to produce a Bill Gates or a Donna Karan any more than a physics professor can guarantee to produce an Albert Einstein or a tennis coach a Martina Navratilova. But give us students with the aptitude to start a business, and we will make them better entrepreneurs.

CRITICAL FACTORS FOR STARTING A NEW ENTERPRISE

We will begin by examining the entrepreneurial process (see Exhibit 1.1). What we are talking about here are the factors—personal, sociological, and

EXHIBIT 1.1   A model of the entrepreneurial process.

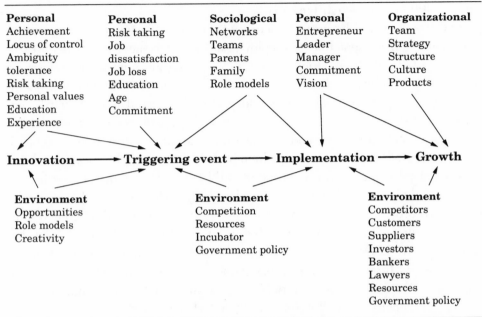

Personal	**Personal**	**Sociological**	**Personal**	**Organizational**
Achievement	Risk taking	Networks	Entrepreneur	Team
Locus of control	Job	Teams	Leader	Strategy
Ambiguity	dissatisfaction	Parents	Manager	Structure
tolerance	Job loss	Family	Commitment	Culture
Risk taking	Education	Role models	Vision	Products
Personal values	Age			
Education	Commitment			
Experience				

Innovation ⟶ **Triggering event** ⟶ **Implementation** ⟶ **Growth**

Environment	**Environment**	**Environment**
Opportunities	Competition	Competitors
Role models	Resources	Customers
Creativity	Incubator	Suppliers
	Government policy	Investors
		Bankers
		Lawyers
		Resources
		Government policy

Source: Based on Carol Moore's model, presented in "Understanding Entrepreneurial Behavior," in J. A. Pearce II and R. B. Robinson, Jr., eds., *Academy of Management Best Papers Proceedings*, Forty-sixth Annual Meeting of the Academy of Management, Chicago, 1986.

environmental—that give birth to a new enterprise. A person gets an idea—an *innovation*—for a new business—either through a deliberate search or a chance encounter. Whether or not he decides to pursue that idea depends on factors such as his alternative career prospects, family, friends, role models, the state of the economy, and the availability of resources.

There is almost always a *triggering event* that gives birth to a new organization. Perhaps the entrepreneur has no better career prospects. For example, Melanie Stevens was a high school dropout who, after a number of minor jobs, had run out of career options. She decided that making canvas bags in her own tiny business was better than earning low wages working for someone else. Within a few years she had built a chain of retail stores throughout Canada. Sometimes the person has been passed over for a promotion, or even laid off or fired. Howard Rose had been laid off four times as a result of mergers and consolidations in the pharmaceutical industry, and he had had enough of it. So he started his own drug packaging business, Waverly Pharmaceutical. And Tim Waterstone founded Waterstone's book stores after he was fired by W. H. Smith.

For other people, entrepreneurship is a deliberate career choice. Sandra Kurtzig was a software engineer with General Electric who wanted to start a family and work at home. She started ASK Computer Systems Inc., which became a $400 million-a-year business.

Where do would-be entrepreneurs get their ideas? More often than not it is through their present line of employment or experience. It has been estimated that 90% of all new high-potential businesses are founded in industries that are the same as, or closely related to, the one in which the entrepreneur has previous experience. That is not surprising because it is in their present employment that they will get most of their viable business ideas. Some habitual entrepreneurs do it over and over again in the same industry. Bill Poduska was a founder of Prime Computer, which he left to form Apollo, from which he retired and subsequently formed Stellar—all firms in the minicomputer industry. Others do it over and over again in related industries. In 1981, James Clark, then a Stanford University computer science professor, founded Silicon Graphics, a computer manufacturer with 1996 sales of $3 billion. In April 1994, he teamed up with Marc Andreessen, to found Netscape Communications. Within 12 months, its browser software, Navigator, dominated the Internet's World Wide Web. When Netscape went public in August 1995, Clark became the first Internet billionaire. Then in June 1996, Clark launched another company, Healthscape, that will enable doctors, insurers, and patients to exchange data and do business over the Internet with software incorporating Netscape's Navigator.

What are the factors that influence someone to embark on an entrepreneurial career? As with most human behavior, entrepreneurial traits are shaped by *personal attributes* and *environment*.

Personal Attributes

About a decade ago, at the start of the entrepreneurial eighties, there was a spate of magazine and newspaper articles that were titled "Do you have the right stuff to be an entrepreneur?" or words to that effect. The articles described the most important characteristics of entrepreneurs and, more often than not, included a self-evaluation exercise to enable readers to determine if they had the right stuff. Those articles were based on flimsy behavioral research into the differences between entrepreneurs and nonentrepreneurs. The basis for those exercises was the belief, first developed by David McClelland in his book *The Achieving Society*, that entrepreneurs had *a higher need for achievement* than nonentrepreneurs, and that they were moderate risk takers. One engineer almost abandoned his entrepreneurial ambitions after completing one of those exercises. He asked his professor at the start of an MBA entrepreneurship course if he should take the class because he had scored very low on an entrepreneurship test in a magazine. He took the course, however, and wrote an award-winning plan for a business that was a success from the very beginning.

Today, after more research, we know that there is no neat set of behavioral attributes that allow us to separate entrepreneurs from nonentrepreneurs. It turns out that a person who rises to the top of any occupation, whether it be an entrepreneur or an administrator, is an achiever. Granted, any would-be entrepreneur must have a need to achieve, but so must anyone else with ambitions to be successful.

It does appear that entrepreneurs have a *higher internal locus of control* than nonentrepreneurs, which means that they have a higher desire to be in control of their own fate. A recent survey of a broadly representative sample of small businesses owners in Britain found that more than 50% said independence was their main motive for running their own businesses. Only 18% said their main reason was to make money, and 10% mentioned other reasons that included enjoyment, challenge, more room for creativity, personal satisfaction. And according to another recent study, more than 80% of 121 Russian entrepreneurs surveyed said they started a business so as to be their own boss, and that having their own business reinforced feelings of autonomy and freedom.

By and large, we no longer use psychological terms when talking about entrepreneurs. Instead we use everyday words to describe their characteristics. The most important characteristics of successful entrepreneurs are shown in Exhibit 1.2.

Environmental Factors

Perhaps as important as personal attributes are the external influences on a would-be entrepreneur. It's no accident that some parts of the world are more entrepreneurial than others. The most famous region of high-tech entrepreneurship is Silicon Valley. Because everyone in Silicon Valley knows someone who has made it big as an entrepreneur, role models abound. This situation produces what Stanford University sociologist Everett Rogers called Silicon Valley fever. It seems as if everyone in the valley catches that bug sooner or later and wants to start a business. To facilitate the process, there are venture capitalists who understand how to select and nurture high-tech entrepreneurs, bankers who specialize in lending to them, lawyers who understand the importance of intellectual property and how to protect it, landlords who are experienced in renting real estate to fledgling companies, suppliers who are willing to sell goods on credit to companies with no credit history, and even politicians who are supportive.

Role models are very important because knowing successful entrepreneurs makes the act of becoming one yourself seem much more credible.

EXHIBIT 1.2   The 10 Ds.

Dream	Entrepreneurs have a vision of what the future could be like for them and their businesses. And, more important, they have the ability to implement their dreams.
Decisiveness	They don't procrastinate. They make decisions swiftly. Their swiftness is a key factor in their success.
Doers	Once they decide on a course of action, they implement it as quickly as possible.
Determination	They implement their ventures with total commitment. They seldom give up, even when confronted by obstacles that seem insurmountable.
Dedication	They are totally dedicated to their business, sometimes at considerable cost to their relationships with their friends and families. They work tirelessly. Twelve-hour days, and seven-day work weeks are not uncommon when an entrepreneur is striving to get a business off the ground.
Devotion	Entrepreneurs love what they do. It is that love that sustains them when the going gets tough. And it is love of their product or service that makes them so effective at selling it.
Details	It is said that the devil resides in the details. That is never more true than in starting and growing a business. The entrepreneur must be on top of the critical details.
Destiny	They want to be in charge of their own destiny rather than dependent on an employer.
Dollars	Getting rich is not the prime motivator of entrepreneurs. Money is more a measure of their success. They assume that if they are successful they will be rewarded.
Distribute	Entrepreneurs distribute the ownership of their businesses with key employees who are critical to the success of the business.

Would-be entrepreneurs see role models primarily in the home and at work. Indeed, if you have a close relative who is an entrepreneur, it is more likely that you will have a desire to become an entrepreneur yourself, especially if that relative is your mother or father. At Babson College, more than half of the students studying entrepreneurship come from families that own businesses. But you don't have to be from a business-owning family to become an entrepreneur. Bill Gates, for example, was following the family tradition of becoming a lawyer when he dropped out of Harvard and founded Microsoft. He was in the fledgling microcomputer industry, which was being built by entrepreneurs, so he had plenty of role models among his friends and acquaintances. The chairman of the British Venture Capital Association recently observed that one of the reasons his nation has relatively few early-stage high-tech startups is that Britain has a scarcity of visible role models compared with the United States, where high-tech entrepreneurs such as Steve Jobs, Bill Gates, and Ken Olsen are household names. One of them, Ross Perot, is so well known that he was the presidential candidate preferred by one in five American voters in 1992.

Some universities are hotbeds of entrepreneurship. For example, Massachusetts Institute of Technology has produced numerous entrepreneurs among its faculty and alums. Companies with an MIT connection transformed the Massachusetts economy from one based on decaying shoe and textile industries into one based on high technology. According to a 1989 study by the Bank of Boston, from the end of the Second World War through 1988, 636 businesses had been established in Massachusetts alone by MIT alums, creating 300,000 jobs and a total income of $10 billion for Massachusetts residents. Annual worldwide sales of those companies totaled about $40 billion in 1988. The neighborhood of East Cambridge adjacent to MIT was termed "The Most Entrepreneurial Place on Earth" by *Inc.* magazine. According to that article, roughly 10% of Massachusetts software companies and 25% of the state's 140 biotechnology companies are headquartered in that square mile.

It is not only in high-tech that we see role models. Consider these examples:

- It has been estimated that half of all the convenience stores in New York city are owned by Koreans.
- It was the visibility of successful role models that spread catfish farming in the Mississippi delta as a more profitable alternative to cotton.
- The Pacific Northwest has more microbreweries than any other region of the United States.
- In the vicinity of the town of Wells, Maine, there are a half-dozen second-hand book stores.

African-Americans make up 12% of the U.S. population, but owned only 3.6% of the nation's businesses in 1992. One of the major reasons for a relative lack of entrepreneurship among African-Americans is the scarcity of African-American entrepreneurs, especially store owners, to provide role models. A similar problem exists among Native Americans. Lack of credible role models is also one of the big challenges in the formerly communist European nations as they strive to become entrepreneurial.

Other Sociological Factors

Besides role models, entrepreneurs have other sociological factors that influence them. *Family responsibilities* play an important role in the decision whether to start a company. It is, relatively speaking, an easy career decision to start a business when a person is 25 years old, single, and without many personal assets and dependents. It is a much harder decision when a person is 45 and married, has teenage children preparing to go to college, a hefty mortgage, car payments, and a secure, well-paying job. A 1992 survey of European high-potential entrepreneurs, for instance, found that on average they had 50% of their net worth tied up in their businesses. And at 45 plus, if you fail as an entrepreneur, it will not be easy to rebuild a career working for another company. But despite the risks, plenty of 45-year-olds are taking the plunge; in fact, the typical CEO of the 500 fastest-growing small companies, the *Inc.* 500, is a 50-year-old.

Another factor that determines the age at which entrepreneurs start businesses is the trade-off between the *experience* that comes with age and the *optimism* and *energy* of youth. As you grow older you gain experience, but sometimes when you have been in an industry a long time, you know so many pitfalls that you are pessimistic about the chance of succeeding if you decide to go out on your own. Someone who has just enough experience to feel confident as a manager is more likely to feel optimistic about an entrepreneurial career. Perhaps the ideal combination is a beginner's mind with the experience of an industry veteran. A beginner's mind looks at situations from a new perspective, with a can-do spirit.

Robert Swanson was 27 years old when he hit upon the idea that a company could be formed to capitalize on biotechnology. At that time he knew almost nothing about the field. By reading the scientific literature, Swanson identified the leading biotechnology scientists and contacted them. "Everybody said I was too early—it would take ten years to turn out the first microorganism from a human hormone or maybe twenty years to have a commercial product—everybody except Herb Boyer." Swanson was referring to Professor Herbert Boyer at the University of California at San Francisco, coinventor of the patents that, according to some observers, form the basis of the biotechnology industry. When Swanson and Boyer met in early 1976, they almost immediately agreed to become partners in an endeavor to explore the commercial possibilities of recombinant DNA. Boyer named their venture Genentech, an acronym for genetic engineering technology. Just seven months later, Genentech announced its first success, a genetically engineered human brain hormone, somatosin. According to Swanson, they accomplished ten years of development in seven months.

Marc Andreessen had a beginner's mind that produced a vision for the Internet that until then had eluded many computer industry veterans, including Bill Gates. When Andreessen's youthful creativity was joined with James Clark's entrepreneurial wisdom, earned from a dozen or so years as founder and chairman of Silicon Graphics, it turned out to be an awesome combination. Their company, Netscape, has distributed 38 million copies of Navigator in just two years, making it the most successful new software introduction ever.

Before leaving secure, well-paying, satisfying jobs, would-be entrepreneurs should make a *careful estimate of how much sales revenue* their new businesses must generate before they will be able to match the income that they presently earn. It usually comes as quite a shock when they realize that if they are opening a retail establishment, they will need annual sales revenue of at least $400,000—to pay themselves a salary of $50,000 plus fringe benefits such as health care coverage, retirement pension benefits, long-term disability insurance, vacation pay, sick leave, and perhaps subsidized meals, day-care, and education benefits. Four hundred thousand dollars a year is about $8,000 per week, or about $1,333 per day, or about $133 per hour, or $2 per minute if they are open 6 days a week, 10 hours a day. Also they will be working much longer hours and bearing much more responsibility if they become self-employed. A sure way to test the strength of a marriage is to start a company that is the sole means of support for your family.

When they actually start a business, entrepreneurs need a host of *contacts,* including customers, suppliers, investors, bankers, accountants, and lawyers. So it is important to understand where to find help before embarking on a new venture. A network of friends and business associates can be of immeasurable help in building the contacts an entrepreneur will need. They can also provide human contact because opening a business can be a lonely experience for anyone who has worked in an organization with many fellow employees.

Fortunately, today there are more organizations than ever before to help fledgling entrepreneurs. Often that help is free or costs very little. The SBA has Small Business Development Centers in every state; it funds Small Business Institutes; and its Service Core of Retired Executives provides free assistance to entrepreneurs. Many colleges and universities also provide help. Some are particularly good at writing business plans, usually at no charge to the entrepreneur. There are hundreds of incubators in the United States where fledgling businesses can rent space, usually at a very reasonable price, and spread some of their overhead by sharing facilities such as copying and FAX machines, secretarial help, answering services, and so on. Incubators are often associated with universities, which provide free or inexpensive counseling. There are numerous associations where entrepreneurs can meet and exchange ideas. In the Boston area, for example, the 128 Venture Forum provides a place where entrepreneurs, financiers, accountants, lawyers, and other professionals meet each month for a two-hour breakfast.

EVALUATING OPPORTUNITIES FOR NEW BUSINESSES

Let's assume you believe you have found a great opportunity for starting a new business. How should you evaluate its prospects? Or, perhaps more importantly, how will an independent person such as a potential investor or a banker rate your chances of success? The odds of succeeding appear to be stacked against you, because according to small business folklore, only one business in ten will ever reach its tenth birthday. This doesn't mean that nine out of ten of the estimated two million businesses that are started every year go bankrupt. We know that even in a severe recession, the number of businesses filing for bankruptcy in the United States has never yet surpassed 100,000 in any year. In an average year, the number is about 50,000. So what happens to the vast majority of the ones that do not survive 10 years? Most just fade away: They are started as part-time pursuits and are never intended to become full-time businesses. Some are sold. Others are liquidated. Only 700,000 of the two million are legally registered as corporations or partnerships, which is a sure sign that many of the remaining 1.3 million never intended to grow. Hence, the odds that your new business will survive may not be as long as they first appear to be. If you intend to start a full-time, incorporated business, the odds that the business will survive at least eight years with you as the owner are better than one in four; and the odds of its surviving at least eight years with a new owner are another one in four. So the eight-year survival rate for incorporated startups is about 50%.

But survival may not spell success. Too many entrepreneurs find that they can neither earn a satisfactory living in their businesses nor get out of them easily because they have too much of their personal assets tied up in them. The happiest day in an entrepreneur's life is the day doors are opened for business. For unsuccessful entrepreneurs, an even happier day may be the day the business is sold—especially if most personal assets remain intact. What George Bernard Shaw said about love affairs is also apt for business: Any fool can start one, it takes a genius to end one successfully.

How can you stack the odds in your favor, so that your new business is a success? Professional investors, such as venture capitalists, have a talent for picking winners. True, they also pick losers, but a startup company funded by venture capital has, on average, a four in five chance of surviving five years—better odds than for the population of startup companies as a whole. By using the criteria that professional investors use, entrepreneurs can increase their odds of success. Very few startup businesses—perhaps no more than one in a thousand—will ever be suitable candidates for investments from professional venture capitalists. But would-be entrepreneurs can learn a lot by following the evaluation process used by professional investors.

There are three crucial components for a successful new business: the opportunity, the entrepreneur (and the management team, if it's a high-potential venture), and the resources needed to start the company and make it grow. They are shown schematically in Exhibit 1.3 in the basic Timmons framework. At the center of the framework is a business plan, in which the

EXHIBIT 1.3   Three driving forces.

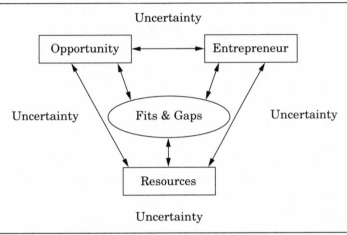

Source: Based on Jeffry Timmons' framework, as presented in Jeffry A. Timmons, *New Venture Creation* (Homewood, IL: Richard D. Irwin, 1990).

three basic ingredients are integrated into a complete strategic plan for the new business. The parts must fit together well. It's no good having a first-rate idea for a new business if you have a second-rate management team. Nor are ideas and management any good without the appropriate resources.

The crucial driving force of any new venture is the lead entrepreneur and the funding management team. Georges Doriot, the founder of modern venture capital, used to say something like this: "Always consider investing in a grade A man with a grade B idea. Never invest in a grade B man with a grade A idea." He knew what he was talking about. Over the years he invested in about 150 companies, including Digital Equipment Corporation (DEC), and watched over them as they struggled to grow. But Doriot made this statement about business in the 1950s and 1960s. During that period there were far fewer start-ups each year; U.S. firms dominated the marketplace; markets were growing quickly; there was almost no competition from overseas; and most entrepreneurs were male. Today, in the global marketplace with ever shortening product life cycles and low growth or even no growth for some of the world's leading industrial nations, the crucial ingredients for entrepreneurial success are a superb entrepreneur with a first-rate management team and an excellent market opportunity.

> The crucial ingredients for entrepreneurial success are a superb entrepreneur with a first-rate management team and an excellent market opportunity.

Frequently I hear the comment that success in entrepreneurship is largely a matter of luck. That's not so. We do not say that becoming a great quarterback, or a great scientist, or a great musician, and so on, is a matter of luck. There is no more luck in becoming successful at entrepreneurship than in becoming successful at anything else. In entrepreneurship, it is a question of recognizing a good opportunity when you see one and having the skills to convert that opportunity into a thriving business. To do that, you must be prepared. So in entrepreneurship, just like any other profession, *luck is where preparation and opportunity meet.*

In 1982, when Rod Canion proposed to start Compaq to make personal computers, there were already formidable established competitors, including IBM and Apple. By then literally hundreds of companies were considering entering the market or had already done so. For instance, in the same week of May 1982 that DEC announced its ill-fated personal computer, four other companies introduced PCs. Despite the competition, Ben Rosen of the venture capital firm Sevin Rosen Management Company, invested in Compaq. Started initially to make transportable PCs, it quickly added a complete range of high-performance PCs and grew so fast that it soon broke Apple's record for the fastest time from founding to listing on the *Fortune* 500.

What did Ben Rosen see in the Compaq proposal that made it stand out from all the other personal computer startups? The difference was Rod Canion and his team. Rod Canion had earned a reputation as an excellent manager at Texas Instruments. Furthermore, the market for personal computers topped $5 billion and was growing at a torrid pace. So Rosen had found a superb team with a product targeted at an undeveloped niche, transportable PCs, in a large market that was growing explosively. By 1994, Compaq was the leading PC manufacturer with 13% of the market.

> In entrepreneurship, as in any other profession, luck is where preparation and opportunity meet.

The Opportunity

Perhaps the biggest misconception about an idea for a new business is that it must be unique. Too many would-be entrepreneurs are almost obsessed with finding a unique idea. Then, when they believe they have it, they are haunted by the thought that someone is just waiting to steal it from them. So they become super secretive. They are reluctant to discuss it with anyone unless that person signs a nondisclosure agreement. That in itself makes it almost impossible to evaluate the idea. For example, many counselors who provide free advice to entrepreneurs refuse to sign nondisclosure agreements. Generally speaking, these super-secret, unique ideas are big letdowns when the entrepreneur reveals them to you. Among the notable ones I have encountered were "drive-through pizza by the slice," "a combination toothbrush and toothpaste gadget," and "a Mexican restaurant in Boston." One computer programmer telephoned me and said that he had a fantastic new piece of software. Eventually, after I assured him that I was not going to steal his idea, he told me his software was for managing hairdressing salons. He was completely floored when I told him that less than a month previously another entrepreneur had visited my office and demonstrated a software package for exactly the same purpose. Another entrepreneur had an idea for fluoride-impregnated dental floss. Not three months later, on a visit to England, I found the identical product in Boots—Britain's largest chain of drug stores and a major pharmaceutical manufacturer.

I tell would-be entrepreneurs that almost any idea they have will also have occurred to others. For good measure I point out that some of the most revolutionary thoughts in the history of mankind occurred to more than one person almost simultaneously. For instance, Darwin was almost preempted by Wallace in publishing his theory of evolution; Poincaré formulated a valid theory of relativity about the same time Einstein did; and the integrated circuit was invented in 1959 first by Jack Kilby at Texas Instruments, and then independently by Robert Noyce at Fairchild a few months later. So the idea per se is not what is important. In entrepreneurship, ideas really are a dime a dozen. Developing the idea, implementing it, and building a successful business are the important things. Alexander Fleming discovered penicillin by chance but never developed it as a useful drug. About 10 years later Ernst Chain and Howard Florey unearthed Fleming's mold. They immediately saw its potential. Working in England under wartime conditions, they soon were treating patients. Before the end of World War II, penicillin was saving countless lives. It was a most dramatic pharmaceutical advance and heralded a revolution in that industry.

> The idea per se is not what is important. In entrepreneurship, ideas really are a dime a dozen. Developing the idea, implementing it, and building a successful business are the important things.

Customer Need

Many would-be entrepreneurs call me up and tell me that they have an idea for a new business and can they come to see me. Unfortunately, it is impossible to see all of them, so I have developed a few questions that allow me to judge how far along they are with their idea. By far the most telling question is, "Can you give me the names of prospective customers?" Their answer must be very specific. If they have a consumer product—let's say it's a new shampoo—I expect them to be able to name buyers at different chains of drug stores in their area. If they are unable to name several customers immediately, they simply have an idea, not a market. There is no market unless customers have a real need for the product—a proven need rather than a hypothetical need in the mind of a would-be entrepreneur. In a few rare cases it may be a revolutionary new product, but it is much more likely be an existing product with improved performance, price, distribution, quality, or service. Simply put, customers must perceive that the new business will be giving them better value for their money than existing businesses.

> Would-be entrepreneurs who are unable to name customers are not ready to start a business. They have only found an idea and have not yet identified a market need.

Timing

Time plays a crucial role in many potential opportunities. In some emerging industries, there is a definite window of opportunity that opens only once. For instance, about 15 years ago, when VCRs were first coming into household use in the United States, there was a need for video stores in convenient locations where viewers could pick up movies on the way home from work. Lots of video retail stores opened up in main streets and shopping centers. They were usually run by independent store owners. Then the distribution of videos changed. National chains of video stores emerged. Supermarket and drug store chains entered the market. Today, the window of opportunity for starting an independent video store is closed. There are simply too many big competitors in convenient locations.

In other markets, high-quality restaurants for example, there is a steady demand that, on average, does not change much from year to year, so the window of opportunity is always open. Nevertheless, timing can be important, because when the economy turns down, those kinds of restaurants are usually hit harder than lower-quality ones, so the time to open one is during a recovering or booming economy.

If the window of opportunity appears to be very brief, it may be that the idea is a consumer fad that will quickly pass away. It takes a very skilled entrepreneur indeed to make money out of a fad. When Lucy's Have A Heart Canvas of Faneuil Hall Market in Boston introduced shoe laces with hearts on them, they flew off the shelves. Children and teenagers could not get enough of them for their sneakers. The store ordered more and more of them. Then demand suddenly dropped precipitously. The store and the manufacturer were left holding huge inventories that could not be sold. As a result the store almost went under.

Most entrepreneurs should avoid fads or any window of opportunity that they believe will only be open for a very brief time, because it inevitably means that they will rush to open their business, sometimes before they have time to gather the resources they will need. Rushing to open a business without adequate planning can lead to costly mistakes.

The Entrepreneur and the Management Team

Regardless of how right the opportunity may seem to be, it will not make a successful business unless it is developed by a person with strong entrepreneurial and management skills. What are the important skills?

First and foremost, entrepreneurs should have experience in the same industry or a similar one. Starting a business is a very demanding undertaking indeed. It is no time for on-the-job training. If would-be entrepreneurs do not have the right experience, they should either go out and get it before starting their new venture or find partners who have it.

Some investors say that the ideal entrepreneur is one who has a track record of being successful previously as an entrepreneur in the same industry and who can attract a seasoned team. Half of the CEOs of the *Inc.* 500 high-growth small companies had started at least one other business before they founded their present firms. When Joseph Crugnale acquired his first ice cream shop in 1977, he already had almost 10 years in the food service industry. Six years later, when he sold Steve's Ice Cream, it was a 26-store operation. He opened his first Bertucci's Brick Oven Pizzeria in 1981 and began expanding it into a chain in 1985. By 1991, he and his management team, with a total of more than 100 years experience in the food industry, had built Bertucci's into a rapidly growing chain with sales of $30 million and net income of $2 million. When the company went public in June 1991, it had a market value of $63 million.

Without relevant experience, the odds are stacked against the neophyte in any industry. An electronics engineer told me that he had a great idea for a chain of fast-food stores. When asked if he had ever worked in a fast-food restaurant, he replied, "Work in one? I wouldn't even eat in one. I can't stand fast food!" Clearly, he would have been as miscast as a fast-food entrepreneur as Crugnale would have been as an electronics engineer.

True, there are entrepreneurs who have succeeded spectacularly with no prior industry experience. Anita Roddick of The Body Shop and Ely Callaway of Callaway Golf are two notable examples. But they are the exceptions that definitely do not prove the rule.

Second to industry know-how is *management experience,* preferably with responsibility for budgets, or better yet, accountability for profit and loss. It is even better if a would-be entrepreneur has a record of increasing sales and profits. Of course, we are talking about the *ideal* entrepreneur. Very few people measure up to the ideal. That does not mean they should not start a new venture. But it does mean they should be realistic about the size of business they should start. Nine years ago, two 19-year-old students wanted to start a travel agency business in Boston. When asked what they knew about the industry, one replied, "I live in California. I love to travel." The other was silent. Neither of them had worked in the travel industry, nor had anyone in either of their families. They were advised to get experience. One joined a training program for airline ticket agents; the other took a course for travel agents. They became friends with the owner of a local Uniglobe travel agency who helped them with advice. Six months after they first had the idea, they opened a part-time campus travel agency. In the first six months they had about $100,000 of revenue and made $6,000 of profit but were unable to pay themselves any salary. In that way, they acquired experience at no expense and at low risk. Upon graduation, one of them made it his full-time business. In 1994, the business had sales revenue of almost $8 million.

Resources

It's hard to believe that Olsen and Anderson started DEC with only $70,000 of startup capital and built a company ranked in the top 25 of the *Fortune* 500 companies. "The nice thing about $70,000 is that there are so few of them, you can watch every one," Olsen said. And watch them he did. Olsen and Anderson moved into a 100-year-old building that had been a nineteenth-century woollen mill. They furnished it with second-hand furniture, purchased tools from the Sears catalog, and built much of their own equipment as cheaply as possible. They sold $94,000 worth in their first year and made a profit at the same time—a very rare feat indeed for a high-tech startup.

Successful entrepreneurs are frugal with their scarce resources. They keep overheads low, productivity high, and ownership of capital assets to a minimum. By so doing they minimize the amount of capital they need to start their business and make it grow. One quarter of the *Inc.* 500 small business stars began with less than $5,000 of capital, half with less than $25,000, and three-quarters with less than $100,000. Fewer than 5% began with more than $1 million.

Entrepreneurial frugality is:

- Low overhead.
- High productivity.
- Minimal ownership of capital assets.

Determining Resource Needs and Acquiring Resources

In order to determine the amount of capital that a company needs to get started, an entrepreneur must determine the minimum set of essential resources. Some resources are more critical than others. The first thing an entrepreneur should do is assess what resources are crucial for the company's success in the marketplace. What does the company expect to do better than any of its competitors? That is where it should put a disproportionate share of its very scarce resources. If the company is making a new high-tech product, technological know-how will be vital. Then its most important resource will be engineers and the designs they produce. Therefore, the company must concentrate on recruiting and keeping excellent engineers, and safeguarding the intellectual property that they produce, such as engineering designs and patents. If the company is doing retail selling, the critical factor is most likely to be location. It makes no sense to choose a site in a poor location just because the rent is cheap. Choosing the wrong initial location for a retail store can be a fatal mistake, because it's unlikely that there will be enough resources to relocate.

When Southwest Airlines started up 25 years ago, its strategy was to provide frequent, on-time service at a competitive price between Dallas, Houston, Austin, and San Antonio. To meet its objectives, Southwest needed planes that it could operate reliably at low cost. It was able to purchase four brand-new Boeing 737s—very efficient planes for shorter routes—for only $4 million each because the recession had hit the airlines particularly hard and Boeing had an inventory of unsold 737s. From the outset, Southwest provided good, reliable service and had one of the lowest costs per mile in the industry. Today, Southwest is the most successful domestic airline, while two of its biggest competitors when it started out, Braniff International and Texas International, have gone bankrupt.

Items that are not critical should be obtained as thriftily as possible. The founder of Burlington Coat, Monroe Milstein, likes to tell the story of how he obtained estimates for gutting the building he had just leased for his second store. His lowest bid was several thousand dollars. One day he was at the building when a sudden thunderstorm sent a crew of laborers working at a nearby site to his building for shelter from the rain. Milstein asked the crew's foreman what they would charge for knocking down the internal structures that needed to be removed. The foreman said, "Five." Milstein asked, "Five what?" The foreman replied, "Cases of beer."

A complete set of resources includes everything that the business will need. A key point to remember when deciding to acquire those resources is that a business does not have to do all its work in-house with its own employees. It is often more effective to subcontract the work. That way it need not own or lease its own manufacturing plant and equipment. Nor does it have to worry about recruiting and training production workers. Often, it can keep overhead lower by using outside firms to do work such as payroll, accounting, advertising, mailing promotions, janitorial services, and so on.

Even startup companies can get amazingly good terms from outside suppliers. An entrepreneur should try to understand the potential suppliers' marginal costs. Marginal cost is the cost of producing one extra unit beyond what is presently produced. The marginal cost of the laborers who gutted Milstein's building while sheltering from the rain was virtually zero. They were being paid by another firm, and they didn't have to buy materials or tools.

A small electronics company was acquired by a much larger competitor. The large company took over the manufacturing of the small company's products. Production costs shot up. An analysis revealed that much of the increase was due to a rise in the cost of purchased components. In one instance, the large company was paying 50% more than the small company had been paying for the same item. It turned out that the supplier had priced the item for the small company on the basis of marginal costs and for the large company on the basis of total costs.

Smart entrepreneurs find ways of controlling critical resources without owning them. A startup business never has enough money. It should not buy what it can lease. It must be resourceful. Except when the economy is red hot, there is almost always an excess of capacity of office and industrial space. Sometimes a landlord will be willing to offer a special deal to attract even a small startup company into a building. Such deals may include reduced rent, deferral of rent payments for a period of time, and building improvements at low cost or even no cost. In some high-tech regions, there are landlords who will exchange rent for equity in a high-potential startup.

When equipment is in excess supply, it can be leased on very favorable terms. A young database company was negotiating a lease with IBM for a new minicomputer when its chief engineer discovered that a leasing company had identical secondhand units standing idle in its warehouse. It was able to lease one of the idle units for one-third of IBM's price. About 18 months later, the database company ran out of cash. Nevertheless, it was able to persuade the leasing company to defer payments, because by then there were even more minicomputers standing idle in the warehouse, and it made little economic sense to repossess one and add it to the idle stock.

Startup Capital

You have reached the point where you have developed your idea; you have carefully assessed what resources you will need to open your business and make it grow; you have pulled all your strategies together into a business plan; and now you know how much startup capital you will need to get you to the point where your business will generate a positive cash flow. How are you going to raise that startup capital?

There are two types of startup capital: debt and equity. Simply put, with debt you don't have to give up any ownership of the business, but you have to pay current interest and eventually repay the principal; with equity you have to give up some of the ownership to get it, but you may never have to repay it or even pay a dividend. So you must choose between paying interest and giving up some of the ownership.

What usually happens, in practice, depends on how much of each type of capital you can raise. Most startup entrepreneurs do not have much flexibility in their choice of financing. If it is a very risky business without any assets, it will be impossible to get any bank debt without putting up some collateral other than the business's assets—most likely that collateral will be personal assets. Even if entrepreneurs are willing to guarantee the whole loan with their personal assets, the bank will expect them to put some equity into the business, probably equal to 25% of the amount of the loan.

The vast majority of entrepreneurs start their businesses by leveraging their own savings and labor. Consider how Apple, one of the most spectacular startups of all time, was funded. Steven Jobs and Stephan Wozniak had been friends since their school days in Silicon Valley. Wozniak was an authentic computer nerd. He had tinkered with computers from childhood, and he built a computer that won first prize in a science fair. His SAT math score was a perfect 800, but after stints at the University of Colorado, De Anza College, and Berkeley, he dropped out of school and went to work for Hewlett-Packard. His partner, Jobs, had an even briefer encounter with higher education: After one semester at Reed College, he left to look for a swami in India. When he and Wozniak began working on their microcomputer, Jobs was working at Atari, the leading video game company.

Apple soon outgrew its manufacturing facility in the garage of Jobs's parents' house. Their company, financed initially with $1,300 raised by selling Jobs's Volkswagen and Wozniak's calculator, needed capital for expansion. They looked to their employers for help. Wozniak proposed to his supervisor that Hewlett-Packard should produce what later became the Apple II. Perhaps not surprisingly, he was rejected. After all, he had no formal qualification in computer design; indeed, he did not even have a college degree. At Atari, Jobs tried to convince founder Nolan Bushnell to manufacture Apples. He too was rejected.

However, on the suggestion of Bushnell and Regis McKenna, a Silicon Valley marketing ace, they contacted Don Valentine, a venture capitalist in the fall of 1976. In those days, Jobs's appearance was a hangover from his swami days. It definitely did not project the image of Doriot's grade A man, even by Silicon Valley's casual standards. Valentine did not invest. But he did put them in touch with Armas Markkula, Jr., who had recently retired from Intel a wealthy man. Markkula saw the potential in Apple, and he knew how to raise money. He personally invested $91,000, secured a line of credit from Bank of America, put together a business plan, and raised $600,000 of venture capital.

The Apple II was formally introduced in April 1977. Sales took off almost at once. Apple's sales grew rapidly to $2.5 million in 1977 and $15 million in 1978. In 1978, Dan Bricklin, a Harvard business student and former programmer at DEC, introduced the first electronic spreadsheet, VisiCalc, designed for the Apple II. In minutes it could do tasks that had previously taken days. The microcomputer now had the power to liberate managers from the data guardians in the computer departments. According to one source, "Armed with VisiCalc, the Apple II's sales took off, and the personal computer industry was created." Apple's sales jumped to $70 million in 1979 and $117 million in 1980.

In 1980, Apple sold some of its stock to the public with an initial public offering (IPO) and raised more than $80 million. The paper value of their Apple stock made instant millionaires out of Jobs ($165 million), Markkula ($154 million), Wozniak ($88 million), and Mike Scott ($62 million), who together owned 40% of Apple. Arthur Rock's venture capital investment of $57,000 in 1978 was suddenly worth $14 million, an astronomical compound return of more than 500% per year, or 17% per month.

By 1982, Apple IIs were selling at the rate of more than 33,000 units a month. With 1982 sales of $583 million, Apple hit the *Fortune* 500 list. It was a record. At five years of age, it was at that time the youngest company ever to join that exclusive list.

Success as spectacular as Apple's has seldom been equaled. Nonetheless, its financing is a typical example of how successful high-tech companies are funded. First, the entrepreneurs develop a prototype with sweat equity and personal savings. Sweat equity is ownership earned in lieu of wages. Then a wealthy investor—sometimes called an informal investor or business angel— who knows something about the entrepreneurs, or the industry, or both, invests some personal money in return for equity. When the company is selling

EXHIBIT 1.4   Sources of seed capital for the *Inc.* 500.

Personal savings	78.5%
Bank loans	14.4
Family members	12.9
Employees/partners	12.4
Friends	9.0
Venture capital	6.3
Mortgaged property	4.0
Government guaranteed loans	1.1
Other	3.3

Source: Inc., October 1992.

product, it may be able to get a bank line of credit secured by its inventory and accounts receivable. If the company is growing quickly in a large market, it may be able to raise capital from a formal venture capital firm in return for equity. Further expansion capital may come from venture capital firms or from a public stock offering.

Most new firms will never be candidates for formal venture capital or a public stock offering. Nevertheless, they will have to find some equity capital. In most cases, after they have exhausted their personal savings, entrepreneurs will turn to family, friends, and acquaintances (see Exhibit 1.4). It can be a scary business. Entrepreneurs often find themselves with all their personal net worth tied up in the same business that provides all their income. That is double jeopardy, because if their businesses fail, they lose both their savings and their means of support. Risk of that sort can be justified only if the profit potential is high enough to yield a commensurate rate of return.

Profit Potential

The level of profit that is reasonable depends on the type of business. On average, U.S. companies make about 5% net income. Hence, on one dollar of revenue, the average company makes five cents profit after paying all expenses and taxes. A company that consistently makes 10% is doing very well, and one that makes 15% is truly exceptional. Approximately 50% of the *Inc.* 500 companies make 5% or less; 13% of them make 16% or more. Profit margins in a wide variety of industries for companies both large and small are published by Robert Morris Associates. Hence it is possible for entrepreneurs to compare their forecasts with the actual performance of similar-sized companies in the same industry.

Any business must make enough profit to recompense its investors (in most cases that is the entrepreneur) for their investment. It must be profit after all normal business expenses have been accounted for, including a fair salary for the entrepreneur and any family members who are working in the business. A common error in assessing the profitability of a new venture is to ignore the owner's salary. Suppose someone leaves a secure job paying $50,000 per year plus fringe benefits and invests $100,000 of personal savings to start a new venture. That person should expect to take a $50,000 salary plus fringe benefits out of the new business. Perhaps in the first year or two, when the business is being built, it may not be possible to pay $50,000 in actual cash; in that case, the pay that is not actually received should be treated as deferred compensation to be paid in the future. In addition to an adequate salary, the entrepreneur must also earn a reasonable return on the $100,000 investment. A professional investor putting money into a new, risky business would expect to earn an annual rate of return of at least 40%, which would be $40,000 annually on a $100,000 investment. That return may come as a capital gain when the business is sold, or as a dividend, or a combination of the two. But remember that $100,000 compounding annually at 40% grows to almost $2.9 million in 10 years. When such large capital gains are needed to produce acceptable returns, big capital investments held for a long time do not make any sense unless very substantial value can be created, as occasionally happens in the case of high-flying companies, especially high-tech ones. In most cases, instead of a capital gain, the investor's return will be a dividend, which must be paid out of the cash flow from the business.

The cash flow that a business generates is not to be confused with profit. It is possible, indeed very likely, that a rapidly growing business will have a negative cash flow from operations in its early years even though it may be profitable. That may happen because the business may not be able to generate enough cash flow internally to sustain its ever-growing needs for working capital and the purchase of long-term assets such as plant and equipment. Hence, it will have to borrow or raise new equity capital. So it is very important that a high-potential business intending to grow rapidly make careful cash-flow projections so as to predict its needs for future outside investments. Future equity investments will dilute the percentage ownership of the founders, and if the dilution becomes excessive, there may be little reward remaining for the entrepreneurs.

Biotechnology companies are examples of this; they have a seemingly insatiable need for cash infusions to sustain their R&D costs in their early years. Their negative cash flow, or *burn rate*, sometimes runs at $1 million per month. A biotechnology company can easily burn up $50 million before it generates a meaningful profit, let alone a positive cash flow. The expected future capital gain from a public stock offering or sale to a large pharmaceutical company has to run into hundreds of millions of dollars, maybe into the billion-dollar range, for investors to realize an annual return of 50% or higher, which is what they expect to earn on money invested in a seed-stage biotechnology company. Not surprisingly, to finance their ventures biotechnology entrepreneurs as a group have to give up most of the ownership. A recent study of venture-capital-backed biotechnology companies found that after they had gone public, the entrepreneurs and management were left with less than 18% of the equity, compared with 32% for a comparable group of computer software companies.

As has already been mentioned, the vast majority of businesses will never have the potential to go public. Nor will the owners ever intend to sell their businesses and thereby realize a capital gain. In that case, how can those owners get a satisfactory return on the money they have invested in their businesses? The two ingredients that determine return on investment are (1) amount invested, and (2) annual amount earned on that investment. Hence, entrepreneurs should invest as little as possible to start their businesses and make sure that their firms will be able to pay them a "dividend" big enough to yield an appropriate annual rate of return. For income tax purposes, that "dividend" may be in the form of a salary bonus or fringe benefits rather than an actual dividend paid out of retained earnings. Of course, the company must be generating cash from its own operations before that dividend can be paid. For entrepreneurs, happiness is a positive cash flow. The day a company begins to generate cash is a very happy day in the life of a successful entrepreneur.

For entrepreneurs, happiness is a positive cash flow.

INGREDIENTS FOR A SUCCESSFUL NEW BUSINESS

The great day has arrived. You found an idea, wrote a business plan, and gathered your resources. Now you are opening the doors of your new business for the first time, and the really hard work is about to begin. What are the factors that distinguish winning entrepreneurial businesses from the also-rans? Rosabeth Kanter prescribed Four Fs for a successful business, a list that has been expanded into the Nine Fs for entrepreneurial success (see Exhibit 1.5).

First and foremost, the founding entrepreneur is the most important factor. Next comes the market. This is the "era of the other," in which, as Regis McKenna observed, the fastest-growing companies in an industry will be in a segment labeled "others" in a market share pie-chart. By and large, they will be newer entrepreneurial firms rather than large firms with household names; hence specialization is the key. A successful business should focus on niche markets.

EXHIBIT 1.5   The Nine Fs.

Founders	Every startup company must have a first-class entrepreneur.
Focused	Entrepreneurial companies focus on niche markets. They specialize.
Fast	They make decisions quickly and implement them swiftly.
Flexible	They keep an open mind. They respond to change.
Forever-innovating	They are tireless innovators.
Flat	Entrepreneurial organizations have as few layers of management as possible.
Frugal	By keeping overhead low and productivity high, entrepreneurial organizations keep costs down.
Friendly	Entrepreneurial companies are friendly to their customers, suppliers, and workers.
Fun	It's fun to be associated with an entrepreneurial company.

The rate of change in business gets ever faster. The advanced industrial economies are knowledge based. Product life cycles are getting shorter. Technological innovation progresses at a relentless pace. Government rules and regulations keep changing. Communications and travel around the globe keep getting easier and cheaper. And consumers are better informed about their choices. To survive, let alone succeed, in business, a company has to be quick and nimble. It must be fast and flexible. It cannot allow inertia to build up. Look at retailing: The historical giants such as Kmart are on the ropes, while nimble competitors dance around them. Three of the biggest retailing successes are Les Wexner's The Limited, the late Sam Walton's Wal-Mart, and Anita Roddick's The Body Shop. Entrepreneurs such as those know that they can keep inertia low by keeping the layers of management as few as possible. Tom Peters, an authority on business strategy, liked to point out that Wal-Mart had three layers of management, whereas Sears had ten a few years back when Wal-Mart displaced Sears as the nation's top chain of department stores. "A company with three layers of management can't lose against a company with ten. You could try, but you couldn't do it!" says Peters. No wonder Ferdinand Piëch, when he became the new boss of Volkswagen, wanted to eliminate seven or eight levels of management as part of his effort to revive the profits of Europe's largest automobile manufacturer. So keep your organization flat. It will facilitate quick decisions and flexibility, and keep overhead low.

Small entrepreneurial firms are great innovators. Big firms are relying increasingly on strategic partnerships with entrepreneurial firms in order to get access to desirable R&D. It is a trend that is well under way. Hoffmann-La Roche, hurting for new blockbuster prescription drugs, purchased a majority interest in Genentech and bought the highly regarded biotechnology called PCR (polymerase chain reaction) from Cetus for $300 million. Eli Lilly purchased Hybritech. In the 1980s, IBM spent $9 billion a year on research and development, but even that astronomical amount of money could not sustain Big Blue's technological leadership. As its market share was remorselessly eaten away by thousands of upstarts, IBM entered into strategic agreements with Apple, Borland, Go, Lotus, Intel, Metaphor, Microsoft, Novell, Stratus, Thinking Machines, and other entrepreneurial firms for the purpose of gaining computer technologies.

Fifteen years ago, IBM stood astride the computer industry like a big blue giant. According to one survey, it was the most respected company in the world. Two suppliers of its personal computer division were Intel and Microsoft. In comparison with IBM, Intel was small and Microsoft was a midget. Today, Intel is ranked 5th on the list of most respected U.S. companies and Microsoft is 7th, with IBM a distant 168th. The combined market value of Microsoft and Intel handily exceeds the market value of IBM. Bill Gates, who was mistaken for an office boy when he first visited IBM in 1981 is the richest person in the United States with a net worth of $18 billion; Paul Allen, Microsoft's cofounder is the 4th richest person with $7.5 billion; and Steven Ballmer, Microsoft's executive vice president is 26th with $3.7 billion. Today, it is Microsoft's Windows 95 operating system and Intel's microprocessors—the so-called WINTEL—that are shaping the future of the computer and the communications industries.

When it comes to productivity, the best entrepreneurial companies leave the giant corporations behind in the dust. According to 1994 computer industry statistics, Compaq and Apple ranked first and second with productivity per employee of $872,300 and $647,000, compared to IBM's $269,000 and DEC's $177,100. No wonder Louis Gerstner of IBM and Robert Palmer of DEC have been busily downsizing their companies. Apple and Compaq subcontract more for their manufacturing, but this does not explain all the difference. Whether you hope to build a big company or a small one, the message is the same. Strive tirelessly to keep productivity high.

But no matter what you do, you probably won't be able to attain much success unless you have happy customers, happy workers, and happy suppliers. That means you must have a friendly company. It means that everyone must be friendly, especially anyone who deals with customers.

"The most fun six-month period I've had since the start of Microsoft," is how Bill Gates describes his astonishing accomplishment in re-inventing his 20-year-old company to meet the threat posed by Internet upstarts. In not much more than six months of Herculean effort, Microsoft has developed an impressive array of new products to match those of Netscape. Having fun is one of the keys to keeping a company entrepreneurial. If Microsoft's product developers were not having fun, they would not be putting in 12-hour days and sometimes overnighters to catch up with the Netscape.

Most new companies have the Nine Fs at the outset. Those that become successful and grow pay attention to keeping them and nurturing them. The key to sustaining success is to remain an entrepreneurial gazelle and never turn into a lumbering elephant and finally a dinosaur, doomed to extinction.

2 OPPORTUNITY RECOGNITION
Jeffry A. Timmons

If an idea is not an opportunity, what is an opportunity?[1] *An opportunity has the qualities of being attractive, durable, and timely and is anchored in a product or service which creates or adds value for its buyer or end user.*

For an opportunity to have these qualities, the "window of opportunity" is opening and remains open long enough. Further, entry into a market with the right characteristics is feasible and the management team is able to achieve it. The venture has or is able to achieve a competitive advantage (i.e., to achieve leverage). Finally, the economics of the venture are rewarding and forgiving and allow significant profit and growth potential.

To repeat, opportunities that have the qualities named above are anchored in a product or service that creates or adds value for its buyer or end user. The most successful entrepreneurs, venture capitalists, and private investors are opportunity-focused; that is, they start with what customers and the marketplace want and do not lose sight of this.

THE REAL WORLD

Opportunities are created, or built, using ideas and entrepreneurial creativity. Yet, while the image of a carpenter or mason at work is useful, in reality

This chapter was excerpted and modified from Jeffrey A. Timmons *New Venture Creation*, 4th ed. (Homewood, IL: Richard D. Irwin Press, 1994).

the process is more like the collision of particles in the process of a nuclear reaction or like the spawning of hurricanes over the ocean. Ideas interact with real-world conditions and entrepreneurial creativity at a point in time. The product of this interaction is an opportunity around which a new venture can be created.

The business environment in which an entrepreneur launches his or her venture is usually given and cannot be altered significantly. Despite the assumptions individuals make about social and nonprofit organizations, they too are subject to market forces and economic constraints. Consider, for instance, what would happen to donations if it were perceived that a nonprofit organization was not reinvesting its surplus returns, but instead was paying management excessive salaries. Or what if a society oriented organization, like the Body Shop, concentrated all its efforts on the social mission, while neglecting profits? Clearly, dealing with suppliers, production costs, labor, and distribution are critical to the health of these social corporations. Thus, social and nonprofit organizations are just as concerned with positive cash flow and generating sufficient cash flows, even though they operate in a different type of market than for-profit organizations. For-profit business operate in a free enterprise system characterized by private ownership and profits.

In a free enterprise system, *opportunities* are spawned when there are changing circumstances, chaos, confusion, inconsistencies, lags or leads, knowledge and information gaps, and a variety of other vacuums in an industry or market.

Changes in the business environment and, therefore, anticipation of these changes, are so critical in entrepreneurship that constant vigilance for changes is a valuable habit. It is thus that an entrepreneur with credibility, creativity, and decisiveness can seize an opportunity while others study it.

Opportunities are situational. Some conditions under which opportunities are spawned are entirely idiosyncratic, while, at other times, they are generalizable and can be applied to other industries, products, or services. In this way, cross-association can trigger in the entrepreneurial mind the crude recognition of existing or impending opportunities. It is often assumed that a marketplace dominated by large, multibillion-dollar players is impenetrable by smaller, entrepreneurial companies. After all, how can you possibly compete with entrenched, resource-rich, established companies? The opposite can be true for several reasons. A number of research projects have shown that it can take six years or more for a large company to change its strategy, and even longer to implement the new strategy since it can take 10 years and more to change the culture enough to operate differently. For a new or small company 10 or more years is forever. When Cellular One was launched in Boston, giant NYNEX was the sole competitor. From all estimates they built twice as many towers (at $500,000 each), spent two to three times as much on advertising and marketing, in addition to having a larger head-count. Yet, Cellular One grew from scratch to $100 million in sales in five years and won three customers for every one that NYNEX won. What made this substantial difference? An entrepreneurial management team at Cellular One.

Some of the most exciting opportunities have actually come from fields the conventional wisdom said are the domain of big business: technological innovation. The performance of smaller firms in technological innovation is remarkable—95% of the radical innovations since World War II have come from new and small firms, not the giants. In fact, another study from the National Science Foundation found that smaller firms generated *24 times as many innovations* per research and development dollar versus firms with 10,000 or more employees.

There can be exciting opportunities in plain vanilla businesses that might never get the attention of venture capital investors. The revolution in microcomputers, management information systems (MIS), and computer networking has had a profound impact on a number of businesses that had changed little in decades. Take, for instance, the used-auto-wreck and used-auto-parts business, which has not changed in decades. Yet, Pintendre Auto, Inc., saw a new opportunity in this field by applying the latest computer and information technology to a traditional business that relied on crude, manual methods to track inventory and find parts for customers.[2] In just three years, he built a business with $16 million in sales.

Other regulatory and technology changes can radically alter the way you think about the opportunities because of the economics of sales and distribution for many customer products, from fishing lures to books to cosmetics to sporting goods. By the mid-1990s, there will be 500 or so cable television channels in America versus 40 to 50 for most markets in 1993. A number of new companies up to $100 million in sales have already been built using "infomercials." A 30-minute program can be produced for $50,000 to $150,000 and a half hour of air time can be purchased today for about $20,000 in Los Angeles or for about $4,000 in smaller cities. Compare that with a $25,000+ cost of a full-page advertisement in a monthly magazine. With a large increase in the number of channels, the cost and market focus will undoubtedly improve. Traditional channels of distribution through distributors, wholesalers, specialty stores, and retailers will be completely leapfrogged. Entrepreneurs will find ways to convert those funds previously spent on the profit margin that went to the distribution channel (30% to 50%) to their infomercial marketing budget and to an increased gross margin for their business.

Consider the following broad range of examples that illustrate the phenomenon of vacuums in which opportunities are spawned:

- Deregulation of telecommunications and airlines led to the formation of tens of thousands of new firms in the 1980s, including Cellular One and Federal Express.

- Microcomputer hardware in the early 1980s far outpaced the development of software. The development of the industry was highly dependent on the development of software, leading to aggressive efforts by IBM, Apple, and others to encourage software entrepreneurs to close this gap.

- Many opportunities exist in fragmented, traditional industries that may have a craft or mom-and-pop character and where there is little appreciation or know-how in marketing and finance. Consider such possibilities as fishing lodges, inns, and hotels; cleaners/laundries; hardware stores; pharmacies; waste management plants; flower shops; nurseries; tents; and auto repairs.

- In our service-dominated economy (where 70% of businesses are service businesses, versus 30% just 25 years ago), customer service, rather than the product itself, can be the critical success factor. One study by the Forum Corporation in Boston showed that 70% of customers leave because of poor service and only 15% because of price or quality. Can you think of your last "wow" experience with exceptional customer service?

- Sometimes existing competitors cannot, or will not, increase capacity as quickly as the market is moving. For example, the tent industry was characterized by this capacity stickiness in the mid-1970s. In the late-1970s, some steel firms had a 90-week delivery lag, with the price to be determined, and foreign competitors certainly took notice.

- The tremendous shift to off-shore manufacturing of labor-intensive and transportation-insensitive products in Asia, Eastern Europe, and Mexico, such as computer-related and microprocessor-driven consumer products, is an excellent example.

- In a wide variety of industries, entrepreneurs sometimes find they are the only ones who can perform. Such fields as consulting, software design, financial services, process engineering, and technical and medical products and services abound with examples of know-how monopolies. Sometimes a management team is simply the best in an industry and irreplaceable in the near term, just as is seen with great coaches with winning records.

Big Opportunities with Little Capital

Within the dynamic free enterprise system, opportunities are apparent to a limited number of individuals—and not just to the individuals with financial resources. Ironically, successful entrepreneurs like Howard Head attribute their success to the discipline of limited capital resources. Thus, in the 1990s, many entrepreneurs have been learning the key to success is in the art of boot-strapping, which "in a start-up is like zero inventory in a just-in-time system: It reveals hidden problems and forces the company to solve them."[3] Consider the following:

- A 1991 study revealed that of the 100 start-ups researched, 77% had been launched with $50,000 or less; 46% were started with $10,000 or less as seed capital. Further, the primary source of capital was, overwhelmingly, personal savings (74%), rather than outside investors with deep pockets.[4]

- In the 1930s, Josephine Esther Mentzer assisted her uncle by selling skin care balm and quickly created her own products with $100 initial investment. After convincing the department stores rather than the drug stores to carry her products, Estee Lauder was on its way to a $3 billion corporation.[5]

- Putting their talents (cartooning and finance) together, Walt and Roy Disney moved to California and started their own film studio—with $290 in 1923. Today, the Walt Disney Co. has a market value exceeding $16 billion.[6]

- While working for a Chicago insurance company, a 24-year-old sent out 20,000 inquiries for a black newsletter. With 3,000 positive responses and $500, John Harold Johnson published *Jet* for the first time in 1942. In the 1990s, Johnson Publishing publishes various magazines, including *Ebony*.[7]

- With $100, Nicholas Graham, age 24, went to a local fabric store, picked out some patterns, and made $100 worth of ties. Having sold the ties to specialty shops, Graham was approached by Macy's to place his patterns on men's underwear. So Joe Boxer Corporation was born and "six months into Joe Boxer's second year, sales had already topped $1 million."[8]

Real Time

Opportunities exist or are created in real time and have what is called a *window of opportunity*. For an entrepreneur to seize an opportunity requires that the window be opening, not closing, and that it remain open long enough.

Exhibit 2.1 illustrates a window of opportunity for a generalized market. Markets grow at different rates over time and as a market quickly becomes larger, more and more opportunities are possible. As the market becomes larger and established, conditions are not as favorable. Thus, at the point where a market starts to become sufficiently large and structured (e.g., at 5 years in

EXHIBIT 2.1   Changes in the placement of the window of opportunity.

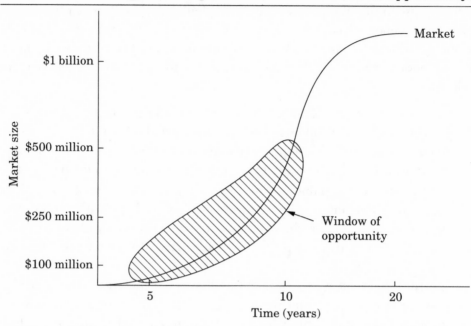

Exhibit 2.1), the window opens; the window begins to close as the market matures (e.g., at 15 years in the exhibit).

The curve shown describes the rapid growth pattern typical of such new industries as microcomputers and software, cellular car phones, quick oil changes, and biotechnology. For example, in the cellular car phone industry, most major cities began service between 1983 and 1984 for the very first time. By 1989, there were over 2 million subscribers in the United States, and the industry continued to experience significant growth. In other industries, such as a mature industry, where growth is not so rapid, the slope of a curve would be less steep and the possibilities for opportunities fewer.

Finally, in considering the window of opportunity, the length of time the window will be open is important. It takes a considerable length of time to determine whether a new venture is a success or a failure. And, if it is to be a success, the benefits of that success need to be harvested.

Exhibit 2.2 shows that for venture-capital-backed firms, the lemons (i.e., the losers) ripen in about two and a half years, while the pearls (i.e., the winners) take seven or eight years. An extreme example of the length of time it can take for a pearl to be harvested is the experience of a Silicon Valley venture capital firm that invested in a new firm in 1966 and was finally able to realize a capital gain in early 1984.

EXHIBIT 2.2   Lemons and pearls.

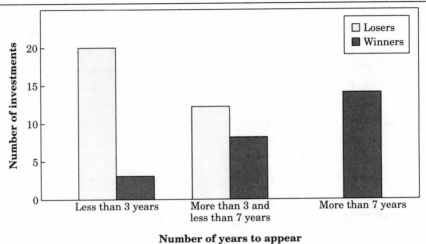

Another way to think of the process of creating and seizing an opportunity in real time can be thought of as a process of selecting objects (opportunities) from a conveyor belt moving through an open window, the window of opportunity. The speed of the conveyor belt changes, and the window through which it moves is constantly opening and closing. That the window is continually opening and closing and that the speed of the conveyor belt is constantly changing represent the volatile nature of the marketplace and the importance of timing. For an opportunity to be created and seized, it needs to be selected from the conveyor belt before the window closes.

The ability to recognize a potential opportunity when it appears and the sense of timing to seize it as the window is opening, rather than slamming shut, are critical. That opportunities are a function of real time is illustrated in a statement made by Ken Olsen, the president and founder of Digital Equipment Corporation, in 1977: "There is no reason for any individual to have a computer in their home." Nor is it so easy for even the world's leading experts to predict just which innovative ideas and concepts for new business will evolve into the major industries of tomorrow. This is vividly illustrated by several quotations from very famous innovators. In 1901, two years before the famous flight, Wilbur Wright said, "Man will not fly for 50 years." In 1910, Thomas Edison said, "The nickel-iron battery will put the gasoline buggy . . . out of existence in no time." And in 1932, Albert Einstein made it clear: "There is not the slightest indication that nuclear energy will ever be obtainable. It would mean that the atom would have to be shattered at will."

RELATION TO THE FRAMEWORK OF ANALYSIS

It is also important to remember that successful opportunities, once recognized, fit with the other forces of new venture creation. This iterative process of assessing and reassessing the fit among the central driving forces in the creation of a new venture was shown in Exhibit 1.3 in Chapter 1. Of utmost importance when talking of opportunity recognition is the fit of the lead entrepreneur and the management team with an opportunity. Good opportunities are both *desirable* to and *attainable* by those on the team using the resources that are available.

In order to understand how the entrepreneurial vision relates to the analytical framework, it may be useful to look at an opportunity as a three-dimensional relief map with its valleys, mountains, and so on, all represented. Each opportunity has three or four critical factors (e.g., proprietary license, patented innovation, sole distribution rights, an all-star management team, breakthrough technology). These elements pop out at the observer; they indicate huge possibilities where others might see obstacles. Thus, it is easy to see why there are thousands of exceptional opportunities that will fit with a wide variety of entrepreneurs, but that might not fit neatly into the framework outlined in Exhibit 2.3.

EXHIBIT 2.3   Criteria for evaluating venture opportunities.

Criteria	Attractiveness	
	Highest potential	**Lowest potential**
Industry and market	Changes way people live and work	Incremental improvement only
Market:	Market driven; identified; recurring revenue niche	Unfocused; one-time revenue
Customers	Reachable; purchase orders	Loyal to others or unreachable
User benefits	Less than one-year payback	Three years plus payback
Value added	High; advance payments	Low; minimal impact on market
Product life	Durable	Perishable
Market structure	Imperfect, fragmented competition or emerging in industry	Highly concentrated or mature or declining industry
Market size	$100 million to $1 billion sales potential	Unknown, less than $20 million or multibillion sales
Growth rate	Growth at 30–50% or more	Contracting or less than 10%
Market capacity	At or near full capacity	Undercapacity
Market share attainable (Year 5)	20% or more; leader	Less than 5%
Cost structure	Low-cost provider; cost advantages	Declining cost

EXHIBIT 2.3 *(Continued)*

Criteria	Attractiveness	
	Highest potential	**Lowest potential**
Economics		
Time to breakeven/positive cashflow	Under 1½–2 years	More than 4 years
ROI potential	25% or more; high value	Less than 15–20%; low value
Capital requirements	Low to moderate; fundable	Very high; unfundable
Internal rate of return potential	25% or more per year	Less than 15% per year
Free cash flow characteristics:	Favorable; sustainable; 20–30% or more of sales	Less than 10% of sales
Sales growth	Moderate to high (+15% to +20%)	Less than 10%
Asset intensity	Low/sales $	High
Spontaneous working capital	Low, incremental requirements	High requirements
R&D/capital expenditures	Low requirements	High requirements
Gross margins	Exceeding 40% and durable	Under 20%
After-tax profits	High; greater than 10%; durable	Low
Time to break-even profit and loss	Less than two years; breakeven not creeping	Greater than four years; breakeven creeping up
Harvest issues		
Value-added potential	High strategic value	Low strategic value
Valuation multiples and comparables	20 × P/E; 8 − 10 × EBIT; 1.5 − 2 × revenue; 8 − 10 × free cash flow	≤ 5 × P/E; 3 − 4 × EBIT; ≤ .4 × revenue
Exit mechanism and strategy	Present or envisioned options	Undefined; illiquid investment
Capital market context	Favorable valuations, timing, capital available; realizable liquidity	Unfavorable; credit crunch
Competitive advantage issues		
Fixed and variable costs	Lowest; high operating leverage	Highest
Control over costs, prices, and distribution	Moderate to strong	Weak
Barriers to entry:		
Proprietary protection	Have or can gain	None
Response/lead time	Competition slow, napping	Unable to gain edge
Legal, contractual advantage	Proprietary or exclusivity	None
Contracts and networks	Well-developed; accessible	Crude; limited
Key people	Top talent; an A team	B or C team

(Continued)

EXHIBIT 2.3   *(Continued)*

	Attractiveness	
Criteria	**Highest potential**	**Lowest potential**
Management team		
Entrepreneurial team	All-star combination; free agents	Weak or solo entrepreneur
Industry and technical experience	Top of the field; super track-record	Underdeveloped
Integrity	Highest standards	Questionable
Intellectual honesty	Know what they do not know	Do not want to know what they do not know
Fatal-flaw issue	Non-existent	One or more
Personal criteria		
Goals and fit	Getting what you want; but wanting what you get.	Surprises, as in *The Crying Game*
Upside/downside issues	Attainable success/limited risks	Linear; on same continuum
Opportunity costs	Acceptable cuts in salary, etc.	Comfortable with status quo
Desirability	Fits with lifestyle	Simply pursuing big money
Risk/reward tolerance	Calculated risk; low risk/reward ratio	Risk adverse or gambler
Stress tolerance	Thrives under pressure	Cracks under pressure
Strategic differentiation		
Degree of fit	High	Low
Team	Best in class; excellent free agents	B team; no free agents
Service management	Superior service concept	Perceived as unimportant
Timing	Rowing with the tide	Rowing against the tide
Technology	Groundbreaking; one of a kind	Many substitutes or competitors
Flexibility	Able to adapt; commit and decommit quickly	Slow; stubborn
Opportunity orientation	Always searching for opportunities	Operating in a vacuum; napping
Pricing	At or near leader	Undercut competitor; low prices
Distribution channels	Accessible; networks in place	Unknown; inaccessible
Room for error	Forgiving strategy	Unforgiving, rigid strategy

SCREENING OPPORTUNITIES

Opportunity Focus

Opportunity focus is also the most fruitful point of departure for screening opportunities. The screening process should not begin with strategy (which derives from the nature of the opportunity), with financial and spreadsheet analysis (which flow from the former), or with estimations of how much the company is worth and who will own what shares.[9]

These starting points, and others, usually place the cart before the horse. Perhaps the best evidence of this phenomenon comes from the tens of thousands of tax-sheltered investments that turned sour in the mid-1980s. Also, as has been noted, a good number of entrepreneurs who start businesses—particularly those for whom the ventures are their first—run out of cash at a faster rate than they bring in customers and profitable sales. There are lots of reasons why this happens, but one thing is certain: These entrepreneurs have not focused on the right opportunity.

Over the years, those with experience in business and in specific market areas have developed rules of thumb to guide them in screening opportunities. For example, one such rule of thumb was used by a firm with approximately $1 billion in sales in evaluating start-ups in the minicomputer industry in the mid-1980s. This firm believed, based on an analysis of performance data relating to 60 computer-related start-ups in the United States from 1975 to 1984, that one leading indicator of the progress of new firms and a good boundary measure of positive performance and a healthy start was sales per employee of $75,000 or more. To this firm, sales of less than $50,000 per employee signaled serious trouble. While there is always the risk of oversimplification in using rules of thumb, it is true also that one can miss the fundamentals while searching for subtleties.

Screening Criteria: The Characteristics of High-Potential Ventures

Venture capitalists, savvy entrepreneurs, and investors also use this concept of boundaries in screening ventures. Exhibit 2.3 summarizes criteria used by venture capitalists to evaluate opportunities. These criteria are used by this group to evaluate a select group of opportunities that tend to have a high-technology bias. As will be seen later, venture capital investors reject 60% to 70% of the new ventures presented to them very early in the review process, based on how the entrepreneurs satisfy these criteria.

However, these criteria are not the exclusive domain of venture capitalists. The criteria are based on plain good business sense that is used by successful entrepreneurs, private investors, and venture capitalists. Consider the following examples of great little companies built without a dime of professional venture capital:

- Paul Tobin, who built Cellular One in eastern Massachusetts from ground zero to $100 million in revenue in five years, has started Roamer Plus with less than $300,000 of internally generated funds from other ventures. Within two years, it grew to a $15 million annual sales rate and was very profitable.

- Another entrepreneur started a small specialty publishing company with minimal capital and grew it to over $12 million in highly profitable sales by 1987. While looking for acquisitions, he discovered that valuations were at an all-time high. Instead of buying, he decided to sell. In 1988, he sold his small firm for over $70 million.

- Morris Alper & Sons was a third-generation, small, traditional food brokerage business with around 40 employees when the founder's grandson joined the firm in the early 1970s. By 1993, financed entirely by internally generated cash flow, they have grown to nearly 350 employees. The company has become an integrated marketing services firm whose clients are 70 of the largest consumer food product companies in North America.

- In 1983, Charlie Butcher, at age 66, had to decide whether to buy out an equal partner in his 100-year-old industrial polish and wax business with less than $10 million in sales. This niche business had high gross margins, very low working capital and fixed-asset requirements for increased sales, substantial steady growth of over 18 percent per year, and excellent products. The result was a business with very high free cash flow and potential for growth. He acquired the company with a bank loan and seller financing, and then he increased sales to over $50 million by 1993. The company continues to be highly profitable. Charlie vows never to utilize venture capital money or to take the company public.

The point of departure here is opportunity and, implicitly, the customer, the market-place, and the industry. Exhibit 2.3 shows how higher and lower potential opportunities can be placed along an attractiveness scale. The criteria provide some quantitative way in which an entrepreneur can make judgments about industry and market issues, competitive advantage issues, economic and harvest issues, management team issues, and fatal flaw issues and whether these add up to a compelling opportunity. For example, *dominant* strength in any one of these criteria can readily translate into a winning entry, whereas a flaw in any one can be fatal.

Entrepreneurs contemplating opportunities that will yield attractive companies, not high-potential ventures, can also benefit from paying attention to these criteria. These entrepreneurs will then be in a better position to decide how these criteria can be compromised. As outlined in Exhibit 2.3, business opportunities with the greatest potential will possess many of the following, or they will so dominate in one or a few that the competition cannot come close.

Industry and Market Issues

Market

Higher potential businesses can identify a market niche for a product or service that meets an important customer need and provides high value-added or value-created benefits to customers. Customers are reachable and receptive to the product or service, with no brand or other loyalties. The potential payback to the user or customer of a given product or service through cost savings or other value-added or value-created properties is one year or less and is identifiable, repeatable, and verifiable. Further, the life of the product or service exists beyond the time needed to recover the investment, plus a profit. And the company is able to expand beyond a one-product company. Take, for example, the growing success of cellular car phone service. At prevailing rates, one can talk for about $25 an hour, and many providers of professional services can readily bill more than the $25 an hour for what would otherwise be unused time. If benefits to customers cannot be calculated in such dollar terms, then the market potential is far more difficult and risky to ascertain.

Lower potential opportunities are unfocused regarding customer need, and customers are unreachable and/or have brand or other loyalties to others. A payback to the user of more than three years and a low value added or created also makes an opportunity unattractive. Being unable to expand beyond a one-product company also can make for a lower potential opportunity. The failure of one of the first portable computer companies, Osborne Computer, is a good example of this.

Market structure

Market structure, such as evidenced by the number of sellers, size distribution of sellers, whether products are differentiated, conditions of entry and exit, number of buyers, cost conditions, and sensitivity of demand to changes in price, are significant.

A fragmented, imperfect market or emerging industry often contains vacuums and asymmetries that create unfilled market niches—for example, markets where resource ownership, cost advantages, and the like can be achieved. In addition, those where information or knowledge gaps exist and where competition is profitable, but not so strong as to be overwhelming, are attractive. An example of a market with an information gap is that of the experience a Boston entrepreneur encountered with a large New York company that wanted to dispose of a small, old office building in downtown Boston. This office building, because its book value was about $200,000, was viewed by the financially oriented firm as a low-value asset, and the company wanted to dispose of it so the resulting cash could be put to work for a higher return. The buyer, who had done more homework than the out-of-town sellers, bought the building for $200,000 and resold it in less than six months for over $8 million.

Industries that are highly concentrated, that are perfectly competitive, or that are mature or declining industries are typically unattractive. The capital requirements and costs to achieve distribution and marketing presence can be prohibitive, and such behavior as price cutting and other competitive strategies in highly concentrated markets can be a significant barrier to entry. (The most blatant example is organized crime and its life-threatening actions when territories are invaded.) Yet, revenge by normal competitors who are well-positioned through product strategy, legal tactics, and the like, also can be punishing to the pocketbook.

The airline industry, after deregulation, is an example of a perfectly competitive market and one where many of the recent entrants will have difficulty. The unattractiveness of perfectly competitive industries is captured by the comment of prominent Boston venture capitalist William Egan, who put it this way: "I want to be in a nonauction market."[10]

Market size

An attractive new venture sells to a market that is large and growing (i.e., one where capturing a small market share can represent significant and increasing sales volume). A minimum market size of over $100 million in sales is attractive. Such a market size means it is possible to achieve significant sales by capturing roughly 5% or less and thus not threatening competitors. For example, to achieve a sales level of $1 million in a $100 million market requires capturing only 1% of the market. Thus, a recreational equipment manufacturer entered a $60 million market that was expected to grow at 20% per year to over $100 million by the third year. The founders were able to create a substantial smaller company without obtaining a major market share and possibly incurring the wrath of existing competitors.

However, such a market can be too large. A multibillion-dollar market may be too mature and stable, and such a level of certainty can translate into competition from *Fortune* 500 firms and, if highly competitive, into lower margins and profitability. Further, an unknown market or one that is less than $10 million in sales also is unattractive. To understand the disadvantage of a large, more mature market, consider the entry of a firm into the microcomputer industry today versus the entry of Apple Computer into that market in 1975.

Growth rate

An attractive market is large and growing (i.e., one where capturing a good share of the increase is less threatening to competitors and where a small market share can represent significant and increasing sales volume). An annual growth rate of 30% to 50% creates new niches for new entrants, and such a market is a thriving and expansive one, rather than a stable or contracting one, where competitors are scrambling for the same niches. Thus, for example, a $100 million market growing at 50% per year has the potential to become a $1 billion industry in a few years, and if a new venture is able to capture just 2% of sales in the first year, it can attain sales in the first year of $1 million. If it just maintains its market share over the next few years, sales will grow significantly.

Market capacity

Another signal of the existence of an opportunity is a market is a market at full capacity in a growth situation—in other words, a demand that the existing suppliers cannot meet. Timing is of vital concern in such a situation, which means the entrepreneur should be asking himself or herself: Can a new entrant fill that demand before the other players can decide to and then actually increase capacity?

Market share attainable

The potential to be a leader in the market and capture at least a 20% share of the market is important. The potential to be a leader in the market and capture at least 20% can create a very high value for a company that might otherwise be worth not much more than book value. For example, one such firm, with less than $15 million in sales, became the dominant factor in its small market niche with a 70% market share. The company was acquired for $23 million in cash.

A firm that will be able to capture less than 5% of a market is unattractive in the eyes of most investors seeking a higher potential company.

Cost structure

A firm that can become the low-cost provider is attractive, but a firm that continually faces declining cost conditions is less so. Attractive opportunities exist in industries where economies of scale are insignificant (or work to the advantage of the new venture). Attractive opportunities boast of low costs of learning by doing. Where costs per unit are high when small amounts of the product are sold, existing firms that have low promotion costs can face attractive market opportunities.

For instance, consider the operating leverage of Johnsonville Sausage. Their variable costs were 6% labor and 94% materials. What aggressive incentives could management put in place for the 6% to manage and to control the 94%? Imagine the disasters that would occur if the scenario were reversed!

A word of caution from Scott W. Kunkel and Charles W. Hofer, who observed that

> Overall, industry structure . . . had a much smaller impact on new venture performance than has previously been suggested in the literature. This finding could be the result of one of several possibilities:
>
> 1. Industry structure impacts the performance of established firms, but does NOT have a significant impact on new venture performance.
> 2. The most important industry structural variables influencing new ventures are different from those which impact established firms and thus research has yet to identify the industry structural variables that are most important in the new venture environment.
> 3. Industry structure does NOT have a significant DIRECT impact on firm performance, as hypothesized by scholars in the three fields of study. Instead, the impact of industry structure is strongly mitigated by other factors, including the strategy selected for entry.[11]

Economics

Profits after tax
High and durable gross margins usually translate into strong and durable after-tax profits. Attractive opportunities have potential for durable profits of at least 10% to 15%, and often 15% to 20% or more. Those generating after-tax profits of less than 5% are quite fragile.

Time to breakeven and positive cash flow
As mentioned above, breakeven and positive cash flow for attractive companies are possible within two years. Once the time to breakeven and positive cash flow is greater than three years, the attractiveness of the opportunity diminishes accordingly.

ROI potential
An important corollary to forgiving economics is reward. Very attractive opportunities have the potential to yield a return on investment of 25% or more per year. After all, during the 1980s, many venture capital funds achieved only single-digit returns on investment. High and durable gross margins and high and durable after-tax profits usually yield high earnings per share and high return on stockholders' equity, thus generating a satisfactory "harvest" price for a company. This is most likely true whether the company is sold

through an initial public offering or privately or whether it is acquired. Given the risk typically involved, a return on investment potential of less than 15% to 20% per year is unattractive.

Capital requirements

Ventures that can be funded and have capital requirements that are low to moderate are attractive. Realistically, most higher potential businesses need significant amounts of cash—several hundred thousand dollars and up—to get started. However, a business that can be started with little or no capital is rare, but they do exist. One such venture was launched in Boston in 1971 with $7,500 of the founder's capital and grew to over $30 million in sales by 1989. In today's venture capital market, the first round of financing is typically $1 million to $2 million or more for a start-up.[12] Some higher potential ventures, such as those in the service sector or "cash sales" businesses, have lower capital requirements than do high-technology manufacturing firms with continual large research and development expenditures.

If the venture needs too much money or cannot be funded, it is unattractive. An extreme example is a venture that a team of students recently proposed to repair satellites. The students believed that the required start-up capital was in the $50 million to $200 million range. Projects of this magnitude are in the domain of the government and the very large corporation, rather than that of entrepreneurs and venture capitalists.

Internal rate of return potential

Is the risk reward relationship attractive enough? The response to this question can be quite personal, but the most attractive opportunities often have the promise—and deliver—a very substantial upside of 5 to 10 times the original investment in 5 to 10 years. Of course, the extraordinary successes can yield 50 to 100 times or more, but these truly are exceptions. A 25% or more annual compound rate of return is considered very healthy. In the early 1990s, those investments considered basically risk free had yields of 3% to 8%.

Free cash flow characteristics[13]

Free cash flow is a way of understanding a number of crucial financial dimensions of any business: the robustness of its economics; its capital requirements, both working and fixed assets; its capacity to service external debt and equity claims; and its capacity to sustain growth. We define unlevered free cash flow (FCF) as earnings before interest but after taxes (EBIAT) *plus* amortization (A) and depreciation (D) *less* spontaneous working capital requirements (WC) *less* capital expenditures (CAPex), or FCF = EBIAT + [A + D] − [+ or − WC] − CAPex. EBIAT is driven by sales, profitability, and asset intensity.

Low-asset-intensive, high-margin businesses generate the highest profits and sustainable growth.[14]

Gross margins

The potential for high and durable gross margins (i.e., the unit selling price less all direct and variable costs) is important. Gross margins exceeding 40% to 50% provide a tremendous built-in cushion that allows for more error and more flexibility to learn from mistakes than do gross margins of 20% or less. High and durable gross margins, in turn, mean that a venture can reach breakeven earlier, an event that preferably occurs within the first two years. Thus, for example, if gross margins are just 20%, for every $1 increase in fixed costs (e.g., insurance, salaries, rent, and utilities), sales need to increase $5 just to stay even. If gross margins are 75%, however, a $1 increase in fixed costs requires a sales increase of just $1.33. An example of the cushion provided by high and durable gross margins is provided by an entrepreneur who built the international division of an emerging software company to $17 million in highly profitable sales in just five years (when he was 25 years of age). He stresses there is simply no substitute for outrageous gross margins, by saying, "It allows you to make all kinds of mistakes that would kill a normal company. And we made them all. But our high gross margins covered all the learning tuition and still left a good profit."[15] Gross margins of less than 20%, particularly if they are fragile, are unattractive.

Time to breakeven—cash flow and profit and loss (P&L)

New businesses which can quickly achieve a positive cash flow and become self-sustaining are highly desirable. It is often the second year before this is possible, but the sooner the better. Simply having a longer window does not mean that the business will be lousy. Two great companies illustrate that a higher potential business can have a longer window. For instance, Pilkington Brothers, an English firm that developed plate glass technology, ran huge losses for over two and a half years before it was regarded as a great company. Similarly, Federal Express went through an early period of enormous negative cash flows of $1 million a month.

Harvest Issues

Value-added potential

New ventures that are based on strategic value in an industry, such as valuable technology, are attractive, while those with low or no strategic value are less attractive. For example, most observers contend, a product technology of compelling strategic value to Xerox was owned, in the mid-1980s, by a small company with about $10 million in sales and showing a prior-year loss of $1.5 million. Xerox purchased the company for $56 million. Opportunities with extremely large capital commitments, whose value on exit can be severely eroded by unanticipated circumstances, are less attractive. An example would be nuclear power.

Thus, one characteristic of businesses that command a premium price is that they have high value-added strategic importance to their acquirer: distribution, customer base, geographic coverage, proprietary technology, contractual rights, and the like. To illustrate, such companies might be valued at four, five, even six times (or more) last year's *sales*, whereas perhaps 60% to 80% of companies might be purchased at .75 to 1.25 times sales.

Valuation multiples and comparables

Consistent with the above point, there is a large spread in the value the capital markets place on private and public companies. Part of your analysis is to identify some of the historical boundaries for the valuations placed on companies in the market/industry/technology area you intend to pursue. The rules of thumb outlined in Exhibit 2.3 are variable and should be thought of as a boundary and a point of departure.

Exit mechanism and strategy

Businesses that are eventually sold—privately or to the public—or acquired usually are started and grown with a harvest objective in mind. Attractive companies that realize capital gains from the sale of their businesses have, or envision, a harvest or exit mechanism. Unattractive opportunities do not have an exit mechanism in mind. Planning is critical because, as is often said, it is much harder to get out of a business than to get into it. Giving some serious thought to the options and likelihood that the company can eventually be harvested in an important initial and ongoing aspect of the entrepreneurial process.

Capital market context

The context in which the sale or acquisition of the company takes place is largely driven by the capital market context at that particular point in time. Timing can be a critical component of the exit mechanism because, as one study indicated, since World War II, the average bull market on Wall Street has lasted just six months. For a keener appreciation of the critical difference the capital markets can make, one only has to recall the stock market crash of October 19, 1987, or the bank credit crunch of 1990–1992. In fact, by the end of 1987, the valuation of the Venture Capital 100 index dropped 43% and private company valuations followed. Initial public offerings are especially vulnerable to the vicissitudes of the capital markets; here the timing is vital. Some of the most successful companies seem to have been launched when debt and equity capital were most available and relatively cheap.

Competitive Advantages Issues

Variable and fixed costs

An attractive opportunity has the potential for being the lowest-cost producer and for having the lowest costs of marketing and distribution. For example, Bowmar was unable to remain competitive in the market for electronic calculators after the producers of large-scale integrated circuits, such as Texas Instruments, entered the business. Being unable to achieve and sustain a position as a low-cost producer shortens the life expectancy of a new venture.

Degree of control

Attractive opportunities have potential for moderate-to-strong degree of control over prices, costs, and channels of distribution. Fragmented markets where there is no dominant competitor—no IBM—have this potential. These markets usually have a market leader with a 20% market share *or less*. For example, sole control of the source of supply of a critical component for a product or of channels of distribution can give a new venture market dominance even if other areas are weak.

Lack of control over such factors as product development and component prices can make an opportunity unattractive. For example, in the case of Viatron, its suppliers were unable to produce several of the semiconductors that the company needed at low enough prices to permit Viatron to make the inexpensive computer terminal that it had publicized extensively.

A market where a major competitor has a market share of 40%, 50%, or, especially, 60% usually implies a market where power and influence over suppliers, customers, and pricing create a serious barrier and risk for a new firm. Such a firm will have few degrees of freedom. However, if a dominant competitor is at full capacity, is slow to innovate or to add capacity in a large and growing market, or routinely ignores or abuses the customer (remember "Ma Bell"), there may be an entry opportunity. However, entrepreneurs usually do not find such sleepy competition in dynamic, emerging industries dense with opportunity.

Entry barriers

Having a favorable window of opportunity is important. Having or being able to gain proprietary protection, regulatory advantage, or other legal or contractual advantage, such as exclusive rights to a market or with a distributor, is attractive. Having or being able to gain an advantage in response/lead times is important since these can create barriers to entry or expansion by others. For example, advantages in response/lead times in technology, product innovation, market innovation, people, location, resources, or capacity make an opportunity attractive. Possession of well-developed, high-quality, accessible contacts that are the products of years of building a top-notch reputation and that cannot be acquired quickly is also advantageous. In fact, there are times when this competitive advantage may be so strong as to provide dominance in the marketplace, even though many of the other factors are weak or average. An example of how quickly the joys of start-up may fade if others cannot be kept out is the experience of firms in the hard disk drive industry that were unable to erect entry barriers in the United States in the early to mid-1980s. By the end of 1983, some 90 hard disk drive companies were launched, and severe price competition led to a major industry shakeout.

If a firm cannot keep others out or if it faces already existing entry barriers, it is unattractive. An easily overlooked issue is a firm's capacity to gain distribution of its product. As simple as it may sound, even venture-capital-backed companies fall victim to this market issue. Air Florida apparently assembled all the right ingredients, including substantial financing, yet was unable to secure sufficient gate space for its airplanes. Even though it sold passenger seats, it had no place to pick the passengers up or drop them off.

Management Team Issues

Entrepreneurial team

Attractive opportunities have teams which are existing and strong and contain industry superstars. The team has proven profit and loss experience in the same technology, market, and service area, and members have complementary and compatible skills. An unattractive opportunity does not have such a team in place or has no team.

Industry and technical experience

A management track record of significant accomplishment in the industry, with the technology, and in the market area, with a proven profit, and lots of achievements where the venture will compete is highly desirable. A top-notch management team can become the most important strategic competitive advantage in an industry. Imagine relocating the Chicago Bulls or the Phoenix Suns to Halifax, Nova Scotia; do you think you would have a winning competitor in the National Basketball Association?

Integrity

Trust and integrity are the oil and glue that make economic interdependence possible. Having an unquestioned reputation in this regard is a major long-term advantage for entrepreneurs and should be sought in all personnel and backers. A shady past or record of questionable integrity is for B team players only.

Intellectual honesty

There is a fundamental issue of whether the founders know what they do and do not know, as well as whether they know what to do about shortcomings or gaps in the team and the enterprise.

Fatal-Flaw Issues

Basically, attractive ventures have no fatal flaws; an opportunity is rendered unattractive if it suffers from one or more fatal flaws. Usually, these relate to one of the above criteria, and examples abound of markets which are too small, which have overpowering competition, where the cost of entry is too high, where an entrant is unable to produce at a competitive price, and so on. An example of an entry barrier's being a fatal flaw was Air Florida's inability to get its flights listed on reservation computers.

Personal Criteria

Goals and fit

Is there a good match between the requirements of business and what the founders want out of it? A very wise woman, Dorothy Stevenson, pinpointed the crux of it with this powerful insight: "Success is *getting* what you want. Happiness is *wanting* what you get."

Upside/downside issues

An attractive opportunity does not have excessive downside risk. The upside and the downside of pursuing an opportunity are not linear, nor are they on the same continuum. The upside is easy, and it has been said that success has a thousand sires. The downside is quite another matter, since it has also been said that failure is an orphan. An entrepreneur needs to be able to absorb the financial downside in such a way that he or she can rebound, without becoming indentured to debt obligations. If an entrepreneur's financial exposure in launching the venture is greater than his or her net worth—the resources he or she can reasonably draw upon, and his or her alternative disposable earnings stream if it does not work out—the deal may be too big. While today's bankruptcy laws are extremely generous, the psychological burdens of living

through such an ordeal are infinitely more painful than the financial consequences. An existing business needs to consider if a failure will be too demanding to the firm's reputation and future credibility, aside from the obvious
financial consequences.[16]

Opportunity cost

In pursuing any venture opportunity, there are also opportunity costs. An entrepreneur who is skilled enough to grow a successful, multimillion-dollar venture has talents that are highly valued by medium- to large-sized firms as well.
While assessing benefits that may accrue in pursuing an opportunity, an entrepreneur needs to take a serious look at other alternatives, including potential
"golden handcuffs," and account honestly for any cut in salary that may be involved in pursuing a certain opportunity.

   Further, pursuing an opportunity can shape an entrepreneur in ways that
are hard to imagine. An entrepreneur will probably have time to execute between two to four multimillion-dollar ventures between the ages of 25 and 50.
Each of these experiences will position him or her, *for better or for worse,* for
the next opportunity. Since it is important for an entrepreneur, in his or her
early years, to gain relevant management experience and since building a venture (either one that works out or one that does not) takes a lot more time than
is commonly believed, it is important to consider alternatives while assessing
an opportunity.

Desirability

A good opportunity is not only attractive but also desirable (i.e., a good opportunity fits). An example of an intensely personal criterion would be the desire
for a certain lifestyle. This desire may preclude pursuing certain opportunities
(i.e., certain opportunities may be opportunities for someone else). The
founder of a major high-technology venture in the Boston area was asked why
the headquarters of his firm were located in downtown Boston, while those of
other such firms were located on the famous Route 128 outside of the city. His
reply was that he wanted to live in Boston because he loved the city and
wanted to be able to walk to work. He said, "The rest did not matter."

Risk/reward tolerance

Successful entrepreneurs take calculated risks or avoid risks they do not need
to take; as a country western song put it: "You have to know when to hold 'em,
know when to fold 'em, know when to walk away, and know when to run." This
is not to suggest that all entrepreneurs have the same risk tolerance; some are
quite conservative while others actually seem to get a kick out of the inherent
danger and thrill in higher risk and higher stake games. The real issue is fit—

recognizing that gamblers and overly risk averse entrepreneurs are unlikely to sustain any long-term successes.

Stress tolerance
Another important dimension of the fit concept is the stressful requirements of a fast-growth high-stakes venture. Or as President Harry Truman said so well: "If you can't stand the heat, then stay out of the kitchen."

Strategic Differentiation

Degree of fit
To what extent is there a good fit among the driving forces (founders and team, opportunity and resource requirements) and the timing given the external environment?

Team
There is no substitute for an A quality team, since the execution and the ability to adapt and to devise constantly new strategies is so vital to survival and success. A team is nearly unstoppable if it can inculcate into the venture a philosophy and culture of superior learning, as well as teaching skills, an ethic of high standards, delivery of results, and constant improvement. Are they free agents—clear of employment, noncompete, proprietary rights, and trade secret agreements—who are able to pursue the opportunity?

Service management
A few years ago, the Forum Corporation of Boston conducted research across a wide range of industries with several hundred companies to determine why customers stopped buying these companies' products. The results were surprising; 15% of the customers defected because of quality and 70% stopped using a product or service because of bad customer service. Having a "turbo-service" concept that can be delivered consistently can be a major competitive weapon against small and large competitors alike. Home Depot, in the home supply business, and Lexus, in the auto industry, have set an entirely new standard of service for their industries.

Timing
From business to historic military battles to political campaigns, timing is often the one element that can make a significant difference. Time can be an enemy or a friend; being too early or too late can be fatal. The crux is to row with tide, not against it. Strategically, ignoring this principle is perilous.

Technology
A breakthrough, proprietary product is no guarantee of success, but it certainly creates a formidable competitive advantage (see Exhibit 2.4).

Flexibility
Maintaining the capacity to commit and decommit quickly, to adapt, and to abandon if necessary is a major strategic weapon, particularly when competing with larger organizations. Larger firms can typically take six years or more to change basic strategy and 10 to 20 years or more to change the culture.

Opportunity orientation
To what extent is there a constant alertness to the marketplace? A continual search for opportunities? As one insightful entrepreneur put it, "Any opportunity that just comes in the door to us, we do not consider an opportunity. And we do not have a strategy until we are saying no to lots of opportunities."

Pricing
One of the most common mistakes of new companies, with high-value-added products or services in a growing market, is to underprice. A price slightly below to as much as 20% below competitors is rationalized as necessary to gain market entry. In a 30% gross margin business a 10% price increase results in a 21% increase in gross margin and will lower the breakeven sales level for a company with $900,000 in fixed costs to $2.5 million from $3 million. At the $3 million sales level, the company would realize an extra $180,000 in pre-tax profits.

EXHIBIT 2.4   Major inventions by U.S. small firms in the 20th century.

Acoustical suspension speakers	Fluid flow meter	Piezo Electronic devices
Aerosol can	Fosin fire airinguisher	Polaroid camera
Air conditioning	Geodesic dome	Prefabricated housing
Airplane	Gyrocompass	Pressure-sensitive cellophane
Artificial skin	Heart valve	Quick frozen foods
Assembly line	Heat sensor	Rotary oil drilling bit
Automatic fabric cutting	Helicopter	Safety razor
Automatic transfer equipment	Heterodyne radio	Six-axis robot arm
Bakelite	High capacity computer	Soft contact lens
Biosynthetic insulin	Hydraulic brake	Sonar fish monitoring
Catalytic petroleum cracking	Learning machine	Spectographic grid
Continuous casting	Link trainer	Stereographic image sensoring
Cotton picker	Nuclear magnetic resonance	

Source: Small Business Association.

Distribution channels

Having access to the distribution channels is sometimes overlooked or taken for granted. New channels of distribution can leapfrog and demolish traditional channels; take for instance, direct mail, home shopping networks, infomercials, the coming revolution in interactive television in your own home, and the Internet.

Room for error

How forgiving is the business and the financial strategy? How wrong can the team be in estimates of revenue, costs, cash flow, timing, and capital requirements? How bad can things get, yet be able to survive? If some single engine planes are more prone to accidents, by 10 or more times, which planes do you want to fly in? High leverage, lower gross margins, and lower operating margins are the signals in a small company of these flights destined for fatality.

GATHERING INFORMATION

The data available about market characteristics, competitors, and so on, are frequently inversely related to the real potential of an opportunity; that is, if market data are readily available and if the data clearly show significant potential, then a large number of competitors will enter the market and the opportunities will diminish.

The good news: Most data will be incomplete, inaccurate, and contradictory, and their meaning will be ambiguous. For entrepreneurs, gathering the necessary information and seeing possibilities and making linkages where others see only chaos are essential.

Leonard Fuld defined competitor intelligence as highly specific and timely information about a corporation.[17] Finding out about competitors' sales plans, key elements of their corporate strategies, the capacity of their plants and the technology used in them, who their principal suppliers and customers are, and a good bit about the new products that rivals have under development is difficult, but not impossible, even in emerging industries, when talking to intelligence sources.[18]

Using published resources is one source of such information. Interviewing people and analyzing data also is critical. Fuld believes that since business transactions generate information which flows into the public domain, one can locate intelligence sources by understanding the transaction and how intelligence behaves and flows.[19]

This can be done legally and ethically. There are, of course, less-than-ethical tactics, which include conducting phony job interviews, getting customers to put out phony bid requests, and lying, cheating, and stealing. Entrepreneurs need to be very careful to avoid such practices and are advised to consult an attorney when in doubt.

Note that the sources of information given below are just a start. Much creativity, work, and analysis will be involved to find intelligence and to extend the information obtained into useful form. For example, a competitor's income statement and balance sheet will rarely be handed out. Rather, they most likely must be derived from information in public filings or news articles or from credit reports, financial ratios, and interviews.[20]

Published Sources

The first step is a complete search of material in libraries and on the Internet. You can find a huge amount of published information, databases, and other sources about industry, market, competitor, and personnel information. Listed below are sources for gathering information to help you get started.

Guides and Company Information

Information is available in special issues of *Forbes* and *Fortune* and in the following:

- *Thomas Register.*
- *Directory of Corporate Affiliations.*
- *Standard & Poor's Register of Corporations, Directors and Executives.*
- *Standard & Poor's Corporation Records.*
- *Dun & Bradstreet Million Dollar Directory.*
- *Dun & Bradstreet Billion Dollar Directory; America's Corporate Families.*
- *Dun & Bradstreet Principal International Businesses.*
- *Dun & Bradstreet Business Information Reports.*
- *Moody's Manuals.*
- *World Almanac.*
- *Encyclopedia of Business Information Sources*, edited by Paul Wasserman.
- *Business Information Sources*, by Lorna Daniels.
- *Directory of Industry Data Sources*, by Harfax.
- *Business Information*, by Michael Lavin.
- *Financial Analyst's Handbook*, by Sumner Levine.
- *Value Line Investment Survey.*
- *Encyclopedia of Small Business Resources*, by David E. Gumpert and Jeffry A. Timmons.

Overviews and General Industry Information

Overviews of American industries, such as:

- *Moody's Investors Industrial Review.*
- *Standard & Poor's Industry Surveys.*
- *U.S. Industrial Outlook,* U.S. Department of Commerce.
- *Current Industrial Reports,* U.S. Department of Commerce.
- Census Information from the U.S. Department of Commerce.
- *County Business Patterns,* U.S. Department of Commerce.
- *Industry Surveys,* Standard & Poor's.
- *Forbes Annual Report on American Industry.*
- *The Wall Street Transcript.*
- *Inside U.S. Business,* by Philip Mattera.

Statistics and Financial and Operating Ratios

Industry statistics listed under the subject heading *statistics* in library catalogs, and under Standard Industrial Classification (SIC) code numbers in publications (see the *Standard Industrial Classification Manual*). Such information also can be obtained from trade associations. There are also guides to statistics, general collections of industry statistics, and sources of composite financial and operating ratios, such as:

- *Statistical Abstract of the United States,* U.S. Bureau of the Census.
- *Encyclopedia of Business Information Sources,* edited by Paul Wasserman.
- *Economic Indicators.*
- *Statistical Reference Index.*
- *American Statistics Index.*
- *Statistics Sources.*
- *Basebook,* Predicasts.
- *Statistical Service,* Standard & Poor's.
- *County Business Patterns,* U.S. Bureau of the Census.
- U.S. Bureau of the Census publications on certain industries.
- Competitive assessments of certain industries in the United States by the U.S. International Trade Administration.
- *Summary of Trade and Tariff Information,* U.S. International Trade Administration.
- Studies of media and markets by Simmons Market Research Bureau, Inc.

- *Industry Norms and Key Business Ratios*, Dun & Bradstreet.
- *Annual Statement Studies*, Robert Morris Associates.
- *Analysts Handbook*, Standard & Poor's.
- *Almanac of Business and Industrial Financial Ratios*, published by Prentice-Hall.

Projections and Forecasts

Projections and forecasts listed under the subject heading in library catalogs and publications, such as:

- *Predicasts Forecasts.*
- *Predicasts F&S Index.*

Market Data

An overall guide to sources of data on consumer and industrial markets can be found in such publications as:

- *Data Sources for Business & Market Analysis*, Scarecrow Press.
- *Basebook*, Predicasts.
- *US Industrial Outlook Handbook.*
- *Findex* (Find/SVP).

Consumer Expenditures

Data on consumer expenditures can be found in such publications as:

- *Editor & Publisher Market Guide.*
- *US Census Reports (Business, Housing, etc.).*
- *Survey of Buying Power*, published by Sales Management, Inc.

Market Studies

Market studies of particular industries and products available from such companies as:

- Predicasts (Cleveland, Ohio).
- Simmons Market Research Bureau (New York, New York).
- Arthur D. Little, Inc. (Cambridge, Massachusetts).
- Business Communications Company (Stamford, Connecticut).

- Frost & Sullivan, Inc. (New York, New York).
- Morton Research Corporation (Merrick, New York).
- Theta Technology Corporation (Wethersfield, Connecticut).

Data Services

A listing of on-line databases appeared in the June 1984 *Personal Software*. Data services and databases, such as:[21]

- Dialog Information Service, Inc. (Knight-Ridder, Inc.).
- CompuServe Information Service Company (H&R Block, Inc.).
- Dow Jones News/Retrieval Service (Dow Jones & Company).
- *Lexis, Nexis, Mesis* (Mead Corporation).
- The Information Bank (Parsipanny, New Jersey).
- Information Data Search, Inc. (Brookline, Massachusetts).
- Economic Information Systems (New York, New York).

Articles

Magazine and newspaper articles published by trade associations, government agencies, and commercial publishers. Lists can be found by consulting periodical indexes and directories, such as:

- *The Directory of Directories.*
- *Predicasts F&S Index.*
- *Business Periodicals Index.*
- *Guide to Special Issues and Indexes of Periodicals.*
- *Public Affairs Information Service Bulletin.*
- *Applied Science and Technology Index.*
- *The Wall Street Journal Index.*
- *New York Times Index.*
- *Encyclopedia of Business Information Sources.*
- *Standard Periodical Directory.*
- Library directories of current periodical publications.

Other Sources

- *Wall Street Transcript.*
- *CIRR: Company & Industry Research Reports.*

- *Encyclopedia of Associations.*
- *National Trade and Professional Associations of the United States and Canada and Labor Unions.*
- *Ayer Directory of Newspapers, Magazines, and Trade Publications.*
- Brokerage house reports.
- Trade association material.
- Books and other material listed in library catalogues under the name of the industry.
- NASA Industrial Applications Centers and several universities, such as Southeastern Oklahoma State University, the University of New Mexico, the University of Southern California, and the University of Pittsburgh provide technically oriented reports, studies, and literature searches.
- Company annual reports.

Biographical

- *Standard & Poor's Register of Corporations, Directors and Executives.*
- *Dun & Bradstreet Reference Book of Corporation Managements.*
- *Who's Who* directories.

Other Intelligence

Everything entrepreneurs need to know will not be found in libraries, since this information needs to be highly specific and current. This information is most likely available from people—industry experts, suppliers, and the like.
Summarized below are some useful sources of intelligence.

Trade Associations

Trade associations, especially the editors of their publications and information officers, are good sources of information.[22] Especially, trade shows and conferences are prime places to discover the latest activities of competitors.

Employees

Employees who have left a competitor's company often can provide information about the competitor, especially if the employee departed on bad terms. Also, a firm can hire people away from a competitor. While consideration of ethics in this situation is important, certainly the number of experienced people in any industry is limited, and competitors must prove that a company hired a person intentionally to get specific trade secrets in order to challenge any hiring legally. Students who have worked for competitors are another source of information.

Consulting Firms

Consulting firms frequently conduct industry studies and then make this information available. Frequently, in such fields as computers or software, competitors use the same design consultants, and these consultants can be sources of information.

Market Research Firms

Firms doing the market studies, such as those listed under published sources above, can be sources of intelligence.

Key Customers, Manufacturers, Suppliers, Distributors, and Buyers

These groups are often a prime source of information.

Public Filings

Federal, state, and local filings, such as filings with the Securities and Exchange Commission (SEC) or Freedom-of-Information Act filings, can reveal a surprising amount of information. There are companies that process inquiries of this type.

Reverse Engineering

Reverse engineering can be used to determine costs of production and sometimes even manufacturing methods. An example of this practice is the experience of Advanced Energy Technology, Inc., of Boulder, Colorado, which learned first-hand about such tactics. No sooner had it announced a new product, which was patented, when it received 50 orders, half of which were from competitors asking for only one or two of the items.

Other

Classified ads, buyers guides, labor unions, real estate agents, courts, local reporters, and so on, can provide clues.

3 ENTRY STRATEGIES

Karl H. Vesper

Setting up a new business collides with the wishes of established competitors, who want all the customer dollars they can get. To get those dollars, they try to give good service, look for new customers and new ways to serve them, take care in pricing not to drive too many customers away, and advertise to remind customers that they are there and anxious to serve. If a competitor comes up with a better offering for customers, they try to match or beat it.

To established companies, a new competitor means any number of unattractive things, such as lost potential sales, lower margins from price cutting, longer hours, loss of key employees, and buildup of inventory that is not moving. At the very least, competitors add worries, keep profits down, and threaten complete displacement from the market; at worst, new competitors can cause bankruptcy. Airlines have gone through such nightmares repeatedly. When deregulation was introduced, entrepreneurs seized the opportunity to start new airlines. Prices dropped. Some major carriers, such as Branniff, failed. The big lines fought back. Most of the entrepreneurs (for example, People's Express and Laker) failed. Then big lines, such as Pan Am, failed. For them the pain from competition has been easy for the whole public to see. At a less visible level competition means discomfort for other companies as well, even when they do not totally fail.

When a new competitor enters, established companies usually fight back. The response may be quick. When Preston Tucker introduced his new automobile in the late forties, the established interests ran him out of business before he had made more than a few dozen cars. Interestingly, they did it not by cutting prices or introducing superior products, but rather by using political influence to bring the government down on him. His company died while he was defending himself from litigation.

Sometimes the response is slower. IBM let Control Data get started and become a well-established mainframe competitor before it struck back. Then it was again slow in responding when Digital Equipment introduced minicomputers, so slow that it had still not caught up after decades. Finally, it let the microcomputer startups get ahead of it by about five years before it finally introduced its PC and started catching up. But then it did so with a vengeance, and scores of microcomputer entrepreneurs were put out of business.

Of course, the entrepreneurs were also putting each other out of business in the meantime. More features, better designs, lower prices, better service, higher reliability, bundled software promotions, and more effective advertising all made entry progressively more difficult as the industry developed. Both capital and customers became harder to get. Consequently, the number of startups that survived became smaller, and the number of attempts to start up also declined. There were just too many competitors, and some of them, such as IBM, Tandy, Apple, and a host of small, low-overhead IBM cloners, had become very tough.

But the startup attempts in microcomputer manufacturing kept on, and some of them became highly successful. One relatively late entrant was IBM, which enjoyed the advantages of its well-established brand name and image of dependable high quality in both products and service. Another late entrant was Compaq, which managed to make headway even against IBM by being equal in quality but higher in performance. Still another was Dell Computer, which found a way to bypass the established channels of distribution, namely computer retailers, by selling direct at low prices both to large single customers and, through mail order, to small ones.

Thus, there was an interplay between the defensive advantages built up by those companies already in business and the *entry wedges* used by new entrepreneurs to crack through those defenses and break into the competitive arena. Such interplay is constantly going on in virtually all industries, with established companies trying to kill each other off and keep new competitors out while entrepreneurs look for entry wedges that will enable them to break in.

Such entrepreneurial entry wedges can be grouped into six types:[1]

- Developing a new product or service.
- Developing a similar product or service—that is, the "better mousetrap."
- Buying a franchise.

- Exploiting an existing product or service.
- Sponsoring a startup enterprise.
- Acquiring a going concern.

This chapter discusses each of these entry strategies in detail. It also notes risks that may be associated with each. Other potentially important dimensions of strategic choice are listed elsewhere, as is description of ways to check out in advance the prospects for pursuing entry wedges.[2]

DEVELOPING A NEW PRODUCT OR SERVICE

The first auto, airplane, radio, life insurance policy, jet engine, TV, plastic plumbing pipe, color TV, microwave oven, microchip, and microcomputer were clearly new products. Some were introduced by existing companies. Others were the basis for forming new companies. Sometimes the products lasted but the startups did not. For example, the first pocket calculator (by Bomar) and the first microcomputer kit (by MITS) were clearly winning products, but the companies they formed the bases for did not have what it took to continue with them.

Dramatically new services are not so easy to name. Some, however, arose to serve markets created by new products. For instance, the microcomputer created opportunities to start repair businesses, disk-copying firms, data-salvaging companies, trade shows, and companies to collect and sell data on the industry. Cellular telephones created similar service startup opportunities. Opportunities for service startups in such things as occupational safety and environmental management were created by new government regulations.

What it takes to start a company around a new product or service includes, most importantly, the discovery of an intersection between the market for that product or service and a way to create one. Sometimes the right person for this is someone working on a technical frontier who discovers a way to accomplish something worthwhile physically or an inventor with a "better idea." Other times it may be a person who comes in contact with a potential market through work or hobbies and either finds a way to satisfy it or teams up with another person capable of solving the product or service design problem.

What Are the Risks?

Risks in applying the new product or service entry wedge include a number of possibilities:

- The design task may be practically impossible for the entrepreneur to accomplish in time.
- The new venture may err in the design.
- Another company with stronger resources may follow and wipe out the startup.
- The startup may not be able to persuade enough people to buy the new product or service either fast enough or at a high enough price to make a profit.

How easy it can be to succeed with a truly new product was illustrated by the experience of Osborne Computer, which was immediately swamped with orders when its product, the first "compact" microcomputer, was introduced. The same company also illustrated how easy it is to fail by doing so within two years of its takeoff as it bungled on design, deliveries, and costs while competitors surpassed it with better designs. Even a company with strong resources and an entrepreneur with a proven successful track record can fail with a startup, as was illustrated by the total failure of Fred Smith's Zap Mail venture.

Most companies with new products that last probably succeed, although nobody has made a count of that particular approach. Among high-technology startups, for instance, the success rate appears to have been about 80% on a five-year time span.[3]

Creating Parallel Competition by Developing a Similar Product or Service

Across a shade of gray from new products and services are those that are not really new but are just different enough to allow a startup to accomplish competitive entry with them. The clones of IBM's PC provide examples of this. They ranged from those that were dramatically cheaper to those of Compaq, which were somewhat more expensive than IBM's but were also a bit higher in performance though not fundamentally different in design. These products, which were similar, but sufficiently differentiated to succeed, enabled entry via what might be termed *parallel competition*, a term coined by Professor Arnold Hosmer of Harvard.

Examples of parallel competition include a restaurant that starts with nearly the same location but a different menu or price structure, another job machine shop, cabinet shop, construction contractor, or advertising agency; these are all types of firms that continually enter competition in parallel. Every city has them. Most are small, but some, such as recent startups in warehouse stores (such as Price Savers and Costco) or home improvement stores (Builders' Emporium, Home Club, and Eagle Hardware, for example), can be quite large.

Eagle Hardware, for instance, started out with public financing made possible by the credibility of its founding entrepreneur, who had previously developed another hardware store chain. Interestingly, the prior chain, Pay 'N Pak, had been sold to a larger firm that proved unable to sustain it; shortly after Eagle opened, Pay 'N Pak went out of business.

Parallel competition is often fierce. By definition it involves firms that lack strong differentiation and therefore tend to compete on price, which drives margins down. A curious exception, up to a point, seems to be local microbreweries, which seem to do better when they have local competitors. Evidently, only then do local beer drinkers take an interest in them.

To succeed in parallel competition certainly requires some degree of differentiation, however. It may be based on price. Filling stations often start with a lowered price. It may also be a different use of advertising, service, personality or contacts of the owner, style of presentation, or convenience features. The toughness of such competition will likely force the entrepreneur to be good at performing the functions of the business. The margin for error in learning and acquiring skill may be vanishingly small. Thin capitalization may also not be tolerable, since margins are thin and competitors may lower prices to keep the new company out of contention.

What Are the Risks?

Risks in applying parallel competition as an entry wedge include the possibilities that the startup's financing may not be sufficient to carry it to profitability and that the owner may simply not be capable of competing with "pros" in the business, who already have their routines polished and their names established. An easy risk to overlook is that competitors will likely take retaliatory action to counter whatever features the new parallel startup attempts to use for differentiating itself. Also easy to underestimate may be the gap in credibility that the new firm will have with customers it is attempting to take from established firms and the strength of customer habits in buying from existing firms.

BUYING A FRANCHISE

Help from an already-established business can be bought through a contract that grants some sort of franchise, usually for a particular geographical territory. This help may include permission to use the established business's name and logo, to sell its products, or to use its methods. The already-established business, called the franchisor, may provide training, accounting services, performance evaluations, assistance in choosing locations and arranging financing, as well as annual meetings where those who have bought franchises—the franchisees—meet and exchange information about what has been working well and what has not in their operations.

Examples of businesses started with the help of franchisors are easy to find in any community or yellow pages. They include fast-food outlets, car dealers, dry cleaners, filling stations, many types of retail stores, real estate offices, insurance offices, tax services, mailing firms, ice cream shops, printing businesses, and other services. One simple way to learn what franchising is like is to visit such firms and ask their owners. Some will likely be very satisfied that they chose franchising as a wedge for competitive entry, and others will be less so. Some franchisees have become very wealthy by building their own chains of outlets, whereas others have gone broke trying to make their franchises work. Countless lawsuits have been conducted by franchisees who claimed that their franchisors did not deliver as promised. One result of these suits has been the enactment of many state laws and regulations to control franchisors.

Customarily, the franchisee begins with a cash payment or a promise to pay a royalty to the franchisor. These, plus capital to equip and operate the franchise, are requisites for the franchisee to get started in business. Usually prior experience in the same line of work is not required, which sometimes makes franchising an attractive way to enter business in a new line of work. Many franchisees are people who have retired from some other job, such as the military.

Some franchisees have become very prosperous by obtaining franchises from franchisors that are just beginning and selling them cheaply to prove themselves, or by obtaining franchises for large territories, where it is possible to develop chains of them and earn large profits from multiple outlets. More often, however, it is the franchisors who make the large profits.

What Are the Risks?

Risks include failure by the franchisor to tell the truth about how likely the franchise is to be successful or to live up to its part of the bargain, such as providing the sorts of help mentioned above. For checking out a franchise there are lists available from the Small Business Administration and in books on franchising. Other risks are that the franchisee will start with too little capital to sustain operations until breakeven occurs and that the franchisee simply may not like the work. Compared to investing the capital required in securities that pay interest or dividends and taking a job that pays a salary, the franchisee may not be ahead financially at all. So a franchisee can end up simply providing the investment for a franchisor to expand and working long hours at routine tasks for low pay.

EXPLOITING PARTIAL MOMENTUM FROM AN EXISTING PRODUCT OR SERVICE

Sometimes situations arise in which the potential for profit is generated by events outside the control of the entrepreneur. Then what is needed is simply to notice that the potential is there and take advantage of it. There are three types of such circumstances: transferring a product or service to a new location, meeting a supply shortage, and capitalizing on unused resources.

Transferring to New Locations

The underlying principle of chains in such businesses as stores, restaurants, and filling stations is that the same type of business is needed in many places. When a new kind of business is created to which this same principle applies, an opportunity exists to transfer that kind of business to many other places. This transfer can be accomplished by independent entrepreneurs as well as chains and franchisors, and it often is. Recent examples of such new businesses have been instant photo shops, copy centers and microcomputer retailers.

Sometimes such startups are subsequently acquired by larger chains as a way of expanding faster. This can generate a substantial cash-out profit to the entrepreneur who spots the geographical transfer opportunity and takes advantage of it early.

What Are the Risks?

To accomplish such a transfer, the entrepreneur must first notice the potential and then either have or be able to recruit the capital and talent to introduce the new type of firm in a new setting. The risk is that the entrepreneur will not have enough of these two advantages to get the new firm started or to sustain it once competition develops.

Meeting a Supply Shortage

There may be a period of time before the sources of supply recognize shortages of desired goods or services that occasionally crop up in the economy. Shortages of housing, for example, may arise in areas with rapidly expanding populations, such as certain areas in the Sun Belt and in areas hit by such calamities as fires and hurricanes. Shortages of water, such as those that occurred in Seattle in 1990, give rise to entrepreneurs who truck in water from other areas to be used for watering lawns when it is prohibited to use city water for doing so.

What Are the Risks?

At the outset, there is usually little risk in undertaking to relieve such shortages, though attempting to gouge on prices can generate hostility and contempt. With time, however, the risk is that the shortage will go away because other sources will be better equipped to supply the needs; competition must be anticipated.

Capitalizing on Unused Resources

The other side of the supply shortage picture is an availability of resources that are not being used. Harvesting industries such as mining and forestry are built on such circumstances. A more recent example of such entrepreneurial opportunity has been the collection and processing of recyclable materials. Another is to process surplus grain and make it into ethanol for use as a gasoline substitute.

Requisite for making a venture in unused resources are to discover them, to see how they might be exploited to make a sale, and to act to bring that about. Devices sometimes used in doing so include buying an option on the resources or obtaining an agency agreement for selling them. These approaches may be able to circumvent the need to invest capital in the resources.

What Are the Risks?

The biggest risk is investing time and capital to take control of resources that turn out not to be salable at a profit after all. The entrepreneur needs to ask himself why the resources were unutilized in the first place. Was it because nobody else could see the opportunity that they contained, or was it because everybody could see that in fact there really was not an opportunity? What is it that the entrepreneur knows that others do not? Such activity inevitably involves speculating, and in speculation there is always risk of loss.

FINDING SPONSORSHIP

A safer bet as an entry wedge may be to take advantage of the willingness of someone to help sponsor the startup in some manner. Typically, the sponsor is a customer, a supplier, or an investor in the startup venture.

- *Customer sponsors.* A potential customer who strongly wants to obtain what the new venture will offer may be willing to provide sponsorship through a substantial purchase order, a contract to buy goods over time, or a cash advance on some purchase.
- *Supplier sponsors.* A supplier who strongly wants to see the venture develop as a user of what she offers may be willing to advance inventory or labor as a way of helping the venture get started.
- *Investor sponsors.* Someone who thinks the prospective venture will become highly successful may advance cash to it as an investor. The purpose usually includes making a profit, but sometimes people advance cash to ventures simply because they like the entrepreneur, think the venture is a "good cause," or want to participate in the adventure of a startup. Less encouraging investor motivations can include the investor's hope that he will be hired by the venture or will be taken on as a director.

A prime requisite for all these types of sponsorship is that the entrepreneur and the venture be regarded by the sponsor as credible and likely to succeed. The strongest basis for this is usually a track record of prior accomplishment and a demonstration that the entrepreneur possesses the capacity to perform the critical tasks of the venture. How good the venture idea looks is also crucial, and it may be helpful for the entrepreneur to develop in writing a clear description of just how it works and how it will be implemented.

What Are the Risks?

Credibility is also important for the entrepreneur to assess personally, because the risk is that sponsorship may be lost if the venture fails, and that can make it much harder to pull off a venture the next time. Even when direct sponsorship is not involved, the entrepreneur requires help from other people in venturing. Suppliers, customers, employees, banks, and government agencies are usually all involved to some degree. The more confidence they have in the entrepreneur and what he is trying to do, the more they are likely to help the venture.

ACQUIRING A GOING CONCERN

The final main entry strategy is to acquire a going concern. This can tremendously simplify the process of getting into business. A business can be viewed as basically a bundle of habits—customers buying, suppliers supplying, employees doing their jobs. In a going concern, those habits are already present. The premises are set up, any necessary permits are in effect, and the cash flow should be giving a fairly clear picture of what the financial needs are. In a startup business, there will likely be a negative cash flow that is hard to predict while the company struggles to break even. Two important needs can be circumvented by the entrepreneur through entering business via acquisition: the need for expertise and the need for capital.

Expertise in a going concern should already be present in employees of the business. Even if it is not, the buying entrepreneur should be able to obtain education and operating help from the selling owner to fill in the expertise needed. Consequently, it is fairly common to find businesses owned by entrepreneurs who bought them with no prior experience in that particular line of work and nevertheless succeeded. This is in stark contrast to a startup. Those who start companies and succeed usually do so with the benefit of prior related business experience unless the business is either such a new type that nobody has such experience or, alternatively, it is so straightforward that little expertise is required. Examples of such simple types are small retail stores and restaurants or services such as housecleaning, painting, or hedge trimming.

The need for capital in acquisition entry is often circumvented by having the selling owner help with financing through leveraging the buyout. The purchaser may be able to borrow against assets of the business to provide for a down payment to the seller and some working capital to continue operations. The seller takes a note for the balance owed, which the buyer pays off over time from earnings of the business. Thus the buying entrepreneur may be able to enter an independent business in a line of work new to her and to make a salary and profit from it right away without putting up any cash at all. There will, of course, be a debt obligation for the buyer, but the odds of succeeding with a buyout of a business, provided it has a history of profitability and is in reasonably good shape, historically appear to have been very high. It is often the most effective way to enter independent business.

Negotiation of price and terms may be the most discussed part of the acquisition, but that may not be the really hard part. Finding a suitable buyout and establishing credibility with the seller are. But it is still necessary and therefore worth thought and possibly some study.

One task that certainly should be part of this process is to develop a checklist of criteria to use in deciding whether to buy the business or not. A general list for this task appears in the more extensive discussion of acquisition entry in *New Venture Strategies,* Chapters 9 and 10.[4] Some questions to be asked and answered are:

- What is the real reason that the seller is willing to sell?
- What assets are to go with the business?

- How much would be required to replicate the business rather than to buy it?
- What elements in the business are key to its survival?
- If the former owner drops out, how would this affect decisions by customers and the conduct of operations in the business?

Another key task is to develop a projected cash flow for the business during takeover and subsequent operations of the business. Consider the following:

- How much cash will the buyer have to have and when?
- How fast will the cash come back in, and what net inflow will occur over time?
- What will be the discounted present value of this flow, and how will that compare to the price of the business?

To answer the last question some sort of discount rate will have to be assumed. Several should be tried, ranging from the interest rate on a secure investment to a much higher rate characteristic of a high-risk investment. Presumably, the appropriate figure will be somewhere in between.

Another assumption, usually critical, will concern the cash drawdown to be taken by the buyer as salary. An appropriate figure here might be the estimated salary appropriate for a manager who might be hired to run the business.

Each of these assumed figures can be adjusted in size to assess the impact of error in estimating the financial future of the buyout. Such adjustments should probably be tried with the help of a personal computer spreadsheet program to generate "what if" scenarios and assess possible consequences of going through with the buyout.

What Are the Risks?

There are two main catches in attempting this method of entry. The first arises from the fact that the approach is so effective. As a consequence, there are far more people who would like to acquire a business than there are opportunities to do so. This tends to make available buying opportunities scarce. They tend to be grabbed up quickly, and they tend to drive the prices of buyouts up, sometimes to the point of financial unfeasibility. To deal with this problem, the entrepreneur should try as many approaches as possible for locating buying opportunities. These include using such lead sources as:

- Classified advertisements (Business Opportunities).
- Business and commercial real estate brokers.

- Professionals (bankers, accountants, attorneys).
- Cold calling.

The second major problem with accomplishing a buyout is to appear adequately credible to the seller. The "ideal" seller is most often a person who is getting older and wants to sell a business *not* because it has problems but rather in order to retire. Such a person will likely care not only that the full purchase price will be paid on time but also that the business, its employees, its name, and its facilities will be well maintained.

To provide this assurance, a buyer is likely to benefit from having developed a reputation for demonstrating high-quality performance in whatever she did, being an honorable person who keeps promises, being competent in controlling costs and managing finances, and being able to set and follow effective priorities. Personal agreeability and compatibility with the nature and idiosyncrasies of the seller may also be important. Sellers sometimes compromise on price and terms for the sake of the comfort they feel in dealing with the buyer and the peace of mind they think they will derive from having that particular person as a debtor and a steward of their business.

CONCLUSION

Which of these entry wedges will fit best for a given entrepreneur has to be decided by the individual. Any of them can work. At a particular point in time none of them may work. At other times it may be possible to combine more than one. Having them in mind and searching continually until something works out may be the most effective individual strategy.

4 MARKET OPPORTUNITIES AND MARKETING

Gerald E. Hills

Entrepreneur R. David Thomas opened the first Wendy's restaurant because he saw an unfilled need in the marketplace.[1] Thus, he started with a *market orientation*. Realizing that many customers wanted more choice and a fresher hamburger than they received at McDonald's, he decided to sell his four Kentucky Fried Chicken franchises and open Wendy's (after his daughter's nickname). Thomas said, "I like a hamburger with mustard, pickle, and onion, and you didn't have a choice at a McDonald's or Burger King. I thought the other ones were . . . just giving you what they wanted to and not what you really wanted." This kind of customer orientation is the foundation for modern marketing. "No one else was doing a very good job, and I wanted a hamburger that was different, made to order so you could choose whatever you wanted to put on it and get out of the heat-lamp and heat-bin syndrome." Thomas did not use frozen patties but ground his hamburger fresh daily, and he let the customers select their own condiments. That provided customers with 256 possible combinations of condiments. The market perceived Wendy's products to be of higher quality and better taste than those of the competition, and Thomas grabbed a piece of the market not exploited by McDonald's and Burger King. Wendy's went on to successfully offer the restaurant industry's first drive-up windows.

The author wishes to acknowledge the contributions of Dr. Robert B. Woodruff and Dr. David W. Cravens to this chapter as previous coauthors with me of *Marketing Management,* published by Richard D. Irwin, Inc.

When Thomas started, McDonald's had 1,298 restaurants. Two years after he started, he had 2 restaurants. He opened 2 more the year after that, then 4 more, then 12 more. In 1973 he sold his first franchise for $5,000; in 1976 there were 300 Wendy's restaurants, and the company went public. Today, Wendy's restaurants number nearly 4,700 with sales over $4.6 billion, and, as Chairman of the Board, R. David Thomas is still the largest stockholder and the centerpiece of their promotional strategy. He demonstrated once again what an entrepreneur can do by perceiving market opportunity and using sound marketing fundamentals.

Marketing is the process of planning and executing the conception, pricing, promotion, and distribution of ideas, goods, and services to create exchanges that satisfy individual and organizational objectives.[2] The Wendy's operation illustrates the definition of marketing. Through convenient distribution of quality goods and services at the right price, Wendy's has created millions of mutually beneficial exchanges that satisfy individuals and attain company objectives. This chapter discusses the critical importance of marketing within entrepreneurship—both as a philosophy and orientation, and as a set of management tasks that together form the marketing plan for a business.

But perhaps the ultimate marketing task for many entrepreneurs is the wealth generating sale of their "baby"—the business that they conceived and guided into maturity.

MARKETING AS A PHILOSOPHY

The foundation for contemporary marketing management and entrepreneurial success is the "marketing concept," which provides an orientation for conducting business, a way of thinking, and a basic approach to business problems. Although the marketing concept may seem obvious, a surprising number of entrepreneurs still fail to grasp its far-reaching implications. The *marketing concept* is a customer-oriented philosophy that is implemented and integrated throughout the business to serve customers better than competitors and achieve specified goals.

> Marketing requires separate work and a distinct group of activities. But it is, first, a central dimension of the entire business. It is the whole business seen from the point of view of its final result, that is, from the customer's point of view.[3]

As Exhibit 4.1 shows, the marketing concept is made up of three components. Starting with *customer needs and wants,* a business owner develops an *organizationally integrated marketing strategy* to accomplish its *goals.* The

EXHIBIT 4.1   The marketing concept and entrepreneurship.

concept begins with the customer: "The principal task of the marketing function . . . is not so much to be skillful in making the customer do what suits the
interests of the business as to be skillful in conceiving and then making the
business do what suits the interests of the customer."[4]

Entrepreneurs have special opportunities and challenges in marketing
new enterprises. Credibility must be established, awareness must be built, and
the perception of newness overcome. There are no established relationships, no
market share, and severe resource constraints. Access to distribution channels
and suppliers may be limited and advertising costs cannot be spread over several stores or high volume sales. Yet all of these challenges also represent opportunities to begin anew with positive communications and perceptions.

Identifying Customer Needs or Desires

Since no businesses have the skills and resources to be all things to all people,
entrepreneurs must identify which customer needs and wants can and should
be met. Deciding which preferences and potential customers to serve is crucial, given any entrepreneur's limited resources and competitive strengths. A
target market is a group of existing or potential customers within a particular
product market toward which the business directs its marketing efforts.

Selectively choosing target markets is an integral part of the philosophy suggested by the marketing concept. The alternative is to try to serve all potential customers in a mediocre fashion and thus to fall short in providing customer satisfaction.

Entrepreneurs who are not market oriented are often technology or product oriented, production oriented, or sales oriented. A *technology or product orientation* often exists in firms that have had a highly successful product. Where such an orientation exists, management implicitly believes that if "you build a better mousetrap, the world will beat a path to your door." It is true that, given enough publicity, a glamorous technological innovation may, for a time, seem to create its own market. Texas Instruments has been accused of being a technology-oriented company because when it was founded, its high-tech products seemed almost to sell themselves. In later years, however, competition and the company's failure to adapt spelled trouble for its entry into new markets.

Entrepreneurs with nontechnical products and services may also fall into the product orientation trap. A lawyer, for example, may strive for a "perfect, risk-free" agreement for a client, a beautiful "product," but destroy a valuable deal for the client. Communicating the reasons to buy a product requires adopting the role of a buyer, not that of an engineer, inventor, or developer. There is obviously a very real need for the development of quality technologies, products, and services. But these should not be developed for their own sake. Peter Drucker captured the essential difference between a product orientation and a customer orientation:

> True marketing starts . . . with the customer. . . . It asks, "What does the customer want to buy?" It does not say, "This is what our product or service does." It says, "These are the satisfactions the customer looks for, values, and needs."[5]

Another orientation that sometimes develops in entrepreneurial businesses is a *production orientation.* Professional service firms such as dentists or accounting firms can become so enamored with how they deliver a service that they lose a focus on the customers' wishes. A cost-cutting efficiency focus in manufacturing operations may also hinder efforts to deliver customer satisfaction.

Finally, an entrepreneur with a *sales orientation* is one who assumes that effective selling can "push" its output into the hands of customers. Even first-rate personal selling, however, is at most one element in a total marketing program. A sales orientation is geared toward converting an existing product into cash rather than beginning with customer needs and responding to those needs. Pushing products is less necessary if a business' products and services fill customer needs better than those of competitors. A new office furniture producer learned this truth because his furniture, prices, and distribution channels were the same as most other firms in the industry. The business owner believed that the key to success was a better group of furniture brokers and more salespeople. The firm went bankrupt within a year, having fallen victim to a sales orientation. For a business to succeed it must, of course, have good products and services, good production, and good selling. But these revolve around creating customer satisfaction in a target market—that is, marketing!

Integrating the Customer Focus throughout the Organization

The second major component of the marketing concept philosophy is *organizational integration* (refer to Exhibit 4.1). Whether an entrepreneur owns a startup company of three people (hopefully with no organization chart) or a rapidly growing firm of 200, she can encounter hurdles as she tries to integrate a customer focus as a philosophy for all people in the company. The technical genius who develops exciting products and services may be rude or incompetent in answering telephone calls from customers. Or a conservative accountant may alienate potential customers in reviewing their credit rating. Or the marketing leader in the entrepreneurial team may not be given equal influence in decisions or, worse yet, may not even be a marketer but rather a salesperson with a narrow perspective. Virtually all the people in a company directly and indirectly affect how customers perceive the firm. There is a unique opportunity in a new enterprise to create the firm's image, in part by everyone acting in a consistent way toward customers. This early-stage philosophy, then, provides the foundation for developing customer-oriented guidelines as the company grows.

Marketing to Achieve Your Goal

The third part of the marketing concept illustrated in Exhibit 4.1 refers to *goal achievement*. Marketing is oriented toward sales volume as a success measure, but it is essential to strive not just for sales, but also for *effective* marketing that contributes to *profitable* sales. Other goals often exist as well, such as developing a specific image for the new business or taking over significant market share from existing firms. For example, Marketplace Business, an entrepreneurial mailing list firm, decided to offer some unique "product" features to potential business clients. Marketplace Business' user-friendly mailing lists are creating a differentiated image in a highly comparative and saturated market, which will likely result in some significant market share gains.[6]

EXHIBIT 4.2   Indicators of customer and marketing orientation.

1. What information do you carefully collect about the exact needs of your customers?
2. Could you consider custom designing your services or products for smaller groups of customers? How?
3. Are your (nonsales) employees specifically trained to represent your company to customers? How?
4. Are customers contacted after the sale to determine their level of satisfaction? How?
5. How do you convert unsatisfied customers to satisfied customers? Do you have any strategy?
6. Is your top marketer in the company a top-level, equal team member?
7. To what extent do you build your strategies around an in-depth understanding of your customers?
8. To what extent are activities of different people (or departments) coordinated to ensure customer satisfaction?

Business owners can look reflectively in the "mirror" shown in Exhibit 4.2 and the questions there can help answer the question "How customer-oriented and marketing-oriented is my business?"

MARKETING MANAGEMENT: CREATE A MARKETING PLAN

Marketing management requires analyzing the environmental situation and the market opportunities, setting marketing objectives, formulating marketing strategies and tactics, and then creating an action plan to implement the marketing practices. Exhibit 4.3 illustrates how marketing is based on the entrepreneur's vision and *mission*. And the macroenvironment—encompassing broad economic, governmental, social, natural, and technological changes—constantly provides new business opportunities as well as threats. For example, the recreational vehicle (RV) industry has been impacted over the past two decades by interest rates, varying levels of consumer confidence, changing gasoline prices, and even gasoline shortages. The author observed the opening of two RV retailers one mile apart a few years ago, but one soon failed. The successful retailer, anticipating substantial gasoline price hikes and consumer uncertainty, minimized the initial investment in facilities and inventory. The unsuccessful retailer ignored the signals from external forces and purchased land, constructed a building, and offered a large RV inventory and a full array of services. The changing environment reduced consumer demand for RVs, and the second retailer was forced to liquidate. The surviving entrepreneur gradually expanded into newly

EXHIBIT 4.3   Marketing management and entrepreneurship.

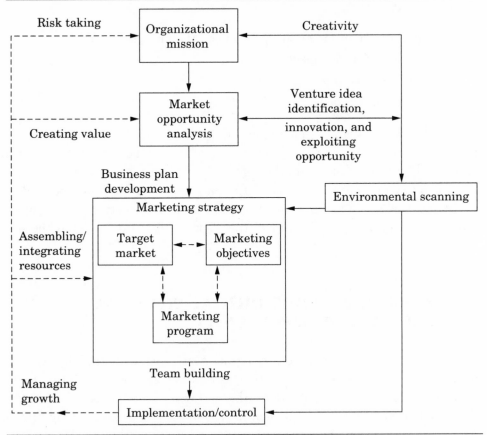

Source: Gerald E. Hills and Raymond W. LaForge, "Marketing and Entrepreneurship: The State of the Art." In *The State of the Art of Entrepreneurship,* Donald L. Sexton and John D. Kasarde (eds.) (Boston, MA: PWS-Kent Publishing Company, 1992), 164–190.

constructed facilities, largely financed from internal cash flow, and still operates successfully today.

Marketing management, as shown in Exhibit 4.3, also captures the elements of a *marketing plan.* The marketing plan is part of a *business plan,* or *strategic plan.* The marketing plan includes a situation analysis that in large part comprises a market opportunity analysis and an assessment of the existing or potential businesses' strengths, weaknesses, threats, and opportunities in the marketplace. Other major elements of a marketing plan include developing specific marketing objectives, determining which target markets to serve, and formulating a marketing program for each target market. Together, the objectives, target market selection, and marketing programming decisions form the marketing strategy for the business. The last portion of a marketing plan is to outline specific actions and a timetable. To summarize, the marketing plan outline is as follows:

1. Analyze the environmental situation and the market opportunity.
2. Develop marketing objectives.
3. Formulate a marketing strategy.
4. Create an action plan.

Entrepreneurs are often immersed in the marketplace, meeting customers every day. "My marketing plan is in my head" is a common statement by successful business owners. Yet the rigor of being more systematic and of casting words to paper nearly always clarifies entrepreneurs' thinking and leads to profitable changes and longer-run strategies. A good marketing plan is "intensive thinking on paper." The rest of this chapter discusses in detail the four steps for creating a marketing plan.

ANALYZING THE ENVIRONMENTAL SITUATION AND THE MARKET OPPORTUNITY

Situation analysis consists of identifying and evaluating uncontrollable external influences, customers, and competition, as well as company capabilities, to determine opportunities, threats, strengths, and weaknesses. This information is then used in preparing and implementing the marketing strategy. A significant part of the situation analysis required for developing a marketing plan is a market opportunity analysis (MOA). *Market opportunity* refers to a situation in which a combination of factors creates the potential for selling the company's product or service. In some ways, conducting an MOA is similar to putting together a jigsaw puzzle. An entrepreneur gathers pieces of information from many sources. Each piece describes some aspect of the customers, the competition, or the environmental forces influencing them. The challenge lies in putting all of the information together to form a picture of the nature and extent of market opportunity. If the entrepreneur has in-depth experience in the industry being entered, this can provide many pieces of the picture and be a huge advantage. This picture becomes the foundation for building a marketing strategy to tap the opportunity.

We need an approach for conducting an MOA that can be used to guide the analysis, particularly in situations where we start with little or no advance understanding of product markets. Exhibit 4.4 provides such an approach.

Because markets exist only for particular products and services, MOAs and marketing plans should be done on a product-by-product, market-by-

EXHIBIT 4.4   The five steps for assessing market opportunities.

1. Identify the business environmental forces.
   - Economic conditions and trends
   - Legal and regulatory situation and trends
   - Technological positioning and trends (state of the art; related R&D)
   - Relevant social changes
   - Natural environment (shortages? vulnerabilities?)

2. Describe the industry and its outlook.
   - Type of industry
   - Size—now and in 3–5 years
   - Types of market segments
   - Industry marketing practices
   - Major trends
   - Implications for opportunity

3. Analyze the key competitors.
   - Product description
   - Market positioning (relative strengths and weaknesses, as seen by customers)
   - Market practices: channels, pricing, promotion, service
   - Estimated market share (if relevant)
   - Reactions to competition
   - Implications for opportunity

4. Create a target market profile.
   - Levels: generic needs, product type, specific brands
   - End-user focus; also channel members
   - Targeted customer profiles
       Who are my potential customers?
       What are they like as consumers/businesspeople?
       How do they decide to buy/not buy?
       Importance of different product attributes?
       What outside influences affect buying decisions?
   - Implications for opportunity?

5. Set sales projections.
   - As many formal or intuitive approaches as possible
   - Comparison of results
   - Go/no go

market basis. This means that an MOA can begin only after the entrepreneur decides on the product for which markets are to be analyzed. Exhibit 4.5 shows typical sources of information for MOAs. Published sources and the Internet are the places to start because they are easily accessible and relatively inexpensive. Interviews with experts, personal observation, and primary marketing research are used to fill in the gaps with information not found in published sources. The costs and time required for an analysis rise dramatically when marketing research is used, so other sources are usually exhausted before a decision is made on whether to conduct such research. If the downside risks are high, this may dictate investing in market research. Yet many entrepreneurs

EXHIBIT 4.5   Source of information for MOAs.

Published sources	Personal observation
Periodicals and newspapers	Of customers
Trade association reports	Of competitors
Standardized information service reports	Of environmental influences
Government documents	**Primary marketing research**
Company reports	Focus groups
Interviews with experts	Concept tests
Managers of suppliers	Cross-sectional surveys
Managers of trade companies	Longitudinal panels
Managers of trade associations	Experiments
Consultants	
Salespersons	

seem to have an uncanny ability to spot opportunities. Their use of intuitive judgment in evaluating opportunities is sometimes remarkable as well.[7] Yet an MOA should still enhance the odds of success.

One of the first steps is to define the product-market boundaries. In some industrial markets, customers can be listed by name. More typically, customers must be classified by various characteristics to give entrepreneurs insight into who makes up product markets. An MOA must sort from the population those people who are most likely to buy and use the products and services. Then the analysis can look for specific groups or market segments. Many characteristics of people have been used to define the makeup of markets. Among the more frequently used are geographic area, demographic characteristics, lifestyles, importance of product benefits, rate of product use, and product preferences.

Analyzing the Customer Profile

Whatever the characteristics, such as demographics, used to define markets, these characteristics provide only a glimpse into the real people. The next task is to build a customer focus to help entrepreneurs understand customers well enough to anticipate their market requirements. *Customer profiles* are intended to describe what these customers are like as people, how they decide what product/brand to buy, and what outside influences affect their buying decisions.

Customer profiling concentrates on learning why demand exists by describing the underlying needs and wants. Here, profile information helps the entrepreneur understand which customers are likely to buy a product. Activities, interests, opinions, decision processes, and demand factors affecting customer preferences for one product type over others are described. The challenge for entrepreneurs is to create a marketing program that effectively appeals to targeted customers in these product markets.[8] The marketing strategy must demonstrate to customers how the company's marketing, including the products and services, meets their requirements.

Discovering What Customers Are Like

Many factors are used for this purpose, including activities, interests, attitudes, experiences with the product, personal tastes, values, and personality. Which ones are best depends on the product and market being analyzed. Learning more about the makeup of customers helps business owners visualize how a product fits into lifestyles (or work styles) and how customers might react to marketing strategies. Already knowing the customer benefits of the company's products, entrepreneurs can search profiles for clues to the customer requirements that the products can best meet.

> Ian S. Leopold was a senior at Hobart College in Geneva, New York, when he started Campus Concepts. The business began with an advertiser-supported free shopping guide for Hobart students and has grown into a nationwide, multi-million-dollar college marketing company that focuses on students' specific needs . . . .
>
> Leopold was president of Hobart's Entrepreneur Club in 1985 . . . . Leopold wrote a business plan for Campus Concepts as an independent-study project. His professor didn't see eye to eye with Leopold and gave him a failing grade, preventing him from graduating with his class. "So I set out to prove the professor wrong," Leopold says.
>
> He stayed in Geneva that summer to redo his paper, and he worked on the second Hobart guide. In four weeks, he sold more than 100 ads and made a $5,000 profit. In the fall he entered Northwestern University's Kellogg School of Management, in Evanston, Illinois, and hired someone to do the next editions. He returned to Campus Concepts full time in January 1990, . . .
>
> The guide reflects Leopold's belief that college students make up a major market and are prime candidates for developing product loyalty. The average student's buying power is about $5,000 a year, he says, which comes to $65 billion a year for the entire U.S. college population . . . .
>
> Leopold expects revenues of about $4.5 million [in 1995] and aims to top $10 million in 1997.[9]

Through his own immersion in the marketplace, Leopold sensed an opportunity to offer a promotion vehicle to businesses that wanted to reach the college student market.

Discovering How Customers Decide What to Buy

Learning how customers make choices among products reveals customer requirements. The decision processes that customers go through help them determine how product benefits match their requirements for purchase. Only a careful search through entire customer profiles will reveal all the market requirements that customers have.

Discovering What Outside Influences Affect Buying Decisions

Demand factors are influences on customer buying decisions that come from outside the market and the industry serving the market and are largely uncontrolled by customers or competitors. Important categories of demand factors that show up in many MOAs are economic, legal, technological, natural, and social influences coming from the environment. For example, government moves to protect national forests have encouraged customers to consider alternative building materials. Rivenite Company products are lumber, extruded from dirty waste plastic that is heated and mixed with sawdust. One major customer, the Florida Department of Transportation, estimates it can replace a hardwood post, which costs $65 and lasts 5 years, with Rivenite, which costs only $1.50 more and will last 44 years.[10]

Attracting Customers to Innovative Products or Services

Entrepreneurs who offer innovative new products and services encounter special challenges in the marketplace. There is evidence that the customer profile of those who first buy innovative products may be different from those who buy the product after it is generally accepted. And the rate of acceptance by customers depends on a number of factors, some of which the entrepreneur can control. The product or service must be adopted (purchased) and diffused throughout the markets and, usually, the faster this happens, the better. *Adoption* is the decision of an individual to use the product. *Diffusion* is the collective spread of individual adoption decisions throughout a population or market. Both pertain to *innovative* new products and services, the result of entrepreneurial efforts. There is usually a limited window of opportunity for new products. Venture capitalists often indicate that their projected sales for a product are more accurate than their timing. It often takes longer than expected to attain projected sales levels. This rate of acceptance often differentiates a tremendously successful product from a disaster. So how can the *rate* of acceptance be increased?

First, consumers usually go through a process of deciding to buy a product. The usual steps in the adoption process, the buying decision process for new products, are

Awareness → Interest → Evaluation → Trial → Adoption

Marketing in the introduction and early growth stages must be oriented toward facilitating the rapid movement of as many customers as possible through this process. The timing of various marketing tactics (informative advertising, coupons, or incentives to try a product, and so forth) becomes critical.

Second, some customers adopt products more quickly than others, which has strategy implications. Individual customers may be labeled according to how quickly they adopt a product, ranging from *innovators* to *laggards,* as shown in Exhibit 4.6. If possible, marketing should be initially directed to the innovators and early adopters, both to develop an early cash flow and to encourage a faster rate of diffusion into the majority of the market. Unfortunately, research has found little consistency of innovator and early adopter demographic or psychographic characteristics across different types of products. Marketers should, however, seek to find common characteristics for early purchasers in their particular product category and, if possible, target their marketing strategy accordingly. Some evidence exists for the general innovator profile (depicted in Exhibit 4.7), but again, those results should be viewed cautiously with respect to specific products.[11]

For example, consider the glow-in-the-dark Nitelite golf balls. Because there are 25 million golfers, Corky Newcomb, cofounder of Pick Point Sports thought, "Some should be selling for me." But in 1989, retailers would not stock his innovative ball. So Newcomb designed a campaign aimed at amateur golfers, by offering a $100 reward to amateur golfers who could persuade their clubs to sponsor a Nitelite tournament. By 1992, sales of the Nitelite golf ball were $10 million. He succeeded in enlisting innovator consumers not only to buy but to help him with his marketing campaign.[12]

EXHIBIT 4.6   Types of adopters by adoption time required.

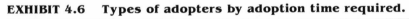

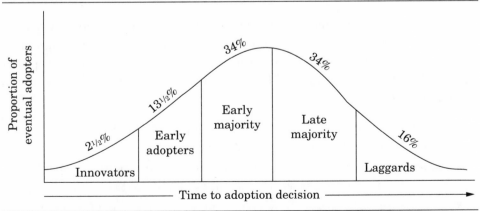

Source: Reprinted with permission of The Free Press, a division of Macmillan, Inc., from *Diffusion of Innovations* (4th ed.), by Everett M. Rogers. Copyright © 1995 by The Free Press.

EXHIBIT 4.7 Comparative profiles of the consumer innovator and the later adopter.

Characteristic	Innovator	Noninovator (or later adopter)
Product interest	More	Less
Opinion leadership	More	Less
Personality		
Dogmatism	Open-minded	Closed-minded
Social character	Inner-directed	Other-directed
Category width	Broad categorizer	Narrow categorizer
Venturesome	More	Less
Perceived risk	Less	More
Purchase and consumption traits		
Brand loyalty	Less	More
Deal proneness	More	Less
Usage	More	Less
Media habits		
Total magazine exposure	More	Less
Special-interest magazines	More	Less
Television	Less	More
Social characteristics		
Social integration	More	Less
Social striving (e.g., social, physical, and occupational mobility)	More	Less
Group memberships	More	Less
Demographic characteristics		
Age	Younger	Older
Income	More	Less
Education	More	Less
Occupational status	More	Less

Third, many diffusion studies have demonstrated that a product's characteristics as *perceived* by potential buyers are extremely important. Marketing activity can be partially directed toward helping to minimize misperceptions and enhancing product strengths. Important perceived product characteristics include the following:

- *Relative advantage* is the extent to which potential customers perceive a new product as superior to existing substitutes.
- *Compatibility* is the extent to which potential customers consider a new product to be consistent with their values, needs, and behavior.
- *Complexity* is the degree to which an innovation is difficult to understand or use.

- *Testability* is the extent to which a new product or venture is capable of being tried on a limited basis by customers.
- *Observability* or communicability, is the ease with which a product's benefits can be seen by, imagined by, or described to potential consumers.

Exhibit 4.8 suggests marketing actions related to each of these perceived product characteristics. Although each of these product characteristics borders on being intuitively obvious, paying systematic and creative attention to them can be critical to the design of effective marketing strategies for new products. Apple Computer's Macintosh personal computer was a good example of a product designed with the above characteristics in mind. Compared to IBM's PC, in this now classic example, the relative price/quality advantage of the Macintosh was assumed to be favorable, and its compatibility and lack of complexity were major advantages.

EXHIBIT 4.8   Marketing implications of important new product/venture characteristics.

Characteristic	Marketing action
Relative advantage	Clearly and credibly communicate the product's advantage.
	Obtain third-party/professional/objective endorsements.
	Price the product to compare favorably with others.
	Construct the product to "deliver" benefits quickly.
Compatibility	Develop an understanding of customer life-styles, behavior, etc., to minimize the required adaptation.
	Make the product fit in with related products.
	Make the product/brand fit customer's social situation.
Complexity	Make the product readily understandable.
	Strive to make the product user friendly.
	Make the product at a complexity level not exceeding that of substitutes.
Testability	Offer money-back guarantee (reduce the cost/risk of trial).
	Make small quantities free or at low price.
	Provide incentives to encourage trial.
	Offer special incentives for durable items (test drives for autos, etc.).
Observability	Encourage visible use by customers.
	Make it easy for others to perceive the product/brand.
	Create incentives for customers to encourage friends to consider trial.

Source: Leon G. Schiffman and Leslie Lazer Kanuk, *Consumer Behavior,* 4th ed. (Englewood Cliffs, NJ: Prentice Hall, 1991).

Analyzing the Industry and the Competition

Opportunity in product markets is influenced as much by competition as by customer characteristics and demand factors. Gaining an advantage over the competition is crucial to a successful marketing plan. So that entrepreneurs can determine what the advantage over the competition should be, an MOA profiles and evaluates the capabilities and actions of competitors serving the same product markets.

When competition comes from only a very few firms, analyzing each of these firms is possible. Typically, however, there are many competitors in the industry, so that analyzing each of them is unnecessarily time-consuming and expensive. So, first, the industry is analyzed. Then key competitors are singled out for in-depth evaluation.

Industry Analysis

Competitors serving the same market can be grouped together into an industry so that conclusions can be drawn about the similarities and differences in the way in which a market is served. Because business owners are concerned with the most direct competition, an industry can be restricted to those firms that sell the same product or service, operate at the same level in a channel of distribution, and sell in the same geographic area. For example, a wholesale wine distributor serving Chicago considers its industry to be all of the wine distributors serving the same area. In contrast, a national wine producer, such as Gallo, views its industry as all the wine producers selling to the nation's markets.

An industry analysis begins with accumulating an information base, or profile. First, the size, growth, and structure of the industry are described. Next, information is obtained on the marketing practices of the industry, including target market coverage, key marketing objectives, and marketing strategies and tactics. Entrepreneurs use industry information to draw conclusions about probable changes in industry size, structure, and marketing practices. They also evaluate industry practices to look for weaknesses or problem areas that can be exploited. For example, Unity Forest Products proclaims that it "is thriving in an industry threatened by a severe shortage of raw material—timber—and depressed by a downturn in housing starts. Yet . . . the company has never had an unprofitable month." One observer says that Enita Nordeck, the principal owner, "runs the company with tactics that are nothing less than revolutionary in the hidebound, unhurried lumber business. . . . What she has is a theory of inventory management and sales and marketing that hasn't found its way into this industry yet."[13]

Key Competitor Analysis

Key competitors are those companies in, or predicted to enter, an industry that are expected to have the most effect on a venture's success. Key competitor analyses begin with the construction of a profile describing the size, growth, objectives, management, technical capabilities, and marketing practices of each key competitor. As noted in Exhibit 4.4, attention should also be given to the market positioning and practices of key competitors, their estimated market share, and their likely responses to our competitive moves. This information is used to predict future changes in the competitor's marketing actions and to evaluate how well the competitor is meeting customer requirements. Through published sources, interviews with those familiar with each competitor, and observation, a picture can be pieced together of the marketing strategies, tactics, and management styles of each key competitor. The crucial factors that influence the marketing strategies and tactics of key competitors are shown in Exhibit 4.9. The purpose of key competitor analyses is to describe these factors and to evaluate their effects on the marketing decisions of key competitors.

As a first step in conducting such an analysis, entrepreneurs should construct a financial picture of each key competitor. There are independent published sources of financial information, such as Dun & Bradstreet, Standard & Poor's, and Moody's. More creative means may sometimes have to be employed to estimate financial strength—counting the number of advertisements run in

EXHIBIT 4.9   Factors influencing the marketing strategy of key competitors.

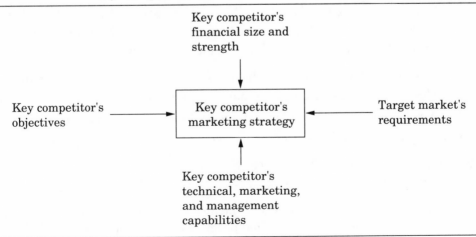

Source: Dr. Robert B. Woodruff, The University of Tennessee.

a certain time period or keeping track of the number of sales personnel in overlapping sales territories. The resulting financial profile can be invaluable as an indicator of a key competitor's ability to sustain a marketing strategy in target markets.

Second, entrepreneurs should pay close attention to key competitors' objectives and capabilities. Competitor characteristics that are ideally profiled are the following:

- Mission and business objectives.
- Market position and sales trends.
- Management capabilities and limitations.
- Target market strategies.
- Marketing objectives.
- Marketing strategies and tactics.

The result is a picture of the way in which a key competitor strives to reach markets and positions itself against competition. The information gathered allows an entrepreneur to evaluate a key competitor's strengths and weaknesses. The entrepreneur considers both the competitor's coverage of market segments and its success in meeting customer requirements. The evaluation of key competitors' respective abilities to meet or exceed customer requirements is concerned with the quality of each key competitor's marketing program. Customer profiles are examined to identify customers' important requirements and then the strategy and tactics used by each key competitor are scrutinized to see how they meet each customer requirement. Judgments can then be formed about how well or poorly each of these requirements is satisfied. This comparison helps entrepreneurs uncover the strengths and weaknesses of each key competitor's technical and marketing strategy and tactics.

Finally, entrepreneurs should predict changes in key competitors' marketing strategies and tactics. But entrepreneurs should not place too much reliance on trend analysis. Other methods include the following:

- Analyzing key competitors' probable responses, given their management styles, to anticipated changes in market conditions.
- Interviewing key competitors' suppliers, distributors, and customers.
- Hiring away key competitors' executives.

One expert comments on the efforts of some companies to familiarize themselves with the key competitors:

> What appears to be vital to effective intelligence activities is that the emphasis be focused on anticipating expected behavior by key competitors. . . . Several firms have successfully institutionalized this emphasis on anticipating behavior

or responses by key players by assigning to line managers the role of a "shadow" competitor. . . . In strategy meetings, it is expected of these "shadow" executives that they be able to present their best judgment as to how their particular "shadow" will respond to strategic moves being considered.[14]

Clearly, to be successful, a new venture's marketing strategy must meet customers' requirements and also effectively position itself against competition. In fact, the essence of planning marketing strategy is to effectively position a company against the competition in the minds of customers. *Positioning* refers to the use of marketing strategy to match the strengths of competition and to exploit its weaknesses, thereby giving customers a reason to buy from your company rather than another. Entrepreneurs can achieve positioning through target market selection by exploiting competitive weaknesses in market coverage. From the industry and key competitor analyses the entrepreneur looks for "holes" in the competitive coverage across the market. A hole is evident when there is more demand in the market, or in a specific market segment, than is being met by competition.

But selecting target markets is only a start toward effective positioning. The marketing strategy must also be creatively employed to build a differential advantage over competition in the minds of customers. Being different from the competition is not enough. The difference must represent an advantage to customers by meeting at least some important customer requirements better than other sellers.

> Boston Beer Co. (BBC) is the country's 10th-largest beer producer. Next to Anheuser-Busch's, Miller's, and Coors's combined 1994 production of 150 million barrels, BBC's 700,000 barrels were a drop in the bucket. But they were enough to spirit the company to the head of the microbrewing niche. But since CEO [Inc./Ernst & Young] and runner-up Entrepreneur of the Year, Jim Koch's arrival on the craft-beer scene, an estimated 500 small breweries and brew pubs have ventured to open, their ranks swelling at the rate of some 50 a year from 1985 on. The success was spurred by as astute and imaginative a promotional barrage as the industry had seen. In addition to handing out the typical T-shirts and coasters, Koch and company peppered Boston and its environs with restaurant umbrellas, pub-menu chalkboards, and gala beer parties—all touting BBC's brands.[15]

But the key to the success of BBC's Samuel Adams beer was a differential advantage over his key competitors in the minds of his target market customers. He quit a $250,000/year job to continue in the footsteps of his family of beer producers.

Careful review of both customer requirements and competitor strengths and weaknesses in meeting those requirements are the cornerstone for differential advantage strategies. The payoff from an MOA comes when the entrepreneur:

- Reviews the information and alternative target markets.
- Determines important customer requirements.
- Reviews competitive strengths and weaknesses for building a differential advantage.
- Decides on which market positioning is best: a niche market.
- Forecasts the sales expected from a marketing strategy.

Customer groups or segments in which buyers have similar customer requirements are identified and separated from segments in which buyers have different requirements. Each segment becomes an alternative target market. The sales generated by a marketing strategy depend to a great extent on how well buyers' expectations are met. Matching company strengths (and not exposing weaknesses) to the market requires understanding exactly what customers want—their requirements. Customer profile information is examined to develop a list of requirements reflecting the benefits and services that customers want. The entrepreneur should consider the relative importance of each of these requirements. For example, President Michael Harris of Deck House, Inc., said, "We felt that forcing standardized homes on customers was infringing on their freedom.[16] But in reality the variety of choices was overwhelming. This was a conclusion based on customer survey responses. As a result, Deck House designed a new line of standardized homes that met most customers' requirements without needing a lot of customization. We are seeing an uptick in business even though the housing market is still flat." For those target markets in which the entrepreneur believes that a strong position can be developed or maintained, the company can position itself against the strengths and weaknesses of the competition. Ultimately, success in markets comes from finding a unique advantage over key competitors. Entrepreneurs are usually more successful in serving well-defined niche markets than mass markets. Market positioning involves finding a "position" in the minds of customers where your strengths satisfy customers better than competitors.

The final step in evaluating market opportunity is forecasting the sales response to the planned marketing strategy. Having selected alternative markets as candidate targets, the entrepreneur plans a marketing program to tap sales from these markets. The plan will show the extent to which their company's strengths can be brought to bear on meeting customer requirements and providing an advantage over the competition. Only then can a sales forecast be made to estimate the sales return from the marketing strategy. The sales forecast is used, in turn, to estimate profits, return on investment, cash flow, and other financial indicators of the worth of alternative target markets.

Target markets are finally selected based on all of these indicators as well as other considerations, such as consistency with the firm's mission, legal constraints, and available resources. Several sales-forecasting methods may be considered for use, and although beyond the scope of this chapter, it is noteworthy that without any past sales data in a new venture, many of the traditional methods are not helpful to the entrepreneur.[17]

A market opportunity analysis is essential as the first step toward developing a marketing plan. With this understanding in hand, the entrepreneur moves on to the second step—setting the marketing objectives for a particular product market.

SETTING MARKETING OBJECTIVES

The next step in developing a marketing plan is to set marketing objectives. Objectives should be stated for each target market in terms of sales, profit contribution, and other qualitative aims, such as building an image. Objectives are sometimes divided into two groups: market performance objectives and marketing support objectives. *Market performance objectives* pertain to specific outcomes such as sales and profits. *Marketing support objectives* pertain to tasks that precede final performance outcomes such as building customer awareness and engaging in educational efforts.

Objectives help shape the marketing strategy for each target market. For example, an entrepreneur seeking to increase sales in a target market by 6% for the coming year would probably make only limited changes in the existing marketing program. Or the marketing effort may be reduced if entrepreneurial growth is becoming uncontrollable. Alternatively, starting a new business requires developing a totally new marketing strategy.

Objectives must, at least to some degree, be measurable; otherwise, identifying progress toward their achievement is impossible. But in marketing, this is no easy task. A support objective could include creating an image in the minds of potential customers—and progress toward that objective could be measured by surveying (even informally) customer perceptions. Objectives should be worded very carefully, with the intention of developing measurable and attainable standards. For example, the following marketing performance and support objectives were used in an early-stage personal computer education business:

- To increase (over last year) the number of student/class hours (unit = one student for one class hour) by 36%.
- To increase class size to an average of 28 (despite a 6% price increase) and thereby to increase profits by 20%.
- To increase awareness of our services to at least 50% of our targeted customers.

- To develop, over the next year, three new class offerings, with high-quality instructors, to serve the personal computer user.
- To develop a targeted, systematic, and coordinated advertising program.

The first two objectives are oriented toward market performance, whereas the last three are market support objectives.

FORMULATING A MARKETING STRATEGY

Marketing strategy is the set of guidelines and policies used for effectively matching marketing programs (products, distribution, prices, and promotion) with target market opportunities and customer requirements in order to achieve the venture's objectives. This is the third step in developing a marketing plan. The development of an overall marketing strategy helps ensure that mutually beneficial exchanges occur, which is part of the definition of marketing. It is oriented toward the long run, composed of fundamental decisions (not day-to-day adjustments), and developed with an eye to competition as well as markets. Developing a marketing strategy includes deciding which customers to target and how to position products and the business relative to competitors in the minds of existing and potential customers.

Developing marketing programs involves identifying alternative combinations of marketing variables (for example, Wendy's higher-quality, higher-priced hamburgers) and then judging how well these combinations match the market opportunity. The key to such matching is forecasting potential customer response to the mix of marketing variables. Then, a program with great potential is implemented! Admittedly, however, this is often more an art than a science.

For example, in starting a new venture targeted to wealthy customers, the guidelines and policies that constitute a strategy could be oriented toward creating the highest-quality image possible. They might include the following:

- A high, narrow pricing range to convey an image of price exclusiveness.
- Products that offer exceptionally high quality and service standards and excellent warranty coverage.
- Advertising media and messages that impart an exclusive, high-quality image.

These guidelines and policies (marketing strategy) narrow the range of marketing actions that are appropriate given the overall marketing objectives (quality image). Basically, a marketing strategy guides how marketing objectives will be achieved. Marketing objectives, part of marketing strategy, were discussed above. Objectives, target market selection, and determination of the marketing program together form the marketing strategy. Making decisions about target markets is one of management's most important tasks. For example, Wendy's decision to go after a subgroup of the population—young adults—with a particular food service was a *target market decision*.

A firm's marketing must consist of an integrated strategy aimed at providing customer satisfaction. To develop a strategy, a firm uses demand-influencing variables that make up the "marketing mix." The marketing mix (or program, as noted above), like a puzzle, has numerous pieces that must be combined for a successful result (see Exhibit 4.10). It includes the following:

- The services or products offered by the firm.
- The distribution channels the firm uses (wholesalers, distributors, retailers) to make the product available to customers.
- The prices the firm charges.
- The promotion (advertising, personal selling, sales promotion, and publicity).

Other terms used to describe the components of the marketing mix are the marketing offer and the Four Ps (product, place, price, and promotion). Each of these four elements in the marketing mix is discussed in detail in the subsections that make up the rest of this chapter.

These variables must be consistent with one another, and ideally they complement one another for a synergistic result. Building a high-quality, prestigious product and combining it with inconsistent mix ingredients such as heavy price discounting would yield a poorly integrated, internally inconsistent marketing program. The mix ingredients would conflict with one another in the minds of customers.

EXHIBIT 4.10 Marketing mix variables.

Product	Distribution	Price	Promotion
Features	Types of channels/	List price	Promotion blend
Quality	middlemen	Credit terms	Advertising
Packaging	Store/distributor	Discounts	Media
Branding	location	Selection and	Copy
Services	Storage	allowances	Timing
Guarantees	Transportation and	Flexibility	Personal selling
Assortment	and logistics		Training
	Service levels		Motivation
			Allocation
			Sales promotion
			Publicity

The creative role that entrepreneurial management must play in moving from knowledge of the market to the formulation of marketing programs is both a major challenge and an opportunity. For instance, Mallards clothing specialty store for men in Chicago provides an excellent example of the development and implementation of a unique marketing mix for a firm's target market. Started in the 1980s, Mallards offers updated versions of classic Ivy League and sportswear-oriented clothing for men, which, because of its traditional styling, avoids quick outdating. The target market is ambitious and active, career-oriented individuals, 25- to 45-year-old college graduates, mostly professionals, with above-average incomes. Yet Mallards customers still value a good buy. The clothing is mostly private label, obtained directly from high-quality producers. This departure from traditional industry practices enables the firm to offer reasonable prices for the quality it provides. The store location projects a quality image and is convenient for the targeted customers. The company engages in limited advertising, relying primarily on location, window displays, and a quality reputation to attract customers. All Mallards employees also project a quality image. They are fully trained in selling techniques, fitting, garment care, fabrics, and styles, allowing them to deal with discriminating buyers. Mallards offers an appealing blend of marketing mix elements.

Building a marketing program for a target market consists of the following:

- Determining how much should be spent on marketing.
- Allocating the budget to the marketing mix variables of the firm.
- Determining how to best use the resources for each marketing mix element.

Given the myriad of possible marketing programs that can be developed for each market, and the difficulty of estimating the likely revenue and cost results of each alternative program, these are complex decisions. Management determines the combination of marketing variables that will yield the most favorable profit contribution, after subtracting marketing costs. Estimating the responsiveness of target markets to alternative marketing mixes is perhaps the greatest uncertainty in all of marketing management.

Finally, the terms *strategy* and *tactics* are often used in marketing discussions. *Strategy* (or strategic) *decisions* provide a broad, long-term framework (a year or usually more) for marketing action. They are fundamental decisions that guide the day-to-day actions. *Tactical decisions* determine how marketing strategies are to be carried out on a day-to-day basis. For Mallards, strategy includes placing an emphasis on quality, private brands, and reasonable prices. The strategy of Mallards is implemented by day-to-day tactical decisions, such as setting the exact prices, deciding whether or not to include prices in advertising copy, and deciding how frequently to offer sale prices.

Product Decisions

Each of the marketing mix elements should be discussed as part of the marketing plan. First, the *product* is anything that is potentially valued by a target market for the benefits or satisfactions it provides, including objects, services, organizations, places, people, and ideas. Making product decisions requires grouping the various meanings of the term *product* into three levels (see Exhibit 4.11). Level 1 comprises the basic *benefits* or *satisfactions* that a particular product delivers. The same product may provide different benefits to different people. For example, to one person a Cadillac is a way to enhance one's status; to another it is a source of comfortable, quiet, and reliable transportation.

Marketers must also understand the linkages between objective, tangible *product attributes* (level 2 in Exhibit 4.11) and subjective satisfactions. The Cadillac brand name, quality, and styling enhance the satisfactions that customers feel. Tangible attributes, however, sometimes receive a disproportionate amount of attention in product decision making.

EXHIBIT 4.11 Customer perception hierarchy.

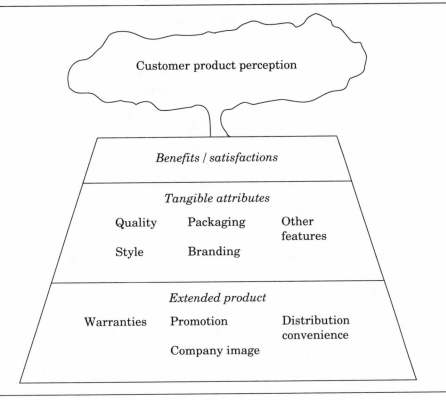

Finally, the *extended product* (level 3 in Exhibit 4.11) comprises marketing elements that go beyond the specific product itself but are valued by customers. The extended product is the broader set of marketing elements within which the product exists. For a Cadillac, it includes such things as warranty service, status-oriented promotion, and delivery arrangements.

These three levels—the extended product, product attributes, and benefits/satisfactions—together create the customer's overall *perception* of a product. The entrepreneur's task is to blend the three levels in a consistent, synergistic manner to meet the needs and wants of well-defined target markets. The levels imply that product perceptions in the marketplace are hierarchical; such perceptions are affected most by the customer benefits derived from products, second by the specific attributes of products, and last by the other marketing elements associated with products. Business owners can adopt this customer-oriented perspective in attempting to create product images for target markets. This is also true for the huge service sector of the U.S. economy. Services are intangible; they blend production and consumption; and they often involve unorthodox distribution channels. Yet the delivery of services involves attributes (e.g., pleasant, smiling personnel) that contribute to the perception shown in Exhibit 4.11.

New Product Development Process

New products and services provide new life for otherwise aging organizations and propel entrepreneurs to the top of new industries. Few decisions in a business are as fundamental, pervasive, and long lasting as those concerning products. Entrepreneurs sometimes face difficulty in taking their business to second and third generation products and services that reduce dependence on their first product. *New* products are those whose degree of change *for customers* is sufficient to require the design or redesign of marketing strategies. A business is usually created with one product or service or, if a retailer or distributor, with one location and one target market. But products eventually die, and without product/service improvements and new products the business will eventually die.

Booz-Allen & Hamilton's research of 700 U.S. companies involved with 13,000 products concluded that most companies use a formal new-product-planning process as shown in Exhibit 4.12. It must be emphasized, however, that they studied few new or smaller businesses and that not all companies use a systematic new-product-planning process. Indeed, Feldman and Page concluded that it is a myth that companies use a new-product-planning process that is orderly, logical, and sequential.[18] Yet they also stated that use of a strategic new-product-planning process is important to success. Entrepreneurs benefit from knowing what the steps are in a formal new product development

EXHIBIT 4.12   New product development process.

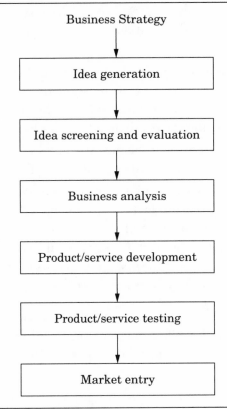

Business Strategy

Idea generation

Idea screening and evaluation

Business analysis

Product/service development

Product/service testing

Market entry

Source: Adapted from Booz-Allen & Hamilton, *New Product Management for the 1980s* (New York: Booz-Allen & Hamilton, 1982), 11.

process, even if they are not followed systematically. Also, once new services and products are in the market, entrepreneurs interacting with customers day-to-day often make major changes to better position their products.

Whether the entrepreneur wants to familiarize the public with the name of the entire business, a group of products, or single products, he should consider building a "brand" image. There are several important reasons:

- To create a market identity. A brand helps position a business' product offering in terms of price level, quality, service, prestige, and other factors that are important to buyers in the firm's target markets. Consumers often use brand image as a proxy for quality and dependability, particularly if they find it difficult to evaluate a product because of its newness or complexity.

- To legally protect a name or symbol for which major promotional expenditures may be made.

- To create a focus for building customer loyalty for a successful business or brand, which can be an important competitive strategy. Repeat sales become more likely, and the position of other company products may also be enhanced.

- To serve different market niches by introducing different brands as a business expands. Similar products, such as soft drinks, with different brand names (Pepsi, Mountain Dew, Orange Crush, Mr. Pibb) can help provide a sufficient array of alternatives to increase sales in many markets.

- To create a brand identity of the business and/or products, which may itself increase margins and profits by enhancing the perception of quality.

- To help ensure that customers will demand the product from distributors, thus strengthening the producer's influence in the channel of distribution. A strong image helps "pull" manufacturers' products through the channel of distribution by establishing recognition and preferences among consumer or industrial end-users. This can also establish powerful bargaining positions with suppliers and distributors.

The entrepreneur should be aware that a "brand" image, at least of the business, is being created in the minds of customers in any event. Careful attention to the special opportunity in a new business to create a strong image can be critical to success.

Distribution Decisions

Another important part of the marketing plan involves distribution decisions. The marketing system is made up of a vast configuration of organizations and individuals, linked together by flows of information, products, negotiations, risks, money, and people. A *channel of distribution* is "an organized network [system] of agencies and institutions which, in combination, perform all the activities required to link producers with users and users with producers . . . to accomplish the marketing task."[19] Each organization in the distribution channel performs particular activities in connecting end-users with desired goods and services.

For example, consider the firms, functions, flows, and relationships involved in transforming a steer on an entrepreneur's Texas ranch into a roast on the dinner table of a family in Washington, D.C. The animal is sold by the rancher to a feedlot operator for fattening and then purchased by a meat packer for processing. The hindquarter of the carcass, or bulk packaged portions, are sold to a large retail food chain, transported from a regional warehouse of the food chain to a supermarket in Washington, D.C., and processed by the supermarket butcher into steaks, roasts, and ground beef that are finally placed in the meat display case. There are several business owners, from producers to the dinner tables.

Marketing intermediaries are organizations that perform the various channel-of-distribution functions necessary to connect producers with end-users. Intermediaries drastically reduce the number of buyer-seller transactions. Suppose 10 customers each wanted to buy a Gant Oxford button-down shirt, a pair of Calvin Klein jeans, an Aigner belt, and Bass loafers. Each person dealing directly with each manufacturer would have to conduct 4 transactions, for a total of 40. Now place a retailer between the 4 manufacturers and the 10 consumers, and the number of transactions is reduced from 40 to 14. By taking advantage of the economies obtainable through specialization and by greatly reducing the number of transactions needed to bring end-users and producers together, middlemen perform functions that are often not possible for manufacturers or end-users.

Business owners in the distribution channel perform various functions—procurement, storage, packaging, financing, transportation, and counseling. A substantial portion of the price paid by consumers for products and services is frequently accounted for by activities performed by these companies. For example, 69¢ of each dollar spent for food is used to pay for distribution and processing activities.[20] The entrepreneur who assumes, without study, that direct distribution will lower costs usually misunderstands the efficiencies offered by distribution systems. The key issue for the entrepreneur is how to perform the functions that are needed cost effectively.

Over time, inefficient intermediaries are eliminated from the marketing system. Yet the competitive marketplace generates new distribution alternatives when entrepreneurs see better ways to provide cost-effective services to buyers and when buyers are willing to consider different levels of customer service. For example, several rapidly expanding distribution methods today are nonstore marketing, including mail, telephone, vending machines, and door-to-door selling. Strategic alliances can also be important:

> Sheila Talton is talking big: Head-to-head competition with IBM Corp. and Andersen Consulting . . . . Are these simply the daydreams of the CEO and founder of Chicago-based Unisource Systems Inc., a 42-employee network integrator specializing in telecommunications that is still under $6 million in annual revenues? Not at all. Sheila Talton is talking about today's business. She is super-structuring her company with strategic alliances.
>
> There are some corporate goliaths standing behind Talton as she discusses Uniscource's current activities companies such as Booz Allen & Hamilton Inc., Sun Microsystems Inc., Computer Services Corp., and Lockheed Martin Inc. Little Unisource, just nine years old, is partnered with each of them in a variety of formal and informal agreements . . .
>
> "What I was lacking was the distribution and the ability to implement and support many of those customers on a worldwide basis. . . . What we said

was that if we were going to stick to our vision [to be the worldwide industry standard for process-manufacturing software], . . . we must partner for distribution, for implementation, and support, but not partner for the building of the product."[21]

Middlemen may be classified by their level in the channel of distribution. Exhibit 4.13 illustrates alternative vertical channels. Closest to consumers and organizational end-users are retailers. Manufacturers may employ salespersons for contacting wholesalers and distributors and sometimes own their own sales offices and branches. If sales personnel cannot be economically justified by a new venture's sales volume, manufacturers often use agents or brokers on a commission basis.

Also, marketers sometimes join together for mutual advantage in voluntary groups and retailer cooperatives. For example, pooled buying groups include independent, entrepreneur grocers who work cooperatively to lower the costs of goods purchased from wholesalers.

Actually deciding which method of distribution to use may be obvious, or it may be a very complex decision process. Michael Dell, in starting Dell Computer, decided to advertise directly to customers and eliminate intermediaries. Dell is now leading a rapidly growing *Fortune* 500 company. His distribution strategy has been a huge success!

EXHIBIT 4.13   Alternative marketing channels.

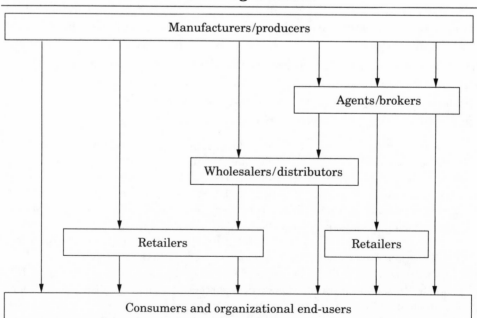

There has also been substantial growth in network marketing in recent years:

> Multilevel marketing (MLM) is the wave of the future, says Wayne McIlvaine, consultant and former marketing director for McCann-Erickson advertising agency. Since manufacturing costs have fallen, distribution today represents 85% of retail cost, according to Paul Zane Pilzer, author of Unlimited Wealth. Therefore, the greatest opportunities in the 1990s await those who reduce the cost of distribution. That is what MLM does. Once the domain of housewives and blue-collar workers, MLM today attracts corporate presidents, stockbrokers, and accountants who are attracted by the possibility of exponential growth with MLM companies such as Nu Skin and Oxyfresh. Industries such as insurance and telecommunications have been assaulted by MLM, and McIlvaine says that virtually any area of the economy is open to the sales method.
>
> It's often assumed that multilevel marketing—sometimes called MLM, network marketing, or multiplex marketing—is a glorified chain letter or pyramid scam. But while the critics have scoffed, a handful of visionaries has quietly set the stage for economic revolution.[22]

Although there is evidence that a very small percentage of new recruits make a substantial profit, the changing economics of distribution have benefited many entrepreneurs.

As business owners consider different distribution alternatives, and selection of intermediaries, they should consider the decision criteria shown in Exhibit 4.14. The method of distribution is often a critical part of marketing strategy, spelling success or failure in new enterprises.

Pricing Decisions

Pricing is often used by entrepreneurs to enhance the image of their business or products, to increase sales through discount pricing, or, in combination with promotion, to build future sales. At times, however, price is an inactive element of the marketing mix, with business owners just using traditional markups over cost or following industry leaders. The use of price as a competitive tool, particularly by new, smaller companies, is often avoided because of fear of retaliation and price wars. But whether pricing is an active or inactive element, it is an integral part of the overall marketing plan.

Price is used in different ways by different companies, depending on the role it plays in the overall marketing program. For example, Service Merchandise, a catalog showroom discounter (and entrepreneurial success story), uses low prices on name brands as its major basis for appealing to customers. In return for low prices, customers are willing to complete an order form and wait until their purchase is obtained from the warehouse. Through operating efficiencies, reduction in customer service, and high volume, catalog showrooms

EXHIBIT 4.14   Channel design decisions and decision criteria.

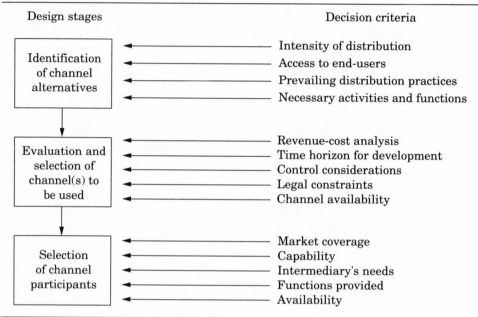

Design stages   Decision criteria

Identification of channel alternatives
- Intensity of distribution
- Access to end-users
- Prevailing distribution practices
- Necessary activities and functions

Evaluation and selection of channel(s) to be used
- Revenue-cost analysis
- Time horizon for development
- Control considerations
- Legal constraints
- Channel availability

Selection of channel participants
- Market coverage
- Capability
- Intermediary's needs
- Functions provided
- Availability

Source: Dr. David W. Cravens, Texas Christian University.

are able to compete with other retailers by using low prices. In contrast, exclusive, high-end furniture stores assign price a very different role. High-priced furniture and fixtures allow attractive margins that make possible a variety of customer services and help support promotional efforts.

Pricing decisions must also be made in light of channel/distributor interests. Palm Beach, Inc.'s pricing strategy for its Evan-Picone line of tailored apparel for women was developed, in part, as a way to strengthen relationships with retailers. Palm Beach management promised retailers designer-quality clothes at prices at least 30% lower than those of other distinguished labels, a price reduction made possible by the company's ability to mass-produce fine garments.

There are four steps to pricing products (or services) effectively.

Step 1: Establish Specific Objectives for Pricing Programs

Many entrepreneurs fail to focus on this step. *Pricing objectives* are specific quantitative and qualitative operating targets that reflect the basic role of pricing in the marketing plan.[23] Examples of pricing objectives for entrepreneurs might include:

- Increase sales or profit growth.
- Maximize short- and long-run profits.
- Discourage entrants.
- Speed exit of marginal competitors.
- Discourage price cutting.
- Stabilize market prices.
- Rapidly establish market position.
- Rapidly recover new product development costs or increase cash flow.
- Contribute to the image of the product and the firm.
- Build traffic.
- Develop a reputation for being fair to middlemen and customers.

New businesses usually have a set of objectives—some primary, others collateral; some short run, others long run.

Step 2: Determine the Extent of Pricing Flexibility

The extent of pricing flexibility is determined by costs, demand, competition, and legal and ethical constraints. Together, these elements establish upper and lower limits for prices.

The writer once consulted for a business owner who, after study, was found to be pricing under cost—hardly a long-term strategy. We joked that he could set prices below cost and make it up on volume! Costs often vary at different volume levels and business owners may not allocate fixed costs appropriately. Hands-on involvement with the financial whiz of the new venture is essential for determining the *floor* for setting prices.

Demand and competition set the *ceiling* for prices, and the expression "what the market will bear" goes to the heart of evaluating demand. The range between the cost floor and the demand and competition ceiling defines the flexibility in pricing available to the entrepreneur. A critical demand consideration is price elasticity; that is, the percentage change in sales (based on the number of units) divided by the percentage change in price. If an entrepreneur reduces a price from $20 to $15 (a 25% cut) and sales volume jumps from 100,000 to 200,000 units (100%), the elasticity is greater than 1, and we say that the demand is price elastic. Conversely, a Chicago entrepreneur who manufactures furniture says, "If it sells well, raise the price!" If he raises the price of a chair 25% and demand drops by only 15%, the elasticity is less than 1 and we say that the demand is price *in*elastic. The more that customers know about competitive products, the less flexibility the business owner possesses with pricing strategy. Determining the likely response of customers in either buying less or more, or in buying competitor's products, is essential to determining the price ceiling.

Step 3: Develop Price Strategies

Price strategies are the guidelines and policies used to effectively guide pricing decisions to match target markets. Price strategies determine, among other things, the following factors:

- Whether prices should vary day-to-day.
- Overall price levels.
- The use of price lining.
- Price stability.
- Pricing relative to stages of the product/service life cycle.
- The use of psychological pricing.

For example, in a new business, it could be decided to minimize day-to-day changes in prices, to set prices slightly above the competition, not to set prices at different levels within a product line, and to use a psychological pricing premium (e.g., a high price for a difficult-to-evaluate product, such as a sound system) to enhance the perceived value of the product.

Step 4: Establish Prices

Setting pricing objectives, determining the extent of pricing flexibility, and selecting price strategies provide considerable direction to management for setting specific prices. But how are prices for specific products actually set? Again, a sound approach to pricing must incorporate cost, competition, and demand factors. Costs establish the floor for a possible price range. Thus, cost-plus pricing often involves simply adding a percentage of the cost to set the price. However, there are many other strategies to setting prices.

Markup pricing

This is a variation of cost-plus pricing in that markups are calculated as a percentage of the selling price rather than as a percentage of the cost. Successful new ventures are sometimes founded on innovative, low-margin pricing, in the hope that high volume selling will provide a good return. For example, in the 1930s, supermarkets shook up the food distribution business using this approach, and in the past decade, the health care industry experienced similar changes. Traditional hospitals and HMOs (health maintenance organizations) faced increased competition from major brand name health care providers, such as Humana, Inc.

Break-even pricing

This is another cost-oriented method; it determines the level of sales needed to cover all of the relevant fixed and variable costs. If fixed costs are $100,000, unit variable costs are $2, and the price per unit is $4, then the firm must sell 50,000 units to break even [$100,000/($4 − 2)].

Target return pricing

Whereas break-even prices just set a pricing floor, target return pricing sets prices at a desired percentage return over and above the break-even point. The obvious weakness of this and other cost-oriented pricing methods is that prices determined according to these methods are without regard to market demand. The actual quantity sold at the determined price could easily be greater or less than the quantity required. Yet using costs as a beginning point helps ensure that prices exceed all costs and therefore contribute to profit.

Going-rate pricing

This method involves setting prices equal to or a certain percentage above or below competitors' prices. Whether or not this method is appropriate depends on several factors:

- The firm's pricing objectives.
- The structure of the industry (for example, oligopoly).
- Whether there is excess production capacity (so the added cost of more production is low).
- The relative production, selling, and administrative costs of competitors.
- Customers' perceptions of the firm's products compared with those of competitors.

Entrepreneurs often use going-rate pricing when retaliatory price changes are likely and when price changes by competitors can have a substantial effect on company sales. Retail owners often employ competition-oriented pricing methods in conjunction with the cost markup method. Retailers often survey competitors' prices on selected items, and adjust prices accordingly.

Demand-modified break-even pricing

This strategy involves setting prices to achieve the highest profit (over the break-even point) in consideration of the amount demanded at alternative prices. Demand-modified break-even pricing requires estimates of market demand at each feasible price; break-even points and expected levels of total sales revenue can then be calculated. The primary challenge in demand-oriented pricing (particularly for new ventures) is obtaining accurate estimates of the price/quantity relationships. One approach is to conduct direct customer interviews, asking customers within a target market a series of questions to measure their likely response at different price levels. This approach is complicated by customers who find it difficult to judge how they would actually respond.

Although it may often seem an insurmountable task, particularly for new firms, some businesses have been successful in gaining a better understanding of their markets' responsiveness to price changes. For example, Approach Software, a startup firm whose only product was a database software for "non-techies," tested three introductory prices for their product on five mailing lists of 50,000 prospective customers. The result provided "statistical proof—sales came in almost as high at $149 as at $129." A price of $199 "crossed a threshold of what people would spend to try a new product through the mail," according to Jaleh Bisharat, Approach's marketing director.[24]

Perceived-value pricing

This strategy is sometimes used to set the prices of industrial products. The price of an industrial (versus consumer) product is probably determined somewhat more by the exact potential benefit that the product offers the buyers. This is especially true when an industrial product faces little direct competition.

For example, one business owner developed a new electronic temperature measurement instrument, and the owner was unsure about how to price it. The variable costs were about $1200. Management usually set a selling price of about four times the variable costs to cover other costs and contribute to profits, but the fixed costs were to be proportionately lower for the new product. Management estimated that a price of $3600 for the new product would cover costs and meet the profit objectives. But then several potential users were asked to rate the new product and directly competitive products on product attributes. Management learned that less accurate competitive instruments were available at $3200. After assessing the product's potential benefit to users and the willingness of users to purchase the product at different price levels, management set the price at $4500. Demand factors ultimately dictated the appropriate price.

Perceived-value pricing is also applicable to consumer products, often being based on a psychological pricing strategy. For instance, branded shirts are priced in part on consumers' perception of their value. This pricing method underscores the behavioral nature of pricing decisions. The willingness of customers to pay a higher price depends on their perception of the fairness of the price and the quality they get for the price they pay. Perceptions sometimes stray from reality, and creatively conducting low cost market research on perceptions as they affect demand can be very useful.

Skimming and penetration pricing strategies

Approaches to new product pricing are particularly relevant to entrepreneurs entering new markets. Pricing objectives for new products have more latitude than those for existing products and pricing flexibility is also greater for new products. For products in the growth, maturity, or decline stages of the product life cycle, there is usually growing competition and a smaller number of acceptable prices. The prices of such products often have to be reduced. New products with little competition usually offer the option of a skimming or penetration strategy.

A *skimming pricing strategy* sets introductory prices at a high level relative to costs so as to "skim the cream" off the market. With price-insensitive customers (in the absence of immediate competition), firms often consider it safe to set initial new product prices high relative to costs and to lower the prices gradually as market conditions dictate. Skimming profits allows entrepreneurs to recover their investment rapidly, though the high margins tend to attract competition. For example, makers of personal computers charged high prices in the early years, but there has been competitive price warfare in recent years.

In contrast to a skimming strategy, a *penetration pricing strategy* sets new product prices low relative to costs. This strategy is usually employed to rapidly acquire a large share of a potential market. Relatively low margins discourage the entry of competitors. The appropriateness of a penetration strategy depends on the firm's ability to retain its desired market share once competition develops.

Establishing the Price Floor

Setting specific new product prices within the strategies selected, given limited competition, normally involves first establishing a price floor through break-even analysis. Unit costs may be high at first, so a long-run viewpoint may be essential in deriving cost estimates. Cost and demand uncertainties are high, so building in alternative cost assumptions and using *sensitivity analysis* to determine important cost thresholds can be very important. Sensitivity analysis answers such questions as:

- What *if* production costs are 10% higher than anticipated?
- What happens to the break-even point?
- What are the odds of achieving the required, higher sales level?

The uncertainty that accompanies new businesses cannot be totally eliminated, and monitoring new product prices is therefore particularly critical.

Nonprice competition is often emphasized in marketing strategies by entrepreneurs, in part because price changes are easy for competitors to counter. It is far more difficult to directly counter a strong brand image with unique product features than to counter a price change. Marketing strategies comprise an array of marketing mix variables, of which the price variable is sometimes best left alone. Yet promotion is virtually always an active part of the marketing plan.

Promotion Decisions

Promotion is considerably more than just advertising. In fact, an entrepreneur can draw on four major tools:

- *Sales promotion* is communicating with an audience through a variety of nonpersonal, nonmedia vehicles such as free samples, gifts, and coupons.
- *Advertising* is communicating with an audience through nonpersonal, paid media.
- *Publicity* is communicating with an audience by personal or nonpersonal media that are not explicitly paid for delivering the messages; the audience is likely to perceive the media rather than the business as the source of messages.
- *Personal selling* is communicating directly with an audience through paid sales personnel.

Together, these tools make up the *promotion mix*. The promotion mix is the combination of promotion tools used by a company to communicate with its markets.

Each major promotion tool includes a wide variety of activities, some of which are listed in Exhibit 4.15. Business owners use all four of these tools to achieve promotional objectives, but place different weights on each of the tools. For example, industrial companies typically spend more for personal selling than for advertising or publicity. In contrast, consumer products companies are likely to place heavy weight on advertising and sales promotion to reach customers.

The use of *publicity* affords an opportunity for entrepreneurs to receive valuable exposure without spending a penny. Creative use of publicity can help

EXHIBIT 4.15   Promotion mix tools.

Advertising		Personal selling
Print ads Broadcast ads Billboard ads Direct mail ads Packaging logos and information		In-person sales presentations Telemarketing

The
promotion
mix

Sales promotion		Publicity
Games, contests Free samples Trade shows Couponing Trading stamps Price promotion Signs and displays		Print media news stories Broadcast media news stories Annual reports Speeches by employees

Source: Dr. Robert B. Woodruff, The University of Tennessee.

offset the small budget often available to business founders. A business startup is often very newsworthy:

> In 1992, Randy Jones, who calls himself the P.T. Barnum of publishing, had the guts to introduce *Worth*, which positions itself as a smart, sophisticated, even in-your-face financial adviser. Since then, circulation has grown to 501,000, and counting. Revenues have risen from $5.4 million in 1992 to $13.7 million [by 1994]. Jones may be having the time of his life, but he cannot claim victory yet—*Worth* still has to turn a profit. Jones rarely misses an opportunity to sell *Worth*. Jones has proved to be a master networker . . . .
>
> Talk about P.T. Barnum: This is the guy who once showed up at an Esquire party for Hollywood celebrities in boxer shorts. The day *Worth* was launched, Jones hired two gorgeous models, dressed in Revolutionary War garb, to hand out copies of the magazine—and 100 Grand candy bars—in front of the New York Stock Exchange. . . .
>
> Fidelity Management Resource Corporation, an investment company that handles about $400 billion in assets, invested in the neighborhood of $25 million in the magazine . . . . "We'll have repaid Fidelity no later than 1997, and that will have been just five years after our launch," [says Jones].[25]

Newspapers and the trade press, particularly in smaller cities or neighborhoods of large cities, are often eager to receive such news items. The keys to success are to (1) try to benefit the media writer and (2) be creative. A cure for cancer would require little more than publicity to be a success. It would be a rare exception and the world would beat a path to the entrepreneur's door. The more innovative and revolutionary the new product or service, the easier it is to obtain publicity. But media writers often *need* stories. The business owner, thinking in terms of the *writer's* needs, can provide a one-page story of 200 to 300 words that helps to make the writer's job easier. Creativity can transform a boring announcement of a new restaurant to that of a "unique restaurant concept with exciting dimensions." The announcement can be mailed to as many outlets as possible. (Use the library and other sources to find lists of media.) Radio or even TV interviews are also possible. The print media often find a high-quality, glossy photograph appealing, particularly if taken creatively. And once the articles appear, copies of a highly credible outlet may be used in other ways to enhance the exposure. What is written or said must be of interest to the media outlet's audience. If this requirement is satisfied, the writers are likely to be interested. A telephone follow-up to letters and news releases often increases the chances of exposure. Even after a business opens and there are no new products or services being offered, creative efforts may yield a great return. Supporting a charitable drive (e.g., offering a free service) can add a noncommercial appeal to gain entry to the media. A now-deceased, famous entrepreneur who started 30 food stores in the Southeast, for example, many times threw live chickens from the roof of a new store to an eager crowd of rural customers. Imagine the free media exposure! Using creative (and appropriate) means to "make news" is often an important entrepreneurial talent.

The entire promotion program—objectives, creative content of messages and format, selection of delivery vehicles, and the budget—should follow directly from marketing objectives and help achieve them. In this way the marketing plan ensures that promotion is coordinated with marketing strategy.

Firms rarely rely on only one of the four tools of promotion. Entrepreneurs can use the following five criteria to determine the role of each promotional tool:

- Cost of reaching an audience member.
- Ability to reach target audiences with little leakage to persons not included in them.
- Ability to deliver a complicated message.
- Ability to engage in interchanges with the target audiences.
- Credibility.

Exhibit 4.16 summarizes how well the four tools compare on these criteria.

EXHIBIT 4.16 Promotion tools' strengths and weaknesses.

Criteria	Advertising	Sales promotion	Publicity	Personal selling
Cost per audience member	Low	Low	Very low	Very high
Focused on target markets	Poor to good	Good	Moderate	Very good
Deliver a complicated message	Poor to good	Poor	Poor to good	Very good
Interchange with audiences	None	None	Low to moderate	Very good
Credibility	Low	Low	High	Moderate to high

Source: Dr. Robert B. Woodruff, The University of Tennessee.

When business owners think about the four promotion tools, it becomes obvious why promotion managers must use a mix. There are clear trade-offs to be made between the tools. A comparison of advertising and personal selling illustrates such trade-offs. Advertising reaches far larger audiences than personal selling for a given total cost. But personal selling is better able to target a particular audience and can develop an interchange with customers, responding to their questions and refuting their objections. Further, complicated messages, such as explaining how a technical product works or how a product may be applied in an unusual way, are much better presented in person than by advertising. Finally, because salespeople can build relationships with customers over time, personal selling has the potential to build much greater credibility with audiences.

Sales Promotion

Sales promotion can be aimed at target markets, but also at distributors and at the company's own sales force. Usually, distributors and the sales force are targets when business owners want to encourage cooperation in a company's total marketing effort. Offering a free vacation to the person with the highest sales volume is a sales promotion activity of this type. Also, grocery manufacturers use price promotions to encourage retailers to lower prices to consumers, arrange special displays of products, and give products a featured position in advertising. Similarly, many manufacturers offer gifts (appliances, vacations) to motivate sales personnel to push particular brands or models.

If there are several target audiences, a company may use a number of sales promotion activities at the same time. A real estate developer selling houses, condominiums, or lots for a development project uses sales promotion tactics that are aimed directly at consumers, as well as sales promotion activities directed at real estate brokers who might steer consumers to the project. The developer's promotion included the following:

- Special events to draw consumers' attention to the development, including family barbecues and picnics.
- Price promotions on slow-moving property.
- Attractive signs at the development site.
- Prizes and other incentives for high-selling real estate brokers.

Sales promotion is usually intended to promote overt actions in target audiences, and well-formulated promotion objectives state exactly what these actions are for each target audience. The objectives differ somewhat for different audiences. An entrepreneur may want customers to:

- Try the product.
- Switch brands.
- Stock up on the product.
- Visit a dealer's showroom.
- Make an inquiry about the company's product.

Sales promotion is a catchall category that encompasses a wider variety of activities than do the other promotion tools. One way to group these many activities is by the way they reach audiences:

- *In-store promotions* are aimed at communicating with customers while they are shopping in a store; they include in-store signs, displays, and brochures.
- *Audience-direct sales promotions* are aimed at reaching audiences directly, through the mail, through advertising media, or through delivery by sales personnel; they include samples, gifts, contests, and cents-off coupons.
- *Trade shows* are events where a number of companies display their wares in exhibits at a central location and invite dealers or customers to visit the exhibits.

Emphasis on sales promotion varies considerably among entrepreneurs. Some firms do very little sales promotion, whereas others spend more on sales promotion than on advertising. Sales promotion budgets have been increasing rapidly in recent years, owing to a new recognition of its effectiveness and the rising cost of other media.

Advertising

A central part of the advertising mission is communicating with specific audiences. One important audience for advertising is "the trade" (resellers in a company's channel of distribution). This audience is reached through trade advertising intended to enlist wholesaler or retailer cooperation in selling the new venture's products. For instance, retail stores may be encouraged to stock the advertiser's product, to participate in a cents-off price promotion, or to buy larger quantities of the product.

How entrepreneurs split spending between trade and customer advertising depends on the type of marketing strategy used. A *push strategy* that emphasizes pushing products through the distribution channel requires relatively more trade advertising. In contrast, a *pull strategy* to build a strong preference for a company's brands among customers must have a higher proportion of consumer advertising. Of course, many marketing strategies fall somewhere in between push and pull and have more balanced allocations.

The primary purpose of advertising is to convey to audiences information about a company and its products. On the basis of this information, customers form beliefs, likes and dislikes, predispositions, and intentions that later influence purchase decisions. In this way, advertising contributes to the total selling effort of a marketing strategy but does not carry the entire burden of generating sales.

The most creative part of advertising is planning an *advertising campaign*. The campaign determines what to say to target audiences and how to say it so that people will listen to and understand the messages and remember them when they make buying decisions.

A marketing plan should provide a "position statement" explaining how a company's product (or service) is differentiated from those of key competitors. A position statement helps advertising managers plan a *selling proposal*. A selling proposal is a statement describing the important facts, images, and persuasive arguments to be communicated to target audiences (Exhibit 4.17).

The next step is to develop a media strategy and tactics. Developing media strategy is complicated because there are many different vehicles are available, each having its advantages and disadvantages. Typically, no one vehicle reaches an entire target audience. Consequently, media planners must

EXHIBIT 4.17   Advertising for a selling proposal.

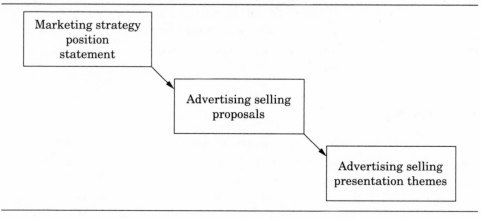

evaluate the many alternatives so as to construct a *media mix* that will meet objectives. The media mix is the combination of vehicles (for example, magazines, newspapers, TV, radio, direct mail, billboards) that will carry advertisements to target audiences.

Further, the timing of advertisements—a *media schedule*—must be determined so that they are properly sequenced when the advertising campaign is run. The media schedule is the combination of specific times (for example, by day, week, month) when advertisements are inserted into media vehicles and delivered to target audiences. The media plan lists the media to be used, the times or issues in which each advertisement is to be carried by each vehicle, and the cost of the media mix. It serves as a blueprint for implementing the delivery of an advertising campaign.

Exhibit 4.18 describes important advantages and disadvantages of various media types. Choosing the best combination of these vehicles and deciding the number and size of advertisements to place in each of them requires careful attention.

Business owners can deal with this complexity by setting criteria for comparison to ensure that the vehicles selected meet advertising objectives and budget constraints. Three particularly important criteria are:

- Overlap of the media audience with target audiences.
- Media communication capabilities.
- Cost.

The success of new ventures depends in part on the availability of cost-effective promotional vehicles to reach the particular market. Launching a new

EXHIBIT 4.18   Advantages and disadvantages of major advertising media.

Media	Advantages	Disadvantages
Television	Reaches large audiences Has visual and audio capabilities Provides great flexibility in getting attention Short lead time needed to place ad	Not easy to reach specific target markets Total cost is high relative to other media Requires production specialists Short exposure time
Magazines and journals	Reach of issues is high for demographic and geographic segments High-quality production Ad lasts as long as magazine or journal is kept Issues are often read by more than one person Credibility of magazine or journal can benefit ad	Must place ad well in advance of publication Provide limited flexibility in gaining attention Provide incomplete control over location of ad in issue
Outdoor advertising	Relatively inexpensive Many repeat exposures	Only very limited message possible Cannot reach well-defined target markets Very short exposure time
Radio	Audio capability Low cost relative to costs of the other media Short lead time needed to place ad Can reach demographic and geographic segments Reaches large audiences Reaches audiences in cars	No visual capability Short exposure time Provides little flexibility in gaining attention
Newspapers	Reach large audiences Can reach segments by locale Short lead time needed to place ad Credibility of newspaper can benefit ad	May be relatively expensive Provide little flexibility for use of creativity Limited reproduction quality (e.g., little or no use of color) Short life carries over to ad
Direct mail	Provides great flexibility in reaching target market segments No clutter from competing ads Easy to personalize copy and layout	Easily thrown away as "junk mail" Obtaining appropriate mailing lists can be expensive

Source: Dr. Robert B. Woodruff, The University of Tennessee.

business often requires a large advertising program initially to build awareness and cash flow.

Personal Selling

Annual expenditures for personal selling in the United States exceed advertising expenditures by as much as 50%. Selling includes:

- Locating prospective customers.
- Planning calls.
- Making sales presentations.
- Relationship marketing—building long term positive ties.
- Closing sales.

In addition, salespeople can collect information on competitive products, prices, customer reactions to product use, and service and delivery problems. Customer service can encompass a variety of responsibilities, including delivery, marketing assistance (for example, promotional and display advice), product application assistance, and repair of products.

The size and characteristics of each target market help determine how personal selling will be used in a firm's marketing mix. When the number of customers is very large, as in mass markets, and the size (in dollars) of the purchase is relatively small, personal selling costs become prohibitive. A sales call is expensive, although its cost is influenced by the salesperson's qualifications, the degree of customer concentration, the size of the territory, waiting time, and the time spent with the customer. The average cost of an industrial sales call exceeds $200. In contrast, a minute of national television advertising during prime viewing time can cost less than $10 per thousand viewing homes. Yet television is often not available to the entrepreneur because of its high cost.

The sales force forms a major part of the marketing mix when customer needs can best be met through personal selling efforts and when there are sufficient margins between the purchase price and the costs to cover sales force expenses. Personal selling is often used in industrial markets since the number of customers and prospects is relatively small (compared to most consumer markets) and the dollar amounts of purchases are sufficient to support salespeople. The same characteristics may exist in some consumer markets, for example, in encyclopedia sales. In other situations, the marketing of consumer products may combine personal selling to channel intermediaries with heavy use of advertising at the consumer level.

The task of the entrepreneur is to select the best combination of marketing mix elements to obtain the desired responses from target markets. The role

EXHIBIT 4.19   Conditions favoring entrepreneurs' use of personal selling as a major element of the marketing mix.

Mix area	Characteristics
Product or service	Complex products requiring customer application assistance (computers, pollution control systems, steam turbines) Major purchase decisions, such as food items purchased by supermarket chains Features and performance of the product requiring personal demonstration and trial by the customer (private aircraft)
Channels	Channel system relatively short and direct to end-users Product and service training and assistance needed by channel intermediaries Personal selling needed in "pushing" products through channel Channel intermediaries available to perform personal selling function for supplier with limited resources and experience (brokers or manufacturer's agents)
Price	Final price negotiated between buyer and seller (appliances, automobiles, real estate) Selling price or quantity purchased enable an adequate margin to support selling expenses (e.g., traditional department store compared to discount house)
Advertising	Advertising media do not provide effective link with market targets Information needed by buyer cannot be provided entirely through advertising and sales promotion (life insurance) Number of dispersion of customers will not enable acceptable advertising economies

Source: Dr. David W. Cravens, Texas Christian University.

of personal selling should be determined in conjunction with that of the other marketing mix components. Several characteristics of marketing programs that may indicate a relatively important role for personal selling are shown in Exhibit 4.19.

Most studies of salespersons' performance have failed to identify factors that are always good predictors of performance. Predicting sales performance is an elusive task, and in the absence of research findings, a great deal of reliance is typically placed on the entrepreneur's judgment and experience. A major problem is pinpointing relevant influences on sales performance, since a number of influences are involved, some of which are interrelated, and the impact of each is often impossible to estimate. Possible determinants fall into the following categories:

- *Aptitude* includes physical factors, such as appearance; mental abilities, such as education and past experience; and personality characteristics, such as empathy, ego strength, and sociability.
- *Skill level* is a learned proficiency at performing the requirements of the job. It includes salesmanship and the interpersonal and technical skills needed in the selling environment.
- *Motivation* is the amount of effort that the salesperson chooses to expend on each of the activities associated with the job.
- *Role perceptions* are the salesperson's perceptions of the activities or behaviors necessary to meet the expectations, demands, and pressures communicated by management, customers, and family.
- *External and constraining factors* are factors that may directly facilitate or constrain performance or interact with other performance determinants. Among such factors are the intensity of competition, the quality of management, and the market potential.

The lead entrepreneur in a new venture is often the lead salesperson, but aptitude and skill-level factors are often used in selecting salespeople when the company expands. Here, the difficulty is that factors in the other three areas may also affect eventual performance. Although some of the determinants of sales performance can be controlled or influenced by training, supervision, and motivational tools, others are uncontrollable. Considering the variety of the possible influences on sales performance and the meagerness of the available research findings, it is not surprising that sales force management places heavy reliance on experience and judgment.

CREATING AN ACTION PLAN TO IMPLEMENT THE MARKETING PRACTICES

The final step in developing a marketing plan is to take the important decisions that have been made and turn them into an action framework. Based on analysis of the environment and the market opportunity, the entrepreneur has developed a marketing strategy that targets well-defined markets, sets quantitative and qualitative marketing objectives, and specifies which elements should form the marketing program. The products and services to offer, the prices, the channels of distribution, and the promotion elements, when combined, will portray the new venture or entrepreneurial firm to the eyes of customers. Customers' perceptions of this mix of marketing elements will contribute to success or failure.

To convert the many marketing decisions into a plan, the final step is to delineate numerous tasks and develop a detailed timetable and budget with an assignment of responsibilities. Although maintaining flexibility is essential, particularly once market feedback begins to flow, it is helpful to identify the major tasks required to implement the marketing plan and establish a timeline to achieve various milestones. Certain tasks, such as advertising, may require detailed scheduling as a subpart of the overall marketing plan.

Too often, entrepreneurs place little emphasis on monitoring and control as the business grows. There is often a tendency to battle intensely through the startup phase, but then place too little detailed attention on marketing control as the enterprise grows. When the business becomes so large that it is beyond the capacity of the founding entrepreneur to manage all of the major elements, it is often necessary to develop a team with the marketing expertise to reach the next development stage.

CONCLUSION

To conclude, marketing is the home for entrepreneurship, and vice versa. In a study of venture capitalists, the importance of marketing management to venture success, was rated 6.7 on a 7.0 scale.[26] They further agreed that venture failure rates could be reduced, by as much as 60%, through better preventure market analysis. Finally, they agreed that entrepreneurs face several unique marketing-related challenges, such as the inability to spread advertising costs, poor access to good-quality distributors, and lack of access to retail shelf space.[27] Several volumes have now been published that provide an in-depth look at many of these issues.[28] But even more important, in a study of highly successful entrepreneurs, the factors cited by business owners as most responsible for their success were high-quality products and services, development of a good customer reputation, and responsiveness to customer desires.[29] This requires adopting the marketing concept as a business philosophy and developing and implementing effective marketing strategy.

5 CREATING A SUCCESSFUL BUSINESS PLAN

David E. Gumpert

When I write about management issues, I try as much as possible to begin on a positive note. That way, even if there are negative points to make, at least I will have gained the interest and involvement of readers, increasing the likelihood that they will be receptive to the inevitable unpleasant matters.

When it comes to the subject of business plans, though, I have come to believe that it is best to make an exception and start with a negative slant. Otherwise, I run the risk of being misleading and, more significantly, of discouraging you from completing the task at hand—creating a successful business plan. By giving you the bad news first, I hope to clear a path for you to get on with what you need to do, which is to write a business plan that will attract the support your business requires.

So here is the straight dope: Writing a business plan is no fun. For many entrepreneurs, the mindset associated with writing a business plan is akin to that associated with root canal surgery or periodontal work. It's not something you look forward to. It's something that goes on for a long while with repeat sessions of agony. The dentist tries to relieve the pain with Novocain.

In one sense, this chapter serves the role of the dentist and relieves the pain. But, fortunately, this chapter is designed to do something much more positive than the dentist does.

When you are finished with the dentist, you breathe a sigh of relief because everything is back to normal, at least until the next visit. But as you complete your business plan, you'll actually begin feeling excited. I know because I've been through the process many times—with my own business and with that of other entrepreneurs—and it's truly exhilarating. The psychological benefits alone are worth the effort. They include a feeling of confidence and a sense of control over your own destiny.

Now that you have the straight story, let's deal with the task at hand. My goals in this chapter are threefold:

1. To get you off on the right foot in writing a business plan.
2. To provide you with a process that makes the writing seem less forbidding.
3. To give you an overview of the information requirements of a successful business plan.

THE BUSINESS PLAN AS A SELLING DOCUMENT

To get off on the right foot, you need to understand the task at hand. How you define the business plan affects your approach to writing it. If you view it as a very complex and boring task, your plan will come across that way—to the detriment of your business.

Indeed, there's a tendency to define a business plan as a roadmap, a statement of strategy, or some other conceptual label. As a result, too many business plans are rambling, dry, and technical, because the entrepreneurs see them as some sort of formal academic exercise.

In my view, the business plan is best defined as a selling document, not unlike sales literature you pass out to customers or a sales pitch you give to prospective employees. Except with the business plan you're not just selling a product or a work environment, *you're selling the entire company as a package.*

If you're really excited about your company, it should come through in the business plan. If you approach the business plan as a document designed to convey, and support, your sense of excitement about the company, you will avoid the dry, convoluted document that too many entrepreneurs produce.

This is not to say that the business plan should consist of a lot of puffery or exaggeration. You need supporting evidence in the form of solid research and experience to back up the excitement and the sales pitch. The point is that the business plan should convey to readers the *excitement* and *promise* that you feel.

Defining a Business Plan

A *good definition:* A business plan is a document that convincingly demonstrates the ability of your business to sell enough of its product or service to make a satisfactory profit and be attractive to potential backers.

A *better definition:* A business plan is *a selling document* that conveys the excitement and promise of your business to any potential backers or stakeholders.

EIGHT REASONS FOR WRITING A BUSINESS PLAN

Why write a business plan? This is a legitimate, indeed essential, question to ask yourself before you plunge in.

If you write a business plan in a vacuum—because you feel it is something you are "supposed" to do—you run the risk of engaging in a painful process of conceptualizing and in the end conveying a sense of aimlessness. But if you write the business plan with one or more specific purposes and audiences in mind, you will likely feel a greater sense of commitment and produce a more focused and practical document.

Your audience most fundamentally consists of those individuals or organizations with a stake in your company's success—those I refer to as *stakeholders.* Here are eight of the most important reasons for writing a business plan, with a description of the stakeholders associated with each:

1. **To sell yourself on the business.** This is a "sanity check." The most important stakeholders in any business are its founders. First and foremost, you need to *convince yourself* that starting the business is right for you—both from a personal viewpoint and an investment viewpoint.

The case of Fred Gibbons helps illustrate this point. Back in the early 1980s when he was considering leaving Hewlett-Packard to start Software Publishing, he was a rising star at the computer giant. Moreover, he would need to take a second mortgage on his house and borrow money from his family to make it work.

Gibbons decided he needed to write a business plan to serve as a "sanity check," to convince himself he was doing the right thing. In other words, he needed to sell himself on committing so deeply to his idea.

2. **To obtain bank financing.** Up until the late 1980s, writing a business plan to obtain bank financing was an option left up to the entrepreneur. Bankers usually took the approach that a business plan helped you make a better case, but wasn't an essential component in the banks' decision-making process.

The bank failures of the late 1980s and early 1990s changed all that. Banks are under greater scrutiny by federal regulators and, as a consequence, are requiring entrepreneurs to include a written business plan with any request for loan funds. Getting bank money is tougher than it has ever been, and a business plan is an essential component of any campaign to sell banks on your company.

3. **To obtain investment funds.** For many years now, the business plan has been the "ticket of admission" to the venture capital evaluation process. Now, though, whether you are seeking venture capital or so-called informal capital from private investors, you will need a written business plan. Rare is the private investor—typically a successful entrepreneur or other well-heeled individual—who will make a financial commitment based entirely on your oral presentation. Even if you get in the door to sell your idea, you will be asked to send along something in writing, namely a business plan. If you attempt a private offering under Securities and Exchange Commission rules and exemptions, you will need a business plan to enable your lawyer to write a private placement or offering memorandum.

4. **To arrange strategic alliances.** Joint research, marketing, and other efforts between small and large companies have become increasingly common in recent years. These efforts, which have come to be known as strategic alliances, have resulted from the need of small and large companies for each other. Small companies need financial support and large companies need innovation.

Despite the mutual needs, though, many more small early-stage companies seek out alliances with corporations than the corporations can ally with. To help them in their selection process, the corporations usually want to see the business plans of prospective small company alliance partners. Indeed, the large companies are more likely to be attracted to a company that volunteers a plan early in the negotiating process, without being asked for one.

5. **To obtain large contracts.** When small companies are seeking substantial orders or ongoing service contracts from major corporations, the corporations often respond (somewhat arrogantly): "Everyone knows who we are. But no one knows who you are. How do we know you'll be around in three or five years to provide the parts or service we might require for your product?"

If, at this point in the conversation, entrepreneurs can pull out their business plans, the corporate representatives will be immediately impressed that the entrepreneurs have thought about the future. More important, the corporate representatives will see that the small company fully expects to be around in three or five years, bigger and stronger than it is now. This can be a powerful argument in the selling process. And in today's selling environment, in which corporations are increasingly looking toward their suppliers as partners, the business plan helps convey that feeling of partnership.

6. **To attract key employees.** One of the biggest obstacles that small, growing companies face in attracting key employees is convincing the best people to take the necessary risk—that the company will thrive and grow during the coming years. Even in today's uncertain job environment, the best executives are still attracted to large corporations. A small company must be as convincing as the corporate officials can be. A written business plan can assure prospective employees that the entrepreneurs have thought through the key issues facing the company and have a plan for dealing with them.

A business plan does something more, though. It helps the prospective employee understand the company's culture and rationale for doing business. Conveying such fundamentals helps ensure that the most compatible people will take the job.

7. **To complete mergers and acquisitions.** No matter which side of the merger process you are on, a business plan can be very handy. If you want to sell your company to a large corporation, a business plan helps you stand apart from the crowd. Corporations searching for acquisition candidates typically examine hundreds of companies. The business plan says to the potential acquirer that you have thought about the future and know where the business is headed.

Similarly, if you are seeking to acquire a company, your business plan can help convince a reluctant seller that your company would be a suitable partner. The business plan in these situations serves almost as an extended company résumé.

8. **To motivate and focus your management team.** As smaller companies grow and become more complex, a business plan becomes an important component in keeping everyone focused on the same goals. Frank Carney, a founder of Pizza Hut, points out that in the late 1970s, when his company was showing signs of foundering, a business plan helped it resume its fast growth. The process of developing and writing a plan helped get everyone thinking about the company's long-range goals. And the final document served as a roadmap over the next year, until the plan was updated.

Beginning to Write: The Bite-Size Approach

The hardest part about trying to write a business plan is getting started. You look at that blank piece of paper or computer screen and you have no idea where to begin. Then you begin thinking about coming up with 30 or 40 pages, and you are understandably discouraged. In such a state of mind, it is easy to move on to a more immediate business task and put off writing the plan.

There is a way around the inevitable anxieties that come up when you are faced with such a seemingly overwhelming task. My approach involves two facets:

1. Posing the right questions or subjects.
2. Providing bite-size answers to those questions.

In my experience, it is a lot easier to write a few paragraphs or even a few pages in answer to specific questions or requests than to begin writing in the abstract. It is also important to keep in mind that the questions need not be completely answered all at once. It is all right to jot down some notes about things that occur to you immediately and think further about other matters that the question suggests. Even in answering focused questions, you often gain insights into additional research you need to do.

With that in mind, let's consider specific questions or issues that should be dealt with in writing a plan.

HOW LONG SHOULD THE BUSINESS PLAN BE?

It often helps psychologically when beginning a writing project to have some sense of the task's scope. So it is with business plans.

From a practical organizing perspective, it helps to have some idea ahead of time about how much written material is expected. That way, discipline can be exerted early rather than later after much work has been done. Too often, business plans are much longer than is necessary or appropriate. As in most areas of writing, it is more difficult to write a concise business plan than to write a long one.

To provide guidance about the size of the task, I categorize business plans broadly into three types: the summary business plan, the full business plan, and the operational business plan. Each type is discussed in the following sections.

The Summary Business Plan: 10 Pages

Summary business plans—running about 10 pages or so—have become increasingly popular and accepted in recent years. This is considerably shorter than the 40 or so pages traditional for business plans. Summary plans obviously require less data and research to complete, so, in some cases, they can be written more quickly than a traditional plan.

Summary plans also tend to be most appropriate for early-stage businesses for the simple reason that they don't have as much history or as many product lines to explain as more mature businesses.

Here are some of the situations in which a summary business plan works best.

Business Launch

A summary plan serves the needs of entrepreneurs in early-state companies because it can typically be completed fairly rapidly, and revised easily. While it may not be the most complete plan possible, in the case of early-stage companies, some plan is better than no plan.

Bank Loan

Though bankers are increasingly demanding written business plans as part of any application for loan funds, the summary business plan will usually serve the purpose. The business plan is often a supplement to some other application and documentation asking for personal financial information, asset valuations, and other such data that wouldn't normally be included in a business plan.

Well-Known Founders

If the founding entrepreneurs are well known in their industries or as celebrities, a shorter plan is likely to be acceptable to investors or bankers. Thus, Fred Gibbons, who was well known in computer circles, was able to raise venture capital based on a business plan of fewer than 10 pages.

Lifestyle Business

This is the term I apply to the bulk of the nation's businesses—those that tend not to seek outside financing, which are intended to provide a nice living to the owners while employing a handful of people. Lifestyle businesses range from the corner dry cleaner and hardware store to the small graphic design and consulting firm. Because these businesses are most likely to want a business plan to help focus the owners on the most important business issues, a summary plan may be the most effective way to get the task completed.

Gauge Investor Interest

Before sending a lengthy business plan to venture capitalists and private investors, entrepreneurs may want to try out their ideas. A summary plan can serve that purpose, enabling them to obtain feedback that can then be applied to a lengthier plan.

And, indeed, venture capitalists increasingly say they prefer to see a shortened version of a plan initially. After all, it saves them reading time as well.

The Full Business Plan: 10 to 40 Pages

This is the traditional plan. It covers all the key subjects in enough depth to allow a full exploration of the key issues, yet it doesn't go on much beyond 40 pages. For a well-established business, dealing with its key issues in 40 pages or less can be a real challenge.

The full business plan is most appropriate in the following two situations:

Seeking a Substantial Amount of Financing

For companies trying to raise several million dollars, a full business plan will likely be required at some point in the fund-raising process, even if a summary plan was used to get in the door. A summary plan unfortunately just doesn't allow entrepreneurs to provide the depth of discussion that professional investors typically demand.

Looking for a Strategic Partner

A small company in search of a corporate partner should likewise expect to complete a full business plan. Because major corporations have so many more such opportunities than they can possibly take advantage of, the corporations understandably want to scrutinize promising candidates as closely as possible. A full business plan allows that process to take place.

The Operational Business Plan: 40+ Pages

I used to feel strongly that executives should do everything possible to keep their business plans from exceeding 40 pages. Plans that extended much beyond that ideal, in my view, were likely to lack focus and discipline.

Once I saw the business plans of some highly successful companies like Celestial Seasonings and Pizza Hut, though, my viewpoint changed. A Celestial Seasonings plan, for example, extended just beyond 100 pages, and, in reading it through and discussing it with Mo Siegel, the company's founder, I realized that the plan actually did a very effective job in accomplishing what needed to be done.

Basically, there are two reasons to have such a long plan:

1. *Company growing quickly.* For companies that are already complex and are growing quickly, a business plan must cover quite a few issues to be truly complete. Such was the case with Celestial Seasonings in the early 1980s.

2. *Part of an annual process.* Equally important in fast-growing companies, the management team must be focused on the same issues. It is easy in such situations for the executives to lose their focus. For the business plan to be effective in keeping everyone on track, though, it must contain a level of detail not necessary in either a summary or full plan. An operational plan must get into the details of distribution, production, and other areas that are essential to making certain everyone understands what is expected. Indeed, managers often welcome such detail so they know clearly what they need to work toward.

WHAT SHOULD THE BUSINESS PLAN COVER?

Once you've decided which type of plan is right for your company, you need to organize it. In my experience, there is no completely right or wrong way to organize the plan, but in general, it includes the following features:

1. **Cover page.** This may seem like an insignificant detail, but in fact, a cover page serves several purposes. It is the place where you include not only the company's name and address, but the name of the main contact (usually the president) and a phone number. You want to avoid the situation in which an investor or banker becomes excited by the plan and then discovers that the phone number is nowhere to be found, except by searching out directory assistance.

The cover page should also warn readers that the material in the plan contains private information and is not to be copied or otherwise transmitted. It can also include a copy number, to convey the message that you keep track of each plan. (For details on composing and handling confidentiality statements and other related matters, consult a lawyer.)

If your company has a product that is especially interesting visually, such as computer graphics or a new type of machinery, your cover could include a photo. If your company's product is a low-cost consumer item, like food, you might want to consider including a sample with the plan you send to outside stakeholders.

2. **Table of contents.** This should be as detailed as possible, with the page numbers of each section included. Some bankers or investors have a preferred way of reading business plans that may not involve starting at the beginning. Some like to begin at the executive summary, while others seek out the marketing section or the financial section. For this reason, you don't want to frustrate readers by failing to include page numbers.

3. **Executive summary.** This is the single most important section of the business plan because most readers turn to it early in their reading for a sense of the entire plan. The executive summary is the heart of the plan and requires much attention; I provide more detail about the executive summary a little later.

4. **The company.** In this section you discuss the company's strategy and its management team. These matters must be evaluated from the perspective of the company's history and current situation.

5. **The market.** Who are the potential buyers? How many of them exist? This section identifies the prospective customers and provides evidence of how many are likely to become real customers.

6. **The product/service.** This is the section of the business plan that most entrepreneurs find the easiest to do. Because most feel strongly about the quality and utility of their product or service, they love to describe its attributes. Here is where such discussion is most appropriate.

7. **Sales and promotion.** Here you explain how sales will be completed. Will there be an in-house sales force? Or manufacturers' representatives? Or will mail order be used? And how will the product/service be promoted? Via advertising? Or public relations?

8. **Finances.** This is the section for the nuts-and-bolts financial issues to be considered and financial results/projections to be included. Generally speaking, three types of financial statements are necessary: cash flow, income/loss, and balance sheet.

9. **Appendix.** Here you can include items that don't fit well within particular sections of the plan—items like executive résumés, product literature, and endorsement letters from customers.

Sample Cover Page

copy number 5

The Company

Chris Smith, President
123 Lincoln Way, Suite B
Chicago, IL 60606
(312) 222-2222

The material in this plan is private information and
is not to be copied or transmitted.

Sample Table of Contents

THE EXECUTIVE SUMMARY: YOUR GUIDING LIGHT

What is the executive summary? It is *not* an abstract, an introduction, a preface, or a random collection of highlights. It is much more than those things. Quite simply, it is *the business plan in miniature*. As such, it should stand alone as a document, almost as a kind of "business plan within the business plan." It should capture the excitement and essence of the business. Someone who has finished reading your executive summary should be able to say, "So that's what these people are up to."

If you have hopes of obtaining any financing from the plan, the executive summary has to keep potential investors or bankers interested. Otherwise, those individuals will not bother to spend time with the rest of the plan.

Writing the executive summary in its final form is an enormous task because it must carry out its duties in *at most two pages*. Any executive summary that goes on longer than two pages dilutes the impact of this segment of the plan simply because the longer it gets, the less of a summary it becomes.

Because the executive summary is of necessity such a concise document, it offers entrepreneurs an important initial writing opportunity. You can begin writing the executive summary, knowing that it shouldn't be longer than two pages. You can also take comfort in the fact that this initial draft can be revised later, after other parts of the plan are completed.

In writing the initial executive summary draft, you will likely make an important discovery. You will begin to see gaps or holes in your knowledge and ideas. This discovery provides direction for the challenge of researching and writing the rest of the plan.

THE COMPANY: WHAT'S YOUR IDENTITY?

The section on the company should address two primary matters: your business strategy and your management team.

Describing Your Business Strategy

Strategy is one of those words that gets misused because it is applied to so many different aspects of business life. It is really a buzzword for your company's overall approach to producing and selling its products/services—and its goals for maximizing success. In describing your company's strategy, though, there needs to be a logical consistency between what you say you plan to do and what the rest of the plan will support.

For example, take the case of a bearings manufacturer that had been in business nine years and had achieved inconsistent results—sales would rise 8% one year and decline 3% the next; one year it would be profitable and the next it would lose money.

In its business plan, though, the company said it had devised a strategy based on new product innovations that would increase sales and profits 15% annually in each of the coming three years. The obvious question a reader might have about this plan was how the company would suddenly change a nine-year pattern of operations. If the strategy had included replacing one or more top managers by someone with a proven record of helping companies achieve such growth, it might have been more believable. As it was, a discrepancy existed between what had happened in the past and what the company projected for the future.

In describing the strategy, therefore, entrepreneurs need to directly address three main areas: the past, the present, and the future.

Analyzing the Company's Past Successes and Problems

For mature companies, the past must be explained as directly and honestly as possible, in both its positive and negative aspects. This may be painful, but it assures stakeholders that the executives are realistic about themselves and their company.

For startup companies, the past can only be dealt with in terms of individual executives. What have they accomplished in managerial terms? Ideally, one or more have been through startup situations that required the sorts of skills that are needed in this venture.

Describing the Company's Current Status

The discussion of the company's current status should answer the following questions:

- Is the company operating profitably or at a loss?
- What have been the recent sales and earnings trends?
- What recent important changes have taken place in the product or service mix?
- Are there any other significant changes?

Note that here the plan may touch on areas considered in greater detail later in the plan, like product or marketing issues, as they relate to overall strategy.

Outlining the Company's Future Goals

At this point, the plan can move on to the future. Of course, this part of the plan is likely to be optimistic. That is fine, but it is essential that the plan's description of future strategy and goals be in keeping with what has happened before. And if there will be significant changes in direction, explain forthrightly how they will occur. Of increasing importance is to try to anticipate the effects of technological change on your business. Few companies and industries are unaffected by technology in today's fast-changing marketplace; it is incumbent on executives to provide in their business plans their view of the most significant technological changes likely to affect their industry and company.

Describing the Management Team

The key issue is whether the people running the company have what it takes to enable the company to fulfill its strategy. Professional investors are fond of saying that they would rather invest in a company with a mediocre product and top people than the reverse.

How do you demonstrate that your company has top people? By bringing aboard individuals with a track record of past accomplishment. Preferably, these accomplishments will have occurred at your company; if you have new managers, determine their track record from what they have accomplished in the past in other positions.

Try to avoid the common management team traps. One trap is putting too much responsibility into the hands of a single leader, which I refer to as "the one-man-band syndrome." Another problem is choosing managers who all have the same background. For example, in high-technology companies, it is common for all the founders to be engineers. This worries professional investors, who want to see expertise in marketing and finance as well.

Describe the management team members in just a paragraph each, if possible. But be sure you are making the most of your resources—using everyone's experience and capabilities to their fullest in your descriptions. This includes listing consultants or part-timers who are key players.

MARKETING ISSUES: WHO ARE THE BUYERS?

Marketing tends to get confused with selling. The two functions are, however, quite distinct, which explains why they are treated separately in the business plan. Quite simply, *marketing* is identifying your customer prospects and determining how best to reach them. *Selling* is convincing those prospects to buy from you.

One way to begin identifying prospective customers is by demographics. For example, if you have a cosmetics store on the north side of Chicago, your prospects may be all of the women ages 16 to 40 with annual incomes above $25,000 living in a two-mile radius. Once you understand those parameters, your choices about trying to reach them become clearer; if you are inclined toward advertising, you might want to select a neighborhood newspaper rather than a citywide daily that reaches lots of people who are not potential customers.

Selling the Benefits of Your Product or Service

An important part of the task of identifying your customer prospects is determining what your company is *really* selling. Entrepreneurs tend to view their companies in terms of the products or services they sell. For example, they think of their companies as selling high-quality pizzas or high-quality graphic design services.

In writing this section of the plan (and in running a business), you must think about your company in terms of the *benefits* you sell to customers. The best benefits are those that help customers make money, save money, or feel good. As much as possible, try to *quantify* the benefits—the amount of money made or saved. Moreover, determine how long it takes for that money to pay for your product or service.

An example helps illustrate this point. When you buy insulation for your home, one of the first questions that you most likely want answered is how much energy it will save you each year. If insulation costs $800 and saves $200 in heating bills annually, it will take four years to recover the cost of the product. Thereafter, the savings are all gravy.

That information is valuable on two counts. First (and most obviously), it helps in *developing a promotional theme* to sell the product. But it also helps in *identifying prospective customers.* What kind of people are most likely to be interested in that kind of benefit? Perhaps better-educated individuals who tend to have a longer time horizon than poorly educated individuals. But also individuals who expect to stay in their homes for many years as opposed to those who plan only a short stay. Additional conclusions are certainly possible, based on the company's location, energy price trends, and so forth. The key point is that looking at your company's products or services from a *benefits* perspective provides important marketing insights.

Of course, customer benefits are not as obvious for many products as they are for home insulation. But by thinking creatively, you can often come up with similar benefits. If a computer software company's $500 package reduces a $25,000-a-year bookkeeper's time expenditure by one-fifth, the system saves the owner $5,000 per year and pays for itself in less than two months. The promise of improved productivity is behind the success of many personal computer software companies.

An interior designer specializing in servicing businesses may be able to save its corporate clients 10% to 15% in space requirements through efficient design. For a corporation paying $200,000 a year in prime city center office rent, saving 10% would be equal to $20,000. If the design fee is $20,000, the corporation would pay for its design in one year and then pocket the $20,000 savings for years into the future.

Not surprisingly, the more quickly your product or service can pay for itself in money saved or made, the more attractive it is to buyers. The calculations you come up with should be clearly spelled out in the business plan.

When a clear financial benefit doesn't exist, there should be other compelling benefits. Many mail-order companies selling everything from clothing to food to flowers have capitalized on the growing desire for convenience. People who can save a trip to a shopping mall have more time to spend with their families.

Simplifying Market Research

Market research is one of those terms that sounds intimidating, conjuring up images of statistical analysis and complex formulas. But it is really quite straightforward. It is a matter of determining, first, whether there are enough potential customers to achieve the growth you want and, second, whether they are increasing or decreasing in number.

Here are some of the key questions that need to be answered:

- What is the market, precisely? Is it all restaurants, or just fast-food restaurants, gourmet restaurants, or wine bars? The more specific you can be, the better off you usually are.
- Is the market growing or shrinking? Obviously, you'll want a growing market rather than a declining market, and the faster it's growing, usually the better off you'll be. (Declining markets can be attractive if you are strong enough financially to outlast competitors falling by the wayside.)
- Is it worth your while? You may have identified a niche market that is growing, but it may not achieve a size that makes it worthwhile. Keep in

mind that no matter how good your product or your promotion, you are unlikely ever to capture more than a significant minority of a total market. Competitors will see to that.

Market research need not be a complicated matter. For example, take the case of two entrepreneurs who owned a stationery wholesaling business and were investigating the possibilities for selling office products directly to large-scale users in the Rochester, New York, area—corporations, midsize businesses, universities, and nonprofit organizations.

The first thing they did was look through a corporate guide and tally up the number of companies that had more than $50 million in annual sales in their region. They also looked through the Yellow Pages and determined how many universities existed and contacted an association of nonprofit organizations for a tally on such organizations in the area.

Then they looked at U.S. Commerce Department statistics along with those from some office products trade associations to determine annual sales of office supplies in their region. From those statistics, they could begin calculating the expected size of purchases per business, university, and nonprofit organization.

To validate such raw data, though, they conducted some telephone interviews to determine not only the actual volume of purchases, but how purchases were being made. Such real-life research enabled the entrepreneurs to determine that corporations were buying a growing percentage of supplies directly from paper and other suppliers. This discovery reduced the entrepreneurs' estimate of the potential market.

The Internet has become an increasingly important resource for market research. It is possible in a matter of minutes to obtain extensive government demographic data, industry statistics, and global trends. It is also possible to obtain detailed information about competitors via their home pages on the World Wide Web.

Assessing the Competition

Entrepreneurs are quick to minimize the significance of competitors. In the entrepreneurs' view, the competitors are flawed in important ways—producing an inferior product or providing poor service. The fact is, if competitors are attracting customers, it is for a good reason.

For a business plan to have credibility, it must analyze the competitors objectively—not just in terms of their weaknesses, but in terms of their strengths. The best business plans I have seen include a complete competitor assessment; they carefully evaluate each competitor on several criteria including sales, number of employees, product or service, and future plans. Given the easy availability of competitive data on the Internet, entrepreneurs now have no excuse for failing to obtain such data.

Effective business plans demonstrate a willingness to learn from competitors. In an early business plan, Ben & Jerry's, the ice cream maker, pointed out that the success of a competitor's ice cream plant forced the company to abandon its focus on several regional plants and conclude that a national plant could indeed serve its needs. Most competitors offer at least a few potential lessons in how to improve your business.

Equally important, an objective analysis of competitors in your business plan helps convince stakeholders that your company is serious in its overall analysis.

Facing the Pricing Dilemma

This is one of the toughest issues any business faces, and I wish I had a magic formula to help deal with it. Unfortunately, I don't, because none exists. Most fundamentally, the pricing decision is the outcome of your marketing research and testing of what your target market is willing to pay for your product or service. Pricing is also partly a function of what the competition is charging, as well as what your costs and margins are.

But in the final analysis, pricing comes down to basic planning issues—balancing your goals on margins versus market share and the attractiveness of your benefits versus those of the competition.

As you agonize over prices, remember that they aren't engraved in stone. You are free to raise and lower your prices and to test out new pricing structures on prospects or certain existing customers. Just try not to lose sight of the ramifications of your changes or testing. If you lower your prices for prospects, you may irritate existing customers who learn about the change. If you adjust your prices downward too often, you may find it difficult to raise them. For example, the auto companies and many large mass-market retailers relied so heavily on rebates or sales during the late 1980s and early 1990s that they eventually found it difficult to sell their products at regular prices.

The business plan should include a well-articulated rationale for your company's overall pricing strategy.

Just as the description of the issues that must be dealt with in the marketing plan constitute the longest single segment of this chapter, so should the marketing section of your business plan be the longest single section of the plan. In general, it should be twice as long as the section that follows, on the product or service.

PRODUCT/SERVICE ISSUES: WHAT ARE YOU SELLING?

This is the area of the business that most entrepreneurs love to talk about. They tend to be wrapped up in the details of their product or service—its uniqueness, high quality, or innovativeness. In this section of the business plan, all important aspects of the company's products or services should be dealt with in detail. The following sections describe some of the most important product/service issues.

How Many Bells and Whistles?

Entrepreneurs tend to get wrapped up in the details of product or service performance. Thus, they want to have as many features and options as possible. They are urged on by product designers, engineers, and salespeople who want the same things.

All the recent attention to quality issues has only added to this tendency. Quality is associated with providing as many attributes that the customer could want as possible.

In reality, though, some attributes are more important than others to customers. And some features that rank lowest on the customer priority list may be among the most expensive to include.

I suggest as part of the planning process that you make a list of all the features you expect your product or service to include. That in itself is often revealing. Then go through the list with an eye to *costs* versus *benefits*. You may find that some low-cost features, like a simplified instruction sheet, may give you more bang for the buck than some expensive electronically controlled accessory that most customers have little need for.

This section of the plan should assess your key product or service features and justify their existence.

Can You Deliver?

One of the worst things any company can do is announce a new product or service and then be unable to provide it when promised. It is equally bad when the company ships the product before all the bugs have been worked out, and initial purchasers are irritated. These have been big problems for producers of computer software, hardware, and accessories.

Such *delivery* problems then become *marketing* problems. Customers have developed an image of the company as having uneven quality or as being untrue to its word.

The business plan should address these delivery issues, especially for new products or services. It should provide not only a schedule of events, but an explanation of steps that will be taken to ensure that deadlines are met.

Who Will Provide Ongoing Service?

It's popular for companies of all sizes to offer guarantees and warranties to attract customers. But how will such offerings be administered and who will pay for them? Once again, the answers may become marketing-related issues. Having a more attractive warranty than competitors may help bring in more customers, assuming that they consider warranties a high-priority item. But an attractive warranty can also eat into profit margins. Some companies have turned after-sales service into a separate profit center.

Whatever decision is made, it should be listed in this section, and the rationale for the decision should be explained.

SALES AND PROMOTION: HOW DO YOU SELL?

Now that you have sketched out your marketing and product/service approaches, you are ready to tackle sales. This is the make-or-break issue for any business. As good as your marketing and product/service strategies may be, they will all be for naught if you can't convince prospective customers to buy.

In my experience, selling is the most difficult single task associated with business success. That helps explain why salespeople are usually the most highly paid individuals in most companies. Enlightened executives understand that salespeople bring in the business and don't mind if they earn even more than the president.

To help you map out the sales section of your business plan, the following sections describe the key issues to address.

What Is Your Selling Approach?

There are many ways to sell products and services—via an in-house sales force, sales representatives, executives, or direct mail. If you sell a consumer product, you may have a *multistage selling approach.* That is, your in-house sales force sells to wholesalers, who in turn sell to retailers. Not only must you be on top of the first stage, but you must find ways to influence the second stage, to ensure that your product is purchased by the retailers and displayed and promoted in the retail outlet for maximum sales.

In this section of the business plan, you need to explain and justify your selling approach or approaches. Different selling approaches entail different costs and other demands. Generally speaking, an in-house sales force costs more to support than outside representatives. But because outside representatives are selling several products or services, your company won't get the same level of attention it would get from its own salespeople.

Increasingly, products and services are being sold via more than one sales vehicle. For example, book publishers sell through retail bookstores and direct mail.

Many companies are tied to particular selling approaches because of tradition. Plumbing supplies are sold through wholesalers because they have always been sold that way. Today's most successful growing companies, though, are open to unconventional ways of selling and distributing their products. The high-flying retailers in stationery supplies, hardware, consumer wholesale clubs, and computer products are testimony to the new possibilities.

Alternative approaches are expanding for two reasons. First, for most products or services, *selling costs* are rising dramatically. Second, *competitive pressures* make it difficult to rely on a single approach, especially if competitors are using two or three approaches. Thus, if you use an in-house sales force, you may want to experiment with direct mail. Or if you use only direct mail, you may want to get into retail outlets.

The sales section of your business plan should explain the rationale for a particular sales approach. It should also provide an assessment of costs. And it should evaluate any alternative sales approaches you may be considering to relieve cost and competitive pressures.

How Will You Motivate Your Sellers?

Because selling is so difficult, salespeople need to be trained, supported, and, above all, motivated. They need sales literature, administrative support to send out promotional material, and presentation graphics. They also need *incentives* that work—the right combination of commissions, prizes, stock, and whatever else you might dream up. What are you doing in these areas and what do you plan for the future to upgrade your selling efforts?

If you plan to use new sales approaches, the motivation becomes even more important because it is difficult to know in the early stages which approaches will work best—commissions, bonuses, prizes, or increased vacation time.

Generally speaking, though, a good rule to follow is that when you find something that works, stay with it, even if it means paying what seems to be obscene amounts of cash. The best salespeople should earn top dollar.

How Will You Promote Your Product or Service?

The real issue here is, how will you identify prospective customers? Your sales force can, of course, make calls to individuals in your target market. But beyond that effort, you will likely want a larger-scale approach to generating sales leads and referrals, based on *advertising* and/or *public relations.* Neither choice is either right or wrong, and some companies choose both advertising and public relations. Generally speaking, advertising provides companies with greater control over the message that goes out to the target market but costs more than public relations.

Public relations involves convincing the media to cover your company and/or its executives. Newspaper articles and radio interviews have more credibility than advertising and may thus be more effective than advertising in convincing prospective customers to buy. Additional opportunities for free exposure have opened up via online publications on the Internet. Equally impressive, such coverage is free. Of course, there is a cost involved in communicating with the media and obtaining its interest. (Chapter 4 provides a detailed discussion of advertising, publicity, and other approaches to promoting your product or service.)

For service companies, in particular, public relations is especially attractive. A big part of selling services involves *creating an image.* This is a tricky issue because the image for many services must be one of trustworthiness and professionalism that advertising tends to work against.

Fortunately, the public relations opportunities for such businesses are tremendous. For example, consultants can serve as experts to be quoted by the press on their area of expertise. Or they can write their own articles for publication in magazines catering to a specific target market. Editors are often in great need of such articles to fill up space, especially if the writer does not have to be paid. The beautiful thing about public relations for service companies is that you can be a one-person business and give the impression of being a national or international firm.

None of this is meant to minimize the public relations opportunities for manufacturers, retailers, and other sellers of products. Companies involved in everything from futuristic technologies to more mundane businesses like machine tools or groceries can obtain publicity—provided they are imaginative and tuned in to the needs of the media.

Once you get mentioned in the press, try to use that success to gain additional publicity. For example, you may be able to leverage magazine articles into radio and television interviews.

The key point here is that *media exposure brings in prospective customers.* The right article or radio mention can generate dozens of leads for salespeople to follow up on. For maximum effectiveness, though, companies must leverage any media exposure.

For example, in telemarketing efforts, it helps a lot after making a cold call if you can offer to send some newspaper or magazine clippings as a follow-up. You can also follow up with existing prospects by using articles that quote the company or its executives. Send them out to individuals who are in a position to recommend customers or to become customers. You can also use such articles in the business plan you intend for investors or lenders, to convince them of your credibility (although the actual article texts are usually best included in the appendix of your business plan).

Whichever promotional choice you make, though, you need a budget. This section of the business plan should explain how much you plan to spend on advertising or public relations.

"Love Letters" and Other Evidence of Success

Another useful promotional tool is a letter of thanks or praise from a customer—commonly referred to as a "love letter." Ideally, you already have some love letters, but if you don't, you can encourage customers to write them. Or you can even write the letters and simply ask customers to sign them.

These can be used to great effect. For example, a Los Angeles store specializing in custom-made men's shirts had a wonderful application of the love letter concept in its store window. Along with displays of shirts were inscribed photos of movie stars. One of Burt Reynolds read, "Thanks always for a perfect fit." Another one of Sylvester Stallone said, "Brilliance!" And a third one of Kirk Douglas had a similar complimentary inscription. That was a brilliant use of love letters.

Another similar tactic, though a bit more tricky, is to use a partial list of clients to give yourself credit. It's tricky because some customers don't take kindly to having their names used publicly, so you have to approach them gingerly.

While love letters and client lists can be excerpted in this section of the business plan, the full texts or lists belong in the appendix.

FINANCIAL ISSUES: HOW ARE YOU DOING?

This section of the business plan covers your financial history and your projections. Ideally, you should look back and ahead between three and five years. You do this with three different types of financial analyses: the cash flow statement, the profit/loss statement, and the balance sheet.

But this section of the plan should also include an explanation or analysis of the numbers. If there have been losses, what do they really signify? If there is much existing debt, how will it be dealt with?

Assembling financial projections has become much easier with the advent of computer spreadsheet programs like Lotus 1-2-3 and Excel. But their very ease of assembly has made many bankers and investors nervous about the projections that entrepreneurs come up with. Some are put off by many pages of such projections, feeling that the numbers have simply been plugged in rather than seriously analyzed.

In any case, this section of the business plan should conform to generally accepted financial and accounting principles. There is no room for creativity. The next sections provide details about the three finance areas entrepreneurs should cover.

Cash Flow: The Business Lifeline

A useful way to learn about cash flow is to view the business as a person. Cash is the nutrient that runs through its arteries and veins.

A famous but unnamed economist once put it aptly when he said, "Cash flow is more important than your mother." A T-shirt that became popular a few years back reads, "Happiness is positive cash flow."

Because your business is an organism with cash for blood, insufficient cash flow leads to death; the thriving organism becomes a skeleton. The point here is basic but often overlooked. Cash flow is different from profit, and, for a smaller business, much more important. It's possible to run out of cash and go broke even as you're making a major sale that will give the business a profit.

Besides being vitally important, cash flow can be used as a planning tool. By monitoring cash flow on a regular basis as cash comes in and goes out, you develop a record that enables you to plan into the future.

That becomes very important, especially if you want to expand or go after new markets: you can quickly calculate the effect of such actions on the flow of cash and determine whether you'll need to seek out a bank loan or other financing, or whether you can support the new activity from internally generated funds.

Technically, cash flow is a record of cash available at different points in time. It's usually monitored on a monthly basis. A cash flow statement may seem complicated when you first look at it, but it's really very simple, and it's extremely important as a planning tool, once you get the hang of it.

You start with the cash on hand at the beginning of the month.

To that you add the receipts during the month from customer payments and any other sources.

From that you subtract the actual disbursements, the cash going out each month in what are generally categorized as fixed and variable expenses. *Fixed expenses* are recurring items that can't easily be changed, such as rent, debt, salaries. *Variable expenses* include advertising, office supplies, promotion, consulting, and other such expenses that can more easily be increased or decreased from month to month.

The result is the amount of cash available at the end of the month. The cash flow is the difference between what the business started and ended with.

The Income Statement: The Bottom Line

The income statement is the one that, for public companies at least, gets all the attention for showing the company's profit or loss.

Actually, it's similar to the cash flow statement. You start with the company's revenues, less any commissions.

From that you subtract direct labor and materials.

The result is a subtotal that is your gross profit or loss. Just as a side note, the percentage of gross profit to revenues can be a very useful number. It's your gross margin, and it can help you to compare yourself to others in your industry, because it immediately tells you whether your labor costs are appropriate.

Next, you subtract from the subtotal indirect labor, administrative labor, and expenses (general and administration), along with depreciation.

The result is another subtotal that is the company's pretax net profit or loss.

From that you subtract a provision for taxes, and the result is, at long last, net income, or the net increase (or decrease) in retained earnings.

The main difference between the cash flow and income statements is one of timing. The cash flow statement is a more accurate barometer of cash on hand at any particular moment.

The Balance Sheet: A Statement of Business Health

The balance sheet is the financial statement bankers like to focus on because they believe it offers the most revealing clues about basic business health by highlighting the state of assets and liabilities at a particular point in time.

On one side of the balance sheet are the company's assets—in terms of *current assets* like cash and accounts receivable, and in terms of *fixed assets* like furniture and computers.

On the other side of the balance sheet are the liabilities—the *current liabilities* in the form of accounts payable and notes payable, and *long-term liabilities* in the form of equity held by investors.

The assets and liabilities add up to the same number.

The balance sheet tends to assume greater importance for manufacturing and other product companies than for service companies because the service companies tend not to have traditional assets like machinery and real estate. Indeed, a balance sheet can be misleading for a service firm, since its primary assets are its people, and it's difficult to measure that in balance sheet form.

Unfortunately, bankers often rely heavily on the balance sheet, using ratios of various assets and liabilities to decide whether a company is creditworthy. Bankers are gradually changing their attitudes, though, as the economy becomes increasingly service oriented.

TARGETING AND WRITING THE PLAN

By this time, you should actually have a fair amount of written material. You should have written a first draft of the executive summary. You should have notes in answer to questions and issues raised about your company, marketing, product, and selling approaches.

Now the challenge is to put it all together into the selling document that is an effective business plan. Two issues need to be addressed in putting together a draft you can begin showing around: targeting and writing.

Who Are the Readers?

As I pointed out early in this chapter, the business plan is meant to influence various stakeholders to support your business. Thus, your business plan should ideally be *targeted at specific stakeholders* most important to your business.

Different stakeholders have different priorities in evaluating businesses; these need to be addressed in the business plan. Sometimes, though, the priorities conflict. For example, bankers tend to be scared by fast growth, while venture capitalists love it.

Taking the targeting need a step further, there is nothing that says you can't have *several* business plans, each targeted to a particular group of stakeholders. These plans need not differ on the basic facts, only in the *presentation* of the company's needs. You may have one plan intended only for senior management, which provides a more candid assessment of the company's various challenges. A second plan, which is oriented more toward selling the company's strengths, can be distributed to investors. To obtain venture capital, a company may say that it will use the money to stimulate fast growth. To obtain a bank loan, however, that same company may say that it will use the money to improve quality and productivity, with a somewhat slower growth rate.

EXHIBIT 5.1   Business plan targeting summary.

Stakeholder	Issues to emphasize	Issues to deemphasize	Length
Banker	Cash flow, assets, solid growth	Fast growth, hot market	10–20 pp.
Investor	Fast growth, potential large market, management team	Assets	20–40 pp.
Strategic partner	Synergy, proprietary products	Sales force, assets	20–40 pp.
Large customer	Stability, service	Fast growth, hot market	20–40 pp.
Key employees	Security, opportunity	Technology	20–40 pp.
Merger & acquisition specialist	Past accomplishments	Future outlook	20–40 pp.

Exhibit 5.1 summarizes the key targeting issues associated with different stakeholders.

How Can You Write an Effective Plan?

Entrepreneurs often get bogged down in the actual mechanics of writing. The material often comes out too conceptual or disorganized, and they don't know how to fix it. Here are some suggestions to smooth the writing process:

Support Your Goals and Claims

One key to effective writing is the use of examples to back up general statements. This is especially true for business plans.

Supporting evidence should include *statistics, studies,* and *examples.* If you say the market is growing by 12% annually, provide evidence for that statement such as market studies or prior history. Feel free to use anecdotal evidence, but in moderation.

Place One Person in Charge

Another way to ease the writing process is to get as many written inputs as possible from partners or subordinates. You may then have one person write the entire plan or several people each write a section or two.

Whatever your approach, place one person in charge of overseeing the process: setting deadlines, reading drafts, and rewriting material. Otherwise, the process can easily get bogged down. People have a way of avoiding deadlines that they do not perceive as very important. Emphasize that this particular deadline is of the highest priority. The person in charge should then set a deadline for getting the material into a readable format for everyone to review.

Designate an Outside Reader/Editor

As a company's executives get ever more deeply involved in writing the plan, they tend to lose perspective and objectivity. They will use industry buzzwords and shorthand expressions that outsiders won't understand.

The solution to this problem is to get an outsider with some editorial expertise to look at the plan critically—a business school professor, another business owner, or an accountant or lawyer. Try for someone who will be candid. The plan is bound to have problems, and you want to learn about them from someone you designate rather than from a banker or venture capitalist.

This person may even have the skills to rework and reorganize the plan, if necessary. It's all right to have an outsider do some writing, as long as the ideas and supporting evidence come from the company.

Rewrite, Rewrite, Rewrite

I always stress that very few people can write finished prose on their first or even second tries. The secret to successful writing is rewriting. Do a small chunk, leave it for a day or two, and come back to it. Rewrite it, fill it in, and add to it. You'll be surprised at how it will change shape over time.

Set some limits, though. Beyond a certain point—and that varies from person to person—the rewriting process becomes counterproductive. When you sense that is happening, give the plan to the designated outsider for reaction.

At some point, you need to declare the plan complete, for now. But keep in mind that the business plan is never really complete. The business is always changing, so the plan must struggle to keep up. To help in that process, I suggest reviewing the plan at least annually, and preferably more often. As market changes speed up, so does the need to adjust the plan.

And that's all there is to it. Good luck.

FINANCIAL PROJECTIONS: HOW TO DO THEM THE RIGHT WAY

6

Bob Ronstadt

Harold Geneen, the former chairman of IT&T, once said that "to be good at your business, you have to know the numbers—cold." Geneen's advice sounds simple and straightforward. If only it were that simple. Unfortunately, business decision makers need to respond to change and unforeseen events. The numbers change because *nothing* ever turns out precisely the way it is planned.

That doesn't mean you should stop planning or ignore the numbers. Quite the contrary, you need to better understand the numerical dimensions of your business so you can respond as best you can to change when it occurs.[1]

Although Geneen's words are oversimplified, they are nevertheless true for both planning new businesses and managing ongoing operations. In all businesses—whether they are new ventures or established smaller businesses or larger corporations—superior management means having a sense for the *future financial implications* of decisions that must be made today. Geneen knew that to ignore the numbers was dangerous. If you ignore the numbers, particularly the numbers that relate to the future, pretty soon your business will begin to ignore you.

WHAT ARE FINANCIAL PROJECTIONS?

Numbers that relate to the future are called financial projections or financial pro formas. These future-oriented numbers differ greatly from accounting numbers, that is, numbers based on past performance. Financial projections differ from accounting numbers in why, how, and by whom they should be constructed.

At the minimum, a good set of financial projections should include a pro forma income statement, balance sheet, and cash flow statement, along with a detailed explanation of the assumptions that underlie the projections.[2] A comprehensive set of financial projections will also provide a separate sales forecast that will include considerable detail about how the sales numbers are derived. Finally, you should use the data in your projections to compute selected key measures, standard financial ratios, and projected breakevens. The latter are necessary for several reasons, but chiefly to see if your projections are fairly accurate. For instance, a set of projections may look fine until you see that the derived current ratio is simply absurd for a startup in your industry.

The purpose of financial projections is to show what a business will realize in sales, gross profits, net profits, net worth, cash flows, and several other measures associated with the income statement, balance sheet, and cash flow. But more specifically, you usually want to know the answers to several questions. Given your assumptions about 50 to 100 different variables (sales growth rates, receivable collections, rent, wage levels, salaries, interest rates, and so on), you need to ask the following questions:

- How much money will my business need to maintain a positive cash flow?
- When exactly will I need this money?
- What kind of money (debt or equity or both) should it be?

Answering these questions is almost impossible when you use a simple set of *stand-alone projections* because venturing is a *dynamic* process. Things change—often quite rapidly. Yesterday's financial projections are often out-of-date today, and creating a new set simply becomes too time-consuming.

The answer to these realities is a set of financial projections that represents a valid financial model of your business. Instead of a stand-alone income statement, balance sheet, and cash flow statement, you need to *link* these different statements together so that they change when the underlying assumptions and their values change. The fact that all the numbers are related or tied to one another is why these linked financial projections are called *integrated financial statements.*

For the record, financial projections are linked, or *integrated,* when your projected income statement, balance sheets, cash flows, and the assumptions underlying these financial projections are linked by formulas. To be valid, these formulas must be consistent with accepted accounting principles. Your statements also should tie out, that is, your balance sheet should still balance whenever you change the assumptions that drive your financial projections.

But you may ask, "Can't I get by with a pasted-up set of stand-alone projections?" The answer is "probably yes." Many investors and bankers don't understand or require integrated financial projections. You may be able to satisfy them with stand-alone projections. But the sharper ones will require linked financials because they know that a new set of conditions will emerge almost as soon as you are out the door. What will you do then? Ignore or misread the financial implications? No, the savvy investor or banker wants to be sure you understand how the numbers in your business are interconnected. They also want to be sure you have the ability to determine the financial implications of unforeseen changes that are likely to occur.

This chapter explains how financial projections should be constructed and why the leaders of a business need to understand these projections if they are ever to take control of their financial decision making. But first the chapter shows:

- Why financial projections are actually quite difficult to construct.
- Why financial projections are rarely constructed properly, even when spreadsheets are used.
- Why financial projections should be constructed by the principal decision makers of a business, despite the difficulty involved.

Although these observations probably sound like a lot of bad news, the good news is that linked financial projections have an ongoing business use. Unlike the one-use, misleading stand-alone projections, linked financial projections stay with you, once they have been created, and can help you make better management decisions.

WHY FINANCIAL PROJECTIONS ARE DIFFICULT TO PRODUCE

"What happens" when "what if" happens? The future is concerned with "what if." As you change basic assumptions about sales growth, wage levels, product costs, and so on, you need to know more than their profit-and-loss (P&L) effect. You also need to understand their effect on cash flow, on your balance sheet, and on a variety of other derived measures (for example, breakevens on selected financial ratios).

In other words, to play "what if" appropriately, you need to know what happens not just to sales, wages, and product costs but also to operating cash flow. For example, how are inventory levels, accounts receivable and accounts payable affected? What happens to profitability, breakeven, and owner's equity? Before long, implementing this "simple" process gets detailed, downright complicated, and, for lack of better words, "intensely muddy."

It also gets exhausting. The point is that before you can simplify your numbers and know them cold, you must first produce literally thousands of numbers. It's an arduous job, even with an electronic spreadsheet. Then, to add insult to injury, you should know that most of the numbers are wrong.

Why does this happen? It happens because of technical errors. First, you need to realize that the real problems associated with producing good financial projections aren't *forecasting errors* of one kind or another. For instance, sales have always been difficult for most ventures to predict, and always will be. No one has a crystal ball, and plans rarely, if ever, work out the way intended because actual sales and cost numbers rarely match budgeted or forecasted numbers. No, the real problem lies in *technical errors*; specifically, the implicit, incomplete, and misleading financial models that most people create when putting together their financial projections, whether they use paper, pencil, and calculator, or an electronic spreadsheet.

WHY FINANCIAL PROJECTIONS ARE RARELY CONSTRUCTED PROPERLY

Why do people serious about making good decisions rely on faulty financial models? There are two reasons, and they reside in two myths:

- *Myth 1:* Most people, especially those schooled in business, believe that they can develop technically correct financial projections.

    The Reality: Most people, including most MBAs, cannot develop anything more than crude, generally misleading, financial projections.

- *Myth 2:* Spreadsheets alone (or with financial templates) make it possible for most people to create technically correct financial projections that can be used for business planning and budgeting purposes, that is, financial decision making.

    The Reality: Only a tiny percentage of spreadsheet users are capable of putting together integrated financial projections, and even they are prone to commit spreadsheet errors. They are a select group who are very advanced in both their spreadsheet skills and their accounting/finance skills. A rare breed indeed.

Consequently, most people don't really "know the numbers," cold or otherwise; they only think they know them. This lack of knowledge isn't simply a failure to "push the numbers." That used to be a problem when calculations were done with paper, pencil, calculator, and eraser. Fortunately, the proliferation of spreadsheets helped to overcome the pure tedium of number pushing. Unfortunately, spreadsheets compounded the problem by giving people the idea that financial projections were now easier than ever to produce. Spreadsheets certainly allow people to push numbers. But, unfortunately, when it comes to financial projections, the folks using spreadsheets rarely derive the correct numbers and only rarely understand the numbers they create so plentifully.

The hard cold fact you must learn to accept is that deriving correct business numbers is impossible when working with financial models that are incomplete more often than not, and that also contain accounting or mathematical errors. To use some software lingo, the resulting financial projections are *internally corrupted.* The numbers are wrong because the implicit models people adopt are technically wrong. To use another software expression, it's classic GIGO: Garbage in, garbage out. And because the underlying assumptions aren't explicit in nine out of ten spreadsheet models, the garbage is nicely hidden from view.

What's So Important about Integrated Financials Anyway?

In life, especially business life, good ideas aren't much help if you can't execute them. And the quality and accuracy of your execution is everything. For planning and budgeting, quality and accuracy means translating your assumptions about different alternatives into a set of financial projections that are linked together into a financial model that reflects your business.

Why is this unique financial model needed? It's needed because everything you know about the first part of Geneen's advice, that is, "to be good at your business," points to understanding the interconnected totality of your decisions. Just as a business is a web of interconnected individuals and resources where every decision impacts everyone to some degree, so the various statements of your financial projections need to be interconnected because they impact one another.

For instance, let's suppose you want to add several employees, buy a piece of expensive equipment, or start or end a sales campaign. In each of these instances, you need to see the likely financial impact of your decisions. And you need to see how these decisions affect not only your income statement, but also your cash flow, balance sheet, and numerous financial measures, including breakevens.

In short, financial projections must be tied together, or *integrated,* to have much utility—not just for strategic purposes but for everyday financial decision making.

Without this total picture, disaster can occur. For instance, projected P&Ls that show healthy profits can mask *negative operating cash flows* and *weak balance sheets* that literally drive a business into the ground. Business leaders need a full representation of their businesses, not an isolated snapshot of an individual projection that shows only part of the story.

Integrated financial projections are especially needed when a business takes a nose dive. Good times can mask all kinds of errors. But when the bad times come, and we all see them at one time or another, there is no room for error. At these difficult moments, integrated financial models are nearly priceless. Hard decisions must be made. What projects get axed? What equipment, property, or other assets must be sold? Which vendors must wait to be paid? How much should salaries be cut? Who gets a pink slip? How soon should these actions and others be taken?

Decisions like these are never easy to make, but it helps immeasurably to know the impact of each decision on the "ending cash balance" of your cash flow projection. Many businesses that will fail in the future can be saved if they have but one tool: a financial model that produces integrated financials.

WHO SHOULD PRODUCE YOUR FINANCIAL PROJECTIONS?

The short answer is that you need to produce and understand your financial projections. The problem, however, with the short answer is that it doesn't reflect the realities of existing deficiencies in your awareness about and skills for developing integrated financials.

A wise friend once told me that the road to truth and knowledge begins by becoming aware of the things you don't know you don't know. If you are aware that you don't know something, that's 80% of the battle. It's those things about which you are totally oblivious that are the real snares of life. Integrated financials represents one such snare.

So first, *you need to recognize that significant obstacles exist when it comes to developing meaningful financial projections.* Despite intellectual muscle flexing by "spreadsheet power users," business consultants, and even some business school professors, the reality is that most people can't put together a valid and useful set of financial projections in a reasonable period of time. The reason is that for mere mortals, they are actually quite difficult to prepare.

Second, *you need to understand the concept of integrated financials and realize its importance for doing everyday financial decision making.* Fudging your financials, or putting together a set of unlinked or stand-alone projections (for example, the income statement isn't linked to the cash flow or balance sheet) simply won't do. A financial model that truly reflects your business is a tremendous decision-making asset. In fact, I have found that it can be the difference between success and failure—not just for occasional planning and budgeting exercises, but, when necessary, for running your venture from day to day.

Given the real difficulties involved, *you will probably need to find someone who will help you to build these financial decision-making models.* The person may be a CFO, financial analyst, or accountant within your own organization. Also, there are financial business consultants who do understand integrated financials and how to implement them, and most importantly how to teach you to modify and use the model.

HOW TO PRODUCE INTEGRATED FINANCIAL PROJECTIONS

The traditional way to produce financial projections is to do the following:

1. Build a sales forecast.
2. Use the projected sales revenue as a basis for deriving a projected income statement—for example, the income statement is produced either by using historical percentage analysis or by simply making assumptions about the relationship of each cost item as a percentage of total sales. For instance, you can assume that future cost of goods sold will be 70% of projected total sales if, for one reason or another the historical cost of goods sold has been 70% of past sales (for the industry, or for other startups during their first year, or based on your own company experience if you have prior history). If forecasted sales are projected to be $1,000,000, then cost of goods sold will be 70% of this total, or $700,000. The same procedure is then used for all other expense items, calculating them individually as a percentage of total sales.
3. Use a similar approach to generate a balance sheet—for example, each balance sheet item can be derived by using its historical relationship to total assets. An alternative method is to use historical ratios (such as the accounts receivable turnover period or the inventory turnover period) to derive the projected balance sheet.
4. Build a cash flow statement using one of several approaches, including:

   - Do a rough approximation of the net cash flows by taking profit after tax and adding back depreciation and other accounting items that are not real cash outflows. (I don't recommend this approach.)

- Calculate changes in beginning and ending balance sheets to derive the net change in cash. (This approach is ok, but it is tough for most practitioners to do.)
- Actually track cash inflows and cash outflows over a *relevant time period.* (For most startups, a relevant time period is a month. For other startups, and most turnaround situations, the relevant time period is often a week. Avoid quarterly and especially annual cash flows since these longer time periods can mask all sorts of potential cash flow disasters.)

This traditional approach for generating financial projections is fine for "quick & dirty" analysis, that is, to get a fast but rough idea about what a business will be like in numerical terms. But the traditional approach has four major deficiencies:

- It generally fails to be explicit about the assumptions that are producing the numbers.
- The individual statements aren't linked together, so the real picture isn't being produced, only (at best) a close likeness.
- Most practitioners don't understand the implications of the numbers, principally because they aren't linked together and because they aren't linked to other measures (ratios, breakevens, industry-specific measures, and business valuations) that help us to understand their implications.
- Major alternatives and unforeseen changes in your business are very difficult to quickly incorporate into these partial models without almost completely redoing them.

Using the traditional approach is a little like riding a bicycle on a freeway. The bicycle is okay for academic off-road games, but it won't do for real world applications. Instead I recommend you travel your business highways in a real automobile, that is, take the time to build an integrated financial model of your business. To build one, you must do the following:

1. **Be explicit about your assumptions by first building an assumptions statement.** (A sample assumptions statement is presented later in Exhibit 6.3 for a retail business.)[3] Remember, an assumptions statement is no less important than your income statement, balance sheet statement, or cash flow statement. It's what produces them. List your sales assumptions, your P&L assumptions, your balance sheet assumptions, your cash flow assumptions, plus other assumptions as they relate to supporting budgets or output analysis such as breakevens; for instance, what percentage of cost of sales is a variable cost?

2. **Make certain you understand the general interrelationships between your assumptions and the sales revenue projection, the**

income or P&L projection, the balance sheet projection, and the cash flow projection. In other words, you need to know how your projected financial statements are related to one another as a group.

3. **Make certain you understand the specific relationships between line items within and across the different statements.** Such knowledge will enable you to make better venture decisions by knowing:

> How the individual components or line items of each financial statement are linked together *within* the same statement;
>
> How the individual components of each financial statement are linked to components with the same or similar names on different statements; for example, how is "cash" on the balance sheet linked to "cash" on the cash flow statement; and
>
> How the individual components of each financial statement are linked to different components in other financial statements.

In the latter two cases, you especially want to know the number of items involved in each linkage and the direction of the association. For example, net income from the income statement and retained earnings from the balance sheet are linked. However, you also need to know that retained earnings is derived from net income, not vice versa. Exhibit 6.1 illustrates these linkages. And you need to know what other variables, if any, are involved (or could be involved) in the calculation; for example, if dividends were declared, they would have to be subtracted from net income and subtracted from ending cash on the cash flow statement.

Once you understand how these specific linkages work, you will better understand not only what it takes to balance your balance sheet, but also how to obtain answers about how much money your business will need, when it will need this money, and what kind of money it can or should be.

EXHIBIT 6.1   A specific relationship between financial statements.

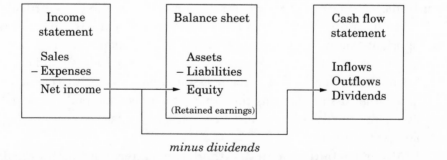

GENERAL RELATIONSHIPS BETWEEN THE PROJECTED FINANCIAL STATEMENTS

Now examine how projected financial statements are linked together as a group. A diagram helps you to visualize these general linkages. Graphically, the relationships between the statements are shown in Exhibit 6.2.

After providing information for an assumptions statement (including optional data for a beginning balance sheet for Period #0), Exhibit 6.2 traces how this information flows to produce the values in the sales forecast, the income statement, the balance sheet, and the cash flow statement. Here's how it works:

- Selected values that are produced in the sales forecast (such as net sales) based on data taken from the assumptions statement flow directly into the income statement for Period #1.

- Beginning balance sheet values for Period #0 (if you have listed them under the *base period* in the balance sheet statement) are combined with information for Period #1 from the assumptions statement, the income

EXHIBIT 6.2   General linkages between core statements.

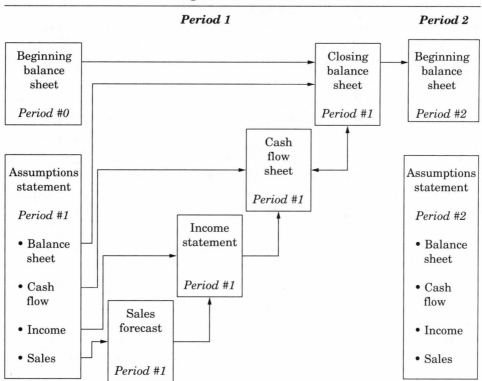

statement, and the cash flow statement to create the values shown in the closing balance sheet for Period #1. [*Note:* The closing balance sheet for Period #1 becomes the beginning balance sheet for Period #2, and the process continues for the total number of time periods being projected. In Exhibit 6.2, the beginning balance sheet (sometimes called the opening, or base period, balance sheet) is shown as part of the balance sheet statement because this positioning is conventional; however, the base period items and values are effectively assumptions that can be listed in the assumptions statement and linked by formulas to Period #1 of the balance sheet.]

- Certain information is also flowing from the closing balance sheet into the cash flow statement. This information is supplemented with data drawn from the assumptions statement and the income statement to produce the values shown in the cash flow statement.

- Then, the process is repeated for Period #2, Period #3, and so on.

SPECIFIC RELATIONSHIPS BETWEEN THE PROJECTED FINANCIAL STATEMENTS

Although *general relationships* exist between projected financial statements, there are many specific ways to configure projected financial statements, perhaps as many as there are different ventures. Some obvious differences exist between industries. However, differences in projected financial statements can also exist within the same industry. Sometimes these differences are minor and at other times they are quite significant in the number of individual items and the way individual items are derived and linked together. Consequently, there are unlimited specific kinds of financial statements and multiple ways to derive the specific linkages across statements. What follows represents but one way. Yet, because many of the variations can be minor, it serves as a blueprint for building and linking together the components of financial projections.

Case Study

Because actual numbers help trace the linkages, let's assume you are planning to expand a small retail venture you recently started. Assume you've just finished completing the assumptions statement shown in Exhibit 6.3. You've also filled out the base period, or beginning, balance sheet column on the balance sheet statement. Your program should then compute your monthly revenue statement, income statement, balance sheet, and cash flow for the next 12

EXHIBIT 6.3 Sample assumptions statement for a retail company.

	1/31/88 Retail	2/29/88 Retail	3/31/88 Retail	4/30/88 Retail	5/31/88 Retail	6/30/88 Retail	7/31/88 Retail	8/31/88 Retail	9/30/88 Retail	10/31/88 Retail	11/30/88 Retail	12/31/88 Retail
Revenue forecast assumptions:												
Annual sales, Store A	$300,000											
Percent of sales allocated / month	4.0%	5.5%	3.5%	5.0%	9.0%	7.0%	5.0%	2.0%	4.0%	9.0%	20.0%	26.0%
Should sum to 100%	100.0%											
Growth rate next year:												
Growth rate Store A	10%											
Income statement assumptions:												
Cost of goods as a percent of sales												
Store A	45.00%											
Store A: Monthly operating expenses												
Store A manager's salary	$2,500											
Salespeople salaries:												
Base salaries	$750											
Commission rate	5.00%											
Advertising and promotion, Store A	3.00%											
Rent, Store A	$1,500											
Supplies, Store A	3.00%											
Telephone, utilities, and insurance	$1,000											
Store payroll tax and benefit rate	18.00%											
Balance sheet assumptions:												
Inventory purchases:												
Enter minimum purchasing lead time, in months to receive inventory	2											
Please review your inventory. You may want to increase or decrease your inventory.												
Enter your adjustments below:												
Inventory adjustments Store A	$6,300	$7,000	$0	$0	$0	$0	$0	$0	$0	$0	$0	$0
Fixed assets purchased:												
Fixed assets Store A	$25,000	$0	$0	$0	$0	$0	$0	$0	$0	$0	$0	$0
Depreciation schedule:												
Store fixed assets (in years)	7											

(Continued)

159

EXHIBIT 6.3 *(Continued)*

	1/31/88 Retail	2/29/88 Retail	3/31/88 Retail	4/30/88 Retail	5/31/88 Retail	6/30/88 Retail	7/31/88 Retail	8/31/88 Retail	9/30/88 Retail	10/31/88 Retail	11/30/88 Retail	12/31/88 Retail
Cash flow assumptions:												
Base period accounts receivable received	100%	0%	0%	0%	0%	0%	0%	0%	0%	0%	0%	0%
Monthly sales collected:												
% collected 0–30 days	80%											
% collected 31–60 days	10%											
% collected 61–90 days	5%											
% collected 90+ days	5%											
Total monthly sales collected	100%											
Base period accounts payable paid	40%	50%	10%	0%	0%	0%	0%	0%	0%	0%	0%	0%
Monthly expenses paid:												
% paid 0–30 days	70%											
% paid 31–60 days	30%											
% paid 61–90 days	0%											
% paid 90+ days	0%											
Total monthly expenses paid	100%	0%	0%	0%	0%	0%	0%	0%	0%	0%	0%	0%
Vendor deposits required	$1,250											
Line of credit:												
Annual line of credit interest rate	12.00%											
Maximum line of credit	$50,000											
Notes payable:												
Annual note interest rate	11.50%											
Term of note in months	60											
Minimum cash balance	$5,000											
Additional funding:												
New equity	$15,000	$0	$0	$0	$0	$0	$0	$0	$0	$0	$0	$0
New debt (notes payable)	$20,000	$0	$0	$0	$0	$0	$0	$0	$0	$0	$0	$0
Projected breakeven assumptions:												
Variable portion of cost of goods	50.0%											
Variable portion of store salaries	20.0%											
Variable portion of advertising and promotions	30.0%											

months. (Each of these statements is presented and discussed in the following sections.) The assumptions made in Exhibit 6.3 can be summarized as follows:

- Annual sales are $300,000 for Store A (eventually, you hope to start two or three more stores).

- The spread of sales shows a strong seasonality factor with 20% and 26% of total sales realized respectively in November and December. Note: The sales formula multiplies $300,000 by each month's seasonality factor, which projects monthly sales; thus, the $300,000 shown in January is not simply replicated across all 12 months for total sales of $3,600,000.

- A 10% annual growth rate is used to calculate 1989 sales, which are used to figure certain 1988 items (for example, purchases) that need to "look into" January and February of 1989 to calculate and derive November and December values.

- Cost of goods is projected at 45% of total sales based on prior experience.

- Operating expenses include the addition of a store manager (so we can subsequently start Store B). Advertising is increased to 3% (from 0%).

- Assets are depreciated over seven years.

- Payroll taxes and benefits have been increased to 18% due to a new employee benefits package.

- Purchases need to be made two months in advance of actual delivery, on average. *Note:* The formula related to the two-month lead time won't show any inventory purchases until Month #3; consequently, you need to enter your assumed inventory purchases for January and February ($6,300 and $7,000, respectively).

- Cash flow assumptions show that 100% of your *prior* accounts receivable will be collected in January. These were a few known customers, who were allowed to charge their purchases. However, you've decided to liberalize your policy to allow more store accounts. You believe collections will be slower (represented by the 80%, 10%, 5%, 5% spread of accounts receivable over 90+ days), but will be more than offset by greater sales compared to last year.

- *Prior* year's payables will be paid over a three-month period with 40% paid in January, 50% in February, and 10% in March.

- Accounts payable incurred in 1988 will be paid faster (70% within 30 days and 30% within 60 days) to improve credit ratings with suppliers so that good terms can be obtained when Store B is started.

- An additional $25,000 in fixed assets will be purchased in January to improve Store A. Some vendor deposits ($1,250) have been made for various deposits.

- Remaining long-term debt ($20,000) is payable over five years or 60 months at 11.50%. You also have a $50,000 line of credit at 12% with your bank where you must maintain a minimum cash balance of $5,000.

- Additional funding is set at zero for both new equity and new debt, so you can determine the minimum cash balance (to be shown in the cash flow statement). This figure will tell you if you need additional funding, and how much you need. The monthly ending cash balance will indicate when you will need these funds. You can then experiment with injecting different amounts of equity or debt into the venture to see what kinds of financial projections are associated with different combinations of debt and equity.

In order to calculate the amount of sales the store needs to break even for different assumptions and financial projections, you also need to make rough estimates to what extent monthly costs are totally variable (100% means these costs vary directly with each incremental sale, that is, the cost is not incurred until the sale is made) versus totally fixed (0% means these costs must be paid even if nothing is sold). For example, salaries (0%) must be paid each month even if there are no sales. Thus, salaries are totally fixed costs. However, advertising and promotion is 30% variable because the promotions portion (30%) is paid *only* when someone buys something. Advertising is 70% of the budget, and it is fixed because you must pay your advertising bill even if you sell nothing.

The Revenue Statement (or Sales Forecast)

The better business plans I've read over the last decade usually did a fairly good job of forecasting their costs. Though it is sometimes tedious, you can generally obtain good ballpark estimates of R&D, marketing, production, and administrative expenses. If these "better plans" had a flaw, it was their estimates of sales revenues or the *top line*.

Before startup, the top line is the most important line for nearly all entrepreneurial enterprises. After startup, other lines may assume greater importance. For instance, a materials-intensive manufacturing enterprise may need to monitor inventory and purchasing of certain materials much more closely than sales (once these are known for some relevant period of time). The reason is that slight variations in materials costs can have a devastatingly negative or incredibly positive impact on profits compared to slight changes in sales.[4] But before venture launch, the top line is usually the hardest line to forecast accurately. (That's why I've separated sales from the income statement and given it the status of a separate statement.)

Unexpected sales growth or sales decline can cause an increase in cash needs that pushes you above the upper limit of your venture's required capitalization. For instance, you need to know the *maximum sales increase* for which you have sufficient cash to cover related increases in costs and cash outflows that may suddenly begin increasing faster than cash inflows. Conversely, you need to know the *maximum sales declines* for which you have sufficient cash to cover decreases in cash inflows that may be occurring faster than the decline in costs and cash outflows.

Exhibit 6.4 illustrates the capital you'll need in different sales scenarios. The shaded portion represents a range of sales. Your ultimate task (in terms of entrepreneurial finance) is to discover what is the appropriate amount of capital that will finance not just likely sales, but the entire range of sales possibilities between pessimistic and optimistic sales forecasts.

The Components of the Sales Revenue Statement

There can be one or many items in a sales revenue statement. There may be no more than a single line (for example, net sales) if you are doing a quick feasibility analysis as is the case for the retail venture described in the case study. Exhibit 6.5 provides a sample retail revenue statement. Of course, many additional line items can be involved for a more detailed forecast of sales. For instance, a slightly more complicated sales forecast may break out sales discounts, deductions, and/or returns. More extensive calculations of sales may

EXHIBIT 6.4   Capital needed for a range of sales.

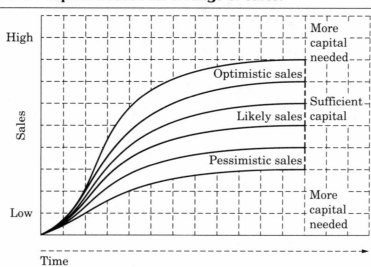

EXHIBIT 6.5   Sample revenue forecast for a retail company.

| | 1/31/88 | 2/29/88 | 3/31/88 | 4/30/88 | 5/31/88 | 6/30/88 | 7/31/88 | 8/31/88 | 9/30/88 | 10/31/88 | 11/30/88 | 12/31/88 | Year 1 |
	Retail	Retail	Retail	Retail	Retail	Retail	Retail	Retail	Retail	Retail	Retail	Retail	Retail
Sales, Store A	$12,000	$16,500	$10,500	$15,000	$27,000	$21,000	$15,000	$6,000	$12,000	$27,000	$60,000	$78,000	$300,000
Net sales	$12,000	$16,500	$10,500	$15,000	$27,000	$21,000	$15,000	$6,000	$12,000	$27,000	$60,000	$78,000	$300,000
Monthly increase/decrease in sales	0%	38%	(36%)	43%	80%	(22%)	(29%)	(60%)	100%	125%	122%	30%	N/A

show units and prices for different products and services. Detailed sales forecasts may disaggregate sales by location (Store A, Store B, and so on), channel of distribution, or many other ways.

The Derivation of the Sales Forecast's Components

For the retail venture, the analysis is fairly simple for the first cut to see if the venture expansion is feasible. The analysis can be refined later. Based on some preliminary work, $300,000 in annual sales represents a realistic top line. The assumptions statement assumes a seasonality spreading of these sales based on discussions with other retailers in related businesses. Consequently, monthly sales in Exhibit 6.5 are derived in the revenue statement simply by multiplying the annual sales assumption by the percent of sales allocated per month (both found in the assumptions statement).

The Income Statement

The income statement presents your venture's performance over a specified period of time (be it a month, quarter, or year) in terms of sales, costs, and profits or losses. A projected income statement's main purpose is to show how much profit (or loss) you hope to earn based on when you make your sales and legitimately incur your costs, as opposed to when you actually collect the cash for the sales or pay for the costs you are obligated to pay.

The Derivation of the Income Statement's Components

In the retail store example, several items (gross profit, total operating expenses, operating profit, and net income before taxes) are calculated internally from other income statement items. Also, you've already seen how one item, net sales, has simply been copied from the revenue statement. The actual values are shown in Exhibit 6.6. The remaining items are all derived as follows:

Note: The source of each item in the following list is shown in brackets when it comes from a statement other than the income statement.

- *Cost of goods* is calculated by multiplying net sales by 45% (the cost of goods as a percentage of sales for Store A [assumptions statement]).
- *Payroll, taxes, and benefits* is calculated by adding payroll to taxes and benefits. First, payroll is derived by adding the store manager's salary [assumptions statement] to the product of net sales on the income statement times the 5% commission rate [assumptions statement]. Then, taxes and benefits

EXHIBIT 6.6   Sample income statement for a retail company.

	1/31/88 Retail	2/29/88 Retail	3/31/88 Retail	4/30/88 Retail	5/31/88 Retail	6/30/88 Retail	7/31/88 Retail	8/31/88 Retail	9/30/88 Retail	10/31/88 Retail	11/30/88 Retail	12/31/88 Retail	Year 1 Retail
Net sales	$12,000	$16,500	$10,500	$15,000	$27,000	$21,000	$15,000	$6,000	$12,000	$27,000	$60,000	$78,000	$300,000
Cost of goods	5,400	7,425	4,725	6,750	12,150	9,450	6,750	2,700	5,400	12,150	27,000	35,100	135,000
Gross profit	6,600	9,075	5,775	8,250	14,850	11,550	8,250	3,300	6,600	14,850	33,000	42,900	165,000
Operating expenses:													
Payroll, taxes, and benefits	4,543	4,809	4,455	4,720	5,428	5,074	4,720	4,189	4,543	5,428	7,375	8,437	63,720
Occupancy	2,500	2,500	2,500	2,500	2,500	2,500	2,500	2,500	2,500	2,500	2,500	2,500	30,000
Advertising and promotion	360	495	315	450	810	630	450	180	360	810	1,800	2,340	9,000
Supplies and other	360	495	315	450	810	630	450	180	360	810	1,800	2,340	9,000
Depreciation	714	714	714	714	714	714	714	714	714	714	714	714	8,571
Total operating expenses	8,477	9,013	8,299	8,834	10,262	9,548	8,834	7,763	8,477	10,262	14,189	16,331	120,291
Operating profit (loss)	(1,877)	62	(2,524)	(584)	4,588	2,002	(584)	(4,463)	(1,877)	4,588	18,811	26,569	44,709
Interest expenses/income	288	476	486	621	665	597	524	496	587	775	920	733	7,168
Net income before taxes	$(2,165)	$(413)	$(3,010)	$(1,205)	$3,922	$1,405	$(1,108)	$(4,959)	$(2,464)	$3,812	$17,890	$25,835	$37,540

are calculated by multiplying base salaries [assumptions statement] by the 18% store payroll tax and benefit rate [assumptions statement].

- *Occupancy* is calculated by adding monthly rent [assumptions statement] plus monthly telephone, utilities, and insurance [assumptions statement].
- *Advertising and promotion* is calculated by multiplying net sales on the income statement by the 3% monthly advertising and promotion rate [assumptions statement].
- *Supplies and other* is calculated by multiplying net sales by the 3% monthly supplies rate [assumptions statement].
- *Depreciation* is calculated by using a straight line depreciation function that is equivalent to rounding the figure for total property and equipment at cost [balance sheet] for Period #1 to $60,000 and dividing it by seven years, the store fixed assets depreciation rate [assumptions statement], and then dividing this total ($8,571) by 12 months to arrive at the $714 of monthly depreciation shown on the income statement.
- *Interest expense/income* is calculated by multiplying the beginning principal balance [cash flow statement] times the 11.5% annual interest rate [assumptions statement] divided by 12 months plus the previous period's line of credit [balance sheet] times the 12% annual line of credit interest rate [assumptions statement] divided by 12 months.

The Balance Sheet

A balance sheet is a statement of a venture's financial position at a specific point in time. It gives a snapshot of the venture's financial position at this time, expressed in terms either of historical costs for an accounting statement or future costs when a balance sheet is used for financial projections. Often the date of a balance sheet coincides with the ending date of an income statement; however, you should remember that the income statement is showing sales, expenses, and profit activity *over a specified period,* whereas the balance sheet is showing the venture's financial position *exclusively as of the ending date.*

Actually, there are at least two balance sheets you need to consider when generating a set of linked financial projections: one is the opening balance sheet, and the other is a closing balance sheet. The *opening balance sheet* contains all prior transactions, and is sometimes called the base period, or beginning, balance sheet. The *closing balance sheet,* as the name suggests, shows the status of your assets, liabilities, and equities at the end of a specified period.

One reason you need two balance sheets on the balance sheet statement is that the other projected financial statements encompass or cross some period of time. However, the balance sheet is different. It shows the status of an enterprise at a specific point in time, for example, on January 1, 1990, when you first committed some significant dollar resources to your venture. It's vital to recognize at least two balance sheets because the comparison of the two statements allows us to understand how an organization changed the size and deployment of its assets and liabilities during the time period.

The opening balance sheet is unique because it represents either:

- A statement of historical fact, for example, I've started working on this venture and here are the assets I've allocated and the liabilities I've incurred, and the equity I've invested up to this point in time; or
- An assumption about the future set of assets, liabilities, and equity I will bring to the initiation of the venture.

If the latter, you may ask, "Then why isn't the opening balance sheet part of the balance sheet assumptions in the assumptions statement?" The answer is that it could be included in the assumptions statement. However, convention and convenience require us to show the opening balance sheet (or at least some base period) on the balance sheet statement so it can be compared easily with other projected balance sheets.

What the initial time point of an opening balance sheet should be for a new venture is a matter of judgment. To be informative, the opening balance sheet should be prepared after some assets have been obtained and deployed. The key point is that every venture has an opening balance sheet. Even if you aren't explicit about its existence, an implicit balance sheet exists. Theoretically, one exists from the time you first had the idea for your venture, even if you had zero assets invested and zero liabilities incurred at that point.

Obviously, listing a balance sheet with zero assets and liabilities is not very informative; consequently, it usually pays to select a base period to mark the beginning point of your business for comparative purposes. The fact that the base period is not necessarily the first balance sheet does not matter for our purposes since a balance sheet captures all that has transpired financially up to that time.

For instance, Base Period #5 in Exhibit 6.7 incorporates all prior balance sheet transactions, covering a 60-day prestartup period for a venture. See if you can explain the transactions that have occurred by the end of each period shown in Exhibit 6.7:

- *Period #1:* The end of Day 1 marks the birth of your venture idea. No financial transactions have taken place yet, but an implicit balance sheet already exists.

EXHIBIT 6.7   Opening balance sheet or base period.

	Idea for venture	Prestartup period (no sales)			60 days later
	Day 1 Period #1	Day 15 Period #2	Day 30 Period #3	Day 45 Period #4	Day 60 Period #5
Cash	$0	$10,000	$20,000	$20,000	$15,000
Inventory	0	0	0	5,000	5,000
Fixed assets	0	0	0	0	5,000
TOTAL ASSETS	$0	$10,000	$20,000	$25,000	$25,000
Trade payables	0	0	0	5,000	5,000
Long-term debt	0	0	10,000	10,000	10,000
Equity	0	10,000	10,000	10,000	10,000
TOTAL LIABILITIES AND EQUITY	$0	$10,000	$20,000	$25,000	$25,000

- *Period #2:* As of Day 15, the following transactions have occurred: $10,000 has been invested in the venture as *equity* and appears as $10,000 in cash on the asset side of the balance sheet.
- *Period #3:* As of Day 30, an additional $10,000 has been borrowed as long-term debt, raising total liabilities and equities to $20,000. Cash is increased to $20,000 on the asset side of the balance sheet.
- *Period #4:* As of Day 45, $5,000 of trade payables have been incurred to finance the buildup of $5,000 worth of Inventory.
- *Period #5:* As of Day 60, no charges occur on the liabilities and equities side of the balance sheet. However, $5,000 is used to purchase (for cash) some fixed assets.

Although these transactions are simple, they reveal two important things about the balance sheet:

- The size of your balance sheet in terms of total assets can increase (as it did in Periods #3 and #4) if you simply increase long-term or short-term debt.
- Shifts in assets and liabilities can occur that will have a definite impact on the amount of cash you end up with.

The Derivation of the Balance Sheet's Components

The retail venture's balance sheet is shown in Exhibit 6.8. The numbers for the opening balance sheet come from either historical data or assumed data that

EXHIBIT 6.8 Sample balance sheet for a retail company.

	Base period	1/31/88	2/29/88	3/31/88	4/30/88	5/31/88	6/30/88	7/31/88	8/31/88	9/30/88	10/31/88	11/30/88	12/31/88
Assets													
Current assets:													
Cash and equivalents	$24,700	$34,893	$5,000	$5,000	$5,000	$5,000	$5,000	$5,000	$5,000	$5,000	$610	$5,000	$19,197
Accounts receivable	12,500	2,400	4,500	4,350	4,875	7,425	7,650	6,450	3,750	3,750	6,900	15,300	22,950
Inventories	7,250	12,875	19,200	26,625	29,325	23,925	17,175	15,825	25,275	46,875	69,825	48,765	21,833
Total current assets	44,450	50,168	28,700	35,975	39,200	36,350	29,825	27,275	34,025	55,625	77,335	69,065	63,979
Property and equipment, net	33,500	57,786	57,071	56,357	55,643	54,929	54,214	53,500	52,786	52,071	51,357	50,643	49,929
Other assets	2,500	3,750	3,750	3,750	3,750	3,750	3,750	3,750	3,750	3,750	3,750	3,750	3,750
Total assets	$80,450	$111,704	$89,521	$96,082	$98,593	$95,029	$87,789	$84,525	$90,561	$111,446	$132,443	$123,458	$117,658
Liabilities and equity													
Current liabilities:													
Accounts payable	$32,456	$31,247	$8,418	$4,584	$3,855	$3,261	$1,938	$2,640	$4,503	$9,066	$11,766	$3,612	$4,604
Accrued expenses	1,850	1,850	1,850	1,850	1,850	1,850	1,850	1,850	1,850	1,850	1,850	1,850	1,850
Current portion of long-term debt	10,000	14,000	14,000	14,000	14,000	14,000	14,000	14,000	14,000	14,000	14,000	14,000	14,000
Line of credit	0	0	1,676	15,702	20,775	14,516	7,835	5,622	15,406	34,852	50,000	31,950	0
Total current liabilities	44,306	47,097	25,944	36,136	40,480	33,627	25,623	24,112	35,759	59,768	77,616	51,412	20,454
Long-term debt	20,000	35,628	35,012	34,390	33,762	33,129	32,489	31,843	31,191	30,533	29,868	29,197	28,519
Stock-holders' equity:													
Contributed capital	20,000	35,000	35,000	35,000	35,000	35,000	35,000	35,000	35,000	35,000	35,000	35,000	35,000
Accumulated earnings	(3,856)	(6,021)	(6,434)	(9,444)	(10,649)	(6,727)	(5,322)	(6,430)	(11,389)	(13,854)	(10,041)	7,849	33,684
Total equity	16,144	28,979	28,566	25,556	24,351	28,273	29,678	28,570	23,611	21,146	24,959	42,849	68,684
Total liabilities and equity	$80,450	$111,704	$89,521	$96,082	$98,593	$95,029	$87,789	$84,525	$90,561	$111,446	$132,443	$123,458	$117,658
Does the balance sheet balance?	Yes	Yes	Yes	Yes	Yes	Yes	Yes	Yes	Yes	Yes	Yes	Yes	Yes

are entered directly into each line item of the base period, just as sales, income, and cash flow assumptions are entered directly into the assumptions statement. [*Note:* In the present model, the only requirement is that the amount of total assets you enter in the base period must equal total liabilities and equities. There is no discretionary balancing, or "plug," figure that automatically equalizes these totals for the base period. The formulas for this model are written to start at Period #1, so you do not necessarily have to enter an opening balance sheet since the equalizing precondition is still satisfied in the base period when zero assets equals zero liabilities and equities.]

The derivation of the numbers for the closing balance sheet is described in the following lists, with the source statement for variables shown in brackets if the variable comes from a statement other than the balance sheet.

Current assets are derived as follows:

- *Cash and equivalents* is derived from the ending cash balance [cash flow statement] for the period in question.
- *Accounts receivable* is derived from the previous period's accounts receivable plus the current period's net sales [income statement] *after* subtracting total cash receipts [cash flow statement].
- *Inventories* is derived by adding purchases [cash flow statement] to the previous period's inventories and then subtracting cost of goods [income statement].

Fixed assets are derived as follows:

- *Net property and equipment at cost* is calculated by adding the previous period's fixed assets at cost plus fixed assets purchased [assumptions statement] minus accumulated depreciation.
- *Accumulated depreciation* is calculated by adding the previous period's accumulated depreciation plus the current period's depreciation [income statement].
- *Other assets* is calculated by adding the previous period's other assets plus vendor deposits required [assumptions statement].

Current liabilities are derived as follows:

- *Accounts payable* is calculated by taking all the previous payables that have not been paid and adding all the new bills or obligations incurred in operating expenses [income statement] *plus* inventory purchases [inventory purchasing statement, not shown here] *plus* fixed assets purchased [assumptions statement] *minus* the bills or obligations that are paid during the month (for example, payroll, taxes, and benefits [income statement]) *minus* noncash expenditures included in operating expenses (for example, depreciation, [income statement]). Exhibit 6.9 illustrates the calculation of a rolling accounts payable balance.

Unfortunately, the formulas used to project your balance sheet are often the most complicated among those in your financial projections. For instance, the specific formula for *accounts payable* for our retail store is calculated by adding the previous period's accounts payable on the balance sheet *plus* inventory purchases [inventory purchasing statement] *plus* fixed assets purchased [assumptions statement] *plus* operating expenses [income statement] *minus* payroll, taxes, and benefits [income statement] *minus* depreciation [income statement] *minus* accounts payable paid from 1987 expenses [cash flow statement] *minus* monthly expenses, inventory, and fixed assets paid [cash flow statement].

- *Accrued expenses* for the retail store are assumed to equal the previous period's accrued expenses. In other situations, you may wish to include new items that are obligations you have incurred legally but have not yet received an invoice or are not yet obligated to pay. If so, the process is similar to accounts payable in which old and new accrued expenses are combined and then subtracted from accrued expenses actually paid during the current period to arrive at a net accrued expenses balance. For example, income taxes are incurred legally for each day you operate. However, you are not invoiced daily or even monthly but are expected to pay quarterly. Perhaps a better example is services you have received

EXHIBIT 6.9   Calculation of accounts payable.

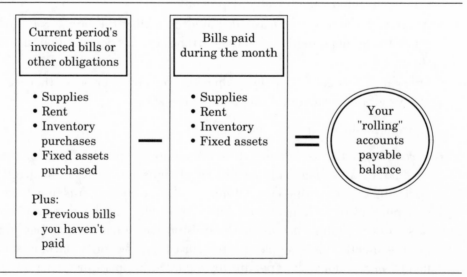

from a lawyer or consultant, who will not send a bill or invoice for three or four months.

- *Current portion of long-term debt* is calculated by taking the previous period's current portion of long-term debt plus the current period's current portion of long-term debt on the balance sheet minus the notes payable principal payment [cash flow statement] *until* long-term debt becomes a zero balance.

Equities are derived as follows:

- *Contributed capital* is derived from the previous period's contributed capital on the balance sheet plus new equity [cash flow statement] from the current period.
- *Accumulated earnings* is derived from the previous period's accumulated earnings on the balance sheet plus net income before taxes [income statement] minus dividends [cash flow statement] for the current period.

How to Get the Balance Sheet to Balance

If you have ever tried to put together a set of financial projections, you probably experienced some trying moments attempting to discover why your balance sheet didn't balance. Don't worry. You're not alone. I've seen experienced CPAs spend hours trying to figure out why a particular set of projections didn't *tie out*, that is, produce a balanced balance sheet.

Despite what people may say, getting your balance sheet to balance isn't easy. You may also wonder, since we're dealing with imprecise future projections, why you need to have a balance sheet that balances. The answer relates to the *interdependent nature of all the statements*. Because the balance sheet is tied to the cash flow and ultimately all other statements, a balance sheet that is out of balance can provide the wrong answers about how much cash your venture needs, when it needs this cash, what form the cash should take, and where you should try to raise the needed funds.

In short, an incorrect balance sheet can mess up your cash flow statement, your ratios and profitability measures, your sales breakeven, and any other analysis that is derived directly or indirectly from the balance sheet. That means just about everything, since the linkages between the statements ensure that errors ripple through all of your projections. In addition, you can't ignore or rationalize away a small error in your balance sheet. Flagging potential errors is important here. It's why Exhibit 6.8 asks a simple "Yes" or "No" question at the bottom of the statement: "Does the balance sheet balance?" Remember, a small error in your balance sheet often gets bigger with each new round of calculations for each successive time period.

The Cash Flow Statement

The income statement and the balance sheet have dominated the attention of stockholders, and, consequently, many managers in the past. The reasons for this domination include the facts that:

- Both statements are important indicators of the organization's past performance and current position; and
- Accountants can reduce and consolidate a great deal of information from other statements into these two statements for presentation purposes.

Both the income statement and the balance sheet also satisfy the needs of managers and stockholders of larger corporations for a relatively accurate picture of an enterprise's future health, especially when these people can focus on a few financial ratios drawn from these statements. For instance, the amount of debt your venture has incurred relative to total equity (the debt/equity ratio) shows the financial commitment of the owners compared to that of outside creditors and bankers. Where nearly all debt is used with very little equity, this shows little financial reason for the owners to stick with the venture when it experiences difficult times. They personally have little to lose by selling the business. They also have little or no further ability to use debt to help the venture through difficult times.

Over the last decade, a third statement—the cash flow statement—has garnered increasing attention among entrepreneurs, and especially owner/managers of smaller businesses. The reason is simple. Cash is what keeps ventures alive and functioning. The cash flow statement tracks the *actual flow of cash into and out of the venture.* The income statement and balance sheet can be misleading about the true existence of cash, and this is especially likely if a venture is new, small, or rapidly growing. For example, at some point *within* an accounting period, a venture may not have sufficient cash to continue operating, even though the income statement shows a substantial projected profit and the balance sheet projects a positive net worth and positive cash for the end of the accounting period (some months away).

This possibility is more likely to have a devastating impact when the accounting period or the projection period is relatively long, (for example, a quarter or especially a year). Annual income and balance sheet projections have been known to show entrepreneurs rich and famous at the end of the year although their ventures actually run out of funds six months before that time. For instance, monthly cash flow projections in the exhibit on page 167 show big negative cash flows in August, September, and October followed by large positive cash flows in November and December. Unfortunately, the venture never sees November unless it raises additional funding of $4,390 in October.

Consequently, the cash flow statement is an extremely important statement for new enterprises. It shows not only *how much* money you need to launch the venture but also *when* you will need it.

The cash flow statement tracks when you actually receive cash and when you pay it out over some specified period of time. In short, its basic purposes are to tell you if you have sufficient cash to continue present and future operations, and, if not, how much cash you will need and when you will need it to keep the venture operating at some designated level.

The cash flow statement is important because it prevents you from equating sales with cash flow unless sales are actually cash sales. It also tells you what your minimum cash point will be over the time period in question. From a projections perspective, the cash flow statement tells you how to manage the cash you have. It gives you the insight and time to react, to decide how to spend (or not spend) cash under a variety of circumstances.

For example, your ending cash position for any particular month can be positive or negative, depending on whether you've received more cash (including your starting cash position) than you've spent. If you cannot offset negative cash flows with additional capital (debt or equity), someone will go unpaid. You may be able to live with this condition for some period of time depending on your creditors. But eventually you will be forced to take action to turn cash flow positive in the future. This action can include a reduction in expenditures as shown on the income statement—that is, reducing wages, salaries, rent, utilities, travel, and so on. Or it can include changes in balance sheet items that free up cash: selling fixed assets, reducing your accounts receivables faster (that is, increasing your collections), increasing your accounts payable (that is, extending the average time you pay vendors and other creditors), or reducing the amount of cash tied up in inventory. Should these and other possible actions prove insufficient to turn cash flow positive, you may have no other choice but to sell or discontinue the venture.

The critical point, however, is that you can use an integrated financials model to test the effects of these actions *before* they happen. This capability allows you to manage financial decisions by evaluating numerous options quickly, using a true "what if" approach to find a viable, if not the best, option available to you.

Many new and fairly new ventures show negative net cash flows from their operations because entrepreneurs and other investors have to spend money to build up the business. These negative positions should be covered by the initial capital invested in the venture and other debt and equity financings that prove necessary. Eventually, however, a venture needs to earn a positive *operating* cash flow so the business can not only stand on its own feet but presumably begin providing a return to investors from the operations

EXHIBIT 6.10   Timing of cash flows.

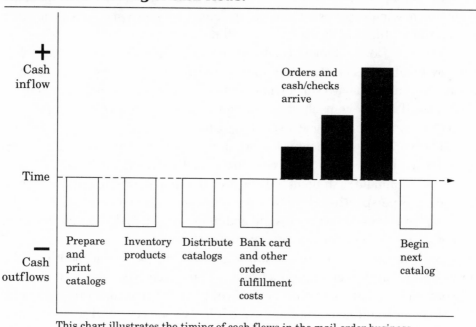

This chart illustrates the timing of cash flows in the mail-order business.

of the venture. For instance, Exhibit 6.10 illustrates the typical situation for a mail-order venture at startup where operating cash flows are negative at first.

Components of the Cash Flow Statement

Cash flow statements are arranged in many different ways. These can be categorized into three basic types in terms of complexity:

1. *The simple cash flow statement,* so called because all items are arranged into only two categories: cash inflows (including your starting cash position) and cash outflows.

2. *The operating cash flow statement,* so called because cash inflows and outflows are limited initially to the cash flows that stem from the venture's ongoing operations, as opposed to the cash flows needed to finance the venture.

3. *The priority cash flow statement,* so called because cash inflows and particularly cash outflows are further classified into any number of priority or discretionary groupings.

Priority cash flow statements are very useful. However their increased utility is often offset by their greater complexity. For our purposes, the operating cash flow statement offers a better trade-off. A slight decrease in complexity is worth the advantage of knowing whether a positive cash flow for a particular month, quarter, or year is being produced from the venture's operations, from financial inflows, or from operating inflows from *prior* periods.

Because of this advantage, I've chosen to use the operating cash flow model with only some slight variations. The fundamental model is shown in Exhibit 6.11, followed by the projected cash flow statement for our retail venture in Exhibit 6.12.

EXHIBIT 6.11   Operating cash flow statement.

	Period #1	Period #2
Cash received:	(Inflows)	
Cash sales	XXX	
Receivables collected	XXX	
Operating cash inflows	XXX	
Cash disbursed	(Outflows)	
Purchases paid	XXX	
Payroll paid	XXX	
Other operating expenses paid	XXX	
Operating cash outflows	XXX	
Net operating cash flow	XXX	
Nonoperating inflows		
Add:		
Beginning cash balance	XXX	
New equity invested	XXX	
New debt invested	XXX	
Nonoperating outflows		
Minus:		
Debt principal payments	XXX	
Interest payments	XXX	
Income taxes paid	XXX	
Fixed assets paid	XXX	
Dividends paid	XXX	
Ending cash balance	XXX	
Cumulative cash flow	XXX	

EXHIBIT 6.12 Cash flow statement for a retail company.

	1/31/88	2/29/88	3/31/88	4/30/88	5/31/88	6/30/88	7/31/88	8/31/88	9/30/88	10/31/88	11/30/88	12/31/88
Cash received (inflows)												
Accounts receivable collected from 1987 sales	$12,500	$ 0	$ 0	$ 0	$ 0	$ 0	$ 0	$ 0	$ 0	$ 0	$ 0	$ 0
Monthly sales collected	9,600	14,400	10,650	14,475	24,450	20,775	16,200	8,700	12,000	23,850	51,600	70,350
Total cash receipts	22,100	14,400	10,650	14,475	24,450	20,775	16,200	8,700	12,000	23,850	51,600	70,350
Cash disbursed (outflow)												
Payroll paid	4,543	4,809	4,455	4,720	5,428	5,074	4,720	4,189	4,543	5,428	7,375	8,437
Accounts payable paid from 1987 expenses	12,982	16,228	3,246	0	0	0	0	0	0	0	0	0
Monthly expenses, inventory, fixed asset paid:												
1–30 days paid	27,472	12,068	10,696	8,995	7,609	4,522	6,160	10,507	21,154	27,454	8,428	10,743
31–60 days paid	0	11,774	5,172	4,584	3,855	3,261	1,938	2,640	4,503	9,066	11,766	3,612
61–90 days paid	0	0	0	0	0	0	0	0	0	0	0	0
90+ days paid	0	0	0	0	0	0	0	0	0	0	0	0
Vendor deposits	1,250	0	0	0	0	0	0	0	0	0	0	0
Total cash disbursement	46,247	44,878	23,568	18,299	16,892	12,857	12,818	17,336	30,200	41,948	27,569	22,792
Operating cash surplus (deficit)	(24,147)	(30,478)	(12,918)	(3,824)	7,558	7,918	3,382	(8,636)	(18,200)	(18,098)	24,031	47,558
Less: interest payments:												
Interest on debt (notes payable)	288	476	470	464	458	452	446	439	433	427	420	414
Interest on line of credit	0	0	17	157	208	145	78	56	154	349	500	320
Less: notes payable principal payment	372	616	622	628	634	640	646	652	658	665	671	677
Add: beginning of month cash balance	24,700	34,893	5,000	5,000	5,000	5,000	5,000	5,000	5,000	5,000	610	5,000
Cash balance before funding	$(107)	$3,324	$(9,026)	$(72)	$11,259	$11,681	$7,212	$(4,784)	$(14,446)	$(14,538)	$23,050	$51,147
Line of credit principal payments	0	0	0	0	6,258	6,681	2,212	0	0	0	18,050	31,950
Dividends	0	0	0	0	0	0	0	0	0	0	0	0
Additional funding:												
New equity	15,000	0	0	0	0	0	0	0	0	0	0	0
New debt (notes payable)	20,000	0	0	0	0	0	0	0	0	0	0	0
Line of credit borrowings	0	1,676	14,026	5,072	0	0	0	9,784	19,446	15,148	0	0
Ending cash balance	$34,893	$ 5,000	$ 5,000	$ 5,000	$ 5,000	$ 5,000	$ 5,000	$ 5,000	$ 5,000	$ 610	$ 5,000	$19,197
Is additional funding required?	No	No	No	No	No	No	No	No	No	Yes	No	No
If Yes, please enter your amount in the "new equity" or "new debt" (notes rows on the assumptions statement)												
Your minimum cash requirement was	$5,000											
The cash to fund your venture is	$4,390											

The Derivation of the Cash Flow's Components

The components of retail store's cash flow are derived from several sources. Some items come directly from the assumptions statement. Others come from the balance sheet or income statement. Again, the source statement is shown in brackets.

The formulas for certain cash flow items are very complex for legitimate technical reasons. In these instances, I've chosen to demonstrate how the calculation works; however, the reader should realize that computing a number in your head or even with a calculator is very difficult. In one or two instances, such calculations are even impossible because they require access to some intermediary calculations that are not shown.

Operating cash inflows are derived as follows:

- *Accounts receivable collected from 1987 sales* are taken directly from the amounts estimated in the assumptions statement.
- *Receivables collected from 1988 sales* are calculated from the sum of the following:

    —*Receivables collected 30 days after sale*, which is derived by multiplying the previous month's net sales [income statement] by the assumed percentage collected in 30 days [assumptions statement].

    —*Receivables collected 60 days after sale*, which is derived by multiplying the net sales [income statement] realized two months ago by the assumed percentage collected in 60 days [assumptions statement].

    —*Receivables collected 90 days after sale*, which is derived by multiplying the net sales [income statement] realized three months ago by the assumed percentage collected in 90 days [assumptions statement].

    —*Receivables collected over 90 days after sale*, which is derived by multiplying the net sales [income statement] realized four months ago by the assumed percentage collected after 90 days [assumptions statement]. Note: In this set of projections, bad debts are part of deductions and subtracted from gross sales. An alternative calculation would be to make receivables collected add up to something less than 100% in the assumptions statement with receivables collected over 90 days incorporating the shortfall (for example, a cumulative receivables collected percentage of 98% gives a 2% bad debt rate).

In some instances, cash sales are assumed to be any sale where cash is received within the first 1 to 30 days. When this assumption is made, cash sales are simply combined with receivables collected instead of being listed as a separate item.

EXHIBIT 6.13   Accounts receivable spreading.

Month	Actual				Projected			
	F	M	A	M	J	J	A	S
Sales	300	200	100	100	200	300	400	400
Cash receipts								
1–30 days (20%)	60	40	20	20	40	60	80	80
31–60 days (50%)	150	150	100	50	50	100	150	200
61–90 days (30%)	120	90	90	60	30	30	60	90
Total receipts from sales	330	280	210	130	120	190	290	370

Source: Adapted from Leon Haller's excellent book, *Making Sense of Accounting Information* (New York: Van Nostrand Reinhold, 1985), 41 (with the author's permission).

Exhibit 6.13 shows how receivables are spread over time. Operating cash outflows are derived as follows:

- *Payroll paid* is taken from payroll, taxes, and wages and benefits [income statement].

- *Accounts payable paid* [from 1987 expenses] is calculated by multiplying the '87 accounts payable of $32,456 [base period of balance sheet] by the base period accounts payable paid [assumptions statement].

- *Monthly expenses, inventory, fixed assets paid* is calculated by *multiplying* operating expenses [income statement] *minus* salaries and wages, *minus* depreciation, *plus* any inventory purchases and any fixed assets purchased [assumptions statement] by a monthly expenses paid rate that is spread over 90+ days.

- *Vendor deposits* is taken from vendor deposits required [assumptions statement].

- *Interest part of debt (notes payable) payment* is calculated by multiplying the beginning principal balance [memo item or cash flow statement, not shown] times the annual interest rate [assumptions statement] and divided by 12 months.

- *Principal part of debt (notes payable) payment* is calculated by subtracting the interest part of payment from the monthly payment amount [memo item or cash flow statement, not shown].

- *Interest on line of credit* is calculated by multiplying the previous period's line of credit [balance sheet] times the line of credit interest rate [assumptions statement] and dividing by 12 months.

- *Add: beginning of month cash balance* is taken from the previous period's cash and equivalents [balance sheet].

- *Line of credit principal repayments* occur when the cash balance before funding [cash flow statement] is above the $5,000 minimum cash balance [assumptions statement]. The exact amount paid is either the total principal due on line of credit borrowings or the maximum amount that will still leave an ending cash balance of $5,000.

- *New equity* is taken directly from new equity [assumptions statement] and is held at zero initially in order to determine incremental cash needs.

- *New debt* is taken directly from new debt [assumptions statement] and is held at zero initially in order to determine incremental cash needs.

- *Line of credit borrowings* are calculated when the cash balance before funding plus new equity and new debt are less than the $5,000 minimum cash balance [assumptions statement]. The amount calculated is whatever amount is needed to make the ending cash balance $5,000 without exceeding the maximum line of credit [assumptions statement] of $50,000.

YOUR ULTIMATE GOAL: POSITIVE OPERATING CASH FLOWS

If happiness is a positive cash flow, then venture ecstasy is a *positive operating cash flow.* One can finance a venture forever and show a positive cash flow by injecting new debt or equity. Yet your business may never be profitable in either an accounting or economic sense because you haven't produced a positive cash flow from the operations of the business.

Under certain conditions, a conscious decision may be made to subsidize a venture (for example, some nonprofit ventures) through donations and other fund-raising activities. For instance, many symphonies and museums operate on this basis in order to keep admission prices affordable. Although they operate in the red every year, a positive cash flow is produced by annual gift giving or periodic capital campaigns.

Most ventures, however, do not fit these nonprofit profiles. The goal of most for-profit entrepreneurs, though it may be unappreciated and unstated, is to earn a positive *operating* cash flow. Only as these operating cash flows increase over time can true wealth be created and equity increased in a venture so that the venture is worth something substantial to you because others place value on it.

KNOWING YOUR NUMBERS COLD MEANS NEVER GUESSING ABOUT THEM UNLESS YOU MUST

This chapter has shown how the initial assumptions you make will produce an interrelated set of projections. These projections start with a revenue statement and culminate in a cash flow statement. Don't worry if you don't understand every interrelationship perfectly at this time. With experience, these linkages will become clearer. For now, it's enough to understand how every element of your financial projections are related to all other elements. There's a saying in business that a change in any part of an organization finds a way of eventually rippling across the entire venture. Your financial projections are no different.

Today's entrepreneurs need to understand how accounting statements and financial projections are created and evolve. Practically speaking, they need this knowledge to plan and execute the startup of their ventures. They also need it for their own peace of mind. The experience of one entrepreneur speaks for many:

> Numbers may be the language of commerce, but it's a dialect few of us speak when we first go into business. That can make for some very anxious moments. I recall being at the mercy of my bookkeeper for seven long years. She was oracular, and I would wait nervously for her to deliver each month's profit-and-loss statement. It took about 15 years before I actually understood the double-entry method of accounting. As much as I pretended to read, comprehend, and comment on P&Ls and balance sheets, I was operating under a thick film of ignorance that I was too embarrassed to admit. It was only later—after I got over both my ignorance and my embarrassment—that I fully appreciated the role numbers should play in the management of a successful business.[5]

What's true about understanding historical accounting statements is doubly true for future-based financial projections. Most entrepreneurs need to control their environments as much as possible given the uncertainty that confronts them. Fortunately, reduction of uncertainty in the area of financial projections is attainable, and you shouldn't have to wait years to experience it. For venturing to be truly a calculated risk, you should be *calculating* likely cash flows, not guessing about them. As someone once said, "Never guess . . . unless you have to. There is enough uncertainty in the universe."

Creating a set of integrated financial projections allows you to take calculated risks. It allows you to limit your guessing. With integrated financial projections you can test and retest your basic assumptions about your business. You can understand the impact of changing many variables simultaneously. As this process evolves, you begin to see the forest, not just the trees, and eventually you truly understand your numbers, as Harold Geneen would say, "cold."

7 VENTURE CAPITAL

William E. Wetzel, Jr.

During the last ten years, most venture capital funds left their traditional role as early-stage investors in young companies. Fund portfolios now include large, later-stage deals, management/leveraged buyout financing, private placements for public companies, and, in some cases, investments in the stock of public companies. For a history of the venture capital industry and a provocative discussion of recent trends, see *Venture Capital at the Crossroads*.[1]

This chapter focuses exclusively on traditional, or classic, venture capital. *Classic venture capital* is distinguished by the following characteristics:

- It requires early-stage equity or equity-linked financing.
- It involves high risk.
- There is a lack of liquidity or marketability.
- Investment returns are primarily from capital gains.
- It is typically provided by patient investors equipped to offer value-added advice.

Classic venture investors are in the business of financing and building businesses that will be worth five to ten or more times the capital invested in

For their critique of this chapter the author extends a special "thank you" to Patricia M. Cloherty (Alan Patricoff Associates, Inc.), Robert J. Crowley (Massachusetts Technology Development Corp.), Peter D. Danforth (Kearsarge Ventures, L.P.), Robert C. McCray (private investor), P. Andrews McLane (TA Associates), Richard E. Morley (private investor), and Stephen G. Woodsum (Summit Partners).

five to ten years. *These investors look for long-term capital gains* on their portfolios and typically invest their financial and managerial know-how as well as their capital. In a very real sense, the decision to bankroll a new venture is the ultimate capital investment decision. It involves finding and funding investment opportunities that are expected to be worth substantially more than they cost.

Venture capital is expensive. Extreme uncertainty surrounding investment outcomes, coupled with the absence of investment liquidity, accounts for the high cost of venture capital. Consequently, the number of investment opportunities attractive to venture investors is limited. This chapter unravels some of the mystery surrounding the exciting but arcane world of venture capital.

WHEN *NOT* TO LOOK FOR VENTURE CAPITAL

Time runs a close second to *cash* on every entrepreneur's list of scarce resources. Don't waste valuable time thinking about raising venture capital until you have convinced yourself that your venture will generate substantial wealth for yourself and your investors. Your goal must be more than self-employment. You must have a burning desire to build an enterprise that will seize every opportunity for *profitable growth* and, ultimately, provide *liquidity for your investors.* Furthermore, the venture must be positioned in markets that provide such opportunities.

In practical terms, that means your vision and your business plan must support expectations that within five years your venture will be generating revenues of at least $10 million and growing by at least 20% per year with a pretax profit margin of at least 15%. Ventures below these thresholds may provide a comfortable income and perks for the entrepreneur, but the prospects for capital gains for investors are unattractive. At the other extreme, entrepreneurs will have the least trouble raising venture capital when their vision and financial projections support expectations of revenues in excess of $50 million within five years, growing at 30% to 50% or more per year and bringing down pretax profit margins of 20% or more.

Reread the previous paragraph. From a venture investor's perspective there are three types of entrepreneurial ventures:

1. *Life-style* ventures have five-year revenue projections under $10 million. These are fine for entrepreneurs driven by life-style motives, but they are of no interest to investors. Life-style ventures account for more than 90% of all startups.

2. *Middle-market* ventures have five-year revenue projections from $10 million to $50 million. These are also fine for entrepreneurs, but they may need venture financing. They can, if properly structured, offer capital gains and cash-out opportunities for investors. These ventures make up the backbone of our entrepreneurial economy. Most will remain privately owned or will be sold. They rely heavily on *bootstrap* financing and financing from individual investors.

3. *High-potential* ventures have five-year revenue projections in excess of $50 million. These are the potential big winners for both entrepreneurs and investors. They typically require several rounds of six- or seven-figure financing. Such ventures should expect to be publicly traded or acquired within five years. They are the next generation's Netscape, Callaway Golf, and Genzyme. They are candidates for financing from venture capital funds. High-potential ventures make up less than 1% of startups.

This chapter will be of interest to entrepreneurs trying to raise early-stage and growth financing for middle-market and high-potential ventures.

TAPPING THE VENTURE CAPITAL MARKETS

There are no hard data on the number of startup and high-growth middle-market and high-potential ventures or their annual capital requirements. Educated guesses place the number of companies growing at rates in excess of 20% per year at about half a million. Companies on the *Inc.* 500 list of fastest-growing private companies are leading examples. The number of start-ups with attractive capital gains potential is in the neighborhood of fifty thousand per year. The annual equity financing requirements of these high-growth and startup ventures are estimated to total some $60 billion per year.

Access to "patient capital" emerged from the 1995 White House Conference on Small Business at the most critical obstacle to the vitality of new high-growth ventures. The need was defined more precisely as seed and start-up capital on the order of $250,000 to $1,000,000.

There are two primary sources of venture financing for these entrepreneurs: one visible and one invisible.

Venture Capital Funds

The *visible* venture capital market is composed of over 500 venture capital funds that manage about $40 billion—not a lot of capital in the grand scheme of things. It is equivalent to the total assets of one good-sized bank, such as the

Bank of Boston. *Pratt's Guide to Venture Capital Sources* is a comprehensive directory of venture capital funds in the United States.[2]

Venture capital funds are investing about $4 billion annually in entrepreneurial ventures. Four billion dollars per year sounds like a lot of money to all of us, but keep in mind that more than $4 billion changes hands before noon every day on the floor of the New York Stock Exchange. Here are two more sobering statistics: Venture capital funds bankroll about 1,000 companies per year, and over two-thirds of these financings are for ventures already in their portfolios. Furthermore, all venture fund portfolio companies started life in the *high-potential* category.

A typical round of financing from a venture capital fund is a later-stage deal in excess of $3 million. If your venture is looking for equity financing, you are on the wrong side of 100-to-1 odds that you will be able to raise it from institutional venture capital investors. To save time knocking on the wrong doors, test your business plan against the high-potential venture criteria discussed in Chapter 2. If it flunks, take a close look at the invisible venture capital market.

Business "Angels"

The *invisible* venture capital market is also the oldest and the biggest. It is made up of over two million individuals, each with a net worth in excess of $1 million, excluding their personal residences. The majority of these individuals are self-made multi-millionaires (first-generation money)-individuals with substantial business and entrepreneurial experience. In 1984, 40% of the *Forbes* 400 richest people in America were entirely self-made. By 1994, 80% of the *Forbes* 400 were self-made. A net worth of $310 million was required to make the cut. They are often referred to as business "angels." Best estimates of the scale of this informal venture capital market suggest that about 250,000 angels invest $10-$20 billion every year in over 30,000 ventures. Bill Gates, number one on the *Forbes* 400 list, is "Exhibit A" on the angel list. For reasons he describes as intellectual as well as financial, Gates has bankrolled several start-up ventures in the biotech field.

For ventures with competent and committed management and a convincing business plan, the odds of raising angel financing are much higher than the odds of raising capital from venture capital funds. A typical angel deal is an early-stage round in the $100,000 to $500,000 range raised from six or eight investors. These co-investors usually are trusted friends and business associates. Find one angel and you have found five or ten.

The better odds are offset by the fact that angels are not easy to find. For obvious reasons, angels keep low profiles. There is no *Pratt's Guide to Angels*, and there are no public records of most angel deals. The resources closest to a

Pratt's Guide are regional venture capital networks. The original, Venture Capital Network, Inc. (VCN), was founded in 1984 as a not-for-profit corporation affiliated with the Center for Venture Research at the University of New Hampshire. VCN moved in 1990 to MIT, where it is now affiliated with the MIT Enterprise Forum of Cambridge. It was renamed Technology Capital Network (TCN) in 1992. There are six or eight similar organized networks in other regions of the country. These networks have proven to be effective in connecting angels and entrepreneurs. However, they are all relatively young and still minor players in the angel market.

Within the next few years look for a national angel network that will link these regional networks, effectively creating a new capital market designed to:

- Increase opportunities for qualified private equity investors to participate in the rewards and risks of financing emerging growth companies.
- Provide entrepreneurs with expanded access to the private equity markets.
- Reduce the cost of raising private equity capital through the use of standard interstate disclosure documents and policies.
- Employ controlled access to the Internet as the vehicle for a new capital market.
- Accomplish the above while maintaining an appropriate balance between venture promotion and investor protection.

Entrepreneurs need to depend on ingenuity and tenacity in their pursuit of angel financing. Here are some tips on how to find prospective angels:

- Look close to home—most angels invest in ventures they can reach in a half-day's drive.
- Look for individuals familiar with your markets or technology—they are the most likely to be interested in your venture.
- Many angels are active in charitable and civic affairs—look for their names in the local press and on the boards of directors and sponsors of such organizations.
- Most angels are risk-takers in their avocations as well as their professions—many are private pilots and sailors, and private aircraft and yachts must be registered with the FAA or the U.S. Coast Guard; these registrations are public information.
- Although it sounds bizarre, use your state motor vehicle department to find the owners of expensive performance cars.
- Use "gatekeepers"—lawyers, patent attorneys, accountants, venture capitalists, and bankers who specialize in serving early-stage and high-growth ventures.

- Above all, start building a roster of potential investors at least six months before you start your search for money.

"Bootstrap" Financing

If your search for financing from venture capital funds or from angels comes up empty, and, realistically, the odds are not in your favor, *don't quit*. Interviews with the founders of 100 companies on the 1989 *Inc.* 500 list attest to the prevalence of *bootstrap* financing. From these interviews it was estimated that more than 80% of the *Inc.* 500 fastest-growing private companies were financed *solely* by founders' personal savings, credit cards, second mortgages, customer advances, extended terms from vendors, and a multitude of other bootstrap techniques. The founders revealed that the median startup capital of the 100 companies was about $10,000. Less than one-fifth of the *Inc.* 500 raised outside equity capital during the five or more years that they had been in business.[3]

A Comparison of the Three Venture Capital Markets

A study of the financial histories of 284 new technology-based firms (NTBFs) founded in New England between 1975 and 1986 sheds light on the role of bootstrap financing,[4] angels, and venture capital funds:

- One hundred seven firms (38%) raised no outside financing.
- The remaining one 177 firms (62%) raised $671 million in 445 rounds of financing.
- Angels financed 120 firms.
- Venture capital funds financed 90 firms.
- Thirty-three firms used both sources.
- The distribution of angel versus venture capital fund financing according to the size and stage of the venture is illuminating: See Exhibits 7.1 and 7.2.

The median size of a round of seed, startup, and later-stage financing provided by angels was $150,000, $150,000, and $200,000, respectively. The median size of a round of seed, startup, and later-stage financing provided by venture capital funds was $450,000, $1,500,000, and $2,000,000, respectively.

The data contrasting angel and venture capital fund financing suggest that these two sources of capital complement each other. The complementary relationship is a function of the size and the stage of the deal. Angels are the most

EXHIBIT 7.1 **Size and source of rounds invested in new technology-based firms.**

Size of financing round	Private individuals		Venture capital funds	
<$250,000	102	(58%)	8	(5%)
$250,000–$499,999	43	(24%)	14	(8%)
$500,000–$999,999	15	(8%)	31	(18%)
≥$1,000,000	17	(10%)	120	(69%)
Total	177	(100%)	173	(100%)

likely source of small amounts of early-stage financing, whereas venture capital funds are more likely to provide larger amounts of later-stage financing.

OBTAINING FINANCING: START EARLY

A successful hunt for angel financing or financing from a venture capital fund normally will take at least six months from start to finish. The Center for Venture Research at the University of New Hampshire asked entrepreneurs who had raised venture financing how long it took to raise funds. The fund-raising process was divided into two stages:

- Stage 1—the elapsed time between the decision to raise funds and the first meeting with an angel or managing partner of a venture capital fund.

- Stage 2—the elapsed time between the first meeting and the receipt of funds.

EXHIBIT 7.2 **Stage and source of rounds invested in new technology-based firms.**

Stage of financing	Private individuals		Venture capital funds	
Seed	52	(29%)	11	(6%)
Startup	55	(31%)	38	(22%)
First stage	29	(16%)	56	(32%)
Second stage	26	(15%)	46	(27%)
Third stage	10	(6%)	19	(11%)
Bridge	5	(3%)	3	(2%)
Total	177	(100%)	173	(100%)

In *Stage 1*, the median elapsed time was one month to find and meet the first angel and 1.75 months to find and meet the first managing partner or senior investment professional of a venture capital fund. This result seems counterintuitive, given the relative obscurity of angels. However, although venture capital funds are easier to find, it may take more persistence to arrange an appointment with a venture capitalist than with an angel. One venture capitalist tests an entrepreneur's persistence by never returning the first three or four telephone calls.

A more significant difference was reported in the elapsed time between the first meeting and the receipt of funds (*Stage 2*). The median elapsed time was 2.5 months for angels and 4.5 months for venture capital funds.

The shorter deliberation time for angels may be due to the fact that angel deals typically involve a close group of co-investors led by a successful entrepreneur who is familiar with the venture's technology, products, and markets. Typically, the lead investor will vary from deal to deal, and each angel's piece of the deal tends to be a relatively small percentage of each investors total assets.

Venture capital funds, on the other hand, typically are involved in larger deals that represent a significant fraction of fund assets. As managers of other peoples' money, venture capital funds have a fiduciary responsibility to their investors. Their organizational structure and decision-making authority involve more people in the approval process.

Entrepreneurs reported that, from start to finish, raising funds from angels consumed about four months compared to six months for capital raised from venture capital funds. In his critique of this section of the chapter, one battle-scarred entrepreneur/angel commented: "I do not believe this is correct. I believe this is revisionist hindsight. I would suspect nine to twelve months from the concept to the check is much more realistic."

BUSINESS PLANS ARE CRITICAL WHEN OBTAINING VENTURE CAPITAL

A comprehensive, investor-oriented business plan will not guarantee success in raising funds, but *the lack of a business plan will ensure failure.* Preparing a winning business plan is a painful, but essential, exercise for two reasons:

1. The discipline of the process forces you to articulate your vision and how and when you expect to achieve it. Anticipate weeks of hard work to do the job right.

2. A clearly written and attractively packaged business plan will raise the odds of getting the attention of serious investors. Because the business plan speaks for the venture, it must speak loud and clear. The ability to articulate goals, objectives, and a strategy for achieving them is characteristic of successful entrepreneurs. Investors look for entrepreneurs who can manage limited resources by objectives as well as by instinct. The Executive Summary is the most critical section in a business plan. This is your bait. To stand out from the crowd, you must craft the Executive Summary with both care and flair.

GET PROFESSIONAL ADVICE

This chapter makes many generalizations that are necessary to cover complex issues in limited space. If you are launching a venture that will be looking for outside investors, you can't afford less than the best legal, accounting, banking, financial, and management advice. One word of caution: don't confuse legal and accounting advice with business advice. Early-stage companies sometimes make the mistake of looking to attorneys to shape their businesses.

Be cautious about whom you choose for advisors. Ask for and check references. Here are some general guidelines on what to look for in each advisor:

- *Attorneys*—Your attorney should be experienced in negotiating, pricing, and structuring venture financing and must also be familiar with state and federal securities regulations.

- *Bankers*—Picking the right banker is as important as picking the right bank. A commercial loan officer who has been through the financing of emerging companies more than once can be an invaluable source of financial advice and contacts. The right banker knows the difference between cash flow and profit. Your banker will be there when it counts if you maintain frank and frequent contact. A brief status report once a month is sufficient.

- *Accountants*—Pick a respected CPA with a firm that specializes in the design of accounting and management information systems for emerging companies. The cost is high, but the sooner you have a full audit of your financial statements, accompanied by an unqualified opinion, the better.

Finally, you should know that successful entrepreneurs are the best single source of advice. Use several you respect on a working board of directors and pay them if you can. The benefits are certain to exceed the costs.

FINDING THE RIGHT INVESTORS

Think of fund raising as a process of *buying capital* rather than *selling stock*. The difference is subtle but important. Venture capital is a commodity. It is available from a variety of sources on a variety of terms. For every venture, some combination of sources and terms will be more appropriate than others and will exert a powerful influence on the future of the venture. Besides the price, the following factors will influence the choice of sources:

- Investors' exit expectations.
- The availability of future financing.
- The quality of management assistance available from investors.
- Investors' experience in dealing with illiquid, high-risk investments.

The final deal should be a partnership of professionals with *complementary resources* and *shared goals*.

As a fund-raising strategy, entrepreneurs should always look for knowledgeable investors. They are the most likely to be attracted to your venture, and whether you ask for it or not, they will provide you with the benefit of their know-how—most of which they acquired by making their own mistakes in business, the way entrepreneurs learn their most valuable lessons. The right investors are *value-added investors*. For first-time entrepreneurs, the know-how available from battle-tested investors can be more valuable than their capital.

Your best investor prospects will be familiar with your markets, products, and technologies. Often these investors have managed or financed a successful startup in a similar field. For your sake as well as theirs, these investors will stay in close touch with your venture. However, there is a fine line between meddling and a productive relationship. Your investors' professional qualifications are necessary but not sufficient for a healthy relationship. Interpersonal chemistry will determine the quality of the relationship. The fit must *feel* right as well as *look* right.

Attention to chemistry and shared goals is especially important when dealing with individual investors. The following comments paraphrase the thoughts of one successful angel. For him success is more than the numbers; it has to do with *values* and *commitment to a shared vision*. While he sits on the boards of directors of his portfolio companies, he describes his role as a *coach* and *mentor*, someone with whom the entrepreneur can share doubts, fears, and vulnerabilities. Creating a company that is so successful that he can sell his shares back to the founders at a reasonable profit is his idea of the ultimate achievement.

Create a compatible structure for the relationship: a seat on a working board of directors, an informal consulting role, or full or part-time employment. Maintain frequent contact with all your investors. Quarterly financial statements accompanied by status reports from the CEO are bare minimums. Contact can mean a simple telephone call or faxed message. Investors like to be touched by short but frequent contacts.

The right investors will be aware of the risks involved in your venture and should be emotionally, as well as financially, able to bear those risks. You don't have time to deal with impatient, inexperienced investors while trying to cope with the inevitable delays and problems that plague all entrepreneurs. Murphy (of Murphy's Law fame) will be your constant companion.

Unless your margins are truly exceptional (more than 20% after-tax), your venture will develop an insatiable appetite for cash if it succeeds. Ideally, your original investors should be prepared and able to provide the additional funds required to finance growth. If not, be sure that they anticipate the need and are realistic about the cost (dilution) of second- and third-round financing. Your pro forma financial statements provide the basis for discussing these issues with your initial investors.

BE PREPARED FOR THE DUE DILIGENCE PROCESS

Once you and your prospective investors have reached a preliminary agreement, your investors will begin what is known as *due diligence.* Due diligence is the homework investors complete before a final investment decision is reached. The process typically includes background checks on the management team, industry studies, analysis of your competition, identification of major risks and other reasons, often intangible, why the investment should or should not be made. In essence, due diligence is a detailed evaluation of your business plan. Expect six to eight weeks to pass before the due diligence is complete.

The most important variables in an investor's decision to finance a venture are the integrity, competence, and commitment of the entrepreneur and his or her management team. But due diligence is a two-way street. Entrepreneurs should be equally concerned about the qualifications of their investors. Ask for the names of your investors' bankers, accountants, and attorneys. Then have your banker, accountant, and attorney check their professional reputations. If they don't have impeccable reputations, you may want to look for other investors. Guilt by association is not conclusive, but it does raise warning flags. If you are dealing with angels, ask for references and résumés describing their professional and educational backgrounds. Talk to each of the references.

Remember that you will be living with your investors through stressful times. Finding the right investors is worth the effort! The most valuable homework you can do is to talk to other entrepreneurs that your potential investors have bankrolled. Ask your investors for a list of their portfolio companies, including those that failed. Contact a random sample. Here are some key questions to discuss with the founders of these ventures:

- Are your investors trustworthy and predictable?
- Do you consider them fair and reasonable?
- Were they difficult to deal with?
- How long did it take to get your money?
- What are your investors like to work with on a consistent basis?
- How active are they in your business?
- Do you consider them meddlesome or helpful?
- What have they done for you besides invest money?
- How have they been helpful?
- Do they act like your partners or your adversaries?
- How did your investors behave during periods of difficulty?
- Who were the investors' representatives on your board of directors?
- If you had to do it all over again, would you raise money from the same investors?

All of these questions focus on the relationship between investors and the management they bet on. They are designed to help you decide whether your investors will make good partners. Satisfying yourself on these issues is part of the subtle distinction between buying capital and selling stock.

One entrepreneur/angel took exception to the list, reacting to these questions as follows: "The key questions seem to be adversarial. Sometimes it's better to have money and excellent advice, and good experience from investors than have them nice people to deal with. Fair and reasonable fall by the wayside when compared to good advice and patient money." Although this experienced investor makes a useful point, "fair and reasonable" are not imcompatible with "good advice and patient money."

THE COST OF VENTURE CAPITAL

Deal pricing is the central mystery of venture capital. Pricing venture capital is part art, part science, and part Yankee horse trading. Risk and, consequently, the cost of venture capital vary substantially over the developmental stages of a new venture. The following generally accepted definitions of the stages of financing are taken from *Pratt's Guide to Venture Capital Sources.*

Early-Stage Financing

Seed Financing

This is a relatively small amount of capital provided to an inventor or entrepreneur to prove a concept and to qualify for startup capital. If the initial steps are successful, this may involve product development and market research as well as building a management team and developing a business plan.

Startup Financing

This money is provided to companies completing product development and initial marketing. Companies may be in the process of organizing, or they may already have been in business for one year or less but not sold their product commercially. Usually such firms will have made market studies, assembled the key management, developed a business plan, and are ready to do business.

First-Stage Financing

This is provided to companies that have expended their initial capital (often in developing and market-testing a prototype) and require funds to initiate full-scale manufacturing and sales.

Expansion Financing

Second-Stage Financing

This financing provides working capital for the initial expansion of a company that is producing and shipping and has growing accounts receivable and inventories. Although the company has made progress, it may not yet be showing a profit.

Third-Stage, or Mezzanine, Financing

This is provided for major expansion of a company that has an increasing sales volume and that is breaking even or profitable. These funds are used for marketing, working capital, further plant expansion, or development of an improved product.

Bridge Financing

This type of financing may be needed when a company is between stages and when it plans to go public in six months to a year. Bridge financing is often structured so that it can be repaid from the proceeds of the next round or a public underwriting. It may involve restructuring of major stockholder positions through secondary transactions.

Estimating the Return on Various Types of Financing

Despite every entrepreneur's confidence in his or her "sure thing," more new ventures fail than succeed. Investors need a few big winners to offset the losers. Depending on the stage of the financing and, therefore, the risks involved, compound rates of return from 25 to 50% or more are not unreasonable expectations. A typical range of risk/return expectations is shown in Exhibit 7.3.

Keep in mind that the figures in Exhibit 7.3 are *anticipated* returns. Seasoned investors know that, no matter how thorough their due diligence, only one venture in five or ten will meet or exceed their expectations. There is no average deal. Investors are fond of saying (with tongue in cheek) that they never made a bad investment—all their losers went bad after the deal was made. In other words one or two big winners are required to offset the inevitable losers.

The rates in Exhibit 7.3 are also *rough approximations*. The unique characteristics of each venture and investor will determine the appropriate rate. The lesson for entrepreneurs is that you must recognize that the lower your investors' *perceptions of risk*, the lower will be their required return on investment (ROI), that is, the lower the share of equity an entrepreneur will have to give up to obtain any given amount of capital. Put another way, the longer an entrepreneur can survive on founders' capital, sweat equity, and bootstrap financing, the lower will be the cost of venture capital.

EXHIBIT 7.3   Risk-adjusted cost of venture capital.

Stage (risk)	Expected returns
Seed	80%
Startup	60
First-stage	50
Second-stage	40
Third-stage	30
Bridge	25

EXHIBIT 7.4   Capital gain/ROI conversion table.

	Exit year				
Multiple	3	4	5	7	10
3 times	44%	32%	25%	17%	12%
4 times	59	41	32	22	15
5 times	71	50	38	26	17
7 times	91	63	48	32	21
10 times	115	78	58	39	26

Investors give value-added advice and accept risk and lack of liquidity, yet realized returns on a successful investor's portfolio of venture deals will seldom be more than five to ten points above the returns on a diversified portfolio of quality common stocks, that is, venture portfolio ROIs of 20 to 25%. Entrepreneurs should keep in mind that if a venture fails, investors typically incur bigger losses than the founders—and if the venture succeeds, the founders typically are bigger winners than their investors. For this reason alone, losing potential investors by quibbling over a few percentage points of ownership seldom makes sense.

Investors tend to think in terms of capital gains multiples rather than rates of return. The conversion is simple and can be done on most hand calculators. Exhibit 7.4 illustrates conversion relationships.

To use Exhibit 7.4, select the exit year (that is, the expected holding period between investment and cash-out). In the *Exit year* column, select the required ROI appropriate for the risk perceived by investors. Risk, and therefore ROI, primarily reflects the stage of the financing. The multiple expected by investors can be found in the *Multiple* column.

EMPHASIZE THE NONFINANCIAL PAYOFFS OF INVESTMENT IN YOUR VENTURE

The influence of *nonfinancial payoffs* is another distinction between the venture capital fund and angel markets. Individual investors frequently look for nonfinancial as well as competitive financial returns from their venture investments.

Nonfinancial considerations fall into several categories. Some reflect a sense of social responsibility, and some are forms of *psychic income* (so-called hot-buttons) that motivate many individuals. The list of influential considerations includes whether your venture can:

- Generate jobs in areas of high unemployment.
- Develop socially useful technology (for example, medical, energy, and environmental technology).
- Assist in the economic revival of urban areas.
- Support female and minority entrepreneurs.
- Provide personal satisfaction derived from assisting entrepreneurs who build successful ventures in a free enterprise economy.

In addition to bringing a certain missionary zeal to the deal, angels (especially cashed-out entrepreneurs) typically look for fun in their investments. Most angels could be described as adventure capitalists.

Entrepreneurs sensitive to the match between the characteristics of their ventures and the *personal tastes* of investors should be able to raise funds on terms that are attractive to both parties.

PRICING THE DEAL: THINK LIKE AN INVESTOR

Based on projected revenues, profits, growth rates, and future financing requirements (dilution), entrepreneurs and investors should arrive at a *shared vision* of the venture's value five to ten years after financing, or at whatever exit date they agree on, and its exit strategy. Think in terms of *dollars* and *value* as opposed to ownership percentage. A business plan based on realistic assumptions is an entrepreneur's best friend at this point in the negotiations.

Four basic principles are involved in the pricing decision:

1. The division of ownership between founders and outside investors is determined by the *expected future value* of the venture and the *share* required to compensate investors at competitive rates—not by the relative dollar investments of the two parties.
2. The longer the track record of a new venture, the lower the risk to an investor, the lower the cost of capital, and the lower the share of equity required to purchase any given amount of capital. Exhibits 7.3, 7.4, and 7.5 illustrate this principle.
3. The more a venture is expected to be worth at any point in the future, the lower the share of equity required to purchase any given amount of capital. Exhibit 7.5 illustrates this principle.
4. The shorter the waiting period to cash out (that is, to harvest), the lower the share of equity required to purchase any given amount of capital. The time to liquidity is very important to investors. This is also illustrated in Exhibit 7.5.

EXHIBIT 7.5   Percentage of ownership required to yield a 40% rate of return on a $1 million investment.

Exit year (holding period)	Future value of the company (in millions)				
	$5	**$10**	**$15**	**$20**	**$25**
2	39%	20%	13%	10%	8%
3	55	27	18	14	11
4	77	38	26	19	15
5	N/A	54	36	27	22
7	N/A	N/A	70	53	42
10	N/A	N/A	N/A	N/A	N/A

N/A = Not applicable; investment would not be made.

Exhibit 7.5 illustrates how future values and holding periods affect percentage of a venture's equity required to yield a 40% return on a $1 million investment. The impact is dramatic: In a venture expected to be worth $25 million in two years an 8% stake would be required, whereas in a venture expected to be worth $15 million in seven years a 70% stake would be required. The lower left-hand corner of Exhibit 7.5 illustrates the fact that over 100% of the equity would be required if holding periods are too long or future values too small.

Most venture investors do not want to own a controlling interest in your venture or tell you how to run the business. Some investors argue that no one should own 50%, and no one should own control, that it should take at least two people to effect a major change in the company's goals, direction, or financing. As Exhibit 7.5 reveals, investors seek more than 50% of a company *only* when they need that much to justify the amount of money invested. Investors expect you and your management team to run the company profitably. Beware of investors who are "control freaks," including former operating managers who assume that they can run the company better than its management.

Take a look at a common approach to pricing a deal. *Pricing* refers to the fraction of the equity your investors will receive for the capital they provide. By focusing on the pricing models and assumptions that determine values in the capital markets, you can avoid some of the emotional biases that creep in during negotiations when the stakes are high or when human relationships are involved. A discussion of the pricing model (that is, its assumptions and probabilities) is bound to reveal differences between entrepreneurs' and investors' perceptions. Reconciling these discrepancies will be useful to both parties. The pricing model is a powerful tool for negotiating and reaching agreement on the appropriate pricing of an investment.

The following simple example employs traditional discounted cash flow techniques, except that it focuses on future values rather than present values using the risk-adjusted rates of return given in Exhibit 7.3.

DEVELOPING A PRICING MODEL: A CASE STUDY

Assume that we are dealing with a startup venture, Goforit, Inc., that needs a single round of financing of $1 million (an unrealistic assumption for a high-potential venture). The venture expects to generate $20 million in revenues after five years with a 10% after-tax net profit. Assume that after five years, the company expects to be growing at 20% or more and plans to go public. Stocks of companies with comparable size and growth rates trade at a price that is 15 times earnings.

Given these numbers and the investors' target ROI of 60% (ten times the investment in five years), the founders will have to provide investors with 33% of the company. See the *Most likely* scenario in Exhibit 7.6.

The pricing model unfolds as follows: $20 million of revenues with a 10% margin yields after-tax profits of $2 million. Using a P/E ratio of 15 for a young, growing company with a thin market for its shares, the equity will have a market value of $30 million. To earn their 60% ROI, investors need 10 times their initial investment of $1 million, that is, $10 million. For their investment to be worth $10 million, they will need to own 33% of the company's total equity value of $30 million.

EXHIBIT 7.6   Goforit, Inc. pricing model.

	Worst case	Most likely	Best case
Assumptions			
Investment	$1 million	$1 million	$1 million
Exit year	7	5	3
Revenue	$10 million	$20 million	$30 million
Net margin	5%	10%	15%
Growth rate	10%	20%	30%
P/E multiple	10×	15×	20×
Total equity value	$5 million	$30 million	$90 million
Investor multiple	15×	10×	5×
ROI	47%	58%	71%
Investor equity value required	$15 million	$10 million	$5 million
Results			
Investor percentage	N/A	33%	6%
Premoney valuation	None	$2 million	$17 million

EXHIBIT 7.7a Pro forma valuation model Chicago method.

Company X

Capital Invested	$500,000
Required Rate	
of Return	40%

	Success	Sideways survival	Failure
1. Revenue level after 2 years			$0
2. Revenue level after 5 years	$20,000,000		
3. Revenue level after 3 years		$5,000,000	
4. Exit strategy	IPO	Acquisition	Liquidation
5. After tax profit margin at liquidity°	15%	10%	0%
6. Earnings at liquidity°	$3,000,000	$500,000	$0
7. Price-earnings ratio at liquidity°	20	12	0
8. Value of company at liquidity°	$60,000,000	$6,000,000	$0
9. Present value of company using 40% discount rate above	$11,156,066	$2,186,589	$0
10. Probability of each scenario	20%	50%	30%
11. Expected present value under each scenario	$2,231,213	$1,093,294	$0
12. Weighted average present value of the company	$3,324,508		
13. Percentage of ownership required to invest capital above	15%		

°Liquidity refers to the point in the Company's growth where the common stock can be sold by investors, either back to the Company or to a third party.

As shown in the last row of Exhibit 7.6 (which shows premoney valuation), these numbers imply that, before the investor's money goes in, the venture has a value of $2 million. This value is the result of the entrepreneur's recognition of a market opportunity and the capital and sweat equity invested to create a venture positioned to capitalize on that opportunity. If the founders' investment one year prior to startup was $200,000, they have generated a return of 900%, on paper, 10 times their investment in one year.

Exhibit 7.6 also contains *best case* and *worst case* scenarios. Both scenarios can be thought of as those outcomes or assumptions for which the probability of occurrence is one chance in ten. By focusing and agreeing on the range of possible outcomes and their probabilities, entrepreneurs and investors can accomplish the difficult task of pricing venture capital with a minimum of subjective debate and hard feelings. Both parties should feel that the pricing outcome is fair and openly arrived at. Recognize, however, that, because of entrepreneurs' optimism and investors' pessimism, it is unlikely that

EXHIBIT 7.7b Pro forma valuation model conventional model.

Company X

| Capital Invested | $500,000 |
| Required Rate of Return | 40% |

	1999	Pro forma	Percent pro forma
1. Revenue level after 4 years	$10,000,000	$20,000,000	50%
2. Exit strategy	Acquisition	IPO	IPO
3. After tax profit margin at liquidity°	10%	20%	50%
4. Earnings at liquidity°	$1,000,000	$4,000,000	25%
5. Price-earnings ratio at liquidity°	12	25	48%
6. Value of company at liquidity°	$12,000,000	$100,000,000	12%
7. Present value of company using 40% discount rate above	$3,123,698	$36,443,149	9%
8. Percentage of ownership required to invest capital above	16%	1%	

°Liquidity refers to the point in the Company's growth where the common stock can be sold by investors, either back to the Company or to a third party.

real agreement will be reached on your projections. Most investors assume that an entrepreneur's *worst case* is, in fact, the *best case.*

Computer spreadsheets are indispensable tools for examining the implications of alternative assumptions. But beware of spreadsheet diarrhea. Investors are more interested in sales/marketing, management, production, and technology. Financial projections are the result of the vision, not vice versa.

Exhibits 7.7a and 7.7b display two pro forma valuation models used to support a successful round of startup financing for a real company, Company X. Company X is a materials handling systems company focused on providing innovative solutions to difficult material handling problems. The company's products are based on patented technology which dramatically reduces manual labor costs, provides significant safety enhancements and eliminates landfill waste problems. The company had no sales in 1995. It projects sales of $10 million by 1999.

In the summer of 1996, Company X raised $500,000 from eight individuals through the sale of 200,000 shares of common stock at $2.50 per share, representing 21% of the company's common equity. Minimum investment was $50,000 and participation was limited to investors who qualified as "accredited investors" under SEC Regulation D (there is more on this in Chapter 10). Investors were required to sign a Shareholder Agreement that restricts ownership rights of common shareholders. It is the company's objective to provide investor liquidity of common shares within 3 to 5 years. The two pro forma valuation models in Exhibit 7.7 were included in Company X's financing proposal.

For examples of pricing models see "The Pricing of a Venture Capital Deal" in *Pratt's Guide to Venture Capital Sources* and *OED Report on Venture Capital Financial Analysis.*[5] A lot of homework on the application of these principles will pay big dividends. The booklets published by national accounting firms are useful summaries. Recommended books include *New Venture Creation* by Jeffry Timmons (Richard D. Irwin, Inc.) *Venture Capital Handbook* by David Gladstone (Prentice Hall) and *Venture Capital: Law, Business Strategies, and Investment Planning* by Joseph Bartlett (John Wiley & Sons).

STRUCTURING THE DEAL—TERMS AND CONDITIONS

If you are dealing with a venture capital fund, once you have reached an oral agreement, but before the legal documents are drafted, you will receive a non-binding commitment letter and a term sheet setting forth the following terms of the deal:

- The amount of the investment.
- The form of the investment.
- The share of the equity represented by the investment.
- The terms and conditions to which you will be asked to agree.

You are, in effect, your investors' agent—"a person empowered to act for another." The terms and conditions are legal obligations designed primarily to protect investors from management behavior incompatible with investor interests. The term sheet is useful for identifying issues that could turn into deal killers if they are not addressed and resolved.

Everything in this life is negotiable, including the terms and conditions governing a venture investment. Don't go shopping for capital until you are familiar with the terms and conditions typically demanded by investors. These will be spelled out in the term sheet. Go over a sample term sheet with your legal counsel and financial advisors before you start the negotiations. Concessions made under pressure to raise cash can lead to ruinous conflicts later. Since most terms are negotiable, it is essential that you understand the terms, identifying those that are most important to investors and those that are and are not acceptable to you. Pay special attention to voting rights, antidilution provisions, board seats, and stock restriction agreements. The ultimate contract should be one in which both parties feel that they have been treated fairly.

Before going over the sample term sheet, do your homework! Never underestimate the wisdom to be found in interviews with other venture founders or the value of libraries, books, and seminars. "The Legal Process of Venture Capital Investment," one of the essays in *Pratt's Guide to Venture Capital Sources,* is an excellent place to start. Other sources include *Start-Up Companies: Planning, Financing and Operating the Successful Business* by Richard D. Harroch (Law Journal Seminars-Press, New York) and *Venture Capital: Law, Business Strategies, and Investment Planning* by Joseph W. Bartlett (John Wiley & Sons, New York).

The types of equity-linked securities used by venture investors range from common stock (typical of angel deals) through convertible preferred (typical of venture capital fund deals) to subordinated debt with conversion features or warrants (typical of Small Business Investment Company—SBIC—deals). (SBICs are privately owned but chartered by the U.S. Small Business Administration.) Angel deals typically are less tightly structured than venture fund deals. Some angels won't do a deal if their agreement with an entrepreneur can't be captured in two pages. Venture fund deals often involve agreements that require 15 pages or more to cover everything the investors (and their well-paid attorneys) insist on reducing to written agreements.

The sample term sheet provided in Exhibit 7.8 (see pp. 206–207) summarizes the terms and conditions of a $1 million convertible preferred stock financing placed by Goforit, Inc. with a venture capital fund. The text under each heading identifies principal features, but it is not a complete description.

The outline in Exhibit 7.8 is far from a complete enumeration of all the terms and conditions that investors and entrepreneurs might wish to impose on a venture investment. At best, the outline is an agenda of issues to be explored with your attorney, financial advisors, and other entrepreneurs who have raised venture capital.

DETERMINING THE HARVEST STRATEGY

Venture capital is "patient money." Returns to investors take the form of long-term capital gains realized after an extended period during which the investment has little or no marketability (liquidity). Because expectations about *timing* and *method* of exit influence investment decisions significantly, be prepared to discuss these issues early in your negotiations with investors. A harvest mentality based on the creation of substantial wealth for founders and investors is central to the fund-raising process.

Successful companies typically require several years to launch and build (although each venture is unique and each industry is unique). The harvest

EXHIBIT 7.8 Sample term sheet for *Goforit, Inc.*

December 31, 1996
Memorandum of principal terms and conditions

Amount: $1,000,000

**Type of
Security:** Series A convertible preferred stock

Price: $1,500,000 premoney valuation. This will result in the following stockholdings after the fully diluted effect of the investment and the addition of management options:

Preferred stock:	40%
Founders stock:	35%
Management options and stock:	25%

Closing: On or before March 1, 1997

Rights and Preferences

Dividends:

Dividends at the rate of 7.5% per share per annum, cumulative after third anniversary of the closing. No dividends payable on common stock unless first paid on the Series A shares.

Liquidation preference:

Original issue price per share plus all accrued but unpaid dividends. Participation in remaining assets on a pro rata basis with common shares. Merger or sale shall be deemed a liquidation.

Conversion rights:

Each Series A share shall be convertible at any time at the option of the holder into one share of common stock. Automatic conversion if voted by a two-thirds majority of the preferred stockholders. Automatic conversion on public offering at a price exceeding three times the purchase price of the preferred, where at least $5 million is raised.

Redemption:

At investor discretion between years 5 and 7 at original price plus 6% interest compounded annually plus accrued and unpaid dividends.

Antidilution protection:

Weighted average antidilution protection. Proportional adjustments for splits, stock dividends, recapitalizations, and similar events.

Voting rights:

Voting rights equal to common equivalent shares. Holders of Series A shares can elect a majority of the board of directors in the case of certain events:
   a. Default in two annual dividend payments.
   b. Default in redemption.
   c. A loss of $25,000 or more in two consecutive quarters.
   d. Company net worth falls below $2,000,000.

Registration rights:
   a. Two demand registrations at Company's expense.
   b. Unlimited piggyback registrations at Company's expense.
   c. Rights may be transferred.

EXHIBIT 7.8 *(Continued)*

Restrictions:

Consent of a majority of Series A shares required to:
  a. Issue any equity security or security convertible into equity.
  b. Approve merger or sale of all or substantially all the assets of the Company.
  c. Approve any liquidation of the Company.
  d. Approve the acquisition of or investment in another company.

First refusal rights:
  a. Preferred shareholders will have a right to maintain their pro rata interest in the Company on a fully diluted basis on any subsequent offering of stock prior to an effective public offering.
  b. Preferred shareholders will have a right of first refusal with respect to any employee's shares proposed to be resold to a third party, which rights will terminate upon a public offering.

Information rights:
  a. Audited annual financials within 90 days of year end and unaudited quarterly financials comparing actual results to budget within 30 days of quarter close. Annual budgets shall be supplied prior to the commencement of each fiscal year.
  b. All other reports prepared by management for the board of directors.
  c. Inspection rights. No more often than once a month, with four days notice.

Board of directors:

The board shall initially consist of five directors. The Series A preferred holders shall have the ongoing right to elect two members of the board of directors. Management limited to two board seats.

Stock restriction agreement:

All present holders of common stock of the Company who are employees of the Company will execute a stock restriction agreement pursuant to which the Company will have an option to buy back at cost the shares of common stock held by such person in the event that such shareholder's employment with the Company is terminated prior to the expiration of 48 months from the date of employment.

Special conditions:
  a. Management shall have entered into two-year noncompetition agreements.
  b. The company shall have obtained key person life insurance on the life of the Chief Executive Officer in the amount of $1,000,000. The policy shall be owned by and payable to the preferred shareholders.
  c. Founders' shares shall vest over five years through nominal price buy-back arrangement.

Expenses:

Company shall pay all fees and expenses of counsel to the preferred shareholders up to a specified amount. Expenses in excess of that amount will be subject to written approval by the preferred shareholders and the company.

strategy should reflect this fact of life by contemplating a medium-to-long time frame, at least three to five years for a high-potential venture and as long as seven to ten years for a middle-market company. A public stock offering, merger, or outright sale of the company are common exit strategies for high-potential ventures. Management and Employee Stock Ownership Plan (ESOP) buyouts are common harvest strategies for investors in middle-market companies.

Patience and shared exit expectations are particularly critical for middle-market ventures, that is, ventures with limited prospects for a public offering or an acquisition by a larger firm within the five-to-ten-year exit horizon of venture investors. If an investor expects to cash out by selling shares back to your venture or its management, be sure that the terms and conditions of the sale are tied to the operating performance and cash flow of the venture and not to some arbitrary multiple of the original investment. For example, if the investors in Goforit, Inc. own 33% of the common stock, the "put" option might read as follows:

> There shall be a "put" provision whereby anytime after five years the holders of the convertible preferred shares may require the Company to purchase the preferred shareholders' equivalent common shares at the higher of the following:

> 1. $1,000,000 cash.
> 2. Book value times 33% ownership.
> 3. Five times pretax earnings for the year just ended times 33% ownership.
> 4. Fifty percent of sales for the year just ended times 33% ownership.
> 5. Ten times operating cash flow times 33% ownership.
> 6. Appraised value times 33% ownership.

Your legal and financial advisors can help design acceptable "put" arrangements.

LESSONS FROM LOSERS

Most entrepreneurs learn lessons the hard way—by making mistakes. However, entrepreneurs can learn some financial lessons from the mistakes of others. For example, the reasons cited by investors for rejecting investment proposals can be instructive. The most common reasons are:

- Lack of confidence in management.
- Unsatisfactory risk/reward ratios.
- Absence of a well-defined business plan.
- The investor's unfamiliarity with products, processes, or markets.
- In the case of angels, the business's unattractiveness to the investor.

The following comments from private investors reflect the range of reasons that investment proposals are rejected:

- "We need to see market dominance. Never invest in 1% of any market. We will invest in 100% of a yet undiscovered market segment."
- "In most cases management did not seem adequate for the task at hand."
- "Simply not interested in the proposed businesses. Saw no socioeconomic value in them."
- "Risk/return ratio was not adequate."
- "Unable to agree on price."
- "Too much wishful thinking."
- "One of two key principals not sufficiently committed—too involved with another activity."
- "Unfamiliar with business."
- "Spouse refused."

CONCLUSION

Entrepreneurs and venture investors are at the heart of the free enterprise system. Just as the 1980s brought financial engineering and the leveraged buyout, the 1990s are bringing the downsizing of large corporations and the emergence of the entrepreneur. Employment of the *Fortune* 500 peaked at 16 million in 1979 and has fallen since then by 25%—a loss of 4 million jobs. In the meantime, *entrepreneurs and their investors have created over 24 million jobs.* All these signs point to an acceleration of this "sea change" in the structure of the U.S. economy. This chapter has been written for the next generation of entrepreneurs with the *integrity, competence,* and *commitment* to build ventures that will create wealth for themselves and their investors as well as the jobs, innovative products and services, export trade, and tax revenues of the future.

Business history in the United States is the history of equity financing. Raising equity is arduous. Multiple rejections are part of the process. But business history and the stock market pay tribute to the entrepreneurs who stuck it out.

8 DEBT AND OTHER FORMS OF FINANCING

Joel M. Shulman

Entrepreneurs at small, growing firms, unlike finance treasurers at most *Fortune* 500 companies, do not have easy access to a variety of inexpensive funding sources. In the entire world, only a handful of very large firms have access to funding sources such as asset-backed debt securitizations, A-1 commercial paper ratings, and below-prime lending rates. Most financial managers of small- to medium-size firms are constantly concerned about meeting cash flow obligations to suppliers and employees and maintaining solid financial relationships with creditors and shareholders. Their problems are exacerbated by issues concerning growth, control, and survival. Moreover, their difficulty in attracting adequate funds exists even when firms are growing rapidly and bringing in profits (this is explored later in the chapter).

This chapter describes various financing options for entrepreneurs and identifies potential financing pitfalls and solutions. It also discusses how these issues are influenced by the type of industry and life cycle of the firm and how management should plan accordingly.

GETTING ACCESS TO FUNDS—START WITH *INTERNAL* SOURCES

Entrepreneurs requiring initial startup capital, funds used for growth, and working capital generally seek funds from *internal* sources. This contrasts with managers or owners of large, mature firms that have access to profits from operations as well as funds from external sources. Internal funds are distinguished from external funds in that internal funding sources do not require external analysts or investors to independently appraise the worthiness of the capital investments before releasing funds. Moreover, since external investors and lenders do not share the entrepreneur's vision, they may view the potential risk/return trade-off in a different vein and may demand a relatively certain return on their investment after the firm has an established financial track record.

Exhibit 8.1 shows a listing of funding sources and the approximate timing of the firm's usage. In the embryonic stages of the firm's existence, much of the funding comes from the entrepreneur's own pocket. For example, in the beginning entrepreneurs will consume their personal savings accounts, credit cards, and other assets such as personal computers, fax machines, in-home offices, furniture, and automobiles.

Soon after entrepreneurs begin tapping their personal fund sources, they may also solicit funds from relatives, friends, and banks. Entrepreneurs would generally prefer to use other people's money (OPM) rather than their own because if their personal investment turns sour, they still have a nest egg to feed themselves and their families. The nest egg phenomenon may be particularly acute if the entrepreneur leaves a viable job to pursue an entrepreneurial dream on a full-time basis. The costs to the entrepreneur in this case include the following:

- The opportunity cost of income from the prior job.
- The forgone interest on the initial investment.
- The potential difficulty of being rehired by a former employer (or others) if the idea does not succeed.

EXHIBIT 8.1   Sources of outside funding.

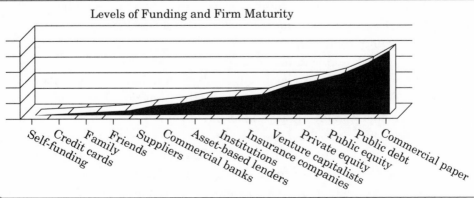

Levels of Funding and Firm Maturity

Self-funding · Credit cards · Family · Friends · Suppliers · Commercial banks · Asset-based lenders · Institutions · Insurance companies · Venture capitalists · Private equity · Public equity · Public debt · Commercial paper

After adding to this the embarrassment of having to beg for a new job while paying off old debts, the prospective entrepreneur quickly realizes that the total cost of engaging in a new venture is very high.

Family and friends may "volunteer" to fund the entrepreneur's project in the early stages, and often will do so without a formal repayment schedule or specified interest cost. However, the funds are far from free. Total costs, including nonfinancial indirect costs—such as family pressure, internal monitoring, and strained relations—are probably extremely high. Moreover, family and friends make poor financial intermediaries since they have limited financial resources, different repayment expectations, and narrow loan diversification. This will contribute to the entrepreneur's desire to get outside funding from a traditional source as soon as possible. The question is, where can entrepreneurs go before banks will give them money?

WORKING CAPITAL—GETTING CASH FROM RECEIVABLES AND INVENTORIES

The timing of receivables collection and payment of accounts payable are key determinants in whether a firm is cash rich or cash poor. For example, an increase in net working capital (that is, current assets minus current liabilities) does not necessarily translate into an increase in liquidity.

Clearly, as a small firm grows, current operating assets will increase. If current operating liabilities do not increase at the same rate as the increase in current operating assets (which is true when an entrepreneur pays suppliers before receiving payment from customers), then the entrepreneur will find that the firm's liquidity will decrease (assuming the firm does not increase its long-term funding arrangements). This may be true even though the firm is generating paper profits.

Accounts receivable are a major element in working capital for most companies. And they are one of the items that gave us reason to assert that *working capital* is not the same as *available cash,* and that the timing of short-term flows is vitally important.

If a company is selling a major part of its output on credit and giving 30 days' credit, its accounts receivable will be about equal to sales of 30 days, that is, to one-twelfth of its annual sales, if sales are reasonably stable over the year. And if the company's collection policies are so liberal or ineffective that in practice customers are paying on an average, say, 45 days after they are billed, accounts receivable are no less than one-eighth of annual sales. Investment in accounts receivable is a use of funds. The company has to finance the credit it is giving to its customers by allowing its money to be tied up in this way instead of being available for investment in productive uses. Therefore, accounts receivable, like cash, have an opportunity cost.

But a company that does not give credit will obviously lose sales, particularly if its competitors offer generous credit. Here, again, there is a trade-off to be made between the cost of *giving credit* and the cost of *restricting credit.* In other words, there are two possible errors that a firm can make. It can incur the cost of being *too conservative* (deny credit to a good customer), or risk being *too aggressive* (grant credit to a poor customer). Most firms choose to exercise caution in granting credit, since the cost of extending credit to a customer who doesn't pay can far exceed the profits lost by not extending credit.

The magnitude of a company's accounts receivable obviously depends upon a number of factors:

- The level and the pattern of sales.
- The breakdown between cash and credit sales.
- The nominal credit terms offered.
- The way these credit terms are enforced through a collection policy.

Although the opportunity costs for accounts receivable may be quite large, the largest current asset balances are usually in inventories. Accordingly, as the entrepreneur's business grows, inventory balances rise, and resulting operating cash flows decline. Consequently, the entrepreneur needs to monitor both accounts receivable and inventories and keep both the levels as low as possible without interfering with profitable sales. This is especially true if the entrepreneur has a shortage of capital or credit limitations.

INVENTORY

Inventory represents the most important current asset of most manufacturing and trading companies. Indeed, for many entrepreneurs, inventories account for an important part of total assets. Yet money invested in inventory does not earn a return. In fact, it costs money to maintain inventories. They must be stored, moved about, insured, and protected from theft and deterioration. Records must be kept, and clerks must be paid to keep those records. In addition, some inventory will be devalued or become a total loss because it deteriorates or becomes obsolete before it can be used or sold. These costs can easily add up to 20% or more annually of the inventory value. Since the money tied up in inventory might otherwise be invested profitably, the real costs plus the opportunity costs of carrying inventory may add up to 30%, 40%, or even more. As with accounts receivable, the dollar amount of inventory depends on when the entrepreneur chooses to recognize profit: Is it at the time of production or the time of sale? A strong argument can be made for valuing inventories at cost or market, whichever is lower. With inventories, there may be a lot of uncertainty as to how much cash flow will actually be generated, so a conservative approach to valuation is recommended.

Entrepreneurs usually want to keep inventory levels as low as possible. Although they are not likely to be directly interested in the more detailed and lower-level decisions (which are usually made by production or purchasing personnel), they must be able to evaluate and influence overall results. Not only does keeping inventory at a minimum reduce inventory carrying charges such as storage costs and insurance, but it also ensures that as little as possible of the entrepreneur's capital is tied up in inventory.

But carrying too little inventory also incurs heavy costs. These include:

- The costs of too frequent reordering.
- Loss of quantity discounts.
- Loss of customer goodwill or plant efficiency due to items being unavailable when needed.

Entrepreneurs must be able to weigh these costs against those of carrying excessive inventory in order to be able to judge what is an optimum inventory level.

The control of investment in inventories is particularly important to *the management of working capital*. Inventories are likely to represent the entrepreneur's largest current investment, and they are likely to be the least liquid of his current assets. Marketable securities can be turned into cash in a matter of hours, and most accounts receivable will usually be collected within the next 30 days. But three months' supply of inventory will take three months to turn into cash, if forecasts of demand or usage prove to have been accurate. If forecasts prove to have been optimistic, even more time than this may be required. The alternative—an immediate forced sale—is hardly attractive. Marketable securities can be sold for their market value, and receivables can usually be sold, or factored, for something like 80% of their face value. But inventories, other than some raw materials for which a ready market always exists, traditionally sell for little more than 10% of their acquisition cost in a forced sale. Thus, controlling a company's investment in inventory is of critical importance to the management of working capital.

SOURCES OF SHORT-TERM CASH—MORE PAYABLES, LESS RECEIVABLES

Entrepreneurs usually do not have all the cash they need all the time. Very often, an entrepreneurial firm needs to build up its inventory, thus reducing cash levels. Or an entrepreneur's customers may place unusually large orders, thus increasing accounts receivable financing or reducing company cash levels. This section describes the many ways entrepreneurs obtain additional short-term cash to restore their cash balances to the required levels.

As a rule, entrepreneurs look for short-term cash at the lowest possible rates. If they cannot obtain cash at no cost or at a very small cost, they begin to explore more expensive sources of cash. For example, an entrepreneur faced with a cash shortage might look first to her company's suppliers and her customers. She would look to suppliers because they extend credit to the company by collecting for goods and services after those goods and services are supplied. The entrepreneur can enlarge this credit by paying bills more slowly. The entrepreneur may also obtain additional cash by collecting from her company's customers more quickly.

Cash from Short-Term Bank Loans

If these relatively low-cost options are unavailable (or if their cost is too high because of the ill will generated), the entrepreneur may next turn to the company's bank for a short-term loan. Entrepreneurs faced with a severe cash shortage may also try to convert into cash two of their working capital assets—accounts receivable and inventory. An entrepreneur may pledge her accounts receivable to a finance company in exchange for a loan, or she may sell them to a factoring company for cash. Similarly, an entrepreneur may pledge her inventory (often using a warehousing system) in exchange for a loan.

Cash from Trade Credit

Trade credit is one important and often low-cost source of cash. Nearly all entrepreneurs make use of trade credit to some degree by not paying suppliers immediately for goods and services. Instead, companies bill the entrepreneur, and the entrepreneur pays in 10 days, 30 days or more. From the time when the supplier first provides the goods or services to the time when the customer finally pays for them, the supplier has, in effect, loaned the entrepreneur money. The sum of all these loans (bills) represents an entrepreneur's trade credit. By paying bills more slowly, an entrepreneur can increase the amount of these loans from his suppliers.

One way an entrepreneur can take more time to pay for his bills (or stretch his payables) is to stop taking discounts. For example, if his company normally takes advantage of all prompt-payment discounts, such as 2% for payment within 10 days, he can increase his company's cash by passing up the discount and paying the bill in the expected 30 days. Of course, this is an expensive source of cash. If he loses a 2% discount and has the use of the funds for 20 more days, he has paid approximately 36% interest (annual rate) for using the money.

However, he might argue that, in practice, the interest cost would not really be 36% because by forgoing discounts and aggressively stretching payables the company would not pay the bill in 30 days. Instead, such a company would stretch out this payable as long as possible and perhaps attempt to pay in 60 days. Now, the equivalent interest rate is only about 15% (50 days' extra use of the money for 2%).

This brings up the subject of late payments. Many entrepreneurs do not consider 30 days (or any other stated terms) a real deadline. Instead, they try to determine the exact point at which further delay of payment will have a penalty. For example, if a company pays too slowly, the supplier may take one of the following actions:

- Require payment in full on future orders.
- Report the company to a credit bureau, which would damage the company's credit rating with all suppliers.
- Bring legal action against the company.

Many cash managers believe, however, that as long as they can pay company bills just before incurring any of these penalties, they maximize their company's cash at little or no cost. The *hidden costs* of this approach include such risks as damaged reputation, lower credit limit from suppliers, higher prices from suppliers to compensate for delayed payment, and the risk of exceeding the supplier's final deadline and incurring a penalty.

Cash Obtained by Negotiating with Suppliers

If an entrepreneur wants more credit and would like to stretch out her payables, she does not always have to incur the risks described above. Very often, she can negotiate with her suppliers for more generous credit terms, at least temporarily. If she and her supplier agree on longer credit terms (say 60 or 90 days), she can get the extra trade credits she needs without jeopardizing her supplier relations or credit ratings. It's important to bear in mind that suppliers are trying to build up their businesses and must compete with other similar suppliers. One way these suppliers compete is through credit terms, and that fact can be used to the entrepreneur's advantage. Just as the entrepreneur solicits several price quotes before placing a major orders, she may also want to encourage competition among suppliers for credit terms.

Some suppliers use generous terms of trade credit as a form of sales promotion. This is especially likely where a distributor is trying to enter a new geographical area and is faced with the need to lure customers away from established rivals. In such circumstances, generous credit may well be more effective than an intensive advertising campaign or a high-pressure sales team. The credit may be a simple extension of the discount or net terms, or it may take a modified form such as an inventory loan.

Cash Available Because of Seasonal Business Credit Terms

If the entrepreneur is in a highly seasonal business, such as many types of retailing, he will find large differences in credit terms in different seasons. For example, as a retailer, he might be very short of cash in the fall as he builds up inventory for the Christmas selling season. Many suppliers will understand this and willingly will extend their normal 30-day terms.

Furthermore, some suppliers will offer exceedingly generous credit terms in order to smooth out their own manufacturing cycle. Consider a game manufacturer that sells half its annual production in the few months before Christmas. Rather than produce and ship most of the games in the late summer, this manufacturer would much rather spread out its production and shipping schedule over most of the year. To accomplish this, the manufacturer may offer seasonal dating to its retail store customers. Seasonal dating provides longer credit terms on orders placed in off-peak periods. For example, the game manufacturer might offer 120-day terms on May orders, 90-day terms on June orders, and so on. This will encourage customers to order early, and it will allow the game manufacturer to spread out production over more of the year.

Advantages of Trade Credit

Trade credit has two important advantages that justify its extensive use. The first advantage is convenience and ready availability; because it is not negotiated, it requires no great expenditure of executive time and no legal expenses. If a supplier accepts a company as a customer, the usual credit terms are automatically extended even though the maximum line of credit may be set low at first.

The second advantage (which is closely related to the first) is that the *credit available from this source automatically grows as the company grows.* Accounts payable are known as a spontaneous source of financing. As sales expand, production schedules increase, which in turn means that larger quantities of materials and supplies must be bought. In the absence of limits on credit, the additional credit becomes available automatically simply by placing orders for the extra material. If the manufacturing process is long and the supplier's payment is reached before the goods have been sold, some additional source of credit will also be needed. But the amount required will be much less than it would have been if no trade credit had been available.

Cash Obtained by Tightening Up Accounts Receivable Collections

Rapidly growing accounts receivable tie up a company's money and can cause a cash squeeze. However, these same accounts receivable become cash when they are collected. Some techniques—such as lockboxes and wire transfers—enable firms to collect receivables quickly and regularly. However, the question is: How can the rate of collection of receivables be increased temporarily during a cash shortage?

The most effective way to collect receivables quickly is simply to *ask for the money.* If the entrepreneur just sends a bill every month and shows the amount past due, the customer may not feel a great pressure to pay quickly. But if the entrepreneur asks for the money, either with a handwritten note on the statement of account, a phone call, or a formal letter, the customer will usually pay more quickly. To take an extreme case, a customer receiving several calls a week from an aggressive entrepreneur may pay the bill just to get the entrepreneur to stop bothering him. Of course, these more aggressive collection techniques also have costs, such as loss of customer goodwill, scaring away new customers, loss of old customers to more lenient suppliers, and the generation of industry rumors that the company is short of cash and may be a poor credit risk.

Stretching out accounts payable and collecting accounts receivable more quickly are really two sides of the same issue. Most entrepreneurs attempt to stretch out their bill payments as long as is reasonably possible and to collect their own bills as quickly as competitively possible. The entrepreneur's objective is to maximize company cash, using both techniques, without antagonizing either suppliers or customers so much that his working relationship with them suffers.

Although the fastest way to collect receivables is to ask for the money regularly, the entrepreneur can also *change his sales terms* to collect cash more quickly. The entrepreneur has several options, including:

1. *Introduce discounts.* A company can initiate a discount for prompt payment (for example, a 2% discount for payment within ten days). Similarly, a company with an existing discount may increase the discount (for example, increase discount from 1% to 2%).

2. *Reduce credit terms.* If competitively possible, an entrepreneur may require payment in full in 15 days, a deposit when the order is placed, COD

orders (in which the customer must pay for goods on delivery), or even full payment with the order. Companies will have difficulty instituting these measures if competitors offer significantly more lenient credit terms.

3. *Emphasize cash sales.* Some entrepreneurs, particularly those selling directly to consumers, may be able to increase their percentage of cash sales.

4. *Accept credit cards.* Sales made on bank credit cards or on travel or entertainment cards are convertible within a couple of days into cash. The credit card companies charge 3% to 7% of the amount of the sale for this service.

5. *Impose a penalty for late payment.* Some companies now charge 1.0 or 1.5% of the unpaid balance per month as a penalty for late payment. Again, competitive conditions may make this approach unlikely.

OBTAINING BANK LOANS THROUGH ACCOUNTS RECEIVABLE FINANCING

One approach an entrepreneur can take to free up working capital funds is to convert his accounts receivable into cash more quickly through aggressive collection techniques. However, when the entrepreneur fears that aggressive collection may offend customers and cause them to take their business to competitors, the entrepreneur may decide to convert his accounts receivable to cash through a financing company. In this form of financing, the entrepreneur can choose between two methods: pledging and factoring. The following sections describe both methods. In practice, finance companies or banks offer many variations on these two financing methods.

Pledging

Pledging means using accounts receivable as collateral for a loan from a finance company or bank. The finance company then gives money to the borrower, and as the borrower's customers pay their bills, the borrower repays the loan to the finance company.

With this form of accounts receivable financing, the borrower's customers are not notified that their bills are being used as collateral for a loan. Therefore, pledging is called *nonnotification financing.* Furthermore, if customers do not pay their bills, the borrower (rather than the finance company) must absorb the loss. Thus, if the customer defaults, the lender has the right of recourse to the borrower.

In general, a finance company will not lend the full face value of the accounts receivable pledged. In determining what fraction of the face value of receivables to lend, the finance company considers three factors:

1. The credit rating of the borrower's customers (because bills that may be paid slowly, or not at all, obviously do not make good collateral).
2. The quantity and dollar value of the accounts receivable (because a small number of large dollar-value receivable is easier to control).
3. The borrower's credit rating (because the finance company prefers having the loan repaid to taking possession of the collateral).

Typically, a company can borrow 75% to 90% of the face value of its accounts receivable if it has a good credit rating and its customers have excellent credit ratings. Companies with lower credit ratings can generally borrow 60% to 75% of the face value of their receivables.

Pledging receivables is not a cheap source of credit. In recent years, when the commercial bank lending rate was between 8% and 15%, the cost of pledging receivables was almost 20%. Moreover, an additional charge is often made to cover the lender's expenses incurred in appraising credit risks. Therefore, this source of financing is used mostly by smaller companies that have no other source of funds open to them.

Pledging with Notification

Another form of pledging is called *pledging with notification,* in which the borrower instructs its customers to pay their bills directly to the lender (often a bank). As checks from customers arrive, the bank deposits them in a special account and notifies the borrower that money has arrived.

With this approach, the lender controls the receivables more closely and does not have to worry that the borrower may collect pledged accounts receivable and then not notify the lender. The company loses under this system, however, because it must notify its customers that it has pledged its accounts receivable, which can reduce the company's credit rating.

Factoring

Factoring is defined as selling accounts receivable at a discount to a finance company (known as the *factor*). There are many variations of factoring, but the following example covers the main points. With factoring, a company usually transfers the functions of its credit department to the factor. That is, the factor takes over credit checking and collection. If the factor rejects a potential customer as an unacceptable credit risk, the company must either turn down the order or insist on cash payment.

An example will demonstrate how this process works. Suppose the W. Buygraves Inc. company (buyer) orders $10,000 worth of exotic wood and marble from the Saleman company (seller). The Saleman company calls its factor to report the order. The factor checks the credit rating of the Buygraves company and, if all is satisfactory, calls the Saleman company with an approval. The Saleman company then ships the goods and sends an invoice to the Buygraves company. The invoice instructs the Buygraves company to pay the factor. At the same time, the Saleman company sends a copy of the invoice to the factor, and the factor sends approximately 85% of the invoice amount ($8,000 in this case) to the Saleman company. The factor must now collect the $10,000 from Buygraves. When the factor actually collects the bill, it may send the Saleman company a small additional amount of money to recognize collections being higher than original estimates.

The fees that factors charge vary widely. These fees include:

- An interest charge, usually expressed on a daily basis (for the time the bill is outstanding) and equivalent to a 15% to 30% annual interest rate.
- A collection fee, usually in the range of an additional 6% to 10% annual rate.
- A credit checking charge, either a percentage of the invoice or a flat dollar amount.

The factor keeps a hold-back amount (which is not immediately paid to the Saleman company) to more than cover these various fees and charges, deducts the total from the hold-back amount, and sends the remainder to the Saleman company.

Recourse

Factoring may be with or without recourse. In the previous example, factoring without recourse means that if the Buygraves company does not pay its bill (that is, is a true deadbeat), the factor must absorb the loss. Factoring with recourse, on the other hand, means that if the Buygraves company does not pay the bill within a prenegotiated time (for example, 90 days), the factor collects from the Saleman company. The Saleman company must then try to collect from the Buygraves company directly.

Naturally, a factor charges extra for factoring without recourse. Typically, a factor adds 6% to 12% (on an annual basis) to the interest rate it charges the Saleman company. For factoring without recourse, factors generally come out ahead because they minimize bad-debt expense by carefully checking each customer's credit. Nevertheless, the Saleman company might prefer factoring without recourse for two reasons:

- The Saleman company does not have to worry that any bills will be returned. In this way, factoring without recourse is a form of insurance.
- The factor expresses the extra charge for factoring without recourse as part of the daily interest rate. This daily interest rate may look very small.

Most factoring is done with notification. This means that the customer company is notified and instructed to pay its bill directly to the factor. Occasionally, factoring is done without notification. In this case, the customer sends his payment either directly to the supplier or to a post office box. In general, factoring is more expensive than pledging. On the other hand, factors provide services, such as credit checking and collection, that a company would otherwise have to carry out itself. For a small company using the factor is often less expensive than providing the services on an internal basis.

OBTAINING LOANS AGAINST INVENTORY

An entrepreneur's inventory is an asset that can often be used as collateral for a loan. In this way, entrepreneurs can get the cash they need while still retaining access to their inventory. There are four basic ways to use inventory as security for a loan, depending on how closely the lender controls the physical inventory. These four ways are:

1. *Chattel mortgage,* in which specific inventory is used to secure the loan.
2. *Floating* (or blanket) lien, in which the loan is secured by all the borrower's inventory.
3. *Field warehousing,* in which the lender physically separates and guards the pledged inventory right on the borrower's premises.
4. *Public warehousing,* in which the lender transfers the pledged inventory to a separate warehouse.

Each method is discussed in the following sections.

Chattel Mortgage

A *chattel (or property) mortgage* is a loan secured by specific assets. For example, a borrower might pledge 5,000 new refrigerators as collateral for a loan. To guarantee the lender's position as a secured creditor (in case of bankruptcy), a chattel mortgage must precisely describe the items pledged as collateral. In the case of the refrigerators, the loan agreement would include the serial numbers of the specific refrigerators pledged by the borrower. If the borrower sells some of these refrigerators or receives a new shipment of refrigerators, the chattel mortgage must be rewritten to include these changes specifically.

Because the chattel mortgage describes the collateral so specifically, it offers fairly high security to a lender. Lenders further reduce their risk by lending only a fraction of the estimated market value of the collateral. This fraction depends on how easily the assets can be transported and sold. In the case of refrigerators, which are easy to sell, a borrower might obtain as much as 90% of their wholesale cost. But a borrower with a highly specialized inventory, such as bulldozer scoops, might get 50% or less of their fair market value because the lender would have difficulty selling the bulldozer scoops to recover the money. Because chattel mortgages describe the collateral so specifically, lenders limit their use to high-value items.

Floating Lien

Instead of naming specific items of inventory to secure a loan, borrowers may pledge all of their inventory. This is a *floating, or blanket, lien.* Because such an arrangement does not describe specific items of inventory, it does not have to be rewritten each time the borrower sells an item from inventory or receives new items into inventory. However, this flexibility makes it extremely difficult for the lender to maintain the security for the loan. For example, the borrower might sell most of the inventory and not leave enough to secure the loan. For this reason, banks and finance companies will usually lend only a small fraction of the inventory's market value when using a floating lien.

Field Warehousing

Field warehousing was invented to fully protect the lender's security. Under a field warehousing arrangement, the borrower designates a section of the premises, often a room or a specific area of the regular warehouse, for the use of the finance company. The finance company then locks and guards this field warehouse area and stores in it the actual inventory that the borrower is using as collateral. The finance company gives the borrower the agreed-on fraction of the fair market value of the inventory and receives in return a warehouse receipt, which gives the finance company title to the inventory. Companies use field warehousing when the inventory is especially bulky or valuable, such as structural steel, bulk chemicals, or diamonds.

Whenever the borrowing firm needs some of the inventory, it repays part of the loan, and the finance company releases part of the inventory. In this way, the finance company guarantees that there is sufficient collateral at all times to secure the loan.

Public Warehousing

Public warehousing is similar to field warehousing except that the actual inventory is moved to an independent warehouse away from the borrower's plant. As with field warehousing, the finance company releases inventory as the borrower repays the loan. Again, this ensures that the collateral is always sufficient to cover the loan.

There are many variations of warehousing. For example, some bonded warehouses accept checks in payment for loans and then forward these checks to the finance company while releasing the appropriate amount of inventory to the borrower. If such an arrangement is acceptable to all parties, it helps the borrower regain title to the inventory more quickly.

Costs of Warehousing

Warehousing companies collect both a service charge and interest. The service charge is usually a fixed amount plus 1% to 2% of the loan itself. This service charge covers the cost of providing field warehousing facilities or of transferring inventory to a public warehouse. In addition, the warehouse company charges interest, usually 10% or more. Because of the high fixed costs of setting up a warehousing system, this form of financing is practical only for inventories larger than about $500,000.

OBTAINING "FINANCING" FROM CUSTOMER PREPAYMENTS

Some companies are actually financed by their customers. This situation typically occurs on large, complex, long-term projects; it includes defense contractors, building contractors, ship builders, and management consulting firms. These companies typically divide their large projects into a series of stages and require payment as they complete each stage. This significantly reduces the cash these companies require, compared to firms that finance an entire project themselves and receive payment on completion. In some companies, customers pay in advance for everything they buy. Many mail-order operations are financed this way.

CHOOSING THE RIGHT MIX OF SHORT-TERM FINANCING

The entrepreneur attempts to secure the required short-term funds at the lowest cost. The lowest cost usually results from some combination of trade credit, unsecured and secured bank loans, accounts receivable financing, and inventory financing. Though it is virtually impossible to evaluate every possible combination of short-term financing, entrepreneurs can use their experience and subjective opinion to put together a short-term financing package that will have a reasonable cost. At the same time, the entrepreneur must be aware of future requirements and the impact that using certain sources today may have on the availability of short-term funds in the future.

In selecting the best financing package, the entrepreneur should consider the following factors:

- The firm's current situation and requirements.
- The current and future costs of the alternatives.
- The firm's future situation and requirements.

For small firms, the options available may be somewhat limited, and the total short-term financing package may be less important. On the other hand, larger firms may be faced with a myriad of possibilities. Clearly, the short-term borrowing decision can become quite complex, but the selection of the right combination can be of significant financial value to the entrepreneur's firm.

TRADITIONAL BANK LENDING: SHORT-TERM BANK LOANS

After an entrepreneur has fully used her trade credit and collected her receivables as quickly as competitively possible, she may turn to a bank for a short-term loan. The most common bank loan is a *short-term, unsecured loan made for 90 days*. Standard variations include loans made for periods of 30 days to a year and loans requiring collateral. Interest charges on these loans typically vary from the prime rate (the amount a bank charges its largest and most financially strong customers) to about 3% above prime.

Very often, an entrepreneur doesn't immediately need money but can forecast that she will have a definite need in, say, six months. The entrepreneur would not want to borrow the required money now and pay unnecessary interest for the next six months. Instead, the entrepreneur would formally apply to its bank for a *line of credit*—that is, an assurance by the bank that, as long as the company remains financially healthy, the bank will lend the company money (up to a specified limit) whenever the company needs it. Banks usually review a company's credit line each year. A line of credit is not a guarantee that the bank will make a loan in the future. Instead, when the company actually needs the money, the bank will examine the company's current financial statements to make sure that actual results coincide with earlier plans.

Banks also grant *guaranteed lines of credit.* Under this arrangement, the bank guarantees to supply funds up to a specified limit, regardless of circumstances. This relieves the company of any worries that money may not be available when it is needed. Banks usually charge extra for this guarantee, typically 1% a year on the unused amount of the guaranteed line of credit. For example, if the bank guarantees a credit line of $1 million and the company borrows only $300,000, the company will have to pay a commitment fee of perhaps $7,000 for the $700,000 it did not borrow.

In return for granting lines of credit, banks usually require that an entrepreneur maintain a *compensating balance* (that is, keep a specified amount in its checking account without interest). For example, if an entrepreneur receives a $1 million line of credit with the requirement that she maintain a 15% compensating balance, the entrepreneur must keep at least $150,000 in her demand account with that bank all year. The bank, of course, does not have to pay interest on this demand account money; so the use of this money is the bank's compensation for standing ready to grant up to $1 million in loans for a year. Of course, when the bank actually makes loans during the year, it charges the negotiated rate of interest on the loan.

Maturity of Loans

The most common time period, or maturity, for short-term bank loans is 90 days; however, an entrepreneur can negotiate maturities of 30 days to one year. Banks often prefer 90-day maturities, even when the entrepreneur will clearly need the money for longer than 90 days, because the three-month maturity gives the bank a chance to check the entrepreneur's financial statements regularly. If the entrepreneur's position has deteriorated, the bank can refuse to renew the loan and, therefore, avoid a future loss.

Entrepreneurs, on the other hand, prefer maturities that closely match the time they expect to need the money. A longer maturity, (rather than a series of short, constantly renewed loans) eliminates the possibility that the bank will refuse to extend a short-term loan because of a temporary weakness in the entrepreneur's operations.

Interest Rates

The rates of interest charged by commercial banks vary in two ways:

- The general level of interest rates varies over time.
- At any given time, different rates are charged to different borrowers.

The base rate for most commercial banks traditionally has been the *prime rate,* which is the rate that commercial banks charge their very best business customers for short-term borrowing. It is the rate that the financial press puts on the front page every time it is changed. Congress and the business community speculate about the prime's influence on economic activity because it is the base line for loan pricing in most loan agreements.

Historically, the prime was a base line for loan pricing; "prime plus two" or "2% above prime" was a normal statement of interest rate on many loan contracts. However, as the banking industry has begun to price its loans and services more aggressively, the prime is becoming less important. Along with the change in the prime, *compensating balances* (that is, the borrower's agreeing to hold a certain percentage of the amount of the loan in a noninterest-bearing account) are becoming less popular.

The current trend in loan pricing is *to price the loan at a rate above the marginal cost of funds* as typically reflected by the interest rates on certificates of deposit. The bank then adds an interest rate margin to the cost of funds, and the sum becomes the rate charged to the borrower. This rate changes daily in line with the changes on money market rates offered by the bank. As liability management becomes more of a way of life for bankers, the pricing of loans will become a function of the amount of competition, both domestic and international, that the banker faces in securing loanable funds. As a result of this competition for corporate customers and enhanced competition from the commercial paper market, large, financially stable corporations are often able to borrow at a rate below prime.

Interest represents the price that borrowers pay to the bank for credit over specified periods of time. The amount of interest paid depends on several factors:

- The dollar amount of the loan.
- The length of time involved.
- The nominal annual rate of interest.

- The repayment schedule.
- The method used to calculate the interest.

The various methods used to calculate interest are all variations of the simple interest calculation. *Simple interest* is calculated on the amount borrowed for the length of time the loan is outstanding. For example, if $1 million is borrowed at 15% and repaid in one payment at the end of one year, the simple interest would be $1 million times 0.15, or $150,000.

When the *add-in interest* method is used, interest is calculated on the full amount of the original principal. The interest amount is immediately added to the original principal, and payments are determined by dividing principal plus interest by the number of payments to be made. When only one payment is involved, this method is identical to simple interest. However, when two or more payments are to be made, the use of this method results in an effective rate of interest that is greater than the nominal rate. In the example above, if the $1 million loan were repaid in two six-month installments of $575,000 each, the effective rate is higher than 15% because the borrower does not have the use of funds for the entire year.

The *bank discount method* is commonly used with short-term business loans. Generally, there are no immediate payments, and the life of the loan is usually one year or less. Interest is calculated on the amount of the loan, and the borrower receives the difference between the amount to be paid back and the amount of interest. In the example, the effective interest rate is 17.6%. The interest amount of $150,000 is subtracted from the $1 million, and the borrower has the use of $850,000 for one year. If you divide the interest payment by the amount of money actually used by the borrower ($150,000 divided by $850,000), the effective rate is 17.6%.

If the loan were to require a compensating balance of 10%, the borrower does not have the use of the entire loan amount; rather, the borrower has the use of the loan amount less the compensating balance requirement. The effective rate of interest in this case would be 20%—the interest amount of $150,000 divided by the funds available, which is $750,000 ($1,000,000 minus $150,000 interest and minus a compensating balance of $100,000). The effective interest cost on a revolving credit agreement includes both interest costs and the commitment fee. For example, assume the TBA Corporation has a $1 million revolving credit agreement with a bank. Interest on the borrowed funds is 15% per annum. TBA must pay a commitment fee of 1% on the unused portion of the credit line. If the firm borrows $500,000, the effective annual interest rate is 16% [(0.15 × $500,000) + (0.01 × $500,000) divided by $500,000].

Because many factors influence the effective rate of a loan, when evaluating borrowing costs, only *the effective annual rate* should be used as a standard of comparison to ensure that the actual costs of borrowing are used in making the decision.

Collateral

To reduce their risks in making loans, banks may require collateral from entrepreneurs. Collateral may be any asset that has value. If the entrepreneur does not repay the loan, the bank owns the collateral and may sell it to recover the amount of the loan.

Typical collateral includes both specific high-value items owned by the company (such as buildings, computer equipment, or large machinery) and all items of a particular type (such as all raw materials or all inventory). Banks use blanket liens as collateral where individual items are of low value, but the collective value of all items is large enough to serve as collateral.

The highest level of risk comes in making loans to small companies, and it is not surprising to find that a high proportion of loans made to small companies—probably 75%—is secured. Larger companies present less risk and have stronger bargaining positions; only about 30% of loans made to companies in this class are secured.

One aspect of protection that most banks require is *key person insurance* on the principal officers of the company taking out the loan. Because the repayment of the loan usually depends on the entrepreneur or managers running the company in a profitable manner, if something should happen to the entrepreneur or key managers, there may be some question about the safety of the loan. To avoid this uncertainty, a term insurance policy is taken out for the value of the loan on the life of the entrepreneur or key managers. If the officer or officers die, the proceeds of the policy are paid to the bank in settlement of the loan.

When making loans to very small companies, banks often require that the owners and top managers personally sign for the loan. Then, if the company does not repay the loan, the bank can claim the signer's personal assets, such as houses, automobiles, and stock investments.

Applying for a Bank Loan

To maximize the chances of success in applying for a bank loan, an entrepreneur should maintain good banking relations. Personal visits by the entrepreneur and other senior officers, as well as quarterly delivery of income statements, balance sheets, and cash flow statements, are useful means of sustaining such relations.

The actual process of obtaining bank credit (whether a line of credit or an actual loan) must be conducted on a personal basis with the bank loan officer. The loan officer will be interested in knowing the following information:

- How much money the company needs.
- How the company will use this money.
- How the company will repay the bank.
- When the company will repay the bank.

Entrepreneurs should be able to fully answer these questions and support their answers with past results and realistic forecasts; if so, they stand an improved chance of obtaining the line of credit or loan that they need.

Restrictive Covenants

Bank term loans are negotiated credit, granted after formal negotiations take place between borrower and lender. As part of the terms agreed to in these negotiations, the bank usually seeks to set various restrictions, or *covenants,* on the borrower's activities during the life of the loan. These restrictions are tailored to the individual borrower's situation and needs; thus, it is difficult to generalize about them. This section introduces some of the more widely used covenants and their implications. All of these covenants are (at least to some degree) negotiable; it is wise for the financial executive to carefully review the loan contract and to attempt to moderate any overly restrictive clause a bank may request.

The restrictive covenants in a loan agreement may be classified as:

- *General provisions*—these are found in most loan agreements and are designed to force the borrower to preserve liquidity and limit cash outflows. They typically vary with the type of loan.
- *Routine provisions*—these are also found in most loan agreements and are normally not subject to modification during the loan period.
- *Specific provisions*—these are used according to the situation and are used to achieve a desired total level of protection.

The following sections describe these restrictions in more detail.

General Provisions

Most common of all general provisions is a requirement relating to the *maintenance of working capital.* This may simply be a provision that net working capital is to be maintained at or above a specified level. Alternatively, when the company is expected to grow fairly rapidly, the required working capital may be set on an increasing scale. For example, the bank may stipulate that working capital is to be maintained above $500,000 during the first twelve months of the loan, above $600,000 during the second, above $750,000 during the third, and so on. If the borrower's business is highly seasonal, the requirement for working capital may have to be modified to reflect these seasonal variations.

The provision covering working capital is often set in terms of the borrower's current ratio—current assets divided by current liabilities—which must be kept above, for example, 3 to 1 or 3.5 to 1. The actual figure is based on the bank's judgment and whatever is considered a safe figure for that particular industry.

Working capital covenants are easy to understand and very widely used. Unfortunately, they are often of rather doubtful value. As discussed in this chapter, a company may have a large net working capital and still be short of cash.

Another widely used covenant is *a limit on the borrower's expenditures for capital investment.* The bank may have made the loan to provide the borrower with additional working capital and does not wish to see the funds sunk into capital equipment instead. The covenant may take the form of a simple dollar limit on the investment in capital equipment in any period. Alternatively, the borrower is often allowed to invest up to, but not more than, the extent of the current depreciation expense. Such a provision may prove to be a serious restriction to a rapidly growing company. And clearly, any company will find such a covenant damaging if the maximum expenditure is set below the figure needed to maintain productive capacity at an adequate and competitive level.

Most term loan agreements include *covenants to prevent the borrower from selling or mortgaging capital assets without the lender's permission.* This may be extended to cover current assets other than the normal sale of finished goods, in which case the borrower is prohibited from factoring accounts receivable, selling any part of the raw-material inventory, or assigning inventory to a warehouse finance company without the bank's express permission.

Limitations on additional long-term debt are also common. The borrower is often theoretically forbidden to undertake any long-term debt during the life of the term loan, though in practice the bank usually allows new debt funds to be used in moderation as the company grows. The provision is often extended to prevent the borrower from entering into any long-term leases without the bank's authorization.

One type of covenant that clearly recognizes the importance of cash flows to a growing company is a *prohibition of or limit to the payment of cash dividends.* Again, if dividends are not completely prohibited, they may be either limited to a set dollar figure or based upon a set percentage of net earnings. The latter approach is the less restrictive.

Routine Provisions

The second category of restrictive covenants includes routine provisions found in most loan agreements that usually are not variable. The loan agreement ordinarily includes the following requirements:

- The borrower must furnish the bank with periodic financial statements and maintain adequate property insurance.
- The borrower agrees not to sell a significant portion of its assets. A provision forbidding the pledging of the borrower's assets is also included in most loan agreements. This provision is often termed a negative pledge clause.
- The borrower is restricted from entering into any new leasing agreements that might endanger the ability to pay the loan.
- The borrower is restricted from acquiring other firms unless prior approval has been obtained from the lender.

Specific Provisions

Finally, a number of restrictions relate more to the borrowing company's management than to its financial performance. For example:

- Key executives may be required to sign employment contracts or take out substantial life insurance.
- The bank may require the right to be consulted before any changes are made in the company's top management.
- Some covenants prevent increases in top management salaries or other compensation.

Restrictive covenants are very important in borrowing term loans. If any covenant is breached, the bank has the right to take legal action to recover its loan, probably forcing the company into insolvency. On the other hand, it may be argued that the covenants protect the borrowing company as well as the lender, in that their intention is to make it impossible for the borrower to get into serious financial trouble without first infringing on one or more restrictions, thus giving the bank a right to step in and apply a guiding hand. A bank is very reluctant to force any client into liquidation. In the event that a restriction is infringed on, however, the bank may use its very powerful bargaining position to demand even tighter restrictions—and some control over the borrower's operations—as the price of continuing the loan.

OBTAINING TERM LOANS FROM INSURANCE COMPANIES

Term lending by insurance companies is much less common than bank term lending. It does, however, offer an unusual range of maturities that span both intermediate- and long-term credit.

Insurance companies—especially life insurance companies—have a particularly stable and predictable business. Their cash inflows (which consist primarily of premium payments on insurance policies) can be forecast accurately. Their principal cash outflows (that is, payment of claims on policies) are also predictable on the average because the unpredictability of individual cases is effectively smoothed out by large numbers. Insurance companies, then, do not have any of the potential problems of liquidity of commercial banks. They can lend funds for a relatively long term.

The shortest-term loans made by insurance companies are for about five years. Ten years is probably about the average, and 15 years is not uncommon. During the 1950s some companies moved heavily into long-term financing and made loans that were virtually permanent capital: a number of term loans with maturities of more than 40 years were granted, and one major company made some 100-year loans. This trend has been reversed, however, and 10- to 15-year loans may be considered typical.

The preferred maturities of banks on the one hand and insurance companies on the other are obviously complementary, and some companies have been able to match term loan funds to their needs very effectively by putting together a package of bank and insurance funds. In such a case the bank advances funds for the first five years; then the insurance company takes over the loan for perhaps a further ten years. The borrower negotiates with representatives of both the bank and the insurance company at the same time, and the restrictive covenants are set at this time to apply to both phases of the loan.

OBTAINING TERM LOANS FROM PENSION FUNDS

The very rapid growth in pension funds has been one of the most striking developments in the financial world in recent years. At the same time, pension funds have a somewhat greater degree of flexibility in the ways they can be invested, and many pension-fund managers have aggressively looked for ways of maximizing their rates of return. One result of this has been an increasing interest in term loan lending. However, availability of loans from this source for very small dollar amounts is limited.

Pension funds have much the same stability and predictable cash flows as life insurance companies, and their managers also prefer the same kinds of longer-maturity loans. The characteristics of pension fund lending, in fact, are almost the same as those for insurance term loans.

It should be added that, when borrowing from both pension funds and insurance companies, the borrower does not usually approach the lender directly. Typically, the first move is for the entrepreneur or key officer of the firm to approach the company's commercial bank. If the bank is not able to supply the company's needs—probably because the funds are needed for a longer period than the bank's maximum maturity—the bank itself may then invite a life insurance company or pension fund to participate in the loan. Alternatively, the commercial bank may introduce the borrower to an investment banker, who will discuss the company's needs and facilitate the private placement of paper through a pension fund or life insurance company.

EQUIPMENT FINANCING

Capital equipment is often financed by intermediate-term funds. These may be straightforward term loans, usually secured by the equipment itself. Both banks and finance companies make equipment loans of this type. The non-bank companies charge considerably higher interest rates; they are used primarily by smaller companies that find themselves unable to qualify for bank term loans.

As with other types of secured loans, the lender will evaluate the quality of the collateral and advance a percentage of the market value. In determining the repayment schedule, the lender ensures that the value of the equipment exceeds the loan balance. In addition, the loan repayment schedule is often made to coincide with the depreciation schedule of the equipment.

One further form of equipment financing that should be considered is the *conditional sales contract*, which normally covers between two and five years. Under such a contract, the buyer agrees to buy a piece of equipment by installment payments over a period of years. During this time the buyer has the use of the equipment, but the seller retains title to it until the payments are completed. Companies that are unable to find credit from any other source may be able to buy equipment on these terms. The lender's risk is small because the equipment can be repossessed at any time if an installment is missed.

Equipment distributors who sell equipment under conditional sales contracts often sell the contract to a bank or finance company, in which case the transaction becomes an interesting combination of equipment financing for the buyer and receivables financing for the seller.

The credit available under a conditional sales contract is less than the full purchase price of the equipment. Typically, the buyer is expected to make an immediate down payment of 25% to 33% of the full cash price, and only the balance is financed. The cost of the credit given may be quite high. Equipment that is highly specialized or subject to rapid obsolescence presents a greater risk to the lender than widely used standard equipment, and the interest charged on the sale of such specialized equipment to a small company may exceed 15% to 20%.

USING EQUIPMENT LEASING AS A FINANCING STRATEGY

Leasing has become popular in recent years because there has been a trend emphasizing the ability to use property over the legal ownership of property. Other reasons often mentioned include the sharing of tax benefits between lessors and lessees. But the big incentive for leasing continues to be the nontax attributes such as flexibility, a hedge against obsolescence and inflation risk, service and maintenance contracts, convenience, lower costs, and off-balance-sheet financing. These advantages are discussed in the following sections.

Use versus Ownership

Many entrepreneurs have come to realize that the use of a piece of equipment is more important to the production of income than the possession of a piece of paper conveying title to the equipment. In fact, if people can use equipment for most of its economic life without having the full legal responsibilities, risks, and burdens of ownership, why should they ever desire to own it? Even farmers, who may have traditionally valued land ownership, now readily acknowledge that the use of land is more important than ownership of it. Many farmers and ranchers lease tracts of land to increase production of cattle or crops.

Tax Considerations

A big boost to leasing over the years has been the sharing of large tax benefits created through accelerated depreciation and investment tax writeoffs. Although the investment tax credit is not currently available, its reenactment would be a tremendous boost to low-income capital/property users. Lessees in low or negative tax positions may not be able to enjoy the full tax benefits of asset ownership and thus look to lessors in high tax positions to share some of the tax benefits through competitive lease pricing.

Nontax Attributes

Although in the past leasing may have gained from the investment credit and other tax benefits, it doesn't depend on the tax code for its survival. Much of the growth in leasing of late has been a result of nontax attributes. Many lease and tax experts generally agree that some companies, especially nonfinancial companies that did leveraged leasing primarily for the tax advantage, will leave the market. They also point out that a principal purpose of leasing is asset use, not ownership.

Leasing provides 100% financing, flexibility in usage requirements and terms, fixed rates, and convenience. Furthermore, from the lessee's perspective, leasing is a source of off-balance-sheet financing, a hedge against obsolescence and inflation risks, and often a cheaper financing source than borrowing. These attributes are particularly useful to lessees, which are often cash-poor companies.

Flexibility of Leases

Flexibility is a major factor in the recent growth of leasing. A short-term cancelable lease offers a firm flexibility, particularly if the leased asset is in an industry undergoing rapid technological advances. If a superior product comes to market, the lessee can cancel the current lease and enter into a new lease with the new product. Many managers mention the ability to specifically structure the financial and usage terms of the lease agreement as one of the major benefits of leasing.

In addition to allowing flexibility provisions, leases seldom contain the restrictive covenants usually found in loan agreements. For example, some loan agreements prohibit future financing of equipment until the loan is paid down significantly; leasing allows further expansion without restrictions.

Obsolescence of Equipment

Another reason use of equipment has been emphasized is that penalties are attached to the ownership of equipment (such as computers) that is developed by high-technology industries undergoing rapid growth. Some computers have even become obsolete between the order date and the delivery date—and who wants to own an outmoded piece of equipment? Short-term, cancelable leases permit firms to avoid the pitfalls of owning obsolete equipment.

If a piece of equipment becomes outdated, the lessee cancels the lease and orders updated equipment. In fact, automatic replacement of obsolete equipment is written into an upgrade lease agreement. A renewable operating lease enables a lessee to transfer the obsolescence risk to the lessor, who presumably is in a better position to resell a product and to forecast the residual value of a piece of equipment. Some lessors, such as Equitable Life Leasing, even specialize in equipment where the risk of technological obsolescence is great.

Cost and Convenience

Some entrepreneurs are attracted to leasing because of lower costs, fewer down payment restrictions, and convenience. Leasing companies generally require down payments lower than other financial institutions. The typical lease requires the first and last rental payments in advance (representing 2% to 4% down), whereas many banks require 10% to 20% as a down payment. In addition, other incidental costs of acquiring the asset—such as sales tax and installation charges—can be included as part of the lease payments rather than (as required by other financial institutions) paid in advance along with the large down payment. Frequently, the opportunity cost of tying up cash in equipment acquisitions is high enough that it almost necessitates leasing as an alternative. This is especially true for small, rapidly growing companies, where available funds are tied up in accounts receivables and inventories. (For example, if a small, growing firm needs a piece of equipment that it cannot afford to buy from funds generated internally, it may be able to lease the equipment immediately.)

Economies of Scale

Certain leasing companies, because of their large size, can effect savings in the form of quantity discounts received from volume purchasing. Such savings can be partially passed on to the entrepreneur. Additional savings from economies of scale may be obtained through the service lease, in which the cost of maintaining the leased equipment is included as part of each rental payment.

Autos, trucks, computers, and office copiers are examples of equipment often accompanied by a maintenance and service contract. Many lessees believe that leasing companies, because of familiarity with the equipment and large size, may be more proficient in servicing the equipment and will therefore pass along any savings. It does not always follow that large size and efficiency go hand in hand, however. Therefore, savings must be ascertained by comparing lease rates charged by competing companies.

Large leasing companies usually have access to secondary markets in which returned equipment may be resold. Since operating leases tend to be short-term, a great reliance is placed on the resale or salvage value. Lessors assume the risk of the resale value and are often willing to wait until the end of the lease term to realize their return objective. Thus, they are able to reduce their front-end cost to the entrepreneur and may charge a lower lease payment.

Off-Balance-Sheet Financing

Operating leases that meet certain accounting criteria are not capitalized on the balance sheet of the entrepreneur. Thus, the entrepreneur can acquire the use of equipment without showing the lease as a payable liability on his balance sheet. This attribute is not as significant as it once was because of stricter reporting requirements and more sophisticated creditors. However, some creditors may not consider leases as debt if they are properly structured. This may enlarge the firm's overall debt capacity.

When examining long-term projects, the entrepreneur needs to make important decisions about the financing of major assets. One obvious choice is to purchase the desired asset with either corporate cash or borrowed funds. Leasing provides an alternative. Leasing is designed to be a flexible financing vehicle. This may someday be helpful to the entrepreneur who anticipates future problems, and presents alternative and flexible strategies.

OBTAINING EARLY FINANCING
FROM EXTERNAL SOURCES

The Small Business Administration

During much of the 1970s and 1980s the Small Business Administration (SBA) provided billions of dollars to small business owners and entrepreneurs through the SBA direct and guaranteed loan programs. However, the direct loan program—in which the SBA works in concert with banks or local agencies to provide loans directly to borrowers—has been strongly curtailed.

The more common approach is for the entrepreneur to receive an SBA-guaranteed loan from the local bank. (See Chapter 9 for more information about the SBA.) The SBA can guarantee up to 90% of the loan (not exceeding $750,000) once a local bank has rejected the loan application. With the SBA guarantee the local bank has less risk; however, the bank must also forfeit part of the interest rate that it might normally charge. Prospective borrowers should recognize that the SBA, as well as SBICs, venture capitalists, and angels, have specific guidelines that they follow in lending money to new business operations.

Business borrowers should be advised to thoroughly prepare for their meeting with their (prospective) bankers. Bankers are likely to demand the following information and documents:

- Pro forma financial statements.
- Personal balance sheet and credit history.
- A list of all equipment/assets and pledged collateral.
- A description of how loan proceeds are being used.
- A description of shareholder and creditor interests.
- Personal business disclosures.
- A detailed business plan.

In addition, entrepreneurs should be able to respond to questions regarding their own salary, spending habits, and willingness to personally cosign a note on any borrowed funds. Moreover, it's also important for the entrepreneur to avoid the appearance of commingled personal and corporate assets and liabilities.

SBICs

The SBA licenses and regulates SBICs (Small Business Investment Companies). The SBA mandates SBIC investments be made to businesses with a net worth less than $6 million and with an average net income after taxes less than $2 million. Moreover, SBICs may not exceed a 20% capital interest in a single business nor more than 33% in a portfolio of real estate investments. These investment restrictions result in many relatively small investments in small companies. For example, from their inception through 1990, SBICs invested almost $9 billion in over 90,000 small firms including such success stories as Apple Computer, Cray Research, Federal Express, Teledyne, and Midway Airlines. At year end 1990, there were approximately 380 SBICs with assets of $3.1 billion.

SBICs draw their initial capital from private sources such as individuals, corporations, and banks and borrow funds from the government or from private financial institutions through government-guaranteed loans. The SBA guarantees enable the SBIC to attract more capital for investment and capital at more favorable rates than it could commercially. As such, SBICs are able to leverage their capitalization by a factor up to three or four.

SBICs make either *equity investments* or *long-term subordinated or unsecured loans* to companies with significant profit potential that otherwise could not qualify for long-term funding from banks or the private equity market. SBICs are regulated under the 1940 Investment Company Act and are required to pay out at least 90% of their net income, exclusive of capital gains, each tax year. Any income retained within the 10% limit is subject to the corporate income tax. Capital gains may be retained or paid out. If retained, they are subject to the corporate income tax. The result of this policy is that the company can only retain a small fraction of its earnings, so that the only manner in which the firm can grow is to either raise new equity capital or increase the firm's financial leverage.

INNOVATIONS AND TRENDS IN BUSINESS FINANCING

Credit Scoring for Small Business

Credit card issuers have applied an automated credit processing system (i.e., credit scoring) for many years as a mechanism to distinguish between good and bad credit risks for small consumer loans. Issuers typically focus on the prior credit payment history of the prospective customer and his or her stability of income, net worth, and lifestyle. Fast decisions can be made with a high degree of reliability as long as the issuer can select among a large population pool with similar income and spending characteristics. This is why many issuers send credit cards to individuals without application. Issuers anticipate a certain level of default and percentage loss that will be offset by profits from credit card interest collections. Until recently, credit scoring has not been used for business loan applications. Now however, many large banks are providing business credit decisions within 24 to 48 hours of the loan inquiry, and can fund requests up to $500,000. Although most lenders that use credit scoring, apply a loan "ceiling" of $100,000, many in the industry suspect that credit scoring levels will rise to $1 million within the next few years. Reasons should be clear: During times of tight credit entrepreneurs are satisfied simply receiving an adequate supply of funds. They are less concerned about arguing about credit terms. However, when credit is loose, entrepreneurs want their funds quickly at a low cost.

Large borrowers already enjoy advantages associated with an aggressive banking industry. Unsolicited bids for their business are not uncommon within the banking industry as bankers compete for a fixed supply of business. Bankers come to them and intentionally undercut their competitors bid, recognizing that their competitors will probably do the same to their choice clients. Borrowers in the smaller loan category (below $1 million) do not enjoy this attention. Smaller banks will tend to compete on customized service rather than price, and larger banks may not know that these customers exist. For example, a "relationship manager" accustomed to only 20 clients in the Middle Market group (borrowers in the $5 million to $20 million category), might find that in the Micro Lending area (borrowers below $500,000) he is now the "advocate" of over 200 clients. Thus, he is much more likely to use common term sheets and conditions for these borrowers, and more likely to conduct more business over the phone rather than with personal visits and active solicitation.

Entrepreneurs seeking a "traditional" banker providing debt levels of $1 million and less are more apt to receive this personalized service from a smaller, local bank rather than from a super regional or national institution. However, with increased consolidation and greater use of the Internet for debt and equity matchmaking, it seems clear that entrepreneurs will have more options in the years ahead. Already, a number of banks are looking to the Internet to solicit new business. Many finance providers offer a simplified loan application and information sheet in the hope of finding a suitable customer. Moreover, several companies currently exist that will attempt to match the borrowers' needs with the most appropriate lender, and some companies enable an entrepreneur to solicit funds from several lenders simultaneously. This trend will no doubt continue to become more efficient in the years ahead.

Bankers do not distinguish between the entrepreneur and his small, growing firm. The banker views the firm and entrepreneur as the same credit risk. Thus, the entrepreneur should be particularly sensitive to personal credit history and personal asset accumulation. Technological breakthroughs make it more difficult to hide from past credit mistakes. For those with an unblemished track record, funds will be made available quickly and inexpensively. These entrepreneurs will have the best chance for financial success with their young, growing company. However, those with a less desirable credit history or personal legal blemish may still find credit available, though finance providers will focus on the quality of the assets and use tight covenants to protect against future adverse situations.

Our financial markets are becoming more efficient. This generally works to the entrepreneur's advantage. During periods of surplus cash, entrepreneurs will find easier credit, simpler terms and more expeditious service. However, during recessionary times entrepreneurs will find that the cold-hearted efficiency of the capital markets also works to their disadvantage. There will be fewer relationship managers to appeal to, and banks may decide to focus on larger, strategic clients that will more likely survive the tough years. Some small, worthwhile ventures might possibly go unfunded. As the markets continue to develop, funds allocated to young, growing firms will become better defined and higher risk/specialty lenders will become more visible. Thus, the likelihood of a strong credit being denied funds in future years will diminish, and the allocation of resources will improve.

EXTERNAL ASSISTANCE FOR STARTUPS AND SMALL BUSINESSES

9

Elizabeth J. Gatewood

There is a wealth of external assistance out there that you have probably never heard of. Federal, state, and local governments and nonprofit institutions together offer a bewildering array of helpful resources. This chapter offers a map for the varied terrain of entrepreneurial assistance.

WHY YOU SHOULD CONSIDER EXTERNAL ASSISTANCE PROGRAMS

External sources of assistance are certainly useful and probably necessary for almost all entrepreneurs because the successful creation of a startup company, or the management of a small, growing company, is a highly complex, time-consuming, and difficult process. You may need all the help you can get.

The stereotypical entrepreneur—the so-called rugged individualist who doesn't need help—may still wince at the thought of government assistance. Some entrepreneurs believe that government regulations (especially in the areas of taxation, employee benefits, and environmental controls) may hinder small business. Nevertheless, many agencies of the government are committed to assisting entrepreneurship, usually because of the potential of small businesses to create jobs.

According to the U.S. Small Business Administration, small businesses create two out of every three new jobs, produce about 50% of the private gross domestic national product, and invent more than half of the nation's technological innovations. Over 22 million small companies (constituting 99% of all businesses in the United States) provide work and income for 54% of the private U.S. work force, and inspire further entrepreneurial activity. Small businesses are central to the U.S. economy, despite the dominance in the business and general press of the corporate giants that make up the *Fortune* 500.

Not all successful companies have required external assistance in their early stages. But many successful entrepreneurs have built their companies with government-guaranteed startup loans, lucrative government contracts, or government-sponsored advice on business plan development. Here are some recent prominent examples:

- Electronic Data Systems (EDS), built by Ross Perot—Some of EDS's early contracts were with the state of Texas and the federal government's Medicare programs.
- Apple Computer, Inc., and Cray Research, Inc., received Small Business Investment Companies capital during their early stages.
- Nike, Federal Express, Compaq Computer, Winnebago Industries, T.J. Cinnamons, and Godfather's Pizza were all assisted by SBA-sponsored programs.

External assistance programs have helped entrepreneurs at all phases of small company growth, in all sectors of industry, at all income levels, of all races, and of both genders.

You should consider external assistance programs because they are available, free, or inexpensive, and often effective in delivering useful services. They can also give you a competitive advantage in the difficult and complex project of starting up a new company or building a small company.

EXTERNAL ASSISTANCE AVAILABLE NATIONWIDE TO ANYONE IN THE UNITED STATES

Getting Advice: Business Development Programs

Most small business owners or would-be entrepreneurs begin with a need for business development assistance. This may involve managerial or technical assistance, for example, identifying and accessing relevant business and technical information, or using such information to evaluate new products, business concepts, and business plans. Many turn to the U.S. Small Business Administration.

The U.S. Small Business Administration (SBA)

Recognizing the importance of entrepreneurial initiative, Congress in 1953 created the Small Business Administration, an independent federal agency, to promote small business. The SBA is the primary federal agency charged with aiding, counseling, assisting, and protecting the interests of small business, although other federal agencies also provide services to this diverse economic constituency. (In 1996, the agency had over 100 offices covering every state, the District of Columbia, Guam, Puerto Rico, and the Virgin Islands, and annual loan guarantee authorization of over $10 billion.

A small business must meet certain size criteria to be eligible for the SBA's services. These services include not only business development programs carried out by the SBA's Resource Partners (discussed later in this chapter), but also loans, procurement assistance, and international trade assistance. The Small Business Administration Act of 1953 defines a small business as "one which is independently owned and operated and not dominant in its field of operation." For statistical purposes, the SBA defines a small business as one with fewer than 500 employees. For business development assistance, loans, and other services, the SBA defines eligibility either by employment size or annual revenue criteria that vary by industry and change periodically.

The SBA uses the Standard Industrial Classification (SIC) manual to define industries, and it periodically reorganizes and clarifies eligibility criteria. The SBA sales and employment size criteria in 1996 were as follows:

- *Services and retailing*—Small if annual sales are not over $3.5 to $13.5 million, depending on the specific industry.
- *Wholesaling*—Small if number of employees does not exceed 100.
- *Manufacturing*—Small if average employment in the preceding four calendar quarters did not exceed 500, including employees of any affiliates; large if average employment was more than 1,500. If employment is between 500 and 1,500, the SBA decides based on a size standard for the particular industry.
- *Construction*—Small if average annual sales for three years preceding application did not exceed $17.0 million, except for specialty contractors, for whom sales may not have exceeded $7 million.
- *Agriculture*—Small if average annual sales range from $0.5 to $3.5 million, depending on the industry.

The SBA has gradually reduced its provision of management and technical assistance to small business firms via its own field representatives. Technical and management assistance is now primarily provided through several innovative partnerships, collectively called the SBA's Resource Partners, described in the next sections of this chapter. The SBA still provides a comprehensive set of useful brochures. In 1995 the SBA distributed more than 3.5 million SBA publications and videotapes. In 1992 the SBA introduced SBA On-Line, an electronic bulletin board that allows anyone with a computer and modem to browse through detailed descriptions of the SBA's services and publications. In 1996, SBA developed a World Wide Web Site with similar information.

Where to Find the SBA

For your district SBA office, look in the Blue Pages, under the U.S. Government listing headed "U.S. Small Business Administration." Or call the 24-hour SBA answer desk at 800-8-ASK-SBA. The SBA On-Line access numbers are 800-859-INFO (for a 2,400 bps modem) and 800-697-INFO (for a 9,600 bps modem). For the hearing-impaired, the TDD number is (703) 334-6640. Web address: http://www.sba.gov

---

As mentioned, the SBA also supports business development efforts through the following "Resource Partners":

- The Small Business Development Center (SBDC) program.
- The Service Corps of Retired Executives (SCORE) program (into which the former Active Corps of Executives (ACE) program was merged in 1982).

These SBA Resource Partners assisted more than 800,000 clients and training attendees in fiscal year 1995 alone. That's still less than 5% of the 22 million small businesses in the country—clearly, they're waiting to hear from you!

Small Business Development Centers (SBDCs)

Congress initiated the Small Business Development Center program as a pilot program in 1977 to make management assistance and counseling more widely available to present and prospective small business owners. Congress enacted the SBDC program into law in 1980 and granted the SBA oversight for the program.

SBDCs offer one-stop assistance to small businesses and startups by providing a wide variety of information and guidance in central and easily accessible locations. They offer free counseling services and reasonably priced seminars and workshops to new and existing businesses. There are now more than 950 service locations organized into 57 SBDC territories—one or more in each of the 50 states, the District of Columbia, Puerto Rico, and the Virgin Islands.

In each state there is a lead organization (often within a state university and sometimes within the state government itself), endorsed by the governor, which sponsors the SBDC and manages the program. The lead organization coordinates program services offered to small businesses through a network of subcenters and satellite locations in each state. Subcenters are located at colleges, universities, community colleges, vocational schools, chambers of commerce, and economic development corporations.

SBDC assistance may be divided into two main areas: free one-on-one counseling and inexpensive classroom-style training. Customized counseling services range from informal detailed evaluations of business plans by an industry-experienced counselor to advising growing companies on expansion plans for new territorial or product markets.

SBDCs sometimes supplement their free counseling services by making referrals on specialized accounting, legal, or technical subjects to professional business services. One SBDC, at the University of Houston, has negotiated a reduced-fee program for these services. The service also offers referrals to potential advisory board members for the small business owner.

SBDC training seminars are usually priced at substantial discounts off commercial rates (for example, $30–60 for a four-hour minicourse on how to write a business plan). They are offered by SBDC staff or recognized local experts. Training seminars cover topics such as:

- Strategic planning.
  —Business planning.
- Market analysis and strategy.
  —Marketing to the government.
  —International trade.
- Product feasibility and development.
  —Technology access.
- Organizational analysis.
- Financial control.
  —Loan assistance.
  —Cash management.
  —Bookkeeping and accounting.

Some SBDCs also feature specialized centers that provide assistance in the following areas:

- Government contracting (procurement).
- International trade (for existing businesses looking for international expansion, or startups focused on international trade).

- Technology transfer and product development—Guidance in commercializing new products or services may include advice on royalty agreements, patent research, and new product evaluations.

Each SBDC center has full-time and part-time employees and recruits qualified volunteers from professional and trade associations, the legal and banking communities, academia, and chambers of commerce to counsel clients. Many SBDCs also use paid consultants, consulting engineers, and testing laboratories from the private sector to help clients who need specialized expertise.

SBDCs maintain strict client confidentiality. Only counselors directly working with you learn details of your company's operations. All advisors—whether staff, paid consultants, or volunteers—have to sign a conflict-of-interest agreement. This prohibits disclosure of information about any client to any non-SBDC personnel or any other client, solicitation or acceptance of gifts from clients, or investment in SBDC clients.

The SBA provides 50% or less of the operating funds for each state SBDC. The matching-fund contributions come from state legislatures, private sector foundations and grants, state and local chambers of commerce, state-chartered economic development corporations, public and private universities, vocational and technical schools, and community colleges. The success of SBDCs is reflected in the increasing tendency of sponsors' contributions to exceed the minimum 50% matching share. Unlike the SCORE (described in the next section of this chapter), which is totally funded by the SBA, SBDCs are more free to develop programs and services independently of the SBA.

Where to Find SBDCs

For a local office, look in the Blue Pages under the U.S. Government listing. The Association of Small Business Development Centers (ASBDC) is located at

1300 Chain Bridge Road, Suite 201
McLean, VA 22101-3967
(703) 448-6124

Service Corps of Retired Executives (SCORE)

SCORE, a volunteer organization founded in 1964, numbers more than 12,000 retired and active executives and small business owners who volunteer their professional management expertise to help current and future business owners and managers. Most SCORE volunteers are retired, but about 18% are still in the work force. SCORE provides business information and management help through confidential counseling, training, and workshops.

SCORE provides the following information and advisory services:

- Short-term startup counseling.
- Longer-term counseling for established clients.
- Team counseling, when several experts are desirable.

SCORE counseling may occur at a SCORE office or at the client's place of business. Its clients have included a wide variety of businesses—for example, graphic arts companies, archaeological consulting firms, and security systems stores. Nearly 40% of SCORE's clients are word of mouth referrals.

SCORE offers a prestartup seminar, one of many topics covered in the 4,291 workshops SCORE provided nationwide for 103,491 people in FY 1995. SCORE is an active participant in the operation of Business Information Centers (BICs). In 1996 there were 36 BICs nationwide, primarily in major cities. BICs typically have a video library; computer services, including on-line research capabilities and applications software; and other business library services for entrepreneurs.

SCORE has helped nearly 3 million people since 1964. In fiscal year 1995 its $3.25 million budget supported 800 counseling locations, providing assistance through its network of 387 chapters.

Where to Find SCORE

For your district SBA office, look in the Blue Pages, under the U.S. Government listing headed "U.S. Small Business Administration." Or call the 24-hour SBA answer desk at 800-8-ASK-SBA. For the hearing impaired, the TDD number is (202) 205-7333. The National SCORE Office (NSO) is located at

409 Third St., S.W., Suite 4800
Washington, DC 20024
(202) 205-6762

Summary of SBA Resource Partner Activities

Exhibit 9.1 shows that for 1995, SBDCs and SCORE counseled almost 400,000 small business owners and prospective small business owners. In the same year, they provided training events that attracted almost 450,000 attendees.

Getting Money: Financial Assistance from the SBA

Debt fuels growth. The entrepreneur promoting a new business venture through a well-prepared business plan and the successful small business proprietor

EXHIBIT 9.1   Business development programs: SBA's resource partners (fiscal year 1995).

	SBDCs	SCORE	Total
Counseling			
Clients counseled	228,424	165,387	393,811
Counseling hours	1,158,916	1,020,139	2,179,055
Hours/client	5.07	6.17	
Training units	18,481	4,291	22,772
Attendees	341,148	103,491	444,539
Training hours	1,610,217	441,978	2,052,195
Attendees/unit	18	24	20

both face the challenge of finding money for startup operations, for working capital, and for expansion and growth. A variety of institutions respond to these needs.

The SBA's financial assistance programs for small companies and start-ups complement its business development programs. SBA guarantees loans made by lending institutions to small businesses, provides venture capital through its Small Business Investment Company Program and provides loans to nonprofit organizations to fund small loans to small businesses. Many SBA loan programs are targeted to specific groups and needs. Borrowers can use different SBA financial assistance programs simultaneously, up to the SBA's statutory loan guarantee limit of $750,000.

Loan Guarantees

The 7(a) general loan guarantee

This is the SBA's principal way of financially promoting small business creation and growth. (The 7(a) name refers to a section of the original SBA law.) It represents more than 90% of the agency's total loan effort. 7(a) loans are made by private lenders to small businesses that cannot obtain credit without an SBA guarantee and are then guaranteed by the SBA for up to 75% (80% if total loan is $100,000 or less) of the amount provided by the commercial lender.

The maximum loan guarantee is $750,000; however, the average loan amount is $178,000. The maximum repayment period for loans is 25 years for land, buildings, and equipment; typically seven years for working capital. Funds can be used for working capital; to construct, expand or convert facilities; to purchase machinery or equipment; to buy land and buildings; for a seasonal line of credit; and for inventory. In some cases the loan may be used for refinancing certain types of debt. In fiscal year 1995 the SBA provided guarantees on 55,590 loans, for a total value of $7.8 billion.

A study by Price Waterhouse reported that businesses that got loan guarantees showed higher growth than comparable businesses. Perhaps only companies with very strong business plans and founding teams can pass the screens of a primary lender and the SBA guarantee evaluation.

The Low Doc Program

This program has extended the SBA's guaranteed lending efforts to loans that most banks previously would have been reluctant to make because they would have considered them too small to be profitable. The Low Doc Program encourages conventional lenders to make loans of $100,000 or less by reducing the amount of paperwork lenders must submit to the SBA. SBA will guarantee up to 80% of the loan. Loan proceeds may be used for purposes specified for 7(a) loans, except for certain types of existing debt. The maximum repayment period is 25 years for fixed assets and 10 years for all other uses for the loan. Businesses that are start ups, or have annual sales of $5 million or less for the past three years, or have 100 or fewer employees qualify for Low Doc loans. Lending decisions are based on applicant character and history.

The CAP Lines Program

This program is designed to improve small business access to working and short-term capital. SBA will provide guarantees up to 75% (80% if total loan is $100,000 or less) on lines of credit extended by commercial lenders for up to five years. The maximum loan amount is $750,000. Interest rates are capped at 2.25 percentage points above prime. Proceeds from the loan can be used for seasonal capital needs; as advances against inventory and accounts receivables during peak seasons; financing the direct labor and material costs associated with contracts; financing direct labor and materials construction and renovation costs; and consolidating short-term debt.

The 504 Certified Development Company Loan Program

This program finances fixed assets with long-term, low-interest funds through certified development companies (CDCs). The typical structure for a CDC funding project would include 50% conventional bank financing, 40% CDC second mortgage, and 10% owner's equity. CDCs are nonprofit economic development agencies, certified by the SBA and licensed by the state to operate in designated counties only. In 1996, there were approximately 290 CDCs nationwide. They raise their funding by selling 100% SBA-guaranteed debentures to private investors.

These loans are generally up to $750,000 (up to $1 million in some cases) at 10 to 20-year maturities. Funds can be used for purchasing land or buildings; constructing, renovating, or expanding buildings; or buying machinery or long term equipment. Collateral and personal guarantees are required. Interest rates are based on 5- and 10-year U.S. Treasury issues plus an increment. Fees are approximately 3% of the debenture and may be financed with the loan proceeds. To be eligible for the 504 program, a business must have neither a tangible net worth greater than $6 million nor an average net income in excess of $2 million after taxes for the previous two years. Businesses engaged in speculation or investment in rental real estate are not eligible. CDCs consider jobs generated or jobs saved in choosing projects to fund.

Defense Loan and Technical Assistance (DELTA) Program
The Delta Program, a joint effort of SBA and the Department of Defense (DOD), provides funding to small companies affected by cutbacks in defense. The loans can be through the 7(a) loan program or a Certified Development Company (CDC). The maximum loan amount for a 7(a) Delta loan is $1.25 million, the maximum for a CDC Delta loan is $1 million. If both types of loans are used, or if the company already has a SBA loan, the total amount is $1.25 million.

Pollution Control Loans Program
SBA provides loan guarantees under the 7(a) program to small businesses that are planning, designing, or installing a pollution control facility. The facility must abate, control, prevent, or reduce pollution. The maximum guarantee amount is $1 million. However, if the company has an existing SBA loan guarantee, this amount is reduced by the outstanding guarantee.

Other Loans

Disaster loans
The SBA offers two types of loans for businesses located in disaster areas designated by the president or the SBA administrator. Businesses suffering uninsured property damage or economic losses from the disaster can obtain long-term recovery loans at low interest rates. Property damage to real estate, machinery, equipment, supplies, or inventory is eligible for physical disaster loans of up to $1.5 million to nonfarm businesses of all sizes damaged in a disaster. Loans of up to $1.5 million for economic losses, for working capital until normal operations resume after the physical disaster, are available to small businesses and agricultural cooperatives that are not able to access credit elsewhere. Interest rates for physical disaster loans are 4%, 8% for business with other sources of credit. Economic injury disaster loans for working capital are 4%. Terms are negotiated with the borrower with a maximum of 30 years, however, businesses with other credit sources are limited to three-year terms. Businesses damaged by Hurricane Andrew and the Midwest floods were beneficiaries of SBA disaster loans.

Micro-loans

The SBA's experimental Micro-Loan Program was distributed through 101 nonprofit organizations (for example, community service and church groups) in 48 states, Washington D.C., and Puerto Rico in 1996. These micro-loans are targeted at women, low-income, and minority entrepreneurs, especially those in areas that have suffered economic downturns. They help entrepreneurs form or expand small, often home-based, enterprises. Individuals should have the skills but not the capital needed to operate a small business.

Micro-loans may range from a few hundred dollars up to $25,000. The average loan is $10,500. Funds may be used for working capital, inventory, supplies, furniture, fixtures, machinery, and equipment. Borrowers seeking more than $15,000 must demonstrate that they cannot obtain credit from other sources at comparable rates. The maximum term of the loan is six years. The interest rate on these loans is no more than 4% above prime.

The Surety Bond Guarantee Program

The SBA provides guarantee bonds for qualified small contractors who are unable to obtain surety bonds through regular bonding markets. For a contractor to be eligible for the program, average annual revenues for the last three fiscal years cannot exceed $5 million.

The SBA guarantees bonds for contracts up to $1.25 million. The guarantees are for 80% or 90%, depending on the amount of the contract or the status of the contractor. Approved socially or economically disadvantaged contractors receive a 90% guarantee for contracts regardless of the contract size; other contractors receive a 90% guarantee for contracts not exceeding $100,000 and an 80% guarantee for those over $100,000.

The small business pays the SBA a guarantee fee of $7.45 per thousand of the contract amount, and when the bond is issued, it pays the surety company's bond premium. In fiscal year 1995 the SBA provided surety bond guarantees to 6,807 contractors with construction contracts worth more than $1.2 billion.

Small Business Investment Company (SBIC) and Specialized Small Business Investment Companies (SSBIC) Program

SBICs and SSBICs are privately owned and managed investment firms that are licensed and regulated by the SBA. They augment their own funds by borrowing at favorable rates with SBA guarantees and by selling their preferred stock to the SBA. They provide equity capital and long-term loans to small businesses. To be eligible, you must qualify as a small business using SBA criteria (see earlier section).

SSBICs operate similarly to SBICs but receive additional leverage from the Federal government because they provide capital to small businesses owned by individuals classified as socially or economically disadvantaged. There are approximately 200 SBICs and 100 SSBICs.

SBA Interest Rate Policy

Interest rates on guaranteed loans are negotiated between borrowers and lenders, although rates cannot be higher than levels set by SBA regulations. Interest rates may be fixed or variable. For fixed rate loans, maturing in less than seven years, rates may not exceed 2.25% plus prime, maturing in seven years or more, rates may not exceed 2.75%. For loans less than $25,000, the maximum is 4.25% and 4.75% respectively. For loans between $25,000 and $50,000, the maximum is 3.25% and 3.75%.

Variable rate loans are based on the lowest prime rate or the SBA optional peg rate, which is calculated quarterly and published in the Federal Register. The lender and borrower negotiate the amount that will be added to the base rate. All guaranteed loans require payment of a guarantee fee by the lender, which varies with the type of loan and may be passed on to the borrower.

How to Apply for an SBA Loan Guarantee

The SBA has the following general credit requirements:

1. The applicant must be of good character and have a good credit history.
2. The applicant must have experience in business management and demonstrate the commitment necessary for a successful operation.
3. The applicant must have enough funds—including the SBA-guaranteed loan plus personal equity capital—to operate the business on a sound financial basis. If the company is a new business, this means enough cash to fund startup expenses and sustain expected losses during the early stages of operation.
4. If the company is an existing business, it must have a past earning record and future prospects to show repayment ability.
5. If the company is a new business, the startup entrepreneurs must provide at least one-third of the total startup capital needed. Therefore, the loan requested should be no more than twice the value of the owner's equity capital in the business.

Borrowers must fully secure the loan with collateral and provide personal guarantees. The SBA normally takes about two weeks to process a request.

Finding an SBA-Approved Lender

About 7,000 lenders nationwide made at least one SBA loan in 1995. Over 950 of these lenders have been designated as either SBA-preferred or SBA-certified lenders. It is worth your while to identify SBA-preferred lenders in your area because they are empowered to apply an SBA loan guarantee to a loan without consulting the SBA in advance. The benefit of dealing with an SBA-certified lender is that the SBA will normally decide whether to guarantee a bank loan within three days. To find out which lenders are preferred or certified, call your SBA district office.

Where to Find the SBA

For your district SBA office, look in the Blue Pages, under the U.S. Government listing headed "U.S. Small Business Administration." Or call the 24-hour SBA answer desk at 800-8-ASK-SBA. The SBA On-Line access numbers are 800-859-INFO (for a 2,400 bps modem) and 800-697-INFO (for a 9,600 bps modem). For the hearing-impaired, the TDD number is (703) 344-6640. Web address: http://www.sba.gov

---

Selling to the Government: The Art of Procurement

The federal government is a big customer. It buys $180 billion worth of goods and services every year from U.S. businesses. The government buys about $43 billion directly from small business and another $22 billion through federally mandated subcontracts between small business and large prime contractors. Nearly 98% of all procurement contracts are for $25,000 or less, although this composes only 20% of all spending.

Procurement Assistance Programs Sponsored by the SBA

The Small Business Act provides for preferential treatment to be granted to small business concerns in the award of government procurement contracts. The SBA has developed cooperative programs with major government purchasing agencies under which proposed purchases are reviewed by purchasing officials and suitable items are set aside, wholly or partially for small business bidders. This system of preferences in contract awards is known as "set-asides." They are aimed at small businesses, disadvantaged small businesses, and small businesses owned by women.

The law also requires large prime government contractors to subcontract work to small businesses. The SBA accordingly develops subcontracting opportunities by negotiating the amounts to be subcontracted to small business concerns by prime contractors undertaking major federal projects.

To achieve these goals the SBA maintains the *Procurement Automated Source System* (PASS), a computerized database that lists small firms and their contracting or subcontracting capabilities. Using computers with modems, procurement officials of federal agencies and major corporations attempt to match their needs to the profiles submitted by participating small businesses. The data base contains approximately 200,000 profiles of small businesses. It is accessed by more than 1,000 authorized users. General information and registration forms may be obtained by calling the PASS hotline at (800) 231-7277.

SBA field officers provide counseling and other services to small business owners seeking to do business with the federal government. Procurement specialists at SBA district offices can help:

- Identify the government agencies that are prospective customers.
- Instruct small businesses about inclusion on bidders' lists.
- Obtain drawings and specifications for specific contracts.

The SBA has its own procurement center representatives (PCRs) stationed at major military and civilian procurement installations. The SBA also provides an appeal procedure when the ability of a low-bidding small firm to perform a contract is questioned.

The SBA also provides surety bonds, whereby it guarantees up to 80% (90% depending upon the status of the borrower or the size of the contract) of losses incurred under bid, payment, or performance bonds issued to contractors on government contracts valued up to $1.25 million. The Surety Bond Guarantee Program was described earlier in this chapter.

Doing business with the federal government has the following advantages:

- Variety—the federal government has a wide range of purchasing needs.
- Creditworthiness.
- The potential for long-term contracts.
- Detailed bidding procedures designed to ensure fairness.

On the other hand, disadvantages include the facts that the competitive nature of the bidding process may reduce profit margins, and its bureaucratic aspects require painstaking attention to involved procedures.

The SBA and minority subcontracting

The SBA is authorized under Section 8(a) of the Small Business Act to enter into contracts with other federal agencies for goods and services and then to subcontract the work to firms owned by socially and economically disadvantaged persons. The 8(a) program is a business development program that helps socially and economically disadvantaged individuals enter the economic mainstream partially through access to federal contracts. The firms must be approved to participate in the 8(a) program by the SBA after demonstrating the nature and source of their disadvantage. The maximum period of eligibility is nine years from initial program certification.

More than half of all federal procurement through disadvantaged firms is channeled through the 8(a) program. In fiscal year 1995 more than 6,600 initial contracts were awarded for a total value of $3.15 billion, with modifications to initial contracts, that amount reached $5.8 billion. In addition the SBA is authorized under Section 7(j) of the act to provide management and technical assistance to 8(a) clients and small businesses in areas of high unemployment (see Exhibit 9.1 for details on the type of assistance offered by various programs).

Procurement Assistance Programs Sponsored by the U.S. Department of Defense (DOD)

Congress has created a national policy stating that a fair proportion of the products and services used by the DOD be purchased from small businesses and small disadvantaged businesses. This policy is grounded in the need to maintain a strong, diversified industrial base and increase competition in defense-related procurement. Defense purchasing officials, therefore, maintain contact with small business firms, small disadvantaged business firms, and small business firms owned by women.

The Department of Defense accordingly supports various procurement counseling services under the *Defense Procurement Technical Assistance (PTA) program.* The PTA is a cooperative program in which the DOD shares the cost of the services with state and local governments and nonprofit organizations. These services (which go by different names in different states) can help entrepreneurs seeking to sell goods and services to the DOD. They also help small businesses identify government agencies—federal, state, county, and municipal agencies that may buy their goods and services—and identify bid opportunities that are currently or prospectively available.

PTAs may offer procurement assistance in the form of technical data, drawings, and the counseling know-how to complete a bid package. They may maintain a library of relevant government specifications, standards, and regulations, including the *Federal Acquisition Regulation* (which describes the basic contracting rules for all federal agencies) and key supplements, plus military specifications and standards. PTAs may access technical data and generate pricing histories on parts, help the client develop quality control manuals, and match by computer the client's business capabilities and products with the millions of items and services purchased by government agencies. PTAs may use computer software to scan the *Commerce Business Daily*, which lists many government bid requests, contract awards, and leads on subcontracting, and the *U.S. Government Purchasing and Sales Directory*, which lists the military and civilian agencies that tend to buy particular products and services. PTAs also assist businesses implementing electronic data interchange (EDI) for the bidding process.

How to Get SBA and DOD Procurement Help

For your district SBA office, look in the Blue Pages, under the U.S. government listing headed "U.S. Small Business Administration." Or call the National SBA answer desk at 800-8-ASK-SBA (827-5722). For the hearing-impaired, the TDD number is (703) 344-6640.

To find whether a PTA program is available in your area, call the nearest Defense Contract Management District (DCMD), administered by the DOD's Defense Logistics Agency.

East: 495 Summer Street
                8th Floor
                Boston, MA 02210-2184
                Telephone: (617) 753-4317/4318
                Toll-free (MA): 800-348-1011
                Toll-free: 800-321-1861

West: 222 North Sepulveda Boulevard
                El Segundo, CA 90245-4394
                Telephone: (310) 335-3260
                Toll-free (CA): 800-233-6521
                Toll-free (AK, HI, ID, MT, NV, OR, WA):
                800-624-7372

International: 209 Chapel Drive
                Navy Security Group Activity
                Sabana Seca, PR 00952
                Telephone: (809) 795-3202

Selling Abroad: International Business in the Global Village

According to the SBA, every billion dollars in U.S. exports generates about 25,000 jobs. Small firms account for almost a quarter of all exporters. Because of the importance of small business in export, the SBA, the SBA's Resource

Partners, the U.S. Department of Commerce, the U.S. Export-Import Bank, and the Overseas Private Investment Corporation (OPIC) have business development and financial assistance programs to help companies involved in exporting.

Export Business Development Programs

U.S. Export Assistance Centers (USEACs)

USEACs are located in major cities in the United States. They integrate services provided by the U.S. Small Business Administration. The U.S. Department of Commerce, the Foreign Commercial Service, the Export-Import Bank, and local international trade programs by providing a single location for access.

The USEACs provide one-on-one counseling to firms to assist them in identifying target markets and developing international marketing strategies. They also provide assistance in areas relating to export finance.

In 1996, there were 13 USEACs located in Atlanta, Baltimore, Cleveland, Chicago, Dallas, Denver, Long Beach, Miami, New Orleans, New York, Philadelphia, Seattle, and St. Louis.

The Small Business Automated Trade Locator Assistance System (ATLAS)

ATLAS, sponsored by the OIT, provides a computerized service useful to exporters. ATLAS provides international marketing and trade information by scanning several large databases. ATLAS can identify the largest markets for specific products ranked by unit sales and dollar volume, five-year trends within those markets, and major sources of foreign competition. The ATLAS system is designed to be useful to businesses that have already identified their target markets. The more specific you are in delineating your product and geographic markets, the more useful the information you will receive.

ATLAS is available free of charge through SBA regional and district offices. SBA will pilot providing the ATLAS information on the internet through the SBA Web site. It will be called Export Access and will be listed under the Office of International Trade. Under an agreement between the SBA and the Federal Bar Association, the Export Legal Assistance Network (ELAN) offers free initial consultations with an experienced international trade attorney on topics ranging from contract negotiation to agent/distributor agreements, export licensing requirements, and credit collection procedures.

International trade centers

The SBA's Resource Partners have a special mission in international trade. Six hundred SCORE members have international trade experience and many

SBDCs offer international trade assistance through their International Trade Centers. These centers can help the client:

- Evaluate the potential for company and product exports.
- Analyze and research potential export markets.
- Define market entry strategies.
- Select distribution networks.
- Manage the logistics of export.

The International Trade Administration

The U.S. Department of Commerce (USDOC) also helps companies expand their international trade capabilities through the International Trade Administration. ITA operates domestic and overseas programs designed to stimulate the expansion of U.S. exports. Major programs include export counseling and assistance.

Through ITA a U.S. business can tap into a worldwide network of:

- Trade specialists who can provide export counseling on a variety of products and industries.
- Country specialists versed in international economic policies and specific markets.
- Industry specialists who help develop trade promotion programs.
- Import trade specialists who can advise domestic industries with regard to unfair trade practices.

The ITA's U.S. Commercial Service can access a network of some 2,500 trade experts located in 67 countries, 68 U.S. cities, and Commerce Headquarters in Washington, D.C. This network covers 95% of the global markets for U.S. goods and services.

The following services are available through your U.S. Commercial Service offices. These services are not free: They range from $35 for the National Trade DataBank discs to $500 to $4,000 per country for the Customized Market Analysis.

- Developing export expertise:
  - —The *Export Qualifier Program* helps firms evaluate their readiness to export through a computerized diagnostic questionnaire.
- Identifying target markets:
  - —The *National Trade DataBank* includes over 100,000 trade-related documents, product-specific market research reports, and trade statistics. Information is collected by 17 agencies, updated monthly, and issued on two CD-ROM disks.

—The *Customized Market Analysis* can assess the competitiveness of your product in a specific market. It involves intensive custom research involving product-specific interviews or surveys. Although potentially useful, this service may be cost prohibitive for small businesses.

- Finding potential partners:

—The *Agent/Distributor Service* can help you locate up to six foreign representatives who, after looking at your product literature, may be interested in marketing your product.

—*International Company Profile* will help you evaluate potential partners overseas, in terms of reliability, creditworthiness, and standing in the local business community.

—*Commercial News USA* is a catalog of new U.S. products and services sent to 110,000 potential overseas buyers, agents, and distributors.

—The *International Buyer Program* brings delegations of overseas buyers from around the world to your exhibit at participating U.S. trade shows.

—The *Trade Opportunities Program* identifies timely sales leads overseas and provides them to U.S. business.

—*Catalog and video/catalog exhibitions* are organized every year for certain industries in selected markets. The Department of Commerce shows U.S. exporter catalogs and videos to potential agents, distributors, and other buyers in each market. Participating exporters often receive up to 50 leads from each exhibition.

—*Trade mission/trade shows* organized with state, local, or private groups help U.S. companies that have representatives visiting their targeted overseas export market to introduce and market their products there.

—*Matchmaker delegations* are introductory missions for firms entering export markets. The Matchmaker program visits more than 15 countries each year. Matchmaker organizers evaluate a product's potential for a market and make introductions to potential buyers or licensees. This program is also for entrepreneurs who are visiting their export market.

—The *Gold Key Service* provides the following services to U.S. businesspeople who are visiting their export market:

Market orientation briefings.

Specialized market research.

Introductions to potential partners.

Interpreter for meetings.

All services are organized by commercial officers located at overseas posts. Typically this service costs $500 per day for in-country time. You need to notify the commercial officer at least six weeks in advance of your arrival.

The Department of Commerce's Bureau of Export Administration issues licenses for the shipment of controlled exports, especially in the areas of computers, electronics, communications, and biotechnology.

Export Financial Assistance

The SBA offers two types of export loan guarantees that protect the lender from default by the exporter. Both must be collateralized with U.S.-based assets. The SBA guaranteed 343 export related loans for $128 million made by commercial lenders in fiscal year 1995.

Export working capital loan guarantees
These are short-term loan guarantees available to small businesses based in the U.S. that are at least one year old. Loans provide working capital to acquire inventory, pay for direct manufacturing costs, to purchase goods and services for export, or to support standby letters of credit. The SBA can guarantee up to 75% (80% if total loan is $100,000 or less). An Export Working Capital loan guarantee may be combined with an International Trade loan guarantee. Loan maturities match a single transaction cycle or generally one year.

International trade loan guarantees
These are guaranteed loans through private lenders that help U.S.-based facilities that engage in international trade or are recovering from the effects of import competition. The maximum guaranteed loan is a combined $1.25 million for fixed assets such as facilities and equipment and working capital. Proceeds may not be used for debt refinancing. The SBA's guarantee may not exceed 75% (80% if total loan is $100,000 or less) of the loan. Loan maturities are up to 25 years for facilities and equipment and up to three years for working capital. The proceeds from the loans may be used for the purposes specified by the 7(a) loan program (see earlier section).

The Export-Import Bank of the United States (Ex-Im Bank)
Ex-Im Bank has three export finance programs of interest to small businesses: working capital guarantees, export credit insurance, and guarantees and loans extended to finance the sale of U.S. goods and services abroad. In the last five years, over 6,000 companies were assisted in their export activities by Ex-Im Bank, over 37% of these were small businesses. Ex-Im transactions benefiting small businesses in 1995 totaled $2.4 billion. This was 80% of all Ex-Im Bank transactions for that year.

Working capital guarantees

This Ex-Im Bank program is very similar to the SBA's Export Working Capital loan guarantees (see page 261). The guarantees cover loans to provide working capital to acquire inventory or pay for direct manufacturing costs, to purchase goods and services for export, or to support standing letters of credit. Guarantees may be for a single transaction or a revolving line of credit. Terms are generally for 12 months and are renewable. Companies need to be based in the United States and in business for at least one year to be eligible for this program. Unlike the SBA, Ex-Im Bank does not require the business to meet the SBA definition of a small business. Ex-Im Bank will guarantee 90% of the loan amount and sets no limit on loan size.

Export credit insurance

Ex-Im Bank offers a variety of insurance policies to protect U.S. exporters from foreign buyers default on payment because of commercial or political risks. One program, geared for the small exporter, offers a short term (up to 180 days) policy that covers 95% of commercial risks and 100% of political risk. The exporter is required to insure all export credit sales, not just specific sales. The program is open to businesses that have an average annual export credit sales volume of less than three million dollars in the previous two years and meet the SBA definition of a small business.

Direct loans and guarantees

Ex-Im Bank provides direct loans and guarantees of commercial financing to foreign buyers of U.S. capital goods and related services. The loans and guarantees cover up to 85% of the U.S. export value, with repayment terms of one year or more. However, there are very few direct loans or guarantees provided each year.

The Overseas Private Investment Corporation (OPIC)

In general, OPIC encourages U.S. business to invest in developing countries and newly emerging democracies and free market economies. OPIC offers a number of programs to insure U.S. investment against political violence, expropriation, and currency risks. It also provides medium- to long-term financing through direct loans and loan guarantees for new investments, privatizations, and expansions and modernizations of existing plants by U.S. investors. If investors contribute additional capital for modernization and expansion, acquisitions of existing operations are also eligible.

Direct loans, generally from two to $10 million, are earmarked for projects significantly involving small businesses or cooperatives. Loan guarantees are generally for loans above $10 million. In 1996, there were 140 countries or areas on the OPIC program list.

Where to Find International Trade Assistance

For your district SBA office and SCORE, look in the Blue Pages, under the U.S. Government listing headed "U.S. Small Business Administration," or call the toll-free hotline at 800-8-ASK-SBA.
Web address: http://www.sba.gov

The Department of Commerce's 800-USA-TRAD is a clearinghouse of international trade sources. For the hearing impaired, the TDD number is 800-TDD-TRAD.
Web address: http://www.doc.gov

You can find Department of Commerce industry and country desk officers at

U.S. Department of Commerce
International Trade Administration
14th and Constitution Avenue, N.W.
Washington, DC 20230
(202) 482-2867

Contact the Export-Import Bank of the United States at
811 Vermont Avenue, N.W.
Washington, DC 20571
(202) 565-3946
Export Hotline: (800) 565-EXIM
Web address: http://www.exim.gov

Contact the Overseas Private Investment Corporation at
1615 M Street, N.W.
Washington, DC 20527
(202) 336-8799

EXTERNAL ASSISTANCE FOR SPECIAL GROUPS, LOCATIONS, AND INDUSTRIES

Business Assistance Programs for Women

According to the SBA, between 1987 and 1992 the number of businesses, excluding 518,000 C corporations, owned by women increased 44%, to more than 5.9 million. Sales for these businesses increased 131% to $643 billion. The SBA estimates that by the year 2000, more than 40% of all businesses will be owned by women.

Despite this explosive growth, few special support programs are aimed solely at women. This has fueled a debate about whether women need special programs or whether they are better served by accessing business assistance programs aimed at the general population.

All SBA offices have a staff member designated as a Women's Business Ownership Representative, whose duty it is to discuss resources that are available for women and to provide assistance for accessing those resources. A program available in nearly all 50 states, designated the *Women's Network for Entrepreneurial Training (WNET),* provides mentoring for small business owners. The mentoring program matches a successful woman business owner with at least five years experience to a woman business owner who has been in business for at least one year and has shown potential for growing her business. The mentoring relationship is for one year.

Another program for women, called the *Demonstration Projects,* has established centers for potential or current women business owners in a number of states. The centers offer counseling and training in management, marketing, and finance. Although open to all women, the program was developed for women who might not normally use services provided through traditional channels.

Where to Find SBA Help for Women

For your district SBA office, look in the Blue Pages, under the U.S. Government listing headed "U.S. Small Business Administration." Or call the 24-hour SBA answer desk at 800-8-ASK-SBA for your district SBA office. Speak to a Women's Business Ownership Representative. For the hearing-impaired, the TDD number is (703) 344-6640.

Assistance Programs for Minority-Owned Businesses

Recent statistics on business ownership from the Bureau of the Census show the changing face of small business in America. (See Exhibit 9.2.) Although the number of minority-owned small businesses in America is still a small percent-

EXHIBIT 9.2   Growth in minority-owned business, 1987–1992.

	1987	1992	Increase (%)
African-American owned	424,000	621,000	46%
Hispanic owned	422,000	772,000	83
Asian, Pacific Islander, Native owned	377,000	606,000	61

age of the total business population, approximately 2 million of 17.3 million in 1992, the growth rate in minority-owned businesses far exceeds that of non-minority-owned businesses. The overall growth rate for minority-owned business was 63 percent between 1987 and 1992 compared to non-minority-owned at 23 percent.

The Minority Business Development Agency (MBDA), an agency of the U.S. Department of Commerce, is the only federal agency specifically created to establish policies and programs to develop the U.S. minority business community. The MBDA sponsors a network of approximately 50 *Minority and Indian Business Development Centers* (MBDCs/IBDCs), located throughout the country in areas with the largest minority populations.

Each center develops and maintains a listing of existing minority-owned firms for inclusion in the agency's *Automated Business Enterprise Locator System* (ABELS). The ABELS system is used by government and private industry purchasing officials to identify minority vendors qualified to supply the goods and services they need. To qualify for ABELS, you must certify that your firm is a nonretail business that:

- Is at least 51% owned, controlled, and actively managed by minority persons.
- Can provide products or services to other businesses, private organizations, and government agencies.

The centers cannot make or underwrite loans because the MBDA has no loan-making authority. MBDCs/IBDCs do engage in business development counseling for a fee. The fee ranges from $10.00 to $60.00 per hour depending upon the gross sales of the business (see Exhibit 9.3). Services typically offered include loan packaging, business planning, marketing, and financial analysis.

The maximum federal funding of each MBDC/IBDC represents not more than 85% of the total cost of the project. Each center is expected to provide the other 15% through private sources of support.

(Other minority assistance programs are discussed in the section on procurement.)

EXHIBIT 9.3   MBDC/IBDC fees.

Gross sales	Cost per hour
< $100,000	$10.00
$100,000 to $299,999	20.00
$300,000 to $999,999	30.00
$1,000,000 to $2,999,999	40.00
$3,000,000 to $4,999,999	50.00
$5,000,000+	60.00

Where to Find the MBDA

The U.S. Department of Commerce
Minority Business Development Agency
14th and Constitution Avenue, N.W.
Room 5053
Washington, DC 20230

To locate the nearest MBDA office, call (202) 482-1936. A recorded message will provide the address and telephone number of a regional MBDA office.

Business Assistance Programs for Veterans

The SBA has a special mission to help veterans get into business and stay in business. In each local SBA office, there is a staff person designated the *Veterans Affairs Officer,* specially trained to guide the veteran seeking business assistance. In addition to SBA Resource Partners' normal business development counseling and training courses (which veterans are welcome to attend), the SBA and its resource partners at times conduct special business training conferences for veterans.

For example, during the Persian Gulf war, SCORE set up workshops to teach businesspeople called up by the Reserves how to cope with sudden and long absences from their businesses. SCORE members also mentored family members and others chosen to manage businesses during the reserves' absences.

Where to Find SBA Help for Veterans

For your district SBA office, look in the Blue Pages, under the U.S. Government listing headed "U.S. Small Business Administration." Or call the 24-hour SBA answer desk at 800-8-ASK-SBA for your district SBA office. Speak to the Veterans Affairs Officer. For the hearing-impaired, the TDD number is (703) 344-6640.
Web address: http://www.sba.gov

Business Assistance for Rural and Agricultural Entrepreneurs

Before describing programs for this group, it should be pointed out that rural is not synonymous with *agricultural.* Not all rural entrepreneurs are engaged in the traditional rural occupation of agriculture. Consider different potential sources of assistance based on your location *and* your line of business. For example, the U.S. Department of Agriculture offers programs that provide management and technical assistance, guaranteed and other loans, and grants and cooperative agreements in areas not limited to traditional agricultural enterprises.

The Agricultural Extension Service

This is the outreach arm of the Department of Agriculture. Although the Agricultural Extension Service has agents in all land-grant universities and nearly all the nation's 3,150 counties, services of interest to businesses vary dramatically by location. It sometimes provides management and marketing assistance to rural businesses, including agricultural and natural-resource-based enterprises, manufacturers, retail businesses, and service businesses. The services are aimed at increasing the profitability and growth of existing businesses, as well as identifying neglected market segments.

How to Find the Cooperative Extension Service

To find what services are available in your area, look under the Blue Pages (U.S. Government) for "U.S. Department of Agriculture" or the Blue Pages (County) for "County Extension Office."

The U.S. Department of Agriculture's Rural Business-Cooperative Service (RBS) Business and Industry Guaranteed Loan Program

This program offers loan guarantees similar to the SBA's for businesses located outside any city with a population of 50,000 or more and its immediately adjacent urbanized area with population density of no more than 100 persons per square mile. Most loans are made in towns with populations of 25,000 or less. Funds can be used for working capital; equipment purchases; improvement, construction, or acquisition of fixed assets (including land and buildings); and, in some cases, debt refinancing.

The maximum loan amount is $10 million, and the average is slightly over $1 million. A minimum of 10% of total capital is required in the form of equity for existing businesses (20% to 25% for startups). The terms are up to 30 years for land and building, 15 years for machinery and equipment, and 7 years for working capital. RBS loan guarantees do not require that you prove your inability to get credit without the guarantee. Interest rates may be fixed or variable and are at competitive banking rates.

The RBS Intermediary Relending Program

This program makes loans to nonprofit organizations, which in turn lend funds to small businesses in their service area. The nonprofit organization may provide up to 75% of each project's cost up to $150,000. The RBS has the following requirements:

- Projects must create new jobs or retain old jobs.
- Funds must be used in rural areas including cities with 25,000 or fewer people.
- Applicants must have been turned down by at least two other sources before applying for this program.

Funds may be used to start a new business or expand an existing one. The interest rate to the nonprofits is 1% for up to 30 years. The nonprofits charge interest at a rate to cover their operating costs, typically around 7% to 9%.

The Alternative Agricultural Research and Commercialization Corporation (AARC)

This program of the Department of Agriculture provides cooperative agreements for the development of nonfood, nonfeed products made from agricultural, animal byproducts, and forestry materials (for example, starches and carbohydrates, fats and oils, fibers, forest materials, animal products, and other plant materials). The cooperative agreements are to fund precommercial development activities such as:

- Identifying viable market needs.
- Designing equipment.
- Scaling up prototypes to commercial scale.
- Obtaining regulatory clearances.
- Conducting precommercial runs.

Private firms, individuals, public or private educational or research organizations, federal agencies, cooperatives, nonprofits, or combinations of the above are eligible to receive funding. Funding is on a competitive basis. In four years of operation, the program has invested $28 million in 66 projects in 32 states. In FY 1996, $6.5 million was available for distribution.

Selection of projects to be funded is based on the likelihood that the projects will result in commercially viable products or processes. Some examples of proposals submitted are:

- Attic insulation from low-grade cotton fibers.
- Biodiesel fuel from waste fat collected by restaurants.
- Ethanol from cellulose material in straw, cornhulls, and grasses.

The program requires matching funds from program recipients. Although the match percentage is not specified, the program requires that AARC funding not exceed two-thirds of the total cost of the project. The AARC requires royalty charges or takes equity positions in the companies it funds.

For More Information

Alternative Agricultural Research and Commercialization Corporation
1400 Independence Avenue, S.W.
Room 0156
Stop 0401
Washington, DC 20250
(202) 690-1633
Web address: http://www.usda.gov/aarc

How to Find Help for Rural and Agricultural Entrepreneurs

Look under the Blue Pages (U.S. Government) for "U.S. Department of Agriculture" or the Blue Pages (County) for "County Extension Office."

Business Assistance for Urban Entrepreneurs

The U.S. Department of Housing and Urban Development (HUD) offers a *Community Development Block Grant (CDBG) Entitlement Program* that awards grants annually to entitled metropolitan cities and urban counties. Cities designated as central cities of metropolitan statistical areas (MSAs), other cities with populations of at least 50,000, and qualified counties with populations of at least 200,000 (excluding the population-entitled cities) are eligible to receive grants. The amount of grants for each community is determined by a formula using several measures of community need, such as the poverty level.

Communities receiving grants are free to develop programs that meet local needs in housing, public works, economic development, public services, acquisition, clearance or redevelopment of real property, or administration and planning concerning urban needs, as long as the activities meet the national objectives of the program. The national objectives are to benefit low- and moderate-income persons, to prevent or eliminate slums or blight, or to meet other urgent community needs. Some communities establish revolving loan pools that may be accessed by startups and small businesses.

Total funds budgeted for the program in fiscal year 1997 were $4.9 billion; however, only about 10% of these funds will probably be used for economic development projects, and an even smaller percentage of funds will directly benefit for-profit businesses.

Where to Find HUD

Businesses should contact their city or county planners to determine whether a CDBG revolving loan pool exists or could be started for funding their projects. City or county planners should contact HUD (look in the Blue Pages under U.S. Government) for more information.

Business Assistance for Entrepreneurs in Distressed Areas

The U.S. Department of Commerce, through its Economic Development Administration (EDA), aims to decrease unemployment and underemployment in economically distressed areas.

For More Information

Businesses should contact their city or county planners to determine whether a Title IX revolving loan pool exists or could be started for funding their projects. City or county planners should contact EDA for more information.

U.S. Department of Commerce
Economic Adjustment Program
Hoover Building, Room 7327
14th and Constitution Avenue, N.W.
Washington, DC 20230
(202) 482-2659

The Economic Adjustment (Title IX) Program (EAP) provides funds to communities that have suffered from long-term economic decline (chronic distress) or from a sudden and severe event, such as a hurricane or plant closing, that has undermined the economic stability of the community. In either case, to be eligible for Title IX funding, the community must demonstrate very high unemployment or very low per capita income. The EAP funding to the community must be used for planning or implementing economic rebuilding.

Some communities have chosen, as part of their rebuilding efforts, to establish revolving loan pools. The funds are then available for targeted small business startups and expansions, business and job retention projects, and the redevelopment of blighted land and vacant facilities.

Engineering and Technical Assistance

According to the SBA, U.S. small businesses in the twentieth century have invented the airplane, the aerosol can, double-knit fabric, the heart valve, the optical scanner, the pacemaker, the personal computer, the soft contact lens, and the zipper. Although building a better mousetrap may not automatically trigger a stampede to your door, technological innovation is a valuable competitive advantage. Recognizing this, a variety of federal initiatives have promoted technological innovation. Unfortunately, these federal technological assistance programs are highly fragmented, the result of many different initiatives over many years.

The federal government provides both business development programs and financial assistance programs. Development programs for technologically oriented businesses include the following:

- Small Business Development Centers.
- National Innovation Workshops.
- Manufacturing Extension Partnership Program.
- The Federal Laboratory Consortium for Technology Transfer.
- NASA Regional Technology Transfer Centers.
- National Technology Transfer Center.
- The National Technical Information Service.
- Federal Research in Progress Database.

Financial assistance programs for technologically oriented businesses include:

- The Small Business Innovation Research Program.
- The Small Business Technology Transfer Program.
- The Advanced Technology Program.

All of these programs are discussed in detail in the following sections.

- Energy Related Inventions Program.
- Innovative Concept Program.

Small Business Development Centers (SBDCs)

SBDCs provide technical services to startups and small businesses. These services provide assistance in product licensing or small business formation based on new product development. Several SBDCs around the nation provide innovation assessments designed to determine a new product idea's potential for commercialization.

More than 80% of SBDCs provide assistance to small businesses in developing Small Business Innovation Research proposals (discussed in the next section). All SBDCs provide links to federal, state, and local sources of technology and technical information.

National Innovation Workshops

The Departments of Energy and Commerce, in partnership with SBDCs, sponsor six to seven innovation workshops each year around the country. The two-day workshops are targeted at inventors and technology-based businesses. The workshops provide information on:

- The availability of federal R&D funding through Small Business Innovation Research and other programs at the federal or state level.
- Technical assistance available through federal laboratories.
- Federal and state sources of technical information.

  They also provide more generic business assistance information.

For More Information

To find the times and places of the next National Innovation Workshops, contact:

The Association of Small Business Development Centers (ASBDC)
1300 Chain Bridge Road, Suite 201
McLean, VA 22101-3967
(703) 448-6124

Manufacturing Extension Partnership

The Department of Commerce and the National Institute of Science and Technology (NIST) fund regional Manufacturing Technology Centers to help small and mid-sized manufacturers compete in the global market place. The Centers encourage the adoption of modern technologies and business practices that result in greater productivity, efficiency, and profitability.

In 1996, there were 60 manufacturing extension centers located in 42 states and Puerto Rico. Each center is a partnership with federal, state and local governments, industry, and educational institutions.

Services vary depending upon the local client base and regional needs. In general, centers provide in-depth assessments of manufacturing and technology needs, assistance in selecting appropriate technologies and processes, and plans for integrating these technologies into company operations. Manufacturing extension centers have a variety of software useful to manufacturers, including computer-aided design (CAD), computer-aided manufacturing (CAM), computer-aided assessment and bench marking tools, as well as PC based hardware systems.

Since 1989 more than 44,000 firms have received assistance ranging from factory floor layout to invoice-handling procedures.

For More Information

Manufacturing Extension Partnership
National Institute of Standards and Technology
Building 301, Room C100
Gaithersburg, MA 20899
(301) 975-5020
Web address: http://www.mep.nist.gov

The Federal Laboratory Consortium for Technology Transfer (FLC)

Federal research and development laboratories received approximately $25 billion in fiscal year 1995 (which was about 38% of total federal R&D investment for that year). Federal laboratories may enter into agreements with individuals or companies to conduct cooperative research. The U.S. government also holds thousands of patents available for licensing. The key to entrepreneurial success may be deciding how to access these resources given the number of federal laboratories and the complexity of their technological resources.

Many individual federal laboratories, such as Los Alamos and Sandia, have outreach programs to help small and medium-sized manufacturers. These programs are subject to annual budget reauthorizations, but they are part of a trend to increase the laboratories' budgets to provide enhanced outreach services. This trend recognizes the need for technology transfer to the private sector from the large number of federal laboratories that are potential sources of technology. Consortium members include all major federal R&D laboratories and their parent organizations, comprising some 500 laboratories belonging to 17 federal departments and agencies.

The FLC provides access for entrepreneurs and small businesses to technology, top-notch scientists and engineers for problem solving, and state-of-the-art laboratory equipment and facilities. FLC members devote approximately 5% of their total laboratory budget to transferring technology out of the laboratories.

For More Information

Federal Laboratory Consortium
P.O. Box 545
Sequim, WA 98382
(360) 683-1005
Web address: http://www.zyn.com./flc/

A request for assistance flows from the entrepreneur or small business person to an FLC regional coordinator to a laboratory representative, and then to the actual technologist who can solve the problem or supply the resource. There is no cost for any of the services.

NASA Regional Technology Transfer Centers (RTTCs)

The RTTC mission is to transfer and assist in the commercialization of NASA and other federal technology. RTTC consultants assist in the identification, evaluation, acquisition, and adaptation of technology to meet specific business needs.

The six RTTCs, which are linked to the NASA field centers, are affiliated with 60 universities and other not-for-profit organizations. They provide access to approximately one million documents in the NASA data bank and to more than 400 other computerized databases. The databases include selected contents for some 15,000 scientific and technical journals.

For More Information

To contact your RTTC, call 800-472-6785.

National Technology Transfer Center (NTTC)

The NTTC helps businesses access NASA and other federal technology resources by matching specific needs of the business with the appropriate NASA or federal resource. The NTTC will search NASA and federal databases and will expedite communication with NASA or federal laboratory experts who may assist with solutions. The NTTC works closely with the Federal Lab Consortium, the NASA Regional Technology Transfer Centers, and other organizations interested in technology transfer for commercialization purposes.

The NTTC also operates a national electronic bulletin board service for the public and private sectors. The free service includes announcement of new technologies, answering of questions on technical problems, and notices of technology transfer conferences and meetings. The bulletin board also includes a number of searchable databases.

For More Information

To contact NTTC, call 800-678-NTTC.
Web address: http://www.nttc.edu

The National Technical Information Service (NTIS)

This is an agency of the U.S. Department of Commerce. NTIS is a national and international information system for technical, engineering, and business-related information. NTIS serves as the central source for federally generated computerized data files, databases, and software. The on-line database system is accessible by modem.

For More Information

Call the National Technical Information Service at (703) 487-4650.
Web address: http://www.ntis.gov

Federal Research in Progress Database (FEDRIP)

FEDRIP is a program of the Department of Commerce. The database contains summaries of U.S. government-funded research projects.

For More Information on FEDRIP

On-line access for a fee can be obtained by calling:

Knight-Ridder Information Inc.
Dialog Online Service
2440 El Camino Real
Mountain View, CA 94040-1400
800-334-2564

Knowledge Express
1235 Westlakes Drive
Suite 210
Berwyn, PA 19312
800-529-5337

In 1996 it included over 160,000 preliminary, ongoing, or final project reports. Each FEDRIP entry includes title, principal investigator, performing and sponsoring organization, detailed abstract, project objectives, and sometimes intermediate findings and funding amount. The summaries provide up-to-date research progress in specific technical areas before technical reports or journal articles are published. Updates to the database are done monthly.

The Small Business Innovation Research (SBIR) Program

Many high-technology companies started up with a government research and development (R&D) contract. If your company has the ability to do technological research and development, you should consider applying to the SBIR program.

The SBIR program is a multiagency federal research and development program coordinated through, but not managed by, the SBA. The SBIR program began in 1982 with the enactment of the Small Business Innovation Development Act. The act required agencies of the federal government with budgets for externally contracted R&D in excess of $100 million to establish SBIR programs. Funding for the program is derived from a fixed percentage of each agency's R&D budget. Under the SBIR program, federal agencies set aside 2.0% in fiscal year 1996 (2.5% after fiscal year 1996) of certain research and development funds for use by small firms.

The SBIR program aims to fund scientifically sound research proposals that will, if successful, have "significant public benefit." SBIR's threefold objectives are:

- To increase small firm participation in federal R&D.
- To foster commercial applications from applied federal research.
- To encourage innovation for public benefit.

The SBIR program involves a competitive three-phase award system that provides qualified small business concerns with opportunities to propose innovative studies that meet the specific R&D needs of the various agencies of the federal government:

- Phase 1: SBIR awardees receive up to $100,000 to evaluate the scientific merit and technical feasibility of an idea. The period of performance normally does not exceed six months. Only Phase 1 awardees are eligible for consideration in Phase 2.
- Phase 2: Awardees receive up to $750,000 to develop prototypes, finalize products, and further expand on the research results of Phase 1. The period of performance normally does not exceed two years.
- Phase 3: Firms try to commercialize the results of Phase 2. Despite its classification as Phase 3, this stage requires the use of private or non-SBIR federal funding. No SBIR funds are utilized in Phase 3. However, Phase 3 may involve production contracts with a federal agency for future use by the federal government.

From the start of the SBIR program in 1982 through fiscal year 1994, the participating federal agencies almost made 33,000 competitive awards totaling $4.6 billion to qualified small business concerns. Many firms of 10 or fewer employees have won funding for their proposals. In fiscal year 1994 small business concerns successfully competed for approximately 3,100 Phase 1 awards and 1,000 Phase 2 awards under the SBIR program worth $717 million. Fiscal year 1995 awards were expected to total $900 million, FY 1996 were expected to be over $1.1 billion.

The end of the Cold War and the associated reduction in defense spending has implications for the SBIR program, especially for the Department of Defense SBIR awards. The Office of Technology Assessment has suggested that the SBIR program may be especially useful to small defense companies in the conversion process to dual-use (military and civilian) manufacturing capability.

In 1996 there were 11 federal agencies that participated in the SBIR program:

Department of Agriculture.

Department of Commerce.

Department of Defense.

Department of Education.

Department of Energy.

Department of Health and Human Services.

Department of Transportation.

Environmental Protection Agency.

National Aeronautics and Space Administration.

National Science Foundation.

Nuclear Regulatory Commission.

SBIR proposals should be 25 pages or less and should follow the specified agency format. Proposals should demonstrate:

- A hypothesis that rests on sufficient evidence.
- Clear use of technical information.
- Familiarity with recent literature or methods.
- Adequate experience or training.
- A realistic proposed effort.
- Technological innovation.
- Good potential commercial application.

Awards have covered a broad range of scientific research, from human habitability and biology in space to airborne datalink cockpit management, and from neural-network-based speech identification to aquacultures.

To be eligible to compete, a business concern must be for profit, at least 51% owned and controlled by individuals who are citizens of, or lawfully admitted permanent residents of, the United States, and, including affiliates, may not have more than 500 employees. The principal researcher for the project must be employed by the business.

The Small Business Technology Transfer (STTR) Program

The STTR program is a relatively new effort of the federal government that encourages innovation by fostering partnership between small businesses and nonprofit research institutions. It is similar to the SBIR program in that it is coordinated through but not managed by the SBA. Five federal agencies are required by STTR to set aside a portion of their R&D budget for awards to small business/nonprofit research institution partnerships. Participating agencies are the Department of Defense, Department of Energy, Health and Human Services, National Aeronautics and Space Administration, and National Science Foundation.

How to Apply for an SBIR or STTR Award

Although the SBA sponsors various SBIR/STTR conferences and seminars in every state, the agency does not distribute copies of SBIR or STTR solicitations. The participating federal agencies responsible for generating SBIR and STTR topics and conferring awards release their own solicitation announcements. However, the SBA collects solicitation information from participating agencies and publishes it quarterly in its electronic Pre-Solicitation Announcement (PSA). PSAs provide the following information:

- The research topics of current interest to each participating agency.
- The opening and closing dates of each solicitation.
- Whom to contact for a copy of the agency solicitation.

For more information contact

U.S. Small Business Administration
Office of Technology
409 Third Street, S.W.
Washington, DC 20416
(202) 205-6450
Web address: http://www.sba.gov

Technical abstracts of past SBIR awards are available through an on-line service of the U.S. Department of Commerce National Technical Information Service (NTIS) known as the Federal Research in Progress (FEDRIP) database (described earlier in this chapter). FEDRIP is also accessible through DIALOG or Knowledge Express, the private information services. About 16,500 projects are currently listed in this database.

Information on each past SBIR project typically includes:

- Company name, address, and telephone number.
- Sponsoring federal agency.
- Funding awarded for Phase 1 and Phase 2.
- A 200-word abstract describing the technical work.
- Commercialization potential.

Free copies of the FEDRIP Search Guide (PR-847) are available by calling (703) 487-4650. For information on the DIALOG Online Service, call 800-3-DIALOG; on Knowledge Express, call 800-529-5337.

The STTR, like the SBIR program, involves a competitive three-phase award system.

- Phase 1: STTR awardees receive up to $100,000 for the exploration of the scientific, technical, and commercial feasibility of an idea or technology. The period of performance is approximately one year. Only Phase 1 awardees are eligible for Phase 2 awards.
- Phase 2: Awardees receive up to $500,000 to expand R&D results and commercial potential. The period of performance is a maximum of two years.
- Phase 3: Firms try to commercialize the results from Phase 2. No STTR funds are available for Phase 3, however awardees may pursue other federal agency funding.

To be eligible for STTR funding, the business must be for-profit, at least 51% owned and controlled by individuals who are citizens of, or lawfully admitted permanent residents of, the United States, and including affiliates, may not have more than 500 employees. The non-profit research institution must be located in the United States. The principal researcher, unlike the SBIR program, does not have to be an employee of the business. Since 1994, federal agencies have issued 436 Phase 1 STTR awards for $40.5 million and 22 Phase 2 awards for $10.7 million.

The Advanced Technology Program (ATP)

The Department of Commerce and the National Institute of Standards and Technology also make awards to businesses or to industry-led joint ventures of businesses, universities, federal laboratories, and nonprofit independent research organizations. These awards are for innovative research and development of cutting-edge, generic technologies that have the potential to improve U.S. economic growth and productivity. Generic technologies underlie a wide range of potential applications for a broad range of products or processes. The technologies can be from any scientific area.

Past awards have ranged from ceramics to metal processing, from optical data storage systems to tissue engineering. The awards support the development of laboratory prototypes and proof of technical feasibility, not commercial prototypes, proof of commercial feasibility, or product development.

Awards to individual firms are limited to $2 million over three years to cover direct R&D costs. Awards to joint ventures are for five years, and the dollar amounts are limited only by available funding. However, NIST funding to joint ventures is capped at less than 50% of total R&D costs. Support for the ATP program has increased over time from a 1990 appropriation of $10 million to an appropriation of $221 million in 1996.

How to Find ATP

Proposals must be submitted to specifically dated solicitations. To get your name on the mailing list for solicitation announcements contact:

Advanced Technology Program
A430 Administration Building
National Institute of Standards and Technology
Gaithersburg, MD 20899
(301) 975-2636

To reach the ATP Hotline for the latest program update call (301) 975-2273.
Web address: http://www.atp.nist.gov

The awards are based on business and technical merit and the potential benefit to U.S. industry. They are highly competitive. Only 280 awards have been made from 2,210 proposals as of early 1996. However, 46% of awards went to small businesses or joint ventures led by small businesses. In addition small businesses make up a significant percentage of membership in ATP joint ventures led by large businesses.

Energy Related Inventions Program (ERIP)

This joint program of the Department of Energy (DOE) and National Institute of Standards and Technology (NIST) was started to assist individuals and small company investors develop nonnuclear energy technologies. NIST evaluates the inventors disclosures. Evaluations are based on technical feasibility, energy conservation or supply potential, and commercial possibilities. Inventions that pass the NIST screen are forwarded to DOE for possible financial support. It is a highly competitive program. For every 1,000 applications received, 20 (2%) are recommended for funding by NIST, and only 16 (1.6%) are funded. Average grant awards are under $100,000. To submit an energy-related invention, ask for an Evaluation Request Form 1019 by writing to:

Office of Technology Innovation and Assessment
National Institute of Standards and Technology
Building 820, Room 264
Gaithersburg, MD 20899-0001
(301) 975-5500
Web address: http://www.nist.gov/techeval

Innovative Concepts (Inn Con) Program

This DOE program provides seed money to individuals, small companies, and university researchers to allow them to determine if their ideas are technically and economically feasible. It also provides linkages to potential technical or commercial partners and other possible funding sources. Inn Con chooses an energy-related topic and solicits proposals for funding in 1 to 2 year cycles. Up to 15 projects per cycle are awarded seed money in the $15,000 to $20,000 range. To add your name to the mailing list for proposal solicitation announcements contact:

> U.S. Department of Energy
> Inventions and Innovations Program
> Forrestal Building EE24
> 1000 Independence Ave., S.W.
> Washington, DC 20585
> (202) 586-1478

EXTERNAL ASSISTANCE AVAILABLE PRIMARILY TO STATE AND LOCAL RESIDENTS

State Resources

State, local, and regional development agencies imitate, support, and expand federal efforts to help startups and small businesses. Like the federal agencies, their services target business development, startup and small business financing, procurement, and international trade. Their clients include women, minorities, entrepreneurial ventures in rural or depressed areas, and technologically oriented startups.

Your first stop should be your *state department of commerce,* a useful starting place for finding other resources, such as those national programs described in this chapter, and other state, regional, and local-sponsored management assistance and financial support programs. This management and technical assistance may range from business planning to licensing, helping firms locate capital, and finding state and federal procurement opportunities. They typically offer state certification programs for businesses owned by minorities and women.

Local Resources

Chambers of Commerce

These are city-based groupings of local businesses that often provide assistance for firms wishing to relocate or start operations in the city. Chambers often provide information packages on local regulations and taxes. They also work closely with economic development organizations to lobby the city government for more favorable business conditions. They have traditionally provided a setting for business leaders, including entrepreneurs, to network and discuss common problems.

Incubators

These organizations nurture several fledgling firms that share services and equipment and occupy building space at a reduced rate. Nationwide there are about 540 incubators, with an average of one added each week. Businesses starting out in incubators have an 80% success rate, which is higher than the average startup success rate. In addition to low-cost shelter and services, one of the biggest benefits provided by incubators is the support and counsel provided by a network of business assistant professionals.

Where to Find Incubators

National Business Incubation Association
20 E. Circle Dr., Suite 190
Athens, OH 45701
(614) 593-4331

University Libraries

Although they have no direct charter to assist startups, many university business libraries, particularly those at public universities, are dedicated to serving the information needs of business. They offer reasonably priced information services, including:

- Photocopies or book loans.
- Government publications.
- Company reports—annual or 10K.
- Scientific or technical information.
- Business management information.
- Market or product studies.
- Reviews of computer hardware or software.
- Tax or legal information searches.
- Patent and trademark searches.

- Technical standards and specifications.
- Consumer profiles and census data.
- Corporate financial information.
- Mailing labels.
- Other search help.

Public Libraries

The business sections of city-funded public libraries also provide useful resources.

10 LEGAL AND TAX ISSUES

Richard P. Mandel

Tony and Jennifer had both worked for the same manufacturer of computer disk drives since their college graduations some five years ago. Their employer manufactured and sold a variety of drives that were powered by the company's own proprietary software. These products sold fairly well, but the company regularly received complaints regarding the slow response time of these drives relative to the computers to which they were linked.

Tony worked in sales at the company and was acutely aware of these complaints. He had often spoken about this problem with Jennifer, who was employed in engineering. After considering the problem for some time, Jennifer was convinced she could solve the problem through new software that could be loaded into these or any company's drives by the end-user.

One night, after work, the two budding entrepreneurs decided to establish their own company to develop and sell this software. Jennifer estimated it would take her six months to develop and perfect the software, and Tony thought he could develop significant sales volume within eight months after that. Tony was additionally convinced he could obtain enough money from his wealthy Uncle Max to keep them going until then. However, they both recognized that when it became time to market and distribute their product on a large scale, they would probably need both bank and investor financing. Furthermore, although the two of them could probably perform all necessary tasks in the short run, they expected that additional programmers, sales

285

professionals, and packing and shipping personnel would be necessary in the long run. Both of them knew of fellow employees who would be perfect for these positions. Excited about their plans, Jennifer and Tony prepared to submit their resignations.

This chapter covers legal issues that an entrepreneur must consider before leaving a position to start a new venture (for example, whether the new firm can legally compete with the former company). The chapter then discusses issues that need to be resolved before initiation of the new venture, including how to choose the legal form of the business (such as a corporation or partnership), how to name the business, and how to avoid potential tax pitfalls related to the initial founders' investment (such as how to negotiate stockholder agreements and handle the disposition of stock). The legal and tax issues involved in hiring employees is covered, as are insurance considerations and tax issues related to financing the venture.

LEGAL ISSUES INVOLVED IN LEAVING A POSITION

Enthusiastic entrepreneurs may be so excited about where they are going that they forget to consider where they have been. Many are surprised to learn that serious limitations arising out of their former employment may be imposed upon their freedom of action. Some of these limitations may be the result of agreements the entrepreneur signed while in the former position. Others may be imposed as a matter of law, without any agreement or even knowledge on the part of the employee.

The Corporate Opportunity Doctrine

The corporate opportunity doctrine is an outgrowth of the traditional obligation of loyalty owed by an agent to a principal. In its most common form, *it prohibits an officer or director of a corporation, a partner in a partnership, or a person in a similar position from identifying a business opportunity that would be valuable to his company and using that information for his own benefit or the benefit of a competitor.*

Thus, a corporate director who discovers that one of the corporation's competitors may shortly be put on the market cannot raise money and purchase the competitive company himself. To discharge his legal obligation to the corporation of which he is a director, he would be required to disclose the opportunity to his board and allow the board to decide (without his participation) whether the corporation will make the purchase. Only after the corporation has been fully informed and has decided not to take advantage of the opportunity may the director use that information for himself. Even then, as the new owner of a competitor, he would be required to resign from his former corporation's board.

The scope of this *duty of loyalty* is normally adjusted by the law to reflect the individual's position within the business. Although the president and members of the board may be required to turn over knowledge of all opportunities that may be in any way related to the business of the company, lower-level employees probably have such an obligation only with regard to opportunities that are directly relevant to their positions. Thus, arguably, a sales manager may be required to inform her company of any sales opportunities she may encounter that are relevant to the company's products. She may not be required to inform the company of a potential business acquisition.

Tony and Jennifer must consider the corporate opportunity doctrine because the opportunity to create a product that more quickly drives the devices made by their employer is directly relevant at least to Jennifer's job. Yet both Jennifer and Tony probably have positions low enough in the company hierarchy that their obligations in this regard are very limited. In addition, the slow pace of the company's disk drives and the fact that such a problem might be solved by more sophisticated software appears to be well known by the company's officers, who have shown little interest in the software side of the business.

Recruitment of Employees from the Former Employer

As Jennifer and Tony delved more deeply into their dreams, they began to identify certain fellow employees who might wish to join their company sometime down the road. This, too, can in some circumstances be problematic.

Another aspect of the duty of loyalty owed by an employee to an employer is the legal requirement that *the employee cannot knowingly take action designed to harm the employer's business.* This is, perhaps, pure common sense. After all, the employee is collecting a paycheck to perform tasks that advance the employer's interests. We would not expect the law to countenance a paid salesperson's regularly recommending that customers patronize a competitor, nor would we expect the law to endorse an engineer's giving his best ideas to another company. Similarly, courts have held that it is a breach of the duty of loyalty to solicit and induce fellow employees to leave their jobs.

Once again, the likelihood that a court would enforce this obligation depends to some extent on the nature of the employee's activities and her position in the company. Neither Tony nor Jennifer need fear reprisals for their having convinced each other to leave. Nor would there be much likelihood of liability if they convinced another employee to leave with them, especially if these conversations took place after working hours.

However, if either Tony or Jennifer worked in the human resources department, where their job descriptions would include recruiting and retention of employees, this activity might well expose them to liability. Furthermore, if their plan included the wholesale resignations of a relatively large number of employees, *such that the company's ability to continue to function efficiently might be compromised,* a court would be more likely to intervene with injunctive or other relief. This is especially true if the defendants' job descriptions included maintaining the efficient operation of the departments they were involved in destroying.

Use of Proprietary Information

Another potential complication involves Tony and Jennifer's use of information or technology belonging to their former employer. Such information need not be subject to formal patent or copyright protection to be protected. *Any valuable information that the company has successfully kept confidential, and that is not otherwise known to outsiders, is likely to be protected by law as a trade secret.* Such information may include inventions and technology, but it may also include such other valuable information as customer lists, pricing strategies, and unique operating methods.

In this case, if Jennifer had developed the software concept that solves the speed problem as part of her job, that concept might well belong to the company and be unavailable to Jennifer and Tony for their new enterprise. Of course, it is not enough for the concept to be developed by or for the company; the concept must be unique and unknown to software engineers outside the company, and the company must have taken steps to keep it that way.

Thus, the company should label any physical manifestations of the information as "confidential" and should restrict its distribution to those who have either a legal or contractual obligation to keep such information private. If, on the other hand, the company had deliberately or carelessly allowed the distribution of the information to outsiders, it has likely lost the right to restrict its use.

Many companies require employees to sign agreements that spell out the employees' obligation to protect trade secrets. This has led some employees to believe that such an obligation applies only to those who have signed such an agreement. This is a misconception. *The obligation to respect an employer's trade secrets and keep them confidential is imposed by law and is not dependent upon contract.* Furthermore, that obligation continues after the employment relationship has been terminated, for whatever reason, and continues indefinitely until the information makes its way into the public domain.

Employers who require a confidentiality agreement from their employees are generally not misinformed about the general applicability of the law but are simply making sure that the employees are aware of their responsibilities in this regard. After all, if an employee, under a mistaken belief about his rights, releases proprietary information to outsiders, it is small comfort to the employer to have the right to sue the employee for damages.

Fortunately for Jennifer and Tony, they appear to have merely identified a need that is known generally to the industry; they have not begun to develop the specific software solution to the problem. On that set of facts, it is extremely doubtful that their new enterprise will make use of any information that legally belongs to their former employer.

Protecting Proprietary Information in the New Business Venture

By the time Jennifer and Tony have developed a product that meets the identified need, they will have created a body of proprietary information of their own. At that point they will be forced to consider the variety of means at their disposal to protect that information from use by competitors and end-users who have failed to pay for the privilege.

A measure of protection is available from the copyright laws and, depending upon the nature of their product, from a patent. Both of these options require disclosure of the information in exchange for the protection granted by the government; thus, they present the risk that others may engineer around the patent or reconfigure the software around the copyright. In such a case, Tony and Jennifer would be unlikely to have resources adequate to bring the necessary lawsuits to protect their rights.

Thus, they may choose to forgo statutory protection and protect their asset by a policy of nondisclosure as a trade secret, accompanied by very tight licensing agreements with customers. Further discussion of these issues and of the relative advantages and risks of these various modes of intellectual property protection is contained in Chapter 11.

Noncompetition Obligations to the Former Employer

Related to the obligation not to disclose proprietary information is *the obligation not to compete with one's employer.* Like most of the obligations discussed already, this is derived from the fiduciary relationship between employer and employee, specifically, the duty of loyalty. How can an entrepreneur justify accepting a paycheck from her employer when she is simultaneously establishing, working for, or financing a competing business?

The law imposes this duty not to compete upon all employees, officers, directors, partners, and so on, while their association with the employer remains in effect. Unlike the obligation to protect proprietary information, however, this obligation does not extend to the period after termination of the relationship. Extension of this obligation requires the contractual promise of the employee. Thus, in the absence of a contract, as soon as Tony and Jennifer quit their present jobs (but not before), they are free to go into direct competition with their former employer, so long as they do not make use of any of the employer's proprietary information.

Noncompetition agreements can be analyzed using many different measurements. To begin with, the scope of the obligation must be examined. In an extreme case, an employee may have agreed not to engage in any activity that competes with any aspect of the business his former employer engaged in, or planned to engage in, at the time of the termination of the employee's association with the company. At the other end of the spectrum, the employee may have agreed only to refrain from soliciting any of the former employer's customers or (somewhat more restrictively) from dealing with any of them no matter who initiated the contact. Such agreements also may be measured based on the length of time they extend beyond the termination of employment and by the size of the geographic area they cover.

Such measurements are important because, in the employment context, many states take the position that such agreements contravene basic public policies, such as encouraging competition and allowing each individual to make the best use of her talents. A few such states actually refuse to enforce all such noncompetition agreements. Most, however, purport to enforce only those agreements that are deemed reasonable under the circumstances. Thus, these public policies are balanced against the employer's recognized interest in protecting its business and goodwill. Only those restrictions which are limited to the extent necessary to prevent harm to the employer's legitimate interests will be enforced.

For example, a medical practice that does business only with customers located within a 25-mile radius would probably not be able to enforce a noncompetition agreement that extends much beyond that geographic area. Furthermore, although a manufacturer may be able to enforce such an agreement against an officer, salesperson, or engineer who has either direct contact with customers or knowledge of the company's processes and products, it might not be able to enforce the same agreement against a bookkeeper, whose departure would have little effect upon the company's goodwill. Even the officer, salesperson, or engineer might be able to resist an agreement that purports to remain in effect beyond the time the employer might reasonably need to protect its goodwill and business from the effects of new competition.

Another factor that may affect the enforceability of a noncompetition agreement is whether the employer agrees to continue part or all of the former employee's compensation during the noncompetition period. In addition, a noncompetition agreement that might be unenforceable against an employee might nonetheless be enforceable against the seller of a business or a major stockholder having his stock redeemed. Finally, employers in some states can take comfort in the fact that some courts that find the scope or length of a noncompetition agreement objectionable, nonetheless enforce the agreement to the maximum extent they deem acceptable. Others take an all-or-nothing approach.

Since in Tony and Jennifer's case there is no indication that they have signed a noncompetition agreement, they need only resign from their current positions before taking any affirmative steps to establish their new enterprise. After resigning, they are under no further noncompetition restrictions.

CHOOSING AN ATTORNEY AND ACCOUNTANT

There is a natural reluctance to incur what are perceived to be unnecessary expenses in beginning a new venture, and many people perceive engaging an attorney and accountant as just such expenses. However, as may already be evident from the discussion so far, the earlier these professionals can be consulted, the more likely the business will be to avoid costly mistakes. One is tempted to repeat the old cliche "either pay me now or pay me later," the latter alternative being much more costly.

Choose a Lawyer Who Is Experienced in Small Business Startups

The choice of an appropriate attorney is complicated by the fact that American law does not officially recognize legal specialties. Thus, in virtually all states, there is only one form of licensing, and, once licensed, an attorney can practice in all areas of the law. In practice, however, the American legal profession has become highly specialized, with many attorneys confining their practices to one or two areas of expertise. Thus, most patent attorneys do very little else, and most good litigation attorneys concentrate on litigating. Few very good corporate attorneys know their way around a courtroom. Just as these legal areas are practiced mainly by specialists, the representation of startups and small businesses is becoming a specialty as well.

Tony and Jennifer would do well to ask their prospective attorney to describe her experience in representing small businesses. The local generalist may not be sufficiently aware of the many technical matters identified in this chapter (and elsewhere in this book). Also, an attorney experienced in the problems of startups will be familiar with the unique cash-flow problems of such ventures. A business's need for legal services may never be so great in comparison with its ability to pay than at the outset. The attorney may be willing to work out installment payments or other arrangements to avoid postponing essential early planning.

Unfortunately, many attorneys practicing in this area have adopted a policy of accepting equity in the new business as part of the fee arrangement. Interestingly, many such attorneys do not lower their fee in exchange for equity but justify taking equity as the price of accepting the risk that their fee may not be paid if the business does not succeed. Such an arrangement may lead to dangerous conflicts of interest in the future, when legal advice affects the value of the company's stock. For example, how can an entrepreneur be confident of an attorney's advice regarding the suitability of the company for a public offering when such an offering would have the effect of creating a market for the same attorney's stock? Tony and Jennifer may wish to avoid such an arrangement.

Choose a Small, Local Accounting Firm

Many of the same considerations inform the choice of an accountant. Although the level of expertise in the national and international firms is unmatched, most of them have little experience with startups such as that proposed by Tony and Jennifer, since their fee structures are inappropriate for the size of such businesses. Many local firms have all the skills necessary to serve the startup and can be sensitive to the cash-flow issues mentioned earlier.

It is important to engage the accountant as early as possible so he can establish the information management systems and recommend the computer software that will get the company's records off on the right foot. This gives the entrepreneur the tools necessary to gauge the success of her efforts against her budget before it is too late to adapt, and it prevents the expensive and frustrating task of reconstructing the company's results from fragmented and missing records at the end of the year.

CHOOSING THE LEGAL FORM OF YOUR BUSINESS

Business Forms

One of the first issues Jennifer, Tony, and their attorney will confront, after weaving their way through the thicket of issues associated with leaving their current jobs, is what legal form they should choose for their new venture. Many choices are available.

The Sole Proprietorship

The most basic business form (and the one that will apply unless an individual entrepreneur chooses otherwise) is the sole proprietorship. This is a business owned and operated by one individual, who is in total control. No new legal entity is created; the individual entrepreneur just goes into business, either alone or with employees, but without any co-owners. This is the simplest of entities but one that will not be attractive to Jennifer and Tony unless one of them chooses to forgo ownership and act only as an employee.

The Partnership

The default mode for Tony and Jennifer is the partnership. This is the legal form that results when two or more persons go into business for profit, as co-owners, sharing profits and losses. Since Tony and Jennifer clearly contemplate sharing ownership and control, they will find themselves in a partnership unless they choose otherwise.

A Corporation

Another choice available to our subjects is the corporation. This form is created by state government, as a routine matter, upon the entrepreneur's filing an application and paying a fee. It is a separate entity, with legal existence apart from its owners, the stockholders. Jennifer and Tony might well choose to form a corporation, dividing its stock between them.

The Subchapter S Corporation

A variation of the corporate option is the so-called subchapter S, or small business, corporation. If a corporation passes a number of tests, it may elect to be treated as such. However, it is essential to understand that such election affects only the tax status of the corporation. In all other respects, a subchapter S corporation is indistinguishable from a standard corporation. For reasons discussed later in this chapter, Jennifer and Tony may also find this business form attractive.

The Professional Corporation and Limited Liability Partnership

The professional corporation is another variation of the corporate form. This choice is typically available only to businesspeople who intend to render professional services, such as medical or legal practitioners, accountants, architects, and social workers. It was created primarily to allow these professionals to take advantage of certain tax opportunities available only to corporations, without granting them the limited liability afforded to normal business corporations.

Over time, however, many of the tax advantages formerly available only to corporations have been extended to sole proprietorships and partnerships, and some of the limited liability formerly associated with business corporations has been extended to professional corporations. Thus, the differences between these forms have narrowed considerably. In addition, many states now allow groups who have practiced as partnerships to obtain limited liability by registering as limited liability partnerships. In any case, Tony and Jennifer will not be practicing a profession, so these business forms will not be attractive to them.

The Limited Liability Company

Over the last decade, virtually all states have enacted legislation enabling businesses to be conducted as *limited liability companies*. These entities are owned by "members," who either manage the business themselves or appoint "managers" to run it for them. All members and managers have the benefit of limited liability (as they would in a corporation) and, in most cases, are taxed in the same way as a subchapter S corporation without having to conform to the S corporation restrictions described below.

The Limited Partnership

Another possible legal form is a hybrid of the corporate and partnership forms known as the limited partnership. Such a business has one or more general partners (who conduct the business) and one or more limited partners (who act as passive investors, similar to stockholders with no other interest in the business). Because both Tony and Jennifer intend to be actively involved in the business, neither would qualify as a limited partner. But Uncle Max may well qualify if he is willing to fade into the background once he has made his investment.

The Nonprofit Entity

A summary of available business forms should not omit the nonprofit entity. Typically, such a business will take the form of a corporation or trust and will elect nonprofit status as a tax matter. Although many startups do not make a profit, nonprofit (or, more accurately, *not-for-profit*) status is available only to certain types of entities, such as churches, educational institutions, social welfare organizations, and industry associations. If an organization so qualifies, its income is exempt from taxation (as long as it doesn't stray from its exempt purpose), and if certain additional tests are met, contributions to it may be tax-deductible. However, since Tony and Jennifer do not intend to operate a qualifying business, they need not explore this option.

Choosing the Form

Faced with all these choices, the budding entrepreneur will want to compare these various business forms on a number of parameters relevant to the needs of his business. Both the attorney and accountant for the business can be extremely helpful at this juncture.

Although these forms may be compared on the basis of an almost endless list of factors, those normally most relevant include control issues, exposure to personal liability, tax factors, and administrative costs. These issues are discussed in detail in the following sections, and Exhibit 10.1 provides an overview of the issues and how they affect each business form.

Control Issues

The *sole proprietorship* is the simplest and most direct with regard to the subject of control. Since there is only one principal in the business, this individual wields total control over all issues. However, that option is not available to Tony and Jennifer.

The simplest option available to them is the *partnership*. In that form, control is divided among the principals in accordance with their partnership agreement. Although a written agreement is normally not legally required, this issue and many of the others that arise in a partnership argue for a written agreement to encourage specificity. The parties may decide that all decisions must be made by unanimous vote, or they may adopt a majority standard

EXHIBIT 10.1   Comparison of various business forms.

	Control	Liability	Taxation	Administrative obligations
Sole proprietorship	Owner has complete control	Unlimited personal liability	Not a separate taxable entity	Only those generic to businesses
Partnership	Partners share control	Joint and several unlimited personal liability	Not a separate taxable entity	Only those generic to businesses
Corporation	Control distributed among shareholders, directors, and officers	Limited personal liability	Separate taxable entity unless subchapter S election	Some additional
Limited partnership	General partners control, limited partners do not	General partners: joint and several unlimited personal liability, limited partners: limited personal liability	Not a separate entity	Some additional
Limited liability company	Members share control or appoint managers	Limited personal liability	Not a separate entity if properly structured	Some additional

(making Uncle Max the swing vote). More likely, they may require unanimity for a stated group of significant decisions and may allow a majority vote for others. In addition, Jennifer and Tony may delegate authority for certain types of decisions to one or both of the active partners.

Regardless of how this power is allocated in the partnership agreement, however, third parties are allowed to rely on the authority of any partner to bind the partnership to contracts relevant to the ordinary course of the partnership's business. Thus, no matter what may have been agreed among them, Uncle Max will have a free hand with third parties, subject only to the consequences of his breaching his agreement with the others. This is also true for the consequences of torts committed by any partner acting in the course of partnership business. The looseness of this arrangement may well be enough to discourage Jennifer and Tony from choosing the partnership option.

A *corporation*, whether professional or business, and regardless of whether it has elected subchapter S status, is controlled by three levels of authority. Broadly speaking, the stockholders vote, in proportion to the number of shares owned, on the election of the board of directors, sale or dissolution of the business, and amendments to the corporation's charter. In virtually all cases, these decisions are made either by the majority or by two-thirds of the shares. Thus, if Tony, Jennifer, and Uncle Max each owned one-third of the issued stock, Tony and Jennifer (if they voted together) could elect the entire board and sell the business over the objections of Uncle Max. Uncle Max would not even be entitled to a minority position on the board. He would, however, be the swing vote should Jennifer and Tony ever disagree, perhaps prompting them to consider nonvoting stock or some similar device for him.

The board of directors, in turn, makes all the long-term and significant policy decisions for the business, as well as electing the officers of the corporation. Votes are virtually always decided by majority. The officers, consisting of a president, treasurer, and secretary at minimum, run the day-to-day business of the corporation and, as such, are the only level of authority that can bind the corporation by contract or in tort.

In this case, one would expect either Tony or Jennifer to be president and the other, perhaps, to be executive vice president and treasurer. Other commonly used titles are chief executive officer, chief operating officer, and vice president of finance. It is not uncommon for the corporation's attorney to act as secretary, since the attorney presumably has the expertise necessary to keep the corporate records of the company in an accurate manner. We might also expect that Tony and Jennifer would convince Uncle Max not to insist upon a title, thus eliminating his power to deal with third parties on the corporation's behalf.

The limited liability company can be operated much like a general partnership. All members can share in control to the extent set forth in a members agreement. However, most states allow the members of a limited liability company to appoint one or more "managers" (usually, but not necessarily members) to control most of the day-to-day operations of the business. In the case of Jennifer, Tony, and Uncle Max, we might expect the three members to appoint Jennifer and Tony as managers to avoid giving Uncle Max the authority to deal with outsiders on behalf of the business.

The *limited partnership* concentrates all control in the general partners, who exercise that control as set forth in the limited partnership agreement (just as such control is allocated in a partnership agreement). Limited partners have virtually no control, unless the limited partnership agreement has granted them some influence over very significant issues such as sale of the business or dissolution. Only the general partners have the apparent authority to bind the partnership in contract or tort with third parties. Since the limited partnership is required to file the names of its general partners with the state, third parties are deemed to know that limited partners (whose names do not appear) cannot have such authority.

Based upon control issues alone, therefore, Tony and Jennifer would likely be leaning away from a general partnership and toward the limited partnership, limited liability company, or corporation. Their decision will, however, be greatly affected by considerations of personal liability.

Personal Liability Issues

If the business should ever incur current liabilities beyond its ability to pay, must the individual owners make up the difference? If so, this could easily result in personal bankruptcy for the owners on top of the loss of their business. And this unhappy result need not occur as a result of poor management or bad business conditions. It could just as easily be brought about by an uninsured tort claim from a buyer of the product or a victim of a delivery person's careless driving.

For both the *partnership,* and the *sole proprietorship,* the business is not recognized as a legal entity separate from its owners. Thus, the debts of the business are ultimately the debts of the owners if the business cannot pay. This unlimited liability is enough to recommend avoidance of these forms for virtually any business, with the possible exception of the one-person consulting firm, for which all liability will be the direct result of the wrongdoing of its owner in any case.

If this unlimited liability is uncomfortable for Jennifer and Tony, imagine what it means to Uncle Max, who apparently has significant assets to lose and who will likely be excluded from meaningful control over the business. This is made even worse by the fact that all partnership liabilities are considered joint and several obligations of all partners. Thus, Uncle Max will be responsible for full payment of all partnership liabilities if Tony and Jennifer have no significant assets of their own.

Uncle Max can gain solace from the fact that in trading away his influence over the operation of the business in a *limited partnership,* he is granted limited liability for its debts. Thus, if the limited partnership cannot meet its obligations, Uncle Max will lose his investment, but his personal assets will not be exposed to partnership creditors except to the extent that he made promises of future investment.

However, the limited partnership does not afford this protection to the general partners. They retain unlimited exposure. Tony and Jennifer may believe they can afford to take this risk, especially if they have no significant assets. Yet even if that is so today, it may not be the case at the time liability is incurred.

The solution to all this lies in the *corporation* and the *limited liability company*, both of which afford limited liability to all owners. None of the three participants in our enterprise would have personal liability for its debts. If the business ultimately becomes insolvent, its creditors will look only to business assets for payment and will absorb any shortfall.

Of course, this solution is not quite as simple as it sounds. To begin with, creditors know these rules as well as the entrepreneurs. Thus, large or sophisticated creditors, such as banks and other financial institutions, will insist upon personal guarantees from the owners before extending credit. In addition, the law has developed a number of theories that allow creditors of corporations to "pierce the corporate veil" and go after the stockholders of a failed corporation under certain conditions. Although it is still early in the history of limited liability companies, it is reasonable to assume that courts will adopt similar theories applicable to them. Generally, these theories fall into one of two categories.

The first of these covers businesses that were initially underfunded, or "thinly capitalized." A business should start out with a combination of capital and liability insurance adequate to cover the claims to which it might normally expect to be exposed. As long as the capital was there at the outset and has not been depleted by dividends or other distributions to stockholders, the protection of the separate entity survives, even after the capital has been depleted by unsuccessful operation.

The second situation that may result in the piercing of the separate entity is the failure of the owners to treat the corporation or limited liability company as an entity separate from themselves. This may be manifest by the entrepreneurs acting in one or more of the following ways:

- Failing to use "Inc.," "Corp.," "LLC," or a similar legal indicator when dealing with third parties.
- Commingling business and personal assets in a personal bank account or allowing personal use of business assets.
- Failing to keep business and legal records and to hold regular directors, stockholders, or member meetings.

After all, why should creditors be required to respect the difference between the business and its owners when the owners themselves have not?

Assuming, however, that Tony and Jennifer will avoid conduct that would expose them to such personal liability, both the corporate and limited liability company forms should look rather attractive to them. No significant business decision should be made, however, without a look at the tax consequences.

Taxation Issues

Once again, the business form that is simplest to understand in regard to taxation is the *sole proprietorship.* The financial results of the business are calculated, and the profit or loss appears on the tax return of the sole owner. He can eliminate much of the profit by taking it out of the business as salary, but that has no tax effect, as it simply increases taxable wages by the exact amount that it lowers profit. The tax rate applied to any profit would be the maximum marginal rate to which the taxpayer is exposed by the combination of this profit and his other taxable income. If there is a loss, the results of the business act as a sort of tax shelter by offsetting an equal amount of the owner's other taxable income, if any.

As one might expect, the *partnership* acts in a manner very similar to that of the sole proprietorship. Since a partnership is not recognized as a separate taxable entity, it pays no taxes itself (although in many cases it is required to file an informational return). Its profit or loss is reported by its partners. The only complication is allocating the percentage of this profit or loss to be reported by each partner. This is normally determined by the allocations of profit and loss set forth in the partnership agreement by the partners themselves, so long as that allocation reflects a "substantial economic reality."

The *limited partnership* is taxed in exactly the same way as the partnership, with profit and loss allocated among *all* partners, both general and limited, in accordance with the limited partnership agreement. Since the business contemplated by Jennifer and Tony is likely to lose money at the outset, the tax-sheltering aspects of both the partnership and limited partnership may be attractive to Uncle Max, who surely has other sources of income he would like to shelter.

Of the two, the limited partnership would be preferable, since by accepting limited partner status, Uncle Max can have his shelter without being exposed to personal liability. He may be tempted to request that the agreement allocate 99% of the losses to him, since he likely needs the shelter more than Jennifer and Tony do. However, unless he is contributing 99% of the capital and will receive a similar percentage of profit (both operating and capital gain), such an allocation might fail the "substantial economic reality" test.

A further obstacle to Uncle Max's taking advantage of the possible tax shelter of early losses is presented by the recently enacted passive loss rules. Simply stated, if Uncle Max is not actively involved in the business (which would, by definition, be the case if he were a limited partner), any losses

distributable to him from the business could be used to offset income generated only by other passive activities (such as investments in other limited partnerships). The losses could not shelter income from salaries, interest, or
dividends from traditional portfolio investments.

Were the business to be organized as a *corporation,* Tony and Jennifer
would doubtless be warned about the bugaboo of "double taxation." This fear
results from the fact that a corporation is recognized as a separate legal entity
for tax purposes, and it thus pays a separate corporate level of income tax. Double taxation arises when the corporation makes a profit, pays tax on it, and distributes the remainder to its stockholders as a dividend. The stockholders must
then pay income tax on the dividend, resulting in double taxation of the same
money.

The same would be true if the corporation paid tax on its profit and then
retained the remainder for operations. When the corporation was eventually
sold, the increased value caused by that retention of earnings would be taxed to
the selling stockholders as a capital gain.

In reality, however, double taxation is more a myth to the small business
than a legitimate fear. In fact, in most cases, it presents an opportunity for significant economic savings. To begin with, most small corporations reduce or
even eliminate profit by increasing salaries and bonuses for their owners. This
can be done up to the point where the compensation of these individuals is
deemed unreasonable by the Internal Revenue Service. If profit is eliminated
in this way, the owners will have removed their money from the corporation
and will pay only their own individual income tax on it.

On the other hand, if it is necessary to retain some of these earnings, the
corporation will pay income tax at a *lower* rate than the stockholders would
have, since tax will be imposed at the lowest marginal corporate rate, rather
than the stockholders' highest rate. When the corporation is later sold, the
stockholders will be taxed at favorable capital gain rates, and the corporation
will have had the use of the money in the meantime to create greater value.
Thus, it is the rare small corporation that will actually pay the much-feared
double tax.

Furthermore, if the corporation meets certain eligibility requirements, it
can elect (under subchapter S of the Internal Revenue Code) to be taxed essentially as if it were a partnership. Whatever profit or loss it generates will appear on the tax returns of the stockholders in proportion to the shares of stock
they own, and the corporation will file only an informational return. To take
advantage of this option, the corporation must have 75 or fewer stockholders,
all of whom are individuals and either resident aliens or citizens of the United
States. The corporation cannot have any subsidiaries, and it can have only one
class of stock.

The *subchapter S* election can be very useful in a number of circumstances. For example, if the business is expected to be profitable and Uncle Max insists on-a share of those profits, Tony and Jennifer could not avoid double taxation by increasing salaries and bonuses. Since Uncle Max performs no services for the business, any compensation paid to him would automatically be deemed unreasonable. But under subchapter S, since there is no corporate tax, a dividend to Uncle Max would only be taxed at his level.

If the business were to become extremely successful, Tony and Jennifer could reap the rewards without fear that their salaries might be attacked as unreasonable, since, again, there are no corporate compensation deductions to disallow. Furthermore, if the business is expecting losses in the short term, Uncle Max can use his share of the losses (determined by his percentage of stock) as a shelter (subject to the passive loss considerations described previously). Even Tony and Jennifer could use their losses against the salaries from their former jobs earlier in the year. An early subchapter S election can also avoid double tax should the corporation eventually sell all its assets and distribute the proceeds to the stockholders in liquidation.

In a perfect world, Tony, Jennifer, and Uncle Max could form a corporation, elect subchapter S treatment, and arrange their affairs such that Uncle Max could make as much use of short-term losses as could be supported by "economic reality" and the passive loss rules. However, since profits and losses in an S corporation must be allocated in accordance with stock ownership, and only one class of stock is allowed, any disproportionate allocation of losses to Uncle Max would be accompanied by a disproportionate allocation to him of corporate control and later profits. More creative allocations of profit, loss, and control could be accomplished in a general or limited partnership, but one or more of the parties would have to accept exposure to unlimited liability.

Limited liability companies were designed for just this circumstance. If structured carefully, they afford the limited liability and tax treatment of the S corporation, while avoiding the S corporation's restrictive eligibility requirements. Freed from these restrictions, limited liability companies can make use of creative allocations of profit and control which would constitute prohibited classifications of stock in the S corporation context. The only caveat to this analysis is the present policy of the Internal Revenue Service to subject to corporate tax companies which exhibit excessive centralization of management, free transferability of interests, and perpetual life. Although the IRS has recently indicated that it plans to abandon this policy, careful drafting of the members agreement will avoid this risk in any case.

It is likely, then, that Jennifer and Tony would favor the limited liability company for the conduct of their business. Such an entity would shield them from personal liability, and, as managers, allow them to exercise control free from undue influence from Uncle Max. And, as long as the company is properly structured, Uncle Max can have the advantage of the maximum amount of short-term loss available under applicable tax rules. Only an undue administrative burden would seem to be sufficient to reverse this decision.

Administrative Obligations

Certain administrative obligations will be required no matter which business form Jennifer and Tony choose. For example, upon entering business, they should obtain a federal identification number for their business. This will facilitate interaction with the federal government, including the filing of tax returns (real or informational) and the withholding of income and payroll taxes.

On the state level, the business should obtain a sales and use tax registration number, to facilitate reporting and collection of such taxes and to qualify for exemption from such taxes when it purchases items for resale. A nonprofit entity has 18 months to file for and secure nonprofit status from the Internal Revenue Service. Furthermore, as described earlier, all business entities will incur a certain amount of additional accounting expense, specifically for the calculation and reporting of taxable profit and loss.

Corporations, limited liability companies, and limited partnerships, however, bring some additional administrative burden and expense. All three must file an annual report with the state government in addition to a tax return. This document usually reports only the business' current address, officers, directors, managers, general partners, and similar information, but it is accompanied by an annual maintenance fee. The fee, which is in addition to any minimum income tax that the state may levy, must be paid to avoid eventual involuntary dissolution by the state.

In addition, corporations are sometimes formed under the laws of one state while operating in another. In particular, the state of Delaware has acquired the reputation of having a corporate law that is particularly sympathetic to management in its dealings with stockholders. Although this is a questionable advantage in the context of a small business, many corporations nonetheless form in Delaware merely for the appearance of sophistication. In such cases, the corporation must pay initial fees and annual maintenance fees not only to the state of Delaware (or whichever state is chosen for formation) but also to each state in which it actually operates. Many large, national businesses pay these fees in virtually all 50 states.

Although Jennifer and Tony could avoid these fees by operating as a partnership, it is likely they will conclude that the advantages of the corporate or limited liability company forms are worth the price.

CHOOSING A NAME FOR THE BUSINESS

The choice of a name for a business may at first seem to be a matter of personal taste, without many legal ramifications. However, since a business's name is ultimately the repository of its goodwill, the entrepreneur must take care to choose a name that will not be confused with the name of another business. If she does not exercise such caution, the entrepreneur may discover sometime in the future that she has expended considerable money and effort enhancing the goodwill of another entity. Worse yet, she may be sued for infringement of another's rights.

Even apart from these concerns, an entrepreneur choosing to operate in the corporate, limited liability company, or limited partnership form must clear her choice of name with the state of organization. Although partnerships and sole proprietorships need not do so, corporations, LLC, and limited partnerships obtain their existence by filing charters with the state. As part of this process, each state will check to see if the name chosen by the potential new entity is "confusingly similar" to a name used by another entity currently registered with that state. This includes entities formed under that state's laws and foreign entities qualified to do business there. Some states will also deny the use of a name they deem misleading, even if it is not similar to the name of another entity.

Passing this test is far from sufficient for the protection of goodwill, however. The fact that no other entity is using your name in your state does not mean that others are not using it in other states. Furthermore, passing the corporate, LLC, or limited partnership name check doesn't guarantee that no one is using or will use your name for a partnership, sole proprietorship, or product name, in your state or elsewhere.

Fortunately, it is possible to discover whether your chosen name is being used by others and to protect it from later use. A number of companies have compiled databases that contain the names of a wide range of entities and products. Virtually all such services contain all corporate, LLC, and limited partnership names from all U.S. jurisdictions. Others add trade and service mark registrations from around the country. Most lawyers have access to a particularly comprehensive data base that includes the preceding lists as well as names from major trade directories, big-city telephone directories, and similar sources. Once a name has passed this test, you can be relatively sure that it is yours if you protect it.

A limited form of protection can be obtained relatively inexpensively by filing the name (and any associated logo or slogan) with the *state trademark registry* in any state in which you intend to use the name, logo, or slogan. If your business provides a service rather than sales of goods, the same protection can be provided by the state's *service mark registry.* The protection provided by these registries extends only throughout the state and will be preempted elsewhere by any federal registration existing or later obtained. Thus, at best, state registration is merely evidence of your prior use of a mark, resulting perhaps in a later federal registrant's being required to allow your continued use of the mark in a limited market area.

The most effective form of protection is a *federal registration.* Such a registration bars future use of the mark within the relevant class of goods or services anywhere in the United States by anyone who has not established rights through prior use. Since this protection is rather draconian, it is not granted without serious examination by the U.S. Patent Office. Registration can be denied, of course, if the name or mark is already in use by others. Protection can also be denied if the name is excessively generic, such that it describes all goods or services in a particular class instead of identifying the goods and services of a particular market participant. Thus, the name Disk Drive Software would likely be denied protection in the case of Jennifer and Tony's business. (Other legal doctrines relevant to trademark registration are described in Chapter 11.)

Once Jennifer and Tony have chosen a name for their business and product and have selected a level of protection with which they are comfortable, they can turn their attention to the initial funding of their enterprise.

POTENTIAL TAX PITFALLS RELATED TO THE INITIAL INVESTMENT OF THE FOUNDERS

Left to their own devices, Tony and Jennifer would likely arrange the issuance of their equity in the company for no tangible investment whatsoever. After all, they intend to look to Uncle Max for working capital in the short run, and their investment will be the services they intend to perform for the business in the future.

Historically, in the corporate form such a plan would have run afoul of some rather anachronistic corporate legal restraints that required consideration for stock issuances to take the form of present property or cash and to at least equal the par value of the stock issued. These requirements were based upon a theory of protection for corporate creditors, who could be assured that the corporation had assets at least equal to the aggregate par value of the shares of its stock that had previously been issued. Stock issued for less than par value was considered "watered stock" and exposed the holder and the directors issuing it to personal liability for the shortfall.

Much of the protection provided by these rules has been eroded over the years, however, by a number of developments. For example, it has long been commonplace to authorize stock with minimal par value (such as $0.01 per share) or even no par value at all. The corporation then issues stock for what it believes to be fair value without risk of failing to cover the aggregate par. In addition, it has long been possible to issue stock in exchange for intangible assets such as past services rendered. However, stock issuance for future services remains illegal under most corporate statutes, although many proposals have been made to legitimize it.

Of more practical concern than these corporate problems, however, is the fact that any property (including stock) transferred to an employee in exchange for services is considered *taxable income* under the Internal Revenue Code. Thus, even were it possible for Tony and Jennifer to be issued stock in exchange for future services under corporate law, they would face an unexpected tax liability as a result.

The solution to all this may be to require Tony and Jennifer to reach into their limited resources and contribute some minimal cash amount to the business in exchange for their ownership. This would avoid the corporate and tax problems associated with issuance for future services. However, as noted above, if their minimal investment was the full extent of the business' initial capitalization, the corporate veil might well be in danger.

Of course, Jennifer and Tony have no reason to fear exposure to personal liability since, at the same time they will be making their minimal investment, Uncle Max will be putting in the real money. Yet the participation of Uncle Max exposes Jennifer and Tony to a danger they may believe they have successfully avoided. Since Uncle Max will be paying substantially more for his equity than Jennifer and Tony are paying for theirs, the Internal Revenue Service will likely take the position that they are being afforded the opportunity for a bargain purchase in exchange for the services they are providing to their employer. Thus, once again, Tony and Jennifer may face an unexpected income tax on the difference between the price of Uncle Max's equity and the price of theirs.

One way to solve this problem is to postpone Uncle Max's investment until a time sufficiently remote from the date of Tony and Jennifer's investment that an argument can be made for an increase in the value of the equity. However, in addition to the essentially fictional nature of this approach, Jennifer and Tony cannot wait that long. To solve this problem, the parties must design a different vehicle for Uncle Max's investment.

In the corporate form, it may seem immediately advisable to create some sort of senior security for Uncle Max, such as *preferred stock* with a liquidation preference of approximately the amount he invested. A similar preferential position can be devised in an LLC. In fact, assuming for a moment that the initial plan was to split the equity equally among the parties, Uncle Max may well insist on such a security; otherwise, Tony and Jennifer could dissolve the business immediately after its formation and walk away with two-thirds of Uncle Max's investment. In addition to having a preference upon liquidation, Uncle Max might insist that he share in the company's growth, but this could be accommodated by allowing him to participate in profits remaining for distribution after dividend and liquidation preferences have been paid.

Demonstrating the sometimes frustrating interrelated character of tax and corporate law, however, is the fact that the issuance of preferred stock to Uncle Max would render the corporation ineligible for subchapter S status, because it would then have more than one class of stock. As discussed previously, the LLC is not bound by any such restriction.

Another solution could lie in the *utilization of debt securities*. If Uncle Max pays for his equity the same price per share as Jennifer and Tony paid, and if he injects the remainder of his investment in the form of a loan, his fellow owners will not face taxable compensation income, and the business will retain the opportunity to benefit from subchapter S, if desired.

Investment as debt also affords Uncle Max the potential for future nontaxable distributions from the company in the form of debt repayment, and he gains priority as a creditor should the company be forced to liquidate. All the while, he protects his participation in growth through his additional ownership of equity.

Of course, as with all benefits, it is possible to get too much of a good thing. Too high a percentage of debt may expose all the owners to the accusation of thin capitalization, resulting in the piercing of the corporate veil. And abusively high debt/equity ratios or failure to respect debt formalities and repayment schedules might induce the Internal Revenue Service to reclassify the debt as equity, thus imposing many of the adverse tax results described earlier.

NEGOTIATING STOCKHOLDER, MEMBER, AND PARTNERSHIP AGREEMENTS

The results of the negotiations among Jennifer, Tony, and Uncle Max regarding their respective investments would normally be memorialized in a stockholders' or members' agreement. In the unlikely event that this business were to be organized as a partnership or limited partnership, very similar provisions allocating equity interests and rights to distributions of profit and cash flow would appear in a partnership agreement. In each case, however, the parties would be well advised to go beyond these subjects and reach written agreement on a number of other potentially thorny issues at the outset of their relationship.

Negotiating Employment Terms

For example, Tony and Jennifer should reach agreement with Uncle Max as to the extent of their *commitment to provide services* and the *level of compensation* for doing so. It would be very unusual for persons in the position of Tony and Jennifer to forgo compensation solely to share the profits of the business with their investor. For one thing, what would they live on in the interim? For another, the profits of the business are properly conceived of as the amount left after payment of the costs of capital (interest on Uncle Max's note) and the expenses of the business (including reasonable compensation to its employees). Thus, Jennifer and Tony should negotiate *employment terms* into the agreement, setting forth their responsibilities, titles, compensation, and related issues.

This is especially important in this case, since each of the three owners holds only a minority interest in the business. Both Tony and Jennifer may wish to foreclose the possibility that Uncle Max may ally with one of them and employ a majority of the voting power to remove the other as a director, officer, manager, or employee of the company. Given the lack of any market for the equity of this company, such a move would essentially destroy any value the equity had for the holder in the short run.

Although a concise description of each party's obligations and rewards is still advisable to avoid dispute, the negative scenario just outlined would be illegal in a *partnership* (in the absence of serious misconduct by the party being removed) since the majority partners would be violating the fiduciary duty of loyalty of each partner toward the others imposed under partnership law. Although no such duty formally exists among stockholders in a *corporation,* many states have recently extended the fiduciary duties of partners to the relationship among founders of a closely held corporation. Similar doctrines may be expected in LLCs. Thus, in many states, were Jennifer to be removed without cause from her employment and corporate positions by Tony and Uncle Max, she would have effective legal recourse even in the absence of an agreement.

Negotiating Disposition of Equity Ownership Interests

As for other items that might be covered in the agreement among Jennifer, Tony, and Uncle Max, many such agreements address the disposition of equity held by the owners under certain circumstances.

Transfer to Third Parties

To begin with, it is probably not contemplated by any of these persons that their equity will be freely transferable, such that new "partners" may be imposed upon them by a selling stockholder or member. Although sale of equity in a closely held corporation or LLC is made rather difficult by federal and state securities regulation and the lack of any market for the shares, transfers are still possible under the correct circumstances. To avoid that possibility, stockholders' and members' agreements frequently require that any owner wishing to transfer equity to a third party must first offer it to the company or the other owners, who may purchase the equity, usually at the lower of a formula price or the amount being offered by the third party.

Disposition of Equity upon the Owner's Death

Stockholders' and members' agreements should also address the disposition of each party's equity in the event of death. Again, it is unlikely that each owner would be comfortable allowing the equity to fall into the hands of the deceased's spouse, children, or other heirs. Moreover, should the business succeed over time, each owner's equity may well be worth a significant amount at the time of death. If so, the Internal Revenue Service will wish to impose an estate tax based upon the equity's value, regardless of the fact that it is an illiquid asset. Under such circumstances, the deceased's estate may seek the assurance that some or all of such equity will be converted to cash so that the tax may be paid. If the agreement forbids free transfer of the equity during one's lifetime and requires that it be redeemed at death for a reasonable price, the agreement may well be accepted by the IRS as a binding determination of the equity's value, preventing an expensive and annoying valuation controversy.

Any redemption provision upon the death of the owner, especially one that is mandatory at the instance of the estate, immediately raises the question of the availability of funds. Just when the company may be reeling from the loss of one of its most valuable employees, it is expected to scrape together enough cash to buy out the deceased's ownership. To avoid this disastrous result, many of these arrangements are funded by insurance policies on the lives of the stockholders or members. This would be in addition to any key person insurance held by the company for the purpose of recovering from the effects of the loss. In structuring such an arrangement, however, the parties should be aware of two quite different models.

The first, and traditional, model is referred to as a *redemption agreement*. Under such an agreement, the company owns the life insurance policies and is obligated to purchase the owner's shares upon his death. The second model is referred to as a *cross-purchase agreement* and provides for each owner to own insurance on the others and to buy a proportional amount of the deceased's equity. Exhibit 10.2 illustrates the primary differences between the two agreements.

The second arrangement poses some serious mechanical problems, but it may be quite advantageous. To begin with, the cross-purchase agreement becomes quite complicated if there are more than a few owners or members,

EXHIBIT 10.2 Comparison of stock redemption agreement and stock cross-purchase agreement.

	Effect on tax basis	Effect on alternative minimum tax	Need for adequate corporate surplus
Redemption agreement	No stepped-up basis	Risks accumulated current earnings preference for corporations	Need adequate surplus
Cross-purchase agreement	Stepped-up basis	No effect	Surplus is irrelevant

since each owner must own and maintain a policy on each of the others. There must be a mechanism to ensure that all these policies are kept in force and that the proceeds are actually used for their intended purpose. Complicated escrow arrangements are often necessary to accomplish this. In addition, if the ages of the owners are materially different, some owners will be paying higher premiums than others. One might ignore this difference on the basis that those who pay most are most likely to benefit from this arrangement, since their insureds are likely to die sooner. An alternative is to equalize the impact of the premiums by adjusting the parties' compensation from the company.

If these complications can be overcome, however, the cross-purchase agreement provides some significant benefits over the redemption agreement. For example, if Uncle Max were to die and the company purchased his equity, Tony and Jennifer would each own 50% of the company, but their cost basis for a later sale would remain at the minimal consideration originally paid for their equity. In a cross-purchase arrangement, they would purchase Uncle Max's equity directly. This would still result in 50-50 ownership, but their cost basis for later sale would equal their original investment plus the amount of the insurance proceeds used to purchase Uncle Max's equity. Upon later sale of their equity, or the company as a whole, the capital gain tax would be significantly lowered.

Another benefit of the cross-purchase agreement is the fact that although the receipt of life insurance proceeds is exempt from income taxation, it can result in a *tax preference item* for a corporation not electing subchapter S treatment. This would expose the corporation to the alternative minimum tax. This tax preference item does not apply to individuals and is thus avoided by use of the cross-purchase model. It also does not apply to S corporations and LLCs.

Finally, the cross-purchase model eliminates the possibility that the corporation will not have sufficient surplus to fund a buyout upon the death of a stockholder. Similar restrictions would be imposed by an LLC's obligations to its creditors. It would be highly ironic if the deceased's life insurance merely funded an earnings deficit and could not be used to buy his equity.

Disposition of Equity upon Termination of Employment

Of course, stockholders' and members' agreements normally also address disposition of equity upon events other than death. Repurchase of equity upon termination of employment can be very important for both parties. The former employee, whose equity no longer represents an opportunity for employment, would like the opportunity to cash in the investment. The company and its other owners may resent the presence of an inactive owner, who can capitalize on their subsequent efforts. Thus, partnership, members', and stockholders' agreements normally provide for repurchase of the interest of a stockholder, member, or partner who is no longer actively employed by the company. This, of course, applies only to stockholders, members, or partners whose efforts on behalf of the company were the basis of their participation in the first place. Such provisions would not apply to Uncle Max, for example, since his participation was based entirely upon his investment.

This portion of the agreement presents a number of additional problems peculiar to the employee-owner. For example, the company cannot obtain insurance to cover an obligation to purchase equity upon termination of employment. Thus, it may encounter an obligation to purchase the equity at a time when its cash position cannot support such a purchase. Furthermore, in addition to the corporate requirement of adequate surplus, courts uniformly prohibit repurchases that would render the company insolvent. Common solutions to these problems involve committing the company to an installment purchase of the equity over a period of years (with appropriate interest and security) or committing the remaining owners to make the purchase personally if the company is unable to do so for any reason.

Furthermore, these agreements frequently impose penalties upon the premature withdrawal of a stockholder, member, or partner. In our example, Uncle Max is relying on the efforts of Tony and Jennifer in making his investment, and Tony and Jennifer are each relying on the other's efforts. Should either Tony or Jennifer be entitled to a buyout at full fair market value if he or she simply decides to walk away from the venture? Often, these agreements contain so-called *vesting provisions* that require a specified period of service before repurchase will be made at full value. For example, a vesting provision might state that unless Tony stays with the venture for a year, all his equity will be forfeited upon his departure. After a year, one-fifth of his equity will be repurchased for full value, but the rest will be forfeited. Another 20% will vest at the end of each ensuing year.

Such provisions, in addition to providing incentive to remain with the company, have complicated tax implications. As discussed earlier, if an employee receives equity for less than fair market value, the discount would be considered taxable compensation. The Internal Revenue Code provides that compensation income with regard to unvested equity is not taxed until the equity is vested. But at that time, the amount of income is measured by the difference between the price paid for the equity and its value *at the time of vesting*. The only way to avoid this result is to file an election to pay the tax on the compensation income measured at the time of the purchase of the equity, even though the equity is not then vested. For Tony and Jennifer, this provision acts as a trap. Although they have arranged the initial investments of the parties such that there is no compensation income at the time the equity is purchased, if it is not then fully vested, their taxable income will be measured at the end of each future year as portions of the equity vest. Thus, they must file the election to have their income measured at the time of purchase to avoid a tax disaster, even though there is then no income to measure. And that election must be filed within 30 days of their receipt of the equity, not at the end of the year, as they might think.

Some agreements go beyond vesting provisions and give incentive to the founders by imposing further penalties on owners who leave voluntarily or are terminated for cause. Thus, the agreement applicable to Jennifer and Tony might provide that vested equity be repurchased for full fair market value if they are terminated involuntarily (including as a result of disability or death) and for only half of fair market value if they leave for any other reason. Of course, involuntary termination without cause is a somewhat remote possibility due to the expansion of the concept of fiduciary loyalty mentioned earlier.

Negotiating Distributions of Company Profits

Stockholders', members', and partnership agreements may also include numerous other provisions peculiar to the facts and circumstances of the particular business. Thus, partnerships, LLCs, and subchapter S corporations often provide for mandatory distributions of profit to the partners, members, or stockholders, at least in the amount of the tax obligation each will incur as a result of the profits of the business. If Uncle Max had agreed to accept nonvoting equity, the agreement might include provisions to resolve deadlocks between Tony and Jennifer on significant issues; otherwise, the 50-50 split of voting power might paralyze the company. Various types of arbitration provisions might be employed to prevent this problem.

Negotiating Repurchase of Equity

Further, some agreements provide an investor like Uncle Max with the right to demand repurchase of his equity at some predetermined formula price at a designated future time, so that he will not be forever locked into a minority investment in a closely held company. Conversely, some agreements provide the company with the right to repurchase such equity at a predetermined price (usually involving a premium) should the capital no longer be needed. The presence or absence of these provisions depends, of course, on the relative negotiating strength of the parties.

LEGAL AND TAX ISSUES IN HIRING EMPLOYEES

From the beginning of this venture, Tony and Jennifer have known that if they are successful, they will have to hire employees for both the engineering and the marketing and sales functions. Thus, they should consider some of the issues raised by the presence of employees.

Obligations of Employees as Agents of the New Company

It should be understood that employees are agents of the company and as such are governed by many of the agency rules that define the relationships of partners to the partnership and officers to the corporation. Thus, employees have the previously described duty of loyalty to the company and obligations to respect confidentiality, to account for their activities, and not to compete.

Yet Jennifer and Tony are probably more interested in the potential of their employees to affect the business's relationships with third parties, such as customers and suppliers. Here the rules of agency require that a distinction be drawn between obligations based on contractual liability and those resulting from noncontractual relationships such as tort actions. Exhibit 10.3 provides an overview of these employee obligations.

Employees can bind their employers to contracts with third parties if such actions have either been expressly or implicitly authorized. Thus, if Tony and Jennifer hire a sales manager and inform him that he has the authority to close any sale up to $50,000, he may wield that authority without further consultation with his principals. He also has the implied authority to do whatever is necessary to close such deals (such as sign a purchase order in the company's name, arrange delivery, and perhaps even alter some of the company's standard warranty terms).

EXHIBIT 10.3   Comparison of employee obligations based on contractual liability and tort action.

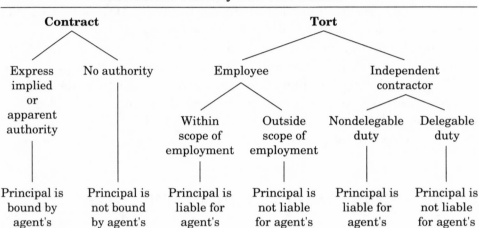

However, the employee's authority often extends beyond that expressly or implicitly given him. To illustrate this, suppose Tony and Jennifer's sales manager decides to close a sale for $100,000 worth of goods. This goes beyond his express authority and is not within his implied authority, since it was expressly prohibited. Yet from the point of view of the customer, the company's sales manager appears to have the authority to close all sales transactions. A customer who has not been informed of the limitation imposed upon the employee has no reason to think that anything is wrong. The law vindicates the customer in this situation by providing that the employee has apparent authority to conclude contracts within the scope of authority he appears to have. Since he was put into that position by his employer, and the employer has not informed the customer of the limits imposed upon the employee, the employer is bound by the employee's actions.

Outside of the contract arena, the employee's power to bind the employer is based on similar considerations. Under the doctrine of *respondeat superior* (or *vicarious liability*), the employer is responsible for any actions of the employee occurring within the scope of his employment. Thus, if the sales manager causes a traffic accident on the way to a sales call, the employer is responsible for damages. This imposition of liability is in no way based on the employer's fault; it is *liability without fault,* imposed as a result of the economic judgment that employers are better able to spread losses among customers and insurance companies. Consistent with this approach, employers are normally not liable for the torts or criminal actions of employees outside the scope of their employment, such as actions occurring after hours or while the employee is pursuing her own interests. Furthermore, an employer is normally not liable for the torts or criminal actions of agents who are not employees (so-called independent contractors) since they are more likely to be able to spread these costs among their own customers and insurance companies.

However, employers should not take this as an invitation to avoid all liability by wholesale hiring of independent contractors. To begin with, the labeling of a potential employee as an independent contractor is not necessarily binding on the courts. They will look to the level of control exerted by the employer and other related factors to make this determination. In addition, many activities of employers are considered nondelegable (such as disposal of hazardous waste). Employers cannot escape the consequences of such activities by hiding behind independent contractors.

Laws Prohibiting Employment Discrimination

In addition to these common law considerations, there are, of course, a number of statutory rules of law that govern the employer-employee relationship. Perhaps the most well known of these are the laws prohibiting employment discrimination. These laws, which include Title VII of the Civil Rights Act of 1964, the Age Discrimination in Employment Act, and laws protecting disabled and pregnant employees, collectively prohibit employment discrimination on the basis of sex, race, national origin, religion, age, and disability. Interestingly, they do not yet prohibit discrimination on the basis of sexual orientation, although a number of state and local laws do.

Prohibited discrimination applies not only to hiring, but also to promotion, firing, and conditions of employment. In fact, sexual discrimination has been found in cases of sexual harassment unconnected to hiring, promotion, or firing, but simply involving the creation of a so-called hostile environment for the employee.

These statutes are exceptions to the age-old common law concept of *employment at will,* which allowed employers to hire and fire at their whim, for any reason or for no reason at all. This rule is still in force in situations not covered by the discrimination acts and, of course, not involving employment contracts. Notwithstanding the rule, however, courts in many states have carved out exceptions to employment at will in cases involving employees fired for refusing to perform illegal acts or employees fired in bad faith to avoid paying commissions or other earned compensations to the employee. Furthermore, courts in some states have been willing to discover employment contracts hidden in employee manuals or personnel communications that employers may not have thought legally binding.

Other Employment Statutes

When they begin taking on employees other than themselves, Tony and Jennifer will encounter a variety of other statutes that regulate the employment relationship and the workplace itself. For example:

- ERISA and the Internal Revenue Code closely regulate the form and amounts of any tax-qualified pension, profit-sharing, or welfare plans that employers may wish to maintain, generally prohibiting discrimination in favor of owners and highly paid employees.
- OSHA and the regulations adopted under that act closely regulate safety and health conditions in the workplace, imposing heavy fines for violations.
- The Fair Labor Standards Act provides minimum wages and overtime pay for employees in nonexempt (generally nonexecutive) positions, as well as prohibiting child labor and other practices.
- Social security and unemployment compensation—The company will find itself contributing to both these funds for each of its employees, as well as withholding social security and income taxes from its employees' wages. With regard to unemployment compensation, the amount of the contribution may depend on the number of employees laid off over the years, causing Jennifer and Tony to contest claims from employees who may have left voluntarily or been fired for cause.
- Worker's compensation—The company will probably be required to carry worker's compensation insurance to cover claims under that system. Although the premiums may seem burdensome, worker's compensation was, at the outset, a welcome compromise between the interests of employers and those of employees. In exchange for avoiding the costs and uncertainties of litigation, employees were assured payment for job-related injuries but lost the opportunity to sue for increased amounts based on pain, suffering, and punitive damages. Employers gave up many common law defenses that formerly could be used against employees but were able to avoid the disastrously high judgments available under common law.

Employment Agreements

In addition to the common law and statutory considerations common to the hiring of all employees, the hiring of persons for professional positions in engineering, marketing, and sales presents a new set of issues. Such persons are likely to demand employment agreements and a piece of the action in some form.

Negotiating the Term of Employment

The attractiveness of employment agreements stems, in the main, from their protection against *firing without cause*. Thus, a major item of negotiation will likely be the term of the contract. Although one might think that, for the employee, the downside of such a provision is that she must make a commitment to stay with a company she may come to dislike, courts have universally held that an employee cannot be forced to work for an employer against her will. Any contrary ruling would, it has been said, amount to a form of slavery! Thus, an employment contract is essentially a one-way street. The employee is promised employment for a period of time, with accompanying salary, bonus, and incentive provisions; but she can leave the company at any time without consequence. As a result, Tony and Jennifer would be well advised to avoid employment agreements whenever possible and, if forced to grant one, at least obtain some benefit for the company.

Negotiating Employee Obligations

Such benefit usually comes in the form of the *noncompetition* and *proprietary information covenants* discussed at the beginning of this chapter. For example, an engineer may promise, in exchange for a two-year employment agreement, not to work in the software industry for a year after termination of his employment. Yet, as mentioned earlier in the context of Tony and Jennifer's former employment, proprietary information obligations exist quite apart from any employee agreement, and it is quite possible that courts would refuse to enforce noncompetition provisions against the employee. Although one could make the argument (in a state that will listen) that the company needs some protection against a former sales manager soliciting the company's customers for a competitor, the argument appears more difficult when applied to a software engineer. This is especially true when one realizes that such an engineer's use of proprietary information learned or developed under a former employer would in any case be prohibited by common law and by contractual prohibitions on the use of proprietary information.

Negotiating Equity Sharing with Employees

In addition to demands for job security, higher-level employees will frequently ask to share in the company's success. This can be easily accomplished by a grant of equity, but Jennifer and Tony would be well advised to resist such a demand, which could upset the company's balance of power and expectations of economic return among the major equity holders. These demands can often be satisfied by an incentive bonus plan tied to the success of the company or, more effectively, to the accomplishment of individual goals set for the employee.

If this is unacceptable to the employee, his return could be tied to the fortunes of the company by the use of *phantom stock, stock appreciation rights,* or similar devices in the LLC context, which simulate the benefits of equity without requiring actual equity ownership. These plans grant the employee bonuses equal to any distributions that would have been made if he had owned a certain percentage of equity, while also rewarding him through payment of any increase in value such equity would have experienced. However, even this type of plan might not be acceptable to an employee with significant negotiating leverage, because it does not give him voting rights. In addition, because the employee does not actually own equity (a capital asset), he cannot report the increase in value as capital gain at lower federal income tax rates. Thus, in certain cases it may be necessary to grant the employee equity in some form.

As previously mentioned, a direct grant of equity to an employee is considered a taxable event. The employee pays income tax on the difference between the value of the equity and the amount paid for it, if any. However, as previously described, the imposition of tax can be postponed if the equity is forfeitable, for example, upon the employee's leaving the employ of the company before the passage of a designated period of time. No doubt Tony and Jennifer would condition the grant of equity to any employee on his remaining employed for a substantial period, so this rule would apply.

The negative side of this rule, of course, is that when the equity is finally vested, the taxable income is measured by the difference between the amount paid, if any, and the value of the equity *at the time of vesting.* Worse yet, this tax will be payable before the employee has received any cash with respect to this transaction. Cash will be available upon sale of the equity; but typically, the employee will not wish to sell at this time, and there will be no market for equity in a closely held company in any case.

Offering Stock Options to Employees

In a corporation, the issuance of stock options is often thought of as a solution to the tax problem. The employee is given the right to purchase stock in the corporation at a fixed price for a significant period of time. Thus, without investing any money, the employee can watch the value of this right increase as the value of the stock increases relative to the amount he would have to pay to purchase it. This right would be much less valuable, of course, if the grant of the option to the employee were a taxable event, but, unless the option is transferable and there is a recognized market for it (which is extremely unlikely in a case like Tony and Jennifer's), the grant of the option is not taxable.

Unfortunately, however, when the employee ultimately exercises the option and purchases the stock, the Internal Revenue Code requires recognition of income in the amount of the difference between the amount paid and the value of the stock at that time. Again, this occurs at a time when the employee has received no cash and likely has little desire or ability to sell.

Recognizing this problem, Congress has provided more favorable tax treatment for employee incentive stock options that meet a number of requirements:

- Incentive stock options (ISOs) must be issued pursuant to a stock option plan approved by the corporation's stockholders.
- The exercise price must be the fair market value of the stock at the time of issuance.
- Each option cannot last more than 10 years, and no more than $100,000 of exercise price may become exercisable in any one year.
- Perhaps most significant, the employee must hold any stock purchased pursuant to the option for the longer of one year after exercise or two years after the grant of the option.

If these requirements are met, the employee is not taxed until he actually sells the stock acquired under the option (and has cash to pay the tax), and the income is taxed at favorable long-term capital gain rates.

The corporation can still require the employee to sell such shares back to the corporation upon termination of employment. The only drawback is that the corporation loses any deduction that would otherwise be available to an ISO for compensation paid to employees. Tony and Jennifer might find this plan to be an attractive way to grant the requested incentive to their key employees in a corporate context.

Exhibit 10.4 compares various ways of handling equity sharing with employees.

INSURANCE

The expenses associated with beginning a business are considerable. The fees demanded by the state and the costs associated with retaining attorneys and accountants have already been described. As employees are added to the organization, social security, unemployment compensation, and other costs increase. As previously mentioned, worker's compensation insurance is required by many states. But this is not the only insurance that should be considered.

EXHIBIT 10.4   Comparison of equity sharing methods.

	Date of grant	Risk removed	Sale of equity
Vested equity	Ordinary income	No income	Capital gain
Risk of forfeiture	No income	Ordinary income	Capital gain
Risk of forfeiture Sec. 83(B) election	Ordinary income	No income	Capital gain

	Date of grant	Date of exercise	Sale of stock
Nonqualified stock option with readily ascertainable value	Ordinary income	No income	Capital gain
Nonqualified stock option with no ascertainable value	No income	Ordinary income	Capital gain
Incentive stock option (ISO)	No income	No income	Capital gain

Property Insurance

To begin with, Tony and Jennifer should consider property insurance for any equipment or inventory that they may have on hand. In fact, should they ever obtain a loan for their business, the lender will likely take inventory and equipment as collateral and insist that it be insured (with the proceeds payable to the lender).

Liability Insurance

Tony and Jennifer should also consider purchasing liability insurance to cover claims against them for product liability and other possible tort claims. As mentioned before, the presence of such insurance often mitigates against claims of undercapitalization by plaintiffs attempting to pierce the corporate veil. Automobile liability insurance is required by many states as a condition for registration of a car. And the dangers of tort liability caused by employees have been discussed earlier.

Key Person Life Insurance

The advisability of purchasing life insurance to cover equity redemptions under cross-purchase or redemption agreements has been discussed. Yet this is not the only role for life insurance in a business. Consider what would result from Tony's untimely death. Not only may Jennifer or the company be required to repurchase his equity, but the operations of the company would likely grind to a standstill while it searched for a new sales manager. If the company owned additional insurance on Tony's life (known as "key person" insurance), it would have funds to tide it over during this business slowdown as well as money to apply to the search for and compensation of Tony's successor.

Business Interruption Insurance

Similar in effect to key-person insurance, is so-called business interruption insurance, which, in many cases of catastrophic business shutdown, will replace some of the company's cash flow. Such a policy is usually quite expensive, however, and may not be within the reach of a typical startup.

Group Life, Disability, and Health Insurance for Employees

As the company grows and adds employees, there will be increasing demand for insurance as part of the employee benefit package. Many companies provide group life insurance or group disability insurance for their employees. The latter can help the business avoid the moral dilemma caused by an employee who is too sick to work. Cutting off his salary may seem unthinkable, but paying another full salary for a long-term replacement may be more than the company can afford. Purchasing a policy with a significant deductible (such as 90 to 180 days) may solve this problem at very reasonable cost. Furthermore, in many industries it has become routine for the employer to provide health insurance as an employee benefit.

These three group policies may be provided to employees tax-free, and the company may deduct the costs of premiums. The only exceptions to this favorable tax result are for the partner in a partnership, member of an LLC, and significant shareholder of a subchapter S corporation, all of whom must report these benefits as taxable income. Thus, one negative aspect of the choice of a LLC or subchapter S for Tony and Jennifer is that any group life, disability, or health insurance provided to them by the company would be included in income. Only 30% of their group health insurance is then deductible.

RAISING MONEY

Thoughts of future hirings will inevitably bring Tony and Jennifer to consider another challenge to the company. Although Uncle Max's money may be sufficient for the short term, other sources of investment will eventually have to be identified. Although financing new businesses is discussed in detail in Chapters 5 through 9, this section describes potential legal and tax implications.

Loans

One source of financing that leaps to mind is debt financing from a commercial bank or other institutional lender. Although these institutions are notoriously loathe to advance loans to startup companies, such a loan may be possible if sufficient collateral or guarantees are available. The loan may take the form of a term note, a line of credit, or some sort of revolving credit plan, depending upon the circumstances. It will almost certainly be the case, however, that the lender will insist upon security for the loan.

Liens

At a minimum, this security will consist of an interest in all of the borrower's assets. In Jennifer and Tony's case, the lender will perfect a lien under Article 9 of the Uniform Commercial Code on the company's property, including:

- Machinery and equipment (computers, filing cabinets, desks, and so on).
- Inventory (copies of their software as well as blank disks, paper, pencils, and so on).
- Accounts receivable.
- All intangible property (copyrights, patents, and trade secrets relating to their product).

Notice of such security interest will be filed under the Code wherever appropriate to perfect this interest such that no future potential lender or purchaser will be misled.

Under the provisions of the Code, such filing will perfect the lender's lien on any new property, including:

- New machinery or equipment purchased after the loan is made, unless such new items are purchased on credit and a lien is granted to the seller or lender.
- Accounts receivable that arise later.
- All new inventory, but any inventory sold to customers in the ordinary course of business will be automatically freed from the lien.

Any further amounts advanced by the lender to the company in the future will be similarly secured.

If the loan ultimately goes into default, the lender may take possession of the collateral and arrange its sale. The proceeds are then applied to the costs of repossession and sale and the amount unpaid under the loan. Any additional amounts would be turned over to any lower-priority secured creditor and ultimately to the borrower or its bankruptcy estate.

Although such a lien might seem to provide adequate security to the lender, most lenders will insist upon guarantees from additional parties. In some cases, guarantees from governmental agencies such as the Small Business Administration may be available (see Chapter 9 for information on how to obtain such guarantees). However, in almost every case, the lender will insist upon personal guarantees from the major owners of the borrower. In our case, this will certainly include Tony and Jennifer, and probably also Uncle Max due to his large share of the company's equity and obviously deep pockets. In many cases, the lender further demands that such guarantees be backed by collateral interests in the private property of the guaranteeing stockholders. Thus, Uncle Max may find that his signature is required both on a personal guarantee and on a second mortgage on his home. Or he may be required to pledge securities held in his personal brokerage account.

It should be noted that these personal guarantees circumvent the limited liability that entrepreneurs hope to achieve through use of the corporate and LLC forms. The abandonment of this protection is unavoidable, however, and extends only to the particular lender. The owners remain protected against other trade creditors and tort plaintiffs.

Tax Effects

As a matter of strategy, the form in which a guarantee is given can have serious negative tax effects if insufficient care is given to structuring the loan transaction. For example, if Tony, Jennifer, and Uncle Max were to approach a small, local bank, they might find that the bank is reluctant to lend to a company under any circumstances. Under these conditions, the three stockholders may choose to borrow the money personally and invest the proceeds in the company themselves. Repayment of the loan would then be made out of the company's profits when they are distributed to its stockholders. As a result of this arrangement, however, the stockholders of a corporation would receive taxable distributions from the corporation (in the form of either salary or dividends) but would receive no compensating deduction for the repayment of a personal loan.

It would be better if they could convince the bank to lend to the corporation and take personal guarantees. Then the corporation could repay the loan directly (deducting the interest as a business loan), and the money would never pass through the hands of the stockholders. Alternatively (but with some additional risk), the stockholders could borrow directly from the bank but grant it a second mortgage as collateral, thereby potentially rendering the interest deductible for them as mortgage interest.

Ironically, if the corporation elects subchapter S treatment, strategy considerations may point in the opposite direction. Since Uncle Max, especially, will wish to see the corporation's short-term losses appear on his personal return, he will be concerned that the amount of loss he may use is limited to his tax basis in his investment. Such basis consists of the amount he paid for his stock, plus any amount he has loaned directly to the corporation. If the company were to borrow from the bank and Uncle Max were merely to guarantee the loan, the amount of the loan would not increase his basis (or his allowable loss) in a subchapter S corporation (although his LLC basis would be increased). If he were to borrow the money from the bank and lend it to an S corporation himself, his basis would be increased. Of course, in either event, the amount of loss he can use may be limited by the passive loss rules discussed earlier.

Legal Issues in the Sale of Securities to Outside Investors

As an alternative to institutional lending, Jennifer, Tony, and Uncle Max may turn to outside investors. Although it may be difficult to attract venture capitalists to such a small startup, other sources of capital, in the form of neighbors, friends, doctors, lawyers, dentists, and other individuals or entities with an interest in ground-floor investing, may be available. If they choose this route, it is crucial that they take note of two common misconceptions.

Although most businesspeople are aware that both federal and state law regulates the offer and sale of securities, most believe that these statutes apply only to the offerings of large corporations, and that small companies are exempt. This is one of the dangerous misconceptions held by many people like Tony, Jennifer, and Uncle Max. In fact, these laws (specifically, the federal Securities Act of 1933, the federal Securities Exchange Act of 1934, and state "Blue Sky" statutes) apply to all issuers.

Further, even many businesspeople who are aware of the scope of these acts believe that they apply only to issuers of equity securities, mainly stock. This, too, is a misconception. These statutes apply to all issuers of "securities," not just issuers of stock. Securities include, in addition to stock, most debt (other than very short term loans), options, warrants, LLC memberships, limited partnership interests, and all other forms of investment in which the investor buys into a common enterprise and relies on the efforts of others for the investment's success. Thus, such disparate items as orange groves, Hawaiian condominiums, and even worms have been held to be regulated securities under the circumstances of their respective cases.

The wide scope of these statutes led some to assert that they include the offering of *franchise opportunities*. Those offering franchises argued that the success of a franchisee is not normally determined solely by the efforts of the franchisor, but requires significant effort on the part of the franchisee. This debate has been rendered moot, however, by the adoption by the Federal Trade Commission of regulations requiring disclosure by franchisors of virtually the same range of information as is required under a securities registration statement. Many states have enacted similar franchise registration laws, requiring dual federal and state registration in most franchise offerings. (Further discussion of franchising can be found in Chapter 12.)

In general, then, the securities laws prohibit the offering of securities to the public without prior (and very expensive) registration with an appropriate government authority such as the federal Securities and Exchange Commission. They also punish fraudulent activities in connection with such offerings, including not only affirmatively false statements, but also mere nondisclosure of material facts about the investment. Because of the complexity and expensiveness of registration, these laws allow exceptions to the registration requirement in specific circumstances, but even these are subject to the antifraud provisions of the laws. Thus, the challenge to our three entrepreneurs is to identify provisions in the securities laws that will offer them an *exemption from registration*, with the understanding that they must still provide sufficient disclosure to potential investors (in the form of a so-called offering circular) to avoid antifraud liability.

One such exemption contained in the Securities Act of 1933 is the *intrastate offering exemption*. Based on the general principle that the federal government can constitutionally regulate only *interstate* commerce, the statute necessarily exempts offerings that are purely local. However, the scope of this exemption is relatively narrow. Not only must all persons who purchase the securities reside in one state, but all offerees must be resident there as well. Furthermore, the company offering the securities must be formed under the laws of that state and do most of its business there. Due to these restrictions, this exemption may be useful only for the smallest of offerings. Besides, the exemption excuses the offering only from registration with the Securities and Exchange Commission (SEC). The state's securities laws may still require expensive and time-consuming state registration.

The more popular exemption from registration under the federal act is the *private placement exemption*, which excuses transactions "not involving a public offering." Over the last decade, the SEC has relied on this exemption, and other provisions in the law, to issue regulations designed to facilitate the raising of capital by small businesses in small offerings. Thus, as of this writing, Regulation D under the act exempts from registration any offering of under $1 million worth of securities. Above that amount, the regulation requires increasing levels of disclosure (still short of full registration, however) and limits the number of offerees to 35 plus an unlimited number of so-called accredited investors. For these purposes, accredited investors include certain institutions, as well as individuals with net worth or annual income levels that indicate a need for less protection. Even apart from the regulation, however, issuers can argue that offerings made to relatively sophisticated investors with prior relationships to the issuer qualify as transactions "not involving a public offering."

Exemption from registration under the federal act *does not* grant exemption under a state act. In fact, offerings made to investors in a number of states require adherence to the Blue Sky statutes of each state. Fortunately, however, virtually all state statutes allow similar exemptions for private placements, typically excusing offerings to 25 or fewer persons.

Thus, Tony and Jennifer will likely be able to seek out the investment they will need without having to register with the federal or state government. However, it cannot be overemphasized that they remain subject to the *antifraud provisions* of these acts. Thus, they will be well advised to seek professional assistance in drawing up a comprehensive offering circular disclosing all that an investor would need to know about their company to make an intelligent investment decision. (See Chapter 7 for further discussion of venture capital.)

CONCLUSION

Considering all the legal and tax pitfalls described in this chapter, one is tempted to ask whether Tony, Jennifer, or any other entrepreneur would choose the road of the startup if she were fully aware of all the potential complications lying in wait. Yet not to be aware of these matters is to consciously choose to play the game without knowing the rules. These issues are there whether one chooses to prepare for them or not. Surely, Tony and Jennifer are much more likely to succeed in their venture for having taken the time to become aware of the legal issues facing the entrepreneur.

11 INTELLECTUAL PROPERTY

Joseph S. Iandiorio

One of the most valuable and fundamental assets of a new small business is its intellectual property. Intellectual property is defined as a business's intangible assets, including patents, trademarks, copyrights, and trade secrets. The rights to such property can be used to prevent competitors from entering your market and can represent a separate source of revenue to the business. All too often, however, they are overlooked or misunderstood, and they are nearly always undervalued. To fully protect and utilize these assets, every entrepreneur, small business owner, and manager, as well as advisers such as management, financial and technical consultants, lawyers, accountants, bankers, and venture capitalists, must be aware of what these rights are and how they are protected and preserved. This awareness is becoming even more critical in a world of global competition and international markets where ideas and information are fast becoming more valuable than products and things. The adoption of two international treaties, the North American Free Trade Agreement (NAFTA) and the General Agreement on Tariff and Trade (GATT) underwrite this concern.

THE BASICS: WHAT IS PROTECTABLE AND HOW SHOULD IT BE PROTECTED?

When a new idea is conceived or a new product or method is designed, one of the first questions that arises is: Can I protect this? Can I keep competitors from copying this? There are very practical reasons for protecting a new idea. Investors are loathe to put money into a venture that cannot establish a unique product niche. Stockholders will challenge a corporation's investment of its resources in a program that can be easily copied once it is introduced to the market. All the time, effort, and money invested in perfecting the idea, as well as advertising and promoting it, may be wasted if imitators can enter the market on your heels with a product just like yours. Moreover, the imitators can cut prices because they have not incurred the startup expenses you had to endure to bring the idea from conception to a mass-producible, reliable, and appealing product or service.

Here are some examples of things that may be protected:

- A new product.
- A new method.
- A process.
- A new service.
- A new promotional or merchandising scheme or approach.
- New packaging.
- A new design.

Once it has been determined that a new idea, product, or method is eligible for one or more forms of protection—a patent, trade secret, trademark, or copyright—the rights should be secured as quickly as possible. Each form of protection is obtained in a different manner and provides a different set of rights. The various forms are discussed in the following sections.

For example, consider a typical modern product—a computer on a stand. The computer has a disk with software on it. The computer includes the usual circuitry, including memory, CPU, and ancillary circuits. It bears the name of the manufacturer and the brand name and is accompanied by a user's manual and a label or tag. What is protectable, and how should you protect it? The next sections provide information to help answer these questions.

Patents

There are three kinds of patents: utility, design, and plant. *Utility patents* are the kind commonly considered when one seeks to protect an invention. They are granted for any new and useful process, machine, manufacture or composition of matter, or improvement thereof, including new uses of old devices or new combinations of well-known components. *Design patents* cover only the new design of an object—its ornamental appearance. *Plant patents* are available for inventions or discoveries in asexual reproduction of distinct and new varieties of plants. This area of patents has become much more important with the growth of biotechnology inventions in the last few years, especially regarding the protection of human-engineered life forms. Most of the following discussion focuses on utility patents, though some special considerations of design patents are also provided.

Utility Patents

Utility patents cover three classes of inventions:

- *Chemical inventions* include new compounds, new methods of making old or new compounds, new methods of using old or new compounds, and new combinations of old compounds. Biological materials and methods, drugs, foodstuffs, drug therapy, plastics, petroleum derivatives, synthetic materials, pesticides, fertilizers, and feeds are all protectable.
- *General/mechanical inventions* include everything from gears and engines to tweezers and propellers, from zippers to fur-lined keyhole appliqués to Jacque Cousteau's scuba regulator. For example, complex textile-weaving machines, space capsule locks and seals, and diaper pins are all protectable.
- *Electrical inventions* include everything from lasers to light switches, from the smallest circuit details to overall system architectural concepts.

  Computer software is patentable in various forms:

- Application programs, such as the software that runs in a computer used to control a chemical-processing plant or a rubber-molding machine, are patentable.
- Software for running a cash management account at a brokerage house or bank is patentable.
- The microcode in a ROM that embodies the entire inventive notion of a new tachometer is patentable.
- Internal or operations programs that direct the handling of data in the computer's own operations are patentable.

Obtaining a utility patent

The basic requirement for a utility patent is that the idea be new and that it be embodied in a physical form. The physical form may be a thing or a series of steps to perform.

Patent protection is established only upon the issue of a patent on the invention. The owner of the patent has the right to exclude others from making, using, and selling, offering for sale or importing the patented invention during the term of the patent. Historically the term of a U.S. patent was 17 years from the date of issue. No longer. Patents issuing from patent applications filed after June 8, 1995, will have a term of 20 years from the date of filing. Patents already issued before June 8, 1992, maintain their 17-year term. Those patents that issue after June 8, 1995, based on patent applications filed before June 8, 1995, have their choice of term: either 17 years from issue or 20 years from filing. Prior to issue there are no rights under a patent.

The effort begins when the inventor or inventors conceive the invention. They or a registered patent attorney on their behalf prepare a patent application and file it in the U.S. Patent and Trademark Office. From the date that the application is filed there is a "patent pending," but this confers no rights or protection. Protection applies if and when the Patent and Trademark Office agrees that the invention is patentable and issues the patent.

The patent application must contain a complete and understandable explanation of the invention. It does not have to be a nuts-and-bolts instruction manual. It is enough to convey the inventive concept so that a person skilled in the art to which the invention relates can make and use the invention without undue experimentation. Further, the explanation must contain a full description of the best mode known by the inventor for carrying out the invention. For example, the inventor cannot use the second best embodiment of the invention as an illustration for the patent application disclosure and keep secret the best embodiment. That will make the resulting patent invalid.

The *timing* of the filing of the patent application is critical. It must be filed within one year of the first public disclosure, public use, sale, or offer for sale of the invention, or the filing will be barred and the opportunity to obtain a patent forever lost. This is known as the one-year period of grace. This may change in the near future to a system in which there is no period of grace (the application must be filed before any activity listed above), to conform with practice in most other countries.

A description of the invention in a printed publication constitutes a public disclosure. A mere announcement is not sufficient, unless it contains an explanation of the invention. It matters not that only a few copies of the publication were made available, so long as it was an unrestricted distribution.

Market testing, exhibitions, or even use by the inventor himself is a public use sufficient to activate the one-year period. An exception is a public use for experimental purposes. The test for whether a public use was an excepted experimental use is rigorous. The inventor must show that it was the operation and function of the invention that was being tested, not the appeal or marketability of the product employing the invention. Further, some evidence of the testing should be established. For example, if samples were sent to potential customers for evaluation, it would be good to show that the customers returned filled-out evaluation forms and that the inventor considered and even made changes based on those evaluations.

A sale will bar a patent even if the invention is embedded so deeply within a larger system that it could not ever be discovered. If the device containing the invention is sold, that is enough. The idea is that an inventor should be given only one year in which to file his patent application after he has begun to commercially exploit or to attempt to commercially exploit his invention. Thus, for an invention embodied in a production machine installed in a locked, secure room, the one-year period for filing a patent application begins the first time a device produced by that machine is sold, even though the machine may never be known to or seen by anyone other than the inventor. And it is not just a sale that triggers the one-year period. An offer for sale is enough, even if the sale is never consummated.

Criteria for obtaining a utility patent

A patent application contains three basic parts:

- Drawings showing an embodiment of the invention.
- A written description of the embodiment referring to the drawings.
- One or more claims.

Sometimes (often, in chemical cases), the drawings are omitted. The definition of the patented invention, the protected property, is not what is disclosed in the drawings and specification portion of the application; this is only the description of one specific embodiment. The coverage of the patent is defined by the third part of the application, the claims.

To qualify for a patent, the claims must be novel and unobvious. *Novelty* is a relatively easy standard to define: either a single earlier patent, publication, or product shows the entire invention, or the invention is novel. *Obviousness* is somewhat more difficult to grasp. Even though an invention may be novel, it may nevertheless be obvious and therefore unpatentable. The test for obviousness is fairly subjective: Are the differences between the invention and all prior knowledge (including patents, publications, and products) such that the invention would have been obvious to a person having ordinary skill in the art to which the invention pertains at the time the invention was made? If so, the invention is not patentable even if it is novel.

The meanings of "novelty" and "unobvious" in the area of patentability can be better understood with an example. Suppose a person is struggling to screw a wood screw into hard wood, and he realizes that the problem is that he cannot supply enough twisting force with the blade of the screwdriver in the slot in the head of the screw. So he gets the bright idea of making the slot a little deeper, so that the screwdriver blade can bite a little deeper and confront more surface area of the slot, thus applying more force to turn the screw. This is a good idea, but it creates another problem. The deeper slot extends much closer to the sides of the screw head. There is less support, and fatigue lines develop, which eventually cause the screw head to crack. The inventor then gets the idea to use a new screwdriver with two shorter, crossed blades, which will give increased surface area contact with two crossed slots in the head of the screw.

But a problem still exists. Although the twin blades do not require such deep slots, there are now twice as many slots, and the screw head is seriously weakened. Now the inventor sees another path: keep the double-blade configuration, but chop off the corners, so that the slots need not extend out so close to the edge of the new screw head.

The result: he has invented the Phillips head screwdriver, for use with a Phillips head screw. Certainly the invention is "novel": no one else has made that design before. It is also "unobvious" and thus patentable. The addition of the second blade and elimination of the corners has resulted in a wholly new screwdriver concept. The concept is patentable.

Now suppose another party, seeing the patent issued on this double-blade Phillips head, comes up with an improvement of her own. Her invention is to use three crossed blades (cutting the head of the screw into six equal areas), with their corners removed. This design is not patentable. Certainly it is novel, but is it unobvious? Not likely. Once the first inventor has originated the idea of increasing the number of blades and eliminating corners, it is obvious to simply add more blades.

Drafting the patent claims

Once it is decided that a patentable invention exists, it must be protected by properly drafted patent claims. It is the claims that the U.S. Patent and Trademark Office examiner analyzes and accepts or rejects in considering the issuance of the patent. It is the claims that determine if someone has infringed on a patent. It is the claims that define the patent property.

Claims are clearly, then, the most important part of a patent. It is no good to have claims that cover the invention yet do not protect your product or process from being copied by competitors. Does this sound contradictory? Study the following example and you will understand.

Suppose an inventor meets with a patent attorney and shows the attorney a new invention for carrying beverages on the slopes while skiing. The invention eliminates the risk of smashing glass, denting metal, or squashing a wineskin, and it also eliminates the need to carry any extra equipment: It's a hollow ski pole. The ski pole has a shaft, a chamber, and a handle. The handle has a threaded hole that communicates with the hollow shaft. Partway down the inside of the hollow shaft is a plastic liner that creates a chamber for holding liquids; this plastic liner is sealingly attached to the shaft. The chamber is closed by a threaded plug, which engages the threaded hole. The inventor wants to patent the pole, so he assists the patent attorney in writing a description of the ski pole. They write the following claim:

"A hollow ski pole for carrying liquids, comprising:
- a hollow shaft;
- a liner sealingly engaging the hollow inside of the shaft to define a chamber for containing liquid;
- a handle on the shaft;
- a threaded hole in the handle communicating with the chamber in the hollow shaft; and
- a threaded plug for engaging the threaded hole."

The patent application is filed. The U.S. Patent and Trademark Office examines the application and issues the patent with that claim. The inventor is happy. But not for long, because a competitor comes out with a similar hollow ski pole that doesn't use a liner. The competitor simply welds a piece of metal across the inside of the shaft to make a *sealed* chamber. The competitor has avoided infringing the patent, because there is no liner, which was one of the specifications of the first patent claim. Another competitor replaces the threaded plug with an upscale mahogany cork. Again the patent is not infringed, because there is no threaded plug.

To infringe a patent, a competitor must infringe a claim of the patent. In order to infringe a claim of the patent, the infringing process or product must include *every* element of the claim.

This problem can be avoided by exploring the various ways in which the product can be built. This may require input from sales, marketing, engineering, and production people as well as the inventor. After a thorough study, a better claim might emerge as follows:

"A hollow ski pole for carrying liquids, comprising:
- a hollow shaft;
- a chamber formed in said hollow shaft for containing a liquid;
- a handle on the shaft having a hole communicating with the chamber in the hollow shaft; and
- a means for closing the hole in the handle."

Someone could still design around this claim by leaving out the means for closing the hole; the skier could use her thumb and hope she doesn't fall. Practically speaking, however, the claim would be good enough to keep others from making a meaningful competing product without infringing. There is a limit to how broadly the claim can be worded, however. Eventually, if the claim becomes broader and broader, and does not specify the ski pole or hollow shaft, it will apply to a bottle or a pot with a cover, and the patent will not be obtainable. Careful claim drafting is critical.

Inventorship

Another important area is inventorship. In the United States a patent must be filed by the inventor(s) and no one else. The inventor is the originator of the inventive concept. A project leader is not by his supervisory position alone an inventor of an invention. Neither is a technician or engineer who may have built the first working model. The inventor may have sold or assigned the patent application to someone else—his employer, a partner in some enterprise, a company he has newly formed, or another inventor. Thus, the original inventors may not be the owners of the patent, but it must still be filed in their names.

Provisional Patent Applications

A new type of patent applications referred to as a provisional patent application is now available. A provisional application requires only a written description of the invention and drawings; unlike a conventional application no claims or oath are required. Its purpose is to allow inventors to get something on file quickly and inexpensively to establish an early filing date that can be relied on by the full patent application, which can be filed up to one year later. Some doubt their effectiveness for either purpose. Provisional applications will be regarded as abandoned in 12 months. The full conventional patent application must be filed within the 12 months and must refer to the provisional application in order to assume the benefits of the earlier filing date. The provisional application must be complete enough to support the disclosure of the later filed full patent application. Otherwise, the filing date is lost and there is a risk of patentable subject matter falling into the public domain.

Design Patents

Hockey uniforms, ladies' dresses, computer housings, automobile bodies, buildings, shoes, and game boards are all protectable with design patents. But this type of patent covers only the *appearance,* not the idea or underlying concept. What you see is what you get. Design patents are generally less expensive than utility patents and in some cases are the only protection that is needed or obtainable.

Design patents have a life of only 14 years from the date of issue but are otherwise generally subject to the same rules as other patents. That is, the new and original ornamental design to be patented must be novel and unobvious and must be filed within one year of the first public use, publication, sale, or offer for sale.

Trade Secrets

Trade secrets cover everything that patents cover, and much more. A trade secret is knowledge, which may include business knowledge or technical knowledge, that is kept secret for the purpose of gaining an advantage in business over one's competitors. Customer lists, sources of supply of scarce material, or sources of supply with faster delivery or lower prices may be trade secrets. Certainly, secret processes, formulas, techniques, manufacturing know-how, advertising schemes, marketing programs, and business plans are all protectable.

There is no standard of invention to meet as there is with a patent. If the idea is new in this context, if it is secret with respect to this particular industry or product, then it can be protected as a trade secret. Unlike patents, trademarks, and copyrights, there is no formal procedure for obtaining trade secret protection. Protection is established by the nature of the secret and the effort to keep it secret.

A trade secret is protected eternally against disclosure by all those who have received it in confidence and all who would obtain it by theft for as long as the knowledge or information is kept secret. In contrast to patent protection, there are no statutory requirements for novelty or restrictions on the subject matter.

The disadvantage of trade secrets compared with patents is that *there is no protection against discovery by fair means*, such as accidental disclosure, independent inventions, and reverse engineering. Many important inventions, such as the laser and the airplane, were developed more or less simultaneously by different persons. Trade secret protection would not permit the first inventor to prevent the second and subsequent inventors from exploiting the invention as a patent would.

The distinction between patents and trade secrets is illustrated in a case in which a woman who designed a novel keyholder immediately filed a patent application. It was a simple design and could be easily copied. While the patent was still pending, she licensed it to a manufacturer for a 5% royalty, with the agreement that if the patent didn't issue in five years, the royalty would drop to 2½%. The patent never issued, and the royalty was dropped to 2½%. Over the next 14 years, on sales of $7 million, the manufacturer's edge eroded as others freely copied the design. The manufacturer repudiated the royalty contract on the ground that it required payment forever for the small jump that the manufacturer got on its competitors, whereas the patent, had it issued, would have allowed only 17 years of exclusivity. The Court held the manufacturer to its requirement to pay. The ruling allowed the inventor to receive 2½% royalty for as long as the manufacturer continued to sell the keyholder. Had the patent issued, royalties would have lasted only 17 years.

Many companies use both approaches, filing a patent application on a trade secret. When the patent is ready to issue, the company reevaluates its position. If the competition is close, they pay the fee and let the patent issue. If not, they don't pay the fee, allowing the patent application to go abandoned, and preserve the trade secret.

Certain trade secrets have been appraised at many millions of dollars, and some are virtually priceless. For example, the formula for Coca-Cola is one of the best-kept trade secrets in the world. Known as Merchandise 7X, it has been tightly guarded since it was invented 100 years ago. It is known by only two persons within the Coca-Cola Company and is kept in a security vault at the Trust Company Bank in Atlanta, Georgia, which can be opened only by a resolution from the company's board of directors. The company refuses to allow the identities of those who know the formula to be disclosed or to allow them to fly in the same airplane at the same time. The company elected to forgo producing Coca-Cola in India, a potential market of 550 million people, because the Indian government requires the company to disclose the secret formula as a condition for doing business there. While some of the mystique surrounding the Coca-Cola formula may be marketing hype, it is beyond dispute that the company possesses trade secrets that are carefully safeguarded and are extremely valuable.

Secrecy is essential to establishing trade secret rights; without it there is no trade secret property. There are four primary steps for ensuring secrecy:

1. Obtain confidential disclosure agreements with all employees, agents, consultants, suppliers, and anyone else who will be exposed to the secret information. The agreement should bind them not to use or disclose the information without permission.

2. Take security precautions to keep third parties from entering the premises where the trade secrets are used. Sturdy locks, perimeter fences, guards, badges, visitor sign-in books, escorts, and designated off-limits areas are just some of the ways that a trade secret owner can exercise control over the area containing the secrets.

3. Stamp specific documents containing the trade secrets with a confidentiality legend and keep them in a secure place with limited access, such as a safe or locked drawer or cabinet.

4. Make sure all employees, consultants, and others who are concerned with, have access to, or have knowledge about the trade secrets understand that they are trade secrets, and make sure they recognize the value to the company of this information and the requirement for secrecy.

Trade secret owners rarely do all of these things, but enough must be done so that a person who misappropriates the secrets cannot reasonably excuse his conduct by saying that he didn't know or that no precautions were ever taken to indicate that something was a trade secret. This is important because, unlike patents, trade secret protection provides no "deed" to the property.

Since there is no formal protection procedure, the necessary steps for establishing a trade secret are often not taken seriously until a lawsuit is brought by the owner against one who has misappropriated them. In each specific case the owner must show that the precautions taken were adequate.

Trade secret misappropriations generally fall into one of two classes: someone who has a confidential relationship with the owner violates the duty of confidentiality, or someone under no duty of confidentiality uses improper means to discover the secret.

Trade secret theft issues frequently arise with respect to the conduct of ex-employees. Certainly, a good employee will learn a lot about the business during his employment. And some of that learning he will take with him as experience when he leaves. That cannot be prevented. The question is, did he just come smart and leave smarter, or did he take certain information that was exclusively the company's?

For example, in one case a company that had been making widgets for the government for many years did not get its annual contract renewal. When the company questioned the loss of the contract, it was explained that a competitor was supplying widgets of equal quality at a lower price. Upon investigation the company determined that the competitor was located in the same town, that the competitor's widgets were uncannily identical in every dimension, and that the competitor was owned by an ex-employee of the company who had left over a year before. Amicable approaches failed, and a lawsuit was instituted during which the company discovered that the ex-employee had copied their detailed engineering drawings to make the widgets; this eliminated all engineering and design costs and enabled the competitor to sell the widgets to the government at a much lower price. But the ex-employee had not stolen anything. It seems the man knew that every year his ex-employer reissued important engineering drawings that had become torn and tattered or that needed updating, and he threw out the old ones. The ex-employee testified that while driving by one day, he saw the old drawings sticking out of the dumpster. He drove in, took them out of the dumpster, put the ones he wanted in his car, and chucked the rest back in the dumpster. That's how he got a widget with identical dimensions. The court held him liable for misappropriation of trade secrets. He had trespassed to obtain the drawings, and he had learned of the ex-employer's practice of disposing of old drawings while an employee with a duty of confidentiality to the company. The court granted an injunction preventing the ex-employee from selling widgets for a period of months equal to the jump he got by not having to develop his own engineering drawings.

But what if the ex-employee had not trespassed to obtain the drawings from the trash? What if he had waited for the trash collector to remove them and then asked if he could pore over the trash? Or what if he had gone to the dump and picked the drawings out of the mud? When does the owner part with ownership of trade secret materials dumped in the trash?

Trade secrets are extremely valuable, often more so than patents, and can form the basis for lucrative licensing programs. Care should be taken to identify and protect them early and consistently.

Trademarks

Trademark protection is obtainable for any word, symbol, or combination thereof that is used on goods to indicate their source. Any word—even a common word such as "look," "life," or "apple"—can become a trademark, so long as the word is not used descriptively. "Apple" for fruit salad might not be protectable. Apple for computers certainly is.

Common forms such as geometric shapes (circles, triangles, squares), natural shapes (trees, animals, humans), combinations of shapes, or colors may be protected. Even the single color pink has been protected as a trademark for building insulation. Three-dimensional shapes such as bottle and container shapes and building features (for example, McDonald's golden arches) can also be protected.

While people generally only speak of trademarks, that term encompasses other types of marks. A trademark is specifically any word or symbol or combination of the two that is used on goods to identify its source. However, a *service mark* is a word or symbol or combination used in connection with the offering and provision of services. Blue Cross/Blue Shield, Prudential Insurance, and McDonald's are service marks for health insurance services, general insurance services, and restaurant services, respectively. Ownership is established by advertising the mark in conjunction with the service, as opposed to trademarks, where advertising is insufficient—the mark must be used on the goods in commerce.

There are also other types of marks. A *collective mark* indicates membership in a group, such as a labor union, fraternity, or trade association. A *certification mark* is used to indicate that a party has met some standard of quality; Quality Court motels, Underwriter's Laboratory, and Good Housekeeping's seal of approval are familiar examples.

If you use any such name or feature to identify and distinguish your products, then think trademark protection. Ownership of a trademark allows you to exclude others from using a similar mark on similar goods that would be likely to confuse consumers as to the source of the goods. This right applies for the duration of ownership of the mark.

Trademarks can be more valuable to a company than all of its patents and trade secrets combined. Consider the sudden appearance and abrupt increase in the worth of trademarks such as Cuisinart, Häagen-Dazs, and Ben & Jerry's. Consider also the increased value that a trademark name such as IBM, Kodak, or GE brings to even a brand new product.

A trademark, unlike a patent, is established without any formal governmental procedure. Ownership of a trademark is acquired simply by being the first to use the mark on the goods in commerce. And it remains the owner's property as long as the owner keeps using it. And keep using it you must, for nonuse for a period of three years constitutes abandonment.

The mark should not be descriptive of the goods on which it is used, although it may be suggestive of the goods. However, it is best to select a mark that is arbitrary and fanciful with respect to the goods. This is because every marketer, including a competitor, has the right to use a descriptive term to refer to its goods. Therefore, exclusive rights to such a mark cannot be secured.

A trademark owner should also take care to prevent the mark from becoming generic, as happened to Aspirin, Cellophane, Linoleum, and other product names. Thus, it is not proper to refer to, for example, simply a Band-Aid, Jello, or Kleenex. The correct form of description is Band-Aid adhesive bandages, Jell-O fruit-flavored gelatin dessert, or Kleenex facial tissues.

It is wise to have a search done for a proposed new mark to be sure that the mark is clear to adopt and use on the goods, that is, to verify that no one else is using the same or a similar mark on the same or similar goods. It is confusing to customers and expensive to change a mark and undertake the costs of all new printing, advertising, and promotional materials when you discover that your new mark has already been used by another.

Registering a Mark

Although there is no need to register a mark, there are benefits associated with registration that make it worthwhile. Registration may be made in individual states, or a federal registration may be obtained. A state registration applies only in the particular state that granted the registration and requires only use of the mark in that state. A federal registration applies to all 50 states, but to qualify, the mark must be used in interstate or foreign commerce. A distinct advantage of federal registration is that even if a mark is used across only one state line, that is, if goods bearing the mark are in commerce only between one state and another state or country, that is enough to establish federal protection in all 50 states. Thus, if you are using your mark in Massachusetts, New Hampshire, and Rhode Island, for example, but do not register it federally, you may later be blocked from using your mark in all other states if a later user of the same mark, without knowledge of your use of the mark, federally registers it. That later user would then have the rights to the mark in all other 47 states even though its actual use may have been only in Oregon and California!

While your common law rights to a trademark or service mark last as long as you properly use the mark, registration must be periodically renewed. Federal registrations extend for 20 years (10 years for registrations filed after November 16, 1989); terms for states vary, but 10 years is typical.

Over the history of trademark law in the United States, registration in the U.S. Patent and Trademark Office followed the common law. That is, to establish ownership of a trademark one had to use the mark on the goods in commerce, and to register the mark in the U.S. Patent and Trademark Office one had to establish that the mark was indeed in use.

That has changed somewhat. Now an application can be filed to register a mark that is not yet in use but is intended to be used. After the U.S. Patent and Trademark Office examines the application and determines that the mark is registrable, the applicant is required to show actual use within six months. The six-month period can be extended if good cause is shown. Nevertheless, before registration, even before actual use, the mere filing of the application establishes greater rights over others who actually used it earlier but did not file an application for registration.

Ownership of a Mark

Care must be taken with trademark properties. A trademark cannot simply be sold by itself or transferred like a desk or car, or a patent or copyright. A trademark must be sold together with the business or goodwill associated with the mark, or the mark will be abandoned. Further, if a mark is licensed for use with a product or service, provision must be made for quality control of that product or service. That is, the trademark owner must require the licensee to maintain specific quality levels for products or services with which the mark is used, under penalty of loss of license. And the owner must actually exercise that control through periodic inspection, testing, or other monitoring that will ensure that the licensee's product quality is up to the prescribed level.

Ownership of a mark is most important in a business. When Cuisinart started selling its food processors, it promoted them vigorously under the trademark Cuisinart. A good part of the business's success was due to the fact that the machines were sturdily made by a proud, quality-conscious French company, Robot Coupe, who had been making the machines for many years before they became popular among U.S. consumers under the mark Cuisinart. When price competition reared its head, Cuisinart found cheaper sources. Robot Coupe owned no patents and had no other protection. When Cuisinart began selling brand X under the name Cuisinart, a wild fight ensued through the courts and across the pages of major newspapers in the United States, but to no avail. The whole market had been created under the name Cuisinart, and Cuisinart had the right to apply its name to any machine made anywhere by anyone it chose. Robot Coupe, whose machine had helped create the demand for food processors, was left holding its chopper.

European Trademark

A "European" trademark registration is now available, known as a Community Trade Mark or CTM, wherein a single registration will cover the entire European Union: with the benefit of a single filing plenary protection is provided. However, there are certain drawbacks. For example, a single user in any country of the Union could block registration everywhere and cost considerations make a CTM filing uneconomical generally unless trademarks are sought in at least three countries.

Copyright

Copyrights cover all manner of writings, and the term *writings* is very broadly interpreted. It includes books, advertisements, brochures, spec sheets, catalogs, manuals, parts lists, promotional materials, packaging and decorative graphics, fabric designs, photographs, pictures, film and video presentations, audio recordings, architectural designs, and even software and databases. Software and databases are protected not only in written form but also as stored in electronic memory.

A utilitarian object such as a hypodermic needle, a hammer, or a lamp base cannot be the subject of a copyright. Yet stained glass windows, software, piggy banks, and a sculpture useful as a lamp qualify for copyright protection.

It is said that a copyright does not protect a mere idea; it protects the *form* of the expression of the idea. But this is broadly interpreted. For example, one can infringe a book without copying every word; the theme is protected even though upon successive generalizations the theme will devolve to one of seven nonprotectable basic plots. This is apparent in the software area, where using the teachings of a book to write a program has resulted in copyright infringement of the book by the computer program. In another case a program was infringed by another program even though the second program was written in an entirely different language and for an entirely different computer.

The form of the expression protected was not merely the actual writing, the coding, but the underlying concept or algorithm—the flow chart. The copyright is a very strong and readily achievable source of protection.

A copyright has a term extending for the life of the author plus 50 years. Legislation is under consideration to extend that 50-year term to 70 years in conformity with certain other countries. For corporate "authors" or works made for hire, the period is 75 years from first publication or 100 years from creation, whichever is shorter. During the life of the copyright the owner has the exclusive rights to reproduce, perform, and display the work.

Establishing Copyright

Historically, under law a copyright was established by publishing the work—a book, painting, music, software, instruction manual—with copyright notice, typically "Copyright," "Copr.," or © followed by the year of first publication and the name of the owner. The notice may appear on the back of the title page of a book, on the face of a manuscript or advertisement, or on the base of a sculpture. It had to be visible and legible, but it could be placed so as not to interfere with the aesthetics of the work. If more than a few copies of the published work appeared without the notice, the copyright was forfeited forever. Works that were unpublished did not need notice. They were protected by virtue of their retention in secrecy. Publication with notice was all that was required; registration with the Copyright Office was not always immediately necessary.

Under the laws enacted in 1976, publication without notice can be rectified if the notice is omitted from only a small number of copies, registration of the work with the Copyright Office is effected within five years, and an effort is made to add the notice to those copies published without it. Notice must be on the work in all its forms. For example, for software the notice should appear on the screen, in the coding, on the disk, and on the ROM, wherever the software is resident or performing. In one case an infringer got away with reading out copyrighted software from a ROM because there was no notice on the ROM, although there was notice elsewhere.

Presently, under an amendment to the current law effective March 1989, no notice is required at all. In order to become a member of an international copyright treaty known as the Bern Convention, the United States had to abolish all formalities required to establish copyright in a work. Now the simple fact that a work was created, whether published or not, is enough to establish the copyright. It is not clear that this removal of the need for notice is retroactive. Thus, new works after March 1989 need not have notice, but those that were required to bear notice before the amendment should, in the exercise of prudence, continue to bear the notice.

Although notice is no longer compulsory, it is a valuable and worthwhile practice since it enables the pursuit of innocent infringers. That is, an infringer who did not have actual notice that the work copied was copyrighted is nevertheless liable if the work bore copyright notice.

Registering a Copyright

Registration also is noncompulsory, but it, too, bestows valuable additional rights. If the copyright owner has registered the copyright, statutory damages of up to $500,000 can be recovered without proof of actual damages. This can be a real advantage in copyright cases where actual damage can be difficult and expensive to prove.

Registration requires filling out the proper form and mailing it to the Copyright Office with the proper fee and a deposit of two copies of the work for published works, or only one copy if the work is unpublished. Accommodations are made for filing valuable or difficult to deposit copies: A deposit for three-dimensional works can be effected using photographs, and a deposit for large computer programs can be effected using only the first and last 25 pages. Further, if the program contains trade secrets, there is a provision for obscuring those areas from the deposit.

Summing Up

Now consider the question posed at the beginning of this chapter: What parts of a computer on a stand are protectable, and how can they be protected? The computer memory, circuits, and CPU, as well as its architecture, could be protected by patents or trade secrets. The software could be protected by patent, too. The software could also be protected by copyright and trade secret. (Software protection is discussed in detail later in this chapter.) The user's manual could also be protected by copyright and trade secret. The company name and the brand name could be trademarks. The housing of the computer as well as the stand could be protected by design patents. The contents or form of the label may be protected by trademark or copyright.

THE INTERNET

Internet activity is placing new pressures on intellectual property practice. Uploading and downloading of copyrighted material on the Internet is copyright infringement. Copyright infringement has also been found in some cases against bulletin board operators and administrators who have received and stored such material.

Webnet addresses are taking on some of the characteristics of trademarks but not enough to make that sort of protection clearly available when there is a similarity between two addresses that is likely to cause confusion. Further, there have been some instances where a party has incorporated a well-known name or mark of another in his own net address. No clear legal theories have evolved yet.

INTERNATIONAL PROTECTION FOR INTELLECTUAL PROPERTY

Obtaining protection for patents, trademarks, and copyrights in the United States alone is no longer sufficient in the modern arena of international competition and global markets. International protection often needs to be extensive and can be quite expensive, but there are ways to reduce and postpone the expense in some cases. Protection must be considered in countries where you intend to market the new product or where competitors may be poised to manufacture your product.

A patent in one country does not protect the invention in any other country: A novel product or method must be protected by a separate patent in each country. In addition, each country has different restrictions that must be met, or no patent protection can be obtained. The first and most important restriction is the *time* within which you must file an application to obtain a patent in a country or else *forever lose your right to do so.*

Patent Filing Deadlines

Not all countries are the same with respect to filing deadlines. For example, as previously noted, in the United States an inventor may file an application to obtain a patent on an invention up to one year after the invention has become public through a publication explaining the invention, a public use of the invention, or the sale or offer for sale of the invention. This one-year period is known as the *period of grace.*

There is no period of grace in many other countries, such as Great Britain, West Germany, Sweden, France, Italy, Switzerland, Belgium, Austria, the Netherlands, Australia, and Japan. And each country has a slightly different view of what constitutes making an invention public. In Japan, for example, public use of an invention before the filing of an application bars a patent only if the public use occurred within Japan, but in France any public knowledge of the invention anywhere bars the patent.

Thus, whereas the United States allows a business *one full year* to test market its new product, most other countries require that the patent application be filed *before any public disclosure,* that is, before the owner can even begin to determine whether the new product will be even a modest success. And meeting this requirement is not inexpensive, especially when the U.S. dollar is down against the currencies of other major countries.

How to Extend Patent Filing Deadlines

However, there are ways around having to file immediately, as provided for by the treaty known as the *Paris Convention.* If you file in the United States and then file in any country that is a party to the convention within one year of the date on which you filed in the United States, the U.S. filing date applies as the filing date for that country. In this way, by filing one application for the invention in the United States, you can preserve your initial U.S. filing date for up to one year. This means that you can file an application in the United States, and then immediately make the invention public by advertising, published articles, and sales. If within one year the product appears to be a success, you can then file in selected foreign countries, even though the prior public use of the invention would ordinarily bar your filing in those countries.

There are other options by which you can postpone the cost of foreign filings while preserving your right to file. Another, more recent treaty known as the *Patent Cooperation Treaty* (PCT) permits a delay of up to 20 or even 30 months before the costs of filing in individual countries are incurred. The PCT option is available if you file and request PCT treatment within one year of your U.S. filing date.

Thus, by filing a PCT application in a specially designated PCT office within one year of your U.S. filing, and by designating certain countries, you can preserve your right to file in those countries without further expense for 20 or 30 months after the U.S. filing date. That will provide an additional 8 or 18 months for test marketing the product. This does introduce the extra cost of the PCT application filing, but if you are considering filing in, say, six or more countries, the extra PCT filing may be well worth the cost for two reasons:

- It delays the outflow of cash that you may not presently have or may require for other urgent needs.
- If the product proves insufficiently successful, you can decide not to file in any of the countries designated under the PCT and save the cost of all six national application filings.

Another cost-saving feature of international patent practice is the *European Patent Convention* (EPC), which is compatible with the Paris Convention and the PTC and which enables you to file a single European patent and designate any one or more of 17 European countries in which you wish the patent to issue.

There are a number of international treaties that affect trademark rights and copyrights as well.

LICENSING AND TECHNOLOGY TRANSFER

A license is simply a special form of contract or agreement. Each party promises to do or pay something in return for the other party doing or paying something. Contracts that deal with the transfer of technology, or more broadly, intellectual property—patents, trade secrets, know-how, copyrights, and trademarks—are generally referred to as licenses. The licensed property can be anything from the right to use Mickey Mouse on a T-shirt or to make copies of the movie *Star Wars,* to the right to operate under the McDonald's name, to use a patented method of making a microchip, or to reproduce, use, or sell a piece of software. Software licenses are just one of the many types of licenses. The basic considerations are the same as for any other license, but specific clauses and language are tailored to the software environment.

Common Concerns and Clauses

The term *license* is typically used to refer to a number of different types of contracts involving intellectual property, including primarily an assignment, an exclusive license, and a nonexclusive license. And this broad reference will be used in this section.

An assignment is an outright sale of the property. Title passes from the owner, the assignor, to the buyer, the assignee. An assignment can take a number of forms:

- It can cover an entire patent, including all the rights under the patent.
- It can apply to an undivided fractional portion of all the patent rights (such as 30% undivided interest).
- It can include all the rights embraced by a patent limited to any geographical part of the United States.

A license is more like a rental or lease. The owner of the property, the licensor, retains *ownership;* the buyer, the licensee, receives the *right to operate* under the property right, be it a patent, trade secret, know-how, copyright, or trademark. An *exclusive license* gives the licensee the sole and exclusive right to operate under the property to the exclusion of everyone else, even the licensor. A *nonexclusive license,* in contrast, permits the licensee to operate under the licensed property but without any guarantee of exclusivity. The licensor can try to find more licensees and license them, there may be others who are already licensed, and the licensor can also operate under the property.

By definition, an assignment is exclusive since the assignee acquires full right and title to the property. Many licensees prefer an assignment or exclusive license because they want a clear playing field with no competitors in order to maximize their revenue from the property and justify the license cost.

Within either of these forms—exclusive license or nonexclusive license—may be included a right to *sublicense,* which is the right of the licensee to license others. This removes part of the licensor's control over the property and extends the licensee's liability to the conduct and payment of all sublicensees. A sublicense is an important and valuable right that is not automatically conveyed with the primary license right; it must be expressly granted. The term *transferable* in a license means that the license can be transferred as a whole along with the part of the licensee's business to which the license pertains; it does not confer the right to sublicense.

Licensors often prefer a nonexclusive license because it spreads their royalty income over a number of diverse licensees, increasing the chances of a successful return. In addition, if the property is freely available to all credible businesses, no one is left out or disadvantaged. All have an equal chance to compete, and the chances are reduced of a lawsuit from a rejected potential licensee.

Defining the Property Being Licensed

Great care must be exercised to clearly define the property being licensed. For example, consider the following questions:

- Is it more than one patent, just one patent, or only a part of one patent?
- Is it just the trademark, or the entire corporate image—names, advertising, and promotional scheme and graphics?
- If it concerns copyright, does it cover just the right to copy a book or other printed material in the same print form, or does it include any of the following rights?
  —Translation into another language.
  —Adaptation for stage, screen or video.
  —Creation of derivative works.
  —Merchandising its characters and events on T-shirts and toys?
- If it involves know-how or trade secrets, where are they defined?

Licensees must be sure that they are getting what they want and need. And a licensor must make clear the limits of the grant. In a software license if the grant is only to use the software, not to modify it or merge it with other software, that must be expressly stated.

Limitations on Licenses

A license may have numerous, different limitations, including time, the unit quantity, and the dollar value of products or services sold. The license can also be limited geographically. Field-of-use limitations are quite common, too. This limitation restricts the licensee to exploit the licensed property only in a designated field or market.

Assigning Value to a License

Perhaps the most universal concern in negotiating a license is, how do you assign a dollar value to intellectual property? First, determine what it *cost* to acquire that property, to build that property. For example, all of the following are hard costs that go into creating a property:

- The research and development cost involved in coming up with a new invention.
- The design cost of coming up with a new trademark or copyrighted work.
- The cost of commercializing the invention.
- The cost of advertising and promoting the trademark or copyrighted work, which can run into millions of dollars a year.
- Incidental costs, such as legal costs, engineering costs, and accounting costs.

Second, determine how this intellectual property affects the *profitability* of the product or the business. Can you charge more because the product has a famous name or because of the new features the invention has bestowed on the product? Can your costs be cut because of the new technology of the invention? If so, determine dollar values for those figures.

You might also determine how much the intellectual property increases gross revenues by opening new markets or by acquiring a greater percentage of established markets. All of these figures can be converted into dollar amounts for valuation.

Royalty Rates

A "typical" royalty rate for a nonexclusive license to a patent, trade secret, or know-how is universally stated to be 5%, but that rule is breached as often as it is honored. Nonexclusive license royalty rates in patent licenses can be 10%,

20%, 25%, or even higher. And exclusive license royalty rates tend to be higher because the licensee receives total exclusivity and the licensor is at risk if the licensee does not perform. Exclusive licensors generally demand initial payments for the same reason. In determining a reasonable royalty as a damage award in an infringement suit, courts have considered the following factors:

- The remaining life of the patent.
- The advantages and unique characteristics of the patented device over other, prior devices.
- Evidence of substantial customer preference for products made under the patent.
- Lack of acceptable noninfringing substitutes.
- The extent of the infringer's use of the patent.
- The alleged profit the infringer made that is credited to the patent.

Negotiating License Agreements

In any commercial agreement in which the consideration promised by one party to the other is a percentage of profits or receipts or is a royalty on goods sold, there is nearly always an implied promise of diligent, careful performance and good faith. But licensors generally seek some way to ensure that the licensee will use its best efforts to exploit the property and maximize the licensor's income. One approach is simply to add a clause in which the licensee promises to use its "best efforts." Another approach is to compel certain achievements by the licensee. The license may require a minimum investment in promotion and development of the property, which may be expressed in dollars, human labor hours, or even specific stated goals of performance or sales. Or the simpler approach of a minimum royalty can be employed: The licensee pays a certain minimum dollar amount in running royalties annually, whether or not the licensee's sales actually support those royalties—not a pleasant condition for the licensee but one that provides a lot of peace of mind for the licensor.

Perhaps the best insurance of performance is a competent, enthusiastic licensee. A little preliminary investigation of the licensee (in terms of net worth, credit rating, experience, reputation, manufacturing/sales capability, and prior successes/failures) can assuage a lot of fears and eliminate risky licensees. A *reverter clause,* which evicts the licensee and returns control to the licensor in the event of unmet goals, is the ultimate protection. Often the licensor's greatest concern is that the licensee might now or later sell one or more competing products, leading to a plain conflict of interest. A *noncompetition clause* can prevent this, but antitrust dangers are raised by such clauses, and licensees do not like this constraint on their freedom. Other approaches are safer, such as specified minimum performance levels.

Confidential disclosure clauses are necessary in nearly all license agreements, especially those involving trade secrets, know-how, and patent applications. Such clauses are necessary to protect not only the property that is the subject of the license, but also all of the technical, business, financial, marketing, and other information the parties will learn about each other during the license term, and even during negotiations before the license is executed.

Foreign Licenses

The aforementioned clauses and concerns pertain generally to all licenses, domestic U.S. as well as foreign. In addition, there are other clauses more peculiarly suited to foreign agreements.

Geographic divisions are important because of the somewhat different treatment of intellectual property in each country. The manufacture and use of the product related to the patent, trade secret, or know-how may be limited to the United States, but sales may be permitted worldwide. Payment must be defined as to the currency to be used as well as to who will pay any taxes or transfer charges. The parties must provide for government approval of the transfer of royalties and repatriation of capital.

A license agreement is a special form of contract in which each party promises to do something in exchange for promises by the other party. It is based on a business understanding between the parties and common sense applied to the attainment of business goals. But it is more complex than a normal contract because of the uniqueness of its subject matter, intellectual property—patents, trademarks, copyrights, trade secrets, and know-how. These properties require special action for their creation and maintenance. And great care is necessary in licensing such properties to maximize their returns and prevent their loss.

SOFTWARE PROTECTION

Protection for computer software has been the subject of debate for many years. At one time there was strong opposition to the awarding of patents for inventions embodied in or involving software. That is no longer the case: Now software is commonly patented. Copyright protection had been considered only for the coding, but that too has changed: Now it is clear that copyright protection covers not only the coding (the literal aspects of a computer program), but also aspects such as the sequence and flow, organization and structure, user interface, and menus. Trade secret protection was formerly available, but only if you kept the software secret, which made it awkward to embrace copyright. Now the Copyright Office has a procedure whereby software copyrights can be registered yet trade secrets contained in the software can be specifically preserved.

Patents for Software

Broad patent protection is available for software. The scope of patent protection extends beyond the coding or routines, beyond the structure and organization, beyond the user interface and menus of the program, to the broad underlying concept or algorithm. All manner of software is protectable by patent regardless of how it is perceived—as controlling industrial equipment or processes, as effecting data processing, or as operating the computer itself.

For example, software implementation of steps normally performed mentally may be patentable subject matter. Thus, while a method of doing business is not patentable subject matter, the software to effect a business activity may be. In one case, the software implementation of a system that automatically transferred a customer's funds among a brokerage security account, several money funds, and a Visa/checking account automatically upon the occurrence of preset conditions, was held to be patentable subject matter. Also, a software method of translating from one language to another (Russian to English) was found to be protectable.

Many patents have been issued on data processing software; following are some examples:

- A system for registering attendees at trade shows and conventions.
- A securities brokerage cash management system.
- An automated securities trading system.
- An insurance investment program for funding a future liability.
- Software for managing an auto loan.
- Software for optimization of industrial resource allocation.
- Software for automatically determining and isolating differences between text files (word processing).
- Software for returning to a specified point in a document (word processing).
- Software for determining premiums for insurance against specific weather conditions.

Software that operates the computer itself is patentable, too. For example, patents have issued on:

- Software for converting a source program to an object program.
- Programs that translate from one programming language to another.
- A cursor control for a pull-down menu bar.
- Software that displays images in windows on the video display.
- A computer display with window capability.

The software may be composed of old routines as long as they are assembled in a different way and produce a different result, for it is well established in patent law that a combination of old parts is patentable if the resulting whole is new. Indeed, most inventions are a new assembly of well-known parts or steps.

Design patents too have been used to protect software. Design patents have been issued for visual features produced on the screen by the computer software, such as various display icons; one example is an icon for a telephone display.

Software Copyrights

Copyright protection for software, though not as broad as patent protection, is nevertheless quite broad. As stated earlier, a copyright protects not just against the copying of the coding but also against the copying of the organization and structure—its "look and feel." If a subsequent developer creates software that "looks and feels" like earlier copyrighted software, there is infringement, whether or not the coding is similar. But courts do differ on the breadth of copyright protection.

All forms of programs are protectable by copyright—flow charts, source programs, assembly programs, object programs. And it makes no difference whether the program is an operating system or an applications program. No distinction is made concerning the copyrightability of programs that directly interact with the computer user and those that, unseen, manage the computer system internally. Protection is also afforded microcode or microprograms that are buried in a microprocessor, and even programs embedded in a silicon chip.

Databases too are protected by copyright. The input of a copyrighted database results in the making of a copy, so there is copyright infringement. It makes no difference if the data copied from indices and graphs or maps is rearranged not as another book or visual aid but as an electronically stored database: It is infringement. And this is so even if new and different maps, graphs, and text are produced from a database by the computer.

Even more subtle copyright problems have occurred regarding databases. The purveyor of a computer program that permits users to access and analyze the copyrighted database of another was found liable for copyright infringement because in order to analyze the data, the program had to first copy portions of the database.

Software Trade Secret Protection

Software may also be protected through a trade secret approach, separately or in conjunction with patent and copyright protection. Normally, all information disclosed in a published copyrighted work is in the public domain. However, the U.S. Copyright Office fully recognizes the compatibility of copyright and trade secret protection, and its rules provide special filing procedures to protect trade secrets in copyrighted software.

HOW TO AVOID THE PRELIMINARY PITFALLS OF PROTECTING INTELLECTUAL PROPERTY

Frequently, when a person thinks of protecting a new idea or product, the thoughts turn to patents, trade secrets, and copyrights. But the game can be won or lost long before one has the opportunity to establish one of those forms of protection. That is why the fundamental forms of protection—confidential disclosure agreements, employment contracts, and consultant contracts—are so important. Whether or not an idea or product is protectable by an exclusive statutory right such as a patent or copyright, there still is a need at an early stage, before such protection can be obtained, to *keep the basic information confidential* in order to prevent public use or disclosure, which can result in the loss of rights and inspire others to seek statutory rights before you.

Confidential disclosure agreements, employment agreements, and consultant agreements have some things in common. They define the obligations of the parties during the critical early stages of development of a new concept, product, or process. They are usually overlooked until it's too late, after the relationship is well under way and a problem has arisen. For proper protection of the business, there must be agreements with employees, consultants, and, in some cases, suppliers and customers to keep secret all important information of the business and to assign to the business all rights to that information.

It is commonly thought that only technical information can be protected. This is not so. All of the following can be protectable information:

- Ideas for new products or product lines.
- A new advertising or marketing program.
- A new trademark idea.
- The identity of a critical supplier.
- A refinancing plan.

And all of these can be even more valuable than the technical matters when it comes to establishing an edge over the competition and gaining a greater market share.

Employment contracts, consultant contracts, and confidential disclosure agreements all should be in writing and signed before the relationship begins, before any work is done, before any critical information is exposed, and before any money changes hands. A business must not be in such a rush to get on with the project that it ends up without full ownership of the very thing it paid for. And the employees, consultants, or other parties must not be so anxious to get the work that they fail to understand clearly at the outset what they are giving up in undertaking this relationship.

Preparing Employment Contracts

Employment contracts must be fair to both parties and should be signed by all employees, at least those who may be exposed to confidential company matters or may contribute ideas or inventions to the business. They should also be short and readable.

Employment contracts, like all agreements, must have considerations flowing both ways. If I agree to paint your house for $1,000, my consideration to you is the painting of your house. Your consideration to me is the $1,000. In an employment contract, the consideration from the employee includes all promises to keep secrets and assign ideas and inventions; the consideration from the business is to employ the employee. Thus, it is best to present these contracts to the prospective employee well before she begins work.

After the job has begun, the consideration will be the employee's "continued" employment, and that sounds a bit threatening. Although "continued" employment is certainly proper consideration, in construing these contracts courts can easily see that the employer usually has the superior bargaining position, and so they generally like to know that when the contract was offered for signature, the employee had a fair opportunity to decline without suffering severe hardship. It is not a good idea to present the employment contract in a packet of pension, hospitalization, and other forms to be signed the day the employee shows up to begin work after having moved the entire family across the country in order to take the job.

Transfer of Employee Rights
to Company Innovations

One of the most important clauses in an employment contract is the agreement by the employee to transfer to the company the entire right, title, and interest in and to all ideas, innovations, and creations. These include designs, developments, inventions, improvements, trade secrets, discoveries, writings, and other works, including software, databases, and other computer-related products and processes. The transfer is required whether or not these items are patentable or copyrightable. They should be assigned to the company if they were made, conceived, or first reduced to practice by the employee. This obligation should hold whether the employee was working alone or with others and whether or not the work was done during normal working hours or on the company premises. So long as the work is within the scope of the company's business, research, or investigation or it resulted from or is suggested by any of the work performed for the company, its ownership is required to be assigned to the company.

This clause should *not* seek to compel transfer of ownership for everything an employee does, even *if it has no relation to the company's business.* For example, an engineer employed to design phased array radar for an electronics company may invent a new horseshoe or write a book on the history of steeplechase racing. An attempt to compel assignment of ownership of such works under an employment agreement could be seen as overreaching and unenforceable. The same may be true of a clause that seeks to vest in the employer ownership of inventions, innovations, or other works made for a period of time after employment ends or before employment begins.

Ancillary to this transfer or assignment clause is the agreement of the employee to promptly disclose the inventions, innovations, and works to the company or to any person designated by the company, and to assist in obtaining protection for the company, including patents and copyrights in all countries designated by the company. The employee at this point also agrees to execute:

- Patent applications and copyright applications.
- Assignments of issued patents and copyright registrations.
- Any other documents necessary to perfect the various properties and vest their ownership clearly in the company.

If these activities are called for after the employee has left the company, she is still obligated to perform but must be paid for time and expenses.

How Employee Moonlighting Might Compromise Confidentiality

Another important concern is moonlighting. While a company that sells CAD/CAM workstations doesn't care if its programmers drive fish delivery trucks on their own time, there are extremely sensitive situations that the company as well as the employee must take care to avoid. In one case a CAD/CAM company discovered huge telephone charges for various lengthy periods from

3:00 P.M. to 8:00 P.M. on most days of the week, including Saturdays and Sundays. The company challenged the telephone bill and found that the calls were indeed made from the company's own phones to a major computer manufacturer many miles away. The computer manufacturer claimed ignorance. But after a lengthy investigation it was discovered that an employee of the company had been hired on a consulting basis by a middle manager at the manufacturer to develop a software system. The employee had been doing his consulting for the computer manufacturer over the telephone lines from his computer terminal while sitting at his desk in his company office. The employee was not short-changing the company as far as hours were concerned; he was working long hours to make up for his moonlighting, and the software he was developing was not in the company's CAD/CAM area. But the revelation was chilling. The mere awareness that an information line existed between this giant computer manufacturer and the company, and what might have transpired over that line, haunted the company's officers and managers for some time afterward.

To prevent this, the employee should agree in the employment contract that during employment by the company there will be no engagement in any employment or activity in which the company is now or may later become involved, nor will there be moonlighting on the company's time or using the company's equipment or facilities.

Noncompetition Clauses

A closely related notion is a noncompetition provision whereby the employee agrees not to compete during his employment by the company and for some period after leaving the company's employ. This is a more sensitive area. It may be perfectly understandable that a company does not want its key salesperson, an officer, a manager, or the head of marketing or engineering to move to a new job with a competitor and have the inside track on his ex-employer's best customers, new product plans, manufacturing techniques, or new marketing program. But the courts do not like to prevent a person from earning a livelihood. Courts do not compel a lifelong radar engineer, for example, to turn down a job with a competitor in the same field and instead take a job designing cellular phones. A person who has spent a life-time marketing and selling drapes and curtains cannot be made to sell floor coverings or used cars.

However, the higher up and more important a person is in the operation of the company, the greater is the probability that that person will be prevented from competing if the employment agreement provides for it. Officers, directors, founders, majority stockholders, and other key personnel have had such provisions enforced against them, but even then the scope of the exclusion must be fair and reasonable in terms of both time and distance. A few months, a year, or even two years could be acceptable, depending on how fast the technology and market is moving. Worldwide exclusion might be acceptable for a salesperson who sells transport planes. In the restaurant business, a few miles might be all that is necessary. A contract that seeks to extend the exclusion beyond what's fair will not be enforced.

One way to ensure that an ex-employee does not compete is to allow the company to employ the person on a consultant basis over some designated period of time. In this way the employee's involvement in critical information areas can gradually be phased out, so that by the time the employee is free to go to a competitor there is no longer a threat to the company, and at the same time the employee has been fairly compensated.

Bear in mind, however, that even if ex-employees are free to compete, they are not free to take with them (in their memories or in recorded form) any trade secrets or any information confidential or proprietary to the company or to use it or disclose it in any way. To reinforce this the employment contract should provide that the employee will not, during employment by the company or at any time thereafter, disclose to others or use for her own benefit or for the benefit of others any trade secrets or any confidential or proprietary information pertaining to any businesses of the company—technical, commercial, financial, sales, marketing, or otherwise. The restriction could also protect such information pertaining to the business of any of the company's clients, customers, consultants, licensees, affiliates, and the like.

Along with this the employment contract should provide that all documents, records, models, electronic storage devices, prototypes, and other tangible items representing or embodying company property or information are the sole and exclusive property of the company and must be surrendered to the company no later than the termination of employment, or at any earlier time upon request of the company. This is an important provision for both the employer and employee to understand. In some states the law imposes serious criminal sanctions and fines for the removal of tangible trade secret property.

Preventing Employee Raiding

Another potential area of conflict is employee raiding, the hiring away of employees by an ex-employee who is now employed by a competitor or who has founded a competing business. This is a particularly sensitive situation when the ex-employee holds a position of high trust and confidence and was looked up to by the employees she is now attempting to hire. And it is particularly damaging when the employees being seduced are critical to operations either because of their expertise or their sheer numbers. In all circumstances such an outflow of employees is threatening because of the potential loss to a competitor of trade secrets and know-how. This can be addressed by a clause prohibiting an employee, during her employment period and for some period thereafter, from hiring away fellow employees for another enterprise.

Employee Ownership of Copyright

One of the most hazardous areas of ownership involves the title to copyrights. If a copyrighted work is created or authored by an employee, the company automatically owns the copyright. But the employee must be a bona fide employee. That is, there must be all the trappings of regular employment. If a dispute arises over ownership between the company and the author, the courts will seek to determine whether the author was really an employee. Was this person provided a full work week, benefits, withholding, unemployment insurance, worker's compensation, and an office or workspace? If the author was anything less than a full employee, the copyright for the work belongs to the person. It does not belong to the company!

This means that if the company hires a part-time employee, a consultant, a friend, or a moonlighter, that person may end up owning the copyright for the work. Thus, when that nonemployee completes the software system that will revolutionize the industry and bring income cascading to the enterprise, the employee, not the company, will own the copyright. The company will own the embodiment of the system that the employee developed for the company, but the employee will own the right to reproduce, copy, and sell the system over and over again. It has happened. A company that spent hundreds of thousands of dollars to develop a software system owned the finished product but not the copyright in the product. The nonemployee owned the copyright and had the right to reproduce the product without limit and sell it to those who most desire it—typically the company's competitors and customers.

This is a chilling scenario but one that is easy to avoid with a little forethought. The solution is easy: Simply get it in writing. Before any work starts, payment changes hands, or plans are revealed, *have the proposed author sign a written agreement* specifying that, whether or not the author is subsequently held to be an employee or a nonemployee, all right, title, and interest in any copyrightable material is assigned to the company. The lack of such a clear understanding in writing can wreck great dreams, ruin friendships and partnerships, and hamstring businesses to the point of insolvency while the parties fight over who owns the bunny rabbit, the book, the software, the poster, or the videotape on how to be a successful entrepreneur.

Moral Rights of Authors or Artists

Another area that must be considered is the moral rights of authors in their works. Under a law effective June 1, 1991, in the United States, moral rights of artists in their visual works are protected. Moral rights are variously defined as the rights of attribution and integrity, or the rights of paternity and integrity. What this means is that an artist has a right to insist that his name be associated with the work, or to refuse to have his name associated with the work if it is mutilated in the artist's opinion, and also to insist that the work not be mutilated; that is, the integrity of the work must be maintained. The moral rights doctrine has been invoked, for example, in an attempt to prevent the removal of a wall containing a painted mural.

The law in the United States that established the moral rights doctrine provides that the artist's moral rights may not be transferred, but may be waived by the artist in a written statement that specifically identifies the work and the uses to which the waiver applies.

Therefore, in every agreement dealing with copyrights it is prudent to include a clause in which the artist in writing specifically refers to the work or works and waives the moral rights for all uses of all the works. It probably would also be wise to refer to Section 106(a) of the Copyright Act, which embodies the moral rights doctrine.

Rights of Prior Employees

There is another issue to consider under employment contracts. When a new employee is to be hired, obtain a copy of the employment contract with the last employer or the last few employers to determine whether this employee is free to work for this company now, in the capacity the employee seeks. Prior employers have rights, too, that can conflict, rightly or wrongly, with the employee's new employment.

Consultant Contracts

Consultant contracts should contain provisions similar to those in an employment contract, along with some additional provisions. A consultant agreement should clearly define the task for which the consultant is hired—for example, to research a new area; to analyze or solve a problem; design or redesign a product; set up a production line; or assist in marketing, sales, management, technical, or financial matters. This is important to show:

- Why the consultant was hired.
- What the consultant is expected to do.

- What the consultant may be exposed to in the way of company trade secrets and confidential and proprietary information.
- What the consultant is expected to assign to the company in the way of innovations, inventions, patents, and copyrights.

A company hiring a consultant wants to own the result of whatever the consultant was hired to do, just as in the case of an employee. But a consultant's stock in trade is the expertise and ability to solve problems swiftly and elegantly in a specific subject area. Sharp lines must be drawn as to what the consultant will and will not assign to give both parties peace of mind.

Consulting relationships by their nature can expose each of the parties to a great deal of the other party's trade secrets and confidential and proprietary information. The company can protect itself with clear identification of the pertinent information and by employing the usual safeguards for trade secrets. It also must limit disclosure to the consultant to what is necessary to do the job, and also limit the consultant's freedom to use the information in work for others and to disseminate the information. Consultants must protect themselves in the same way to prevent the company from misappropriating the consultant's special knowledge, problem-solving approaches, and analytical techniques.

An often overlooked area is the ownership of notes, memos, and failed avenues of investigation. False starts and failures can be as important as the solution, especially to competitors. Related to this is the question of the ownership of the raw data. Raw data may be extremely valuable in their own right but also may be used to easily reconstruct the end result of the consultant's work, such as a market survey.

Confidential Disclosure Agreements

Whenever an idea, information, an invention, or any knowledge of peculiar value is to be revealed, a confidential disclosure agreement should be signed by the receiving party to protect the disclosing party. The disclosure may be necessary for any of the following reasons:

- To interest a manufacturer in taking a license to make and sell a new product.
- To hire a consultant to advise in a certain area.
- To permit a supplier to give an accurate bid.
- To allow a customer to determine whether or not it wants a product or wants a product modified.
- To interest investors to invest in the business.

Domestic agreements are important not only to protect the knowledge or information itself, but also to preserve valuable related rights such as *domestic and foreign patent rights*. These agreements should be short and to the point.

Basically, the receiver of the disclosure should agree to keep confidential all information disclosed. Information is defined as all trade secrets and all proprietary and confidential information, whether tangible or intangible, oral or written, and of whatever nature (for example, technical, sales, marketing, advertising, promotional, merchandising, financial, or commercial).

The receiver should agree to receive all such information in confidence and not to use or disclose the information without the express written consent of the discloser. It should be made clear that no obligation is incurred by the receiver for any information that it can show was in the public domain, that the receiver already knew, or that was told to the receiver by another party.

The receiver should be limited to disclosing the information to only those of its employees who need to know in order to carry out the purposes of the agreement and who have obligations of secrecy and confidentiality to the receiver. Further, the receiver should agree that all of its employees to whom any information is communicated are obligated under written employment agreements to keep the information secret. The receiver should also represent that it will exercise the same standard of care in safeguarding this information as it does for its own, and in no event less than a reasonable standard of care. This latter phrase is necessary because some businesses have no standard of care or a very sloppy attitude toward even their own important information.

Provision should be made for the return of all tangible embodiments of the confidentially disclosed information, including drawings, blueprints, designs, parameters of design, monographs, specifications, flow charts, sketches, descriptions, and data. A provision could also be included preventing the receiving party from entering a competing business or introducing a competing product or service in the area of the disclosed information. Often a time limit is requested by the receiver, after which the receiver is free to disclose or use the information. Such a time period could extend from a few months to a number of years, depending on the life cycle of the information, tendency to copy, competitive lead time, and other factors present in a particular industry. Strong, clear language should be used to establish that no license or any other right, express or implied, to the information is given by the agreement.

While such confidential disclosure agreements between the discloser and receiver are the ideal, they are not always obtainable. The receiver may argue that no such agreement is necessary, saying in effect, "Trust me." Or the receiver may flatly refuse on the grounds that it is against its policy. Some large corporations turn the tables and demand that their own standard *non*confidential disclosure agreement be signed before the disclosure of any information.

Under a nonconfidential disclosure agreement, often referred to as *idea submission agreements,* the discloser gives up all rights to the information except as covered by a U.S. patent or copyright. Outside of those protections the receiver is free to use, disclose, or do whatever it wishes with the information. This is not due simply to arrogance or orneriness. A large corporation has many departments and divisions where research and development of new ideas are occurring unknown to other areas of the corporation. In addition, in a number of cases courts have held corporations liable for misappropriation of ideas and information when no written agreement existed, and even where a *non*confidential disclosure agreement purported to free the receiver from any restriction against dissemination and use of the idea.

If no agreement can be reached or if the nonconfidential disclosure agreement counteroffer occurs, the discloser must decide whether to keep the idea under the mattress or take a chance on the honesty of the receiver; however, in such a case it is wise to reduce the initial disclosure to a minimum to cut the losses should a careless or unscrupulous receiver make public or misappropriate the idea.

A middle ground that courts have recognized is an implied confidential relationship evidenced by the actions of the parties. In one case a letter soliciting a receiver's interest in a particular field and indicating that the matter was confidential, resulted in a face-to-face meeting between the discloser and receiver, where the full idea was revealed. Later, when the receiver came out with a product using the idea, the discloser sued and won. The letter set up a confidential relationship which the receiver did not reject, but rather accepted by meeting with the discloser and accepting the idea without any comment or exclusion. The letter was not signed by the receiver, but it bound the company nevertheless under the totality of the circumstances.

CONCLUSION

These basic forms of protection—employment contracts, consultant contracts, and confidential disclosure agreements—need not be complex or lengthy, but they are essential at the earliest stages of idea generation to protect and preserve for the business some of its most valuable and critical property.

12 FRANCHISING
Steve Spinelli

In the United States in 1995, some 663,000 franchised outlets had total sales of over \$1 trillion, accounting for 40% of all retail sales.[1] The International Franchise Association believes that number will rise by more than 12% in 1996. There are another 90,000 franchised outlets internationally. Franchising experienced a 127% growth in the 1980s. The sheer size of what is called franchising makes it worth investigating.

WHAT IS FRANCHISING?

Over the years franchising has been much maligned as anything from a pyramid scheme to just another form of employment. However, the criticism is seldom warranted. Some of the confusion exists because franchises come in many forms. Robert T. Justis, Professor of Franchising at the University of Nebraska, defines franchising in general as

> a business opportunity by which the owner, producer, or distributor (franchisor) of a service or trademarked product grants exclusive rights to an individual (franchisee) for the local distribution of the product or service, and in return receives a payment or royalty and conformance to quality standards.

The most widely recognized method of franchising is the business format franchise. *Business format franchising* is defined as a contractual, ongoing business relationship between a franchisor and franchisee. The business format concept includes a marketing plan, documented and enforced procedures, process assistance, and business development and innovation. Business format franchising is an overall method of doing business and is a more complex relationship than franchising solely for the purpose of product distribution. The relationship in a business format franchise must be as dynamic as the marketplace to survive.

HISTORICAL BACKGROUND

Few business practitioners or students have not heard about the McDonald's story and its founder, Ray Kroc. Although their contribution to franchising is monumental, the history of franchising dates much further back.

The extensive "pub" network in the United Kingdom may be the oldest franchise system in the world. During the Roman occupation of Britain, the major supplier of food, drink, and accommodations for the traveler was the Church. Religious tenets of the time dictated that two days' food and lodging be supplied free to any traveler. Abuses of these privileges resulted in the growth of commercial enterprises around 740–750.

By 957 King Edgar decided there were too many alehouses and decreed a limit of one per village. As a part of that decree some common standards were instituted. The business format required a standard measure, limited quantities, and a prohibition of sales to priests. A monitoring system was established and fines levied against violators. Franchising was born.

The population steadily grew, and evolving consumer and economic realities forced consolidation of the industry. The national brewers recognized a need to secure market share. "Publicans grappled with the difficulty of keeping pace with fast moving events and the ever-increasing demands of various kinds."[2] More and more pub owners allied with brewers. By the early nineteenth century, half of all alehouses were tied by some form of agreement. The House of Commons Committee on Public Breweries in 1818 noted that tied houses were "of much higher order" than free houses.[3] Franchising was here to stay.

Franchising in the United States began in the 1840s and continues to grow today.[4] Two distinct types of franchises have developed. The first, *product franchising,* was created by makers of complex durable goods who found existing wholesalers either unwilling or unable to market their products. These manufacturers built their own distribution systems and created franchise systems as alternatives to the high cost of company-owned outlets. The second type, *business format franchising*, was created in the 1950s when it became evident that the outlet itself could be a vehicle for entrepreneurial activity.

A franchise system can be a combination of franchisor-operated outlets and franchisee-operated outlets or only franchisee-operated outlets. Eighty-seven percent of the outlets in U.S. franchise systems are operated by franchisees. Types of businesses generally included in business format franchising are restaurants, food and nonfood retailing, and business services. Not included in business format franchising are gas stations and soft drink bottlers, for example. Midas and Dunkin' Donuts are two examples of business format franchises. A consumer electronics retailer of Sony would be a product franchise.

BECOMING A FRANCHISEE VERSUS STARTING A STAND-ALONE BUSINESS

The issues pertinent to success in a franchise are the same as for any other business. The difference is that the array of factors responsible for a franchise's success are tried and true, and there is a proven ability to transfer this system of excellence to varied and dispersed locations. Therefore, the franchise model is predicated on the assumption that *value has been developed* through the careful operation, testing, and documentation of a commercially viable idea. Given that this has been accomplished (which your own diligence must verify), the initial success of the system lies in the ability of the franchisor to communicate this system to qualified franchisees. The long-term success of the system is uniquely tied to the franchisor's ability to receive and assimilate process feedback from the franchisees and use this feedback to modify the system.

The choice of becoming a franchisee or starting a stand-alone business hinges on your answers to two important questions:

- Is risk sufficiently mitigated by the trademark value, operating system, economies of scale, and support process of the franchise to justify a sharing of equity with the franchisor (vis-à-vis the franchise fee and royalty payments)?
- Is my personality and management style amenable to sharing decision-making responsibilities in my business with the franchisor and other franchisees?

For those who need to quantify the choice between a franchise and a stand-alone business, I offer the following:

Franchise fee + PV of royalty = PV of the increased net income from
the value of the franchise trademark

where PV is the present value of a sum of money. (For an explanation of PV, see Chapter 13 and the glossary.) You must also apply a "discount rate" to both the royalty and the proposed increase in net income. The discount rate represents your confidence in the income stream. The more established the franchise the lower the discount rate. If your analysis reveals this equation to be true, or if the right-hand side of the equation is greater than the left-hand side, the franchise decision is appropriate.

Much of this chapter focuses on the quantity and quality of the services and systems that a franchise offers. The choice of a franchise versus stand-alone startup is a question of due diligence, of evaluating the competitive advantages offered by the franchise. Those advantages must exist in sufficient quantity to justify the cost in franchise fees, royalties, and management encumbrances. The foundation for due diligence lies in the contract between the franchisee and franchisor.

THE FRANCHISE CONTRACT

The most refined franchise relationship develops into a partnership between the franchisor and the franchisee, and among the franchisees. However, a contract is necessary to ensure an understanding between the parties of their rights and obligations and the associated costs. In franchising, this contract is usually called a license agreement or a franchise contract. Within the context of individual state franchise laws or under the umbrella of contract law, the license agreement is integral to the legal relationship.

In a mature franchise the trade name and trademark are the most valuable assets owned by the franchisor. In the business format franchise the documented operating system is integral to the trade name and trademark. Together they are responsible for the market value of the franchise. In some cases building specifications, equipment design, and secret formulas or recipes may be important parts of the franchisor's assets. (For example, the Colonel adamantly believed his "secret recipe" was integral to the product and image of Kentucky Fried Chicken.) Some assets may be patented or copyrighted.

Consideration of franchising by a company or due diligence by a franchise prospect requires an intimate understanding of the license agreement. Franchising is a legal specialization, and some firms concentrate their entire practice in this field. An attorney's review of the license agreement is a necessary cost of franchising. As a part of the legal review, the attorney should prepare a lay-language brief of the license agreement. In the development or review of a license agreement, business issues will be woven into the legalese. The more practical the detail in the license agreement, the better the chance for a healthy long-term relationship. However, implementing the license agreement will require the franchisor to incur monitoring costs, which must be considered along with other costs of the relationship such as litigation expense and quality concerns.

This chapter focuses primarily on the license agreement, or franchise contract. Understanding the terms of the license agreement is an integral part of the risk management process vital to all franchise endeavors. The following sections highlight the normal operating parameters in a franchise contract with special attention to the pitfalls. Proper evaluation of the franchise opportunity rests in assessing the value and cost of the franchise in relation to expected profits from going it alone.

Services Provided by the Franchisor

This section of the contract is invariably briefer than that detailing the franchisee obligations. However, a few key references will be sufficient to indicate the franchisor's positive intent and obligation. The services provided by the franchisor are separated into initial and continuing services. The type of business will heavily influence the services the franchisor supplies. As a rule of thumb, the prospective franchisee should discount any personal knowledge or experience in the industry and then ask the question, will the magnitude of the initial services establish the franchisee business in a manner appropriate to efficient operation on the day of opening?

Real Estate Development

Because many business format franchises include a real estate ingredient, site selection and construction specification and supervision are extremely important. Such slogans as "Location, location, location," "Just around the corner from success," and "a 'B' site will get you an 'F' in profitability" are not exaggerations. The real estate on which an outlet is located is often the point of sale and usually cannot be changed without severe economic stress. Most franchisors will approve the location, but not all will actually search for a site. Even fewer will take *responsibility* for finding a site.

The key aspects of site location include a thorough understanding of the primary target audience (PTA), your most likely customer, and the propensity of the PTA to patronize your franchise under varying environmental conditions. An important part of the franchisor's value lies in the accumulation and processing of data from the operating units. Although the franchisor cannot and should not give out information regarding specific stores, compilations with analysis are usually available. This is how the PTA information is gathered. If it is the franchisee's responsibility to locate a site, there must be clearly documented processes linking the PTA to the location specifics. General location parameters include cost, population, traffic volume, traffic patterns, visibility, zoning and permits, and ingress and egress; each of these factors is discussed in the following sections.

Cost

A Holiday Inn franchise requires at least a $2 million investment, much of which is in the real estate. While this is at the extreme in franchise real estate costs, it illustrates the central role of real estate in the success of a franchise. A long-established retail venture may decide to franchise, and a thorough analysis of the site characteristics will reveal certain location standards for successful expansion. A problem can soon surface, however, if the current real estate's market value is not known or is calculated on the existing operation's occupancy cost.

A franchised location under the current market values may not be viable. Contact a large commercial real estate broker and review the site specifications. Gather examples of recently sold or leased property with comparable specifications. Do the property or occupancy costs correlate with the franchisor guidelines? This process should also be followed by the franchisor, especially when expansion into new geographic territories is contemplated. Even if purchase prices are the same, lease terms and conditions can vary over time and among regions. Make sure that the "cap rates" used in calculating lease cost are comparable. The capitalization rate is the percentage return the landlord can expect her property to yield on the value of the asset (in this case, land and building) that is being leased. The term of a lease, the amount of time the lessee contractually holds the property, should match the term of the license agreement.

Population

How many PTA members—not members of the general population—in how wide a market area are prescribed by the franchisor? For example, Service-Master lawn care tracks dual-income homes in their trade areas. Cross the minimum PTA number with the franchisor pro forma market share and sales projection:

3-mile radius
50,000 population, 20,000 PTA
10% market share

2,000 PTA × 3 visits per year = 6,000 customers

Franchisor's sales projections/6,000 = Average ticket price

Do a spreadsheet analysis ramping up volume to equal these sample numbers. Are your projections reasonable and in line with the numbers projected by the franchisor? Will existing outlets' performance validate these projections?

Traffic Volume

Volume is quoted as pedestrians or vehicles per day. Many franchisors will prescribe a minimum volume, usually quoted on a 12- or 24-hour basis. Take note of the outlets the franchisor has singled out or the outlets of franchisees who have expressed satisfaction with their sales volume. Most state departments of motor vehicles, registry, or public works have traffic flow information.

Traffic Patterns

Corner location, the home-bound versus work-bound side of the road, and speed of traffic are but a few of the critical issues related to traffic patterns. A donut franchise may require the work-bound side of the road. Customers are less likely to stop for morning coffee if they must cross traffic when rushing to their jobs. This is an example of the fine distinction between a marginal return and a substantial return—or worse, the difference between failure and success.

Visibility

Visibility is especially important for products bought on impulse. When it is noon and you are hungry, you may act on impulse in reaction to a fast-food sign. Finding a preschool (a growing area of franchising) is probably a more considered choice and not an impulse purchase.

Visibility is a three-prong issue, including the elements of sign, building, and property entrance. At the top speed of the vehicles traveling the road of the proposed location (not to be confused with the posted speed), how many feet and seconds pass from the first view of each of these criteria to the entrance of the site? Is there sufficient time from the initial sighting of the location variable for a driver to comfortably turn into the location? A location that provides adequate turning time with respect to all three visibility variables has the highest ranking in this area.

Seasonality has an impact on visibility. A site as viewed in the winter may yield dramatically different results from the same site in the spring, with trees in full leaf.

Zoning and Permits

The cost and time requirements relating to zoning can vary dramatically from state to state and among local municipalities. Often a land use attorney is required for the process, as well as architects, surveyors, civil engineers, and traffic specialists. Increasingly, environmental impact studies are mandated by state regulation. Estimate the cost of these professionals as a part of due diligence.

Usually the franchisee is required to bear these costs up front. If the franchisor bears the costs, they are often capitalized in the real estate development expense and will be reflected in the outlet rent. In particularly complicated zoning affairs the cost may inflate the project well beyond the ultimate market value and potentially beyond the occupancy cost projected in the franchisor's financial pro forma.

Ingress and Egress

This is real estate jargon for entrance to and exit from the site. Checkers drive-in restaurant, launched in 1986, requires most site plans to have two drive-through windows in the flow of ingress and egress. Planning boards frequently modify a site plan even at the last minute. A quick change in entrance and exit layout can dramatically alter site acquisition criteria.

Summing Up: Don't Ignore Location Success Factors

If franchising is the vehicle chosen by a currently operating firm for expansion, it is critical to match the existing location success factors to the business format developed for sale to a franchisee. To neglect this is a fatal flaw, especially if the franchisee is responsible for finding the new location. It is extremely difficult to overcome location flaws and often impossible to change them.

In rapidly growing franchise systems there is a greater propensity to compromise on the development of individual stores in a rush to gain market share. Often the decision to franchise is made as a result of the desire to grow quickly. This cannot be allowed to dominate good business practice if long-term stability is an objective.

It is mutually beneficial to the franchisor and franchisee to have franchisor professionals provide detailed input in the real estate development. Some franchises typically locate in a mall—T-Shirt *plus*, for example. The same attention to location and demographic issues applies. A successful outlet will yield profit for the franchisee and capital for expansion. The franchisor will gain larger royalty payments. If the franchise is operated poorly and it ultimately fails, the franchisor can turn over the unit quickly, operate it as a company store, or sell the property to an unrelated third party only if the real estate has been carefully acquired and developed.

Investing in the real estate is a separate business venture from the franchise for both the franchisor and the franchisee. In evaluating the franchise opportunity, calculate the occupancy cost on a *market rental rate*. This can be done by multiplying the market square footage rental cost by the size of the proposed project. Alternatively, use the *market lease factor*—8% in a depressed market (August 1992 in New England), 11% in an expansive market (New York, 1987)—applied to the total project cost. The market lease factor is the rate the landlord will charge based on the current demand in the marketplace.

A franchisor who wishes to be the realty holder or lessor will need to negotiate the rental relationship. Some franchisors use what is called "percentage rent" to calculate the occupancy cost for the franchisee. There are a number of methods to implement percentage rents. The simplest is to charge a constant percentage of top-line sales. This can be beneficial in the startup phase but can result in above-market rents for the exceptionally performing location. This is particularly true for businesses with rapidly escalating costs and pricing, and can result in squeezed franchisee margins. This rental formula may seem attractive at the outset but could become burdensome. The variations in the use of percentage rents are limitless. Other methods include charging base rent, a minimum amount each month plus a smaller amount of top-line sales, or an amount slightly less than market rent plus a percentage of top-line sales over the projected break-even sales volume. Some franchisors will offer a variety of options; some will not. The franchisee should negotiate the options as a result of pro forma analysis and in congruence with risk mentality.

Established expertise in interpreting crucial real estate variables is included as part of the franchise purchase. Therefore, the franchisee must be sufficiently convinced that the necessary expertise is in place, available, and utilized.

Construction Specification and Supervision

Upon preliminary qualification of the site, the franchisor should integrate its construction department into the process. The franchisor usually has a standard set of blueprints. Most states require modification to meet state building code with the stamp of an architect from that state. Further modification may be required by local municipalities. Some franchisors modify plans even to the local level, but most do not. The level of sophistication of the model plans will greatly impact modification cost and efficiency. Very general plans leave much room for architectural inventiveness, resulting in diminished standardization, loss of efficiency, and reduced market value of the real estate.

Beyond the physical blueprints, the franchisor may provide construction supervision. Bidding contracts, draw approvals, construction monitoring, and final punch list are the categories of construction supervision. Beware of the franchisor who controls the construction process without independent bidding. There is nothing wrong with construction as a profit center if it also accrues benefits to the franchisee. This is best monitored through the marketplace of contractors. The franchisee should be involved in the construction process even if it is totally supervised by the franchisor. The franchise operator will understand the building better and live with it in greater harmony. Minor examples of building aspects the operator must be familiar with include the heating, ventilation and air conditioning, and basement sump pump operation.

Training

Training is a vital initial service and is also helpful on a continuing basis. The license agreement must define the *specific* form in which this franchisor responsibility will be carried out. It should extend significantly beyond a manual and the classroom. Training will vary with the specifics of the franchise but invariably should include organized and monitored on-the-job experience. Well-established and stable franchise systems require operational experience in the system for as long as a year prior to the purchase of a franchise. However, this is not the norm. Once the franchise is operational, the franchisee may be expected to do much or all of the on-site training. Manuals, testing, training aids such as videos, and certification processes are often provided by the franchisor.

As discussed previously, the trade name and mark are the most valuable assets in a franchise system. This is the result of delivery of the product on a consistent basis to consumers who acknowledge the value through paying a price that includes a profit margin. A poor training regimen will inevitably dilute the standardized, consistent delivery of the product and reduce trade name value.

Preopening Support

The foundation of the support services program is the level and sophistication of preopening support. Preopening support is a concentrated, multifunctional program to launch the new franchise. Inventory and equipment purchase and setup, staff hiring and training, and startup marketing are key variables. Built upon a sound location program, preparedness at launch can create the momentum for success. The franchisor who has the expertise in place to provide sophisticated startup assistance likely has the capability to provide the contractually required continuing services. A poor opening experience is an ominous sign concerning the quality of the franchise.

Continuing Services

Many license agreements define royalties as payment for the use of intellectual property. However, the continuity of the franchise relationship often rests on the cost/value rationalization of the royalty payment by the franchisee to the franchisor. Not only must the franchisor create a marketplace basket of services, but in the provision of services the system must be sustained and nurtured.

The actions of each franchisee affect the value of the trademark and thus the value of each individual franchise. The actions of the franchisor also affect franchise value. Both parties are necessarily interdependent and have a vested interest in actively supporting the system. A franchise agreement that acknowledges and addresses this interdependence is advantageous. The franchisee's performance is somewhat dependent on the quantity and quality of franchisor support. Conversely, the degree of franchisor support is usually inversely related to franchisee performance; more attention is usually provided the underperforming franchisee. Although this is a reasonable response to a threat to trademark value, balance in the application of franchisor resources is a key ingredient for success.

Performance and Standards Monitoring

By developing an array of statistical and financial monitoring devices, the franchisor can identify both the exceptional performer and the potential failure. Application of resources against identified problems maintains a stable system. Operational systems or marketing programs are often changed in a franchise system because of the exceptional performer. The best franchise systems not only compile data but analyze and efficiently distribute the information to franchisees for feedback. Sophisticated computer interfaced management information systems are rapidly becoming a franchise standard. Such systems are very expensive and provide franchises a significant competitive advantage over stand alone competition. Does the contract provide for this informational conduit role?

Field Support

The license agreement should provide for scheduled visits to the franchisee's place of business with prescribed objectives. An efficient agenda might include performance review, field training, facilities inspection, local marketing review, and operations audit. The reality is that some franchisors use their field role as a diplomatic or pejorative exercise. The greater the substance of the field function, the easier it is for the franchisee to justify the royalty cost. Additionally, in a litigious environment a well-documented field support program will mute franchisee claims.

One means of understanding the franchisor's field support motive is to investigate the manner in which the field support personnel are compensated. If field staff are paid commensurate with franchisee performance and ultimate profitability, then politics will play a diminished role. Warning signals are bonuses for growth in the number of stores versus individual store sales growth and pay or bonus for franchisee product usage. Tying arrangements will be discussed later. However, the field support system is a part of the practical application of the influence strategy the franchisor has chosen.

Operational Research and Development

Economies of scale for research and development is a principal benefit in franchising. These economies are best achieved through the centralized, monitored, and standardized franchisor. Research of a franchise should track operations-level changes in franchised stores over a period of two to four years. How are changes in the system encouraged, cultivated, harvested, and communicated? A practical mechanism should be referred to or specifically outlined in the license agreement.

This is a difficult and delicate area for the franchisor. The franchisor must ensure standardization but also must encourage change. This paradox is resolved by realizing that change will occur but must be managed. Franchising provides the mechanism for the efficient management of change. Customer needs, the legal environment, competition, and most of all the entrepreneurial fervor of franchisees will stretch the envelope of standardization.

Recognizing this, the franchise must provide rules in the license agreement for optimizing efforts in the search for betterment of the system. In franchise systems where the franchisor does not operate a number of company-owned stores, the existing franchise body or representative group should play a part in reviewing and approving issues of product or operational change. These kinds of changes are sometimes covered in the marketing services section of the license agreement.

Marketing, Advertising, and Promotion

This is one of the most sensitive areas in the ongoing franchise relationship. Marketing imprints the trade name and mark in the mind of the consumer. If delivery of the product validates the marketing message, the value of the franchise is enhanced. Store growth increases budgets and spreads marketing costs, optimizing the marketing program for the system.

There are a number of mechanisms to fund and implement a marketing program. Typically, a national advertising fund is controlled by the franchisor.

Each franchisee contributes a percentage of top-line sales. The franchisor then produces materials (television, radio, and newspaper ads; direct mail pieces; and point-of-sale materials) and, depending on the size of the fund, buys media time or space. As it is virtually impossible to allocate these services on an exactly equal basis among franchisees, the license agreement will specify the use of "best efforts" to approximate equal treatment, or some such language. "Best efforts" invariably leave some franchisees with a little more and others with a little less advertising. Over time, this should balance but must be carefully monitored.

The second level of marketing, advertising, and promotion in franchising is regional. This is often structured on the basis of an "area of dominant influence," or ADI. All the stores in a given ADI—Greater Hartford, Connecticut, for example—would contribute a percentage of top-line sales to the ADI advertising cooperative. The cooperative's primary function is usually to buy media using franchisor-supplied or -approved advertising and to coordinate regional promotions. If the franchise has a regional advertising cooperative requirement in the license agreement, it should also have standardized ADI cooperative bylaws. These bylaws will outline such things as voting rights and define expenditure parameters. A single-store franchisee can be disadvantaged in a poorly organized cooperative. Conversely, a major contributor to the cooperative may find voting rights disproportionately low.

The final level of advertising is typically dubbed local advertising or local store marketing. At this level the franchisee is contractually required to make direct expenditures on advertising. There is a wide spectrum of permissible advertising expenditures, depending on the franchisor guidelines. However, the license agreement will probably not be specific. Franchisors will try to maintain discretion on this issue for maximum flexibility in the marketplace. Company-owned stores should have advertising requirements equal to those for the franchised units to avoid franchisor free-riding. Historical behavior is the best gauge of reasonableness.

It is important that the franchisor monitor and enforce marketing expenditures. A customer leaving one ADI and entering another will have been affected by the advertising of adjacent regions. Additionally, advertising expenditures not made are marketing impressions lost to the system. The marketing leverage inherent in franchising is thus suboptimized.

Product Purchase Provision

In many franchise systems, a major benefit is bulk buying and inventory control. There are a number of ways to account for this in a license agreement. Most franchisors will not be bound to best-price requirements. Changing markets, competitors, and U.S. antitrust laws make it impossible for the franchisor to ensure this. The franchise should employ a standard of best efforts or good faith to acquire both national and regional product contracts.

Depending on the nature of the product, regional deals might make more sense than national ones. Regional contracts may provide greater advantages to the franchisee because of shipping weight and cost or service needs. The clever franchisor will recognize this. When this is true and the franchisor doesn't act, the franchisees will fill the void. The monthly ADI meeting then becomes an expanded forum. The results of such ad hoc organizations can be reduced control of quality and expansion of franchisee associations outside the confines of the license agreement. Advanced activity of this nature can fractionalize a franchise system or even render the franchisor effectively obsolete. In some cases the franchisor and franchisee-operated buying coops peaceably coexist, acting as competitors and lowering the costs to the operator. However, dual buying coops usually reduce economies of scale and dilute system resources, as well as providing fertile ground for conflict.

For purposes of quality control, the franchisor will reserve the right to publish a product specifications list. The list will very clearly establish the quality standards of raw materials or goods used in the operation. From those specifications a subsequent list of approved suppliers is generated. This list can evolve into a franchise "tying arrangement," which occurs when the business format franchise license agreement binds the franchisee to the purchase of a specifically branded product. This varies from the product specifications list because brand, not product content, is the qualifying specification. The important question here is, does the tying arrangement of franchise and product create an enhancement for the franchisee in the marketplace? If so, then are arm's-length controls in place to ensure that pricing, netted from the enhanced value, will yield positive results? This is impossible to quantify exactly. However, if the tying arrangement is specified in the license agreement, the prospective franchise owner is advised to make a judgment before purchasing the franchise. A franchisor should make a clear distinction of value or abandon the tying arrangement.

Less overt tying arrangements occur when the license agreement calls for an approved suppliers list that ultimately lists only one supplier. If adding suppliers to the list is nearly impossible, there is a de facto tying arrangement. Another tying arrangement occurs when the product specification is written so that only one brand can possibly qualify. A franchisor should disclose any remuneration gained by the franchisor or its officers, directly or indirectly, from product purchase in the franchise system. The market value enhancement test is again proof of a credible arrangement.

In some franchise systems, franchises in a geographic region may form buying cooperatives. This results from either franchisor neglect or because of the nature of the product being purchased, such as a supply with exorbitant shipping costs.

The Operations Manual

The business format is documented in a manual or series of manuals. The fact that it is documented should be noted in the license agreement. The operations manual is the heart of the franchise asset, as it delineates the manner in which the trade name and mark are to be delivered to the customer. The franchise purchase should be made on the basis of the business's effectiveness in the marketplace. However, to remain viable, the operations manual must be a dynamic instrument. In 1984 Ray Kroc said, "I don't know what we'll be serving in the year 2000, but I know we'll be serving more of it than anybody else."

The research and development previously discussed must be documented in the operations manual before being implemented. The method of change is crucial to the health of the system, again emphasizing the delicate line between standardization and change. Some license agreements will contain a clause stating that the franchisee must adhere to the operations system as outlined in the "current operations manual," which may change from time to time. Given that the system should change to maintain a competitive advantage, the franchisee must be comfortable that this change will take place for valid commercial reasons and be willing to live with less personal control of the operational techniques.

Specialist Support

The franchisor's organizational design must be congruent with franchisee support needs. If real estate is a system variable, there must be sufficient real estate expertise in the franchisor organization to meet the demand created by the sale of franchises. This should occur in all management disciplines.

Territorial Rights

It is very difficult to establish a protected geographic area that is fair to both the franchisee and the franchisor. Demographics are a constantly evolving factor, and hence the true market area will inevitably change. A territory suitable for one site today may support three sites tomorrow because of a road change or mall development. The newer the franchise system, the more pronounced the problem.

If likely market penetration cannot be judged, then how can geography or customers be allocated? On the sale of a single franchise the address is sometimes the only protected territory. This allows the franchisor to ensure that the market is fully developed, but it provides little protection for the franchisee. When the individual outlet reaches a preestablished market share (measured by sales dollars, customers, or units of output), the franchisor will conclude that customer demand is not being fully met. Its concern is that unfilled customer needs create an opportunity for competition. Because of the market leader's advertising and promotion, a "copycat" operation can propel its startup through the leader's market exposure. Indeed, this is a viable market strategy for some franchisors. Fast-food operators have been known to purposefully locate directly adjacent to the market leader.

One way to handle this problem is to formalize the criteria for market share in an individual location to give the operator the opportunity for a return commensurate with existing franchisees. Penetration within the agreed band of market share for a given period of time triggers the creation of another location for development. The franchisee in the first location has the right of first refusal of the second location. This right may be qualified based on balance sheet and operational standards. This solution allows for the full exploitation of the marketplace, with the performing franchisee having an equally exciting upside.

Related to the territorial issue is the "relocation clause." This item may be separate or contained within the exclusive territory clause, or operations clause. It may give the franchisor the right to compel a franchisee to relocate the business under specific economic or demographic conditions. Typically, a relocation clause is not found in a franchise contract when the franchisee is required to make a real estate investment.

European franchising has considerably different legal considerations. If the franchise company is large enough to affect trade between nations, the European Community competition laws may come into effect. These laws were established to regulate contracts or practices that may be anticompetitive. Exclusive territory agreements are generally barred in the EC. However, block exemptions can be granted, and a properly structured franchise exclusive territory will likely qualify for this exemption.

Term of the Agreement

Generally, the franchise relationship is established on a long-term basis. A 15- or 20-year agreement is normal, but some can be as short as 5 years. The key is renewal rights. If the terms of the agreement have been met, the franchisee may reasonably expect the relationship to continue. In some states the renewal right is legislated, and in others there is legal precedent for court-enforced renewal.

A franchise prospect should be wary of an agreement that does not address renewal. It may be an indicator that the franchisor is predisposed not to grant renewals. Legally enforced renewal will be expensive, or the franchisor may impose substantial renewal fees as a condition for continuing the relationship. Many franchise systems do not have a long history, and renewal is not an easily researched issue. Therefore, it should always be contractually stipulated.

Sale of the Business

The good franchisor spends considerable time establishing the basis for choosing franchisees. It is understandable that they want to have some control over who their partners will be. The franchisee is motivated by the ownership of a business and accruing the benefits of that ownership and, at the end of the experience, a capital gain. All issues regarding control of the sale of the existing franchisee company should be covered in the license agreement. Additionally, the procedure by which the controls are implemented must be clearly defined.

Three other clauses will affect the franchisee's ability to sell the business.

1. *Right of first refusal*—Some license agreements give the franchisor this right. If so, the price should be equal to or a premium of the bona fide third-party offer. A right of first refusal will typically hinder a sale. The prospective buyer may not be willing to spend time or money on a deal that might be pulled out from under him by the franchisor—hence the premium requirement.

2. *Buyout formula*—At the beginning of the franchise relationship the franchisor has an advantage in understanding the ultimate value of a successful franchisee company. Franchisors have been known to set a buyout formula in the license agreement.

3. *License agreement*—Some agreements call for the buyer of an existing franchise to sign the "then current form of license agreement." Of course, the new franchisee has no way of knowing what future changes will be incorporated, and the franchisee is not bound to modify his license. Therefore, the value of the franchisee company in the marketplace can be significantly altered by a unilateral decision of the franchisor. The value will, of course, be diminished if the new form of agreement changes the fee structure, institutes tying arrangements, or modifies the protected territory or term.

Death or Incapacity of the Franchisee

Most license agreements are signed personally. This generally means that the franchisee must devote all or a majority of her professional life to operating the franchise. Also, the economics of the relationship are guaranteed by the individual(s) who sign the license agreement. Usually, the personal attention of the franchisee is impossible to monitor. However, upon death or disability the franchisee or his estate may be forced into an uneconomic sale of the company or even the loss of the franchise rights. The proper stipulation is for the franchisor to render short-term assistance in operating the franchise (for a fee) until it is sold or transferred to a qualified heir.

Arbitration

The cost of litigation is often too high for a single-outlet operator to bear. The franchisor will sometimes exclude an arbitration clause because it may afford a small franchisee the opportunity to air a grievance and receive redress she otherwise might not be granted. Conversely, such a clause reduces the likelihood of petty arguments. Arbitration is done in private proceedings with an issue judged by an individual who usually has special knowledge of the subject in dispute. Arbitration can be binding or nonbinding. It is usually to the advantage of the smaller franchisee but is gaining support among franchisors also.

License Agreement Termination

Issues of default must be specifically delineated in this section. Important is a reasonable right to remedy a default, provided the breaches are not recurring. Termination means that the franchisee must cease using the trade name and mark, and other property rights of the franchisor. Practically, this means taking down the sign, changing the name of the operation, and returning all manuals and marketing and promotional materials.

In some cases, the franchisor will tie the property lease to the license agreement. Termination of one can mean voiding of the other. This tie can occur even when the franchisor does not own the property vis-à-vis an "assignment and assumption" agreement. This agreement is signed as an addendum to the lease and states that the termination of the license agreement triggers the right, but not obligation, of the franchisor to assume the franchisee's position in a lease. The lessor must be a party to the assignment for it to be valid.

NONCONTRACTUAL CONSIDERATIONS OF BUYING A FRANCHISE

Financial Analysis

The dream of entrepreneurship can become a nightmare if your financial well-being is threatened. An advantage of franchising is a track record that can be scrutinized. The prospect can and should make an in-depth analysis of the offered franchise. The franchisor is wise to package the offering in a manner that assists this due diligence. The franchisor who demonstrates a keen financial understanding gains a pricing advantage in the franchise sales marketplace, attracts a more sophisticated franchisee, and offers that franchisee an advantage in the capital marketplace.

U.S. law requires franchisors to disclose pertinent details of the offering. The federal requirement is fulfilled through the Uniform Franchise Offering Circular (UFOC), which is filed with the Federal Trade Commission and is a matter of public record. The UFOC must be given to the franchisee the sooner of 10 days prior to the franchisor's accepting a fee or the first personal meeting. Many states have similar but usually more stringent disclosure requirements.

A vast majority of franchisors adhere to disclosure laws. A franchise search that reveals the slightest deviation from FTC or state rules should be abandoned. The disclosure will have pro forma financials based on actual franchisee experience. These are not designed to apply to any individual investment; they are an average of the composite operations. Assuredly, the new operator will find variances in the actual statements from the disclosure pro formas. The next sections focus on the areas of likely variance.

Estimating Startup Costs/Initial Investment

If there is a real estate component to the franchise, it is often treated as a lease or rental and not included in the startup calculation. If owning the real estate is a part of the franchisee's strategic plan, it must be accounted for separately from the franchise investment. The basics included in this section are leasehold improvements, furniture and fixtures, machinery and equipment, and tools. Even so-called turnkey arrangements will have some startup expense associated with the leasehold interest. Equipment can sometimes be leased also. This is especially true in restaurant franchises.

Low initial investment may dramatically affect operating expenses. A lease is simply a way to leverage your startup cost. Startup losses should be funded in the initial capitalization but are not always included in the disclosure. Assume a worst-case scenario. Even in franchising, undercapitalization is a major reason for failure.

Calculating Profit and Loss/Income Statement

All the numbers should be adjusted by the prospective franchisee to reflect the realities of the area where operation is planned. For example, New York City will be more expensive to operate in than Pocatello, Idaho, but income will probably be higher also. Decisions about owner's compensation should be incorporated into the pro forma (or into the cash-flow projections, discussed later). The disclosure will typically show the average manager's compensation, and not any remuneration to the franchisee. The franchisor will assume the franchisee is the manager. If the ownership of the franchised company is spread over more than one individual, the issue of compensation is best answered up front.

Remember the discussion of lease versus buy. If leasing is the leverage decision, its costs should be incorporated here. Also, a disclosure pro forma may not include interest payments. The franchisor takes the position that capitalization methods vary so dramatically as to render an average impractical.

Another item sometimes neglected in pro forma projections is depreciation and amortization. These noncash items represent the cost to the business of the decreasing value of fixed assets. Understanding depreciation and amortization will allow for better pricing decisions and more accurate calculation of profit margins.

Pro forma income statements are often annualized. The ramping up of sales and the accrual of expenses on a *monthly* basis will prove invaluable in the first year of operation. Many financial institutions require 36 months of pro forma statements. Although some franchisors will generate or help generate the additional monthly projections, many will reasonably avoid this out of fear of misleading a franchisee and incurring some liability. What a franchisee sees as help in the startup may be remembered as a promise years later, especially in a courtroom setting.

Constructing a Balance Sheet

The long-term health of a franchisee company can be significantly aided by constructing a strong opening balance sheet. Too often small businesses focus solely on the income statement and ignore the balance sheet. Business format franchises are heavily weighted in the service and particularly retail segments of the economy. Strong understanding of working capital management in a retail environment, depending on the business, can mean advantageous supplier terms along with cash payments from customers. This may provide you with significant short-term leverage. As with the income statement, franchising gives you the unique opportunity to use pertinent historical data in the balance sheet to lay a sound foundation in your company through proper capitalization.

There is a whole series of financial ratios that should be constructed for the ideally positioned franchisee company. In general, everyone should be aware of liquidity, capital, debt, and trade ratios as they apply to the franchisee requirements. In theory, liquidity is measured to assess a company's ability to generate operating capital or meet sudden credit demands. The level of optimal liquidity varies dramatically by industry. Franchising allows you to know the details and risks prior to startup, and the astute franchisor will make this analysis readily available. The Initial Investment section of the UFOC, modified for your specific needs, will define your capital requirement but will not specify the form of capital. Use historical numbers from the franchisor to generate stability ratios to help answer this question. This is particularly important if there is a tying arrangement in the franchise, even if the arrangement is informal. Also, when the franchisor is a key supplier, inventory estimates will be very precise. However, conflicts of interest by the franchisor should be carefully avoided, such as excessive startup inventory requirements.

Cash-Flow Projections

Happiness is a positive cash flow no matter what commercial vehicle you choose. However, profitability does not equate to positive cash flow; a profitable business can suffocate and fail due to insufficient cash flow. Cash-flow projection should also be done on a 36-month basis to match the income statement and balance sheet pro forma. Often omitted in the franchisor's cash-flow projection will be the prospect's franchise search cost, professional consultant expense, and the site search and acquisition costs. Failure to consider these will strangle cash flow even before startup.

Financing a Franchise

Financing requirements for a franchise are no different than for any other business startup. Acquisition or alteration of business premises, fittings and fixtures, machinery and equipment, and working capital are all included in the list. Cash flow shortages due to business cycle may be added later. The advantage of franchise financing is the added variable of the franchisee. The franchisor packages a proven product and business methods. The franchisee is a "partner" in the deal who brings additional capital and entrepreneurial commitment. This should provide greater comfort to the financing institution. Properly exhibiting the transferability of the success factors is the principle function of the loan request. Existing operations that are profitable makes access to a lender's ear easier.

A franchisor will systematically meet with large banks or leasing companies to help build confidence in the concept and clear initial hurdles for franchisees. Structuring a debt proposal should utilize much of the due diligence included in the franchise search. In general, the franchise system and the outlets operating in it should be presented both as an integrated organization and as a stand-alone operation. This will promote the franchisee as one who is independently capable of success but whose prospects are dramatically enhanced by being a part of a system. A banker will likely define the long run as the amount of time debt is outstanding. If the successful operation of the franchise system exceeds the term of the loan, the lender will have a higher comfort level.

From the franchisee's perspective, a franchise is a risk management tool. The increased prospects for success will allow for a more secure loan for the bank. Examples of the franchise system's changing to meet the demands of the marketplace will be helpful in projecting future success. The franchisor's organizational chart and support role is appropriate material to review with a banker. It gives depth to the not-as-yet-operating franchisee organization, an advantage the solo startup doesn't have. Pressing the franchise advantage at startup might yield a more competitive loan and more serviceable debt, compounding the advantage over the nonfranchised competitor. Even with these advantages, the personal commitment of the franchisee in the form of cash invested in the business is inevitably required. The financial analysis done in the investigative stage will be helpful in the search for capital. For the purposes of securing debt, add the proposed loan and subsequent debt service to the projections.

The terms in the loan will vary by specific business, franchisor strength, franchisee strength, and general economic conditions. Loans for the substantiated initial investment can run as high as 80%, but 50% to 67% is more likely. Machinery and equipment will have a 3- to 7-year term with a corresponding amortization. The franchisor can help boost the loan-to-value ratio if a market for used machinery and equipment can be demonstrated. Real estate will likely have a 3- to 5-year term with a 15- to 20-year amortization. A few franchisors will provide some financing, and a few more will assist in placing debt. However, a franchisor should not be expected to be a vehicle for acquiring capital.

A problem the franchisor must be cognizant of is franchisee underinvestment. Many franchisees are required to invest a substantial portion of their wealth in the franchise. Theoretically, this could result in a burdensome risk perspective that might cause the franchisee to pass on a favorable opportunity. Franchisee underinvestment is interwoven with the issue of protected territory and expansion rights. Some franchisors include expansion requirements where rights are given. This is especially true when a geographic territory is sold to a franchisee. Often a development schedule is agreed on in advance. Failure of the franchisee to build out the territory under the terms of the agreement (sometimes called an "area development agreement") results in loss of the exclusivity.

HOW SELLING A FRANCHISE IS REGULATED

The United States has an extensive statutory regulatory system governing franchising. In essence, the sale of a franchise is subject to the same scrutiny as the sale of a security. On the federal level, the government mandates extensive disclosure through the Uniform Franchise Offering Circular, developed by the American Securities Administrators Organization. The document must include a copy of the license agreement, an area development agreement if applicable, and a laundry list of standard disclosure items.

Details of the costs and ongoing payments and product tying arrangements follow. Typically, the document opens with a narrative description of the franchise. The franchisor must also list details concerning litigation, bankruptcy and store transfer, acquisition, and termination. There is also a summary of the franchisee's responsibilities and the services provided by the franchisor. There is usually a pro forma compilation of financial statements taken from franchise operating histories. If the UFOC does not present financial information, any statement about the economics of the franchise by the franchisor must be disclosed to the prospective franchisee in an "earnings claim document." If the claims are made in a public fashion, such as in the newspaper, then the earnings claim document is required regardless of UFOC content and use.

The franchisor is required to file the UFOC with the Federal Trade Commission. Any change to the license agreement or any executory document must be filed at least five days prior to signing. The prospective franchisee is asked to sign a receipt for the UFOC, which the franchisor keeps on file. Although the FTC dictates disclosure requirements, it does not editorialize or approve the quality of the content.

A number of state governments have passed legislation specific to franchising that also requires a disclosure document. Financial and termination disclosure is often more extensive than under federal requirements. Franchisors face a morass of complicated laws and must be mindful of the legal costs when contemplating a national expansion program.

LIMITATIONS OF FRANCHISING

The franchisor must recognize that "equity" in the business is being sold when a franchise is sold. Rapid growth and a highly motivated management team are born, but a partner, not an employee, is created. That partner, the franchisee, will risk time, energy, and capital and will expect a return. Because of the long-term nature of the license agreement, the franchisor is bound to this partnership for many years. Anyone who considers expansion through franchising must understand that the benefits of a "system" must endure the test of time.

Sources of Conflict

As a part of understanding the implications of franchising, one should note the potential sources of conflict in the relationship. As discussed, the franchisor builds a prototype operation, completes system documentation, establishes support overhead, complies with regulatory requirements, and then sells the first franchise. Typically, a large amount of capital has been used before any franchise fees or royalties are received. Therefore, a high percentage of the franchisor's costs are necessarily fixed. As the system of franchisees and outlets grow, the franchisor's costs are spread over an increasing base. The average cost to the franchisor for providing services per franchisee decreases as the number of outlets increases.

On the revenue side, the franchisor is motivated to maximize system sales. The franchisor's continuing income is derived from franchisee royalty payments, a percentage of top-line outlet sales paid to the franchisor. System growth in terms of the number of outlets and individual outlet sales results in higher franchisor revenue applied against lower per-unit support costs.

The franchisee, on the other hand, aspires to achieve optimal unit sales (not necessarily maximum sales) to maximize profit. An important aspect of optimal sales is the optimal number of outlets in the market (again, not necessarily the maximum). The franchisee's operating model has more variable expense than the franchisor's. The implication is that there may be sensitive discussion in the areas of pricing, promotion, and the development of outlets. The potential for conflict is exacerbated by the phenomenon of larger, more sophisticated franchisees. With today's heightened level of competition in the marketplace, franchisees are necessarily more educated, with more capital, entrepreneurial drive, and organizational skills, and are capable of building fully integrated companies.

The Future of Franchising

With the vast amount of information available in franchising for due diligence and regarding structure, it might be thought to be a "science." It is not. Franchising is an alliance between a franchisor and its franchisees and can take any form which enhances the alliance. Some franchisors have begun or acquired a number of systems. Pepsi owns such well-known franchises as Taco Bell, Kentucky Fried Chicken, Pizza Hut. Likewise, multiple franchise ownership by franchisees is increasingly common. Other innovations include "clustering" different franchises on a single property and creative "points of access," such as mall kiosks and push carts.

CONCLUSION

Franchising might best be described as the combination of a unique association of corporate organizations and a unique form of raising capital. For franchising to work best, the franchisor and franchisee goals must be congruent. The relationship must be highly interactive and dynamic. Although the license agreement is the focal point of franchising, if it is strictly interpreted, the probability of conflict being resolved through litigation is heightened. The franchise system that understands that interdependence is a reality has a higher probability of optimizing return.

13 ENTREPRENEURS AND THE INTERNET
Julian E. Lange

The Internet has captured the imagination of the world. It is the new frontier of the millennium. It has grown from a little known communication vehicle for scientists and "techies" to a tool that provides access to a seemingly limitless array of information to anyone with a computer, a modem, and a telephone line. Virtually all manner of information is available on the Internet—including stock market quotations, product literature, government statistics, news stories, and video clips from the latest movie releases. But what are the opportunities for entrepreneurs on the Internet? How realistic are they and how can they be identified and developed? How are they likely to change over time?

This chapter provides an introduction to the Internet for entrepreneurs. We will explore what tools are available, how to use them, and how to get connected to the Internet. Those readers who are already Internet-savvy may want to turn to the section on "How an existing business can benefit from the Internet," which explores the *why* of being on the Internet and looks at how it can be utilized to further the goals of existing businesses as well as providing opportunities for the development of new products and services. The Internet is incredibly dynamic. The Internet is changing so rapidly that it is challenging to keep up. This chapter offers a way of doing that by providing specific references to Internet sites and institutions that you should visit often.

WHAT IS THE INTERNET AND WHERE DID IT COME FROM?

Although the term Internet (the Net) is familiar to most people, the exact definition may be unclear. The Internet is a vast network of networks connecting millions of computer networks and individual computers around the world. Estimates of the total number of users vary, but at the time of this writing it is believed to be in excess of 100 million. The Net is growing at an astonishing rate, with the number of users increasing by 10% to 20% every month (Exhibit 13.1). The number of hosts in Exhibit 13.1 refers to the number of computers acting as servers, that is computers with which other computers can connect to exchange data. There are approximately 10 users for each host computer. Although the growth rate will inevitably decrease, there is no denying the recent phenomenal growth in the number of hosts and users, a 1300% increase over the past four years.

Once connected to the Internet, a user can communicate with a computer across the room or across the globe with equal facility. Familiarity with computers and the Internet presently provides a competitive advantage to entrepreneurs, but such knowledge will soon be a necessity for conducting business effectively.

EXHIBIT 13.1   Internet hosts 1989–1996.

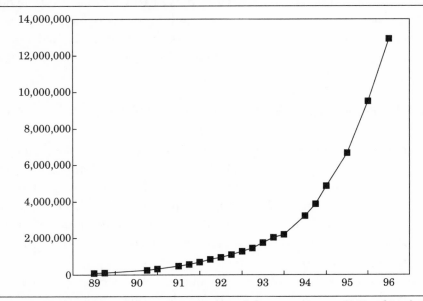

Source: A. M. Rutkowski, General Magic Corp., internal document, August, 1996 and Mark Lottor, *Network Wizards*, August, 1996.

The Internet began almost thirty years ago as a project sponsored by the Department of Defense. In the depths of the Cold War, it was thought essential to have a network that could connect key military and scientific computers in the United States. Such a network would be useful as a means of exchanging information in the scientific community as well as in the event of a nuclear disaster. To fulfill this mission, the ARPANET was born, funded by the Defense Department's Advanced Research Projects Agency. It was initially modest in scope, involving only a handful of scientific sites at major research universities, and it remained the province of academics and the military into the early 1980s. The military portion of the network was split off in the mid-1980s, but there were still significant restrictions on commercial use because the network continued to be funded by the government. Ordinary nontechnical business users were discouraged from using the network because of the often obscure "computerese" commands that needed to be learned in order to use what was by now known as the Internet. The user interface was also "text-based," consisting of line after line of computer jargon, devoid of the point-and-click ease of use of the Apple Macintosh or Microsoft Windows-based personal computers.

That was all changed by the introduction of the World Wide Web (the Web). A group of scientists led by Timothy Berners-Lee of CERN, the European Particle Physics Laboratory, decided that it would be desirable to develop a user interface that incorporated graphics, sound, and video as well as text, and would also link data from various sources around the world on a single screen of information. Subsequently, in the early 1990s, the National Center for Supercomputing Applications at the University of Illinois sponsored the development of the first computer program, called a browser, which implemented these ideas and provided nontechnical users with a graphically-based tool which ushered in the age of multimedia on the Internet.

INTERNET BASICS: PRINCIPAL FEATURES

There are a variety of tools and applications available to users that facilitate information acquisition and exchange on the Net. These tools provide a means to create an Internet presence for an entrepreneurial business that can enhance its growth and effectiveness. If you are new to the Net, you should take some time to get accustomed to the environment. Browse the computer section of a good bookstore and you will find a plethora of introductory "how-to" books about the mechanics of navigating the Net.

We will give you a general overview of the tools so that you can determine which ones seem relevant to your needs. You do not have to learn every tool or technique all at once. Do some Net surfing—exploring the different tools and

Net destinations. See what others are doing and get familiar with the territory. Then, you will be better able to see the possibilities that the Internet offers for your business and, being entrepreneurial, some of you will no doubt invent some new capabilities for your business and others.

E-Mail

Perhaps the most familiar and universal business tool of the Internet age is electronic mail or e-mail. Although used by relatively few people ten years ago, today there are more than 40 million e-mail users worldwide. (As with most of the demographic statistics mentioned here, this number will no doubt increase by the time you read this.) E-mail permits users to send text messages to recipients anywhere in the world. Most systems also permit the sending of attachments containing data in binary form. Such data may include spreadsheet files, database files, word processing documents, and even sound or video files, and allows the sharing of documents in their original format, so that they can be edited or added to by others. In addition to e-mail sent by direct connection to the Internet, there are many e-mail users who exchange electronic messages through on-line providers like America Online or CompuServe as well as within systems proprietary to a particular company. Most of these latter systems also have connections to the Internet, allowing users to correspond electronically with users outside their own e-mail system.

E-mail provides a low cost, simple, and direct way to exchange information. It has all the advantages of phone mail in terms of convenience and "time shift"—allowing you to leave and retrieve messages when convenient for you— as well as having the additional advantage of being content rich. Rather than a brief summary phone mail message, you can send someone a complete document or spreadsheet analysis, which they can then work on and respond to while you are doing something else. E-mail also provides a simple way to tell recipients more about you and your company through the use of signature files. Signatures consist of a few extra lines of text that can be appended to every message that you send. These messages should contain essential information, such as your company name, street address, zip code, telephone and fax numbers, as well as your e-mail address and a short description of your company's product or service. Signatures should be kept to a few lines to be effective; they are a useful tool in creating awareness of you and your company.

The World Wide Web

The immense upsurge of interest in the Internet is no doubt directly related to the growth of the World Wide Web (the Web). The Web is the part of the

Internet that allows the use of multimedia—graphics, audio, and video, as well as text. The Web also makes extensive use of hyperlinks that permit the user to jump from the document being viewed to another document that may reside on another computer in a different city or possibly on a different continent.

In order to access the Web, you will need to use a program called a *browser.* Browsers permit you to view Web documents that have been created especially to incorporate the Web's multimedia capabilities. Such documents are constructed using a computer language called HTML—hypertext markup language. Hyperlinks transform Web documents into dynamic vehicles for displaying related information in a variety of forms. For example, many businesses have created Websites called *home pages,* in which they present information about their companies of interest to customers, potential customers, suppliers, employees, shareholders, job applicants, the press, and others. Through the use of hyperlinks, an electronic visitor to your home page can jump to other areas they may wish to explore (and which you may want to encourage them to explore) about your company, such as product descriptions, job responsibilities and pictures of key employees, tech support information, or a message from the president.

Equally important, you can gather data about the visitor that can be useful in gaining feedback about your products or services, both through directly surveying visitors or simply gathering information about the time of their visit, which parts of the home page they viewed, and how long they stayed. This interactive aspect of the Net is one of its essential features and potentially the most important reason to include the Web in your business strategy. Keeping close to customers and the marketplace has emerged as an important theme for businesses in the 1990s, and the Web and the Net in general provide many excellent opportunities for doing so.

The leading browsers are Netscape's Navigator and Microsoft's Internet Explorer. The browsers are rapidly incorporating add-on features and capabilities far beyond their original versions, such as free linkages to on-line newspapers and search engines and data security features. At this writing, Netscape has the lion's share of the market (estimated at greater than 80% with more than 40 million copies distributed), but the competition from Microsoft (with 10% of the market and growing) is getting very intense. Versions of both browsers can be downloaded free as of this writing from the home pages of Netscape and Microsoft (listed below). Since the competition will no doubt continue to intensify and the vendors will continue to add features and content to their offerings, you should download and try out both products and decide which best meets your needs. You may choose to use both.

The success of Netscape's browser in capturing a huge market share is a good example of the new possibilities opened up by the growth of the Internet.

Netscape attained its market share by giving its product away via the Internet. The cost of distribution was negligible to Netscape and primarily borne by the users, in terms of paying for the connection and the download time. This strategy made Netscape the de facto browser standard. Prior to the growth and widespread use of the Internet, the introduction of a new product and attempt to create a standard was a costly and time-consuming process involving significant marketing and distribution costs. But Netscape's experience proved that the growth of the Internet has created new alternatives for marketing and distributing products. Microsoft is counter-attacking using a similar strategy. They are including their product free with Windows 95 and encouraging users to download it without charge from a variety of Internet sites.

Telnet

Telnet is an Internet tool that allows you to use your computer to log on to a remote computer, that is, a computer other than your own somewhere else in the Internet system. To do so, the telnet program turns your computer into a terminal, a devise capable of communicating with other computers over a network.

In order to log on, you need to have a valid account and password on the remote computer. When you log on, you can use most of the capabilities of the remote computer. You can access directories, files, and programs, and perform most of the operations that you normally perform on your own computer. But you will only be able to access those files that would normally be available to you. For example, if you log on to your company's computer and are not cleared to access the payroll records, you will be restricted from doing so when you log on remotely as well.

A second important restriction is that you may not be able to run programs very efficiently from a remote computer. The reason for this is technical and has to do with the limited bandwidth of a remote log-in. Bandwidth can be thought of as the diameter of the pipe through which you are accessing the remote computer. The amount of data that can be transferred over telephone lines using even the fastest modem is far less than that which can be transferred internally on your own computer or even over your business's local area network (LAN). Consequently, most programs will run too slowly when accessed remotely using telnet. Nevertheless, telnet remains a very useful tool for reading e-mail, accessing files, and uploading and downloading them.

Telnet is a tool that does not require you to be connected to the Web. However, the bad news is that you need to use what is called a command-line interface (a series of "computerese" instructions). The good news is that they are the same instructions that you are accustomed to using when you log on to the computer normally. For example, if you are logging on to your office computer during a business trip to read your e-mail, you use the same commands to access your mail as you do when you are in the office. Although not necessary, you may find it more convenient to access telnet through your Web browser. Most browsers offer this capability, and you may find that the visual interface of the browser is simpler and easier to work with.

FTP

Often, the administrators of a computer installation do not want outsiders to log on and roam around the system, but are happy to have remote users access certain data files. The tool for this sort of situation is called file transfer protocol (FTP). It is a means of allowing you to upload and download files from other computers on the Net. The computers on the Net contain vast numbers of files, and it is important to be able to transport those files to your computer in order to view their contents and work with them. FTP permits you to do this by following a series of instructions presented to you by the remote computer. FTP is often used in conjunction with a program called Archie, which facilitates FTP searches through an index of FTP files and servers throughout the Net. As with telnet, you do not need to be on the Web to use FTP, but since most Web browsers include an FTP capability, you might prefer to use the browser interface.

Many educational institutions, government agencies, libraries, and businesses maintain FTP sites to facilitate the downloading of files. And in keeping with the interactive theme of the Internet, FTP allows uploading of files to remote computers. FTP facilitates the sharing of information among large numbers of users. While sharing is a truly useful aspect of the Internet, it is also important to add a word of caution about viruses. When downloading files from an unfamiliar source, you should always check them for viruses. You can do so fairly easily by purchasing one of the several commercial antivirus programs. You should also determine whether the source of the downloaded files scans them for viruses. While many sites have such a policy, it is a good idea to check the files yourself.

Gopher

Gopher is an Internet tool that enables users to locate and download files of interest on a wide variety of topics. It is a non-Web-based system that employs menus and keywords to guide the user. Gopher can be utilized in conjunction with additional application tools to enhance the search process. For example, through the selection of key words, a program called Veronica can be used to narrow a search to the gopher servers on the Web most likely to contain the information that the user is seeking. As with other non-Web tools, a gopher capability is offered with most browsers, and the graphical browser environment is preferred by many users. The original gopher program was developed at the University of Minnesota. Whoever named the program gopher no doubt had a double meaning in mind: The obvious meaning is that of a program that will fetch data, or be a "go-fer." A second meaning, perhaps less obvious outside the confines of the University of Minnesota and its sports rivals, is the reference to the burrowing animal that also happens to be the mascot of University of Minnesota's sports teams. The program certainly facilitates the task of burrowing through the Internet for information relevant to the user's request.

Usenet

Usenet is a system of discussion groups centered around a particular topic of interest to its members. There are approximately 10,000 such newsgroups in existence involving millions of people. You need to use a program called a *newsreader* to access Usenet. There are many such programs available to be downloaded from the Net. Additionally, many browsers contain newsreaders. You can locate newsgroups of interest by consulting references like the various Internet yellow pages compilations published and updated frequently and available in the computer section of your favorite bookstore. You can also search for various newsgroups or mailing lists on the Net itself (for example, see http://www.liszt.com). After you have joined a newsgroup through use of your newsreader, you will receive messages posted (i.e., sent to) the newsgroup. Newsreaders have the ability to filter the messages, and you can follow what are called *threads* (messages related to a particular topic). There are two basic types of newsgroups, *moderated* and *unmoderated.* In unmoderated groups, all messages posted to the group are forwarded to all members of the group. As the name implies, in moderated groups posted messages are first reviewed by a moderator for relevance, and some messages are screened out through this process.

While newsgroups vary in content and focus, there are certain unwritten but generally understood rules governing their use. The most important rule from the standpoint of business users is that advertising is not considered acceptable by many newsgroups. Not all groups ban advertising. This is particularly true of business-oriented groups, but you should check out the group's policy before posting any advertising-oriented material. Most groups have a file called FAQ, which stands for frequently asked questions, that covers the major ground rules of the group. You should read that file before beginning to contribute to the group.

If advertising is permitted, it is important to understand that the kind of advertising that is welcome on the Net is high in information content and very low in hype—soft sell versus hard sell. You should be forewarned that violating this rule is considered an unacceptable intrusion by newsgroup members and will result in your being *flamed*, that is, sent a large number of unpleasant messages pointing out your error. Since the purpose of advertising is to win new customers, activities that violate the sensitivities of newsgroup members are worth taking pains to avoid.

Mailing Lists

Mailing lists are similar to newsgroups but with some important differences. Mailing lists utilize e-mail as the medium for exchanging ideas. You join a mailing list by "subscribing" to the list. Subscribing is a simple matter of sending your e-mail address and a request to be included on the list to the list administrator, which usually is a program called a listserver. Cancelling your electronic subscription is just as easy—simply send a request to the listserver to delete your name from the subscription list. Mailing lists are unmoderated and you do not need special software to read the postings. Perhaps because of the ubiquitousness of e-mail, there are many more mailing lists than newsgroups. The rules for advertising through mailing lists are the same as those for newsgroups. Be sure to check whether any advertising at all is acceptable, and then follow the custom. If you do advertise, try to include as much content as possible in your posting.

IRC

Internet Relay Chat (IRC) is a kind of instantaneous newsgroup. This tool allows the user to send electronic messages concerning particular topics of interest to other users with those interests. But, unlike newsgroups, the messages and responses take place in real time. Participants may be from anywhere in the world (and often are), and the response time for communication is limited only by the other electronic traffic in the channel. The messages and responses are public and include anyone who has joined the chat. At present, the business use of this tool has been limited, given the public nature of the communications, but that is changing. There are mechanisms for holding private chat sessions with invited participants only, and this aspect of the IRC capability allows business participants to hold conference calls for which there is a written record of what was said and who said it. There are also commercial firms that set up and moderate such conference calls, and the utilization of this feature is likely to grow in the future.

Search Engines

Search engines are tools that allow the user to search for information on topics of interest. A number of such tools have been developed for the World Wide Web including:

lycos: http://www.lycos.com

altavista: http://www.altavista.digital.com

magellan: http://www.mckinley.com

excite: http://www.excite.com

webcrawler: http://www.webcrawler.com

yahoo: http://www.yahoo.com

infoseek: http://www.infoseek.com

InterNIC Whois facility: http://rs.internic.net/cgi-bin/whois

These tools can be reached directly from your Web browser. Some browsers have incorporated several search engines in their menu systems, making it that much simpler to utilize them. For example, Netscape's Navigator 3.0 has a menu item called "search." When you click on it, a choice of five different search engines appears—Lycos, Yahoo, Excite, Magellan, and Infoseek. You can then enter a one word or several word description of the information that you are seeking, and the search engine will process the request, often almost instantly, and display a series of choices that best match your request. The choices are presented as a list of hyperlink references. If one looks interesting, you can click on the text and jump directly to the location of that item on the Net and view and retrieve the file for storage on your computer.

For example, in writing this chapter, it was important to include data on the number and growth rate of users on the Internet. Using Netscape Navigator 3.0, we clicked on the search tool (in this case the Lycos search engine) and then entered "Internet statistics" as the topic we were researching. A number of hyperlinked references appeared. After checking out several, we located the home page of General Magic, Inc., which contained an item called "Internet trends." We then viewed "Internet trends," which consisted of a series of presentation slides describing the growth of Internet host computers and domain names (unique user names). Next, using the Lycos engine and refining our search to "Internet statistics genmagic," we found a reference to the underlying Microsoft Powerpoint file which had generated the presentation slides. The site, maintained by General Magic, is an FTP site, which means that by hyperlinking to that site, we could download the file directly into our computer. This process took just a few minutes. It illustrates the power of the search engines, and also how you can get up-to-date information right now while you are reading this chapter.

GETTING CONNECTED: ON-LINE SERVICES VERSUS DIRECT CONNECTIONS

There are two basic ways to set up your Internet connection:

- A direct Internet connection through an Internet service provider (an ISP).
- A connection through an on-line service.

Choosing which alternative is best for you depends on a number of factors including the amount of time you expect to spend on the Internet per month, your potential usage of other features that on-line services offer, and whether you intend to transact business using the Internet or at least have your own home page presence.

The more extensive you expect your Internet usage to be, the more beneficial it is to have a direct connection. The cost of such a connection depends on the service provider. A simple direct connection (either a SLIP or PPP connection[1]) can vary from $15 to $30 per month, before any additional charges for a home page presence. On-line services' monthly fee structure usually includes a minimum charge for a given number of hours of connect time both to the service and to the Internet through the service. If you will be connecting to the Internet for more than a few hours per month, it quickly becomes more economical to have a direct connection through an ISP, although this situation is beginning to change as the on-line services respond to competition from the ISPs. While opinions vary on this issue, many people find a direct connection to be faster, in terms of both making the initial connection and throughput of data while you are connected. Some of the on-line services have their own browsers, but most are now also providing versions of popular browsers such as Netscape Navigator and Microsoft Internet Explorer for Net surfing while connected through their services.

As a counterbalance to these considerations, it is important to keep in mind that the on-line services offer many other features besides connection to the Internet. These services offer e-mail capabilities, flashy user interfaces, easy menu-based access to news, financial and company data, and technical and customer support from myriad hardware and software companies. Perhaps their most popular offerings are their *forums,* which are similar to usenet newsgroups in their focus on a wide variety of topics of interest to their users. The on-line services are working very hard to justify their value-added to their customers, and no doubt will continue to offer additional capabilities as a means of attracting users. Additionally, some of these services are also moving in a direction that will make them accessible directly through the Internet in the near future.

The choice ultimately becomes one of your willingness to experiment and create your own Internet experience versus having menus and services packaged for you. You may decide to do both for a time while you are determining your ultimate strategy. The key point to remember is that the more you explore the Internet, the greater the probability that you will understand the current opportunities it provides to support and grow your business, and more importantly, the greater the chances that you will see *new* possibilities to develop Internet opportunities for your current business and perhaps for a new Internet business as well.

STAYING IN TUNE WITH THE INTERNET CULTURE

While considering how best to use the Internet in your business, it is important to take heed of the culture of the Net. Just as companies have their individual cultures that entail norms of behavior, standard operating procedures and the like, the Internet too has a distinctive and sometimes demanding set of rules of conduct, in part stemming from its origin as a scientific and technical medium for exchanging ideas and information. First among these is that "content is king." This is important to remember for both positive and negative reasons. Whether you are posting a comment to a newsgroup or designing your home page, Internet users are focused on content and have little patience for fluff and communications that they deem to be a waste of their time—particularly in the case of newsgroups, where your message will go out to hundreds or thousands of users. They are also often intolerant of the mistakes of new users, but you shouldn't let that discourage your explorations.

You should never send a general advertising message to thousands of users on a mailing list (a procedure known as *spamming*). Users do not like their e-mail boxes filled up with the electronic equivalent of junk mail.

Does this mean that you can never advertise on the Internet? Not at all. It just means that you need to get to know its customs and act accordingly. The growth of the Web has somewhat blurred the distinction between information, advertising, and entertainment and this is likely to continue to evolve. More and more users new to the Net do not come from the original "techie" community and will no doubt affect the Internet culture over time. Business users are also clearly amenable to sales and advertising, and they will exert additional influence in shaping the future of the Net. Nevertheless, it is likely that the maxim "content is king" will continue to dominate the Net culture for some time. Your experience with all of the exciting possibilities of the Net will be dramatically improved if you tailor your initiatives to the opportunities presented by the Net's unique culture.

HOW AN EXISTING BUSINESS CAN BENEFIT FROM THE INTERNET

Three outstanding characteristics about successful entrepreneurs are that they are fast, focused, and flexible.[2] In many ways, the Internet holds out the promise of making the playing field more level for startups and smaller, emerging businesses. An attractive, compelling home page is often judged on its own terms and can appear to be the work of a much larger established company. An Internet presence can also help businesses get closer to customers and other stakeholders like suppliers, investors, and professional services providers. Certain tasks, like requests for product literature, can easily be automated, and thus contribute to a company's reputation for a fast response capability.

Before you commit to setting up an Internet presence, it is important to put the decision into perspective. The Internet should be considered as one possible avenue for achieving your company's objectives. It is important to specify those objectives clearly and to think through how your Internet strategy is consistent with and complementary to your overall business strategy. An Internet presence will cost both money and effort. It is a potentially high maintenance activity and not one to be undertaken lightly. But is also has an intangible benefit as well: that of positioning your business as a cutting edge company conversant with the latest technology. When deciding on a Web presence, the following checklist will be helpful.

- What are your company's business objectives, short-term and long-term?
- What resources are realistically available?
- Can the company make a long-term commitment to this effort?
- What is the likely benefit/cost ratio of the overall effort or of distinct components?
- What results can be reasonably expected at particular cost and effort levels?
- What is the realistic time frame to accomplish the task?

Some of the traditional business tasks that are being supplemented through an Internet presence include:

- Customer service/support.
- Technical support.
- Data retrieval.
- Public and investor relations.
- Selling products and services.
- Security and payment issues.
- Cutting costs.
- Obtaining advice/information.

All of the tools we discussed in the previous section are important for deciding on the type and extensiveness of the Web presence that you desire. Having an FTP site and a gopher can enhance your value to customers. Some companies even start their own newsgroups. Almost all provide for e-mail communication with company stakeholders. As usual, things are changing so quickly on the Net that Internet presence is quickly coming to mean having your own Website or home page. While maintaining an FTP site or gopher is still useful for many companies as a means of distributing data, such capabilities are fast being included as part of the Website presence. Let's look at some of these activities in more detail.

Customer Service/Support

There are a number of customer support activities that can be accomplished quickly and efficiently using a Website. Current and new product literature, upgrade information, and short descriptions of common problems and solutions can all be handled easily. It is important to remember that one of the great strengths of the Internet is that it is an *interactive* medium. While you are expeditiously addressing customers' needs, you can also gather information about your customers. This can be done by tracking the number of customers who visit particular areas of your Website and by directly surveying visitors. Surveying should be done with caution, however, lest the questions become a nuisance and discourage customers from visiting your site. Survey participation should be optional, and surveys should be short and to the point. One popular feature is a customer feedback capability in which customers can e-mail their comments to the appropriate executive at your company. Not only does this capability empower customers, it also provides a very useful channel for learning more about how your products are being received in the marketplace. Website support will not completely replace human contact, but it can greatly reduce the number of issues that require the intervention of your staff.

As an example, look at Netscape's home page (Exhibit 13.2). If you type in Netscape's address on your browser (http://home.netscape.com), you will see product descriptions, new product announcements, statements concerning major sales to large customers, and a visionary essay by the co-founder. You will also see some value-added features designed to keep you coming back to the site. There is a "What's Cool?" and "What's New?" area with hyperlinks to any of those sites that interest you. There is also an area for downloading evaluation copies of product add-ons (called *plug-ins*). The site is visually attractive and attention-getting. Netscape also follows the most important rule of Website design: new content is being added at frequent intervals to give users a reason to return to the site often.

It is instructive to look at Microsoft's home page for the same date (Exhibit 13.3). There are hyperlinks to a download page for the new browser version, statements countering Netscape's arguments on "Why Internet Explorer Has a Long Way to Go," an essay by Microsoft's cofounder on Internet censorship, and

EXHIBIT 13.2 Netscape's home page.

NETSCAPE DELIVERS STREAMING AUDIO

NOVEMBER 8: To experience standards-based, high-quality streaming audio and synchronized multimedia in real time on your network, download the beta 3 versions of Netscape Media Server 1.0 and Netscape Media Player 1.0 now.

Act now to get Personal SportsPage delivered to your in-box every day. To take advantage of this special offer and a variety of other great services, visit In-Box Direct.

Rapid adoption of Netscape intranet technology by *Fortune* 1000 customers has already resulted in significant savings for Netscape's enterprise customers. According to a recent study by International Data Corporation, Netscape produced a remarkably swift time-to-payback for companies, with savings and return on investment beginning as early as six weeks after intranet deployment.

Lotus. Lotus announced it will ship Netscape Navigator 3.0 with selected products, including the Notes client family and Lotus SmartSuite.

Netscape Internet Foundation Classes offer a set of powerful Java classes for creating robust enterprise applications. As part of Netscape ONE, IFC provides the foundation for open intranet application development.

MORE NEWS: Netscape launches new column series ... Prudential Securities adopts Netscape software ... Netscape Directory Server 1.0 for Unix available ... Proxy Server 2.5 unveiled ... Get the latest version of Netscape Navigator.

DOWNLOAD OR PURCHASE THE LATEST NETSCAPE SOFTWARE

Select here and click below
JavaScript Enabled

GENERAL STORE SPECIAL

Server special offer expires today. Purchase FastTrack and get a free book + CD called *Running a Perfect Website*. Save $75 on 10-packs of Navigator 3.0.

NETSCAPE COLUMNS

Keep up with current Internet issues and trends: Read Netscape Columns for first-person insights from leading executives, designers, technical experts, journalists, and analysts. Add your comments and thoughts to the discussion in the Netscape Columns newsgroup. This week we're launching a new column series, "Intranet Executive," and rerunning popular columns by Netscape's Jim Barksdale and Marc Andreessen.

EXHIBIT 13.3   Microsoft's home page.

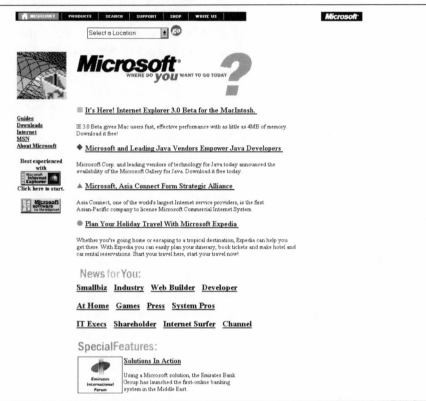

Copyright 1996 Microsoft Corporation. Screen shot reprinted with permission from Microsoft Corporation.

a host of hyperlinks to products, support, guides, downloads, the Microsoft Network, and a general statement describing the company. These two home pages illustrate many of the possibilities of communicating with customers on a Website. The sites are content-rich, address competitor's products directly in a content-based advertising context, and provide users with the opportunity to download products free of charge without human intervention and the costs associated with it, thus transferring much of the cost of distribution from the product developers to the users. This look at the "browser wars" is an example of how quickly the competitive landscape can change on the Internet, aided and abetted by the capability for almost instantaneous product distribution.

Technical Support

Tech support is another fruitful area to be considered for inclusion on your Website. If your company sells technology-based products, customers will frequently have questions concerning installation and proper product functioning.

Many of these can be handled by customers downloading a word processor document file describing the problem and solution in detail. This Website feature means that your company is open 24 hours a day to solve customer problems. This procedure can also save dollars by reducing the amount of tech support reps' time spent on simple questions, and allows your staff to focus their efforts on more complex problems.

Many companies maintain tech support capabilities on forums offered by the on-line services. These provide for the downloading (and sometimes uploading) of software, e-mail discussions by users, and a facility for asking questions of company tech support reps and receiving answers by e-mail. But companies are moving in greater numbers to develop their own Web presence for these purposes in addition to, or perhaps instead of, use of the on-line forums.

Data Retrieval

There are many types of information that can be useful in growing your business, including data pertaining to:

- Customers.
- Competitors.
- Industry trends.
- Suppliers.
- Economic conditions.
- Financial data.
- Forecasts.

The Internet is a vast repository of such information. The challenge is discovering how to find the data you want.

We have already seen how a Web presence offers opportunities for useful interactions with customers. Feedback from customers about products and observing what product information they are requesting provides data on customer preferences. Data on competitors is readily available by visiting their home pages (if they have them). As illustrated in the comparison of Netscape's and Microsoft's home pages, there is much to be learned about competitors' positioning of products and approach to marketing by frequent observations of their home pages.

There are many sources on the Internet for gathering "traditional" data on industry trends and economic conditions. Among the best places to look are the gophers of academic libraries. For example, the Babson College gopher (gopher://gopher.babson.edu) has compiled lists of sources (both on-line and otherwise) for industry analyses, overviews, and forecasts, industry statistics, brokerage house reports, trade association data, and market research reports. The FedWorld Website (http://www.fedworld.gov) is a central source of U.S. government data maintained by the Commerce Department. The Securities and Exchange Commission's EDGAR database (http://www.sec.gov/edgarhp .htm) is a good source for any filings that public companies are required to make with the S.E.C., including items such as annual and quarterly reports and initial public offerings. Additionally, you can check on the constantly changing environment for IPOs (Initial Public Offerings) by visiting NASDAQ's home page (http://www.nasdaq.com). If you want to check on the progress of legislation, you can find the full text of pending bills at http://thomas.loc.gov (named for Thomas Jefferson, a champion of public education and dissemination of information). You should also be aware that many business newspapers and periodicals are going on-line. For example, *The Wall Street Journal* has recently made available an on-line electronic edition, *The Wall Street Journal Interactive Edition,* (go to http://www.wsj.com to subscribe) which features in-depth coverage of topics from the regular paper edition. The service will require a paid subscription, but free trial subscriptions are available as of this writing. The use of hyperlinks simplifies the process of locating and retrieving the data from all of these sources.

Another valuable information source is Open Market, Inc.'s Commercial Sites index. You should consider listing your Website here as well as with the various search engines listed earlier if you decide to have a home page. You can also check on information about companies or individuals through the InterNIC (the Internet Network Information Center), the organization that maintains the set of unique domain names on the Internet. A domain name is part of the URL (Uniform or Universal Resource Locator). For example, if your Internet address is jsmith@yourcompany.com, your domain name is yourcompany .com. It is a good idea to register your preferred domain name with the InterNIC as soon as possible, in order to preserve the simplest way for people to locate you. The current charge is $50 per year for two years paid in advance. Be forewarned that you will not be able to register trademarked names like fedex.com. But if someone gets there first and takes your preferred name, you will be out of luck.

You should also be aware of the data available through the on-line services. The easy access to proprietary databases is one of the strengths of the on-line services. For example, the following are some of the data sources available through Compuserve:

- The Disclosure II database is a convenient source of data on public companies.

- Business Demographic Reports is a service which provides market analysis data based on U.S. Census reports.
- Iquest offers access to more than 450 databases containing information concerning business, government, and research, as well as sports and entertainment.
- Magazine Database Plus provides for the retrieval of full text articles from more than 250 publications.

These sources entail usage charges over and above the usual connect-time fees, sometimes charging by the hour and sometimes by the article or report. One trend to watch is the availability of these data sources directly through the Web. As users are signing up for direct Web connections in greater numbers, many database providers are presenting their wares directly on the Web as well as through on-line services. This trend continues to challenge the on-line services to develop new value-added services in order to justify their existence.

Public and Investor Relations

It is just a small jump from customer service and tech support activities to the realm of public and investor relations. CEO's of companies with Websites often use the home page as a vehicle for conveying the company culture and leadership position (or hoped-for leadership position) in an industry. The product literature and the public statements on company vision (for example, Marc Andreessen's statement on Netscape's home page in Exhibit 13.2) can easily be read by securities analysts as well as the company's other constituencies. The Internet provides a very inexpensive way to distribute product announcements and collateral marketing materials, and its instantaneous availability is a plus for analysts and investors seeking the information.

Selling Products and Services

The potential for selling goods and services on the Web is one of its great fascinations for entrepreneurs. It levels the business playing field for many companies. Since the Web is a virtual world, the argument goes, to paraphrase the movie *Field of Dreams,* "if you build it they will come." The potential is certainly great, but as with most things, it's not as easy as one might hope. Let's look at some of the issues and choices.

The basic decision involves whether your company wants to open its own Website storefront or open a store in another company's virtual mall. Both strategies involve up-front costs, but being in the cyber-mall usually entails monthly rent and payments of a percentage of sales, similar to a physical mall. Your decision rests partly on whether you think that a standalone site will attract sufficient traffic or whether you will benefit from the spillover traffic from other sites in a mall. The decision depends very much on the design of the mall by the developer. Ideally, you would want the demographic profile of mall shoppers to be very similar for as many of the sites as possible, thus encouraging virtual shoppers to follow the hyperlinks among mall Websites.

Alternatively, you can choose to rent "virtual space" from an Internet Service Provider and go it alone. You don't even have to build the site yourself unless you are adept at programming, and even then you would do well to hire a professional Website developer to implement the software and concentrate your efforts on refining and attracting the primary target audience.

An Example: The Internet Fashion Mall

Ben Narasin is the founder and CEO of the Boston Prepatory company, which manufactures high quality affordable men's sportswear. From his vantage point in the fashion industry, Narasin saw an opportunity to develop a virtual mall specializing in fashion. Targeting both the mass market and the fashion trade, the Internet Fashion Mall (IFM) provides Fashion Assistants to aid customers with their purchases. A Fashion Assistant incorporates a database containing past purchasing patterns and preferences, coupled with a complete knowledge of the merchandise available for sale in the mall.

Within a year of its startup, the Internet Fashion Mall was averaging more than 200,000 hits (visits) a day from customers and potential customers. IFM is a classic example of a knowledgeable entrepreneur seizing an opportunity to apply new technology to a field with which he or she is already familiar. As you read this chapter, IFM's story is being written. Why not visit IFM yourself and see what you think? (http://www.fashionmall.com)[3]

Factors to Consider in Designing Your Commercial Website

Because Websites are an electronic and software creation, a potential customer is just a mouse click and a split second away from leaving your site for another. Consequently, you should follow a few simple principles in implementing your Website storefront:

- Make sure your Website is content-rich with content and products geared to pique the interest of your target customer(s).

- Make sure the content changes frequently so that your customers and potential customers will want to return often to your site.

- Design your hyperlinks to keep the customers at your site, particularly at the beginning of their visit. It does not make sense to fill your first Web page with hyperlinks to an area of their interest at some other site. They may never return.

- Be sure to incorporate a means of interaction with your site visitors. Do not be overbearing about it. Initial surveys often turn off visitors, and you should generally allow visitors to bypass surveys if they choose. Alternatively, you can hold a contest, have visitors solve a puzzle or even guess the answers to trivia questions and thus engage their attention and encourage them to return to the site.

- Include an e-mail response mechanism so that you can get feedback from your customers.

- Install some form of tracking software, so that even if visitors decline to participate in surveys and puzzles, you will be able to determine which areas of your site hold the most interest for your customers.

- Make sure to register your Website on as many search engines and catalogues as possible. If you are offering your site through an Internet Service Provider, make sure that your site is on its "What's Cool?" and/or "What's New?" hyperlink connection.

- Consider re-designing and updating the user interface periodically, in order to add novelty to the experience of the virtual customers.

Security and Payment Issues

Many people have been heretofore reluctant to send private payment data over the Internet (for example, credit card and bank account numbers). Part of this apprehension is based on the inherent openness of the Internet, deriving from its origins as a medium for the free exchange of information. Additionally, there have been numerous instances in which computer hackers have broken into systems, many times as a prank but sometimes with the intent to use the information to fraudulently purchase goods and services. Fortunately, these issues are being dealt with in a number of ways. However, it is important to point out that, despite claims to the contrary, most security systems can be defeated by someone skilled and determined enough to do so. The real question is what is an acceptable level of security—how much security is enough?

One of the simpler methods of facilitating the ordering of products from Websites and CyberMalls is to have customers call an 800 number and give their payment information over the telephone. This brings up an interesting question of just how secure traditional telesales transactions are. In fact these transactions are only as secure as the honesty and care with which the payment information is treated. In the early days of mail order selling, security concerns were raised about this process, but over time the public has become comfortable with it despite the occasional problem.

Some innovative technical solutions are emerging. The browser producers are developing and implementing methods to protect the privacy of Web-based communications. Netscape's Navigator, for example, warns the user if information is being transmitted on a nonsecure channel. You can then decide whether to proceed with the transaction. Companies such as CyberCash (http://www.cybercash.com) and Digicash (http://www.digicash.com) have developed systems for protecting users while facilitating transactions. Although each company takes a different approach to the implementation of secure payments, the systems generally involve your opening an account with the company and establishing a secure, encrypted means of identifying you as the person who wants to effect an on-line transaction. Once this is done, verification of your identity becomes a simple matter. Open Market, Inc. (http://www.openmarket.com) is another company working in this area. Hence, the security issue is rapidly being addressed and is much less likely to be a stumbling block to on-line sales by the time you read this.

Cutting Costs

Revenue-increasing activities are not the only way to use the Internet to enhance your business. Reducing the costs of providing essential support services will also enhance the bottom line. As an example, consider FedEx's experience with package tracking.

As part of its operations strategy, FedEx installed a system of bar-coding packages and entering them into portable devices which would convey the information to its data-processing system. A customer could then call a support line to check on whether a package had been delivered and if not, what its estimated time of arrival was. Recently, FedEx instituted a Web-based tracking system. Using a browser, a customer could jump to FedEx's Website (http://www.fedex.com/cgi-bin/track_it), enter the package number, and observe the progress of the item through the various steps on the way to its ultimate destination. It has been estimated that FedEx will save more than $10 million a year through this system, since each tracking inquiry costs approximately $6.00 and the volume of inquiries exceeds 140,000 per month. The beauty of the system is that FedEx has transferred the cost of the transaction to the customer (who needs to have a computer and the appropriate software) while improving the quality of its customer service at a negligible incremental cost. And the impact on the bottom line is far from trivial.

Another development to watch in the category of cost cutting and improving efficiency is the growth of *intranets,* the use of Internet technology and protocols for internal communications within private companies. While this trend is at a relatively early stage in its development, the growth of intranets promises to have a great impact on intracompany operations.

Obtaining Advice/Information

In addition to the data sources which we have explored above, the Internet offers a number of opportunities for entrepreneurs to obtain advice and practical know-how about management and general business issues. Through on-line forums, newsgroups, mailing lists, and dedicated Websites, entrepreneurs have many resources to use. The following list represents a sample of these resources:

- The Babson Center for Entrepreneurial Studies Home Page (http://www .babson.edu/entrep/index.html). Babson College has long been a leader in entrepreneurship, and the home page describes the various programs, courses, outreach activities, research, and teaching initiatives being undertaken at Babson. The Babson gopher (gopher://gopher.babson.edu) is an outstanding source of materials helpful to entrepreneurs in starting and growing their businesses.

- The Ewing Marion Kauffman Foundation Home Page (http://www .emkf.org) is a very useful Web address for entrepreneurs. In addition to the on-going programs described on its home page, the Kauffman Foundation is introducing its EntreWorld Internet site, which has been designed to provide a wealth of useful information for both practicing and aspiring entrepreneurs. By the time you read this, the site will be up and running and will be well worth checking out (http://www .entreworld.org).

- The NetMarquee Website (http://www.nmq.com) specializes in providing resources for emerging businesses and family businesses. The site includes news articles, guest columnists, hyperlinks to University-based entrepreneurship and family business centers, and a search engine for articles of interest to entrepreneurs and executives of family businesses.

- The Lowe Foundation (http://www.lowe.org) has a website that provides valuable information for entrepreneurs.

- The U.S. Small Business Administration gopher (gopher://www.sbaonline .sba.gov) contains a great deal of information concerning SBA programs, as well as general resource materials for small businesses.

- The entrepreneurship gopher at St. Louis University (gopher://avb.slu .edu) has several top ten lists for entrepreneurship resources tailored for practicing entrepreneurs, students, and journalists.

- Newsgroups and mailing lists are an additional source of entrepreneurship information. The Liszt Directory of E-Mail Discussion Groups (http:// www.liszt.com/) contains a search engine through which you can locate both mailing lists and usenet newsgroups focused on entrepreneurship. Once having subscribed to a few mailing lists or having joined some newsgroups, those discourses will lead to further sources elsewhere on the Net. In addition, when you first set up newsgroups on your browser, you can join a few newsgroups for new users (for example, news .announce.newusers, news.newusers.questions, and news.answers) which can point you in the direction of newsgroups of interest.

- The MIT Enterprise Forum (http://web.mit.edu/entforum/www/) and the MIT Entrepreneurs Club (http://www.mit.edu:8001/activities /e-club-home.html) are sites with a number of hyperlinks to information about starting new businesses, venture capital, and business plans. The hyperlinked references relevant to marketing and advertising on the Web on the Entrepreneurs Club home page are particularly useful.

- Various forums on the commercial on-line services (for example, Compuserve and America Online) cater to entrepreneurs' interests. On Compuserve, use the keyword "go small business square." On America Online, take a look at the area accessed by the keyword "your business" or "inc online."

- Additional Websites of interest to entrepreneurs include:
  Wall Street Journal Interactive Edition (subscription):
      http://www.wsj.com
  Library of Congress: http://www.loc.gov
  Ziff-Net (computer magazine source): http://home.zdnet.com
  On-line bookstore: http://www.amazon.com
  CNN Interactive: http://www.cnn.com/
  AT&T 800 Directory: http://www.tollfree.att.net/dir800
  Telephone directory: http://www.switchboard.com
  Real Audio (source of streaming audio program):
      http://www.realaudio.com
  White House: http://www.whitehouse.gov
  Postal rates: http://www.usps.gov/consumer/rates.htm
  Land's End (mail-order retailer): http://www.landsend.com
  City Net (information on various cities): http://www.city.net

Internet Shopping Network: http://internet.net

Travelocity: http://www.travelocity.com

INTERNET-RELATED OPPORTUNITIES FOR THE CREATION OF NEW BUSINESSES

The rapid growth of the Internet has resulted in an environment where opportunities abound for entrepreneurs to create software and hardware products and goods and services to meet market needs.

Netscape is probably the most dramatic example of the achievement of enormous success by Internet software entrepreneurs. The company was created to develop a commercial version of the mosaic browser which had been created by the National Center for Supercomputing Applications. Barely eighteen months after its founding, the company launched a successful IPO which put its market value at more than $2 billion! While Netscape's experience is not the norm, there are numerous opportunities for software applications relating to the Internet, including:

- The development of new plug-ins—programs that provide additional features like sound capability to browsers.
- The creation of tools for Internet software developers.
- The development and refinement of increasingly powerful search engines.
- The implementing of enhancements to compression technology.
- The creation of consumer applications (for example, do-it-yourself home pages).
- The development of telephony capabilities for the Net.
- The creation of advanced security and encryption techniques.

Opportunities also exist in creating advances in the hardware necessary to provide Internet capabilities to companies and individuals. Advances in multimedia capabilities demand accompanying hardware improvements in the throughput of data. Areas where creative entrepreneurs can make significant contributions include:

- The development and refinement of high-speed modems.
- Advances in network technology.
- Improved cable technology.

A third area of opportunity lies in providing services to Internet users. Among those services are:

- Creating and maintaining Websites.
- Developing virtual malls.
- Providing technical and design consulting services to Internet users.
- Furnishing of services by Internet Service Providers for direct connections to the Net.

CONCLUSION

Although we have explored the rich variety of opportunities that the Internet offers for entrepreneurs, both for existing businesses and new enterprises, we have barely scratched the surface. The hypergrowth of the Internet in the recent past and the rapid changes that continue to take place will provide a fertile environment for business creation and growth for the foreseeable future. Whether you and your company are ready to create a full Web presence depends upon your particular circumstances. It is important to keep in mind that getting involved with the Web is a continuum. At the very least, it is a great resource for information relevant to the management and growth of your business. In the tradition of the entrepreneurial spirit, we urge you to go out and explore the Net and the Web. That is the best way to learn about the opportunities it offers to enhance the operations of your business and to develop ideas for new Internet-based products and services as well.

14 HARVESTING
William Petty

The year was 1986. It had been 15 years since Bill and Frances Griffin had started their single restaurant establishment. They now had a chain of 84 restaurants throughout Texas, Oklahoma, Arkansas, and Colorado; the one in Colorado had revenues exceeding those of any other restaurant in the state. Amazingly, all 84 units were profitable. Bill and Frances had started the company largely on borrowed money to finance one small restaurant in Texas. For the first seven years, the couple worked seven days a week to make a go of the business. By 1986 revenues were in excess of $50 million.

On several occasions they had been approached by other companies or individuals interested in buying the Griffins' business. Bill was always willing to listen, saying that he invariably learned something about his company in the process. However, he had no interest in selling. In 1981 a firm from England approached him about selling his company. After several meetings, they offered the Griffins $32 million for the company, and they asked Bill to stay on as president to run the company for at least five more years. Faced with such an offer, the Griffins decided to sell their company. The date was set for the closing. The Griffins went to London, signed the papers, and collected their money.

The day after the sale, the Griffins flew back to the States. On the return trip, Bill began having some regrets for selling his business. By the time he arrived in New York, he was convinced that he had made a big mistake. Instead of continuing the trip home to Texas, the Griffins stayed in New York for the night. The next day they caught the first flight to England for the purpose of buying back their company. They offered to pay $1 million for the buyer to cancel the contract, but the acquiring company had no interest in selling. The Griffins returned home, but instead of feeling a sense of accomplishment, they felt mostly disappointed for no longer owning their business.

Today, over 10 years later, the Griffins still regret selling their company. They feel it is the greatest mistake they have ever made. They had spent 15 years developing and growing the company into what they wanted it to be, only to lose it. The money, though nice, became a burden in one way. Managing the money was not nearly as enjoyable to them as managing the company. Although they had envisioned the good they could do with the money, they had not fully realized how much good they were doing through their company. In their eyes, they had lost their "base" for accomplishing many things they wanted to do, both within and outside of the company. To make matters even worse, they soon discovered that they had significant philosophical differences with the buyer in terms of how to run a business—differences that to them were not merely opinion or judgment, but matters of principle. Within two years, the Griffins left the firm in search of a new opportunity, which they eventually found, but still with deep regrets for having abandoned their "child."

Another entrepreneur, the owner of a successful sunglasses company, had the opportunity to sell his firm for $28 million but decided not to do so. At the time, he did not believe the offering price was adequate. Afterwards, the industry became increasingly competitive, almost to the point of being brutal, and he came to regret not selling. He no longer found running the company to be fun, and there were other things he wanted to do. However, because the industry was in a slump, there was not the opportunity to sell on terms as favorable as had existed earlier. The window of opportunity had closed, at least for the time being.

It was three years after the opportunity to sell for $28 million that this entrepreneur once again had the chance to sell—this time for $21 million. Was he disappointed at the lost opportunity to sell at the higher price? Certainly. But is it detracting from his enjoyment from having the time to spend on other priorities in his life—ones that he believes are significant for his family and the community? Not at all, mostly because he knows what is important to him at this time in his life.

Both of these stories, which were real events, have something to say to us in our study of entrepreneurship. They occur more frequently than you might expect. There is a real chance that an entrepreneur will be disappointed with the final phase of the investment process, which comes when he tries to harvest the venture. In the first case, the Griffins did achieve the harvest, and in a way many of us would consider totally successful. However, for them, the outcome proved to be a disappointment. The second entrepreneur failed to realize the harvest opportunity when it was within reach, and had to wait several years for it to come again and at a lower economic value to him. The moral of the story: An entrepreneur needs to understand the *why* and *when* of the harvest. For the venture to be ultimately successful in the eyes of the entrepreneur, there must be an effective and rewarding end. In other words, the availability and effectiveness of the exit strategy ultimately determines the value—both economic and emotional—to be realized from the venture.

This chapter is devoted to an examination of the final outcome, often called the harvest. The chapter covers three issues:

- The need for a *strategy* in harvesting the opportunity.
- The *financial value* of the harvest.
- *Options available* for harvesting a company.

THE NEED FOR A HARVEST STRATEGY

In formulating a strategy for harvesting a business opportunity, we should first clarify exactly what is meant by the term *harvest*. The harvest is the owners' and investors' strategy for achieving the terminal after-tax cash flows on their investment. It does not necessarily mean that the entrepreneur will leave the company; it merely defines how she will extract some or all of the cash flows from the investment to be used for other purposes. Nor should it totally disregard the personal and nonfinancial aspects of the transaction.

The harvest could involve selling the company for cash, or it could mean intentionally not growing the firm and instead using the cash flows generated by the business for personal needs. Likewise, a harvest can provide some of the managers who have been impact players in the venture with the opportunity to buy all or part of the founder's ownership in the company. Thus, harvests come in many forms, allowing the entrepreneur and the investors to achieve their respective goals.

Steven Covey, in his book *The Seven Habits of Highly Effective People*, says that one of the keys to being effective in life is "beginning with the end in mind."[1] According to Covey, we should visualize the end and then develop a plan to make it happen. Although Covey is speaking of one's personal life, the statement is also true with respect to a venture. If the entrepreneur is to take full advantage of an investment opportunity, it is essential not only to evaluate the merits of the opportunity at the outset, but also to anticipate the options for exiting the business. If the entrepreneur's goal with the venture is only to provide a living, then the exit or harvest strategy is of no concern. But if the goal is to create value for the owners and the other stakeholders in the company, a harvest strategy is absolutely mandatory. Then the exit becomes more than simply leaving a company; it is the final piece necessary in creating the *ultimate value to all the participants in the venture,* especially the owners, managers, and employees.

Harvesting the venture brings both excitement and trepidation to most entrepreneurs, particularly if it takes the form of going public or being acquired by another firm or a private investment group. Few events in the life of the entrepreneurial firm, as well as in the life of the entrepreneur, are more significant. Even so, many entrepreneurs refuse to think about the harvesting of their company. They simply choose to ignore the issue, assuming that there will be ample time to make such decisions later on. Besides, who can predict how it will all end? They contend that attention needs to be focused on the daily operations and growing of the company, not on some distant event that may or may not occur. Despite such an attitude, the fact remains that few events will have a greater personal and financial effect on the entrepreneur's life as the harvesting of the company. Thus, an understanding of the different aspects of a harvest is no small matter for the entrepreneur.

The harvest is also of prime importance to outside investors. Such investors typically have a priori expectations about their investment that include the firm's either going public or being acquired by other investors.[2] The investors, be they professional venture capitalists or private informal investors, have an obvious interest in the exit mechanism used to liquidate their investment. Though the harvest will not have the same personal significance to the firm's investors as it does to the entrepreneur, its effectiveness will in large part determine the after-tax cash flows to be received, which in turn determine the return earned on their investment. For an investor there is no issue more important than the rate of return. This rate is the driving force for most, if not all, of the investor's decisions.

Whatever the final decision by the entrepreneur and others regarding the harvest strategy, several words of advice and caution are appropriate.

Set Personal Goals and Objectives

For most entrepreneurs, the company is a dominant part of their lives. Thus, the decision to harvest a venture cannot effectively be made apart from the entrepreneur's personal goals and objectives. Without an understanding of what is important in his life, the entrepreneur is apt to make a bad decision when it comes to harvesting a firm.

Plan Your Exit and Harvest Strategy

The time will come when the entrepreneur will need to harvest the venture. The circumstances will differ from case to case, but it will happen, sooner or later. Ignoring this eventuality will most likely cause problems, either for the entrepreneur or for other family members. Mistakes will be made either because of a lack of forethought or because of lost opportunities.

Work to Anticipate the Consequences of Decisions Made Today on the Ability to Harvest the Firm in the Future

In the event the firm is successful, thereby creating value for its owners, you want to maximize the chance that the value created can be effectively harvested. For example, you would not want to make any decision today that might preclude harvest options in the future. Sahlman illustrates this point well:

> Some startup companies raise capital from a major participant in the industry. Although doing so may provide necessary capital and some expertise or marketing, it may also mean that no other large competitor of the original founder will even consider an offer later on. A startup can thus lose the option to market the company to the highest bidder in the industry.[3]

Keep in Mind That the Window of Opportunity for Harvesting a Venture Can Open and Close Quickly

Opportunities to sell or take the company public come and go with the conditions of the economy and the industry. One of the most striking examples of the window of opportunity closing occurred in the late 1980s. A young entrepreneur specializing in land speculation in the northern part of the Dallas metropolitan area developed a net worth exceeding $30 million. Only 28, he had accomplished this feat in a matter of four years. He had started with a small amount of capital but with a willingness to take risks and work hard. However, his business depended totally on the ability to borrow the money to do the deals. He had developed good relationships with several savings and loan institutions that were ready to loan him money. A single event changed everything. One afternoon the federal regulators told the S&Ls they were not to make any more real estate loans. The debt markets that provided the financing for these deals evaporated in a matter of hours. The market for land speculation was killed instantly. The young man lost all of his holdings in a matter of months, barely avoiding bankruptcy.

Don't Harvest Too Soon

Although it is good to be sensitive to the opening and closing of a window of opportunity, it is also wise to be patient. It usually requires at least 7 to 10 years for a company to develop to a point that allows the founders and early investors to realize attractive returns on their investment. Rarely does a company allow the entrepreneur the opportunity to get rich quickly. It generally takes longer than expected to develop the sales base needed to create sustainable firm value, which is the key for an attractive harvest opportunity.

Beware of the "Experts"

Advisors, especially those whose income depends on your firm being sold or taken public, can develop biased perspectives, sometimes to your detriment. These advisors provide a useful service in the right situation, but their advice needs to be balanced with that of others who have been through the same process. Seek out other entrepreneurs who have gone through the "rapids" of harvesting a venture. Also, where possible, use advisors whose fee is not based on a deal being consummated, but who get paid regardless of the outcome.

Make Certain That All the Players in the Venture Have the Same Vision for the Harvest Strategy

One entrepreneur who had raised $5 million in venture capital had always conceived of "his" company being acquired by one of the larger players in the industry. The only problem was his failure to convince the venture capitalists of the merits of an acquisition. They believed a public offering would be in their best interest. The entrepreneur was unrelenting in the matter. He was determined to be acquired. Without a word of warning, the venture capitalists appeared at the business one morning, informing the entrepreneur that he was no longer in charge. They were exercising their right to remove him as president. He had antagonized them one too many times. Even though they did not own a majority of shares in the business, the terms of their agreement specified that they could replace the president at will.

Plan Your Harvest Carefully

In conclusion, let there be little doubt as to the importance of achieving an effective harvest strategy. Ignoring the issue or making bad decisions in this regard can have significantly detrimental consequences, both financially and personally. Much of the strategy for harvesting a venture depends on the assessment of the value of the company. Thus, we will next consider some of the basics in valuing a firm.

VALUING THE HARVEST OPPORTUNITY

Valuing a firm is a difficult task even in the best of circumstances. Nevertheless, the effectiveness of the harvest strategy depends to a large extent on being able to assess the value of the business. We simply cannot have confidence in the harvest strategy if we lack an understanding of the firm's economic value.

Valuing the Firm: The Conventional Wisdom

The number of possible approaches for determining a company's value is almost legion. However, most investors in entrepreneurial firms rely on some multiple of earnings, be it net income, operating income, or operating income before depreciation and amortization (EBITDA), to value the business at the harvest. For instance, a multiple of EBITDA plus the firm's cash is often used to estimate firm value. Outstanding debt is then subtracted to determine the value of the equity. Many firms, for instance, are valued at somewhere between four and six times EBITDA, with the actual multiple used depending on the firm's riskiness and growth potential—and the relative negotiating strengths of the buyer and seller.

Using a multiple of earnings or cash flows, while simple on the surface, begs an important question: What *should* determine harvest value? Here we can take one of two basic perspective in answering the question. We either use the accountant's "map of the territory," or that of the economist. The accountant would tell us that earnings drive firm value—the larger the earnings, the greater the firm value. The economist's map of firm value, on the other hand, is based on the present value of future cash flows.

To the extent that a willing buyer is prepared to pay some multiple of earnings for a firm, value, at least from all appearances, is based on earnings. But, there is little in the way of an economic rationale or any empirical evidence to suggest that firm value is closely linked to earnings. Instead, our best thinking would tell us that value ought to be determined by finding the present value of future cash flows discounted at the opportunity cost of funds for the given level of risk. Nevertheless, the conventional wisdom that earnings matter continues to carry the day for most investors.

Valuing the Harvest: Asking the Right Questions

The issue of the harvest value is premised on a fundamental question, that being, "Will economic value be created with the capital that is being invested in the venture?" Given that a start-up company is not traded publicly, we cannot depend on the capital markets for that information. Even so, firm value can correctly be represented as the capital invested in the business plus any value created by earning economic rates of return that exceed the cost of capital; or stated negatively, firm value is equal to the capital invested less the value destroyed by earning rates of return less than the firm's opportunity cost of funds. This notion of creating value by earning a rate of return greater than the cost of capital is not novel; it has been with us since the beginning of economic theory. But seldom do you see it applied at the firm level; more often, owners and managers give excuses as to why it cannot or should not be applied to their company—at the expense often times of destroying value.

As a firm moves in time toward the harvest, there are two questions that are of primary importance: First, are the current owners/managers being effective in creating firm value? The answer to this question can be answered easily from historical financial data by estimating the economic value added (EVA) over time. The economic value added from a firm's operations in year t, EVA_t, could be estimated as follows.[4]

$$EVA_t = (\text{Return on capital}_t - \text{Cost of capital}_t) \times (\text{Invested capital}_t)$$

where return on capital is measured as *economic* income divided by the amount of capital (cash) invested in the company over its life, and cost of capital is the investors' opportunity cost of funds—a concept that is almost totally alien to most entrepreneurs. This single measurement of economic value added, which is seldom considered by large companies (much less smaller companies), can tell us a great deal about the value-creating ability of a company, an issue of import if there is to be any value to harvest.

The second and related question is: Could new owners do more with the company than the founding owners? If so, then the firm would have greater value in the hands of new owners. That is, growing a venture to the point of diminishing returns and then selling it to others better able to carry it to the next level is a proven way to create value. How this incremental value will be shared between the old and the new owners largely depends on the relative strengths of each party in the negotiations, that is, who wants the deal the most.

Free Cash Flow Valuation: A Suggested Approach to Valuing the Harvest

The process of valuing a business depends in part on who is doing the valuation. As already noted, some would take the firm's operating earnings before interest, taxes, and depreciation and apply a multiple to ascertain value. Others would identify similar companies that have publicly traded stock and apply the price-to-earnings multiples of these firms to our own company. Still others might value the individual assets owned by the business and sum these values to get their estimate of firm value.

The above approaches, however, have more of an accounting view of the world, and in the view of some, are not the best way of attacking the problem. Instead, it can be correctly argued—as already done—that value is created only when a venture more than earns its cost of capital. In this context, firm value is the same as the present value of the company's future free cash flows, discounted at the cost of capital. We then subtract the outstanding debt from the firm value to determine the shareholders' value. This process is explained in the sections that follow, beginning with an explanation of what is meant by the term *free cash flows.*[5]

Measuring Free Cash Flows

Free cash flows are the cash flows generated from a firm's operations that are available for distributing to all the firm's investors, both debt and equity. Free cash flows are important because it is these cash flows that may be used to satisfy the investor's rates of return.

You would measure a firm's free cash flows in year t, FCF_t, as follows:

Free cash flows = Operating income

 − Taxes on operating income (Tax rate × Operating income)

 + Depreciation and other noncash charges

 − Increase in net working capital during the year

 − Capital expenditures for the year, both for replacement investments and for investments required to support growth in the company's sales

Determining the Value of the Free Cash Flows

To value a firm's future free cash flows (and thereby value the firm itself), you project future cash flows and then determine the present values of these flows. You could conceivably do as one Japanese firm reportedly does: Develop a strategic plan for 250 years, estimate the expected cash flows, and then find the present value of these amounts. Alternatively, you should:

1. Decide on a planning period, preferably one that approximates the expected duration of any competitive advantage that the firm enjoys. Within this time period, the firm should expect to earn rates of returns from its investments in excess of its cost of capital.
2. Make assumptions about the cash flow stream beyond the planning horizon, such as assuming that the cash flows will continue in perpetuity, either as an annuity or increasing at a constant rate each year.

3. Assume that there is a relationship between future growth in sales and increasing asset requirements. To project future asset requirements as sales increase, you might rely on the historical relationships of assets to sales.

You then find the present value of the free cash flows during the planning period and the present value of the cash flows beyond the planning horizon (the residual value), and then sum these two values to estimate the present value of all future free cash flows. That is, the present value of the free cash flows from operations would be the sum

Present value of planning-period cash flows + Present value of residual value

where the present value, PV, of the planning-period cash flows (FCF_t) through year T is

$$PV = \sum_{t=1}^{T} \frac{FCF_t}{(1 + K)^t}$$

where K is the discount rate, or the firm's cost of capital.

To find the value of the residual cash flow stream beginning in year $T + 1$ and continuing in perpetuity, you must make an assumption about the growth rate of these future cash flows. If you assume that the cash flows beginning in year $T + 1$ will increase at a constant growth rate g, the present value of this cash flow stream as of year T may be reduced to the following equation:[6]

$$PV_T = \frac{FCF_{T+1}}{K - g}$$

You would then find the present value of PV_T effective today as follows:

$$PV = \frac{PV_T}{(1 + K)^T}$$

Thus, the present value, PV, of the combined free cash flows, for both the firm's planning period and the residual, may be expressed as follows:

$$PV = \sum_{t=1}^{T} \frac{FCF_t}{(1 + K)^t} + \frac{PV_T}{(1 + K)^T}$$

Let's look at an example of free cash flow valuation.

Case Study

The Griggs Corporation had sales last year of $5 million; its operating profit margin (operating profits divided by sales) has been 10%, which should continue into the future. You expect sales to grow at 12% for four years and at 5% thereafter. The firm's tax rate is 30%. Typically, fixed assets as a percentage of sales is 25%, and current assets to sales is 15% net of any "spontaneous financing," such as accounts payable. Also, the amount of the firm's depreciation has approximated the cost of replacement equipment. The firm's outstanding debt is $1,200,000. The company's cost of capital is 15%.

Given these assumptions, the free cash flow value of the firm would be determined as follows:

1. Estimate the firm's free cash flows for each year in the planning horizon—in this case, four years. Next, compute the free cash flow in the first year only of the residual period (year 5). These computations are shown in Exhibit 14.1 and are based on the following logic:

   - Sales are assumed to increase at 12% for four years and then at 5% in year 5.
   - Operating profits are 10% of sales.
   - Taxes equal 30% of operating profits.
   - Since depreciation is assumed to equal replacement assets, do not add back any depreciation, but neither should you subtract for any cash flow used to purchase replacement equipment. Given the assumption,

EXHIBIT 14.1   Measuring free cash flows.

			Planning horizon ($T = 4$)			Beginning of residual period
	Year:	1	2	3	4	5
Sales		$5,600,000	$6,272,000	$7,024,640	$7,867,597	$8,260,977
Operating profits		$ 560,000	$ 627,200	$ 702,464	$ 786,760	$ 826,098
Taxes		168,000	188,160	210,739	236,028	247,829
Profits after taxes		$ 392,000	$ 439,040	$ 491,725	$ 550,732	$ 578,268
Incremental investments in:						
Net working capital		90,000	100,800	112,896	126,444	59,007
Fixed assets		150,000	168,000	188,160	210,739	98,345
Total investments		$ 240,000	$ 268,800	$ 301,056	$ 337,183	$ 157,352
Free cash flows		$ 152,000	$ 170,240	$ 190,669	$ 213,549	$ 420,916

they would be a wash. Thus, the cash outflows for assets (incremental investments) would only be the increases in assets corresponding to sales increases.

- The incremental investment in assets equals the change in sales times the relationship of assets to sales. For example, in year 1, sales have increased $600,000 from the prior year. The increase in net working capital is therefore $90,000 ($600,000 × 15%).

- The free cash flows in any year are then computed as

  Operating income − Taxes on operating income − Incremental investments

The resulting amount of free cash flows may be distributed to the firm's investors.

2. Compute the present value of the free cash flows. First, find the present value of each year's free cash flows for years 1 through 4 and sum them. The answer is $508,365, estimated as follows:

$$\text{Present value} = \frac{\$152,000}{(1+.15)^1} + \frac{\$170,240}{(1+.15)^2} + \frac{\$190,669}{(1+.15)^3} + \frac{\$213,549}{(1+.15)^4}$$

$$= \$132,174 + \$128,726 + \$125,368 + \$122,097$$

$$= \$508,365$$

Then find the value of the free cash flows beginning in year 5 and continuing in perpetuity at a 5% growth rate. The value as of year 4, the end of the planning horizon, would be

$$PV_4 = \frac{FCF_5}{K-g} = \frac{\$420,916}{.15-.05} = \$4,209,160$$

The present value today of an amount worth $4,209,year 4 would be

$$PV = \frac{\$4,209,160}{(1+.15)^4} = \$2,406,603$$

3. Compute the total value of the firm, which equals the present value of the free cash flows during the planning horizon (years 1 through 4) plus the present value of the residual value:

Total firm value = $508,365 + $2,406,603 = $2,914,968

4. Calculate the value of the firm's equity:

Equity value = Total firm value − Value of outstanding debt

= $2,914,968   − $1,200,000 = $1,714,968

The Free Cash Flow Valuation: A Commentary

Valuing a firm is not easy, but it is an important issue to an entrepreneur for a number of reasons, one of which is the development of an effective harvest strategy. Although the free cash flow method for estimating value may be hard to apply in some cases, it gives the best framework for approaching the issue. As an entrepreneur, you should be more concerned about the *cash flows* generated from the business than with *profits*. Only by receiving after-tax cash flows do you receive a return on your investment. It is no different than a savings account at a bank. The rate of return on your savings account depends on the cash that accrues in the account, not on some reported earnings based on generally accepted accounting principles. Valuing a firm is the same in principle, although the application is harder.

The discussion of the free cash flow method illustrates what matters in determining the value of an investment (in this case, a business). The driving forces of *value* include the following items:

- The beginning sales.
- The estimated rate of growth of sales, both for the planning period and beyond.
- The time duration of the sales growth.
- The expected operating profit margins.
- The firm's tax rate.
- The projected ratio of operating assets to sales.
- The firm's weighted average cost of capital.

These variables have come to be known as the *value drivers*, in that the value of a firm is driven by changes in these items.

Al Rappaport provides an excellent graphical representation of what determines a firm's value. See Exhibit 14.2. Beginning at the bottom of Exhibit 14.2, management makes certain operating, investment, and financing decisions. These decisions affect the firm's value drivers, which in turn determine the firm's free cash flows and the cost of capital (discount rate). If effective decisions are made by management, the consequence is the creation of shareholder value; however, if bad decisions are made, value could be destroyed. The value created then determines the availability of cash flows to the stockholders in the form of dividends and capital gains. The final result also dictates the options and the eventual outcome of the harvest strategy. If no value is created, there will be no meaningful harvest.

You should now have a basic understanding of firm value, which has serious implications on an entrepreneur's harvest strategy. The next section looks at some of the choices for implementing the harvest strategy.

EXHIBIT 14.2   Firm valuation.

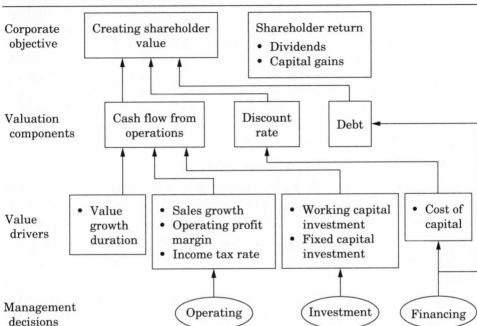

Source: Adapted from Alfred Rappaport, *Creating Shareholder Value* (New York: The Free Press, 1989), 76.

THE OPTIONS FOR HARVESTING

The structuring of a harvest strategy depends to a significant extent on the set of feasible options available to the entrepreneur. Not all options will be available to all firms. The following presentation looks at the more common ones, beginning with the most likely and continuing to the least likely. The strategies to be presented are as follows:

- Increase the free cash flows.
- A management buyout (MBO).
- An employee stock ownership plan (ESOP).
- Merging or being acquired.
- An initial public offering (IPO).

Increase the Free Cash Flows

Most of us remember Aesop's fable of the goose and the golden egg. The story went something as follows:

There was once a poor farmer who had a pet goose. One day the farmer discovers a glittering golden egg in the goose's nest. At first, he thinks it to be a trick. However, when he takes the egg to the assayer, he is told it is pure gold, much to his excitement. Every morning he goes to the nest, and every morning he finds a beautiful golden egg. Over time, he becomes wealthy, more wealthy than he ever imagined possible. But also with time, he becomes increasingly impatient and greedy. He wants all the eggs—now. So he devises a plan to kill his prized goose, open it up, and take all the eggs; and so he does. But when he opens up the goose, there are no eggs. He not only loses the goose, but also any chance for more eggs.

Even Aesop has something to say to the entrepreneur (farmer). The goose may be seen as representing the entrepreneur's company (the productive asset), and the egg is the cash flow generated by the company (the production). In a firm's early years, everything goes to grow the company (the goose) and ensure that it is healthy (strong production capability). As much cash as possible is reinvested in the company to increase sales and, it is hoped, generate additional future cash flows.

At some point, however, the entrepreneur may use discretion about the amount of cash to retain within the business. Rather than reinvesting all the cash flows back into the company, the owner could begin taking some cash out of the business for personal needs and desires. Then only the amount of cash required to maintain the firm (the goose) in reasonably good health would be retained within the company; the rest of the cash flows would be harvested. Of course, if the entrepreneur is interested only in the short term, he or she would run the plant at full capacity while reducing maintenance expenses to a minimum and eliminating employee training and other such "discretionary" expenses, choosing instead to go for all the cash (eggs) now. However, doing so could well kill the goose (liquidation or even bankruptcy of the firm).

Enough of Aesop. Let's restate the case in the language of the twentieth century. The golden goose analogy illustrates one means of harvesting the company. In the discussion of the free cash flow valuation approach, the case study assumed that the Griggs Corporation could increase the company's sales at 12% per year (see Exhibit 14.1). To accomplish this, the firm had to make sizable investments in new assets, both working capital and fixed assets. Then, in year 5, the growth rate is reduced from 12% to 5%; the result is a significant decrease in investment requirements and an equivalent increase in free cash flows. Specifically, free cash flows increased from about $214,000 in year 4 to almost $421,000 in year 5. As a result of the reduction in the firm's growth rate, the firm's free cash flows almost doubled in one year. Thus, restricting a company's growth can be a viable strategy for harvesting the venture, given, of course, you have some time. *The strategy is one of retaining within the firm only the amount of cash necessary to maintain current markets* and not trying to grow the present markets or expand into new markets.

Advantages

Increasing the firm's free cash flows has two real advantages:

- You retain the ownership of the company if you are not ready to sell. The story of the Griffins at the beginning of the chapter might have been different had they chosen this strategy instead of selling their restaurant chain.
- The strategy does not depend on finding an interested buyer and going through the time-consuming and at times energy-draining experience of negotiating the sale. In this regard, it can be less risky.

Disadvantages

There are, however, some disadvantages as well:

- Negative tax implications—In harvesting the business, you want to maximize the after-tax cash flows to the company's owners and investors. If the firm simply distributes the cash flows as dividends, the income will be taxed as *corporate income* and again as *personal dividend income* to the stockholders. Preferably, the cash should be distributed so that it is taxed only as corporate income or as personal income, but not both. There are ways, within limits, to accomplish this objective, but it may not provide the entrepreneur with as much discretionary cash flow as an outright sale would. Here the entrepreneur needs the counsel of a good tax accountant or attorney, and well in advance of the harvest.
- Shrinking competitive advantage—Another disadvantage of this strategy is the chance that you may not be able to sustain your competitive advantage while you are harvesting the venture. It is common for an entrepreneur to hold on to the business too long. The conditions that made the venture attractive at the outset may cease to exist, or the competition may become so intense that the rates of return on the investment are unacceptable. The entrepreneur tries to ride the same horse too long and ends up having to shoot it (a Texas euphemism here). The computer industry is an apparent example of this danger.
- Patience and time are required—Finally, for the entrepreneur who is simply tired of the journey, harvesting the venture by siphoning out the free cash flows over time may take too much patience. Unless there are

individuals within the company who are qualified to provide the needed managerial leadership, the strategy may be emotionally infeasible.

Management Buyout

The 1980s will long be remembered, not so favorably by some managers and employees, as the decade of the raiders and takeover artists, including such notables as Carl Icahn and T. Boone Pickens. These paragons (or parasites, some might say) popularized financial engineering. They would attempt to buy a company for the purpose of restructuring it and selling it off in pieces to the highest bidder. To finance the deal, they used heavy amounts of debt, with as much as 90% being high-yield debt. But they knew that the servicing of the debt could not be sustained by the company for the long haul. Their usual strategy was to sell off some of the firm's assets to reduce the debt and then rely on the firm's free cash flows to pay down the remaining debt—thus the name *leveraged buyout* (LBO).

On some occasions the leveraged buyout was performed by a small group of the managers within the company. Such a transaction came to be called a *management buyout* (MBO). When the managers had little in the way of capital, which was usually the case, they had to borrow the money to buy the company's stock, just as the raiders did.

Advantages

The leveraged buyout, and often the management buyout, came to be perceived by many in the financial community in a negative context. There is, however, considerable evidence that some good came from these financing arrangements, namely, a new incentive structure for the managers to act more like owners.[7] Also, it probably brought increased attention to using the MBO as an exit mechanism for an entrepreneurial firm's founders and investors.

Disadvantages

As already noted, the MBO generally involved a lot of debt financing. Moreover, for MBOs that were designed to buy out the entrepreneur and some of the investors, this debt came from two sources: private investors brought into the deal by financial institutions and the sellers themselves. Thus, in these situations the entrepreneur was at times exposed to considerable risk—the risk that the lenders may call the debt if the new owners should fail to abide by the terms of the loan, and the risk that the new owners may not be able to pay the money owed to the seller.

Although the 1980s, or the decade of the deals, is now over, the use of MBOs is still a perfectly noble strategy for harvesting an entrepreneurial venture. The managers within many entrepreneurial businesses often have a strong incentive to buy the firm. However, the use of large proportions of high-yield debt is no longer an option in most situations. The debt markets for this purpose have, for all practical purposes, disappeared. If the MBO is to be used, the managers buying the firm must have a large proportion of the money available personally, or the selling parties must be willing to accept debt as full or partial payment of the purchase price.

When the entrepreneur accepts debt in consideration for the company, an added complication must be resolved. The deal must be structured to minimize any agency problems. Specifically, if the new owners have placed little or none of their own money in the deal, they may be inclined to take risks that are not in the best interest of the selling entrepreneur; they have nothing to lose if the company fails. Also, if the terms of the deal include an earnout, where the final amount of the payment depends in part on the subsequent profit performance of the company, the buying owners have an incentive to do things that will lower the firm's profits during the earnout period. Thus, the entrepreneur needs to take great care in structuring the deal; otherwise, there will most likely be some disappointment with the outcome. Some good advice here could be well worth the money.

Employee Stock Ownership Plan (ESOP)

The owners of small and middle-sized firms are increasingly turning to employee stock ownership plans, or ESOPs, when they are ready to sell their firms. At least half of all ESOPs are used to create a market for the shares of departing owners of closely held companies. The remaining ESOPs are created either to provide a supplemental employee benefit plan or as a way for a company to borrow money. As noted by one tax accountant, "ESOPs often work best in circumstances where the owner is getting out of the business or where there already is the expectation or reality of some level of public ownership within the company."[8]

An employee stock ownership plan is designed primarily to provide a retirement plan for the firm's employees. At the same time, however, an ESOP can facilitate the financing of the company, as well as provide the entrepreneur with a vehicle for harvesting the company. Whereas most other retirement plans *limit* the amount of an employer's stock that can be bought by the plan, an ESOP is intended to allow employees to *invest primarily* in such stock. The combination of being able to invest in employer stock and take advantage of some significant tax savings not available with other plans makes the ESOP potentially attractive as a way to harvest the venture.

If the primary purpose of the ESOP is to provide a retirement plan for the employees, the arrangement usually takes the form of an *unleveraged ESOP.* In this case, the company makes an annual contribution to the ESOP for the employees' retirement; the ESOP then uses the money to buy stock from the company and, on frequent occasions, from some of its stockholders. With the unleveraged ESOP, the amount of stock purchased in any year is limited to the company's annual contribution to the ESOP. As a result, an unleveraged ESOP is not particularly attractive for the entrepreneur who wants to sell a sizable number of shares within a short period.

A *leveraged ESOP* better fits the needs of an entrepreneur wanting to harvest a venture. With this type of ESOP, money is borrowed to buy the company's stock. With access to borrowed money, the leveraged ESOP can make large purchases of the stock at one time. In fact, the ESOP could conceivably purchase the entire company, which means buying all the shares of the current owners.

Exhibit 14.3 presents a flow chart of the sequence of events in the use of a leveraged ESOP to provide an employee retirement plan and, in conjunction,

EXHIBIT 14.3 Owner stock sale using leveraged ESOP.

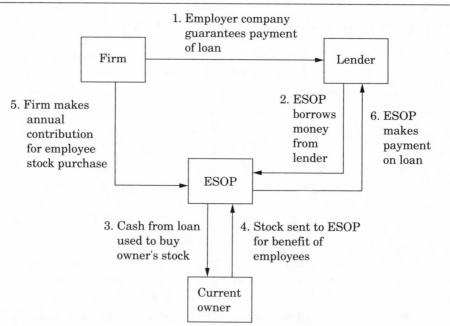

Source: Adapted from Daniel R. Garner, Robert R. Owen, and Robert P. Conway, *The Ernst & Young Guide to Raising Capital* (New York: John Wiley & Sons, 1992), 282.

to allow the present owners to sell their stock. First, the firm establishes an ESOP and guarantees any debt borrowed by the ESOP for the purpose of buying the company's stock. Next, the ESOP borrows money from a lender, and the cash is used to buy the owner's stock. The shares are held by a trust, and the company makes annual tax-deductible contributions to the trust so it can pay off the loan. As the loan is paid off, shares are released and allocated to the employees.

Advantages

Although an ESOP benefits the owner by providing a market for selling stock, it also carries some tax advantages that make the approach attractive to owner and employee alike. Some of the benefits are as follows:[9]

- A company can deduct both principal and interest payments on an ESOP loan.
- If the ESOP owns at least 30% of the firm after purchasing the shares, the seller can avoid current tax on the gain by using the proceeds to buy stocks or bonds of another U.S. industrial company.
- If the ESOP owns more than 50% of the company, those who lend money to the ESOP are taxed on only 50% of the income received on such loans. Thus, the lender can afford to offer a lower interest rate, usually about 1½ percentage points below a company's normal borrowing cost.
- The dividends that a business pays on the stock held by the ESOP are allowed as a tax-deductible expense; that is, they are treated like interest expense when it comes to taxes.

ComSonics, Inc. is an example of owners using an ESOP as a means to sell their stock. Warren Braun was the former owner of the Harrisonburg, Virginia firm, which manufactures and repairs equipment for the cable TV industry. Braun offered an ESOP to the employees in 1975 to allow them to participate in the ownership of the company. The purchase was completed in 1985, when the trust borrowed money to buy Braun's remaining shares. In the words of Dennis Zimmerman, the new president of ComSonics, "The ESOP has been very successful in our organization. It empowers the person on the line to work as an owner."[10]

Disadvantages

Despite the advantages ESOPs offer, they are not appropriate for all companies. For instance, if the entrepreneur does not want the employees to have control of the company, an ESOP is not an option. Also, the ESOP must cover all employees, and the owners are required to disclose certain information about the company, such as its performance and its key executives' salaries, which for some entrepreneurs is not palatable. Finally, using an ESOP can place the employee in double jeopardy, where both her job and her retirement fund depend on the success of a single business. However, even with these potential negatives, an entrepreneur should give serious consideration to an ESOP when crafting a harvest strategy.

Merging or Being Acquired

As commented earlier, the 1980s was a time of unfriendly takeovers, which many instinctively felt to be wasteful and harmful. (There is remarkably little evidence either to support this view or to refute it.) The "merger mania" has come and gone. In the 1990s, the number of transactions has been down significantly, with the value of the transactions falling even a far greater amount. However in 1995 and 1996, the downward trend was reversed although the deals are much smaller.

　　The turmoil in the financial markets during the latter 1980s and early 1990s, including the collapse of the junk bond market, eliminated the primary source of high-debt financing frequently used in acquiring other companies. Financial buyers were frozen out of the credit markets. Yet not all was bad in the 1980s. The merger and acquisition activity of the decade allowed shareholders of a significant number of privately held companies to realize the value locked up in their companies via a market-based transaction.

　　By 1995 *debt* was out and *equity* was in when it came to financing a company acquisition. Also, practice moved away from financial strategies designed to turn a quick profit and from purchasing a company in a different industry. Instead, by the mid-1990s we witnessed more *strategic corporate consolidation of close-fitting companies*. Along with this change, the financial structure of the 1990s acquisitions were clearly different from those of the later 1980s. The prices as a multiple of EBITDA became lower—frequently five or six times compared to seven or eight earlier; and equity as a percentage of the total capital structure in the leveraged buyouts increased from 5–10% to 20–30%. Complementing these trends, record share prices for publicly traded companies relative to private companies served as an encouragement for the larger firms to use their stock as the currency for acquiring smaller companies. Also driving much of the merger activity was a trend toward consolidation in a number of industries. One strategy that has come into use by a number of buyout firms is a *buy-and-build* approach. This approach involves the identification of a fragmented industry with a number of small to medium-sized firms, none of which are dominant. Working with one or more experienced operating managers with industry expertise, the buyout firm purchases a company in the target industry that serves as a platform for further leveraged acquisitions of firms in the same industry. In the beginning of this chapter, we told of an entrepreneur who sold his business of 25 years for $21 million. The firm, the Bonneau Corporation, is a wholesale distributor of sunglasses. It was acquired by Benson Eyecare to serve as the platform from which to acquire a number of businesses in the eyewear industry.

There have been a significant number of studies trying to explain the rationale for mergers and acquisitions and to examine the financial consequences of the transaction on the respective buying and selling shareholders.[11] Most of these studies ask the question, "Is there any value created by a firm's management acquiring another company?" In other words, can management do anything that the stockholders could not do for themselves, possibly even more easily? Although such studies may be of interest to acquisitive managers and their shareholders, they offer little to the entrepreneur attempting to sell a company. The purpose of merging with another company or being acquired makes perfect sense—to capture the value that has been created through the venture.

Advantages

Although the idea behind harvesting the venture ought to be about releasing the value locked up in the firm for the benefit of the owners and investors, the specific impetus for doing so will understandably vary. In the case of merging with another company or being acquired, the most prevalent reason relates to estate planning and the need and opportunity to diversify one's investments. A second reason is the need for financing growth, where the firm or the owner does not have the capacity to provide the needed funds. Many others simply want a change, mostly for personal or family reasons.

Pitfalls

The financial issues related to selling a firm are basically the same for any exit strategy:

1. How should the company be valued for the purpose of the sale?
2. How is the payment to be structured?

However, the financial matters, though not insignificant by any means, are not the only issues of importance when it comes to selling the firm, and they may not even be the primary concern. What the entrepreneur believes to be important when going into the acquisition process is often not what is important after the sale. Most entrepreneurs lack experience in negotiating the sale of their firm and are a bit naive in their expectations about the eventual outcome. Although selling the company does provide the long-sought-after liquidity, there may be some negative consequences during and after the sale.

What can go wrong during the process of selling a company? Several possible entrapments come to mind. First, sellers are often disappointed in the advice they receive from "experts" during the negotiations. After the fact, they may wish they had talked more with other entrepreneurs who had been through the experience of a company sale.

A second problem occurs when significant energy and resources have been committed to selling the firm, and the bidder walks out in the final negotiations. Entrepreneurs describe, with some emotion, the difficulties resulting from failure to consummate the sale. The negotiations may extend over a six-month period, during which time management's focus shifts from company operations to completing the sale. Also, some members of the existing management may expect to be promoted after the acquisition. When the deal is canceled, they have difficulty recapturing their enthusiasm for the existing firm; some eventually leave. When all is said and done, it can take several months for the firm to regain its prior momentum.

To avoid some of these pitfalls, consider the following pointers from an entrepreneur who sold his company:[12]

- You only sell your firm once. Whoever is acquiring your company may buy businesses repeatedly. Therefore, prepare thoroughly and leave nothing to chance.

- Selling your company is a personal affair. You cannot delegate the responsibility to someone else, including a business broker. A family company is you.

- If you want liquidity and you do not want your assets tied up in someone else's company, sell for cash.

- Negotiate with two or more willing buyers at the same time. However, approach potential buyers discreetly to avoid tainting the company with a shopped-around image.

- Carefully select those companies that your firm will appeal to most, and then develop a substrategy for contacting them.

- Plan on 18 months to complete the sale, especially if you must locate the buyer.

- Once you negotiate the framework of the deal, select a lawyer who will negotiate the details in a style compatible with your own personality.

- Stay alert and healthy. The process is stressful.

- Avoid becoming complacent about the transaction. After you have reached an agreement in principle, the hard work has really just begun. A company is not sold until the money is in your bank account.

Once the firm has been sold, there may still be some unresolved issues for the entrepreneur. If stock was accepted in the trade, the entrepreneur's fortunes are linked directly to the successes and failures of the acquiring company. Until the stock can be sold, the entrepreneur is still exposed to considerable risk—a position that can only be improved through diversification of the portfolio of risky assets. For the risk-averse person, which includes even most entrepreneurs, there is merit in diversifying as soon as feasible.

Also, if the entrepreneur continues in the management of the company after the sale, but under the supervision of the acquiring owners, disillusionment may eventually occur. Some selling entrepreneurs perceive a real change on the part of the buyer after the sale—mostly for the worse, in their eyes. Also, the differences in corporate culture can become a significant problem for both companies involved in the transaction, but more so for the entrepreneur.

The next section looks at the option for harvesting the venture that most entrepreneurs would love to attain, but few do.

The Initial Public Offering (IPO)[13]

Conventional wisdom tells us that for many going public is generally the preferred choice for harvesting a firm, if at all possible. The rationale for going public, vis-à-vis other exit mechanisms, rests largely on the contention that IPOs provide higher valuations than what an entrepreneur could expect from other avenues. If a better price can be realized from going public rather than from being acquired or merging, the IPO is obviously the logical choice. Such a position is particularly popular in times of "hot" IPO markets of 1995 and early 1996, and it is hard to argue with the successes experienced during these periods.

Although IPOs are attractive in many ways for a firm needing access to the equity markets, the fact remains that many privately held firms will never find themselves in a position to go public. They simply will not qualify, because of their size, because they are not in the right industry, or because they lack the requisite management. Also, if liquidity is a important issue, it may be several years before an entrepreneur could sell any of the newly issued public shares, owing to legal restrictions placed on such stock. Finally, it may well be that taking a firm public is the preferred choice for many when the IPO markets are booming; however, these markets are unpredictable even for the best

IPO candidates. When the IPO market cools, it can be an anxious time for a firm in the IPO "rapids." Nevertheless, an IPO is a possible alternative and one of considerable appeal for many an entrepreneur who aspires to take the company public, and as such it deserves our attention here.

Understanding the IPO Market

If contemplating a public offering, management needs to have an understanding of the basic nature and peculiarities of the new-issues market. There are three facts that need to be understood:

1. New stock offerings tend to be under priced relative to their trading price in the market. On average, a new stock will increase by 10% to 15% on the first day the stock is traded publicly. These results are even more pronounced for smaller, younger companies going public than for their older, more established counterparts. For instance, the average initial return on IPOs with an offering price of less than $3 was found to be an amazing 42.8%, whereas the average initial return on IPOs with an offering price of $3 or more was only 8.6%.[14]

2. There are cycles in both the volume of new issues and the size of the underpricing just mentioned. The periods of high average initial returns and high volume are known as "hot issue" markets. Thus, timing is terribly important when taking the firm public.

3. New issues tend to underperform for up to five years after the offering, both in terms of the firm's stock price performance relative to the S&P 500 Index and with respect to the firm's earnings performance after the stock offering.[15] These results are even more pronounced for younger firms than for established firms.

Ibbotson, Sindelar, and Ritter, three researchers in this area, nicely summarized a description of the IPO markets:[16]

> The empirical evidence on the pricing of IPOs provides a puzzle to those who otherwise believe in efficient capital markets. We argue that [the three characteristics of the IPO market] are interrelated in the following sense: periodic overoptimism by investors creates "windows of opportunity" during which many firms rush to market, which results in disappointing returns to long-term investors when the issuers fail to live up to overly optimistic expectations. In contrast, firms that issue during low-volume periods typically experience neither high initial price run-ups nor subsequent long-run underperformance. . . . The above patterns, moreover, are much more pronounced for smaller, younger companies going public than for their older, more established counterparts. This finding is consistent with other evidence suggesting inefficiencies in markets for smaller-cap stocks.

In short, the IPO market has somewhat a personality of its own and one that acts a bit different from the rest of the capital markets—a fact that needs to be understood by an entrepreneur wanting to take a firm public.

Understanding the IPO Process [17]

Taking a firm public appears on the surface to be a logical process. Here's a brief but factual description of this process:

> The entire process can take as little as six months to complete, but some companies take eighteen months or longer to go public. In some cases, where the corporate structure is poorly organized and additional financing is required to position the company for a more beneficial public offering, the process can take two years.
>
> During that time, a minimum of one and preferably two or more officers of the corporation will spend much of their time interfacing with attorneys, auditors, underwriters, and financial printers, collecting information for the reams of documentation that need to be submitted.
>
> As the effective date approaches, roadshows—a means for showing off the company and of improving the potential price performance in the after-market—will have to be prepared and then executed. The CEO will spend a fair amount of time making presentations to brokers and institutional investors. Slide shows, product brochures, and possibly videos will have to be produced and distributed. Trips must be planned to make the presentations nationally and, possibly, internationally. [18]

During this process, the firm's owner and managers will be answering such questions as

- What do we need to do in advance of going public?
- What are the legal requirements?
- Who should be responsible for the different activities, and how should we structure our "team" to make it all happen?
- How do we choose an investment banker?
- How do we determine an appropriate price for the offering?
- How will life be different after we are a public company?

Although the preceding description cannot be faulted for being factually inaccurate, it does not capture the essence of the journey. Taking a company public is one of the most exhilarating, frustrating, stimulating, and exhausting experiences owners and managers will ever encounter. They are exposing themselves to the vicissitudes of the capital markets and to the world of investment bankers, which few entrepreneurs understand, much less appreciate. The cost of the process seems excessive and exorbitant. The owners find themselves having little influence in the decisions being made, which becomes most disconcerting to them. Disillusionment with the investment bankers, and with much of the entire process itself, may develop for the company's owners. At some point the owners may wonder where they lost control of the process. Although it may be of little comfort, these feelings are not unique but are shared by many who have participated in a public offering.

Exhibits 14.4 and 14.5 provide an overview of the IPO process, first as most entrepreneurs expect it to be, and then more as it really is. Exhibit 14.5 presents the chronology of the IPO events, beginning with an entrepreneur's decision to begin the process. The entrepreneur then selects an investment banker to serve as the underwriter, who in turn brings together a group of investment houses to help sell the shares. With the help of the underwriter and a host of other experts, the entrepreneur prepares a prospectus, the legal document used

EXHIBIT 14.4   The initial public offering process: A partial view.

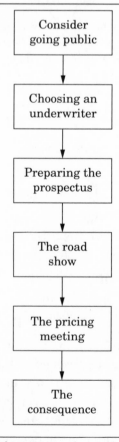

Source: "Teaching Notes, CML (B) and (C)," Copyright 1985 by the President and Fellows of Harvard College (Boston: Harvard Business School, 1985).

EXHIBIT 14.5   The initial public offering process: The complete view.

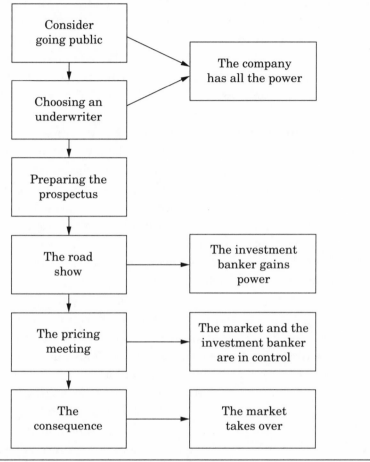

Source: "Teaching Notes, CML (B) and (C)," Copyright 1985 by the President and Fellows of Harvard College (Boston: Harvard Business School, 1985).

to satisfy the SEC that he is telling the whole truth and nothing but the truth to prospective investors. The managers, along with the investment banker, go on the road to tell the firm's story to the brokers who will be selling the stock. At the very end—actually, the day before the offering is released to the public—the decision is made as to the actual offering price. To this point, any discussion of the price of the stock has been tentative. Then all the work, which by now has been months, comes to fruition in a single event—offering the stock to the public and waiting for the consequence.

Exhibit 14.4 does not provide the complete story. A missing element that needs to be anticipated is the shift in power that occurs during the process. Exhibit 14.6 shows what really occurs. When the chain of events begins, the company's management is in control. They can dictate whether or not to go public and who the investment banker will be. However, after the prospectus has been prepared and the road show is under way, the firm's management, including the entrepreneur, no longer has primary responsibility for decision making. Now the investment banker has control. Finally, the marketplace, in complement with the investment banker, begins to take over, and ultimately it is the market that dictates the final outcome. So it behooves the entrepreneur to understand this loss of power as the events play out; otherwise, total frustration will occur.

In addition to the issue of who controls the events and decisions in the IPO process, one other matter is important. Whenever you are negotiating, it is always good to know the underlying motivation for the other side. In this case, you need to understand the investment banker's incentives for assisting with an IPO. For instance, who is the investment banker's primary customer here? Clearly, the issuing firm is rewarding the underwriter for the services performed through the fees paid and a participation in the deal. But the economics for helping with an IPO is not as rewarding as other activities performed by investment bankers, such as their involvement with corporate acquisitions. The banker is also selling securities to its customers on the other end of the trade. Some would argue that herein lies the reason IPOs are underpriced. Is this being done to benefit their customers buying the stock? This ongoing debate will not be resolved soon, but regardless of its outcome, unless you understand how the investment banker and others in the process are compensated, your expectations as to what they will do for your firm may be grossly exaggerated.

Even with the negative aspects associated with the initial public offering, it is a dream come true for most entrepreneurs. I would not advise against pursuing such a dream, as long as the entrepreneur comes into the deal with realistic expectations and asks candidly and honestly, "Does it really make sense?" If so, go for it!

WHAT NEXT?

Once the firm has been sold, taken public, or merged with a larger corporation as part of a strategic alliance, and once the money or stock has changed hands, the entrepreneur is a free person. No longer are there concerns about losing market share, being sued, or not being able to service the firm's debt. The unending and at times chaotic schedule is at last put in order. You now have the financial means to do essentially what you want to do when you want to do it. You can begin relentlessly working to improve your golf game; you can spend a lot more time at the lake enjoying your favorite pastime, fishing; or you and your spouse can spend time traveling. On the other hand, you may find the *good life* is not everything you thought it would be. There may even be some regrets for having separated yourself from something that was such a dominant part of your life.

Two disappointments frequently mentioned by entrepreneurs who have sold their companies are as follows:

- The entrepreneur may lose some focus and direction in life, focus that had been provided by owning a company. Even for those with a basic value system that reminds them that they are not their work, there is a real chance of some emotional down time. Some wish they had never sold their company, even though they received what was to them a fair price. They came to realize that the firm served as the base for much of what they did, both in and out of the business arena.
- Managing the liquidity resulting from the company sale becomes a burden for some. They find managing money more difficult and less enjoyable than they had expected, and less rewarding than operating their own company.

If the loss is too great, chances are you will soon be back working to build a company, either on your own or as a private investor supporting a son or daughter or some other aspiring entrepreneur. Whatever the decision, the key is knowing what is important to you; this was true when you began the entrepreneurial process, and it is equally true in the harvest.

CONCLUSION

Harvesting a business venture is both an economic and emotional decision. While the goal is to build and harvest a business to create value for its founders and investors, the business also is a way of life. The entrepreneurial dream is as much about an ideology as it is about making a living.

A rewarding harvest can come only if you have built a company of value. If the business has provided a good life-style but not created value, there will be no harvest. The only option then is liquidation, or even possibly bankruptcy. That is, the only option is no harvest, which will not be particularly attractive when the time comes to leave the business. Thus, contrary to what you might be inclined to do, anticipating and even planning for the harvest is the only viable choice. Making this decision effectively is, to a large extent, dependent on an understanding of what you value and what is important to you—a deep and genuine understanding. Otherwise, you will be disappointed with the end result. So make a good decision for you and enjoy the fruits.

15 ENTREPRENEURSHIP ECONOMICS

Bruce A. Kirchhoff

The 1980s are often referred to as the "decade of entrepreneurs." But who are the entrepreneurs? To some, entrepreneurs are those who form new businesses that prosper and create new employment. Examples are Bill Gates at Microsoft, Michael Dell of Dell Computer Co. and Mitch Kapor at Lotus Development, Inc. But others view entrepreneurs as unscrupulous business owners and managers who cheat America out of millions of dollars. The Wall Street mogul Michael Milken and California savings and loan promoter Charles Keating are well-known examples. A third perspective is that entrepreneurs are corporate managers who achieve outstanding success with their firms. For example, Lee Iacocca with Chrysler Corporation and Jack Welch with General Electric are frequently mentioned as entrepreneurs.

With such a broad definition, the 1980s was surely the decade of entrepreneurs, but then so were the 1970s, the 1960s, and every decade before and after the 1980s. Clearly, if the 1980s were somehow a unique period of entrepreneurial activity, not all of these definitions can be correct. Not every businessperson who draws media attention can be an entrepreneur. Sorting out the uniqueness requires the application of some systematic thought about what makes entrepreneurship special to the U.S. economy.

Economic theory provides a basis for systematic thought and a definition of entrepreneurship that clarifies its special importance. The economic theory definition gives entrepreneurs a sense of purpose and accomplishment.

And economics provides the explanation for why the 1980s became the decade of entrepreneurs. As will be demonstrated in this chapter, the economics of entrepreneurship are surprisingly important to the economic development, market competition, and social welfare of the United States.

ENTREPRENEURSHIP ECONOMICS

Economic theory is concerned with two major questions about society:

- How does a society *create new wealth*? Without new wealth, as population increases, per-capita wealth declines. Thus, any society that wants to improve its standard of living must find ways to continuously increase its overall wealth.
- How does a society *distribute wealth* among its members? Unless there is some form of equitable wealth distribution, less fortunate members of the society will be dissatisfied, and the society will not be stable.

Obviously, wealth creation and distribution are fundamental to social progress. And, as will be shown here, entrepreneurship is a major mechanism for ensuring both wealth creation and distribution.

To understand entrepreneurial economics, it is useful to look back to the early development of capitalist economic theory. After all, entrepreneurship is not new in economics. The term has been used for at least 150 years, and the concept goes back over 200 years. Looking back to early observations will provide a perspective on the experience of the 1980s and help to explain the sudden surge in attention that entrepreneurship has received worldwide since 1980. Following this look backward is a description of the newly emerging economic theory of entrepreneurship. This leads into a discussion of the social contributions of entrepreneurs during the 1980s, followed by a discussion of the economic options that aspiring entrepreneurs face as they choose their directions.

How Classical Capitalism
Spawned Entrepreneurship

Capitalism is an economic system characterized by the private ownership of property—not only land and buildings, but also machinery, telephone cables, transportation equipment, patents, information, and so forth—that is used by owners *to create profits for themselves.* In a pure theoretical sense, capitalism is also a system where opportunities to exchange goods and services exist in open, uncontrolled markets accessible to all buyers and sellers. The capitalism concept was first formulated in a relatively complete theory by Adam Smith in his book *The Wealth of Nations,* published in 1776. Smith perceived the "capitalist" as an owner-manager who combined basic resources—land, labor, and capital—into a successful industrial enterprise. Smith described how capitalists were essential ingredients to the growth and distribution of wealth in society. Smith's book is the foundation of "classical" capitalist economic theory.

The next 100 years saw a bevy of economic theorists expand and modify Smith's original theories. Sometime during the middle of the nineteenth century, the French word *entrepreneur* (meaning "to undertake") began to be used to identify the owner-manager of a new industrial enterprise. Later, around the turn of the twentieth century, the role of the entrepreneur and the term's definition became more succinct. This further refinement actually arose from the development of another body of theory, called "neoclassical economic theory."

Neoclassical Theory's Deletion of the Entrepreneur

Neoclassical theory owes its development to the work of Walras and Marshall in the late nineteenth century. Following Sir Isaac Newton's development of logical and mathematical analysis, Leon Walras (in 1874) and Alfred Marshall (in 1890) separately developed similar models of capitalist economics that incorporate a rigorous logical framework and provide a foundation for mathematical description. The key component of this theory is the specification that markets consist of many buyers and many sellers who interact so as to ensure that supply equals demand. When supply equals demand, the market is said to be in "equilibrium." Equilibrium is achieved by fluctuations in prices. For example, if demand rises but supply does not, prices will rise so that demand will be discouraged by higher prices, the available supply will suffice, and equilibrium will be attained. Economists call neoclassical markets "perfectly competitive," meaning that such markets perfectly match the theoretical definition.

Economists note that commodity markets operate much like perfectly competitive markets. For example, the Chicago Board of Trade operates with many buyers and sellers who meet on the trading floor with offers to buy and sell. Prices fluctuate to reflect the variations in supply and demand for various commodities. Since these markets are nearly "perfectly competitive," economists refer to them as "efficient" or nearly perfect.

Expressions such as "free markets" derive from this neoclassical formulation of market characteristics. Ideas such as the equating of supply and demand in markets where prices are free to move up and down stem from this theory. Several characteristics of the neoclassical definitions of markets are essential to achieving "equilibrium" market operations:

- There must be many buyers and many sellers; no single buyer or seller can influence market price.
- Prices are set by the operation of the market—not by buyers or sellers, but by transactions or sales.
- Products and services must all be equivalent in content so that they differ only in price.
- All buyers and all sellers must know of all transactions that take place.

Perfect competition is the mathematically precise, theoretical model of equilibrium markets.

The practical application of market equilibrium economic theory emerges from its ability to predict the outcome of economic events. With predictive ability, economists can recommend actions on the part of government to encourage positive or avoid negative economic effects. Neoclassical theory has been developed into a useful body of knowledge, called "general equilibrium theory," for such prediction and recommendations. General equilibrium theory is the mainstream economic theory in America.

But the neoclassical model, unlike the classical model, does not incorporate the owner-manager as an active cause of economic activity. The neoclassical perfect market cannot allow any supplier to create a product different from all other products. No supplier is allowed to control or set market prices. Instead, suppliers (owner-managers) must behave as passive, responsive participants as the market sets prices and determines demand. As prices rise, suppliers produce more; as prices fall, they produce less. So, although the perfect market provides a solid foundation for economic predictability, it achieves this sophisticated capability *by eliminating the unpredictable behavior of entrepreneurial owner-managers* who thrive on upsetting market activities by introducing innovative products and services. Entrepreneurship, then, is assumed to be only a minor occurrence in an otherwise equilibrium-dominated market. This assumption allows general equilibrium theorists to predict overall market behavior (or overall economic performance).

An example of the importance of product-service uniformity may help here. The Chicago Board of Trade (which, as noted, is a reasonable representation of the neoclassical market) would not operate very well if one trader suddenly introduced a new commodity. What if some trader unilaterally decided to trade rhinoceros horn contracts? The contracts may be of interest to other traders, and there might be a surge in trading activity. But the trading floor would be tossed into confusion as word of the new commodity caused other traders to shift their buying and selling habits. Still others would demand clarification of the characteristics and size of the horns. Very quickly, the offending innovative trader would be removed from the floor.

New commodities are introduced at the Board of Trade only after careful examination and analysis by the Board. Individualistic behavior, where one trader brings in a new commodity, is forbidden here and in all equilibrium (perfect) markets. In fact, commodities are traded with very detailed and explicit standards for their composition so that price is the only variable at the time of a transaction. For example, the moisture content of grain is defined in trading standards so that all grain is of a standard quality. Thus, all grain is equal in every way, and price alone is the market variable. It is important for the Chicago Board of Trade to ensure a nearly perfect market where price serves as the market-equilibrating factor so that trade is carried out in an orderly fashion.

Government policies designed to discourage inflation, stimulate economic activity, and reduce the deficit all have their roots in the neoclassical theory of perfect markets. And general equilibrium theorists argue that their theory works "pretty well," even though they recognize that it is flawed. These flaws became glaring faults when entrepreneurship emerged as a major factor in economic growth. As such, the 1980s represent a turning point in the character of the U.S. economy and a serious challenge to mainstream economic thought. This radical departure from general equilibrium theory is the reason the 1980s stand out as the decade of the entrepreneur.

How Neoclassical Theory Views Wealth Distribution and Creation

Neoclassical theory is carefully crafted to demonstrate that capitalism—characterized by perfect markets and unfettered by outside interference—will equitably distribute wealth among buyers and sellers through the intricate operations of markets that adjust fluctuations in demand and supply by variations in prices. The process of wealth creation and distribution is, of course, a major component of this economic theory. The wealth distribution function of the neoclassical equilibrium market theory is described by tracing the flow of income that occurs with the creation of new demand for a product. The increase in demand becomes an increase in product manufacturing activity as suppliers expand production to satisfy the new demand and earn more profit. As suppliers' revenues and profits increase, they add more workers, thereby increasing overall employment and total wages paid. Workers spend their increased wages, and owners spend their increased profits. The net result is that an increase in sales of products causes an increase in suppliers' and workers' income. Thus, the overall level of economic activity rises because of a rise in the demand for goods and services, driven by the increased spending of workers and suppliers. Since wealth is defined as the storage of income, the increase in economic activity adds to the overall wealth of society as some of the increased income is saved.

Thus, the neoclassical model shows that the market mechanism of many buyers and many suppliers operating so that prices are set by the functioning of the market as supply and demand fluctuates, results in the equitable distribution of income among suppliers and buyers, owners and workers. Although the explanation here is overly simplistic, neoclassical theory is logically consistent and demonstrates that capitalism equitably distributes income within society.[1]

But neoclassical theory does not postulate the origin of "new demand." The theory simply assumes an increase in demand without detailing how such new demand occurs. Yet new demand is the source of new wealth creation. It is the absence of a specific mechanism for creation of new demand that many economists perceive as neoclassical theory's greatest weakness. Another group of theorists, the Austrian school, contend that the entrepreneur is the source of new demand.

Schumpeter's Reaffirmation of the Entrepreneur

Neoclassical theory has always had its critics. Around the turn of the twentieth century, many classical economists (especially those associated with educational institutions in Austria) objected to the absence of entrepreneurship from the neoclassical model. Austrian economists argued that entrepreneurship was far too important a part of capitalism to ignore for the sake of achieving predictability through logical and mathematical rigor.

The Austrians advanced their arguments in theoretical terms. In the meantime, neoclassical theorists developed more and more useful mathematical prediction tools and accumulated hard, statistical evidence to demonstrate the value of their theory. The scientific nature of neoclassical theory was particularly appealing to the emerging American economic discipline, so neoclassical theory grew to dominate American economic thinking.

Joseph Schumpeter was a student of the Austrian school who came to the United States early in his career and wrote most of his books here. He saw innovation—the use of an invention to create a new commercial product or service—as the driving force for creating new demand for goods and services. An innovation is a new idea brought to the market, where buyers find it so appealing that they expand their purchases to include this new product or service. Every innovation successfully introduced by business firms, large or small, new or old, creates new demand for goods and services and therefore creates new wealth.

But Schumpeter disagreed with neoclassical theory about the mechanism of wealth distribution. He argued that neoclassical perfect markets with many buyers and many sellers do not exist. All but a trivial few markets are dominated by a few sellers, who often collude to control the market functions. The concept of free exchange is unreal, he states; instead, suppliers control the market for their own benefit, not the buyers' benefit.

Instead of neoclassical competitive markets functioning systematically to achieve equilibrium between supply and demand, Schumpeter observed *chaotic markets* driven by the regular appearance of entrepreneurs who enter the markets using innovations that challenge the established few suppliers who dominate the markets. Entrepreneurs, by definition, are owner-managers who start new, independent businesses to exploit innovations. Entrepreneurs begin their firms with little personal wealth but the ambition to create wealth for themselves. They develop innovations and struggle to achieve success in the market. If successful, they expand the overall market as buyers increase their purchases to include the new product or service offered. As overall demand increases, new wealth is created. The entrepreneurs gain market share and new wealth for themselves.

At the same time, their innovations destroy the structure of existing markets and cause established firms with older products or services to decline. The entrepreneurs acquire the market shares once held by the older firms, thereby acquiring some of the older firms' wealth. The older firms lay off employees, and some declare bankruptcy. Their creditors, employees, and shareholders lose some of their wealth. At the same time, the entrepreneurs hire new employees, pay increased dividends to their shareholders, and increase their purchases from suppliers. New wealth is created through new demand, and both new and old wealth is distributed to the entrepreneurs and their employees, shareholders, and suppliers.

Entrepreneurs, Schumpeter argues, are the mechanism of wealth creation and distribution in capitalism. Schumpeter called this process *creative destruction* because entrepreneurs create new wealth through the process of destroying existing market structures.

Schumpeter derived his theory of creative destruction through observations of the real world during the first half of the twentieth century, but it is still evident in the United States. Examples are easy to find in the highly innovative computer markets. Apple Computer Company brought the microcomputer to markets that were dominated by a few manufacturers of minicomputers and mainframes. Within 15 years the structure of these markets was irrevocably changed. Minicomputer companies such as Digital Equipment Company and Data General Corporation have declined. Prime Computer was acquired, and Wang Computer experienced severe financial difficulties and emerged as a shadow of its former self. Still others have disappeared.

But creative destruction did not stop with the microcomputer innovation. Another wave of marketing and distribution innovations surged through this industry in the late 1980s as Dell Computer Company brought direct mail sales to a microcomputer industry dominated by retail sales outlets. Even "big blue," IBM Corporation, has experienced loss of market share to these "mail-order techies" and experienced declining profits in response to this new form of competition. In the meantime, once-small firms with minimal resources have become giant firms with many wealthy shareholders, employees, and suppliers.

An especially important aspect of Schumpeter's economic theory is that *innovations create new demand* and *entrepreneurs bring innovations to the market*. This means entrepreneurs are central to wealth creation and distribution. Entrepreneurs are owner-managers of new, independent firms that bring innovations into existing markets. They destroy the existing markets as their innovations increase demand and create new wealth. And entrepreneurs distribute wealth as a new set of shareholders, workers, and suppliers experience increases in income and an old set experiences declines. Once entrepreneurial firms become large and wealthy, they become prey for new entrepreneurs.

Good examples of this process are again found in the computer industry. Digital Equipment Company was formed as an entrepreneurial venture in 1957. Data General was formed by entrepreneurs in 1968. Both manufactured minicomputers that gradually took over the market share of several mainframe computer manufacturers. General Electric and RCA exited the computer hardware business in the late 1960s and early 1970s. But both DEC and Data General became victims of the next wave of innovative computers: microcomputers introduced by Apple Computer Company. The cycle of creative destruction goes on endlessly.

Schumpeter's theory of creative destruction, with innovative entrepreneurs as central actors in creating market chaos, stands in sharp contrast to neoclassical theory, with its systematically operating markets with passive, reactive buyers and sellers responding to price fluctuations to adjust demand and supply and achieve equilibrium. The two theories defy systematic comparison. Neoclassical theory depicts the market as *static*, with changes occurring only as movement from one equilibrium condition to another. In Schumpeter's theory the market is *dynamic*, depending upon continuous changes in buyer and supplier behavior. But, the scientific appeal of neoclassical theory with its predictive power overwhelmed the theories of Schumpeter and emerged as the dominant theory in American economic thought—until the decade of the entrepreneur.

Entrepreneurship prior to 1980

If Schumpeter is correct and entrepreneurs play such an important role in society, why wasn't this recognized prior to 1980? The answer lies in America's popular belief systems. After World War II American society was dominated by the belief that large corporations were the source of wealth creation and distribution. In 1956 William Whyte observed the emergence of this popular perspective in American society in his book *The Organization Man.* He suggested that the widespread exposure of Americans to poverty during the depression and military training during World War II created a behavioral norm of accepting employment within and obedience to bureaucracies. Thus, America had become conditioned to believe in the large corporation as a preferred source of employment.

This admiration of large corporations led to a theory of how society would eventually come to be dominated by these corporations. In 1967 John Kenneth Galbraith published *The New Industrial State,* wherein he expressed the belief that large corporations would work in coordination with big government and large labor unions to run the nation. This would occur because large organizations, with their large-scale, efficient operations, had professional managers who held similar values centered upon organization life. Entrepreneurs are notably absent from Galbraith's "new industrial state."

Views of society as being dominated by large corporations are consistent with neoclassical theory, which includes *economies of scale* as a necessary component. "Economies of scale" means that as the size of a firm increases, the cost of production per unit declines.[2] This is due to the increase in specialization of labor and machinery that evolves as production organizations become larger. Henry Ford's invention of the assembly line to produce low-cost automobiles is a familiar example of production cost reduction through increasing the size of production plants. Ford's low-cost production of the Model T allowed it to dominate the automobile market for 20 years.

The principle of economies of scale specifies that larger firms have lower costs of production than smaller firms. This is a very practical, intuitively appealing principle of economics. Neoclassical theory proceeds further by arguing that large firms are more profitable than small firms because large firms have lower production costs. This conclusion is logically consistent for perfect markets, where all suppliers sell at the same price.

Thus, both social observers and mainstream economists find society's respect for large firms to be consistent with their theories and a logical condition for society.

Growing Dissatisfaction with Neoclassical Economics

Researchers have had great difficulty finding evidence that economies of scale exist. Few economists doubt the existence of economies of scale because considerable production management information exists to validate the theory.

Most engineers can run through calculations that show larger manufacturing plants are more cost-efficient than small plants.

But researchers have difficulty finding real-world examples to demonstrate that larger producers are *more profitable*. Neoclassical theory requires not only that firms have lower costs of production but also that market prices be equal for all producers. Only when prices are equal does the lowest-cost producer earn the greatest profit. If market prices are not equal and products are differentiated, then smaller, less efficient firms can have higher prices and be more profitable.

Furthermore, large manufacturing plants that take advantage of specialization of labor and machinery in order to lower production costs become somewhat inflexible. Thus, when entrepreneurs enter markets with new technologies, existing large-scale plants may have difficulty adjusting and can actually fail as they lose market share. Manufacturing costs are a small part of market dynamics in an entrepreneurial economy, and production efficiency does not directly translate into profitability. In other words, *equilibrium markets do not exist, and economies of scale is not a dominant economic factor.*

Still, throughout the post-World War II era, discussions of entrepreneurship's role in American capitalism were relegated to a few academics involved in the study of "small business." The dominant perception of entrepreneurs is summed up in the joke "Entrepreneurs are people who start their own business to avoid getting a job." Then, in 1979, David Birch published results of an economic analysis demonstrating that *small firms dominate job creation and economic growth in the United States.* Economic theory and society's perceptions of entrepreneurs were irrevocably changed.

EMERGING THEORY OF ENTREPRENEURSHIP ECONOMICS

In 1979 David Birch created a furor in the economic establishment by publishing the results of research based on a data file of all U.S. firms and their employment from 1969 through 1976. His research concluded that small firms, those with 100 or fewer employees, created 81% of the net new jobs in the United States. ("Net new jobs" is defined as total new jobs added minus total jobs lost during the time period.) Since net new job creation is a widely accepted measure of economic growth, Birch's findings mean that small firms created most of the economic growth. In 1987 Birch provided a more complete assessment of his findings in a book entitled *Job Creation in America.*

Birch's work was largely discounted by mainstream economists at the time because it is counter to the conclusions reached using methods derived from neoclassical theory. But economists who replicated his work in the United States and other nations have verified his conclusions. In response to Birch's work, the U.S. Small Business Administration (SBA) established a long-term project to create and maintain a data file similar to Birch's beginning with 1976. The SBA continued his dynamic analytical methodology and has provided further evidence that small firms do indeed create new jobs in excess of their share of overall employment.

Evidence that Small Firms Dominate Economic Growth

The SBA's database includes all firms in the United States over the period from 1976 to 1990. The SBA calculates the respective shares of jobs created by small and large firms on a biennial (two-year) basis and publishes these statistics in the annual report *The State of Small Business*. A summary of Birch's and the SBA's findings on the small-firm share of net new jobs is shown in Exhibit 15.1.

Exhibit 15.1 shows that small firms do not produce the majority of the net new jobs in every biennial period. Period-to-period variations in small-firm share are due to fluctuations in the overall economy. During periods of economic recessions (1981–82, 1989–90) and in the first period after such recessions (1977–78, 1983–84), small firms demonstrate substantial contributions to net job creation. Late in the periods of expansion following recessions (1979–80, 1985–88), the small-firm share falls to lower levels.

EXHIBIT 15.1 Small firms' share of net new jobs: Comparison of Birch and SBA results.

Period	Birch	SBA	Static share
1969–72	82%		
1973–74	53		
1975–76	65		
1977–78		57%	36%
1979–80		37	35
1981–82		92	36
1983–84		65	36
1985–86		44	35
1987–88		33	35
1989–90		100	44

Small firm: ≤100 employees

Source: Bruce A. Kirchhoff, *Entrepreneurship and Dynamic Capitalism,* © 1994 by Bruce A. Kirchhoff, Figure 1, Quorum Books, an imprint of Greenwood Publishing Group, Inc., Westport, Ct. Reprinted with permission.

Interestingly, these wide swings in employment growth shares are due primarily to variations in the hiring/firing practices of the 15,000 firms that have more than 500 employees and constitute 50% of the private-sector work force. During recessions, large firms frequently experience overall net declines in employment (job losses exceeding job additions) or only minimal net gains. Small firms, on the other hand, continue to show net gains in employment during recessions and therefore account for a much larger share of net new employment. In fact, the stable, regular net job creation of the small-firm sector regardless of the condition of the overall economy is an important strength of the U.S. economy.

Statistics for longer-term net job creation (four to eight years) show that, on average, small firms create more net new jobs per employee than large firms, and they typically produce more than half of the total. These data make it clear that small firms are the primary job creators in the United States.

Entrepreneurial Growth and Neoclassical Theory

The impact of these findings on neoclassical economic theory (and general equilibrium theory) is profound. First, the results provide convincing evidence that economies of scale do not dominate economic growth since small firms, not large firms, create most of the growth. Second, it suggests that Schumpeter's theory of creative destruction offers a better description of the overall economy. These findings cast doubt on neoclassical theory as an appropriate model for American capitalism. Without economies of scale and with entrepreneurial suppliers as active participants in the economy, general equilibrium theory is without a solid foundation and without predictive powers.

Since 1979 the job creation research has made entrepreneurs into heroes:

- Entrepreneurs are the creators of wealth through innovation.
- Entrepreneurs are at the center of job and economic growth.
- Entrepreneurs provide a mechanism of wealth distribution that depends on innovation, hard work, and risk taking. This is widely respected as an appropriate basis for wealth distribution. Thus, entrepreneurs provide a "fair and equitable" method of wealth redistribution.

Michael Milken and Charles Keating are not entrepreneurs. Nor is Lee Iacocca or Jack Welch. These men did not form new, independent firms with innovations and destroy existing market structures.

Entrepreneurship is now recognized as an important contribution to U.S. society. Employment in a large corporation is no longer considered the preferred objective of all who seek gainful work. Galbraith's "new industrial state" is no longer perceived as the ultimate form of society. "Going it alone" has a uniquely American, individualistic appeal, and with success the "loner" becomes wealthy while contributing to the nation's overall economic progress. To become economically independent through one's own efforts—entrepreneurship—is the ultimate expression of the American ideal of individualism.

The economics profession is now in a state of theoretical turmoil as the dominant neoclassical theory is experiencing increasing pressure to accommodate entrepreneurship. But the neoclassical perfect market cannot incorporate entrepreneurs.

A new economic theory explaining capitalism with such clarity that it allows prediction is now needed. Schumpeter's theory of creative destruction does not meet this need. It cannot be modeled mathematically or used to predict economic events. Rather, it describes capitalism as directionless, driven by the random, unpredictable phenomena of entrepreneurship. Creative destruction offers no methods to forecast the next innovation, the next successful entrepreneur, or the next economic expansion or recession. The theory's absence of predictive power leaves economics without a substitute for neoclassical economics. Much work is required to build a new theory.

A TYPOLOGY OF ENTREPRENEURS: DEFINING SURVIVAL AND SUCCESS

Economists are now working to construct a new theory to incorporate entrepreneurs into capitalism. Typology development is one step toward the development of a new theory. *Typologies* organize existing knowledge into categories that help explain relationships and guide theory development. Furthermore, typologies can provide guidance to policy development and entrepreneurial choices even in the absence of full theory development. This is important because the absence of a fully developed theory does not remove society's need to identify entrepreneurial opportunities and design economic policy to promote entrepreneurial activity. And, given the nonentrepreneurial policy prescriptions emanating from general equilibrium theory, development of a new basis for guiding pro-entrepreneurial activity is desperately needed to ensure the continued vitality of an entrepreneurial economy.

Business firms, including small businesses, have long been classified for decision analysis. Traditional classification criteria are business size, industry type (product or service produced), ownership type, age, and location. None of these provides adequate information to identify the few creative destroyers among the millions of small businesses that exist. Creative destroyers emerge from all industries, all sizes, all ownership types, all ages, and all locations.

To develop a new theory or typology for entrepreneurs, economists need to:

- Identify creative destroyers.
- Determine where innovative market entry opportunities exist.
- Clarify what the entrepreneurs need.
- Guide economic policy so as to improve entrepreneurs' success.

So far, research has established that small firms excel in job creation and innovation. There are millions of small firms,[3] and most of these stay small while producing only one or a few innovations and contributing little or only modest economic growth per firm. Birch observed that small firms create most of the net new jobs, but the vast majority of the new jobs are created by less than 10% to 12% of all small firms. This observation suggests that a small percentage of the small firms are the creative destroyers.

Furthermore, by Schumpeter's definition, entrepreneurship means new firm formation and growth, whereas the job generation statistics measure the job creation of *all* small firms—old, middle-aged, and new. Statistics show that approximately 500,000 to 700,000 new small firms are formed every year. In a small-business sector that includes 7 to 9 million firms, this amounts to an 8 to 10% annual increase. Creative destroyers are among these new firms, as well as among the existing firms, especially the ones that are still young. But not all newly formed or young firms are, or are intended to be, *high-growth firms* that challenge the giants in their markets. Most of these firms have limited growth ambitions. The owner forms and grows the business to the point where it provides a satisfactory standard of living and allows time to enjoy the benefits.

It is useful to describe and understand the phenomenon of new firm formation. Of all the important dynamics that occur in a capitalist system, *firm formation* is paramount. The more firm formations, the greater the potential economic growth. Firm formation is also the phenomenon of greatest interest to aspiring entrepreneurs. Entrepreneurs want to know:

- What are the chances of survival, failure, and growth?
- How can the chances of success be improved?
- What are the odds of achieving huge success such as that experienced by Microsoft, Sum Microsystems, or Dell Computer?

Economists are beginning to answer these questions. But this requires putting entrepreneurs into categories, categories that are related to theory—into a typology.

The following paragraphs present a useful typology and report the results of analysis of one group of new firms as they age and grow. But first it is necessary to dispel the "fiction of firm failure" that dominates the thinking about new small firms.

Survival Rates of Entrepreneurial Firms

Economists and politicians often quote a widely believed statement about small firm failure; "Four out of five small firms fail in their first five years." Administrators (CEOs) of the SBA have used this alliteration to express their concern about the health of small firms, and mainstream economists have used it to express their disdain for small firms. However, this claim has no basis in fact; no statistical sources or analyses report such high failure rates. In fact, there is good evidence that *more than half*—rather than one-fifth—*of all new small firms survive for eight or more years.*

These failure statistics are especially important to aspiring entrepreneurs concerned about their future success. A description of failure is necessary for a full understanding of the survival statistics for new small firms. There is considerable difference between death and failure.

The Difference between Death and Failure of an Entrepreneurial Venture

Every year between 8% and 10% of all businesses terminate operations. Large corporations terminate as large a percentage of their plants and offices every year as do small firms. The difference is that most small firms have only one plant or office, so the termination of a small firm's only plant means the termination of the firm. Large firms, on the other hand, have multiple plants and offices, so the termination of a plant does not eliminate the firm.

Examination of the net effect of closings on employment reinforces this evidence. Over a period of several years, the large- and small-firm sectors lose the same percentage of their total employment because of plant and office closings.

Whereas large firms are required to publicly announce plant and office closures in advance, small firms are not. Thus, small firms terminate operations without an announced or recorded rationale. This makes identification of small-firm deaths far more difficult. There is limited research on the reasons for small-firm closures, but one source of information, Dun & Bradstreet Corporation (D&B), records when firms fail for financial reasons. D&B operates the nation's largest commercial credit rating service, so it promptly notes a firm's default on debts to creditors.

D&B defines business "failure" as business termination with losses to creditors. This is an appropriate definition because it distinguishes the firms that fail because of financial distress and the firms that terminate operations by the choice of the owners. Those familiar with small-firm owners will not be surprised to learn that most firms terminate operations *voluntarily*. In fact, D&B reports that only 20% to 25% of all small-firm terminations are failures as defined by closure with losses to creditors.

The other 75% to 80% of small-firm terminations are due to reasons other than failure:

- Some small-firm owners simply grow tired of the business, pay the creditors, and close the doors. They retire, obtain employment elsewhere, or move on to another business.

- Other owners sell their businesses to new owners.

- Still others change their type of business. For example, an owner of a photo shop may decide to convert it to a videotape rental store.

Here are some statistics substantiating these statements. There were 814,000 new small firms formed in 1977 and 1978. Eight years later, 28% of these firms were still in existence with their same owners. U.S. Department of Labor statistics show that, on average, every year 3.3% of all businesses change ownership. For reasons that originate in data collection methods, ownership changes are largely recorded as *terminations* (sale of a firm) and *subsequent formations* (new owner acquisition of an existing firm) in the statistical data used to calculate survival rates. Thus, we need to add back 8 times 3.3%, or 26%, to the survival percentage. This gives an eight-year survival rate of 28% plus 26%, or a total of 54%. In other words, over half of all small firms formed in 1977–78 survived for eight years. (We do not have data beyond eight years.)

Of those firms that were recorded as being terminated during their first eight years (72%, including ownership changes), D&B states that *only 20% to 25% of these were failures*. Twenty-five percent of 72% is 18%. Thus, of the 814,000 firms formed in 1977–78, *only 18% terminated with losses to creditors* within eight years. A pie chart summarizing the destinies of these new firms after eight years is provided in Exhibit 15.2.

These statistics clearly show that new small firms are far more resilient and capable than is popularly believed. The chances of success for an entrepreneur starting out in the United States are surprisingly good. Certainly, from a lender's perspective, the probability of losses from lending to new businesses is far less than that implied in the statement "four out of five (80%) fail in five years." The survival rate of the small firm, including ownership changes, is one out of two, and 28% survive with their original owners.

EXHIBIT 15.2   Eight-year destinies of all small firms formed in 1977–78 (814,000 firms).

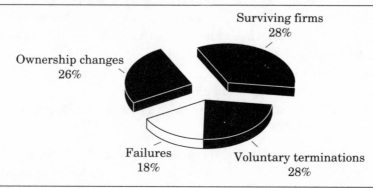

Surviving firms
28%

Ownership changes
26%

Failures
18%

Voluntary terminations
28%

Source: Bruce A. Kirchhoff, *Entrepreneurship and Dynamic Capitalism,* © 1994 by Bruce A. Kirchhoff, Figure 2, Quorum Books, an imprint of Greenwood Publishing Group, Inc., Westport, CT. Reprinted with permission.

Factors Affecting Survival Rates of Entrepreneurial Ventures

By relating a variety of demographic factors to firm survival rates, research has determined which factors are most likely to influence survival. The factors examined are:

- Type of business activity (industry).
- Geographical area (state) where the firm is located.
- Size of the firm at birth.
- Degree of growth experienced by the firm.
- Extent of competition in the region (state) where the firm operates.

Results of this research are very encouraging for aspiring entrepreneurs.

Type of Business Activity

This factor is very important in determining survival. For example, manufacturing firms have a greater survival rate than construction firms. In fact, manufacturing firms have the greatest survival rate of all types of business.

Firms that change their business activity during the first eight years are more likely to survive. This is especially interesting because it means that business experience teaches startup entrepreneurs what is right and wrong with their business, and survivors are able to adapt their products/services based on this knowledge.

Company Size

The size of the firm at startup also has considerable influence on its chance of survival. The larger the firm (number of employees) at birth, the greater its odds of survival. Firms with 1, 2, or 3 employees at birth have a much lower survival rate than larger firms. Interestingly, firms with 5 employees at birth have the same survival rate as those starting with 10, 20, or more employees.

For reasons as yet unknown, only firms with fewer than five employees at birth experience lower survival rates. It is probable that the number of employees at birth is actually a surrogate measure for the extent of resources at birth. In other words, a firm beginning with five or more employees is likely to also have more startup capital and a wider variety of knowledge and skills available than a firm with only one or two employees.

Degree of Growth

Growth of the firm greatly increases its survivability. The degree of growth need not be large; the addition of only one employee after birth makes a great difference in survival rate. It is interesting to note, however, that the majority of firms show no growth for the first six years. Slightly more than 50% of surviving firms show growth after six years. Thus, growth takes much longer to achieve than most entrepreneurs expect at the time of the firm's birth.

Competition

Several of the factors examined have no effect on survival rates. The extent of competition (whether there are many competitors or only a few) makes no difference to survival. The neoclassical economic competition theory suggests that the existence of competitors will make the success of a new firm more difficult. However, Schumpeter's theory says that new firms enter with innovations that provide the opportunity for growth. Thus, Schumpeter's theory, not neoclassical theory, is supported by this finding. Entrepreneurs can rest assured that with the right innovation, they can achieve success in spite of the number of competitors.

Geographical Location

Geographical area also has no effect on survival. In other words, the chances of a small firm's survival are as good in one state as in any other. This is not good news for the state economic development specialists who busy themselves with recruiting firms from other states on the grounds that their state is a better place to be. It is good news, however, for entrepreneurs because it means that they can start their businesses where they live.

However, an important relationship exists between location and type of business. Firms in the *same type of business* tend to locate near each other. For example, computer manufacturing firms tend to cluster in California, Texas, and the Northeast. Thus, locating a computer firm in Kansas may increase your risk of termination since the clusters of computer-knowledgeable and experienced personnel and investors are not in Kansas. Of course, there are exceptions, as evidenced by the success of Gateway 2000 Corporation, a major manufacturer of microcomputers located in South Dakota.

Entrepreneurs' Control over Potential Survival of the Firm

Overall, the general pattern revealed by this survival analysis is that entrepreneurs largely control the factors that influence their chances of survival. The type of business (and changes thereto) and size of firm are decisions made by the entrepreneur. Entrepreneurs may not have complete control over the growth of their firms, but they can influence growth.

Therefore, to ensure survival, entrepreneurs need to carefully pick their type of business, adjust the type according to market needs, define birth size, and work hard to achieve growth. And they need not move out of state or away from competitors to survive. If you are interested in starting a firm, remember these rules. Also remember that more than half of all new firms will survive for at least eight years.

DYNAMIC CAPITALISM TYPOLOGY: UNDERSTANDING ENTREPRENEURSHIP'S CONTRIBUTIONS TO ECONOMIC GROWTH

Survival is not itself indicative of success or economic contribution. Most business owners measure success in terms of *survival and growth*. As mentioned earlier, of those 814,000 firms formed in 1977–78, less than half of the survivors (with their original owners) experienced any growth in employment during the first six years. Growth comes slowly, not during the first year, as most entrepreneurs hope, but in six to eight years.

In a dynamic capitalist economy, entrepreneurs enter existing markets using innovations. Thus, it is logical to expect that the number of innovations created by a firm will be related to the firm's growth rate. On the other hand, it is apparent that the direct relationship proposed by Schumpeter between innovation and firm growth through creative destruction is not correct. Not all innovations are successful, so some firms that create a large number of innovations will not experience high growth. And some innovations are far more successful than others, so some firms with only a few innovations will achieve high rates of growth. This complex relationship between the rate of innovation and the rate of firm growth can be expressed in a matrix called the *dynamic capitalism typology*, illustrated in Exhibit 15.3.

The typology matrix is divided into four main categories: economic core, constrained growth, glamorous, and ambitious. Each category designates businesses with common characteristics that reflect their creative destruction capability. The matrix represents a simplification of the real world, because it lists only the extreme cases registering either high or low on each scale. As noted later in this chapter (in the discussion of the statistical evidence), the vast majority of businesses lie in the middle ground, between the extremes. Still, the matrix describes categories that add to our understanding of entrepreneurship's contributions to economic growth.

EXHIBIT 15.3 Dynamic capitalism typology.

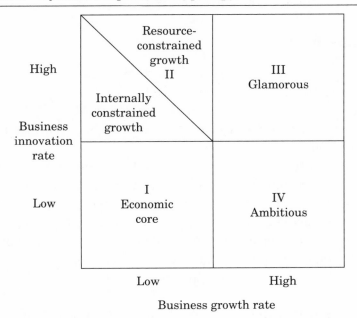

Source: Bruce A. Kirchhoff, *Entrepreneurship and Dynamic Capitalism,* © 1994 by Bruce A. Kirchhoff, Figure 3, Quorum Books, an imprint of Greenwood Publishing Group, Inc., Westport, CT. Reprinted with permission.

Economic Core Firms

Economic core firms dominate in total numbers. There are more low-innovation and low-growth firms in the U.S. than any other kind. Most of these firms satisfy their owners' needs and therefore continue to operate successfully and fulfill their functions in the marketplace without achieving significant growth. No doubt, these firms achieve a degree of growth shortly after their formation, but once they achieve a size that meets the owners' needs, growth stops. Small, independent retail stores, service firms, and repair shops are economic core firms. Such firms are truly ubiquitous—there are probably 5 to 6.5 million of them—and they provide numerous goods and services necessary to the functioning of the U.S. economy.

The economic core also includes hundreds of thousands of firms that are small temporarily. Owners of these firms are ambitious; they want to grow into big businesses. But, to the outsider, these firms look like all other economic core firms—small, independently owned, and struggling. For example, Sam Walton's first Gibson Discount Store looked like most rural discount stores until he found the right formula for growth, changed the name to Wal-Mart, and became the world's largest retailer. To some degree, the massiveness of the economic core hides the ambitious entrepreneur until success causes the growing firm to leap into the realm of ambitious firms.

Ambitious Firms

Ambitious firms achieve high rates of growth with one, or a combination of a few, initial innovations. A single new product or service can provide growth for many years, especially in a large market such as the United States. Growth comes as the innovative product or service takes over the market share of older, established competitors.

Examples of this type are easy to find. Dell Computer Company developed an innovative method of distributing and servicing microcomputers, through direct mail. It used this initial combination of innovations to gradually acquire more than 5% of a very large market within eight years. Of course, it continued to bring out new versions of computers, but none of these was a significant product innovation because microcomputers had become essentially standardized. Its distribution innovation worked best because of this standardization.

So high growth can be achieved without high rates of innovation. However, an ambitious firm's growth will eventually decline *unless it develops additional innovations,* because markets do not remain static. New entrepreneurs will enter the market with product or service innovations, and the once-ambitious firm will experience loss of market share. A good example of this is Wendy's International, founded in 1968. Its original innovation—"hot and juicy hamburgers"—was extremely successful. But after 10 years, its growth rate slowed, and it searched for additional innovations in fast food to continue its growth. Unfortunately, it has never found another innovation that would allow it to achieve the high growth rates of the 1970s.

Glamorous Firms

High growth rates can be achieved over the long term only with high rates of innovation. I call firms with these characteristics *glamorous* because they attract news media attention and receive local and national awards for their successes. Most of these firms are rooted in technology-based product businesses, products that lend themselves to continuous development and spawn innovation after innovation. Microsoft is a good example of a product-manufacturing firm that has created an endless stream of innovations in the software business. It began with the now universal operation system called Microsoft DOS. Then it expanded to include a spreadsheet program, word processor, graphics, and other features, and today it is the world's largest software company.

Constrained-Growth Firms

Many glamorous firms emerge only after a period of *constrained growth*. Lacking the proper resources, these firms have high rates of innovation but do not achieve high growth. Unless revenues grow rapidly to support the expensive innovation efforts, these firms experience financial failure. Owners of such firms fall into two classes: those who make decisions that constrain their firm's growth and those who choose growth but are unable to acquire the needed resources.

Internally Constrained Firms

Owners of these companies deny that they choose to constrain their growth, insisting that growth is constrained by the reluctance of the providers of resources to supply the firm. But, in truth, these owners place such burdens on the suppliers of resources that they are unable to cooperate. Thus, the inventor who refuses to sell more than 10% of her firm's stock in order to raise a million dollars is to blame for her lack of capital. And the owner who refuses to offer a key manager a significant share of the firm's stock to keep the manager constructively employed is also constraining the firm's growth.

Resource-Constrained Firms

Other entrepreneurs are willing to give up reasonable shares of ownership, but they are unable to find or attract the capital or personnel necessary to grow the business. These are the truly resource-constrained businesses. Such businesses represent a major problem in the United States because there is a shortage of capital for investment in early-stage, highly innovative small firms. Without early-stage capital, many constrained-growth firms never have the opportunity to demonstrate the value and contribution of their innovations. Because innovation is expensive, such firms do not last very long. They either cease innovation and become economic core firms or they terminate.

A greater danger threatens constrained-growth firms' continued existence. Innovations (especially patented inventions) are easy prey for better-financed competitors. Highly innovative firms that do not pursue high growth may find their innovations copied and markets devoured by competitors that gobble up market share for themselves. Inventors believe that patents will protect them from such competition, but this belief is false. An issued patent actually exposes the technology to all competitors. If a competitor copies the technology, it is assumed that the courts will punish the offending firm. But the cost of bringing a patent infringement case can be afforded only by firms with good revenue and profit streams. And even if the infringement suit is successful, the courts rarely require offending firms to remove their products from the market and give up their market share. Instead, such firms pay a fine and are awarded licenses to the patent, so they continue their products and maintain their market shares. The inventor owns the patent rights, but the competitor owns the market.

Because of these forces, the constrained-growth category of firms is small in comparison to the economic core. Either firms grow or they die.

Entrepreneurs Can Apply This Typology to Classify Their Own Firms

What is interesting about these four classes of firms is that they do not depend on industrial sector, business size, age, or location. For example, ambitious manufacturing firms share many problems, needs, and opportunities with ambitious construction firms and service firms of different sizes and in different locations. At the same time, ambitious firms have little in common with economic core firms in the same industry or state. The typology also makes it clear that firms in the same industry are not the same in terms of their ambitions and goals. This is true regardless of age, since firm ownership changes sufficiently often that a firm's age tells nothing about the ambitions and goals of the owners. Even the transfer of ownership among family members (for example, parent to child) may create a new set of ambitions. This typology identifies the firm behaviors that indicate the true ambitions and goals of the owners and defines their contribution to economic growth.

Aspiring entrepreneurs need to realistically assess their personal ambitions and where they wish to be in this typology. Not everyone wants the traumas and chaos of starting and running an ambitious firm. Once a modicum of growth is achieved, many formerly ambitious owners suddenly discover that achievement of their ambitions is too costly to their personal lives, and they decide to settle for less. For example, many local retail and restaurant chains have the potential for national growth but choose to remain local. The owners decide that the costs in money and time necessary to achieve national growth are simply more than they want to commit.

Few aspiring entrepreneurs have the drive for innovation and growth that is required to build a glamorous firm. Many inventors have an initial interest in becoming the next Microsoft or Compaq Computer Company, but they lack the necessary business savvy or capital.

This leaves the *economic core as the bastion of entrepreneurs* who have moderate ambitions and those who had greater ambitions but decided to settle for less. Some constrained-growth firms reduce their innovation rates and settle for low growth, thereby becoming a part of the economic core. This does not mean, however, that the economic core is a refuge for failed ambitious and glamorous entrepreneurs. These entrepreneurs find niche markets where they provide goods and services that are preferred by a variety of buyers. The very existence of so many small firms in all industrial sectors demonstrates their success in meeting market needs. Their contribution to overall economic activity and growth is considerable because even a small rate of growth among 5 million businesses creates a lot of new jobs annually.

This contribution to growth is not just a belief. It can be measured and, as shown in the next section, it is considerable.

Measuring Growth Contributions of Entrepreneurs

The dynamic capitalism typology provides a basis for measuring the relative contributions of the four types of entrepreneurs to overall economic growth. In Schumpeter's original theoretical formulation, new small firms that have been formed to exploit innovations create economic growth. Therefore, measurement of dynamic capitalism focuses on newly formed firms. This approach understates the total contributions of all small firms because it considers growth attributable to only a small group of newly formed firms. The approach does, however, isolate the dynamics of new firms in a direct test of the dynamic capitalism typology and creative destruction.

To accomplish this task, Bruce Phillips and I identified all firms formed in the United States between December 31, 1976, and December 31, 1978. For practical purposes, this includes all firms formed during 1977 and 1978. This cohort of firms was followed for the next six years, until the end of 1984. Measures of the number of employees in each firm were taken at the time of birth and at the end of 1984.

The cohort consists of 814,190 small firms formed during 1977 and 1978. Of these, 312,804 survived with the same ownership through 1984. We divided these firms into the four typology classes. We calculated the growth in employment of all firms and defined *high growth* to include the 10% with the greatest growth rates. *Low growth* included the 10% of all firms with the smallest growth rates.

We defined *high innovation* as comprising all firms in a selected group of industries where business activity is characterized by above-average employment of scientists, engineers, and technical professionals. Such industries also display above-average expenditures in research and development. (This is a common research definition of "high-technology" industries.) We selected another group of industries with the opposite characteristics and defined firms in these industries as *low innovation* (low technology).

Success of High-Innovation Firms

Growth rates differed significantly among typology classes. As suggested earlier, glamorous firms showed the greatest growth of all classes. More than 16% of the high-innovation firms became high-growth firms. But only 9% of the high-innovation firms survived as low-growth firms (constrained growth). As discussed earlier, growth is essential for the survival of high-innovation firms because of the cost of innovation. Overall, however, the survival rate of high-innovation firms was as good as that for low-innovation firms. These statistics are shown in Exhibit 15.4.

Success of Low-Innovation Firms

Not surprisingly, only 9% of the low-innovation firms achieved high growth to become ambitious firms. This is significantly lower than the 16% reported for high-innovation firms. But, more than 10% of the low-innovation firms reported low growth. These statistics are shown in Exhibit 15.5.

EXHIBIT 15.4   Six-year destinies of high-innovation firms formed in 1977–78 (58,714 total births).

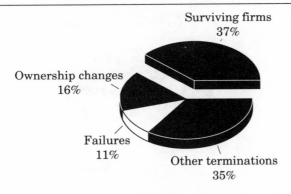

All High-Innovation Firms

Surviving Firms

Source: Bruce A. Kirchhoff, *Entrepreneurship and Dynamic Capitalism,* © 1994 by Bruce A. Kirchhoff, Figure 4, Quorum Books, an imprint of Greenwood Publishing Group, Inc., Westport, CT. Reprinted with permission.

Overall Survival of Entrepreneurial Ventures

In summary, it is apparent that overall survival of newly formed small firms does not depend on innovation rates. Thus, the risk of starting a high-tech firm is no greater than that of starting a low-tech firm. However, the chances of achieving high growth are almost twice as great for high-tech firms as for low-tech firms. Still, among high-tech firms, terminations take a greater toll, as low-growth firms are unable to hang on for as long as low-tech firms.

Given these statistical results, it is somewhat surprising that so few high-tech firms are formed relative to low-tech firms. Low-tech firm formations outnumbered high-tech formations 5 to 1. This fact has significant import concerning the overall job creation contribution of the two-year cohort of newly formed firms. The total employment of the 312,804 surviving firms at the end of 1984 was actually 25% less than the birth employment of the 814,190 firms

EXHIBIT 15.5   Six-year destinies of low-innovation firms formed in 1977–78 (number of firms formed = 280,305).

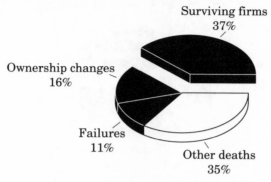

Surviving firms
37%

Ownership changes
16%

Failures
11%

Other deaths
35%

All Low-Innovation Firms

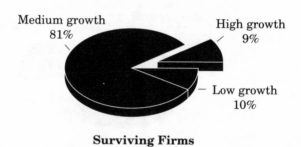

Medium growth
81%

High growth
9%

Low growth
10%

Surviving Firms

Source: Bruce A. Kirchhoff, *Entrepreneurship and Dynamic Capitalism,* © 1994 by Bruce A. Kirchhoff, Figure 5, Quorum Books, an imprint of Greenwood Publishing Group, Inc., Westport, CT. Reprinted with permission.

in 1978. In 1978 the total cohort employment was 4.5 million. By 1984, this had declined to 3.4 million. This is due largely to the departure of 502,000 firms during the six years. Among the 312,804 surviving firms, total employment increased 75% over birth employment. However, some of the surviving firms also suffered declining employment.

Employment changes differ considerably among typology classes. Among high-innovation firms, total employment increased by 14%. That is, the 21,603 surviving firms employed 14% more workers than the entire birth cohort of 58,714. This means that the surviving firms increased their employment by 169%. Eighty percent of this job growth occurred within the glamorous class of firms. Obviously, glamorous firms are the big job creators among new small firms.

Among low-innovation firms, total employment decreased by 31%. A comparison of birth and 1984 employment of the survivors showed an employment increase of 67%. Seventy percent of this job creation activity was concentrated in the ambitious firms. Although not spectacular, 67% growth in employment over a six-year period is an average of more than 9% compounded annually. This far surpasses the average growth in the employment, which is at most 3% annually. Furthermore, these low-innovation survivors produced 380,000 net new jobs. Because there are so many more of these than high-innovation firms, low-innovation firms outproduced high-innovation firms in net new jobs by over 2 to 1. In summary, high-innovation firms are more efficient job generators and more aggressive growers than low-innovation firms, at least during their first six years. But so many more low-innovation firms are started that these firms produce more net new jobs.

It is likely that few of these firms achieved full growth in their first 6 years. Only after analyzing their performance for 10 to 20 years can we identify the full job creation potential of these firms.

These firms had a significant net impact on the U.S. economy. Between the end of 1976 and the end of 1984, the formation and growth of this cohort of firms added 3.5 million net new jobs.[4] Since the total private-sector employment during this time was about 90 million, these firms increased total employment by nearly 4%.

We have examined only one two-year cohort of newly formed firms. Another 800,000 firms were formed in 1979–80, another 800,000 in 1981–82, and so on. If each of these two-year cohorts contribute 4% of the net new jobs, then the average effect is a 2% contribution annually to new employment in an economy that creates 3% to 3.5% new jobs annually. This is how small firms create the largest percentage of net new jobs in America.

ECONOMIC ADVICE FOR ASPIRING ENTREPRENEURS

The typology and research data and their implications for the economic theory of dynamic capitalism provide some advice for aspiring entrepreneurs.

Be Innovative

There are no a priori economic reasons for not starting a new firm using an innovation. In spite of dire warnings from mainstream economists, economies of scale are easily overcome by innovations. But be sure your innovation is significant enough to overcome any economies of scale that exist within the markets you are entering.

For example, small retailers are being ravaged by large firms entering with computerized inventory control systems. These systems allow firms to track daily sales to determine what items are and are not selling. With such control, they can ensure adequate stock on their retail shelves while maintaining a minimum of backup stock in their warehouses. This reduces the cash invested in inventory and frees it for use in advertising, store refurbishing, or salary increases for successful sales personnel. Unless you have a retailing innovation that overcomes this computer advantage, entering retailing is a high-risk venture. On the other hand, there may be entrepreneurial independent wholesalers who are willing to link their warehouses to their small retailers' computerized cash registers to give these retailers the advantages now possessed by larger firms. This may be the innovation the small retailers need. Perhaps you are the entrepreneur capable of developing and marketing this innovation.

Don't Worry about Geographical Location

Location is not an impediment to entrepreneurial success. You can start your firm in any location regardless of tax rates, living conditions or other touted advantages. One state is as good as another, although few state and local departments of economic development will agree with that statement. If you like where you live, stay there. Do not let someone convince you to move to start your business. If you really have doubts about this, I have the telephone number of a successful small computer firm in Spalding, Nebraska (population 635). Try to find Spalding on a map.

Choose Your Business Type Carefully

Highly innovative firms have greater chances for high-growth success but less staying power if early success is not achieved. You do not have to be a scientific genius to start a highly innovative firm. The list of highly innovative firms includes many services such as business consulting and environmental consulting.[5]

Furthermore, high innovation is not the only route to success. Firms with low rates of innovation can and do succeed. The restaurant business has seen a host of successful innovations in the last 20 years, and restaurants basically serve the same food. Most restaurant innovations have been in marketing. For example, Domino's Pizza is home-delivered, hot, and on time. Little Caesar's Pizza is pickup and inexpensive. Both are highly successful and definitely low-technology innovations. With a good marketing gimmick and a willingness to work, you can become a national restaurant franchisor.

Join with Three or More Partners to Start Your Firm

The larger your business is at startup, the better your chances of survival. It takes a wide variety of skills to start a new firm, and few individuals possess all the skills needed. So round up some partners to round out your skills—and to provide the early-stage startup capital.

Don't Be Intimidated by Competitors' Size and Proximity

A good innovation finds an initial small market segment and grows it into a major market share. Large competitors are especially slow to respond to an innovation. One firm I started entered a market where there was one dominant competitor with over 75% market share. And this firm had a history of copying all new products that entered the industry. But it rarely copied a product until five to seven years after its successful introduction. That is a long enough time for a new firm to start up and earn enough money to fund a patent suit.

Be Proud of What You Are Doing

It has been said that an entrepreneur is someone who starts a business because he cannot keep a job. This is not true. Most entrepreneurs want to achieve success through their own efforts. And successful entrepreneurs are very important to America's economic growth. Every new firm creates new jobs. Every successful, growing new firm creates lots of new jobs and new wealth and redistributes wealth. Entrepreneurship is America.

Furthermore, it is becoming more obvious that large firms cannot guarantee lifetime employment. Younger Americans are beginning to recognize that dependence on one's own abilities through owning and managing a business is an attractive option to being booted out when the large corporation begins to experience market share decline, decline that is often attributable to entrepreneurial activity.

Be Ever Alert for Other Entrepreneurs

Once your firm becomes established in an attractive market environment, some entrepreneur is going to take aim at you. With any luck, the entrepreneur's attack and your positive response will result in a growing market big enough for both of you. Remember, even IBM earned considerable profits initially from Apple Computer's introduction of the personal computer by rapidly creating its own competing standard in the market. Unfortunately for IBM, it was unable to sustain its dominant market share in the face of a variety of entrepreneurial attacks from Compaq, Dell, and Gateway 2000. A well-planned "me too" response to an entrepreneurial entry can ensure your continued involvement in the market.

Keep Your Eye on Foreign Firms

Entrepreneurs are not always independent small American firms. Foreign corporations are equally powerful in entering and gobbling up market shares. This is especially evident in automobiles and home electronics, where Japanese corporations have entered and now dominate. When this happens, the U.S. economy suffers losses of jobs and wealth. Thus, the decline of the domestic automobile and home electronics industries can be viewed as a failure of U.S. entrepreneurship: If U.S. entrepreneurs had entered these industries before the Japanese entrepreneurs, these industries might still be U.S.-dominated. Prior to World War II, nations had relatively closed market borders. But today, creative destruction travels easily across national boundaries.

CONCLUSION

It is now apparent that entrepreneurial entry benefits buyers by providing products and services with lower prices, better quality, and more features than were previously available. In fact, it is these characteristics of entrepreneurial innovation that make the entrepreneurs so successful. People do not buy entrepreneurs' new products or services because they like entrepreneurs; they buy these innovations because they provide greater buyer satisfaction. *Buyer satisfaction drives the success of entrepreneurs.*

For this reason, entrepreneurship is now recognized as the engine of competition and economic growth. It is the mechanism by which new products and services enter the economy and create growth. A logical extension of this reality is that the more entrepreneurship an economy produces, the better are its chances of remaining competitive in domestic and world markets.

SUGGESTED READING

David Birch, *Job Creation in America* (New York: The Free Press, 1987).

Bruce A. Kirchhoff, *Entrepreneurship and Dynamic Capitalism* (Westport, CT: Quorum Books, 1994).

GLOSSARY

Accounts payable: Money the company owes to vendors who supplied it with goods or services on credit. A measure of the average time taken to pay suppliers is the number of days payable, which is (accounts payable/annual credit purchases) × 365.

Accounts receivable: Money owed to a company by customers who have bought goods or services on credit. Accounts receivable are a current asset on the balance sheet. They are a liquid asset inasmuch as they are converted to cash in a relatively short time. If payment terms are net 30 days, then in principle every account receivable will be paid in 30 days or sooner. In practice, customers take longer. A measure of the average time taken is the number of days receivable, which is (accounts receivable/annual sales on credit) × 365.

Acid-test (quick) ratio: Current assets minus inventories divided by current liabilities. This ratio indicates a company's ability to meet its current liabilities with its most liquid (quick) assets.

Additional paid-in capital: Money received by a company from the sale of common stock that is in excess of the par value of the stock. If the par value of a share of common stock is $0.10 and investors purchase stock from the company at a price of $1.00 per share, the additional paid-in capital is $0.90 per share. (See *par value*.)

Adjusted book value (of a company):   The book value on the balance sheet after assets and liabilities are adjusted to market value (synonymous with modified book value).

Agency costs: An agency relationship occurs where one party (the principal) rewards another (the agent) for taking decisions on its behalf. Contract design plays an important role in ensuring that the agent acts in the interest of the principal. Agency costs occur because contracts are costly to write and enforce. They include the costs of structuring, monitoring, and bonding a set of contracts among agents with conflicting interests, plus the residual loss incurred because the cost of the full enforcement of contracts exceeds the benefits.

Agency theory: A branch of economics dealing with the behavior of principals (for example, owners) and their agents (for example, managers).

American Stock Exchange (Amex):   Stock exchange located in New York, listing companies that are generally smaller and younger than those on the much larger New York Stock Exchange.

Angel: Wealthy individual who invests in private companies. (See *invisible venture capital.*)

Antidilution (of ownership):   The right of an investor to maintain the same percentage ownership of a company's common stock in the event that the company issues more stock. (See *dilution.*)

Asked: The price level at which sellers offer securities to buyers.

Asset acquisition: Means of effecting a buyout by purchase of certain desired assets rather than shares of the target company.

Audited financial statements: A company's financial statements prepared and certified by a certified public accounting firm that is totally independent of the company.

Balance sheet: Summary statement of a company's financial position at a given point in time. It summarizes the accounting value of the assets, liabilities, preferred stock, common stock, and retained earnings. Assets = Liabilities + Preferred stock + Common stock + Retained earnings. (See *pro forma statements.*)

Basis point: One-hundredth of a percent (0.01%), typically used in expressing yield differentials (7.50% − 7.15% = 0.35%, or 35 basis points). (See *yield.*)

Bear: A person who expects prices to fall.

Bear market: A period of generally falling prices and pessimistic attitudes.

Best efforts offering: The underwriter makes its best efforts to sell as much as it can of the shares at the offering price. Hence, unlike a firm commitment offering, the company offering its shares is not guaranteed a definite amount of money by the underwriter.

Bid: The price level at which buyers offer to acquire securities from sellers.

Big Board: See *New York Stock Exchange.*

Blue sky: Refers to laws that safeguard investors from being misled by unscrupulous promoters of companies with little or no substance.

Book value (of an asset):   The accounting value of an asset as shown on a balance sheet is the cost of the asset minus its accumulated depreciation. It is not necessarily identical to its market value.

Book value (of a company):   The common stock equity shown on the balance sheet. It is equal to total assets minus liabilities and preferred stock (synonymous with net worth and owners' equity).

Break-even point: The sales volume at which a company's net sales revenue just equals its costs. A commonly used approximate formula for the break-even point is Sales revenue = Total fixed costs/Gross margin.

Bridging finance: Short-term finance that is expected to be repaid relatively quickly. It usually bridges a short-term financing need. For example, it provides cash needed before an expected stock flotation.

Browser: A computer program that enables users to access and navigate the World Wide Web.

Burn rate: The negative real-time cash flow from a company's operations, usually computed monthly.

Business plan: Document prepared by entrepreneurs, possibly in conjunction with their professional advisors, detailing the past, present, and intended future of the company. It contains a thorough analysis of the managerial, physical, labor, product, and financial resources of the company, plus the background of the company, its previous trading record, and its market position. The business plan contains detailed profit, balance sheet, and cash flow projections for two years ahead, and less detailed information for the following three years. The business plan crystallizes and focuses the management team's ideas. It explains their strategies, sets objectives, and is used to monitor their subsequent performance.

Call: A contract allowing the issuer of a security to buy back that security from the purchaser at an agreed-upon price during a specific period of time.

Capital gain: The amount by which the selling price of an asset (for example, common stock) exceeds the seller's initial purchase price.

Capitalization rate: The discount rate K used to determine the present value of a stream of future earnings. $PV = $ (Normalized earnings after taxes)$/(K/100)$, where PV is the present value of the firm and K is the firm's cost of capital.

Carried interest: A venture capital firm's share of the profit earned by a fund. In the United States, the carried interest (carry) is typically 20% of the profit after investors' principal has been repaid.

Cash flow: The difference between the company's cash receipts and its cash payments in a given period.

Cash-flow statement: A summary of a company's cash flow over a period of time. (See *pro forma statements*.)

Chattel mortgage: A lien on specifically identified property (assets other than real estate) backing a loan.

Collateral: An asset pledged as security for a loan.

Common stock: Shares of ownership, or equity, in a corporation.

Compensating balance: A bank requires a customer to maintain a certain level of demand deposits that do not bear interest. The interest forgone by the customer on that compensating balance recompenses the bank for services provided, credit lines, and loans.

Conversion ratio: The number of shares of common stock that may be received in exchange for each share of a convertible security.

Convertible security: Preferred stock that is convertible into common stock according to a specified ratio at the security holder's option.

Corporation: A business form that is an entity legally separate from its owners. Its important features include limited liability, easy transfer of ownership, and unlimited life.

Cost of capital: The required rate of return of various types of financing. The overall cost of capital is a weighted average of the individual required rates of returns (costs).

Cost of debt capital: The interest rate charged by a company's lenders.

Cost of equity capital: The rate of return on investment required by the company's common shareholders (colloquially called the hurdle rate).

Cost of goods sold: The direct cost of the product sold. For a retail business, the cost of all goods sold in a given period equals the inventory at the beginning of the period plus the cost of goods purchased during that period minus the inventory at the end of the period.

Cost of preferred stock: The rate of return on investment required by the company's preferred shareholders.

Covenant: A restriction on a borrower imposed by a lender. For example, it could be a requirement placed on a company to achieve and maintain specified targets such as levels of cash flow, balance sheet ratios, or specified capital expenditure levels in order to retain financing facilities.

Cumulative dividend provision: A requirement that unpaid dividends on preferred stock accumulate and have to be paid before a dividend is paid on common stock.

Current ratio: Current assets/Current liabilities. This ratio indicates a company's ability to cover its current liabilities with its current assets. (See *acid-test ratio.*)

Deal flow: The rate at which new investment propositions come to funding institutions.

Debenture: A document containing an acknowledgment of indebtedness on the part of a company, usually secured by a charge on the company's assets.

Debt service: Payments of principal and interest required on a debt over a given period.

Deep pockets: Refers to an investor who has substantial financial resources.

Default: The nonperformance of a stated obligation. The nonpayment by the issuer of interest or principal on a bond or the nonperformance of a covenant.

Deferred payment: A debt that has been incurred and will be repaid at some future date.

Depreciation: The systematic allocation of the cost of an asset over a period of time for financial reporting and tax purposes.

Dilution (of ownership):   This happens when a new stock issue results in a decrease in the preissue owners' percentage of the common stock.

Discounted cash flow (DCF):   Methods of evaluating investments by adjusting the cash flows for the time value of money. In the decision to invest in a project, all future cash flows expected from that investment are discounted back to their present value at the time the investment is made. The discount rate is whatever rate of return the investor requires. In theory, if the present value of the future cash flows is greater than the money being invested, the investment should be made. (See *discount rate, internal rate of return, net present value, and present value.*)

Discount rate (capitalization rate):   Rate of return used to convert future values to present values. (See *capitalization rate, internal rate of return, and rate of return.*)

Doriot, General Georges: Founder of the modern venture capital industry, Harvard Business School professor, and one of the creators of INSEAD.

Double jeopardy: The case where an entrepreneur's main source of income and most of her net worth depend on her business.

Due diligence: The process of investigation by investors into a potential investee's management team, resources, and trading performance. This includes rigorous testing of the business plan assumptions and the verification of material facts (such as existing accounts).

Dun & Bradstreet (D&B):   The biggest credit-reporting agency in the United States.

Early-stage financing: This category includes seed-stage, startup-stage, and first-stage financing.

Earnings: This is synonymous with income and profit.

Earnings before interest and taxes (EBIT):   See *operating income.*

Earnings per share (EPS):   A company's net income divided by the number of common shares issued and outstanding.

Elasticity of demand: The percentage change in the quantity of a good demanded divided by the percentage change in the price of that good. When the elasticity is greater than 1, the demand is said to be elastic, and when it is less than 1, it is inelastic. In the short term, the demand for nonessential goods (for example, airline travel) is usually elastic, and the demand for essentials (for example, electricity) is usually inelastic.

Employee stock ownership plan (ESOP):   A trust established to acquire shares in a company for subsequent allocation to employees over a period of time. Several possibilities are available for structuring the operation of an ESOP. Essentially, either the company makes payments to the trust, which the trust uses to purchase shares; or the trust, having previously borrowed to acquire shares, may use the payments from the company to repay loans. The latter form is referred to as a leveraged ESOP and may be used as a means of providing part of the funding required to effect a buyout. A particular advantage of an ESOP is the possibility of tax relief for the contributions made by the company to the trust and on the cost of borrowing in those cases where the trust purchases shares in advance.

Employment agreement: An agreement whereby senior managers contract to remain with the company for a specified period. For the investing institutions, such an agreement provides some measure of security that the company's performance will not be adversely affected by the unexpected departure of key managers.

Equity: See *owners' equity.*

Equity kicker (or warrant):   An option or instrument linked to the provision of other types of funding, particularly mezzanine finance, which enables the provider to obtain an equity stake and hence a share in capital gains. In this way, providers of subordinated debt can be compensated for the higher risk they incur.

Exit: The means by which investors in a company realize all or part of their investment.

Expansion financing: Working capital for the initial expansion of a company that is producing and shipping products and has growing accounts receivable and inventories.

Factoring: A means of enhancing the cash flow of a business. A factoring company pays to the firm a certain proportion of the value of the firm's trade debts and then receives the cash as the trade debtors settle their accounts. Invoice discounting is a similar procedure.

FAQ: Frequently asked questions—a computer text file that contains answers to common questions about a topic.

Filing: Documents, including the prospectus, filed with the SEC for approval before an IPO.

Financing flows: Cash flows generated by debt and equity financing.

Firm commitment offering: The underwriter guarantees to raise a certain amount of money for the company and other selling stockholders at the IPO.

First-round financing: The first investment made by external investors.

First-stage financing: Financing to initiate full manufacturing and sales.

Five Cs of credit: The five crucial elements for obtaining credit are character (borrower's integrity), capacity (sufficient cash flow to service the debt), capital (borrower's net worth), collateral (assets to secure the debt), and conditions (of the borrowing company, its industry, and the general economy).

Fixed and floating charges: Claims on assets pledged as security for debt. Fixed charges cover specific fixed assets, and floating charges relate to all or part of a company's assets.

Flame: A highly negative electronic message objecting to the actions of or opinions expressed by another user, often in response to a breach of Internet etiquette.

Floating lien: A general lien against a group of assets, such as accounts receivable or inventory, without the assets being specifically identified.

Flotation: A method of raising equity financing by selling shares on a stock market, and often allowing management and institutions to realize some of their investment at the same time. (See *initial public offering.*)

Forum: An electronic discussion group of computer users on an online service (e.g., America Online or Compuserve) that is centered around a particular subject area of interest to the participants.

Franchising: An organizational form in which a firm (the franchisor) with a market-tested business package centered on a product or service enters into a continuing contractual relationship with franchisees operating under the franchisor's trade name to produce or market goods or services according to a format specified by the franchisor.

Free cash flow: Cash flow in excess of that required to fund all projects that have a positive net present value when discounted at the relevant cost of capital. Conflicts of interest between shareholders and managers may arise when the organization generates free cash flow. Shareholders may desire higher dividends, but managers may wish to invest in projects providing a return below the cost of capital. (See *cost of capital and net present value.*)

FTP: File transfer protocol—an Internet tool that allows you to upload and download files from other computers on the Internet.

Future value: The value at a future date of a present amount of money. $FV_t = PV \times (1 + K/100)^t$, where FV_t is the future value, PV is the present value, K is the percentage annual rate of return, and t is the number of years. For example, an investment of $100,000 must have a future value of $384,160 after four years to produce a rate of return of 40%, which is the kind of return that an investor in an early-stage company expects to earn. (See *net present value, present value, and rate of return.*)

Gearing: British term of leverage. (See *leverage.*)

Going concern: This assumes that the company will continue as an operating business as opposed to going out of business and liquidating its assets.

Golden handcuffs: A combination of rewards and penalties given to key managers to dissuade them from leaving the company. Examples are high salaries, paid on a deferred basis while employment is maintained, and stock options.

Goodwill: The difference between the purchase price of a company and the net value of its assets purchased.

Gopher: An Internet tool that enables users both to locate and download files from other computers on the Internet.

Gross margin: Gross profit as a percentage of net sales revenue.

Gross profit (gross income, gross earnings): Net sales revenue minus the direct cost of the products sold.

Guarantee: An undertaking to prove that a debt or obligation of another will be paid or performed. It may relate either to a specific debt or to a series of transactions such as a guarantee of a bank overdraft. For example, entrepreneurs are often required to provide personal guarantees for loans borrowed by their companies.

Harvest: The realization of the value of an investment. (See *exit.*)

High-potential venture: A company started with the intent of growing quickly to annual sales of at least $30–50 million in five years. It has the potential to have a firm-commitment IPO.

Home page: A document on the World Wide Web which serves as the introductory menu for that Web site.

HTML: Hypertext markup language—a computer language that enables the construction of documents that can be viewed on the World Wide Web.

Hurdle rate: The minimum rate of return that is acceptable to investors. (See *return on investment.*)

Hyperlinks: Dynamic references to other computer-based documents which facilitate the rapid movement between documents.

Income statement: A summary of a company's revenues, expenses, and profits over a specified period of time. (See *pro forma statements.*)

Initial public offering (IPO): Process by which a company raises money, and gets listed, on a stock market. (See *flotation.*)

INSEAD: The European Institute of Business Administration located in Fontainebleau, France.

Interest cover: The extent to which periodic interest commitments on borrowings are exceeded by periodic profits. It is the ratio of profits before the deduction of interest and taxes to interest payments. The ratio may also be expressed as the cash flow from operations divided by the amount of interest payable.

Internal rate of return (IRR): The discount rate that equates the present value of the future net cash flows from an investment with the project's cash outflows. It is a means of expressing the percentage rate of return projected on a proposed investment. For an investment in a company, the calculation takes account of cash invested, cash receipts from dividend payments and redemptions, percentage equity held, expected date of payments, realization of the investment and capitalization at that point, and possible further financing requirements. The calculation will frequently be quoted in a range depending on sensitivity analysis. (See *discount rate, present value, future value, and rate of return.*)

Internet: The vast network of networks connecting millions of individual and networked computers worldwide.

Inventory: Finished goods, work in process of manufacture, and raw materials owned by a company.

Investment bank: A financial institution engaged in the issue of new securities, including management and underwriting of issues as well as securities trading and distribution.

Investment flows: Cash flows associated with purchase and sales of both fixed assets and business interests.

Invisible venture capital (informal venture capital): Venture capital supplied by wealthy individuals (angels), as opposed to visible venture capital, which is supplied by formal venture capital firms that make up the organized venture capital industry.

IRC: Internet Relay Chat—an Internet tool that enables users to send and receive electronic messages in real-time over the Internet, thus facilitating interactive conversations among many users.

ISP: Internet Service Provider—a company that provides direct connections to the Internet for computer users.

Junior debt: Loan ranking after senior debt or secured debt for payment in the event of a default.

Junk bonds: A variety of high-yield, unsecured bonds tradeable on a secondary market and not considered to be of investment quality by credit-rating agencies. High yield normally indicates higher risk. Michael Milken, the king of the U.S. junk bond industry in the 1980s, served time in federal jail after pleading guilty to several felonies relating to the junk bond market.

Key person insurance: Additional security provided to financial backers of a company through the purchase of insurance on the lives of key managers who are seen as crucial to the future of the company. Should one or more of those key executives die prematurely, the financial backers would receive the insurance payment.

Lead investor: In syndicated deals, normally the investor who originates, structures, and subsequently plays the major monitoring role.

Lemons and plums: Bad deals and good deals, respectively.

Leverage: The amount of debt in a company's financing structure, which may be expressed as a percentage of the total financing or as a ratio of debt to equity. The various quasi-equity (preference-type shares) and quasi-debt (mezzanine debt) instruments used to fund later-stage companies means that great care is required in calculating and interpreting leverage or gearing ratios.

Leveraged buyout (LBO): Acquisition of a company by an investor group, an investor, or an investment/LBO partnership, with a significant amount of debt (usually at least 70% of the total capitalization) and with plans to repay the debt with funds generated from the acquired company's operations or from asset sales. LBOs are frequently financed in part with junk bonds.

Lien: A legal claim on certain assets that are used to secure a loan.

Limited liability company: A company owned by "members," who either manage the business themselves or appoint "managers" to run it for them. All members and managers have the benefit of limited liability, and, in most cases, are taxed in the same way as a subchapter S corporation without having to conform to the S corporation restrictions.

Line of credit (with a bank):   An arrangement between a bank and a customer specifying the maximum amount of unsecured debt the customer can owe the bank at a given point in time.

Line of credit (with a vendor):   A limit set by the seller on the amount that a purchaser can buy on credit.

Liquidation value (of an asset):   The amount of money that can be realized from the sale of an asset sold separately from its operating organization.

Liquidation value (of a company):   The market value of the assets minus the liabilities that must be paid of a company that is liquidating.

Liquidity: The ability of an asset to be converted to cash as quickly as possible and without any price discount.

Listing: Acceptance of a security for trading on an organized stock exchange. Hence, a stock traded on the New York Stock Exchange is said to be listed on the NYSE.

Listserver: A computer program that handles the administration of subscriptions to electronic mailing lists by computer users.

Loan note: A form of vendor finance or deferred payment. The purchaser (borrower) may agree to make payments to the holder of the loan note at specified future dates. The holder may be able to obtain cash at an earlier date by selling at a discount to a financing institution that will collect on maturity.

Management buyin (MBI):   The transfer of ownership of an entity to a new set of owners in which new managers coming into the entity are a significant element.

Management buyout (MBO):   The transfer of ownership of an entity to a new set of owners in which the existing management and employees are a significant element.

Market capitalization: The total value at market prices of the securities in issue for a company, a stock market, or a sector of a stock market, calculated by multiplying the number of shares issued by the market price per share.

Mezzanine financing: Strictly, any form of financing instrument between ordinary shares and senior debt. The forms range from senior mezzanine debt, which may simply carry an interest rate above that for senior secured debt, to junior mezzanine debt, which may carry rights to subscribe for equity but no regular interest payment.

Middle-market company: A company that has sales revenue of $5–20 million and modest growth. In contrast to a high-potential company, it does not have the potential to float an IPO, but it may be a candidate for an acquisition, LBO, MBI, MBO, or ESOP.

Multimedia: The combination of text, graphics, audio, and video within a single computer application or presentation.

Multiple: The amount of money realized from the sale of an investment divided by the amount of money originally invested.

Murphy's Law: What can go wrong, will go wrong. An unexpected setback will happen at the most inconvenient moment.

National Association of Securities Dealers (NASD): Organization for brokers and dealers in OTC stocks.

National Association of Securities Dealers Automated Quotation (NASDAQ): An electronic system set up by NASD for trading stocks. It is commonly referred to as the OTC market.

Net income (net earnings, net profit): A company's final income after all expenses and taxes have been deducted from all revenues. It is also known as the bottom line.

Net income margin: Net income as a percentage of net sales revenue. In a typical year an average U.S. company has a net income margin of about 5%.

Net liquid value: Liquid financial assets minus callable liabilities.

Net present value: The present value of an investment's future net cash flows minus the initial investment. In theory, if the net present value is greater than 0, an investment should be made. For example, an investor is asked to invest $100,000 in a company that is expanding. He expects a rate of return of 30%. The company offers to pay him back $300,000 after four years. The present value of $300,000 at a rate of return of 30% is $105,038. Thus, the net present value of the investment is $5,038, so the investment should be made. (See *free cash flow, future value, present value, and rate of return.*)

Net profit: See *net income.*

Net worth: See *book value.*

New York Stock Exchange (NYSE): The largest stock exchange in the world, located in New York. Also known as the Big Board.

Offering circular: See *prospectus.*

Operating cash flows: Cash flows directly generated by a company's operations. The cash flow from operating activity equals net income plus depreciation minus increase in accounts receivable minus increase in inventories plus increase in accounts payable plus increase in accruals. (See *financing flows and investment flows.*)

Operating income: Earnings (profit) before deduction of interest payments and income taxes, abbreviated to EBIT. It measures a company's earning power from its ongoing operations. It is of particular concern to a company's lenders, such as banks, because operating income demonstrates the ability of a company to earn sufficient income to pay the interest on its debt. (See *times interest earned.*)

Out of cash (OOC): A common problem with entrepreneurial companies. The OOC time period is cash on hand divided by the burn rate.

Over the counter (OTC): The purchase and sale of financial instruments not conducted on a stock exchange such as the New York Stock Exchange or the American Stock Exchange. The largest OTC market is the NASDAQ.

Owners' equity: Common stock plus retained earnings. (See *book value of a company.*)

Paid-in capital: Par value per share times the number of shares issued. Additional paid-in capital is the price paid in excess of par value times the number of shares issued.

Partnership: Legal form of a business in which two or more persons are co-owners, sharing profits and losses.

Par value: Nominal price placed on a share of common stock.

Piggy-back registration rights: The right to register unregistered stock in the event of a company having a public stock offering.

Pledging: The use of a company's accounts receivable as security (collateral) for a short-term loan.

Portfolio: Collection of investments. For example, the portfolio of a venture capital fund comprises all its investments.

Pratt's Guide to Venture Capital Sources: Annual sourcebook for the venture capital industry.

Preemptive rights: The rights of shareholders to maintain their percentage ownership of a company by purchasing a proportionate number of shares of any new issue of common stock. (See *antidilution, dilution, and pro rata interest.*)

Preference shares: A class of shares that incorporate the right to a fixed dividend and usually a prior claim on assets, in preference to ordinary shares, in the event of a liquidation. Cumulative preference shares provide an entitlement to a cumulative dividend if in any year the preference dividend is unpaid due to insufficient profits being earned. Preference shares are usually redeemable at specific dates.

Pre-money valuation: The value of a company's equity before additional money is invested.

Prepayment: A payment on a loan made prior to the original due date.

Present value (PV):   The current value of a given future cash flow stream, FV_t, after t years, discounted at a rate of return of $K\%$ is $PV = FV_t/(1 + K/100)^t$. For example, if an investor expects a rate of return of 60% on an investment in a seed-stage company, and she believes that her investment will be worth \$750,000 after five years, then the present value of her investment is \$71,526. (See *discount rate, future value, net present value, present value, and rate of return.*)

Price-earnings ratio (P/E ratio):   The ratio of the market value of a firm's equity to its after-tax profits (may be calculated from price per share and earnings per share).

Prime rate: Short-term interest rate charged by a bank to its largest, most creditworthy customers.

Private placement: The direct sales of securities to a small number of investors.

Profit: Synonymous with income and earnings.

Pro forma statements: Projected financial statements: income and cash-flow statements, and balance sheets. For a startup company, it is usual to make pro forma statements monthly for the first two years and annually for the next three years.

Pro rata interest: The right granted the investor to maintain the same percentage ownership in the event of future financings. (See *antidilution and dilution.*)

Prospectus: A document giving a description of a securities issue, including a complete statement of the terms of the issue and a description of the issuer, as well as its historical financial statements. Also referred to as an offering circular. (See *red herring.*)

Put: A contract allowing the holder to sell a given number of securities back to the issuer of the contract at a fixed price for a given period of time.

Rate of return: The annual return on an investment. If a sum of money, PV, is invested and after t years that investment is worth FV_t, the return on investment $K = [(FV_t/PV)^{1/t} - 1] \times 100\%$. For example, if $100 is invested originally, and one year later $108 is paid back to the investor, the annual rate of return is 8%.

Realization: See *exit.*

Redeemable shares: Shares that may be redeemable at the option of the company or the shareholder or both.

Red herring: Preliminary prospectus circulated by underwriters to gauge investor interest in a planned offering. A legend in red ink on its cover indicates that the registration has not yet become effective and is still being reviewed by the SEC.

Registration statement: A carefully worded and organized document, including a prospectus, filed with the SEC before an IPO.

Retained earnings: The part of net income retained in the company and not distributed to stockholders.

Return on investment: The annual income that an investment earns.

Running returns: Periodic returns, such as interest and dividends, from an investment (in contrast to a one-time capital gain).

SBA: Small Business Administration.

SBDC: Small Business Development Centers (supported by the SBA).

SBI: Small Business Institutes, run by universities and colleges with SBA support.

SBIC: Small Business Investments Companies.

SBIR: Small Business Innovation Research Program.

Schumpeter, Joesph A.:   Moravian-born economist whose book *The Theory of Economic Development,* written in Vienna in 1912, introduced the modern theory of entrepreneurship, in which the entrepreneur plays the central role in economic development by destroying the static equilibrium of the existing economy. Excellent modern examples are the roles played by Steve Jobs, Bill Gates, and Dan Bricklin in creating the microcomputer industry in the late 1970s. By the beginning of the 1990s, microcomputers (personal computers) were the principal force shaping the computer industry, and the old companies manufacturing mainframe and minicomputers, which dominated the computer industry until the mid-1980s, were in distress, ranging from outright bankruptcy to record-breaking losses.

SCORE: Service Core of Retired Executives, sponsored by the SBA to provide consulting to small businesses.

Search engine: A computer program that facilitates the location and retrieval of information over the Internet.

Second-round financing: The introduction of further funding by the original investors or new investors to enable the company to grow or deal with unexpected problems. Each round of financing tends to cover the next period of growth.

Securities and Exchange Commission (SEC):   Regulatory body for investor protection in the United States, created by the Securities Exchange Act of 1934. The supervision of dealers is delegated to the self-regulatory bodies of the stock exchanges and NASD under the provisions of the Maloney Act of 1938.

Seed financing: A relatively small amount of money provided to prove a concept; it may involve product development and market research but rarely involves the initial marketing of a product.

Sensitivity analysis: Examination of how the projected performance of the business varies with changes in the key assumptions on which the forecasts are based.

Short-term security: Generally an obligation maturing in less than one year.

Sole proprietorship: A business form with one owner who is responsible for all the firm's liabilities.

Spamming: The simultaneous sending of the same advertising message indiscriminately to a large number of Internet users—a practice viewed very negatively by the Internet community and which often results in retaliatory "flames" directed at the offending message sender.

Startup financing: Funding provided to companies for use in product development and initial marketing. Companies may be in the process of being organized or may have been in business a short time (one year or less), but have not sold their product commercially. Generally, such firms have assembled the key management, prepared a business plan, made market studies, and completed other preliminary tasks.

Stock option plan: A plan designed to motivate employees, especially key ones, by placing a proportion of the common stock of the company under option at a fixed price to defined employees. The option may then be exercised by the employees at a future date. Stock options are often introduced as part of the remuneration package of senior executives.

Subchapter S corporation: A small business corporation in which the owners personally pay the corporation's income taxes.

Subordinated debt: Loans that may be unsecured or, more commonly, secured by secondary charges and that rank after senior debt for repayment in the event of default. Also referred to as junior debt or mezzanine debt.

Sweat equity: Equity acquired by the management team at favorable terms reflecting the value to the business of the managers' past and future efforts.

Syndicate: A group of investors that act together when investing in a company.

Term loan: Debt originally scheduled to be repaid in more than one year, but usually in 10 years or less.

Term sheet: Summary of the principal conditions for a proposed investment by a venture capital firm in a company.

Times interest earned: Earnings before interest and taxes, divided by interest (EBIT/I). The higher this ratio, the more secure the loan on which interest is paid. It is a basic measure of the creditworthiness of a company.

Underwrite: An arrangement under which investment banks each agree to buy a certain amount of securities of a new issue on a given date and at a given price, thereby assuring the issuer of the full proceeds of the financing.

Underwriter: An institution engaged in the business of underwriting securities issues.

Underwriting fee: The share of the gross spread of a new issue accruing to members of the underwriting group after the expenses of the issue have been paid.

Unsecured loans: Debt that is not backed by a pledge of specific assets.

URL: Uniform (or Universal) Resource Locator—the unique address through which users can be located on the Internet.

Usenet: An Internet-based system of discussion groups centered around particular topics of interest to their members.

Valuation (of a company):   The market value of a company. (See *market capitalization.*)

Value-added (by investors):   Many venture capital firms claim that they add more than money to investee companies. They call it value-added, which includes strategic advice on such matters as hiring key employees, marketing, production, control, and financing.

Venture capitalist: A financial institution specializing in the provision of equity and other forms of long-term capital to enterprises, usually to firms with a limited track record but with the expectation of substantial growth. The venture capitalist may provide both funding and varying degrees of managerial and technical expertise. Venture capital has traditionally been associated with startups; however, venture capitalists have increasingly participated in later-stage projects.

Vesting period: The time period before shares are owned unconditionally by an employee who is sold stock with the stipulation that he must continue to work for the company selling him the shares. If his employment terminates before the end of that period, the company has the right to buy back the shares at the same price at which it originally sold them to him.

Virtual mall (cybermall):   The electronic equivalent of a physical shopping mall, in which stores consist of Web pages that display goods and services that can be purchased over the Internet.

Visible venture capital (formal venture capital):   The organized venture capital industry consisting of formal firms, in contrast to invisible venture capital or informal venture capital.

Vulture capital: A derogatory term for venture capital.

Waiver: Consent granted by an investor or lender to permit an investor or borrower to be in default on a covenant.

Warrant: An option to purchase common stock at a specified price. (See *equity kicker.*)

Warranty: A statement of fact or opinion concerning the condition of a company. The inclusion of warranties in an investment agreement gives the investor a claim against the company if it subsequently becomes apparent that the company's condition was not as stated at the time of the investment.

Web pages: The menus and information offered for users to browse through and interact with at a World Wide Web site. (See *home page.*)

World Wide Web: The part of the Internet that enables the use of multimedia—text, graphics, audio, and video.

Yield: Annualized rate of return on a security.

CHAPTER NOTES

Chapter 2: Opportunity Recognition

[1] See Jeffry A. Timmons, *New Business Opportunities* (Acton, MA: Brick House Publishing, 1989).

[2] Barrie McKenna, "More than the Sum of its Parts," *The Globe and Mail*, February 23, 1993, p. B24.

[3] Amar Bhide, "Bootstrap Finance," *Harvard Business Review*, November-December 1992, p. 112.

[4] Edward B. Roberts, *Entrepreneurs in High Technology: Lessons from MIT and Beyond* (New York: Oxford University Press, 1991), p. 144, Table 5-2.

[5] Teri Lammers and Annie Longsworth, "Guess Who? Ten Big-Timers Launched from Scratch," *Inc.*, September 1991, p. 69. © 1991 by Goldhirsh Group, Inc., 38 Commercial Wharf, Boston, MA 02110.

[6] Ibid.

[7] Ibid.

[8] Robert A. Mamis, "The Secrets of Bootstrapping," *Inc.*, September 1991, p. 54.

[9] See J. A. Timmons, D. F. Muzyka, H. H. Stevenson, and W. D. Bygrave, "Opportunity Recognition: The Core of Entrepreneurship," in *Frontiers of Entrepreneurship Research: 1987*, ed. Neil Churchill et al. (Babson Park, MA: Babson College, 1987), p. 409.

[10] Comments made during a presentation at Babson College, May 1985.

[11] Scott W. Kunkel and Charles W. Hofer, "The Impact of Industry Structure on New Venture Performance," *Frontiers of Entrepreneurship Research: 1993*. Reproduced with permission.

[12] J. A. Timmons, W. Bygrave, and N. Fast, "The Flow of Venture Capital to Highly Innovative Technological Ventures," a study for the National Science Foundation, reprinted in *Frontiers of Entrepreneurship Research: 1984*, ed. J. A. Hornaday et al. (Babson Park, MA: Babson College, 1984).

[13] For a more detailed description of free cash flow, see "Note on Free Cash Flow Valuation Models: Identifying the Critical Factors that Affect Value," HBS 288-023, Harvard Business School, 1987.

[14] William A. Sahlman, "Sustainable Growth Analysis," HBS 9-284-059, Harvard Business School, 1984.

[15] R. Douglas Kahn, president, Interactive Images, Inc., speaking at Babson College about his experiences as international marketing director at McCormack & Dodge from 1978 through 1983.

[16] This point was made by J. Willard Marriott, Jr., at Founder's Day, Babson College, 1988.

[17] Leonard M. Fuld, *Competitor Intelligence: How to Get It; How to Use It* (New York: John Wiley & Sons, 1993), p. 9.

[18] An excellent resource is Fuld, *Competitor Intelligence*. See also David E. Gumpert and Jeffry A. Timmons, *The Encyclopedia of Small Business Resources* (New York: Harper & Row, 1984); *Fortune,* "How to Snoop on Your Competitors," May 14, 1984, pp. 28–33; and information published by accounting firms, such as *Sources of Industry Data,* published by Ernst and Whinney.

[19] Fuld, *Competitor Intelligence,* pp. 12–17.

[20] Ibid., p. 325.

[21] Gumpert and Timmons, *The Encyclopedia of Small Business Resources,* pp. 376–79.

[22] Ibid., pp. 46 and 48.

Chapter 3: Entry Strategies

[1] Karl H. Vesper, *New Venture Strategies* (Englewood Cliffs, NJ: Prentice Hall, 1990).

[2] Karl H. Vesper, *New Venture Experience* (Seattle, 1996, pp. 77, 133–55).

[3] Vesper, *New Venture Strategies.*

Chapter 4: Market Opportunities and Marketing

[1] This discussion is based on Wendy's International Inc. (1996). Taken from "Corporate Profile" section of Wendy's Official Worldwide Web Site (August 1996). and John Gorman, "Wendy's: A Made to Order Hamburger Empire," *Chicago Tribune,* 10 March 1986, Business section, 1, 5, 6.

[2] "AMA Board Approves New Marketing Definition," *Marketing News,* 1 March 1986, 1. Published by the American Marketing Association.

[3] Peter F. Drucker, *Management: Tasks, Responsibilities, Practices* (New York: Harper & Row, 1974), 63.

[4] J. B. McKitterick, "What Is the Marketing Management Concept?" in *The Frontiers of Marketing Thought and Science,* ed. Frank M. Bass (Chicago: American Marketing Association, 1957), 78.

[5] Drucker, *Management: Tasks, Responsibilities, Practices,* 64.

[6] Susan Greco, "Desktop Target Marketing," *Inc.* (April 1992): 118.

[7] Gerald E. Hills, "Opportunity Recognition by Successful Entrepreneurs: A Pilot Study." in *Frontiers in Entrepreneurship Research,* (Wellesley, MA: Babson College, 1996), pp. 236–51.

[8] Gerald E. Hills and Raymond LaForge, "Research at the Marketing Interface to Advance Entrepreneurship Theory," *Entrepreneurship Theory and Practice,* Vol. 16, No. 3, pp. 1–27.

[9] Janet L. Willen, "Targeting College Spenders," *Nations Business* (September 1995): 14.

[10] Andrea Trank, "From Animal Feed to Lumber," *In Business* (Summer 1991): 28–29.

[11] Leon G. Schiffman and Leslie Lazer Kanuk, *Consumer Behavior,* 4th ed. (Englewood Cliffs, NJ: Prentice Hall, 1991), 680.

[12] Susan Greco, "Users Get Sales on Course," *Inc.* (November 1992): 29.

[13] Jay Finnegan, "Against the Grain," *Inc.* (November 1992): 116.

[14] Ian C. MacMillan, "Seizing Competitive Initiative," *Journal of Business Strategy* (Spring 1982): 45.

[15] Robert A. Mamis, "Market Maker," *Inc.* (December 1995): 54–64.

[16] Teri Lammers, "The Smart Customer Survey," *Inc.* (November 1992): 133–135.

[17] Donald R. Lehmann and Russell S. Winer, *Analysis for Marketing Planning,* 2nd ed. (Homewood, IL: Richard D. Irwin, 1991).

[18] Laurence P. Feldman and Albert L. Page, "Principles versus Practice in New Product Planning," *Journal of Product Innovation Management* (January 1984): 44.

[19] Reavis Cox and Thomas F. Schutte, "A Look at Channel Management," in *Marketing Involvement in Society and the Economy,* ed. Philip R. McDonald (Chicago: American Marketing Association, 1969), 100.

[20] "What Keeps Food Prices High and Rising," *Citibank* (June 1980): 4.

[21] Theodore B. Vinni, "Enlisting Goliath," *Industry Week* (June 1995): 37–38.

[22] "Magic Marketing. Is Network Selling About to Revolutionize the Way We Live and Work?" *Success* (March 1992): 21–33.

[23] Alfred R. Oxenfeldt, "A Decision-Making Structure for Price Decisions," *Journal of Marketing* 37 (January 1973): 48–53.

[24] Susan Greco, "Smart Use of 'Special Offers,'" *Inc.* (February 1993): 23.

[25] Geoffrey Brewer, "The Greatest of Ease," *Sales and Marketing Management* (November 1995): 48–58.

[26] Gerald E. Hills, "Market Analysis in the Business Plan: Venture Capitalists' Perceptions," *Journal of Small Business Management,* vol. 22 (Jan. 1985): 5.

[27] Gerald E. Hills and Alvin D. Star, "Marketing Strategy Elements for New Venture/Early Stage Firms as Perceived by Venture Capitalists," in *Frontiers of Entrepreneurship Research,* eds. John Hornaday, Edward B. Shils, Jeffry A. Timmons, and Karl H. Vesper, (Wellesley, MA: Babson College, 1985), 215.

[28] These volumes are all published annually by the Institute for Entrepreneurial Studies, University of Illinois at Chicago. Each volume is entitled *Research at the Marketing/Entrepreneurship Interface.* Editors of the volumes are 1987, Gerald E. Hills; 1989, Hills, Raymond W. LaForge, and Beverly J. Parker; 1990, Hills, LaForge, and Harold P. Welsch; 1991, Hills and LaForge; 1992, Hills and LaForge; 1993, Hills,

LaForge, and Daniel F. Muzyka; 1994, Hills and Mchan-Neill; 1995, Hills, Muzyka, Omura and Knight; 1996, Hills, Romano and Teach.

[29] Gerald E. Hills and Chem L. Narayana, "Profile Characteristics, Success Factors and Marketing in Highly Successful Firms," in *Frontiers of Entrepreneurship Research*, ed. Robert H. Brockhaus, Sr., Neil C. Churchill, Jerome A. Katz, Bruce A. Kirchhoff, Karl H. Vesper, and William E. Wetzel, Jr. (Wellesley, MA: Babson College, 1989), 23.

Chapter 6: Financial Projections

[1] Portions of this article and Exhibits 6.1–6.12 have been excerpted with permission from Robert Ronstadt, *Entrepreneurial Finance: How to Take Control of Your Financial Decision Making* (Wayland, MA: Lord, 1989).

[2] This chapter makes the assumption that the reader is familiar with the basic purpose and components of an income statement, balance sheet, and cash flow statement. If the reader needs to review these statements, please refer to Chapter 5 of Eliza Collins and Mary Anne Devanna, eds., *The Portable MBA* (New York: John Wiley & Sons, 1990).

[3] The integrated model used as an example in this chapter was produced using *Ronstadt's Financials* (Wayland, MA: Lord, 1989), Version 2.0, which is DOS-based software for the IBM PC and compatibles with minimum 640k of RAM, or internal operating memory. Models for nonretail businesses accompany the software for manufacturing, contract service, professional service, wholesale distribution, real estate, and other businesses.

[4] See Chapter 5 of Robert Ronstadt, *Entrepreneurship: Text, Cases, & Notes,* (Wayland, MA: Lord, 1984), specifically the discussion of high-variable-cost ventures versus high-fixed-cost ventures.

[5] Paul Hawken, "Mastering The Numbers," *Inc.* (October 1987): 19.

Chapter 7: Venture Capital

[1] W. D. Bygrave and J. A. Timmons, *Venture Capital at the Crossroads* (Boston: Harvard Business School Press, 1992).

[2] J. Morris, S. Isenstein, and A. Knowles, eds., *Pratt's Guide To Venture Capital Sources* (New York: SDC, 1992).

[3] Amar Bhide, "Bootstrap Finance: The Art of Start-ups," *Harvard Business Review* 70(6): 109.

[4] J. Freear and W. Wetzel, "Who Bankrolls High Tech Entrepreneurs?" *Journal of Business Venturing* 5(2): 77.

[5] James L. Plummer, *QED Report on Venture Capital Financial Analysis* (Palo Alto, CA: QED Research, 1987).

Chapter 12: Franchising

[1] International Franchise Association and Horwath International, *Franchising in the Economy 1990* (Evans City, PA: IFA Publications, 1991), 1.

[2] H. A. Monckton, *The History of the English Public House* (London: Bodley House Publishing, 1969), 87.

[3] Ibid., 88.

[4] International Franchise Association and Horwath International, *Franchising in the Economy 1990*.

Chapter 13: Entrepreneurs and the Internet

[1] SLIP stands for Serial Line Internet Protocol, a set of rules (a protocol) for allowing your computer to access the Internet with an ordinary telephone line and a modem. PPP stands for Point to Point Protocol and is considered superior to SLIP because of its error-checking capabilities. For this reason PPP is superseding SLIP as the preferred means of connecting to the Internet.

[2] Jeffry A. Timmons, *New Venture Creation, 4th. ed., rev.*, Burr Ridge, IL: Irwin, 1994.

[3] For further information on IFM, see the case *Internet Fashion Mall, LLC*, published by the Center for Entrepreneurial Studies, Babson Park, MA 02157-0310, 1996.

Chapter 14: Harvesting

[1] Steven R. Covey, *The Seven Habits of Highly Effective People* (New York: Simon & Schuster, 1989), 95.

[2] See J. Freear, J. A. Sohl, and W. E. Wetzel, Jr., "Raising Venture Capital: Entrepreneurs' Views of the Process," *Frontiers of Entrepreneurship Research* (Wellesley, MA: Babson College, 1990).

[3] William Sahlman, "Aspects of Financial Contracting in Venture Capital," *Journal of Applied Corporate Finance* (Summer 1988): 33.

[4] For a complete discussion of the concept and procedures for measuring a firm's economic value added (EVA) as developed at Stern-Stewart & Co., see G. Bennett Stewart, III, *The Quest for Value*, New York: Harper Business, 1991, pp. 136–40.

[5] For an in-depth presentation of free cash flow valuation, see T. Copeland, T. Koller, and J. Murrin, *Valuation: Measuring and Managing the Value of Companies*, New York: John Wiley & Sons, 1996.

[6] For a more complete explanation of the logic of this equation, see a corporate finance text, such as David Scott, Arthur Keown, John D. Martin, and J. William Petty, *Basic Financial Management* (Englewood Cliffs, NJ: Prentice Hall, 1996).

[7] For example, see Amar Bhide, "The Causes and Consequences of Hostile Takeovers," *Journal of Applied Corporate Finance* (Summer 1989): 36–59.

[8] Joan C. Szabo, "Using ESOPs to Sell Your Firm," *Nation's Business* (January 1991): 50.

[9] Ibid.

[10] Ibid.

[11] P. Asquith and E. H. Kim, "The Impact of Merger Bids on the Participating Firms' Security Returns," *Journal of Finance* (December 1982): 1209–28; and K.

Aiginger and G. Tichy, "Small Firms and the Merger Mania," Small Business Economics 3, no. 2 (June 1991): 83–101.

[12] Michael G. Berolzheimer, "The Financial and Emotional Sides of Selling Your Company," *Harvard Business Review* (January-February 1980): 6–11.

[13] Many of the ideas in this section come from Roger G. Ibbotson, Jody L. Sindelar, and Jay R. Ritter, "Initial Public Offerings," *Journal of Applied Corporate Finance* (Summer 1988): 37–45.

[14] A. Chalk, and J. Peavy, "Initial Public Offerings: Daily Returns, Offering Types and the Price Effect," *Financial Analyst Journal*, Vol. 27, No. 4 (1987), pp. 65–69.

[15] See J. Ritter, "The Long-run Performance of Initial Public Offerings," *Journal of Finance, 46:* 3 (1991), pp. 3–27; and B. Jain, and O. Kini, "The Post-Issue Operating Performance of IPOs," *Journal of Finance,* forthcoming.

[16] R. G. Ibbotson, J. L. Sindelar, and J. R. Ritter, "The Market's Problems With the Pricing of Initial Public Offerings," *Journal of Applied Corporate Finance,* 7: 1 (Spring 1994), pp. 66–74.

[17] For a relatively complete presentation of the process of going public, see David P. Sutton and M. William Beneddetto, *Initial Public Offerings* (Chicago: Probus, 1990).

[18] Ibid., 21.

Bibliography

J. C. Van Horne, *Fundamentals of Financial Management,* 8th ed. (Englewood Cliffs, NJ: Prentice Hall, 1992).

L. J. Glitman, *Principles of Managerial Finance* (New York: Harper Collins, 1991).

ABOUT THE AUTHORS

William D. Bygrave is the Frederic C. Hamilton Professor for Free Enterprise and Director of the Center for Entrepreneurial Studies at Babson College, and visiting professor at INSEAD (The European Institute for Business Administration). As a practitioner, he founded a Route 128 venture-capital-backed high-tech company, managed a division of a NYSE-listed high-tech company, cofounded a pharmaceutical database company, and was a member of the investment committee of a venture capital firm. His company won an *IR100* award for introducing one of the 100 most significant new technical products in the United States in 1977. As an academic, he teaches and researches entrepreneurship. He and Jeffry Timmons are the authors of *Venture Capital at the Crossroads,* which examines the venture capital industry and its role in the economy. It was published by the Harvard Business School Press in 1992. He is co-editor of *Realizing Investment Value,* published by Financial Times/Pitman in 1994. He is co-editor of one entrepreneurship journal and serves on the review board of another. He holds doctorate degrees from Oxford University and Boston University, an MBA from Northeastern University, an MA from Oxford University, and an honorary doctorate from the University of Ghent.

Elizabeth (Betsy) J. Gatewood is Executive Director of the University of Houston Small Business Development Center, an organization that provides training and consulting services to small businesses in the greater Houston region. Dr. Gatewood is also a research professor in the Department of Management at the University of Houston's College of Business Administration. Previously, Dr. Gatewood served as Director of the Center for Business and Economic Studies at the University of Georgia, a position she held from 1983 to 1989. Dr. Gatewood also served as chair for the Entrepreneurship Division of the Academy of Management from 1992–93. Additionally, she is a member of the editorial review boards for *Entrepreneurship: Theory and Practice and the Wisconsin Small Business Forum.* Dr. Gatewood received an Advocate award for Outstanding Contributions to the field of Entrepreneurship from the Entrepreneurship Division of the Academy of Management in 1996. Dr. Gatewood has written over 50 articles, papers, and book sections on entrepreneurship, innovation, strategic management, and financial analysis. She received her doctorate and master's in business administration from the University of Georgia and her bachelor's in psychology from Purdue University.

David E. Gumpert is an expert on entrepreneurship, marketing, and other areas of business management. His company, David E. Gumpert Communications, Inc., of Needham, Massachusetts, specializes in marketing communications services, providing newsletters, booklets, and public relations services on the management of small and midsize companies. He is former senior editor of *Inc.* Magazine and associate editor of the *Harvard Business Review.* His articles on business management have appeared in the *Harvard Business Review* and many other publications. He is also the author of three recent business books—*How to Really Start Your Own Business, How to Really Create a Successful Business Plan,* and *How to Really Create a Successful Marketing Plan*—all from Inc. Publishing. In addition, Mr. Gumpert has spoken extensively on business planning and management. He received his BA in political science from the University of Chicago and his MS in journalism from the Columbia University Graduate School of Journalism.

Gerald E. Hills is holder of the Coleman/Denton Thorne Chair in Entrepreneurship and Professor of Marketing at the University of Illinois at Chicago. His doctorate is from Indiana University. Dr. Hills has written and edited seven books and written more than 70 articles in such journals as the *Journal of Marketing, Business Horizons, Journal of Technological and Social Change, Entrepreneurship: Theory and Practice, International Journal of Small Business,* and the *Journal of Business Venturing.* He is past president of the International Council for Small Business, was first president of the United States Association for Small Business and Entrepreneurship, and recently served as the elected head of the education/professor division of the American Marketing Association.

Joseph S. Iandiorio is a partner in a law firm in Waltham, Massachusetts. The firm specializes in patents, trademarks, copyrights, trade secrets, licensing and litigation of intellectual property matters, employee and consultant contracts, confidential disclosure agreements, and other, related areas of intellectual property. Mr. Iandiorio has over 35 years of experience, including a period as an examiner in the U.S. Patent and Trademark Office. He is actively involved in fostering the creation and growth of small businesses and high-technology companies. He was chosen as the SBA's Lawyer Small Business Advocate of the Year. He is Director and Treasurer of the Massachusetts Technology Development Corporation, a venture capital fund; Chairman and Director of the Smaller Business Association of New England; a member of the Massachusetts Small Business Advisory Council and the Science and Technology Advisory Board; and on the Board of Trustees of National Small Business United.

Bruce A. Kirchhoff is Distinguished Professor of Entrepreneurship at New Jersey Institute of Technology. His prior credentials include service as Chief Economist for the U.S. Small Business Administration and as Assistant Director of the Minority Business Development Agency in the U.S. Department of Commerce. He was Director of the Center for Entrepreneurship and Public Policy at Fairleigh Dickinson University and Director of Research in Babson College's Entrepreneurship Center, and he served as Director of the Babson Entrepreneurship Research Conference in 1987 and 1988. Dr. Kirchhoff has published over 100 articles and papers on entrepreneurship, economic development, and business strategy. His book *Entrepreneurship and Dynamic Capitalism* describes how small firms contribute to economic growth. Dr. Kirchhoff earned his PhD in Business Administration and an MBA from the University of Utah. He has extensive consulting experience, having supervised and conducted consultations with over 200 small businesses in the United States and Latin America. He has received six awards for excellence in small business consulting from the U.S. Small Business Administration. Drawing together his business experience and his academic interests, Dr. Kirchhoff joined with two others to found SCT, Inc. in 1984 to manufacture computer-based theft deterrence systems for retail stores. In 1979 he cofounded Pathfinder Systems, Inc., a manufacturer of guidance systems for farm tractors.

Julian E. Lange is an Assistant Professor of Entrepreneurial Studies at Babson College. He is also founder and president of Chatham Associates, a management consulting firm which assists businesses in building competitive advantage. He was president and CEO of Software Arts, Inc., creators of the first electronic spreadsheet (Visi-Calc), and was a founding trustee of the Massachusetts Software Council. He has assisted firms in strategic planning and developing and implementing harvest strategies, including negotiated sales and IPOs. He has been a management consultant to start-up, mid-sized, and *Fortune* 500 companies, and has developed and taught training programs for companies in fields including computer hardware and software, financial services, and health care. He is co-author of *The Construction Industry: Balance Wheel of the Economy* and of articles including "Pricing High Growth Firms: Arbitrage Opportunities in the Inc. 100" in *Frontiers of Entrepreneurship Research 1996*. Lange received his AB from Princeton University and his MBA from Harvard Business School; he earned his AM and PhD from Harvard as well.

Richard P. Mandel is Associate Professor of Law and Chairman of the Finance Division at Babson College, where he teaches a variety of courses in business law and taxation. He is also a partner in the law firm Bowditch and Dewey, of Worcester and Framingham, Massachusetts, where he specializes in the representation of small businesses and their executives. Mr. Mandel has written a number of articles regarding the representation of small businesses. He holds an AB from Cornell University and a JD from Harvard Law School.

J. William Petty, Professor of Finance and the W. W. Caruth Chairholder of Entrepreneurship, teaches at Baylor University. One of his primary responsibilities is teaching entrepreneurial finance, at both the undergraduate and graduate levels. He has also taught Financial Management of the Small Firm at the University of Texas at Austin. His research interest include corporate restructuring, financing of small and entrepreneurial firms, shareholder value-based management, and acquisitions of privately-held companies. He has served as the co-editor for the *Journal of Financial Research* and currently serves as the editor of the *Journal of Entrepreneurial and Small Business Finance*. He has published in numerous finance journals and is the co-author of the following textbooks: *Basic Financial Management, Foundations of Finance, Small Business Management,* and *Financial Management of the Small Firm.*

He has served as a consultant for oil and gas firms and consumer product companies. He is particularly interested in the application of financial strategy for small and middle-market companies as it relates to economic value creation. Petty received his undergraduate degree in marketing from Abilene Christian University, and both his MBA and PhD in finance and accounting from the University of Texas at Austin. He is a CPA in the state of Texas.

Dr. Robert Ronstadt is Professor of Entrepreneurship at Pepperdine University and the author of numerous books, articles, and cases about entrepreneurs. He is the founder or cofounder of several businesses and the originator of *Ronstadt's Financials*, a powerful software program equipped with the financial and accounting expertise to empower people to produce integrated financial projections that are timely and technically correct. He received his undergraduate degree from the University of California at Berkeley, his master's degree from the University of Oregon, and his doctorate in business administration from Harvard Business School.

Joel M. Shulman is the Robert Weissman professor of finance at Babson College, where he teaches Financial Strategies, Working Capital Management, Investments, and Financial Management. He has previously taught Portfolio Management, Taxation, Securities Analysis, Managerial Finance, Cost Accounting, and Special Topics in Finance at Harvard University, Michigan State University, and Wayne State University. He has a PhD in finance and is also a Chartered Financial Analyst (CFA), Certified Management Accountant (CMA), and Certified Cash Manager (CCM). His publications include a number of scholarly articles in his field as well as seven coauthored books published by American Management Association: *Leasing For Profit, Alternatives to Conventional Financing, Planning Cash Flow, How to Effectively Manage Corporate Cash, A Manager's Guide to Financial Analysis, The Job of the Corporate Controller,* and *How to Manage and Evaluate Capital Expenditures.* He has consulted for many small, entrepreneurial firms as well as Coldwell Banker, First Albany, Ford Motor, Freddie Mac, Kmart, Loomis Sayles, Merrill Lynch, Raytheon, Rockwell International, Salomon Brothers, Sears, and UNISYS.

Stephen Spinelli, Jr. was a founding shareholder of Jiffy Lube International and the founder, chairman, and CEO of American Oil Change Corporation, where he had chief executive responsibility for 47 Jiffy Lube service centers in Massachusetts, Connecticut, and New York. He is the Jack E. Muller Professor of Entrepreneurship at Babson College, and he has given seminars on franchising to MBA students at INSEAD and the University of London's Management School and to undergraduate students at the American College in London. He has also conducted conferences on entrepreneurship at Ernst & Young, Siemens, and Lucent Technology. He has an MBA from Babson College and a BA in economics from Western Maryland College; he earned his doctoral degree in economics from the University of London's Imperial College Management School.

Jeffry A. Timmons is internationally recognized for his work in entrepreneurship. He is the Franklin W. Olin Distinguished Professor of Entrepreneurship at Babson College. He was the first to hold a joint appointment at the Harvard Business School, as the first MBA Class of 1954 Professor of New Ventures, and at Babson College, where he was first to hold the Frederic C. Hamilton Professorship. He heads the Price-Babson College Fellows Program. He has authored or coauthored several books, including *New Venture Creation*, 3rd ed., 1990 (Richard D. Irwin) and *Venture Capital at the Crossroads*, 1992 (HBS Press). He is cofounder, investor, or director of several companies, and is an advisor to a $285 million growth capital fund and Ernst & Young's National Entrepreneurial Services Group. A special advisor to the Ewing Marion Kauffman Foundation of Kansas City, he also serves on the board of the foundation's Center for Entrepreneurial Leadership and as a Trustee of Colgate University, his alma mater. He received his MBA and doctorate from the Harvard Business School.

Karl H. Vesper, BSME, MSME, earned a Ph.D. from Stanford and an MBA from Harvard. He is a Professor of Business Administration, Mechanical Engineering, and Marine Studies. His latest book is *New Venture Experience*. Others include *New Venture Mechanics, The Washington Entrepreneur's Guide, New Venture Strategies, Frontiers on Entrepreneurship Research* (with others), *Encyclopedia of Entrepreneurship* (with Kent and Sexton), and *Entrepreneurship and National Policy*. From 1982 to 1985 he served as Chairman of the Management and Organization Department at the University of Washington, where he has been on the faculty since 1969. He has held visiting appointments as the Schoen Professor of Entrepreneurship at Baylor University in 1980 and as the First Babson Professor of Entrepreneurship at Babson College in 1981. During the 1986–87 academic year he was on leave at the University of Calgary, where he held the first endowed professorship in the Faculty of Management. He was a Fulbright Distinguished Lecturer at Trinity College in Dublin in 1989.

William E. Wetzel, Jr. is Professor of Management Emeritus at the Whittemore School of Business and Economics, University of New Hampshire and Director Emeritus of the Center for Venture Research where he remains active. Prior to his retirement in 1993, he held the Forbes Professor of Management chair at the Whittemore School. During the 1987/88 academic year he served as the Paul T. Babson Visiting Professor of Entrepreneurial Studies at Babson College. Professor Wetzel's professional and research interests include the role of the entrepreneur in economic development, the financial management of high-growth private companies and the informal venture capital markets. Professor Wetzel has authored articles and published a wide variety of management and entrepreneurship publications, including the *New England Journal of Business and Economics, Business Horizons, Sloan Management Review, The Financier,* the *McGraw-Hill Encyclopedia of Economics,* the *Encyclopedia of Entrepreneurship,* and others. He serves on the Editorial Boards of the *Journal of Business Venturing, In Business,* the *Journal of Small Business Finance,* and *Frontiers of Entrepreneurship Research.* Professor Wetzel is a founding member of the New Hampshire High Technology Council and a past President of the Council. In 1993 he received the Council's Lifetime Creative Vision Award. He founded Venture Capital Network, Inc. in 1984. He is a member of the Smaller Business Association of New England (SBANE) and served on its Board of Directors from 1983 through 1986. Professor Wetzel also serves on the Boards of Directors of Yankee Equipment Systems, Inc., C.I.M. Industries, Inc., M.I.T. Technology Capital Network, Inc., New Hampshire Business Development Corp., RVA Associates, Inc., Venture Resources, Inc., Zero Emissions Technology, Inc., and on the Advisory Board of Kearsarge Ventures, L.P.

INDEX